For Cecilia and John's grandchildren:

Anne, Ellen, and Nancy Hendricks
Arthur and John DeCamp

CONTENTS

EDITOR'S NOTE

Cecilia Hendricks's letters to her family number in the thousands. Initial research into the correspondence isolated all the topics thought to be of more than passing interest. What emerged finally, after several cuttings, is a very selective narrative. The letters are reproduced verbatim; the only changes are those made to delete duplications and bring rare inconsistencies into line. Brackets and footnotes are used occasionally to bridge deleted material or to explain an item not previously introduced.

When Cecilia Hennel Hendricks stepped off the morning train in the bleak little northwest Wyoming town of Garland in January 1914, she was a new bride who had never been away from her family circle, with a husband she had seen only three times before their wedding day. On December 30, 1913, she had married John Hendricks, a seriously wounded veteran of the Spanish American War who had homesteaded in the Shoshone Valley in northwestern Wyoming in 1911, not long after the new irrigation project was opened.

From the day the newlyweds left Bloomington, Indiana, on their honeymoon journey, and through the seventeen years that followed, Cecilia wrote letters home — daily and sometimes twice a day for the first several years, and then, as responsibilities and activities with her husband and children increased, at least twice weekly. She described all the facets of her life in Wyoming for her mother, who never could be persuaded to travel west to visit her daughter, for her father, who visited briefly twice but whose catholic interests elicited the wide-ranging descriptions his eldest daughter sent to him, and for her two younger sisters.

The great wealth of this family correspondence was saved by the Hennel family to become a valuable narrative of John and Cecilia's life together and a commentary on a woman's role in homesteading. Most of the letters are typewritten; all are dated. The few handwritten letters, when she was sick in bed or away from home and typewriter, are in a clear, firm, blackboard script that never changed as she grew older. The letters represent a place and a time and a family—a picture of Honeyhill Farm in northwest Wyoming developing from raw desert to full bloom. They are filled with detailed descriptions of every phase of the honey-producing business; cooking for hired hands and work crews; menus and recipes and products used; the garden and canning; clothing construction, remodeling, and mending; weather; descriptions of the valley and the mountains; their neighbors' personalities; participation in community and statewide activities; the worsening economic situation; and all the classic problems of the farmer.

If there were doubts, or fusses, or desperation, those things never showed in the letters. John and Cecilia were self-confident people, happy with each other, never losing sight of what could be. They were dedicated to their family and to their perceived responsibility in community affairs. Some of their neighbors no doubt considered them authoritarian, self-righteous, overbearing, and conceited; but their alliances with those neighbors and friends were strong and lasting, and their interdependence apparent.

In a newspaper piece written for the fiftieth anniversary of the Shoshone Project, Cecilia noted:

The early settlers of the Garland Division were far above the average of people usually found in rural areas. All of them were intelligent, ambitious, and industrious enough to have moved to a new place. They had studied the literature on the new national conservation movements and had chosen Wyoming. They had saved enough to back the move financially. They were prepared to live simply and inconveniently until they could get established. They had the stuff that makes pioneers. Most of them had education far beyond that of the average farmer of the early part of the century. I recall an early meeting of the East End Club at the home of Mrs. J. L. Werts. Someone mentioned that she had been a teacher before coming to the Flat. Another said she had too, and another and another. So we took a poll and discovered that of the 23 women present, 17 had taught school in the grades, in high schools, or in colleges. All of them had some college or normal school work, and some were graduates with not only one but two degrees. I doubt if such a record could be found anywhere than among the first settlers of a reclamation project. It indicated a group of people interested in education and in intellectual as well as in agricultural topics. The number and high quality of the magazines subscribed to by early settlers is another evidence of their interests beyond mere existence.

While there was scattered settlement in most parts of Wyoming in the nineteenth century, the development of irrigation on a large scale in the early years of the twentieth century opened vast new areas. In 1894, Congress had voted to donate 1,000,000 acres of public land in each of the arid states to the states themselves, to be reclaimed at the hands of the respective states or through contract with private corporations. In 1902 President Theodore Roosevelt signed the Reclamation Act into law and established a special fund to be used for the storage, diversion, and development of waters for the reclamation of arid and semiarid lands.

The completion in 1910 of the federally funded Shoshone Dam in the canyon which cuts through Rattlesnake Mountain just west of Cody, Wyoming, impounded water to irrigate initially 132,000 acres of land in the northwest corner of the state, and gave the unfailing supply of water which assured crops of many kinds.

Although the brochures published by the U.S. Reclamation Service spoke in glowing terms of the qualities of the soil, only one crop of grain could be produced on the new farms before it was necessary to plant several years' rotation of crops that produced heavy root growth to add humus and to aerate the soil. One of the plants most suitable for this purpose was sweet clover, and the presence of hundreds of acres of blooming clover attracted professional beekeepers. One of the earliest in the Powell-Garland division of the Shoshone Project was John Hendricks, who entered his homestead at Powell in February 1911, on Farm Unit E, about a mile southwest of Garland and five miles east of Powell.

John Hendricks came of a pioneering family. His paternal grandparents came to the United States in 1838 from Germany and settled on a southern Indiana farm at West Franklin.

John's maternal grandfather left Holland in the early 1800s. On board ship he met a Dutch girl, and by the time the ship reached New Orleans they were married and ready to start out in search of a home. They went up the Mississippi and Ohio rivers by steamboat and also settled near West Franklin.

Here, two generations later, in 1874, John Hendricks was born. He had an older brother named Pacific, for the biggest steamboat on the Ohio River, and a younger brother named Abraham Lincoln. John was just plain John. His two sisters were Carrie and Anna. When John was nine, his father died, and since no high school was available when John finished the local grade school, he assumed adult responsibilities at the age of fifteen, helping support his mother and the family. When the Spanish-American War began, he enlisted with patriotic fervor in Company E of the 16th U.S. Infantry. The regiment was sent to Cuba almost immediately, and at the Battle of San Juan Hill, in his first day of action, John suffered a gunshot wound that grazed the sciatic nerve in his groin, left him permanently in need of a crutch to support the leg, and affected his health for the rest of his life.

He spent much of the next ten years in and out of the U.S. Veterans Hospital in Washington and took as many correspondence courses as possible to improve his education. Unable to obtain relief for his wound, he finally went back to his home in southern Indiana, where, unable to do regular work and affected by the humid climate, he developed a small apiary as a hobby. In 1909 he decided to try a drier climate and made an exploratory trip throughout the West, from Texas through Wyoming to Idaho and Washington. He found the climate in Wyoming gave the best promise for health for him, and the bulletins of the U.S. Reclamation Service were compelling.

Early in February 1911, he loaded an immigrant car at Mt. Vernon, Indiana, and started west by rail through Missouri and Nebraska for Wyoming. In the immigrant car were 108 colonies of bees, valued at four dollars per colony, bee equipment, a tent, bed and bedding, a dresser, table and chairs, a stove, and a few cooking utensils and dishes.

One of John's friends at the Veterans Hospital in Washington had been Will Thuman, a young man from Evansville, Indiana. When John went home to West Franklin on his first recuperative furlough in the fall of 1898, he resumed the friendship and often went with Will to visit relatives in and around Evansville. On one visit, sitting quietly in back of the stove while Will chatted with his sister Anna and her husband Joseph Hennel, John was introduced to Cecilia and Cora Hennel. He remembered the meeting; they did not.

Joseph Hennel's parents, immigrants from Strasbourg, France, and Switzerland, came to Evansville in the late 1840s. Joseph was born in 1842 and was a teacher until the Civil War began. He enlisted in the Indiana Volunteer Infantry and served for three years, chiefly in Virginia. Upon his return to Evansville he began teaching again and then opened an abstract of title office and ran a real estate business. He married Anna Thuman in 1882, and by the early 1890s they had three daughters, Cecilia Barbara (1883), Cora Barbara (1886), and Edith Amelia (1891). The family lived on a farm west of Evansville, and the two older daughters went through grade and high school together, graduating from Evansville High School in 1901.

The Hennel family was never separated for more than a few days at a time, and even on short trips they wrote each other daily. When Cecilia and Cora were teaching at country grade schools ten miles from home and seeing some family member once or twice a week, they both made many tear-stained entries in their diaries concerning their terrible homesickness.

Cecilia and Cora taught in country schools for two years to save enough money to attend college, and in the fall of 1903 they entered Indiana University. A year later they persuaded their parents to move to Bloomington and found a rental house for them across the street from the campus, where the Hennels rented their extra rooms to coeds and followed the interests of all three daughters. The two older girls received their A.B. degrees in 1907 and their master's degrees in 1908, Cecilia in

English and Cora in mathematics. Both girls began teaching at the university that year, and Cora received her Ph.D. in 1911. Edith majored in botany, received her master's degree in 1912, and served as a teaching fellow in her department until September 1913.

The Hennel girls loved their college experience and began a lifetime association with Indiana University. Their proudest claim was that all three were elected to Phi Beta Kappa, two of them as charter members of the Indiana University chapter. They were immersed in campus activities and their home was a gathering place for students and faculty alike. Anna Hennel served as a surrogate mother for many a lonesome student, and Pater, as Joseph was now and henceforth called, managed all his women and kept them "at home where they belonged." It was Anna, "Mamma," who wrote all the letters from 822 East Third Street in Bloomington to their daughters. Pater commanded and demanded and was a practicing hypochondriac; but Mamma, whose grammar and syntax were only mediocre, wrote loving, gossipy, informative letters.

In late 1911, when they were both teaching, Cecilia and Cora went to a classmate's wedding in Terre Haute. Cecilia noted in her diary:

> The most astonishing thing is that when we pulled the favors from the wedding cake, Co got the dime and I got the ring. Imagine!

Two weeks later a related item appeared in her diary:

> The wedding ring I got at Dr. Dan's wedding seems bound to produce something. I got a letter today from someone who signed himself John Hendricks, asking me if I would consider a proposal of marriage from him. The letter came from Garland, Wyoming. I don't know the person; he is, so far as I know, "A puffect strangeh to me." So far as I am concerned he'll probably remain so. I should like to know who he is and how he got my name, however. It's either a joke from some of our crowd, or somebody pretty "fresh." Anyway, it makes me sort-o'-weary.

A diary entry, April 21, 1912:

Discovered from Aunt Lena that the letter from the West is from
Uncle Will's old friend. I wrote a letter, therefore. I declined his
invitation.

And on May 26, 1912:

I received another letter from Wyoming. Poor man. He is
dreadfully lonesome. The letter was surprising to me. He said
he had loved me for years, but how could one in a position such
as mine think even of a man like him. If he is the man Aunt
Lena says he is, position counts nought. I never had a letter
that made my heart ache so. I answered it in a couple days,
asking how he knew me, and suggesting he loved an ideal rather
than a real person. Today the annual sermon to the soldiers was
given at our church. As I saw the old soldiers march in, and
then the Spanish-American veterans, I couldn't help thinking of
him and of the difference between these men who got only as far
as Tampa and him. That he is a real hero, his life in Cuba and
more especially since has shown. It seemed to me that if anyone
deserved honoring on Memorial Day it is he. Consequently I
wrote him a Memorial Day letter. It's more worthwhile to send
flowers to a live hero than to a dead one.

And so began a correspondence that culminated in the
wedding on December 30, 1913, of John and Cecilia — the fourth
time they saw each other. John had come to Bloomington in
the fall of 1912 to meet the family and to ask formally for her
hand in marriage, and that visit nearly ended in disaster. John
arrived on a morning train and went to a downtown hotel to
await the formal arrival of Cecilia's father. He waited through
the long afternoon hours and no one came. Finally deciding
that his suit was being rebuffed, he checked train schedules and
was about to leave and never contact the Hennel family again
when Joseph Hennel arrived, flurried and fussed because he
had spent the afternoon trying to reach John at another hotel,
thinking that was the hotel that had been agreed on in
correspondence as the meeting place.

The letters of 1912–1913 when Cecilia and John were getting acquainted by mail are the only ones missing from the many years of family correspondence, although a letter she wrote in 1914 to a college friend sheds some light on the reasons she found for accepting his proposal.

It isn't so much what you would see at first sight — though he is good to look at — as what you would see after you know him. He is almost six feet tall and very broad of shoulder, weighs one hundred and eighty pounds, has a rather massive head with dark brown hair enough for a football player, a broad, large face with firm chin, high forehead, the usual amount of nose and mouth, and blue eyes under which tiny pain wrinkles still show what he has gone through. What counts, however, is not the outward appearance. You remember that when old Buffon was asked what style is, he answered: Le style est l'homme. When you ask me what is the reason for my dropping out of unity with the sisterhood of singles, I shall have to say in like manner: La raison est l'homme.

We first met when I was a youngster way down in high school. He had just returned from a sojourn in a military hospital in New York after being severely wounded in the Battle of San Juan, having been led into the war by his sympathy for the oppressed, ill-treated Cubans. Though our homes were not many miles apart, we had not known each other until we met at my grandmother's, where Mr. Hendricks often stopped in to see my Uncle Will. I thought nothing of the acquaintance, but it was otherwise with him, and though he said nothing, he made his plans accordingly. His wound seemed to get along all right, and he went to Northwestern to start in on the medical course. Before the year was over, his leg gave way, and he suffered a complete nervous breakdown. He had to quit school. By the next fall he was better, and tried again, but had to give up before the year was out. Later he tried again at another school, but with no better success. It looked as if fate were against him, and that the plans he had made about the little high school girl would never be realized. But he would not give in. With indomitable courage he held out against it all and by sheer force of will, slowly, very slowly, began to climb the great hill towards recovery. While he was unable to work he took up beekeeping as a pastime. He also did what he could to make up for the college work he was missing. He read, read, read, all his weakened nerves could stand. Slowly, but surely, he began to get better. Then he became interested in the West both for the health and the wealth it promised. He came out and investigated, and then filed on a homestead in this irrigation project. In this wonderful country his health grew by leaps and bounds. With health, the possibility of carrying out his plans grew bigger. The business opportunity in beekeeping, too, proved excellent. During all this long fourteen years he had gone on without one word of encouragement from her who was his goal, in order that he might spare her the suspense of waiting and the sorrow of disappointment should the struggle be in vain. Not until success was assured, till health was gained, till what he considered as a suitable home was provided, did he tell. Then he came to her with the story. That was two years ago. Answer me now, you scoffer. Wouldn't you have listened? And wouldn't you have loosened your heart strings just a little, just enough to peep over the bars into the new country that lay before you? Honest, wouldn't you?

Even though I have listened to my heart as well as my head that does not mean that I have ceased to use my head. I am not blinded. I would not argue that he is the greatest man in the world, or the most powerful or the most brilliant, or the greatest genius. I am none of these things in my sex. But I do say that to me he is the best man in the world, in terms of courage, of sincerity, of sympathy, of strength of purpose—in general, in live-ableness-with. Our ideas and our ideals, we find, are scarcely different from each other's. We get pleasure from the same things—from work and play and nature and books and men and little children and music and pictures. Together we are not less individual, but more so, since each of us has gained so much from the other. Above all, we can work together without friction, at the same or at different tasks, in the same or in different fields, always with interest in and sympathy for what the other is doing. And that is what counts: That, I take it, is what love means.

Well, this is our story. You ask me why I'm here. In the words of the old round, and I can give you no better answer, "We're here because we're here, because we're here."

And among Cecilia's papers, copied in her own hand, is a paragraph from one of John's letters that must have been a determining point in their relationship.

In getting a companion there are two things that I have always wanted: first, that my wedding day should mark the real beginning of my love making, and not the beginning of the end of it as it so often seems to be the case; and, second, that such a companion should be an independent, Christian character, one whose devotion to him should be second to her devotion to Him who overcometh all things. Likewise I want my devotion to my companion to be patterned after Him whose influence has kept environment from forming my character. It seems to me that if two persons who are trying to build a home would first enthrone Christ in their home they could not fail to build a home where peace and contentment would reign; where the burdens of life would not weigh heavily; where the destroying spirit would not enter, and where sorrow would never outweigh joy. I do not want to be the ruling spirit in my home, but prefer to follow a more wise Leader.

And so Cecilia Hennel left her secure family circle and moved to the strange, raw country of the Shoshone Valley. Her friends were critical, telling her she was wasting a perfectly good education and a fine career to become a farmer's wife. Years later, when she told the story, she always added, "They were wrong. I needed that education and I used it every day of my life!" The environment in Wyoming, the first territory to approve women's suffrage, where the opportunities were as wide open as the landscape, suited this modern, independent woman who, while she was not a militant fighter for women's rights, simply assumed that she would take equal responsibility in the marriage and the management of family and business, and proceeded to do so.

From the time she began teaching in country schools Cecilia yearned to be a writer. She enrolled in mail order courses in writing, took all the college courses she could get, and utilized her writing skills to keep the family solvent during bad years. Her marketable material was always along practical lines, but she continued to write small pieces of fiction and some poetry, and she poured all her writing skills into the long letters home. The letters now become her main work. She always wanted to be a writer, and she always *was*.

Cecilia Hendricks Wahl

First of all I want to tell you that the sun is shining.

BEGINNINGS

1

1914–1915

First of all I want to tell you that the sun is shining. We have been traveling along the Mississippi River. You ought to see how pretty the water looks with the sun shining on it. We have evidently picked out a good day to travel, for we have this whole coach to ourselves, and have had since we left Chicago. That makes it pretty nice for we have all the room we want to put our things. We are now occupying what would be four berths—two upper and two lower.

There isn't any use sitting with a typewriter under the seat and writing longhand, is there? We simply untied the string and took off the string and paper, and here you are. We bought the typewriter, an Underwood, in Chicago, just like new, with tabulator. We didn't want to pay quite as much as this one was, but decided it was a wise investment. The price was $34, which includes some supplies. The salesman fixed it up so we could carry it along on the train—that saved three dollars or so in shipping charges.

The next thing of importance I have to tell is about dishwashing. You all heard yourself the drastic statement John made about washing dishes. This noon on the train, after we had finished eating, I packed the eatables back in the basket. When the dishes were all gathered up, he calmly took them and said, "While you finish packing up, I'll take the dishes down and run the hot water over them." I said nothing and off he went. When he came back with them all hot and clean, I got out the towel and wiped them. As I sat there wiping them, a "got" expression slowly stole over his face, and he owned up to the fact that he was so used to washing dishes he did it before he knew what he was about. So you see all you have to do with a man is to let him alone. Edith and Cora, take notice; I'm giving you some information that may come in handy later.

We had a good dinner. We had buns and two kinds of sausage—metwurst and liverwurst, butter, stuffed olives, canned pineapple, cakes, and nuts. We have plenty of bread and butter and sausage and herring and cakes and fruit with us, besides olives, baked beans, and chicken soup. As we can get all the hot water we want, we can have hot soup, and hot beans if we want them.

It seems strange to have a whole car to ourselves. You didn't know we could afford to charter a car for our wedding trip, did you? It's much pleasanter riding where there is not a lot of talking and noise.

Billings, Montana
January 12, 1914

We got in here at 12:20 and leave at 7:00 A.M. Then we have about four hours till we get to Garland. The trip has been delightful.

While the porter was making up the berth last night he said, "I guess you won't teach no more school now!" When I asked who told him about me he pointed toward the end of the car where John was and said, "He did." Then he said, "I bet you wuz an awful nice teacher, sure; you are so pleasant looking." You can guess from what the porter said that John had tipped him.

Tonight we are to go to the lecture course at Garland. John says I'll attract more attention than the musicians — it is to be a musical number. I guess I'll wear my brown satin. How's that for playing safe on costume. John isn't much help. He can't tell what sort of clothes the women wear on these occasions — only he thinks they dress up, sort o'.

I'm glad the trip is about over. While the train is running you can't help thinking how far it is, and that is rather conducive to — you know what. After we get home and get to work, I'll forget the distance, especially when I get the letters. I haven't heard from you for nearly a week. Won't I be glad to get the mail that is waiting for us!

We arrived all right this morning. Mr. Werts and Mr. Pease were both at the train to meet us. As we got off the train we were greeted by a monstrous shower of rice, not from the men but from three young ladies. One of them looks after the telephone exchange, one is in the post office, and I don't know the domestic relations of the third. We heard later that these girls have met the train for four days to be sure to get us.

Mr. Werts took us in his buggy right to his house. Mr. Pease got the baggage, trunks and all, and then came also to the Werts'. The Werts had invited Mr. and Mrs. Pease, who are our nearest neighbors, and Mr. and Mrs. Hancock were also there. She is a daughter of the Werts. They were all too nice to us for any use. Of course we had a fine dinner. After dinner we sat and talked a while, and about two o'clock Mr. Werts brought us home, and Mr. Pease came with the baggage. Mrs. Pease came with him and helped me get the bed made and the house straightened. She is just lovely. The first thing I found when I got in the house was a bumpy lot of something on the kitchen table covered with an embroidered towel. Under the towel was a great loaf of bread, a pound of butter, a big platter of cookies and a huge mince pie. What do you think of that? People here are so nice.

You ought to see the view from here. In the daytime it is gorgeous. The mountains have the loveliest color. And the night! I never knew what a moonlight night was till tonight. I never saw such stars as we have out here. The strange thing is that they are the same stars I've always seen.

Of course I needn't tell you that occasionally my voice doesn't work right and I have to survey the distant horizon instead of looking at the person near me. I can't talk very steadily about Indiana or things like that yet. But you know I'd be homesick if I were in Ellettsville, five miles away, and you were all at Bloomington. It does seem pretty far away here, but we'll soon get used to that. Everything is so fine and the prospects are so good one couldn't help being happy. And most of all, there is

John. So I am not repining, though I may weep occasionally.

How is everything going at school? We thought of you this morning. We left Billings at seven o'clock which was eight o'clock by central time. We thought of Toah and Edif* trotting across Third Street before the chimes struck. At six o'clock here, seven there, I thought of Pater getting the fires started. Well, it is nearly time to go, and I must yet put on my brown satin dress. I wonder if John can get the combination.

January 13, 1914

After supper last night we went to the lecture course number at Garland. The numbers are given in the Methodist church. The church is an oblong building with one room. The entrance door is at the back of the room. The seats are arranged across the room facing the front, with an extra section in front at the left side where the platform does not extend clear across the room. As we came in, people turned and looked. Evidently they were waiting for us. When they saw who we were, they began clapping. John was taking off his overcoat at the door, and we stood still. I had gumption enough when I found the clapping was for us to stand still facing John and with my back to the room till the applause and the encore had ceased. Then the usher came to show us to a seat. The only seats he could find were clear in the front, half facing the main part of the audience. I think he must have been in on the scheme. Everybody stared and stared at us. Finally the performers came in, and then we had someone to divide attention with us. The entertainment was quite good. The troupe consisted of a reciter, a violinist, and a soloist. The violinist played the piano and played for the soloist. The soloist played the violin accompaniments. All were women. The reciter was very good on impersonations, especially of children. The vocalist had a very sweet, high voice, and was wise enough not to try to do things she couldn't. The violinist was

*Cora is variably called Co, Toah, and Tody; Edith as Edif, Bady, or Baby, all obviously childhood names.

pretty good. She had swing and go even if the tones weren't always the clearest.

We had been warned during the day to look out for a charivari that night. It was about eleven when we got back home, so we thought surely no one would come that late. Sure enough, they did, though. We were ready for them, however, as you very well know. We served the cookies and apples, and they all looked pretty well pleased. We used Olive's brass tray to serve the apples on, and you can guess it looked nice. There were about two dozen in the crowd. The racket they made wasn't so bad, as they used discs from harrows and the sound made was quite sweet and full. Of course some had guns and tin pans and cans. They stayed in the house about half an hour. John introduced them to me, but of course I wouldn't know many of them again. When they started to go, they formed in line and shook each of us by the hand, wishing us good things. Most of the younger fellows were pretty embarrassed while going through this part of the performance, and simply blurted out: Congratulations. They said the same to John and then to me. I don't think I was excited. At least I didn't feel that way. It was a little odd to be in a room with about twenty-five men, and no other woman in sight.

Well, I guess we have been properly welcomed into the neighborhood, with the rice at the station, the applause at the church, and the charivari itself. People here are pretty nice, as you can see.

The mailman is coming so I shall have to stop. Write often to us for a little while, for your letters keep me from getting homesick. After a while you won't need to write so often.

January 16, 1914

I often look at the clock as I do different things about the house and wonder what you are doing at the same time. Of course when you have class work I can place you all right. Just at this minute, for instance, you are teaching your two-o'clock class, Cora, and Edith's people are having a lecture — or is it a quiz?

One thing that seems so strange here is that there is nothing here by which to regulate your clock. If your clock doesn't keep exact time you never know it till you go some place. There are no whistles or bells that we can hear. The train goes by, but that is hardly accurate enough to time a clock by. We think now we are half an hour fast. My watch is not sure, for I have not tested it since it has been fixed, and John's watch gains a little. At all events, I don't believe he has wound his watch since day before yesterday, so that doesn't help. As soon as we get correct time again we shall have to keep all our pieces going for a while until we find out what is what.

January 18, 1914

Today is our first Sunday in our home. We went to church at Powell this morning. Everybody was very lovely to us, and especially to me. I have an invitation to the Ladies Aid for Wednesday. For the present, this lady will aid a bit at home before starting out anywhere else. The service is a good deal like ours at home. The hymns are the same, the commandments, etc., at the beginning, and the responsive readings at the back. There are not so many hymns, that is all. Of course, I got to feeling pretty homesick a time or two during the service. That was only to be expected. Next time it won't be quite so hard, and after a while I guess I won't feel it enough to make me blue. The chief difference I noted this morning is that, as in all smaller and especially rural churches, there is not the air of quiet and solemnity you find at home or in the larger churches. Children are allowed to go out and come in during the service, and I caught two paper wads myself. Maybe I was especially honored, being new. Of course the older folk are very quiet and attentive, but the children are not, and even the young people are not very much so. I guess the difference is partly because there were so many young boys and girls, and they sat together instead of with their families.

We feel today for the first time as if we were really begin-ning to live. Of course you know the house is not finished. The woodwork is just natural and the wallboard uncolored. The floors were awfully dirty and dusty. Yesterday we scrubbed the floors in the living room and kitchen and bathroom, and when the floor was dry we laid some strips of grayish-white rag carpet in the places we walk the most. The house now looks clean and as if somebody lived in it. It will be lovely when it is really finished as we hope to have it in the next couple weeks. The scrubbing yesterday was very easy to do, as we scrubbed with a broom, and mopped up with a "mob" using a mop bucket we ordered from Chicago. The bucket has rollers on it to wring the mop, so you don't have to touch your hands to the water at all. The bucket paid for itself yesterday.

There is one thing I want to tell you about, not because I am afraid you will need it for any unfortunate reason, but because there might arise some business or other reason why you might want to know. It is in regard to reaching us quickly. To send a letter takes four days from you to us. That is, it gets here to the house by rural delivery the fourth day from the day you mail it in Bloomington. From us to you, if we put the letter in our box, takes five days, as the mail goes out of Powell on the train before the rural delivery man gets back in the evening. If we take the mail to Powell or to Garland the time is only four days, the same as from you here. The rural delivery man waits till the mail train comes into Powell each day before he starts out. He does not leave the office till twelve o'clock. Now in case you should need to reach us in a hurry, a telegram sent to Powell to get there *before twelve o'clock noon* would reach us the same afternoon at about three o'clock or shortly thereafter. A night letter sent from Bloomington ought to reach us the next afternoon. It would be wise to mention in sending the telegram or night letter that it is to be delivered on a rural route, Powell No. 2. A message that arrives in Powell after twelve o'clock would not reach us till the next day in the afternoon.

It is five o'clock here now. That means it is six with you. You are about having supper, you all with Edward* for the last

---

*Edward E. Ellis, fiance of Edith, a student at Indiana University.

Sunday he will be there for a while. It will be hard for him to dig out and work now. I know, for I have just gone through what he will have to this week. Really, the *going* is not the hard part. It is the staying after you get there. I don't mean that you would want to start back, but you don't realize until you are settled just what it means to *stay away*. Fortunately Edward's stay will not need to be so long. At least we hope so. The first week will be the worst, too. I am feeling lots better now. I am beginning to take root and don't feel so much now like a big tumble weed blown by the wind. I can't realize that we are so far apart. This morning I saw a buggy coming up the road, and before I knew what I was doing I was thinking, "Maybe that is some of the homefolk coming to see us." I guess I feel the way I did when I was at Grossman's teaching, and you used to come to see me. I knew before I came out here that John is good. How good and dear he is I am just beginning to find out. I think it will take me all my life long to understand fully.

January 20, 1914

I had two callers yesterday — two of the neighbor women came to see me. They wanted to see the house, of course, and seemed very much taken with the kitchen and bathroom. They seemed surprised when we told them this was just half the house. I appreciated very much their coming.

There are a couple things I want. One is my old corset, if it isn't in the freight box. I have only this good new one with me, and I don't want to get it spoiled. Another thing I want is an eraser for the typewriter, just a regular pencil eraser. I tried to get them here, and they wanted five cents for the penny ones, and they were so hard they wouldn't rub. One thing else I want. I want to know the dimensions of the holes in the seat back in the yard. The carpenter here made the holes entirely too small and not the right proportion. Please send me the width from side to side and from front to back, and the distance from the front of the seat to the front edge of the hole.

I am wild about the mountains. We can see such pretty ones from here. It is so odd to me to see the clouds come down over the mountains and run up the valleys between the ranges without ever coming near here. This morning there was a big, dark cloud in the west, just the kind that would bring a good thunder storm in Indiana. The cloud was all fringy at the lower edge and parts of the cloud were trailing low down. It looked quite near, but it just sailed off down a near canyon and didn't come near us. The sun kept on shining all the time. For two days I haven't been able to see the two far mountains. One of the nearer ones has got a new coat of snow on a part of it. The funny thing is that the snow is not on the top but on one slope rather near the bottom of the mountain. Directly south of us in the range of foothills that forms our southern horizon there are two peaks that are exactly like gateposts. The space between looks just like an entrance-way into this part of the country. Yesterday morning there was a cloud just over this gateway that looked exactly like a Japanese pagoda, or temple. The whole effect was like looking out of your gate across the way at a big temple.

Mr. Pease, our neighbor, is putting up ice. We should like to put some up, but are not prepared this year. Next year we hope to. You can get the ice at the reservoir, twelve miles away, at twenty-five cents a ton, ready-cut and easily loaded. This is pure water ice. At the gravel pit, three miles away, you can get it for fifty cents a ton, but this is alkaline. People here put up ice in coal slack, which they get at the mine for the hauling. Mr. Pease goes about six miles for the slack. It seems funny to put ice in coal, but they say it keeps better than in sawdust or any other packing. You may be interested in knowing that ice will keep here if put in a pen made of straw. Two pieces of chicken wire are put eight or ten inches apart, with posts between. This space is packed with straw and chaff. The ice is packed with coal slack and covered with more straw. Some people just pile baled straw into a house around the ice. It will keep that way, too.

January 23, 1914

Pater, will you please attend to some business for us? I should like to have three of the Evansville bonds turned into cash as soon as possible. We did not borrow as much money in Evansville as we at first thought we would, and we will need some of mine. We have a lot of lumber coming in next week that is to be paid for on arrival and unloading of the car. The lumber comes from a Seattle firm that pays the freight on carload lots. Two neighbors went in with us to get the carload. The lumber is largely for the bee fixtures. We shall need $300. I want to leave at least five hundred dollars untouched at Evansville. We want always to have enough on hand for an emergency of any kind, and five hundred ought to do. Beyond that, it seems rather foolish to keep money in the Evansville bonds at four per cent and pay seven per cent interest or, out here, twelve per cent at the bank, or ten from individuals. Right now is when we can use our money to best advantage in the business and in planting a few trees on the farm and getting things in shape.

We can not begin to thank you for all you have done for us. You have helped us so much already we hate to ask you to be looking after things for us still, but we know no one else can do it as well as you can, and we also know that you like to help us. Only we don't want to ask too much of you.

January 30, 1914

I had a letter yesterday from Ralph Murphy* and a nice letter from his girl today thanking me for the letter I wrote in answer to hers of last week. I didn't tell her much of anything, except that if a girl loves a man well enough to marry him, then whatever his work is must be hers too. I told her I knew it was hard to go away from home for I had just learned from experience, but that after all the biggest thing was making a home of your own for the man that loved you. The girl asked

---

*An Indiana Club friend.

me to try to persuade Ralph to give up the idea of going out of the country to do mission work, but I simply said that even so good a friend as I had no right to mix in in a man's life work. I could tell him to go slow and be sure, but no one but he and she had any right to have anything to say about deciding what the work should be. Maybe she will have a mind of her own and make it up for herself, even if her parents do not want her ever to go away. It's all right for parents to want to do things for their children and try to help them all they can. But the children have to grow up some day. I'm mighty glad that our family has always given each of us a right to think for herself, even if the result did mean separation to us in my case. True love in a family allows for individuality, and does not try to make one mind control all.

February 1, 1914

I added another accomplishment (?) to my repertoire last night. I shaved the back of John's neck. I did it all right, too. I didn't whack out any neck or leave any hairs. I guess the credit must go to the good razor Edward gave John and the stone for honing it.

I must tell you that I churned the other day. Our new churn came with the stuff from Montgomery Ward, and of course I was anxious to try it. We have enough milk for milk, cream, and butter. The churn is a glass one, holds a gallon, and works like an ice cream freezer without the tub. You can lift the lid any minute without having the cream run down the sides of the jar outside. The churn works very easily. Well, as I was saying, I churned. I got the cream soured about to what I thought was right, and had it about as warm as I thought it ought to be. I poured it into the churn, got a new magazine, and sat down at five minutes of four to churn. By the time I had read one measly little article, or in other words at ten minutes after four, I had butter. In about a half an hour from the time I began I had a pound and a quarter of butter all churned, washed, and made into a roll. That does not use up much time, does it? And the work is fun. I don't know when I enjoyed anything as much as getting that butter. I didn't know whether I could make butter or not, and it was a circus to have it all come out right. I just grinned like a silly all the while I was finishing up the work after the butter came. The fun is with this glass churn you can see all the time what is going on. The butter, I should state, is first class butter, too.

The other day Mr. Werts and Mr. Pease were both here helping John and of course were here for dinner. I wanted them to know that John had not drawn an absolute blank when it came to cooking, so I planned the dinner with extra care. Of course I didn't want to do anything elaborate, for I didn't want to look as if I were showing off. First we had tomato soup, then roast beef and gravy, potatoes, and baked corn en casserole, and hot muffins; then we had rice pudding baked with apples in it and served with thick cream. Everything was fine, if I do say so myself. I didn't have to say so myself that day, nor since when John was around. He was as tickled as I was because it was all right. Of course cooking is nothing new, but doing all the planning, the preparation, the cooking, the serving, and the table setting, besides eating with the company, keeps a fellow hustling. Especially when dinner is ordered for noon, and at half past eleven the man comes in and says they will be ready much sooner than they thought.

February 3, 1914

There certainly is one convenient thing about living in a place like this. As I sit here at the machine near a north window I can see all over the surrounding country. I can see the road over which the mail man comes, and watch him approaching for half a mile to the corner and a couple miles on the east and west road. I can see the road down which John just went to Garland and watch him on the straight road for a mile and then see him most of the way for the rest of the 3/4 mile of the cross road. When John goes to town to Powell, I can see him coming from the south for half a mile, and I can see him on the east and west road for about the same distance before he turns the corner. When it is about meal time I can start to finish the meal when he is about to heave in sight, and have it all ready when he has the horse unhitched.

I see John coming about a mile down the road. I'd better get at the dishes. Love to all.

February 5, 1914

Our blizzard came all right. Last night about sundown the wind got strong—it had been blowing fairly hard from three o'clock on—and then it began to turn colder. All night the wind just howled. This morning the thermometer was 20 below. By ten this morning it had come up to −15, and now, at half past one, it is 12 below. I guess that is about as high as the mercury will rise today. The wind is still blowing, though not quite as hard as it did early this morning. The sun is shining pretty brightly. The windows on the south side are all melted clear. Even now the window on the north is still pretty frosty even though we have had a fire in the room all morning. We used an extra cover last night, but had no trouble in keeping warm. We have on our bed only the double blanket and the two woollen comforts. Last night I added a cotton comfort.

We do not have any trouble keeping the house warm even today if we keep the fires up. Of course if we let the fires die down the rooms soon get cold. We do not have any fire in the bedroom at all, and keep the door closed between that room and the middle room. I guess we would have trouble today trying to warm the bedroom and this room with the one fire. Ordinarily we can do it easily if we want to.

I am baking bread today. I got a start of yeast from Mrs. Pease, who brought it to me yesterday afternoon when she came to visit. It is bottle yeast, but not like what we had. I don't think I shall like it as well, though the yeast itself is lovely. I think it is too expensive. To use it, you take the yeast and as much water as you will want in your bread, and make a batter with that and the flour—nothing else. You let this rise till it is light, and then take out of this the starter for next time. But in the starter you must put about half a cup of sugar—

quite a good deal, isn't it? After the starter is taken out, then you put in the yeast, the salt, lard, etc. for the baking. You must never put any salt in what you want to save for a starter, or it will kill the yeast. I think I like better the kind that is started with potatoes, as we did at home. At any rate, we have plenty of potatoes, and sugar is dear to buy. Besides, I don't like the bread as sweet as this makes it. I think I shall get some regular yeast foam or the like and start some of the other kind.

I am sorry to have to tell you some very bad news about our honey crop for the past season. John expected it to be gone when we got here. It was not, as you know. Then last week came the order to ship. He got help and loaded the car as soon as it arrived. Just as they had finished loading our honey in the car and the car was sealed ready to send, John got a telegram from Denver countermanding the order. The person in Texas who had ordered the car had rescinded his order.

Tuesday we got a message saying we had better unload as there was no immediate prospect of a sale. Yesterday morning John went to the station and unloaded the car. Fortunately he was able to get room to store the honey for the time being in the old freight station. That saved hauling it clear back home. The chief difficulty with the whole matter is that there is a very great danger that now there will be no sale for the honey at all, as the season is so far advanced that every firm that would use a car is already supplied.

You can easily see that if the worst comes and this crop can not be sold we are up against it. We needed all we could have got from the sale to get the things we wanted. Now we shall have to go extremely slow. John is about heartbroken to think that I should have to live as closely as we shall have to for a while, and says if he had known this we should not have started yet. Of course I do not mean to say he does not want me here. Together we can face this lots better than one alone. I am not afraid of the outcome, but we shall have to put off doing a good many things we wanted to do this year.

This certainly is some cold weather. Last night the thermometer went to thirty below. The only thing we were worried about was the cellar. We put the lantern in it yesterday when we found the temperature in the cellar was getting dangerously low, and it brought it up all right. We were a little afraid to leave the lantern in all night for fear of fire, though it's rather foolish to be afraid of such a thing. We had the lantern hanging on a hook where nothing could touch it. This morning the cellar was all right, but we left the lantern in to be sure. Part of the time yesterday the temperature of the cellar went down to 27, which we thought a bit too low for safety. The lantern brought it above freezing all right, and that is all we cared for. With the outside temperature – 30 and that in the cellar 32, there was a difference of 62 degrees as it was, and that is quite a difference.

I want to ask you about washing. You soap the clothes and soak them in warm water. You dissolve some soap to put in this, don't you? How much? Then when you wash the clothes the first time, do you use the water in which they were soaked, or do you wring them out of this and use all clean water? If you wring them dry you lose the soap in which they were soaked, don't you? Then after they are washed, you boil them. How much soap do you put in each boiler? Our clothes seem to get clean, but when we are washing we don't seem to be able to get soapsuds in the water the way we had at home. I don't know whether I don't use enough soap or whether the water here is somewhat to blame. The water has some alkali in it. Mrs. Pease says she always clears her washing water with lye, but that some lye will make the clothes yellow. You have to be careful what brand you get. I don't much like to use the lye, as it may hurt the clothes as well as my hands. Tell me how much soap you use in the washing and when and where.

I stopped right in the midst yesterday of telling you about the loss of the sale of the honey. I don't know, though, that there is much more to tell. The trouble is, you see, if this honey is not sold, that we shall have nothing coming in, except John's pension checks, till about next December. That is the difficulty of a business where the whole year's returns come in at once — when they come. This probably means that we shall have no ready money at all. Most of the supplies needed for the business John intended to get on time and that can likely be done. But there are some things for which ready money is needed. When you send to Mont. Ward you have to send cash; and when you buy stamps at the post office you can't get them on time.

As far as living is concerned we are not worried, as we have a good warm house and all the furniture we need. We have a good supply of potatoes and canned tomatoes, peaches, apples, and plums, and apple butter. We have all the milk and eggs and honey we can use. But of course this is not all we shall have to have as time goes on. We shall send again to Mont. Ward for some groceries, as we can get them so much cheaper it is a big saving in the long run. The thing that we hate most is that we can not pay some of the notes that John expected to pay off this month and get out of the way. This will mean that we shall be in debt a year longer than we expected, and probably have to wait several years longer to get what we hoped to have next year in the way of house and fruit trees and shade trees and the like. For the house I am not going to worry. This house is lovely and is all we actually need at present. The old house, which John built when he homesteaded, adds as much as two more rooms to this house. Its closets give all sorts of storage room and in it we can do a lot of work we should otherwise have to do in here.

If this were in a neighborhood where everybody else had all they wanted the case would be worse. But there isn't a family living around here that isn't living close — perhaps closer than we shall have to. Of course we didn't expect to have to be quite so saving when we came, but we won't be noticeable if we do. And anyway, happiness isn't dependent on material possessions. We are together, and that counts for more than anything else. We are both glad we are here, and I am sure we shall come out all right and have the most fun in the world all the time. So don't worry about us. I am sorry to have to tell you all this, but I promised we would let you know just exactly how things were going all the time.

Every time I have written I have meant to tell you about the canned goods that John had as a surprise for me. Here is what John had had put up: 84 quarts of tomatoes, 60 quarts of peaches, 45 of plums, 15 gallons of canned apples, 3 or 4 gallons of apple butter, and 21 glasses of jelly. How's that to start housekeeping on. Isn't it lovely? You see, a part at least of our table problem for the next year is solved. We have the butter, eggs, milk, and potatoes to go with this. All we need is a little flour for bread. We also have noodles and macaroni, and butter beans, kidney beans, and barley to last for a long time. If we can't get sugar, we have plenty of honey. I reckon we won't starve, do you? John bought the peaches and plums and had a neighbor woman can them. The woman who canned the apples, apple butter, and jelly had the apples. John furnished the cans. The tomatoes he got from a family that was moving away. He traded honey for tomatoes, ready canned. They cost fifteen cents a can. That surely is cheap enough for home canned tomatoes, including the glass jar. Jars are pretty dear here — about a third higher than at home. It seems strange to can tomatoes in glass, but when you think that a glass jar lasts for years and is not much more than twice as dear in the start, while a tin can can hardly be used a second season, it seems rather sensible to use the glass.

I just wish you could come into our kitchen and see what a fine workplace it is. Of course the walls are not yet done, but the rest is fine. With one step from the end of the range I can reach any cooking utensil. It is three steps from the sink to reach anything in the closet and about two and a half steps from the range to the sink. From the range to the work table is two steps and from the work table to the sink is one. I wash the dishes at the sink, move one foot one step and put all the silver ware and kitchen spoons, pancake turner, etc. away as I wipe it. When I clear the table I carry the dishes on the kitchen work table. When I stand at the sink I can reach them without stepping. I just turn around, get a handful, put them in the dish pan, wash them, step three steps to the stove for the tea-kettle, rinse them, wipe them and set them either on the drain board or the table.

The shelves in the closet reach clear from the door at the china closet and even to the door at the right of the range. In the kitchen utensil end I keep the skim-milk and sweet cream bucket, any open jars of fruit or vegetables, salt jar, sugar, pepper, spices, cocoa, soda, baking powder, tea, lard, cooking butter, and on the top shelf, scales and meat chopper. Thus I can reach anything I need in cooking without stepping more than two steps from the stove. The flour is kept in one drawer of the work table, the bread in the other. I tell you, if the domestic science lady who is coming to visit this week doesn't say something nice about my kitchen when she comes I'll fix her. Work fairly does itself here.

There is just one thing that takes some of the pleasure out of things here, and that is that none of you can see the things. Of course John and I have great joy in them, but there is no one else to show them to, for of course I would not show them to the neighbors even if they happened in. If only some or all of you could come in every little while to see the house and the things we have done and the things we have received, our pleasure in them would be doubled. It makes one feel so selfish to have them all to one's self.

I must tell you about our Jersey cow. She now gives about a gallon of milk a day, or maybe a little more. She will be fresh in May. We use all the milk and cream we can—sometimes a whole milking for drinking and on fruit or cereals. The milk is not skimmed closely for I have only an ordinary hand skimmer to work with, and then I do not try to take every bit of cream out of the skim milk for drinking. Yet besides all this we made 3½ pounds of butter in a little less than nine days.

You will be glad to hear that maybe we shall come out better than we could expect on the honey. We have an offer from an excellent Chicago commission firm to handle it on commission. While that is not as good as selling outright ordinarily, it may turn out even better than the Texas sale might have, for the freight to Chicago is not more than a third as much as to Texas and we run the chance of getting as good a price. We hope that the difference in freight will about pay the commission. The disadvantage of selling to a commission firm is that you can't tell when your money will come in. Still it is better than having the honey stand here and granulate in the comb and have to be rendered. The advantage is that with such nice honey as this is there might be a chance for an even better price than we could have got by selling outright.

It is quite warm here again. Today the thermometer went over forty. The sun was very warm, and we let the fire go out in the heater and left the kitchen door open a good part of the afternoon.

We are "at home" now. Today was the first day. One of John's friends near Powell to whom we sent an announcement said they were thinking of coming to see us last Sunday but thought they'd better wait till after the tenth. Five weeks ago today *it* was. It certainly was a nice wedding, if I do say so myself. The corpse usually doesn't say such things.

I really must go to bed. I wish you had a loaf of the bread I made today. I can make bread, that's certain. Since we have plenty of skim milk, I make it with that. One might as well have all the food value possible in what one eats. What's the use of eating water when the milk is worth so much more? The bread has a brown crust over a quarter of an inch thick. It isn't burned one speck anywhere—just a beautiful brown. Talking about it makes me hungry. I am afraid I shall have to eat a piece before I go to bed.

February 12, 1914

Our house is beginning to look like a house now and less like a makeshift. We have the floors all waxed and the drugget down in the living room. The mission desk, table, chairs and rocker look scrumptious with the mission woodwork. I just wish you could see them all. That is all that is lacking to make me fully satisfied. I got the windows washed yesterday and the curtains up. The plain cross bar looks just right with the mission furniture. I am so glad that I got these curtains.

John sure is a peach when it comes to having things convenient. When he built the cistern he remembered that in the summer we should have to hang our cream there to keep cool, and what did he do but put two openings and two boxes, so that we could use one for drawing water without having to dodge the cream bucket, and the other for hanging the cream in without having to bother it. He has a coal oil can with a faucet at the bottom, so that all you have to do is to hold your lamp under and turn the faucet. No bother to that. Lamps are no bother to take care of anyway, if you clean the chimneys when you do up your morning work, and fill them every other day. That does not take long. The chief objection I have to the whole business is the price of oil. We have to pay $1.50 for five gallons of coal oil. I think that is pretty dear. I asked John if we couldn't get a cheaper grade, but he says the cheaper grades smoke the lamp so badly they are not satisfactory.

February 14, 1914

You will be glad to hear that the honey has been sold. It goes to Minneapolis, a much better deal than the Texas one as the freight is much less. It is also better than the Chicago deal as this brings immediate payment while the Chicago one would have been a commission sale.

I guess Providence is still aware of my whereabouts. I hadn't doubted it any of the time. I knew if we'd just give it time enough things would all come out all right. Maybe my change of residence hadn't been recorded until now.

We have had the best time today you ever heard of. Yesterday Professor and Mrs. Sylvester Loy from the University of Wyoming who are staying with us while they give lectures at the Institute in Powell came on the 1:30 train. John borrowed a surrey from one of the neighbors, so he met them in good style. I intended to have a chicken dinner for last night, but while John was gone Mr. Fowler, who owns the ground south of us and lives in Billings, came by. When he said he would be here a day or two, I invited him to come to dinner today.

For dinner today we had a rather nice dinner party. This Mr. Fowler is a graduate in English and philosophy from Oklahoma University. He filed on a farm near here and with his mother lived long enough to get the title. He and his mother bought the school land that was sold a few months ago just south of here. About a year ago he went to Billings and got a position on a newspaper. After a little while he was made city editor, and in a little while longer he was given the position of secretary of the Chamber of Commerce, which in a land town like Billings is quite an important position in advertising the country round about and booming the town. He certainly is one of the most interesting chaps I ever met. We had a great time. He is quick and full of life, and bright — my, he is bright.

Today we had tomato soup for the first course, with Susie's pretty salt cellars on the table and the crackers served in the lovely dish from Myrtle. Then we had roast chicken, raisin dressing, gravy, mashed potatoes, macaroni with tomato sauce baked in the casserole, apple jelly, honey in Mrs. Schram's jar, and then we had ice cream. As it was so near Valentine Day I thought we would have to take some notice of it. So when I made the ice cream yesterday I packed some of it in a small bucket. This morning I turned it out, cut it in slices, cut each slice in heart shape, and wrapped them in oiled paper and packed them again. Then for dinner I turned the hearts out on the gold rimmed plates from the Sunday school, put this on a small sized white plate, and served this way. The people were as tickled as could be. They said they couldn't tell that they were not in a city.

The place cards each had a wee Kewpie on it and a verse. They were of very nice red art board I swiped from a calendar pad and they stood up, with a heart shape at the top. On each I wrote a verse that I thought was suitable. For myself I had:

> She is not fair to outward view
>   As many maidens be;
> Her loveliness I never knew
> Until she smiled on me.
> O then I saw her eye was bright,
>   A well of love, a spring of light.
>   —H. Coleridge.

John's they all thought was pretty neat, as Fred would say. It was from Samuel Rogers, written in the 18th century.

> Mine be a cot beside a hill;
> A bee-hive's hum shall soothe my ear;
> A willowy brook that turns a mill,
> With many a fall shall linger near.
>
> The swallow, oft, beneath my thatch
> Shall twitter from her clay-built nest
> Oft shall the pilgrim lift the latch,
> And share my meal, a welcome guest.

For Professor Loy I put this from Byron:

> Oh fame! — if I e'er took delight in thy praises
> 'Twas less for the sake of thy high sounding phrases,
> Than to see the bright eyes of the dear one discover
> The thought that I was not unworthy to love her.

Mrs. Loy was very much delighted with this by an unknown 17th century author:

> Love me not for comely grace,
> For my pleasing eye or face,
> Nor for any outward part,
> No, not for my constant heart, —
> > For those may fail, or turn to ill,
> > So thou and I shall sever;
> Keep therefore a true woman's eye,
> And love me still but know not why —
> > So hast thou the same reason still
> > To doat upon me ever.

Mr. Fowler was the only unmarried person present, so I thought he ought to have some wise advice to attend upon the good example he saw before him in the rest of the company. So on his I put this from Herrick:

> Gather ye rose-buds while ye may,
> > Old time is still a-flying;
> And this same flower that smiles today,
> > Tomorrow may be dying.
>
> Then be not coy, but use your time;
> > And while ye may, go marry;
> For having once but lost your prime,
> > You may forever tarry.

Well, that brought down the house. Of course the folk insisted that each person read his verse out loud. When we were through they all clapped and just shouted. We had dinner about two o'clock. We sat at the dinner table till half past three, and had the most fun. Mrs. Loy is Phi Beta Kappa, and of course the men insisted they were in highbrow company. I showed the folks the book of views, and they went into ecstacies over our campus.

I can't tell you how much I have enjoyed having this company. They are perfectly natural people who enter right into everything. Mrs. Loy helps in the kitchen all along, and we have just talked as two of us would have in our kitchen at home—about everything under the sun. I'll be sorry to see them go away in the morning.

Mamma, I got your letter about how to wash. I am certainly glad to find out how to do it. I have sent to Mont Ward for some ammonia powder, and that I think will do the work all right as you say. The powder is just like the liquid, but easier to handle by freight. I think the trouble was that I didn't put in anything but the soap. When we wash this week I shall use some washing powder.

February 17, 1914

I must tell you a good story we heard on one of the merchants at Powell who always uses the gag about high freight when anyone complains at his prices. A farmer was buying a sacking needle and objected to paying twenty-five cents for it, which was the price asked. "Well," answered the merchant, "you know freight is awfully high here." When the merchant handed out the package he asked if the man didn't want anything else. "Well," said the farmer, "I did want to get a crow bar today, but I guess I can't. I've just got fifty dollars with me." John got the story from a dealer at Garland who gave him a sacking needle the other day when he shipped some beeswax.

I did a pretty good day's work yesterday. The Loys went off on the nine o'clock train. I did not go to the station with them, as I thought there was no need. After they had gone I cleaned up the house, washed the dishes, looked after the milk, and soaked the clothes. When John came back from the train he did an errand at Dow's and then got home about half past ten. He built a fire in the work house and put on two kettles of water. I finished up the work in the house and about half past one I got at the washing. John carried all the water for me, and helped with all the lifting. I did all the rest. By six o'clock the washing was all done, and most of the clothes were dry. I was never so surprised in my life as at the way they dried. I always wash the calicoes in the water after the clothes have been washed the first time. I can then get them out of the way while the others are boiling. I also wash any carpets or overalls or the like, and then clean out the machine well before washing the white clothes the second time. At the end of the washing the machine is then clean, and needs only a rinsing. Well, I hung out the calicoes — my black and white house dress, an apron, two petticoats, stockings, and overalls. When I got ready to hang out the first white clothes, not more than twenty minutes later, I thought I would look to see if the calicoes would dry by evening, or if I would have to hang them in the kitchen. They were hanging quite stiffly, and I supposed they were frozen. I went up and caught hold of them, and bless you, weren't they *dry*.

I hadn't intended to hang out the white starched clothes for fear they would freeze. I was going to hang them in the shop. When I saw this you can guess I hustled and got everything out. All the linen towels dried about as fast as I could hang them up. In fact, by the time I was ready to hang up the second boilerful the towels in the first boiler were dry. By dark almost everything was dry. I left the dish towels hanging, however, as I thought it would do them good to get thoroughly dry in the morning sun. All I had to take into the kitchen to finish drying was a linen tablecloth, two good shirts, and of course, the woollen underwear which I did not want to get cold at all. I tell you when this sun gets started, something happens.

February 18, 1914

I must tell you that I, me, myself, *moi*, was able to teach the domestic science lady some things she did not know. She thought it was such a good idea to have a pair of canvas gloves hanging beside the stove to slip on when you fixed the fire! She also did not know that you should not put hot water on hot meat after it is browned ready to roast. But the best of all was about the omelet. She told me that she did not like eggs and that she did not eat them at all except perhaps a little in an omelet. In spite of this, I decided to have hot muffins and omelet for Monday morning breakfast. I made the omelet the way I always do, and filled it with the hamburger that was left from

Saturday night supper. When she came to the table the lady took a small helping, and in a little bit she backed up her cart. She said the omelet didn't have the egg taste she didn't like, and wanted to know how I did it. I explained that I use a teaspoon of flour and about a third of a cup of milk to each egg, beating the whites first, then adding the yolks and beating, then adding the flour and milk together. She had never heard of this. This increases the size of the omelet, too, very appreciably, which is of some importance when eggs are high.

You ought to see the self control I am developing. I stood in the yard the other day talking to a neighbor and there were at least a dozen bees on me, three of them on my hands. I have not quite got to the point when I can keep from dodging if they come at my head, and when they want to sit on my ear, well, I don't feel quite that well acquainted either. I was filling the big lamp the other day, which is so heavy you have to hold it under the faucet with both hands, and along came a bee who wanted to sojourn on the tip of my left ear. I was in a dilemma. If I knocked the bee off, I'd probably spill some oil and have to clean the bowl of the lamp. What did you say? O yes, I cleaned the bowl all right.

February 20, 1914

I got up about seven this morning. John discovered when he had put on his stockings this morning that one of them had developed a ravelling place at the toe. As the stocking is a woolen one the place needed immediate attention. Consequently the first thing I did was to darn. After I got the darning done I put away the milk, and then made the ice cream for dinner. That was quite a little work, as I made chocolate mousse. The chocolate had to be cooked and have the gelatine added, then cooled and beat till it was frothy. The cream had to be whipped, and that took quite a while to whip nearly a quart. I used rather thin cream, too, as I did not want the ice cream too rich. Then the two mixtures had to be whipped together. I used the glass churn to whip the cream and to whip the two mixtures. Then I crushed the ice, whipped the mixture a little more, put it in a lard bucket with a tight cover, packed it in the ice and salt, and the thing was done.

Next I cleaned the house from front to back. I swept and dusted and then mopped the kitchen floor and the border around the drugget in the living room, and the part of the bathroom between the doors. When this was done and the stove board wiped up, I was ready to turn my attention to the dinner. It was then a little after half past ten. I put the macaroni on to cook and peeled the potatoes. The kidney beans were already cooked. I did them yesterday on the heating stove. Then I opened a can of tomatoes and put them on, part for soup and part for the macaroni. Then I cleaned the fish, which had been soaking since yesterday. Then I made the fire for oven heating and made the muffins and got them in, and also the macaroni with tomato sauce. Next I made the soup, and put it over hot water to keep hot till I was ready for it—regular tomato soup made with milk. Then I fried the fish, and saw that everything was going all right. I had set the table in between times of all this, so that at the end all I had to put on was crackers and butter and honey that had been warming. Dinner was on the table at twelve—that is, the soup course. I have discovered that if I give myself a small dish of soup I can sit down with the rest of the people, apparently at leisure, eat all my soup, excuse myself, and dish the dinner while the men finish their soup. I dished the potatoes, beans, put the casserole in the holder, dished the fish, and had this all ready to take in by the time they were ready. Then I took their soup plates and put on the dinner. While they passed the things I poured the tea and milk, all on the brass tray at my place. By the time I got started to eat they were about half through, which gave me about as much time as I needed to eat my dinner and get away and dish the ice cream by the time they were ready. It would not rush you nearly so much if you did not eat with the folk, but when you do that "things has got to hustle some," especially if you want to sit apparently at ease without a care on your mind and discuss crops and chicken raising and the neighbors with the people at the table. John likes me to eat with the company, and I guess he is right. He doesn't want folk to think all he got was a cook or a servant. I thought today when there would be so many (I was expecting six) I wouldn't. He came in when I was ready to set the table, and when he saw that I set just enough plates for the men, he said, "Can't you eat with us? I'd lots rather you did." I guess it makes him feel sort o' settled like to sit at the head of the table and have me at the other end.

February 22, 1914

You asked about our going to church. Yes, we go when we can, and we always want to. Only when the weather is so bad we think it's rather foolish to run any risk by going, much as we want to. I don't feel quite right if I don't get to church, and yet one has to use some judgment in the matter. I guess you can serve the Lord better by being well seven days a week than by going to church one day and being sick the other six — and maybe grouchy. I sent my letter in a week or so ago. I did not get to church the day the new members were taken in, as it was during that very cold spell. That Sunday there were 18 persons taken in, about half by letter and the rest by confession. This church is called "Union Presbyterian" because its membership is made up of people of about a dozen denominations. It is a mission church and is working on the principle of less denominations and more members. This minister is a dandy one for the place.

February 25, 1914

I wish you could see the sunrise preliminaries that filled the eastern sky a few minutes ago. The sky looked like the window display for some gorgeous jeweled fan. At the place where the sun will appear in a little while there was spread a great pink fan of thin cloud radiating from the central point at the horizon. On either side of this were thin streamers of pink tulle, draped against a background of sky-blue-pink velvet. On the lefthand side near the front was a snow-covered mountain whose snow was like a heap of pearls. The other mountains in the foreground were covered with the sky-blue-pink velvet. Floating against the velvet background like suspended fairies were little irregular masses of gold-tipped pink cloud.

February 26, 1914

If it isn't too much trouble, I wish you would save my letters for future reference. I haven't time to keep a diary since I am running a dairy and a house, but I would like to have some record of what we are doing. If you could put the sheets in one of those manila files (the fifteen cent kind at Bowles) they could be easily kept. Maybe Pater could find time to stick the letters in after they have been read. I'd be much obliged if you could.

Yesterday we were honored with a call from the minister and his wife. They and the deacons and elders were invited to Werts for dinner, and they came an hour early and visited here. The lady was muchly surprised at our house. "Why," she exclaimed, "you have a *modern* house." People seem to think that kitchen sinks and washstands and bathtubs belong with city streets and sewer systems and the like. They don't seem to realize that a sink will go wherever you put it. I was much interested in a report the minister gave of a meeting he had just attended at Denver where the question of over-churching was considered. The Methodists want to come into Powell, and there really is not a place for them. There are now an Episcopal and a Baptist church, very small, and the Union Presbyterian, which takes in all sorts of denominations — people of twelve denominations now belong. This church is quite large for a town of 400 people. Sunday before last there were 175 people at the morning service and over 200 at the evening. The church is doing the work, without question. It is a mission station, as half the money comes from the home mission board and half is raised locally. There is a community called Ralston some miles west of Powell where there is a little Methodist church supplied always with circuit rider preachers. This church is not able to keep a minister, and they seem to think that if they can get a start in Powell they can keep their denomination going. The strange thing is that the former Methodists who now belong to the Pres. church do not want the Meth. church to come into Powell, and say whether it does or does not they will stay where they are.

February 27, 1914

I have discovered that John has just loads and loads of nice tissue paper that the wax foundation for the comb honey comes packed in. As the foundation is clean and no doubt packed by machinery without hands touching it, this paper is better than all the paper napkins you can buy. Some of it is pure white, some is straw color, in sheets about 8 x 16. I cut them in half, and keep a bunch hanging behind the range all the time. When I have a greasy pan, I just wipe it out with the paper and put the paper in the stove. If I want to set a pan on the kitchen table, out comes a piece of the paper to set it on. If the lamp chimney gets smoked, wiping out the smoked place with the paper saves the lamp cloth. I use it a score of times every day. We also use it for toilet paper, for shaving paper, for packing paper, and almost everything else you could think of. The paper has on it the faint impression of the hexagonal wax cell foundation and has the most fragrant and delicate odor of the wax. If anything spills and burns on the stove, wiping it up with this paper kills the unpleasant odor and substitutes for it the sweet wax smell. I tell you, this is a find. We can't run out of it for there is a box here now enough to last a year, and the new supply will be here in a few weeks.

We got a load of coal yesterday from the mine. One of the neighbors hauled it for honey. Coal here comes rather dear, counting the hauling. It costs two dollars and a half a ton at the mine, and the hauling about three dollars a ton. We could get coal for five dollars at the cars at Garland, but it would not be worth fifty cents a ton for John to have to haul it, and besides, the miner will take honey in payment for the coal and the man who hauls it likewise takes honey for his work. I was amused to think we can get a load of coal for a can of honey. The load we just got weighed 4800 lbs., — 2.4 tons. That cost just six dollars, or what a can of honey is worth.

March 1, 1914

I who am about to step over the milestone of another year — my 30th — salute you. One day last week when we were making plans for the work for the next couple weeks John mentioned tomorrow, Monday, and said that was a holiday and we'd best not count anything for that day. I cudgelled my brain for what national holiday it might be, and finally had to ask what day it might be. Of course I knew all the time it was my birthday, but you see I had never before been where I was of so much importance I determined the days. We have been alone this afternoon and evening, and we are both selfish enough to think it feels good. We have had so much company the last couple weeks that we are glad to be alone a little.

I must tell you about something that happened this morning at church. In the interval between Sunday school and church, Mrs. Werts introduced me to some of the ladies I had not yet met. Among them was a rather dignified one who sings in the choir. I was standing close beside Mrs. Werts, and as I put out my hand to shake hands with the lady being introduced, in some way the fur tail of Mrs. Werts' fur collar got in the way and got out ahead of my hand. I don't know whether I pushed it or whether Mrs. Werts did. At any rate, the first thing I knew the dignified lady was shaking the fur tail instead of my hand. Naturally I was tickled, and I am sure I giggled as I said I was glad to meet her. It was really funny to see her grip that tail. I wonder what sort of a fish, flesh or fowl she thought I was when she got hold of that.

Tonight I make my debut in Wyoming society. I have put my hair up again and hope to look not quite a fright. I shall wear my blue silk waist and blue serge suit. The party is a surprise farewell party for the Dows.

Tomorrow night is the meeting of the Farmer's Union, a national cooperative association we ought to get into. The local branch is only a few months old. This union was organized in the South by the farmers of a district to look after the advantageous disposal of their cotton crop. It proved of value and grew. At present almost all the southern and western states have state headquarters for the various branch unions, and all together a good deal of influence is wielded over the markets. The main thing is that what the union does is to bring the buyer from one district into direct touch with the seller in another, and thus dispense with a middleman's or commission man's fee. Then, too, it brings the farmers of a community into working harmony with each other, and that is worth a good deal. The husband's membership includes the wife, and there is always a social part of the evening. The order is a secret one, but not as secret as a fraternal organization. Each meeting night there is a regular program dealing with matters of interest and including papers on local problems by the members, as well as interesting subjects of current events in general and more or less literary programs added. Music is also used whenever securable. Wednesday afternoon is the fortnightly meeting of the Ladies Aid. I have meant each time to go, and think I shall really have to this time or people will think I am just a talker. They have invited me so many times and with such special invitations I must really appear. If we go to the party tonight, the Dow's sale tomorrow and Union tomorrow night, and I go to the Aid Wednesday, we'll sure make a gadding week of this.

I found out yesterday morning how high the farther mountains are. About an hour after sunup yesterday morning the eastern sky was filled with clouds at least a third of the way up. The sunlight did not come through at all. To the west and the north the near mountains, which are pretty big, were in the shadow. But behind these the far mountains stood out in the full bright sunlight. You wouldn't think they were so much taller just to look at them, for the near mountains stand up higher in appearance. But the far ones are so far that they are really lots taller than they look. Yesterday the light showed right to light up the vast snow fields that lie on the slopes of some of the mountains. There are places where you can see from here what looks like twenty or thirty mile stretches of unbroken snowfields. They are lovely to look at. When the east was all dark and cloudy yesterday morning the north and west were the most beautiful sky-blue-pink, with light golden clouds sailing airily across the blue—just little bits of cloud. The clouds in the east were so low that the sun just shone right over them to the mountains.

March 5, 1914

We went to the Dow's sale yesterday, and it was surely interesting, especially in a new country. There were about a hundred and fifty people there, about one third of them women. I think a lot of the women came just to have some place to go where there would be other women. I met quite a number of the neighbor women I have been wanting to know. There was one woman there whom Mrs. Pease said could do as much work as a man in any kind of farm work. You'd never guess it from seeing her. She sat at the sale the other day crocheting a most elaborate pattern macrame doiley, and looked as domestic as anything you could think of. She had an awful lot of sense when it came to doing housework, as was very evident when we helped get the lunch ready.

The way they serve lunch here is interesting to me. They put each portion in a paper sack and then a man just grabs a sack and has it all at once. The articles included sandwiches on buns, cheese, ginger snaps, and coffee. The coffee was in a washboiler, and each man was supposed to bring his own cup. The auctioneer brought about fifty tin cups. I thought the lunch was pretty small, for each sack had in it only one sand-

wich, a piece of cheese, and four or five little ginger snaps. I ate
two sandwiches myself, but no cookies or cheese. How a live,
hungry man felt when he got on the outside of one bun was a
debatable question with me. Of course when there are so
many people it is a big expense to provide eats. As it was I
guess the things cost ten dollars or more. There really was an
awful lot to eat, but there were so many people to eat it. One
of the store men from Powell had a stand set up where he sold
candy and cigars. If anybody couldn't stand his hunger, he
could patronize that.

Things sell extremely well at sales here — too well, in fact.
John wanted to get a garden wheel hoe, but when the price ran
up to nearly the market price of the article new, he backed out.
The cattle always sell well. Mr. Dow's cattle were very good,
nearly all of them purebred Jerseys, though not registered as
yet. The year-old heifers sold for prices ranging around seventy
dollars. The cows sold from eighty to a hundred dollars. He
did not sell any horses but bought some more to take back to
Illinois. The household stuff sold extremely well. A little
rocking chair sold for eighty cents. The kitchen range, which
originally was a very good stove, worth about forty dollars new,
but now in rather a dilapidated condition, sold for $22.50. I'd
lots rather have our range than that one, and ours didn't cost
any more than that price. The heating stove is in good condition. It was worth about twenty-five new, and sold for $20.25.
The man who is moving in bought both these. I guess he paid
a little more on that account than he otherwise would have,
and yet Mrs. Dow told me the night before she hoped the two
stoves would bring in at least forty dollars. One thing didn't
sell very well, and that was the surrey. It is in good condition,
a double seated surrey with curtains. It brought only about
seventy dollars.

Yesterday afternoon I went to the Ladies Aid meeting at
Powell. I have been wanting to go, in order to get acquainted
with some of the women of the church. I won't feel so stranded
when I know more people. I found that the joining fee was a
quarter and that the dues each time you attend are ten cents.

This pays running expenses and the lunch that is served each time. All the society makes is then on hand to be used for their work. They do a good deal here, as the church is not yet self supporting. At present they are paying for having the church tinted and decorated. They do a lot of sewing. The market for aprons is very good among the women of the government reclamation service. They usually buy all that the Aid can make. Yesterday there was also a quilt on hand to quilt and a table cloth to hemstitch. I quilted. The refreshments were peanut sandwiches, escalloped corn, pickles, and coffee. There is a fine for serving more than three articles, evidently not counting the drink. Two or three members are the hostesses each time, even though the meeting is held in the church basement. They prepare the eats. The basement is a fine place to have the meeting, as there is plenty of room and light for all sorts of work, and a kitchen and supply of dishes for serving. Most of the houses are so small around here that it is almost impossible to have a crowd and room enough to put up a quilt. I enjoyed myself very much. The meetings are fortnightly. I am going to the Garland Aid meeting Friday afternoon with Mrs. Pease. I want to go to this society too, as the members are closer neighbors. It really is a neighborhood society, only instead of calling itself that or a woman's club or a sewing club, it is called the Aid of the Garland church. Most of the Presbyterian women who live around here go to this Aid too. The way people pay little attention to denominational lines out here is lovely. In the Presbyterian Aid meeting yesterday I sat next to a woman who goes to the Episcopal church. The women have a missionary society and study class. Last time it met at the home of one of the women of the Baptist church.

March 14, 1914

We had the greatest day yesterday. How we wished you could have been along. We left here about half past eight in the morning, when the air was a little chilly but not at all unpleasant. We went in the big wagon, but as the wagon is a spring wagon, with springs under the body as well as under the seat, it is really more comfortable riding than a buggy which has the springs only under the body and none under the seat. First we drove to Blackburns, down on the Shoshone River, about six or eight miles from here. Part of the way we followed a trail over the real desert, where nothing but sage brush of different kinds grows. Here and there you could see the skeleton of a coyote or lamb or prairie dog that the coyotes had picked clean and the sun had bleached as white as snow.

We reached Blackburns about ten o'clock. Mrs. B. is as typically English as Mr. B. She also drops her h's in the most adorable manner. " 'Iram is my only son," she said, as a great tall, mischievous looking chap came in. " 'Iram, this is Mrs. 'Endricks." She flattens her a's and draws out her i's and puts her h's where they do not belong. I love to hear her talk. She is a rather short, stout woman, with the typical English expression and round face. She and Mr. B. were both in the cotton mills in England before they came to this country. He was an overseer and she was a spinner. He went into the mills when he was eight years old. He did not know his letters till he was nineteen, and an overseer in the factory. Now he does quite a bit of business for the Mormons. He is an important officer in the church, keeps records, and does the work of a notary and is a surveyor. He writes wills and contracts and does a lot of things of that sort — even to divorce papers.

We had a good dinner, of course. We had real roast beef, only it was more veal than beef. At all events it is the first meat that we have had since we have been here that was really good.

Well, to proceed with my tale of yesterday. The real reason for our making the trip was to look after the bees in the yard near Byron on Mr. Nauser's place. After dinner we started out to go to Nauser's. This Mr. Nauser is a Swiss who talks German and fairly shakes with delight if anybody will talk German to him. He is getting to be a rather old man and is not able to do much farming. Fortunately for him his farm is in the gas and oil region and he now has his farm leased to an oil company for $400 a year, with the prospects of getting a good well on it, and therefore enough to live on the rest of his life. On the way from Blackburns to Nausers we again followed a sort of trail, as the main road was some distance away. We had to ford a number of creeks and ditches running into the Shoshone. One place where the creek was pretty wide we saw, when we got to the shore, that the ice was broken in the middle. There was water under the ice, but as John knew, or thought he knew, that the creek was shallow, we drove right on. When we got out in about the middle, the horses went through the ice, as we expected, but as we did not expect, they went in almost to their bodies. Of course they gave a lunge and swam a stroke, and got up on the ice again. The wagon gave a plunge after them, then a lurch, and the front right wheel went down through the ice as far as the hub. The other wheels were on top of the ice. Naturally that made the wagon stand at a rather odd angle. The horses stopped when the wheel caught on the ice, and for a minute we thought maybe we would get a plunge bath in the creek.

As fast as I could I climbed out over the front wheel on my side and John did likewise on his, after he had helped me clear of the wagon. The ice when we stepped on it was mushy, and I thought once I was going through myself. I hustled for the shore, and then when I found I had not gone through I promptly went back and we considered how to get the wagon out. Well, we found a pole some little distance down stream, with which John broke the ice for six inches or so ahead of the submerged wheel, until he reached the solid ice. Then we coaxed the horses several times till they pulled hard enough in spite of the bumps the wheel encountered to get the front wheel out. The back wheels then went in but they were not so hard to pull out. After the wagon was on the opposite bank, John quieted the horses and soon we were driving merrily on with the memory of a rather exciting and enjoyable ten minutes. The only unfortunate result was that John skinned one of his knuckles using the pole.

John has had several laughs at the incident and something connected with it. Mr. Nauser being German, John suggested when we planned to go there that we take him a bund kuchen. After the ice incident yesterday, John suddenly began to laugh, and when I wanted to know what was funny, he said he knew we were taking Mr. Nauser a bund kuchen to break the ice but that he did not know it would be so powerful as to make the wagon break through the ice. I told him I knew the kuchen wasn't quite so good as some I had made, but I did not think it was that heavy.

The kuchen did break the ice, all right. John invited Mr. Nauser to come and take dinner with us some time, any time, when he makes his weekly trip to Garland. He has not yet come. We found yesterday — not in so many words, of course — that the gentleman was rather afraid to come because he heard I was a university teacher and he did not know how I would take all the neighbors. Well, after I gave him the bund kuchen and talked German to him a little while, there was no more ice, and he fell all over himself accepting the invitation to dinner the next time he comes to Garland, which will be Monday. He did come out far enough then to say that he thought maybe we were fine folks and would not want an old bachelor in our new house. I assured him that we were just folks and told him that I had been saving a real German wurst made by a German butcher to cook into Kartoffel bruh when he came here to dinner. He was quite moved by the statement, and I guess he won't think anything more about highbrow.

I had my first experience in a bee yard yesterday. I put on a veil and sleeves and went right in with John. I puffed the smoker most of the time for him. We were fairly surrounded by bees. I thought I would be a little scared, but I was not at all. I think I shall be able to go right in the yard any time, provided I feel sure that the veil I have on is whole. Mr. Nauser was surprised that I should go into the yard. "You ought not take a nice young woman like that in among the bees," he admonished John. John assured him that I wanted to go. When we came out I told the man I had not been hurt or frightened, and he said he guessed that John told the bees I was his wife, and that they must not hurt me. He says the bees always do what John tells them. They know John and mind him. Mr. N. speaks the cutest German-English you ever heard. His face is long and striking—in fact, the line from his forehead to his chin down the nose is very striking, being concave on the left side, due to the fact that it was once struck by a mule and knocked out of plumb. He has the reputation of being the homeliest man on the Flat.* I don't think he is so homely. He has a strong face full of interesting character. A little irregularity adds interest to a person's appearance.

I made what I think is a very important discovery while we were at Nauser's. His place is along the river. Right past the bee-yard a creek whose banks are lined with great cotton-woods flows into the river. These tall trees, some of them fifty feet high, are covered in some cases to the tops with a vine that if my eyes do not deceive me is a clematis paniculata, the white kind that grows on the campus walls. The flower pods and feathery fluff, the leaves, the stems, the tendrils, the main stems, everything is as nearly clematis as anything I have ever seen. If that is the case, and the clematis grows wild there at the river where the temperature is always about five degrees lower in the winter than here on the hill, maybe we won't have clematis vines, one every fence post.

I wish you could have been along yesterday to see the different kinds of plants we saw. I asked about forty questions a minute. The day was so warm after the sun came out well and the wind died down, that you could not have found a finer day in summer for a trip. I can't begin to tell you how much I enjoyed the whole day. It was like a picnic from beginning to end. If only you could have been along, we would have had nothing to wish for. We took our gun along and scared up several rabbits, but could not get a shot. We saw prairie dogs basking in the sun at their burrows. We passed cliffs standing straight up in the plains a hundred feet, with all sorts of queer formations resembling all sorts of animals and persons; and one place we saw an eagle's nest sixty or so feet high on a cliff.

---

*The irrigated valley is often called "The Flat."

When we got home your letter was here. We were so glad, as we had not heard from you for several days. When we opened it up and found that two of you are actually coming this summer, we just "yumped for yoy." It took us both to hold each other by the time we got through with the letter. Honestly, I can't tell you how I have been going on since your letter got here. The two of you together can have so much fun on the way and can have so much more fun here. O dear, there are so many things I could think of that we shall do that I don't know how to stop or to go ahead.

John put out a box of ground wheat for the bees to work on and a little while ago he called me to go with him to see them. There were thousands and thousands of them, just digging into that feed as fast as they could load their legs and pollen baskets. They made a hum you can hear for half a block. I tell you, they mean business. We sat and watched them quite a while and saw all sorts of things in their industry — finished house, automobile, etc. The bees are certainly in fine condition. I am surprised at myself for not being afraid. We sat within two feet of the box and the bees were all around us. We had no veils, either. First thing you know I'll be training them to eat out of my hand! I guess not!

Hurrah! Todie and Bady are tuming to see us.

March 15, 1914

The team of horses we have will give out in another year. Then we think we'll get an auto, for it will be so much better. For instance, take the trip we made Friday. It is a good two hours' drive to the bee yard at Nauser's. That means four hours of driving each day that John goes there, or a half day's work spent on the road. This trip must be made once a week during the season, and sometimes oftener. With an auto the trip could be made in half an hour or three quarters at the most. When you think of the time spent on the road each day you realize that John could attend to almost twice as many bees if he could use half or three fourths of that time in the yards. He could also place yards at greater distances, and thus get better pasture.

Ever since we have been here we have been hoping one of you at least, if not more, would come out this summer to take with us a trip we have planned to the big reservoir and dam near Cody. It is about thirty miles to Cody and about seven beyond there to the dam. This reservoir supplies this whole section of the country with irrigating water. The reservoir is enormous—I haven't any idea how big—and the dam is likewise. The rocks rise sheer from the dam on one side to the height of 2,000 feet. It is a wonderful sight, we are told. We are planning to drive, taking about three days for the trip. Of course we could go on the train to Cody and get an auto or buggy to take us out but the trip overland will be so much more good fun. Think of sleeping in the wagon and of cooking your meals by the wayside on a fire that you make right there.

You ought to see how scrumptious our bookcase looks. It is all done except the typewriter door and swinging part. The shelves are six feet long, stained mission oak finish. On the top of the top shelf stands a small Venus de Milo in the center. On either side of that is one of our lovely candlesticks. Then near the right hand end, rather far back, is a small statue of the Three Graces, and at the lefthand end is a small vase—the one with two handles that used to be on the parlor shelf at home. The case is made in regular mission style, with the ends of the shelves run through the end pieces and fastened with pins of wood. On the top one of these—where the shelf comes through— there is just the right place to set that little statue of Cupid and Psyche. Just over the bookcase hangs the American authors from Aunt Lena; just to the left and coming down a little lower than the top shelf is the picture John's brother and wife gave us. On the north wall just to the right of the case is the Return from Labor—the brown picture I had of the man with the pitch fork and the girl with the basket over her head. On the north wall over the desk, on the other side of the window from that is Madame LeBrun and Daughter. On the east wall hangs the Dance of the Nymphs. On the south wall will be put one of the paintings from Florence. On the west wall where the light falls just right on it is the watercolor Edward gave us. This is to the left of the door. The door into the bedroom is near to the south wall. You ought to see how lovely the brown pictures look with the mission finish woodwork and bookcase and moulding. All the pictures are the sepia brown except the two watercolors in gold frames, which give just enough color to keep the room from being monotonous. Over the desk, low, hangs the brown Kansas Ag. calendar from Mary Harmon, and on the lefthand side of the desk at the back stands the tray from Johnstons. This also gives a little color. Really, the bookcase and the pictures look fine. We are quite proud of the room. It is all in keeping and the furniture all matches.

March 22, 1914

I am so glad you girls are coming out this summer to get acquainted with John. He is the biggest monkey. He is always saying funny and clever things. If I am about to get the better of him in an argument he is keen enough to say something nice about me, and of course I succumb. I got ahead of him the other day, though. We were talking about old maids and he said 25 was the dividing line. I said the age had been increased to 30 lately; he wanted to know who was the authority for the change. I asked who had been the authority for the old age of 25. He said he thought it was Antiquity. I said I believed then it was Miss Ann who had changed her mind recently and decided on the new age—anyway, how old is Ann? We are regular kids together. The silliest little thing will set us to giggling, just as we did at home. It really looks funny to see myself call him John in the letters. I hardly call him that once a week here. I usually call him Johnny, or some other youngster name. He usually calls me by a queer pronunciation of mamma, something like mah'-me.

Thereby hangs a tale. When he came out here three years ago, his little niece, then about three years old, was much concerned about his going away alone. It seemed awful to her to go away from home and mother. Finally she asked him very seriously without of course understanding the joke she was making, "Uncle John, aren't you going to take a mamma along with you when you go away?" Of course the folks teased him quite a lot about it and he enjoyed the joke himself. The queer pronunciation is the one she used. As a result of this joke he calls me Mah-me a good deal of the time, and I call him sonny or some other crazy name.

April 30, 1914

When we got to the beeyard today we looked into about fifteen colonies and were delighted with what we found. The majority of the colonies are in almost as good condition now as they were four weeks later than this last year. We think we can have a great crop this year, if the honey flow is what it usually is. The rains we have been having are fine in the promise of good honey flow. So that all around the outlook is fine — finer than we expected even, and better than either year John has been here. It would be great if we could have a bumper crop this year, for it would be so lovely if we could get right away a good many of the things we want — the house, auto, new shop, increased business facilities. Of course the thing we shall do in any event is to build up the business first, for there is where the money will be giving returns right along. The bees are in such good condition we did not disturb many of them. And O, the new brood we did find. Three frames of brood at this time of year is considered good. Every one that had a queen had at least three frames, and most of them had from four to six. Only one colony was without a queen. There has been practically no winter loss this year. What loss there is is due to loss of queen or drifting away to another hive. The total loss will not be over ten percent from the present outlook. Last year it was about 33% and the year before that about 50% of entirely lost colonies with the rest so weakened that the loss really amounted to about 75%. That was due to about six weeks of weather in which the thermometer went to zero or lower every night. So you see we feel pretty good.

After we finished looking into the hives we wanted to inspect, John finished up a little more work in the yard while I got dinner. He had set up the stove before and it works fine. You don't get your cooking vessels black from smoke when you use the sheet iron on the bolt legs. I french-fried potatoes, cooked coffee, and fried eggs. We also had store and home-made cheese, bread, butter, jelly, milk, canned peaches, and cake. It was a good dinner, I tell you. We sat on a box and used another box for a table. The place where we ate was a little clearing right on the river bank. The bank on which we were is quite steep, in fact almost perpendicular, about eight feet high. We sat facing the river, only a few feet from the edge of the bank. On the other side were farms and houses and on behind that the mountains. The river ran on to our left, on into Montana. Behind and around us were tall cottonwoods and among them a thicket of rosebushes and buffalo berry bushes, with paths leading through. When the roses get in bloom the place will be lovely. The river runs quite swiftly with a good deal of fall, and the music it makes is fine. I don't think I was ever happier in my life than when with all that beautiful scenery around us we sat down side by side on the box with the simple dinner before us, and bowed our heads as John said grace. The grace seemed so fitting in a place like that. Uncon-sciously he lowered his voice in keeping with the quiet beauty of the place.

We saw a bird new to me except by name—the magpie—which is very common along the river. It is nearly as large as a crow, black with a white band about two or three inches wide around its breast and over its back just at the shoulders. The wings have a white band in them, too. It is a most striking bird.

The tail is very long — six or eight inches, very straight and slender. The meadows are full of meadowlarks and red-winged blackbirds. They look very natural to me.

You ought to see the bouquet that John brought me yesterday morning. No, it isn't violets. I haven't seen any here and don't know yet whether they grow around here, though I suspect they do in the mountains. This flower is beautiful, about the color of the everlasting sweet pea, and also the same shape, but smaller. The foliage is just like a locust foliage and the blossom is like the locust blossom. But this is a low bush and not a tree or even a shrub. The foliage is a lovely dusty sage green in color that blends beautifully with the pink of the blossom. The plant is not as good as the flower appears; in fact, the flower is the best part, for the plant is the loco weed, on which horses "go loco." Even if the weed has such bad habits it is certainly lovely for a bouquet.

We have been working pretty steadily today, making follower boards for in the supers. The follower board is a board that is put in on either side of the comb honey sections. If you put the sections clear to the edge of the hive, the bees will not fill out the sections clear to the edge and you will have a lot of culls. If you keep the sections from touching the side of the hive, the bees will fill them out. These follower boards are made of a strip of 5/8 inch dressed lumber 17 inches long and about 4¼ inches wide. On this you lay at each end and in the center a strip of wood as long as the other strip is wide, and about 3/4" wide. On top of this you lay a thin board, 17" long and about the same width as the bottom board and only about 1/8 inch thick. On this you lay three more little strips, at each end and in the center immediately on top of the other little strips under the thin board. Then you drive two nails in each end through the boards and the strips, at each end and in the center immediately on top of the other little strips under the thin board. Then you drive two nails in each end through the boards and the strips, and one nail in the center. Then you turn the thing over and clinch the nails. John and I made about 700 of these today. We have 750 of this kind to make, and then 750 more just like them except that these will have another thin board on top of the second layer of little strips. We can make them at the rate of about one a minute, or ten in eleven minutes. Each of us working separately can do that. I can make them as fast as John can—in fact, every time we ran races I beat him. Of course I "hate to go above him," but he said he wouldn't feel bad if I made three to his one. His "endless" finger is always a nuisance to him when he is nailing, as it makes it difficult to pick up nails. I don't believe anybody can turn these out much faster than we did today. To lay together eight pieces of material, start in five long nails, lift the thing out of a frame, drive the nails clear through, turn the thing over and clinch the nails, is somewhat of an operation to perform in one minute.

May 14, 1914

I have been initiated now. Yesterday at the bee yard at the river I got about ten stings. The stings do not bother more than a few minutes. At first there is a sharp scratch, like that of a pin. It doesn't hurt very much. Then the poison gets into working order and for about two minutes there is real pain. Then it is all over. The first sting I got was right under my wedding ring. I told John the bees wanted to remind me first of all that the ring was the cause of all future stings. This sting developed a white spot that lasted for an hour or so. The funny thing is that of all the stings I got, only one got sore. Just why it should have got sore is strange. It was in the middle of the back of my right hand. Ten stings for 106 hives wasn't bad, was it? This morning we went through 36 hives and I got only one sting. The only place I can get stung is on the hands. The bee veil covers my whole head and neck and arms way down on the hand. I have been wearing my bloomers as an under petticoat

and am not afraid of sitting on the bees as we work. I am
going to make me a pair of muslin bloomers, as the heavy ones
are too hot. It is a good deal of comfort to know that bees can't
crawl up your legs while you are working. The bee veils are
made of screen wire and muslin. A piece of screen wire about
ten inches wide and long enough to make a circle about twelve
inches in diameter is fastened together in circular form. In one
end is sewed a piece of muslin for the top. Out of muslin I
made jackets — each one like the top half of a shirt except that
the collar is missing and the shoulder seam is much longer and
less slanted, and the sleeves are about ten inches long. The top
edge of this jacket affair is then sewed to the lower edge of the
wire cloth circle, then a piece of elastic and tape is fastened
inside to the top to make the thing sit straight on your head. You
put the "veil" on as you would a shirt — over your head. It
differs from a shirt in that it has a "hat" on the top instead of a
collar opening. The men put the shirt in their overalls; I tie an
apron over mine to keep the bees from getting up from the
bottom. Then you have an extra pair of sleeves about long
enough to reach halfway from the elbow to the shoulder, with
elastic in the top and two rows of it at the wrist. These sleeves
hold the short sleeves of the veil shirt from slipping up and also
protect the forearm and wrist. Your hands are bare. A person
makes an imposing sight done up in one of these veils.

May 17, 1914

We finished going through the bees Friday and have now a
complete record of the way they are at present. We are
devising a system by which we can keep the record of each
colony straight through the summer by setting the hives in rows.
We expect to have 260 colonies in shape to do good work as
soon as the honey flow begins. If the season is as good as the
first two out here, it is possible to produce a three thousand
dollar crop this year. Of course there must be a good honey
flow all season, as there was the first years, and no drop in
price as there was last year. We have every reason to believe,
however, that the big crop is possible and probable.

John came home last night all puffed up. The local editor had just told him that he looked fifty per cent better since he is married. I told him that I thought that twenty-five percent of the fifty was due to — and there I paused to give emphasis. Before I could go on, Johnny appeared in the door of the living room and pointed to his collar and tie, thus saving me the trouble of saying the words. Then I went on to say that the other seventy-five percent was due to — and again his face appeared at the door and he pointed to his freshly shaven face, saying "Every day." I told him he didn't need a wife to tell him what to do; all he needed a wife for was to jack him up once in a while into doing what he knew. We had a lot of fun over the affair. About half an hour later when we sat down to read, about the first thing I bumped into in the Northwest Farmstead was an article warning girls not to marry old bachelors, as the bachelors would not dress neatly or take any pains with their appearance. I giggled as I read it and then passed it over to Johnny. Of course I teased him a lot about the article before I explained that what I meant was that the writer of the article had better just speak for herself, John, and not for everybody.

May 19, 1914

There is a bird here that I should like to know the name of. It is about as big as a cat bird, but is not the same shape or color. It is deep black with white shoulders and a white rim about its tail.* The tail is not long like a catbird's. In song this bird is more like a cat bird or mocking bird, too; it flies and sings on the wing with darts and dashes and swoops the way a mocker does. It has the wide variety of songs. There is one that sits on our fence posts and sings for fare you well. It will fly up in the air and then dart down to the post again, singing all the time. They are here in great numbers. I wish we had a good bird manual. If you get a chance to pick up one second hand at the book store don't miss the chance.

---

*The bird is a Lark Bunting.

We are going to have the mostest fun tomorrow. We are going down to the river beeyard tomorrow afternoon, work that afternoon, camp out all night and work the next day. Won't it be fun to camp out over night and sleep in the wagon? What we are going for is to work at night moving the bees. They are now in winter quarters, three or four hives together packed with earth and straw up to the top. We are going to take the packing away tomorrow afternoon and then at night move them out, one in a place. We are also moving them about a quarter of a mile farther west than the place where they were all winter. This moving has to be done at night while the bees are all in the hives, or some of them would be lost when they came back home if they happened to be out when the moving was done. Then early in the morning, just as soon as it is light, you have to go to each hive and rap on it till some bees come out. If you do that, they will know where they are and not get lost after they leave the hive. If you don't call their attention to the change, they will be likely to dart away from the hive when they leave during the day, without noticing that the hive is in a different location. You don't have to call out a great many bees—just a few will do. Honest, I'm not fooling you. If you don't go around and rap on the hives, the bees will get lost during the day. Evidently the bees who do come out notice the change, and then they set the guards to telling all the bees as they leave that the place is a new one.

The buffalo gnats have arrived. If you don't know what they are you won't be here long before you find out. They are about as big as a pin point and can bite as hard as a Jersey mosquito. They are really the worst nuisance here in the summer time. They are not so bad right now, but they are a bother. You girls want to be sure to bring along a good chiffon veil, or something like that. You will need it especially if we take any trips.

We had our first spring supper last night. I went to Powell in the afternoon to look after some business. I got some asparagus at the store. On the way home I got out of the buggy to get some sunflower plants that were growing along the roadside and found a big, fine dandelion bush on the ditch bank. The leaves were at least ten inches long and were blanched a fourth of the way up. There were buds on the bush, deep down in the heart, but no blossoms. The buds were white and tender. That bush was as big around at the bottom as my wrist. It made a great dish of salad. I made mayonnaise and used green onion and a boiled egg with it. My, but it did taste good. Besides the asparagus and salad we had bacon and browned potatoes, fresh bread and canned plums. Today for dinner we had a slow steak and more asparagus. I got one bunch of asparagus, ten cents. There were about forty-five stalks in the bunch, nice thick stalks.

May 22, 1914

I am such a swell person today I don't know whether or not I'll write a letter. I am sure I would not write with a pen. I would not consider that for a minute. I may not even use the typewriter. I guess what I'll have to get is a secretary. You see, it is like this: When we were at the bee yard at the river we put numbers on the hives before we moved them so we would know which was which when we got them scattered out in the summer yard. The bees evidently didn't like their houses numbered; they evidently thought that would be too much like the numbers on the cells in a prison. So one bee did what a Frenchman would have done to avenge the insult to her house. She left her card in my hand. She was not in a very good humor, naturally. Evidently she thought she was saving the honor of the house. The place where she got me was on the back of the hand. Now I do not know what the difference is between the front of my hand and the fingers and the back of the hand, but I do know that last week I got ten stings, nine of them on the fingers or thumbs, and one on the back of the hand, and that one, the one on the back of the hand, got sore, while the nine in the fingers did not. This time the sting did more than make a sore place. It made the hand swell and swell and swell (like Mr. Finney's turnip) as long as it was able. The hand swelled up to the wrist and to the tips of the fingers. I couldn't get my ring as far as the middle of the finger, much less over the knuckle. The back of the hand was worst; from palm to back it must have been over two inches thick. Naturally it did not feel particularly comfortable. When we were at the river I kept a plaster of mud on it; that helped to take out the fever. When we got home I bathed it in hot water with vinegar in it. That helped. Then I dosed it well several times with McLean's Liniment. I also put some Mentholatum on it.

John says he won't let me go in the yard with him if the stings are going to hurt me like that. Poor John had to wash and wipe all the dishes last night and this morning, and I am very much afraid he will have to help again this noon.

We had a great time camping. All my life I have wanted to sleep outdoors in a wagon, and at last I got to. Of course no one would try to argue that a wagon bed is as soft as a regular bed, even with hay and carpet to sleep on, but then in a regular bed you can't be lulled to sleep by the sound of the water in the Shoshone River or peep up through a hole in the canvas of the roof and see trees and clouds. Nor can you lie awake in the morning and hear dozens of birds singing within a few feet of you. I had a great time. To add to the interest of the occasion it rained, and we could hear the raindrops patter patter on the canvas over us. We put the high sideboards on the wagon and put the canvas on top of that. That gave us a place like a tent. Then when we got up in the morning, to be out in the open with the blue sky and the white clouds and the green trees was wonderful. John got up about four o'clock and went to work moving bees before they should be stirring. I was awake but did not get up. I took another nap and got up about six. While I was building the fire to get breakfast, Mr. Nauser came down. I had just got some chips from under a log—dry chips—to start the fire. He wanted to know if I had any coal oil and fairly insisted on getting me some to start the fire with. I told him I did not need any. He said he knew he could not build a fire like that and what he couldn't do no one else could. I said nothing, but struck a match and put it to my fire, then went about making biscuits. The fire just went merrily on and burned right along. He looked in amazement at the fire there and said, "Well, it might do that for a young lady, but it wouldn't burn like that for an old man."

Things go on about the same as usual. Of course nothing very important happens, but something is happening all the time.

It is now nearly eight o'clock in the morning. I have cooked breakfast, milked the fresh cow, fed the calf, fed the little chickens, and washed the breakfast dishes. I do not usually milk, but John has a cut on one of his fingers that makes it hard for him to milk. I want to do a number of things this morning, chief among which are washing my hair and trimming my hat and folding about a thousand sections for John, not to mention getting dinner on time, as usual. I don't know what you'll say when I say that I haven't washed my hair since I have been here. I have been meaning to a number of times, but something always came up to interfere. The hairs don't really look as if they needed washing, for they are as fluffy and not a bit greasy, but I am sure the scalp ought to be washed. At first I was afraid to wash my hair for fear the water might hurt them, but John's hair gets as fluffy and nice so I don't see why mine shouldn't. He does the funniest thing—he washes his hair with the soap paste (like Skiddoo). When he did it the first time I was horrified, but it worked beautifully. He was troubled with dandruff and this took it all out and left the hair as pretty and shiny and fluffy as could be. Of course I don't intend to emulate his example with my hair for I don't know what might happen if I got my long hair mixed with the paste, but it surely works with short hair.

The hat I am going to trim is the straw turban with the white lace and black velvet edging. Almost everybody around has been wearing straw hats for ages, but I haven't as my green velvet goes best with my white serge, and my little gray hat with the cerise under the brim with my gray suit and the silk waist with the cerise ribbon on the front. But as I am going to the Ladies' Aid this afternoon, I decided I'd better have a straw hat or they'd be taking up a collection to get me one. It *is* almost June.

June 3, 1914

Iam going to pay some social calls this afternoon and clear up the calls I owe. Thursday we are going to make two more, both of us together, and then we'll be straight with the world on calls. I'd rather stay at home this afternoon and do some work that ought to be done here—in the garden, for instance— but the calls must be paid. Mrs. Pease scolded me the other day when we went to Aid about staying at home all the time. She said that if I kept up the way I'd started by the time I was married as long as she was (14 years) I'd never get out of the house. I just told her that if she had been living the rushed life I have for the past ten years she would count it a real luxury to be able to stay at home. I guess maybe I'll get over the feeling after a while, but as I said the other day, it is fun not to have to go places if you don't really want to.

We are still thinking of things for you to bring. This time it is a summer laprobe for the buggy. We don't care for a real "boughten" laprobe with a bunch of flowers done on it in pink and green crewels, but anything that will serve the purpose. It ought to be tan or dust color, I think. There is one job we are leaving till the girls come. Who speaks up for painting the wagon? Or will you do the dishes, etc., while I paint? I have finally succeeded in getting the buggy painted, though the paint that was supposed to make two coats had to be hurried to make one. I have put new imitation leather on the back of the seat and will cover the cushion as soon as I can find time.

June 9, 1914

The idea of telling me to keep cool when you say you are coming a full week before we thought you could get away! I have been dancing jigs and all other sorts of performances since your letter came yesterday. We have been watching the flowers along the road and over the prairie and have been wishing you would get here to see the best of them. Just yesterday morning we discovered a great many new kinds, prettier than any we had before found. We did so hope the flowers would not be out of bloom by the time you got here. Now we are sure you will get here in time to see the best. The cactus is just starting to bloom down near the river. The blossoms remind one of a water lily, only they are more cup-shaped and not so flat. The color is a clear yellow, changing into a pink-orange as the flower gets older.

We have an extra man working for us at present to get the work up to date. The bees need attention and it does not pay to let them go unattended now. Yesterday we found six swarms in the yard at the river and evidence that three more had already gone. As each swarm is worth five dollars, you can see that attention is the necessary thing. We prevent swarming by giving the colony so much room it does not feel the need of getting out into a new place, and also by killing the cells in which they are raising queens.

June 11, 1914

It keeps a fellow hustling here to get a variety to cook. We get very little fresh meat, maybe once a week, and maybe not more than once in two weeks. We have ham on hand, and salmon. I always have some kind of meat for dinner. Yesterday we had ham, potatoes, gravy, creamed cabbage, macaroni with tomato sauce, and rhubarb pudding. For supper we had fried potatoes and noodles with eggs and homemade cheese, with peaches and fresh rolls for dessert. Today we had salmon with mayonnaise, potatoes, gravy, butter beans, and salad, with oatmeal-bread pudding with plums in it. I forgot to say that yesterday we had lettuce also for dinner. I served it in individual dishes, putting the lettuce on my gold banded plates and having sliced hardboiled egg, onion, and mayonnaise on each serving. Today's salad was canned tomato on lettuce leaves, with chopped onion and mayonnaise. John said he had never tasted anything fixed like that and that it was awfully good.

Just as we were sitting down to dinner a heavy shower of rain came up—the water stood half an inch deep in the yard. It came just at the right time for us. We finally got the grass seed sown in the yard yesterday afternoon. I am so anxious to have a pretty yard. We have the natural situation all right. If the grass will only grow we can have one of the prettiest places in the country. At present we have seeded to grass only the part south and west of the house. Later, when we get the new shop built about a block east of the house and get the part of the old shop moved and the rest put at the side of the yard for a wash house, we'll have the rest of the yard seeded to grass. We are counting on having space then for a croquet ground in the back yard and room for any sort of game. Of course it will take a few years to get everything the way we want it, but we are sort o' making permanent plans right from the beginning.

The queen bees we have bought are beginning to arrive and we are glad of it because we need them. We have ordered 180 from the Conneaut Lake Bee Co. at Duncan Falls, Ohio. They are to arrive from ten to twenty-five at a time from now till the middle of July. Each queen comes in a separate box about two inches wide and an inch thick, and four inches long. The box is made by taking a block of wood the size mentioned. From one side three augur holes about an inch wide are bored three-fourths of the way through the block. From each end a hole about three-eighths inch is bored in to meet these other holes. Over the top and ends screen wire is nailed. The queen, with a few workers as escort, is put in the cage, and the hole at one end filled with queen cage candy, made by mixing honey and sugar till it is stiff. The workers feed the queen and take care of her. Each cage costs two cents to send by mail. Yesterday ten came and the day before that fifteen. We think we got very good rates, as we got the 100 for $75.

We are going to try this summer to rear some queens ourselves. A queen ought not be used more than two years, and it is often best to use a queen only one year. When rearing queens yourself you can rear them only in the strong colonies that have the best traits—gentleness, prolificness, large honey production, good color, etc. Then you can let only other good colonies produce drones for them to mate with, and unless you are too close to other beekeepers you can be pretty sure to have good queens. It is as necessary to have good queens as to have good poultry or good hogs for breeding purposes. In fact, the whole thing in bees depends on the queen.

June 22, 1914

Well, the girls didn't come this morning. We really did not expect them and did not go to meet them, but after I heard the train come in I kept my eye peeled down the road to be sure to see them if they should come walking out. I rather think they are leaving Denver this noon. In that case they will get into Billings about six o'clock tomorrow morning and can get out of Billings between seven and eight, arriving here at 11:01.

Don't worry about my doing a lot of work getting ready for the girls. One of the neighbors who was here a little while ago said when she heard the girls were coming, "O, then you will have plenty to do in the next week or so if you are expecting company." "Not much," I said, "I don't go to a lot of work for the girls. I know them too well and they know me too well for that." All I want is to have the house reasonably clean. I didn't give it much of a cleaning Saturday because I wanted to wait till today. I told John the other day when you said in your letter that I shouldn't work hard getting ready for the girls, "I'll wait till they get here and let them help."

June 25, 1914

The girls are here. I am so tickled I can hardly do anything straight, so if there are all sorts of mistakes in this letter you will know the reason why. Yesterday we got a card from them saying they couldn't get here till tomorrow if they stayed all night in Billings. So this morning we didn't meet the train. I kept a lookout down the road all right, but it happened that the people at Garland showed them the wrong road to come, and they came in the back way. John saw them coming down the east road and went to meet them and brought them to the back door, sneaking quietly into the living room where I was sitting sewing. It was about twelve o'clock. We were planning to have dinner about two, and here they walked in.

July 10, 1914

I am all alone. The girls are going to Yellowstone Park today (that is, if the train ever comes to take them.) I got back just a little while ago from taking them to the station at Powell. The train was an hour and a half late, so I didn't stay with them. It is now two o'clock and the train has not passed here yet. Of course they will be met at Cody no matter what time the train comes in, for there is but the one train a day and all the Park passengers have to come on that train.*

July 17, 1914

The girls are evidently having a better time in the Park even than they expected, for they are not yet back. They thought when they started out that they would be back today. The other day I got a letter from them saying that they thought they would be back Friday, as intended, but that they might not come till Saturday. They will have to come tomorrow, however, or stay over Sunday, for there is no Sunday train. I am glad they are having such a good time.

I guess the girls think it is strange for us not to be able always to get anything we want the way we used to do at home. Cora seemed to think it was dreadful that we felt we couldn't afford to get the stuff to develop the pictures we had in the camera. Well, it would have cost about a dollar to get everything I needed, and I decided it would be cheaper to send the

---

*Yellowstone Park tourists traveled from the end of the railroad line at Cody by horse-drawn bus the sixty miles to the park's east entrance and then around the circuit to the various scenic attractions, camping at the several Park Service lodges.

film back to Wiles and have a few prints made than to buy enough to do the work myself. It is a little different to have to count your money more carefully and to be more economical than we used to be, but we have never suffered for anything that we really needed or that made any real difference in our happiness. Out here no one has any great amount of ready money, and everybody is investing what he has. We feel that it is more to our benefit to invest whatever we can in the business and let a few other things go for a few years than to spend the money for other things now. After a while when the returns of the investment begin to come in we'll have all we want to spend for all sorts of things. It is quite different to live on a salary than to have a business of your own. When you are on a salary, a certain amount comes in at regular intervals, and you know just what to count on. But when you have a business of your own you may have a great deal of money on hand at one time and less than nothing at another. It depends on the demands of the business at any given time. In the long run you will probably come out better with your own business than with a salary, for all the profits are your own and you can increase the business whenever you have the opportunity. Of course if we were in a city we would have to do a great many things we don't have to out here in the country. When I see the way most folk around us are living and the kind of houses they are living in, and the way they are working to pay for their farms and build up their dairy herds and their implements, I feel that we are more than well off, which indeed we are. Very few people out here have such a business as we have. If things do not go wrong from now on, it is possible for us to get returns of more than two thousand dollars on this season's crop.

August 23, 1914

We have been very fortunate this year in getting nearly everything we need in trade for honey. We are getting apples from a Mormon at Byron, who will trade us all the fruit we want for honey. We shall get crab apples from him, big red ones or big yellow ones, also red plums and winter apples. We got 120 pounds of potatoes last week and shall get more later. They are the finest potatoes I ever saw. The price was two cents a pound. We are getting hay for honey, too. As our whole farm is in sweet clover and grain we do not have any alfalfa ourselves. The hay costs $6.50 a ton delivered. We are in hopes of making a trade later whereby we can get celery and cabbage and onions, and any other winter vegetables, for honey. We have nice salsify ourselves. Our onions are lovely, but we haven't enought to last us all winter.

We have an ad in the Powell paper now, not for honey to trade, but to sell. The ad advises people to can fruit with honey. It reads:

CHEAPER THAN SUGAR

Do your canning with honey. Use one half to two thirds as much honey as sugar. NEW CROP EXTRACTED HONEY now ready. Price 10 cents per pound. A book of recipes free with each sixty pound order.

JOHN HENDRICKS   POWELL, WYOMING

We have sent for some recipe books. They cost ten cents each in small quantities. We can get them for 4½ cents with our ad on the cover by getting as many as a hundred. We don't need that yet. We have also sent for a lot of folders on the use of honey, which contain some recipes. We shall give one to each purchaser of any amount. The larger ones we shall give only to those who buy sixty pounds. The sale around here for canning will be mainly extracted honey. We would rather sell the extracted locally and the comb honey by the carload. Of course we sell a good deal of the comb locally and trade a lot of both kinds.

We have been casing the comb honey the past few days and have about eighty cases ready. John has given me the position of grader and caser. I told him it was strange for me to be doing the expert work while he does the less important. He and Acy, the hired man, clean the sections and I grade and case. There are three grades: first, choice, and second. The first must weigh not less than 12½ ounces net, which means

13½ gross, must be white or amber in color, and must have no uncapped cells except in the row next to the wood. It must be firmly attached to the wood. The choice must weigh not less 11 ounces net, other specifications the same as first. The second grade must weigh not less than 10 ounces net and have not more than fifty uncapped cells on both sides. Most of the second class is much heavier than the minimum and goes in this class because of a few uncapped cells. Our honey is running splendidly. About eleven percent is second. The first runs 56%, the choice 32%. In casing, you use a case with glass in the front. The case holds 24 sections, in two layers of twelve each. In the bottom of the case you put a layer of paper and corrugated paper. This same protection goes between the layers and on top. Each separate section must be stamped with the net weight, in accordance with the new interstate commerce law. The exact weight does not have to be marked, but the "not less than. . . ." I have a scale that weighs by half ounces. I weigh each section and put it in the proper box. When the first layer of twelve is in a box, I stamp each of the twelve with a rubber stamp giving the minimum for that grade. This takes less than half a minute to do the twelve so you see the time for marking each section really scarcely counts. After you work a while you do not have to weigh nearly all of the sections. You get so you can tell by lifting the section whether it weighs less than 13½ or more. John does not like to do the grading, as it makes him tired to stand long at a time. Besides, he is so swift at the cleaning that he can do most of that. He can clean five cases an hour.

If the frost holds off three or four weeks yet we'll get a pretty good crop. The returns will not be as much as John hoped for early in the season, however, because the bees swarmed so much this summer. Almost every beekeeper has the same story to tell. Nearly every report in the bee journals says "excessive swarming this summer."

September 17, 1914

You will be interested in the total count of our comb honey crop. We have it all done now: No. 1 — 369; Choice — 175; No. 2 — 99, for a total of 643. We have already shipped about 12 cases of No. 1. We have about $100 worth of culls and about 600 lbs of unfinished comb to render into extracted.

September 29, 1914

It is a quarter after eleven now, which means that you are all at home for dinner and telling all the things that have happened and the people you have met and what they have said. I wish I could be there for a while and hear it all. Enrollment day is always full of excitement and news. How are your classes, Cora? Do you have to give half the poor freshmen away after they sat on the steps half the night waiting for you to get there so as to be sure to be in your class? John asked me this morning if I wouldn't rather be back starting in with a big new lot of nice freshmen. I told him the freshmen were nice all right, but as for me, give me this little house and Wyoming. No, I wouldn't change for anything and start in again today teaching after being here these nine months.

October 4, 1914

The canning is all done now and the dishes resulting all washed. There were eleven pans, by actual count. Yesterday we canned 37 quarts of prunes and nine of peaches. This morning we did 20 quarts and eight pints of peaches — Late Crawfords and Virginia Seedlings. The first were much the nicer. They were so red cheeked and the skin was so thin. There were about the same number of each in a box — 64 and 65 — and they were so large that five made a quart can. I had to put them in rather carefully to get ten in four pint cans. I cooked them just enough to cook them through, taking them off before the edges got ragged. The peaches weighed from five to six and a half ounces each. We have all told now 46 cans of prunes and 43 quarts and eight pints of peaches. You ask what we are going to do with all the fruit. Just ask the girls. Ask them how many peaches they two could eat at a meal. O, no, they would never do it in Indiana, I know, but out here it is different. In the long run, fruit is as cheap a thing as we can get and is certainly the best thing to lend variety and appetite to one's table. We always have fruit for supper and usually some fruit dessert for dinner. For breakfast John always eats whatever fruit is left from the day before. So I guess we won't have to hurry to eat what we have canned.

October 7, 1914

Tomorrow we'll be threshing and I know I won't find time to do any writing, as I expect to go to Pease's rather early in the morning.

She will have about ten or twelve men for dinner tomorrow — maybe a few more. Of course John and the man that is working for us will have to go there if I am there helping. She got my dishes the other day — plates, knives, forks, side dishes, platters, bowls, teaspoons, cups and saucers. I shall take her some pitchers tomorrow. Mrs. Wallace offered to lend her her dishes, but as they are a set of Haviland china that cost over fifty dollars, Mrs. P. didn't want to have the worry of taking care of them. If one of ours is broken there is little harm done.

October 9, 1914

Well, we got the threshing done yesterday and the result is almost too poor to talk about — 99 bushels of wheat and 192 of oats. There must have been sixty or seventy acres in the fields. There is no use raising grain out here till the land is in shape for it, and that means a building-up crop of alfalfa or sweet clover. I am sorry for Peases, for they needed a good crop this year — the same as we did, for that matter. We think the sweet clover we have planted on our place is just the thing, both for a building-up crop and a profit crop, as well as for bee pasture. There is not half an acre in the two patches we had out and we got nearly a bushel of sweet clover seed. The seed is worth about ten dollars a bushel. At least half the seed in this lot was shattered before it was threshed, as the clover had grown all summer without being topped, and since it has been cut it was just stacked up and the wind and rain have knocked out a lot of seed. Sweet clover will be in demand for a couple years yet and the price will no doubt stay up. A great many seed houses could not supply their orders and in nearly all the farm papers and bee journals there were ads for sweet clover seed, offering good prices. The Mormons this year near Byron are going through all the waste land and cutting the sweet clover, tying it in bunches and hauling it home to be threshed. One man in this part of the country made over two hundred dollars last year in a couple week's time by cutting the sweet clover along the ditches and roads and having it threshed for the seed.

October 12, 1914

John has a new song. I sang to him yesterday, "And this the burden of his song forever used to be. . . ." But John's song is a mighty good one; it is, "The Honey's sold! Hurray!" Isn't that a pretty meaningful sentence? Last year it was almost spring before it moved; this year it is sold the first part of October. We haven't heard yet at what prices, but as the market is holding up well, we are not worried about that. It will probably move this week or next. The manager of the Association from Denver, Mr. Rauchfuss, will be here to inspect it as it is loaded. The letter we had Saturday said that maybe the general manager himself would come.

We have a man working for us now who is the funniest fellow you ever saw. He came here a few weeks ago from the Ozarks in Missouri, and as Preachin' Bill would say, "He shore does look it." He is rather small and wiry, very thin as to face, rough as to appearance and absolutely minus when it comes to table manners. The first day he ate here I positively stared, unmannerly as that may be. He doesn't chew his food, he merely rolls his tongue over it once and swallows it. I know he has teeth, too, for you can hear his spoon click against them each time he puts it to his mouth. He reaches anywhere across the table and never asks to have anything passed. Neither does he do without. I was fairly amazed to silence to watch him. After he had gone out, John said with a grin, "His table manners aren't much to speak of, are they." I didn't think of it at the time, but I suppose the proper response would have been like the little boy's when he was retelling a story about the rabbit, which the teacher had concluded: the rabbit has no tail to speak of. You remember the little boy said, "And the rabbit has a tail, but you mustn't talk about it." I said this morning I would be mortified if he were at the table when the Denver man comes. John said we'd just explain he was from the Ozarks, and that would be enough. John calls him Ozarks, though he calls himself Acy.

October 19, 1914

I had a great surprise at church last night. After the service a young man walked up to me and said how do you do. And who do you think it was but our old college friend Ernest Richards. I did not know he was within 1800 miles of here. He is looking around, with somewhat of the idea of settling on a place out here, either homesteading or buying. He has a brother in Idaho and he will look around there too. I invited him out to see us and he said he would come.

November 2, 1914

I wish you could have seen the results of the Hallowe'en pranks at Garland. Yesterday afternoon when John and I drove to Garland to mail the letters we found the road at one place almost closed with planks and logs and such almost across it. We thought at first something was wrong with the road. Then we saw that the road where it crosses the railroad track near the station was shut off with rails built into a fence across the road. We supposed that the bridge had not yet been rebuilt where it had been taken down for the dredging machine to pass through. Then we saw that the bridge was all right. Finally John said, "Hallowe'en!" And that is what it was. The wagons and vehicles from the implement store were carried all over the town; some were across the railroad track out on the commons. Some were on the sidewalk blocking the doors of the store. A wheel barrow adorned the top of the town pump. A disc harrow stood in the middle of the street, with another wheel barrow as a cap. Wagons and various farm implements were strewn across the street where it crosses the tracks and the rest of the space filled in with a fence made of fence posts. A carload of fence posts had just been unloaded a day or so before. These had been used, and all of them, too. Besides the fences built in various directions there was a regular little house made of the posts, in log cabin style. It was quite well done. The whole thing was exceedingly well arranged and the effect quite stunning.

It seems that the boys did more than this, however. If they had done only this the marshal would not have riz in his dignity the way he has. Unfortunately they went on to use printers ink to make some comments on the town and the inhabitants thereof. For instance, on the door of Early's drug store appeared the label, Owl Saloon. Now of course everybody knows that such is the case, but it sort o' hurts a man's feelings to have the thing stare him in the face when he looks at the pride of his life, his fine place of business. There were some similar labels elsewhere and some remarks not especially complimentary to King, the man who owns Garland and runs the town, to the extent of running everyone else out. Naturally King was not overly pleased. One thing the boys did that was not appreciated was put printers ink on the door knobs of the stores and houses. The innocent householder who put his hand on the knob of his own door the next morning found the door-knob's print in his hand. Mr. Pease said that this is the first year the boys have not put Mr. Adam's wagon on top of the shed at the lumberyard. This year he was wise enough to take it home with him and put in in the yard where the presence of a great big dog was somewhat of a hindrance to Hallowe'en celebraters.

Ernest Richards was here to call the other day. He has just about decided to buy the Lowry farm near Garland (about a mile north of us). It is just north of the Jones place across the road west from Adams'. He seems to like the land around Garland better than that nearer Powell. He will buy rather than file so as not to use up his homesteadright.

November 12, 1914

We have been celebrating over the fact that two more states — Montana and Nevada, have joined the suffrage ranks, and that four more — Oregon, Washington, Arizona, and Colorado, have become prohibition. Things aren't as bad as they sometimes look, are they?

November 20, 1914

Well, the Aid meeting here is over and the dishes are all washed and put away, thanks to Johnny's aid. There were eleven women and two children here. Do you remember, Co, why I did not want to have the Aid in the summer time? When the children are not in school the mothers take the whole family along, big and little. You remember at Kilgore's there were twenty women and twenty children, and at Lovercheck's, nineteen women and eighteen children. That was before school began. At Lampman's, the day you went with me, there were at least a dozen children. I decided that when I had the Aid, I wanted women and not children, for of course each youngster requires just the same refreshments as a grownup. Since the weather has been so cold not so many people come, and of course the children are all in school.

The eats were fine, if I do say so myself that made them. For the first course we had fruit salad and cheese crackers. The salad was made of fresh apples, with canned peaches and black currants. The second course was currant ice and cookies.

You ought to see how nice the house looks. Wednesday John helped me clean the windows. He did the outsides and I the insides. Yesterday he mopped the kitchen and the border in

the living room and I did up the curtains and cleaned the
house, and today we feel it is a good thing to have company
once in a while to get the house really clean.

November 23, 1914

Mrs. Pease's mother and sister came Saturday, and Mrs.
Pease and I are going to give a reception for them next
Friday afternoon here at our house. I suggested it, and Mrs. P.
was delighted, also the newcomers. We are inviting all the
neighbors, and the people in Garland that we both know or
that are closely associated with Mrs. P. in church work. I am
also inviting a few people whom I owe social debts. I wrote the
invitations last night. I didn't have much to go on. I think I
did right well considering that I was so far away from any base
of supplies. No one would know that the seals on the invitations are cut from a piece of wrapping paper that came around
some glass jars one of the neighbors returned last spring. I
saved the paper, thinking it might be useful in an emergency,
and it sure is.

We are sending out nearly fifty invitations and you can
guess that number is somewhat a crowd for a house as small as
ours. We do not expect more than thirty, but we may be
surprised. We can't plan to do much, for there isn't room for
anything elaborate. I think we shall use some progressive conversation, without having the people sign up for it. We shall
give them slips with the topics on, and then every three or four
minutes blow a whistle (the one mamma gave me when I came
out here) and ask them to change persons to whom they are
talking. It will at least help to keep them stirred up. I have
thought of some topics: My Favorite Recipe, Christmas Presents,
the Ladies Aid Bazaar, the Dorcas Class Play, Woman in 1950,
a Woman on the School Board, What I Am Thankful For. The
third and fourth are by way of advertisement of their respective
subjects; the sixth is a subject I am agitating out here. I have
found out enough about the running of the schools to know
that a woman is needed, a woman who knows something about

school work. John says to go ahead: they'll put me on. I told him I didn't care if they did, something was needed. They have no uniform school book law here, and in the Garland high school they are actually using texts twenty years old.

We are going to serve just ice cream and cake for refreshments. Mrs. P. will make the cream and I will make the cake. I shall make the usual cream-honey chocolate cake with chocolate icing. I'll bake it in the big bread pans, and I think two will be enough. For favors we'll use the turkey pattern. I think we'll just use brown cardboard and mark the feather slightly with black and put in red wattles. Mrs. P.'s sister is good at watercoloring, however, so we may do more. We did not put the invitations in envelopes, but just wrote the names on the outside—they form their own envelopes.

We are going to Powell tonight for the first number of the lecture series—Ole Theobaldi, the Norwegian violinist. He is called the successor of Ole Bull. He ought to be good, for he is the possessor of sixty-two gold medal decorations and has been royal chamber musician to the King of Sweden and to two Czars of Russia. He won the diamond crown of Osirius at the great congress in Rome in 1896. He has toured all over Europe and this country.

We are looking for our honey check this week. We are anxious to see how large it is. It will probably be less than we had expected, for we have found that the freight rate over the new road is not as much lower as one would expect. Evidently the company wants to pay for the road with the freight profits. When the check comes in we'll have money for a little while, at least, but not long. We want to pay up all our bills and order next season's supplies. When you pay for two season's supplies, the building of a new shop, and a bee cellar and an ice house, all out of one season's returns, you can't expect the money to last long.

We are renewing our periodicals now—the ones that expire at present. We are getting them through a friend of Mr. Roach's who is crippled and supports himself by magazine subscription work. We are planning to take this coming year the following list: Everybody's, the American, the Literary Digest, LaFollette's, the Geographical Magazine, the Vindicator, and, thanks to Bady for her two-year subscription last year, The Woman's Home Companion. Then of course we take the local papers, two farm papers, and three bee journals. I guess that much will keep us busy, don't you? We are dropping the Worlds Work and the Review of Reviews for the Literary Digest. I like the weekly better than the monthlies. One is more likely to read the articles in smaller doses than when they come all at once only once a month. Then too, one gets the news sooner and out here where we do not have any real newspapers, that is quite an item.

We went to church and Sunday school yesterday. We went to our own Sunday school but did not stay there to church. An anti-saloon man was to hold forth there so we went to the Baptist church whose new minister we have been wanting to hear. John is not at all in sympathy with the anti-saloon work, as the Anti-Saloon League does not work for real prohibition at all, and fights the prohibition party.

As I said, we went to the Baptist church. The new minister is a man of about sixty-five almost on the verge of the place where he ought to be superannuated. His sermon had one good point in it, his main point. He talked all he had to say on that point, then talked of something else, then said it over, then of something else, then summed up what he had said on the point, and then talked some more about other things. John said he was beginning to think a committee would have to be appointed to tell him he was done. I was about to remark at the last change of topic that he had put in another record, but I was afraid that might not be polite to say in a strange church. The sermon was one of the kind that appeals to your sympathies—

gets on your nerves, John calls it. "And we won't go there any more, any more, etc."

We sent in our order for stain for the house when we sent to Sears Roebuck the other day. We had hoped to get the staining done this fall, but we did not have the stain or the time. We shall do the work in the spring, sure. We were somewhat surprised when our order amounted to about forty-one dollars. That seems a whole lot; but when you think that we got ten dollars worth of groceries, two dollars worth of sugar, all sorts of harness repairs, notions, household supplies, clothing, bolts, screws, toilet articles, writing supplies, paint, and Christmas candy, you can see that if we just went to the stores whenever we needed the things we would pay out a great deal more and never notice it. These things will supply us for months—practically all winter. The 25 pounds of sugar we get for a dollar with the ten dollar grocery order will last all summer. We haven't used nearly that much in the eleven months I have been here.

December 6, 1914

The play I coached for the Dorcas class at the Garland church came off all right. It was such a poor play there wasn't any climax to it at all and when it was over the audience just sat still, waiting for more and not knowing that the end had come! I was so tickled I didn't know what to do. But we had to do something. The youngsters wanted me to get up and make a speech and tell the audience it was time to vamoose, but I did not hanker after the honor. Finally I got the whole cast shoved on the stage to make a bow as the curtains were pulled. Well, they all got there and the curtains were pulled. Then they all waited, each for the other, and all stood there like dummies. I was watching through the side curtain and I heard someone count: one, two, three, and decided someone was counting for the others to bow together. But at three nothing happened, and they still stood there. Finally I poked my head out the front of the dressing room and shouted to the curtain man—in a stage whisper—Pull the curtain! He did so after much trouble, and we all were simply overcome with laughter. I leaned against the wall (actual fact) and the audience roared. That was the funniest thing in the whole evening and the audience went home satisfied. The admission charge was only twenty-five cents for grown-ups and fifteen for children. It was enough, for that play. Even at those prices the proceeds amounted to about thirty dollars, and of course there was practically no expense. I guess a dollar would cover all the expenses. They want to give another play in March and have asked me to choose the play. I am thinking of "The Work House War," "Spreading the News," and "The Pot o' Broth."

We got all the bees in the cellar Friday morning—just in time, too, for from the looks of things tonight we are going to have some weather. The clouds have hung low all day, right down on the bench and in the Pryor Valley. It has surely been snowing on the bench and in the mountains today.

The temperature at which we want to keep the cellar is forty-five degrees. Before we put the bees in it was forty. After they were in, the temperature went up to forty-eight, when both outside and inside doors were shut. With two sets of doors it will be easy to regulate the temperature and give good fresh air. There are six ventilators, four inches square, set in the ceiling and reaching outside above, and one fresh air duct 8 x 10 inches running out for about thirty-five feet through the ground and coming out on the hillside. If the cellar works, we shall feel mighty good. Of course we do not know now just how it will turn out, but it makes us feel mighty good to go into it and see the 454 colonies placed there in regular rows and stacked up five tiers high. We have 110 at the river yard. Even if the cellar does not winter any better than the outdoor wintering, it will be less expensive in the long run.

December 8, 1914

It is quite cold this evening. By five o'clock the thermometer was down to ten. I hung out the towels about four o'clock and they froze stiff as fast as I could hang them up. I had to

pull each one straight as I hung it, or it would be too stiff to do anything with. I did not try to hang the starched clothes outdoors as they would have no starch in them after freezing the way they would. The woolen underwear of John's I dried indoors; the gowns and cotton underwear, the overalls and jumpers, and the towels are stiff and straight out on the line now. I'll leave them there all night, as there is no wind. Since the weather has turned so cold I am mighty glad I have all the washing done for another two weeks. I got pretty cold hanging up the towels. I did not catch any cold, but I feel a sort o' stiffness across the shoulders. I shall take a piping hot bath tonight and hop in bed immediately. That will fix it all right.
P.S. I did and it did.

December 10, 1914

Well, the Garland Aid Bazaar is over. I haven't heard just how the Aid came out, as we went home a little after ten just after the auction of remaining items had started. I guess if we had stayed I could have got some things rather cheap, for they had a number of aprons and such things that they were going to sell. I don't need any of those things such as dust caps, clothespin aprons, corset covers, drawers, and so I did not care much about staying longer. Our fishpond went like hot cakes. We could have sold a lot more, especially if we could have got things for boys. Next time we'll know a little more about what and how much to get. The men were worse than the women and the boys worse than the girls for fishing. Some of the grown-up men fished three or four times and the young men half a dozen, even after we put in a lot of articles from the general sale (aprons, dust caps, calendars, ties, paper sachet bags) and raised the price to ten cents. What the girls seemed to like best were the heart-shaped sachet bags. I think they sold those for fifteen cents. There was not much sale of aprons and such articles. Most of us folk make our own of such things and can't afford to pay for having the Aid make them. We ate our supper at the bazaar. They served baked beans, sandwiches, pie, cake, and coffee, at five cents per. You could get as many helpings as you wanted to pay five cents for.

I am going to a party at Werts this afternoon to talk over the proposed club that is to be founded soon. I want to go as I want to have a word to say about plans. What I want to see is something that will give us a chance to exercise our heads and not just our stomachs. I am interested, too, in the book idea, of having each member who wishes get a new book for trading around with others who have books. I am going to suggest that before we all buy new books we trade around those we have that others have not read. For instance, last Christmas I got two new books that I am sure people here haven't read. Why should we buy a new book so long as we have these on hand? Then, too, I am going to offer any of our books to anyone who wants them. I'll fix up a catalogue scheme for recording loans and then let anything go. I thought at first I wouldn't lend some of my best bound ones, but what is the use of having a lot of books here that no one has ever looked into just to keep the bindings clean. If a book isn't used it isn't worth anything.

We had our meeting at Werts Friday afternoon to talk over the new club. There were ten or so ladies there. We talked over our ideas and then elected officers and appointed a committee to report at the next meeting on organization and program. They asked me what my idea was for the club and I said I thought what we needed was something to exercise our brains and not our stomachs. They all seemed to think that was right — at any rate they made me president, when we came to elect officers. We didn't make any definite plans for programs, but everybody thought the best thing to take up would be some culinary problems, or household science subjects. My idea is to combine something of current interest and the household problems. The club is to meet every other Thursday and then one time a month during the winter to entertain the husbands in the evening. This evening affair is to be in addition to the regular meetings and is to take the form of just a good time, with program, games, contests, etc., and very light refreshments. We actually discussed not serving refreshments at all in the afternoon. I rather think that during the cold weather one ought to have something hot, though, before starting home in the late afternoon. I think that what we'll do is limit the afternoon refreshments to one article besides a drink. That would make possible sandwiches and coffee, or cake, or fruit, or candy, or pie, and coffee, but it would cut out ice cream and cake, though ice cream could be served, and it would also cut out salads, etc. Afternoon tea isn't at all common out here. I hesitate to start it, because lemons are too expensive to be afforded.

The Aid made about forty dollars at the bazaar—maybe a little more.

December 20, 1914

If the mails are late, as they are likely to be at this time of year, you won't get tomorrow's letter by Friday. I guess therefore I'd better make this a Christmas letter, and wish you all a very merry Christmas and a most happy new year.

So far as I know now, we shall spend the day at home and alone. At least I'd rather. We shall have a grand opening in the morning, of the box you say you are sending, and the one John's mother is sending, and of any small parcels that may arrive up to that time. We won't even take out the tree ornaments before that time. Then we can spend part of the morning trimming the tree. As there are no youngsters here we won't have to have the tree done by the break o' day. I haven't decided yet what we'll have for dinner that day. If the weather is pleasant the fore part of the week, we may butcher. Then we may shoot what John calls a white-tailed bear, and we may have that. Of course we'll have fruitcake, for that is ready. Our Sears Roebuck order will surely be here by then and we'll have some things in that. One thing is a box of chocolates John is getting me for Christmas. It is too bad to know about it, but it couldn't be helped.

I sent out the main lot of our Christmas cards yesterday. The ones that go farthest we had mailed at various times before. I have a few to mail in the morning. We sent out seventy-three cards, and letters to Edward and Grandpa.

The lecture course number we went to the other night was really good. The entertainers were Mr. and Mrs. Dietric. He did magic and unusual musical instruments, she did reciting, imitating, whistling, and piano playing. She could whistle so well, and her piano playing was dandy. She sang tenor of a rather good quality and also assisted him in the magic. He did a number of quite good tricks, some with cards, some with balls, and some with regular magician's apparatus, such as a seemingly empty chest from which he drew all sorts of things. He got a little boy from the audience to help him and made a lot of fun with the youngster. Of course the audience roared at that. He had the boy drink water and then, examining him carefully, said it had gone to his brain, but that he would fix him. Then with an apparently empty funnel held to the boy's ear, he worked the lad's arm like a pump handle and brought a stream of water from the funnel. He did some shuffling of cards that was pretty neat. One shuffle he said was the Frannie shuffle, and he went on to explain that he had learned that when he spent a year in Frannie — this morning. His line of small talk was certainly great, and much of it local.

December 21, 1914

A year ago John started east. He told me this morning all about the things he did and the feelings he had as he started. The feelings weren't all entirely pleasant, for he had a little boil on the place where he usually sits down, and that made sitting somewhat uncomfortable. That was a pretty unfortunate state of affairs with which to start out on a three day's sitting trip, wasn't it?

We went calling yesterday afternoon. We started to Pease's about three o'clock, intending to stay half an hour or so, and then come home and have dinner. We took some letters down for the children to mail when they went to school this morning, and wanted to tell Mr. P. about getting us a Christmas tree when he goes to the Pine Bluff coal mine this week about eight miles from here. There was no one at home, so we left the letters and a note about the tree. As we started home John suggested we go to call on the new family that has built just the other side of Bygrens. They were here one day last week to get some honey, but I was not at home that afternoon and did not meet them. We cut across the vacant farm just south of us and thus took the diagonal of a half mile square instead of walking around. The seepy place was frozen and safe to cross. We had a lovely time visiting. The family is named Murray. He was a teacher in the Philippines for seven years and she for four. They are splendid people. They have a fine collection of curios. We looked at curios nearly all the while we were there and did not see nearly all of them. Their furniture is made of beautiful wood they brought with them from the islands. It is a good deal like rosewood only a little lighter. They have one boy, two years old. They have been back in the States the past four years.

John just came home from Garland with part of the freight order from Sears Roebuck. The first thing he brought in was the box with the clock in it. This is our Christmas present to each other. It is a beauty. It is 10½ inches high and about 13 wide, and is made of oak. The top is rounded and on either side of the dial there is a column of the oak with a brass cap and base. The dial is a bull's eye effect one, with a brass rim. The oak matches our furnishings better than anything else, though it is light or golden oak, and beautifully finished. Of course we stopped right off to unpack the clock and get it runing. It strikes the hours on a gong and the halfs on a bell. I think we'll like it immensely, and we sure do need a clock.

Our beautiful Christmas day will soon be over. It is now eight o'clock by our new clock. The silvery notes have just sounded. I shall spend a while with you now.

We have had a lovely day. We just loafed all day and did just what we wanted to. Since the weather has been so cold we have been sleeping in the sitting room. John got up about seven this morning and did the chores. Before eight he was all ready to have a grand opening. He knew I was making him something for Christmas, and when he got to the point in his dressing that a tie was the next article to be put on, he came to the bed and remarked, "I think a new tie would be nice to wear today with these new trousers from Sears Roebuck." You see he guessed that what I had made him was a tie, as I had been saying I was going to make him some. We both like the white four-in-hand wash ties best on him for everyday wear. I laughed and told him that what I had made he would not want to wear in the daytime. As soon as he was dressed I told him where to find his gift, and he went and got it. He looked at the crocheted edge about the yoke and neck and inquired in a grieved tone why I hadn't put lace around the tail! Then he got my Christmas present, which was a two-pound box of chocolates. The candy is a round marshmallow simply slathered thick with halves of peanuts, until the nuts stick way over the edges, and then the whole dipped in chocolate. Yum, yum. He brought the box to the bed, and I sat up and opened it. We sampled the contents and then I got up and dressed and made up the bed as fast as I could while he opened a box from his mother and got the lid off the box from you.

Then we had a grand opening. My, O, but all the lovely things you got in that box. It was fine of you, knowing our desire for an auto, to gratify our desire at this time when we couldn't get one for another year at least. Thank you very much [for the toy auto]. And the bug! As soon as we saw his antennae sticking up in the box we both just "yumped for yoy." I am so glad to get "The Egoist," and you know I have been wanting all year the "Natural Law in the Spiritual World." John began to read that today and read till he almost went to sleep in his chair. The gingham is so good and there is so much of it, and the lace collars are lovely. The gray silk scarf is so pretty and John likes the gloves immensely. And the candy... O my! We fairly reveled in it all day. (Excuse me while I get a piece now.) Heretofore I have always had a hand in the making—now I know why people who got our boxes of candy always carried on so. The cans of nuts are mighty good, and the dates, too.

I'll just have to give a separate paragraph to the Christmas tree things. When we opened that big box and saw all the lovely glittering things I just did a dance. They are simply scrumptious. The ones from the tree at home I wanted to hug, they looked so good. I am so glad to get the angel. I can't remember when that wasn't on our tree. The big piece with the several angels was always a favorite of mine, though I really believe the title of that was vested in Edith. It's sort o' unfair to her to send it to us. The new ornaments are dandy. While we were trimming the tree, Mr. Pease came up for their things that were in the Sears Roebuck order, and I asked him if they had plenty of bright shiny things for their tree. He said they did not have anything like these, so I just sat down at once and made up into ornaments the tinsel you sent and used balls for centers. I think I sent down fifteen. Mrs. P. told me this evening how lovely they were and that she was going to put them away for next year. I do wish you could see our tree. Really, I never saw a prettier. It is a pine tree, about five feet high, with a spread of nearly four feet near the bottom, and almost perfect in symmetry from bottom to top.

Your Christmas letter came yesterday, Cora, and today we had another good one from Edith. My, how we did enjoy them both. I had a notion to tell you that I was homesick, to see if you would keep your promise of coming out and pounding me. I'd let you do it if you really came. But I must confess that I have not been homesick enough to talk about today. I had a pretty hard spell at Thanksgiving, the first that bothered me since you girls were here, and I was afraid that I might suffer another attack at this time. But I really couldn't be so bad, when everybody is so good to me. It would be ungrateful. Honest, though, I have not had to fight against it, either. We have talked of you all day, too. We have had a lovely day. As I said, we just loafed. We trimmed the tree this morning, and I took my lazy time about getting everything straightened up after the grand opening. Then when the house was clean and we read and loafed some more, and—shall I say it—we just "spooned" all day. I guess we get worse as time goes by. We didn't even have a full meal—we wanted to eat all the candy and cakes and nuts we wanted to, not to mention apples.

December 27, 1914

I said I would tell you about our Christmas gift from Denver. The Colorado Honey Producers' Association, being a co-operative association, admits as members only those persons who buy at least one share of stock at ten dollars. The expenses of running the business are taken from the five per cent commission charged on honey sold. Then at the end of the year the amount of this five per cent not actually needed in the running of the business is rebated to the members whose honey has been sold. Half the rebate is paid in money and half in stock. Rebates are paid once a year, in December, along with the ten per cent dividend on the stock. Consequently this year we expected the rebates on both last year's and this year's crops and the ten per cent dividend on the seven shares of stock we own. Altogether we did not expect more than about sixty dollars all told, thirty in stock and thirty in cash. Well, when the letter came the day before Christmas there were six shares of stock and a check for fifty-three dollars and some cents. Maybe we weren't tickled. It was a fine Christmas present. The letter containing the check for this year's crop came the day after Thanksgiving, on John's birthday; that was a birthday present and this is a Christmas present.

While I am waiting for the men to come to dinner I'll start a letter. We are butchering today. They have just finished the dressing of the beef—or the undressing. They have the carcass cut in two now and will surely be in to dinner in a few minutes. It is nearly one o'clock, but they did not want to stop till they were through. I guess they want to let the halves hang a while before cutting up the meat.

The men are simply astonished at the excellent condition of the beef. The cow has been running on the grainfield since threshing time. We intended to use the whole cow ourselves, or rather, to pickle and can and freeze, etc., but John says the body looks so big he is beginning to have his doubts as to whether we'd better keep it all. Of course Mr. Pease and Mr. Thompson, who are doing the butchering, will take their pay in meat. We have had plenty of chances to sell what we don't want to keep, so if we decide to sell some we won't have any trouble.

Mr. Fowler is in these parts these days to see about his school land that he bought some time ago. He is going to have the irrigable part surveyed off into several tracts and then rent out the pieces this year. We thought that by next year we might be able to undertake that. Sweet clover is a good investment, there is no doubt about it. The price of seed is so high now that it surely won't go low enough in the next couple years to spoil the profits, and the yield of seed is so sure and so large that there is very little risk. The farm papers and agricultural colleges and everything connected with up-to-date farming is boosting sweet clover so that there is certain to be a demand for it at least for three years to come. Some of the farmers in the middle states in the corn belt are beginning to use sweet clover for green fertilizer. In that way they do not raise their own seed, as they plow it under before the seed comes. Of course sweet clover seed can be grown anywhere. It is not like alfalfa in that respect. Alfalfa seed cannot be grown in the east. The season must be just right, which means very warm and dry at the latter part, and plenty of moisture up to a certain point. Of course in an irrigated country this can be controlled. But in a rainy country it cannot and a shower or rain at the wrong time will start the whole alfalfa field to growing and spoil entirely the seed production.

Tomorrow it will be a year. My, but it has been a fine year. If all the rest are as good as this we'll surely be most wonderfully blest. We think the years will be, too, or better even. Of course we have been living over the days last year as they have come this week. No. Toa, we haven't left you all out. You are all in it, and mighty importantly in it, too. We have been wondering how to celebrate tomorrow and have about decided that we'll celebrate by putting on our wedding finery tomorrow evening just all for ourselves and each other. Of course John gets to wear his suit often, but I don't get to wear my dress, and I don't want it to lie there forever without being put on. So imagine us in our svelte duds tomorrow night.

December 30, 1914

We have just had dinner on our first wedding anniversary. Mr. Pease and Mr. Thompson, who are cutting up the meat today, were here. You could never guess what we had for dinner. Well, we decided that nothing could be quite as suitable for a wedding anniversary as heart, so we had baked heart for dinner. I stuffed it and roasted it, and then had potatoes cooked in the same pan. How's that for a suitable feast for the occasion? It is as much in keeping as turkey for Thanksgiving, isn't it? We also had baked beans, gravy and dressing, applenut salad, corn bread, and rice pudding and Herbet cakes.

I wish you could see the meat we have. And I also wish you could have all you could use of it. My, but it is fine. The men worked all morning cutting it up. Some I shall roast and can, and some we'll hang up and let freeze and keep that way. The meat will stay frozen here till way in March after being once frozen. The steaks are so good looking you want one right away. The same with the roasts, and in fact, with every part. We also want to cook the tongue right off, and the brains, etc.

But we can't possibly eat it all at once so we'll have to hold our appetites. We are going to make the pickle at once for the meat we want to pickle. We shall corn the brisket and some other pieces and pickle some of the round to smoke. I think some chipped beef will be good. A good deal we'll hang now, and then put it in a weaker pickle when it will no longer stay frozen. That way we can have fresh meat till way in the summer. Then we'll have the canned meat to use later in the summer and fall. We had a roast last spring from Mr. Nauser that had been pickled, and it was quite good. Of course it had to be well soaked to get the salt out before it was roasted and then salted very sparingly if at all.

December 31, 1914

I told you the other day to imagine us sitting on the evening of our wedding anniversary dressed in our wedding clothes. I couldn't tell you then to imagine the rest of the picture, because I didn't know anything about it. We got dressed about half past six and sat down in the living room. We talked a while, and then got to reading. We read a while and then talked some more, and had a generally good time, when we heard a knock at the door. Now we were sort o' expecting that Fowler would call during the evening, for we knew he was still here and that he would go home today. So John opened the door, and there stood Mr. and Mrs. Werts. We had invited them up to see our tree, so we were not yet very suspicious, though somehow, when I heard their buggy cross the bridge I thought, without knowing who it was, that most likely we would have some callers, and perhaps a number of them. When John took their wraps, he started to put them in the bedroom. I stopped him, and told him to lay them on the couch in the living room, or they would be so cold when they needed them again. John remarked, without really meaning it, that maybe there wouldn't be room enough in the living room if we put the wraps there. Still, neither of us were on. After a while we heard a wagon drive up. Then we winked at each other and guessed the rest.

Peases and Thompsons came in. Mrs. P. came in the kitchen door, while the rest of the folk entered the front door. Then I was certain. Mrs. Werts had not brought any bundle of any sort, so I was not suspicious then. After a while in came the Hancocks, he carrying a big box. Then there was no question.

I found out some time ago that Peases and Werts had planned a reception for us when we first got here, but that unexpected incidents had spoiled their plans several times and they had to give it up. This last night was a sort of carrying out of plans made a long time ago for a different kind of party. Last night, they told me, they invited only the folk we cared most about, as they found that if they began with the neighbors they would not be able to find a stopping place — just as we found when we had the reception for the Thompsons. Of course the bug performed, to the great edification and amusement of the whole crowd. The bug would get near the edge, and somebody would grab for him to keep him from falling off, and he would calmly turn around and proceed on his way. Then the crowd would give the person the laugh. It was not just the youngsters in years who would try to keep Mr. Bug from hurting himself; the older youngsters were just as bad. I forgot to say that Fowler was here, too. After a while Mrs. Hancock produced a contest which is a dandy. I found I was stumped on several of the numbers. Mr. Werts and I got the most; we were just about even. After this they handed me a bundle of envelopes. As this was the paper anniversary, they suited the gifts to that. In each envelope was a handmade booklet with a lot of recipes in it, or other advice to a husband and wife. I read the advice, and the names of the articles whose recipes were given. Some of the booklets had water color covers; some had postcard covers; some were handwritten and some were typewritten. Wasn't that lovely of them? The recipes are, of course, their favorite ones, and some of them ones I have been wanting. After a while more Mrs. P. and Mrs. W. and Mrs. H. went out into the kitchen and proceeded to fix up what they had planned. They cooked coffee and had chicken sandwiches and cake. I did go out to tell them where the dishes were that they wanted, but that is about all. I was company. So I went back in the living room. After the refreshments they washed up all the dishes they had used. How's that? They all stayed till about twelve. We had a lovely evening. We do appreciate it so much, wouldn't you?

We asked Fowler to stay all night with us, and as he said, having neither chick nor child to call him to his own house, he did so. He stayed to breakfast, too, of course, and went off about half past nine, as he had some things to attend to and wanted to catch the eleven o'clock train for Powell, and then take the train on its return to go to Billings.

He had a spell over the breakfast. It wasn't so much, but it really was good. He said it wasn't a country breakfast, but one at the Great Northern Hotel in Billings. I don't see why, for everything we had was homemade or home produced, or produced on the Flat. We had fresh porterhouse steak, and it was the real article. It wasn't even the T-bone, but just real porter-house and nothing else. It was as tender as the proverbial butter. Then we had French fried potatoes and gravy, and bread and raisin bread, cocoa, and currents with whipped cream, and fruit cake. He thought we were extravagant to have whipped cream for breakfast. I told him we had it any meal and most of the time.

January 4, 1915

I wonder if I ever told you about what Mrs. Pease told me of the talk of the neighborhood before I came. When the people found out John was to marry a school teacher, they all went about saying "Poor Mr. Hendricks." To bring a school teacher out here on a farm, and especially to bring a college teacher. That was even worse. "Poor Mr. Hendricks." They all knew he was bad enough off living by himself, but they thought this would be even worse. Sympathy for him was fairly running down the roads and through the ditches. Then when I came and they met me and found out that I was human and could even wash dishes and cook cocoa and even make bread, they didn't know what to think. Mrs. Pease frankly acknowledged that she never was so beat in her life as she was about John Hendricks' wife! I've had a lot of fun teasing poor Mr. Hendricks about his wife. I am wicked enough, too, sometimes, to show off a little to the neighbors. O no, I never do it visibly. I am as innocent as a year old baby. I just merely mention having done something, just as casually as if it were taking breath or seeing the sun rise. For instance, when we were speaking of making soap from the tallow, Mr. P. asked me if I could make soap. He asked it in such a half-awed-half-unbelieving way that I was amused as could be. Of course I answered in the most offhand fashion that I could, though I never in my life made a batch of soap alone. The other day when Fowler was here we were speaking of making soap and he said, in much the same tone that Mr. P. had used, "Can you make soap?" I said, "Why, yes." He looked at me about a half minute and then, "By George," he said, "what can't you do?" John and I managed to wink at each other with one eye and keep the other next to him perfectly normal. John makes believe to scold me sometimes when I show off a little, but of course he really is as tickled as I am and believes me perfectly justified in so doing when I am tempted the way I am.

January 5, 1915

We are going to the river today and want to start before long, so I won't have time to write much of a letter. It is now about eight o'clock. While I'm eating my brown bread and cream I'll be hitting the keys.

John has already eaten his toast and milk. All the while he has not been working so hard he gets himself what he wants in the morning. No, it is not because I am not up, for I usually am by the time he eats, nor is it because I don't want to do it. It's because he likes to do it himself. He tried to tease me one morning about a poor married man's having to get his own breakfast, and I told him he was lucky to be allowed to do so, for lots of women wouldn't have their men rummaging around after anything they wanted. I'd like to have seen Grandpa try to make himself toast and drop crumbs or bits of butter anywhere when Aunt Lena was running the ranch. No, I wouldn't.

We have been having lots of fun about the toasting fork. John never had a long handled toasting fork before, and always burned his fingers using a short one. He said the other day he believed if he had known he could get a long handled toasting fork when he was living alone he wouldn't have been so helpless and dependent on a desired wife for his meals. I told him it was too bad you folks didn't know that, for when he first began to come around I was sure you would gladly have furnished him with a toasting fork if that would have lessened his desire to get me here. I thought you would have considered yourselves as getting off cheap!

January 7, 1915

I have the joke on John now. I am not the only bell sheep in the family. At the meeting of the local branch of the national organization of the Farmers' Union the other night he was elected president. So now I call him bell sheep, too, though he says it must be bell ram. The Farmers' Union is for the cooperation of members. It helps find a market for what the farmers have to sell and makes it possible for the farmer to buy cheaper by buying in quantity. Last spring the Union got a carload of fence posts and saved 2½ cents a post. The Powell Union is constantly buying carloads of lumber for members at a great saving. Next fall we hope to get a car of fruit—peaches, apples, prunes. It is a great help. There are branches all over the west and south, and local, state, and national organizations.

January 11, 1915

Just a year ago at this very minute or thereabouts, we were being showered with rice as we alighted from the train at Garland. The date was the 12th, which is tomorrow, but the day was Monday, which is today. My, O, but my feelings were various and strange as we got into Mr. Werts' buggy and started for his house. John and I had a little celebration a few minutes ago over the anniversary, and especially over the fact that it was a year ago that it happened and not today. I sure am glad that I do not have to go through now the next month as it was a year ago. Homesickness sure is an acute malady when it hits one hard. I reckon I shed more tears in the first three weeks I was here than in the three years previous. It makes me weep to think about it. But the hard time is over now and the good time is here, and we hope the better still to come.

January 14, 1915

Boo hoo. I don't really know how bad I ought to feel about the matter, but the fact is that the Powell post office burned last night, according to a report we got this morning, and all the mail that came in for us on yesterday's train is burned up. The mail comes in now on the afternoon train and is not sent on the rural routes till the next day. As a result of last night's fire we don't get any mail today. Of course the worst part is that we'll never know what we should have got. Maybe someone who hadn't written for years wrote us a letter that came yesterday and when we do not answer will think we don't care. Maybe some of the faculty people in B. wrote me a nice letter and it is burned up. Boo-hoo-hoo. John will no doubt get the details while he is in Powell.

We went to a lecture course in Powell last night. My, but it was the real article. There were four girls in the company — or rather three young girls and one about 25 or 30. One of the girls was only about 16 and was the first violinist in the company. She played just as birds sing, and with apparently no more difficulty. She did not seem to be concerned about getting things right — they just naturally came right. Her touch was sure both on string and bow. John said after we had heard her play one number that the great Theobaldi ought to take some lessons of her. Of the other members of the company, one played the cello and sang alto, one played the second violin and sang contralto and did the accompanying for the special musical numbers by cello and violin and voice, and the other did the accompanying when the whole company played, and did the reading. Her imitations were excellent. She was also the soprano soloist of the crowd, and she really could sing. She and the alto sang one number from Hoffman's Tales — Beauteous Night, that was as good as anything I have heard anywhere. The audience just sat spellbound during it and when they finished people said, I wish they'd sing the same thing again. I don't know when I have enjoyed an evening so much. John and I both said on the way home that if we could hear things like that oftener we wouldn't miss David Warfield so much and others of that class.

January 22, 1915

We went to Club yesterday afternoon, though there was an extremely cold and bitter wind blowing. There were only a dozen or so women there as the day was so cold. When I went to Brown's in the morning to help her get dinner for the hay balers, I wore my heavy coat over my corduroy suit, and was not too warm. I wore a scarf right over my head and face like a veil. Of course I couldn't see through it very well, but it was a protection from the wind. When we went to the meeting we tied the horse in the shelter of one of the old hotels in Garland and then walked to the house where the meeting was to be held — about two blocks away. By the time we got there we were almost winded, so strong was the wind. When the meeting was over the wind had died down some, and we didn't get at all cold coming home, even though the thermometer was no higher than fourteen.

January 26, 1915

Mr. Pease is hauling slack today for packing the ice. He has plenty at his house so is just hauling it up here from there. He will begin hauling ice tomorrow. John has bought fourteen tons of ice. If it won't all go in the ice house we'll put the rest in the cistern. Lots of folk fill their cisterns with ice out here. We got the ice for twenty-five cents a ton. The price is usually higher than that but a man near Penrose who is anxious to go into the business on a bigger scale came and offered that price to those who would pay in advance so he could send at once and get an ice plow. The ice is from good water, not alkaline. I don't know just how John is going to divide up the cost between us and Peases. Pease offered to do a good deal of the hauling and furnish the slack if we could let him go in with us in putting up the ice, as he does not have any good place to keep it. He put up a lot last year and it melted long before the summer was over. It is absolutely necessary to have ice here in the summer if you want to make butter. It will be quite handy to have ice any time we want it, especially for a man who is as fond of ice cream as John is. We had ice cream yesterday and today. We generally make the freezer full, and that lasts a couple days.

John will be working this week sawing out bee fixtures. You have no idea how much material is needed to be ready to handle five hundred colonies. Each colony needs two hive bodies and six supers in order to be fully prepared. Each hive body takes ten brood frames and each of these frames is made of four separate pieces of wood, twelve nails, two staples, and about two yards of wire. Each super requires two flat tins on each end, seven section holders, and one follower board. The section holders are made of wood, each piece grooved. To prepare the boards for the hive bodies and supers, each side piece must be handled through the machine three times and the end piece four times. Then, of course, they must be assembled and nailed together. Mr. Pease will do all the nailing together of the hive bodies and the supers. We are making three hundred hive bodies and six hundred supers, 3000 brood frames, 300 bottom boards and 300 covers for hives. The bottom boards and covers also require nailing together, as do the brood frames.

It is quite warm here now and there is scarcely a bit of wind. We can hear the river as plainly as you can hear the trains at 822. It seems so strange to me to think of hearing the noise of the water of a river three or four miles away and on the other side of very broken country with hills.

This morning Mr. Murray came for me because Mrs. Bygren is very sick. They came for Mrs. Murray during the night, and she went right over and was there when the doctor arrived. Mr. Murray wanted to know if I couldn't go up this morning so Mrs. Murray could get some rest during the day, in case it would be necessary to stay up again tonight. I went right over, sent Mrs. Murray home, and stayed till she came back about half past twelve. I got dinner and got the house cleaned up. She got back in time to serve the dinner and I came on home. I got my bread baked and did whatever else needed doing and then went back to Bygren's about six. Mrs. B. is much better this evening, and the doctor thinks the danger is over. She was seriously threatened with miscarriage, but the worst is probably averted now. She sure has been having a time, for her three children — six, four, and two years old, have all been sick with colds and such. Mrs. Murray and I are going back in the morning to get things straightened up for the day and get dinner. Then probably he can manage all right the rest of the day.

If I owned property in Powell I wouldn't let the post office come anywhere near it. Night before last there was another fire in Powell and the post office was again entirely destroyed. This fire was even worse than the other one, for that took only one big store and one little store, while this one took a hardware and implement store, a harness shop, a tailor shop, the post office, the butcher shop, the ice house, and a restaurant. In fact, half a block was destroyed. Most of the mail was saved — last time it was all saved. It happened this way: The girl who works in the post office was one of the first ones at the fire then. She had her keys with her and calmly went inside the post office, locked the door, gathered up all the mail from the racks and from the private boxes and everywhere else, then unlocked the door and told the crowd to carry out the fixtures. This time she was not there as early, and the crowd just broke in the door and carried out the fixtures with the mail right in the boxes. Naturally some of the mail got spilled out and lost in the mixup. I don't believe we lost any, for we got letters and also second class mail the next delivery. I hope none of the outgoing mail was lost, for we sent off a lot of letters that day — valentines, among other things. If you don't get a letter Saturday with a valentine enclosure, let me know. The thing that aroused us to the fact that there was something wrong was the dynamite blasting they did in hopes of saving some of the buildings. We heard this noise, and at first thought it was thunder. The second report was evidently not thunder, however, and we sat up in bed to see if we could see anything. As soon as we did this we saw the fire out the west windows, nearly five miles away. We could tell at once that it was an awful fire. This was about five o'clock in the morning, and the fire had evidently begun about four.

You ask how I can the beef. I wash it, and do not wipe off the water that clings to it. Then I salt and pepper it well and roast it in the oven, but without flour, and with no more water than that which clings to it from the washing. I use a good deal of suet with it so as to have plenty of broth to cover it when it is canned. When it is done, I cut it in slices as for the table, taking out all the bones. Then I let it get right hot again, usually on top of the stove, and then can it in glass jars. I have been using quart cans, but they hold so much I like pints better. I press the meat close down in the jar, using a stick about an inch square. I put in a lot of meat and several spoonfuls of broth, then press the meat down well. I keep this up till the jar is full when I run a fork down the sides to let the air up, the same as in canning fruit. Then I fill the jar to overflowing with the broth, and put on the rubber and lid, and seal tight. I set the jar upside down for a little while to be sure it does not leak, but turn it right side up in a few minutes so it can cool right side up. The jars and lids should be dry when the meat is put in. I set them on the stove shelf while I am roasting the meat so they will be warm when I fill them. Then they will not break. I think the only important things are to use only what water clings to the meat when it is washed, to have the cans dry, and to press the meat down well so that it is completely covered with the broth. When the meat cools it is then packed so well together it cannot be got loose without heating. In fact, if you want to get it out of the jar, you have to heat the jar to do so.

February 14, 1915

The Ladies Aid served lunch at the Michael sale the other day and made about fourteen dollars. I think they will do the serving at sales whenever they can, for they make more that way than any other.

There are lots of sales this month and next — six or seven. There is always a good deal of changing in a new country. It has been said that Iowa and Nebraska were settled three times — that the land changed hands three times before the people stayed permanently. Some of this changing here is due to the fact that people just homesteaded in order to sell out as soon as they had proved up. That is, they didn't come with the intention of staying. Then the man who is selling today is going farther west for his wife's health, and also because he has a good job on a project in Idaho, running some kind of a machine while the project is being made. He has not sold his farm here, and most likely will come back here after a while. He is just selling out his personal property and farm machinery, as he does not intend to farm in Idaho.

February 25, 1915

We went to Mrs. Sutton's funeral yesterday afternoon. There was quite a large crowd there. We did not go to the cemetery, but just to the house. One thing that was a shock to me was the news that there is not a hearse on the Project, and that an ordinary spring wagon or express is used for the conveyance of the coffin. John says it was very common in Posey County not to have a hearse, but I have never seen a funeral of a grownup person where there was not a regular hearse.

Yesterday at the funeral there were a few persons whom I did not know. Among them was a man whom I supposed to be the undertaker. After the service was over, we were standing in the yard while the coffin was being put in the wagon. I pointed out the man in question, and asked John if that was the undertaker. "Yes," he said, "Tucker." Well, that was irresistible. Of course I responded, "Did you say he was the undertucker?" Then he told me I ought to be ashamed of myself—that is, he did as soon as he could get his face straight enough to say anything.

February 28, 1915

The other night we were reading an article in the current *Everybody's* on the present day industrial situation. John read it to me—we do nearly all our reading out loud to each other. Later in the evening I happened to go into the kitchen, and with that article in mind noticed the kitchen table. There were two dishes of butter, maybe a couple pounds, a pan of eggs, a pan of milk, and on the sink drain board the day's baking of bread. We couldn't help thinking that we had a whole lot to be thankful for. Here were eggs, milk, butter and bread, and we had been just sort o' taking them for granted. I guess there would be lots of families who would like to see such a layout on their tables. They wouldn't exactly take them for granted. There are lots worse places to live than in the country, that's certain.

Mrs. Bygren has been very sick again. We didn't know of it till on the way home yesterday afternoon. I stopped in a little while. She is over it now, and told me when I got there, "Well, it's all over now." They don't seem to feel at all bad about losing the chance of a baby. Mr. Pease told us this morning that Mrs. Lovercheck has been very sick, too, and when I was out he told John she had had the same thing as Mrs. Bygren. The other day at the funeral someone backed a horse where she thought it was going to run into her. She climbed into a wagon to get out of the way and hurt herself in doing so. She felt a pain right away and the next day she had the trouble. It's too bad.

Mr. Roach and his bride are expected back the latter part of this week to the house nearest to us. The people are playing a joke on him. He has been working for the government in the summers, and has been boasting to his brother-in-law, Hoffman, for a long time about how fine the government bunks are. He even insisted that they were so fine for a married man, because he could sleep in his own bed and his wife in hers. The bunks are built a la sleeping car style, only they are exceedingly narrow—just wide enough for one person. Well, what did Hoffman do but get some other of the neighbors to back him up, and went to the government men and begged the loan of two bunks, telling them the situation. Of course they were as willing as could be, and they have put up the two bunks in Roach's house, taking his bed clear off. He won't know anything about it till he brings the bride home, which will probably be late in the evening, after they have had dinner and spent the afternoon at Hoffmans. It's sort o' a mean joke, but I guess Roach deserves it.

Mamma, we were amused at your remedy for cooling the bee cellar by using ice, and yet I guess we ought not laugh, either, for one of the best beekeepers in the country, Dr. Miller, of Illinois, tried that way to his very great sorrow. It isn't so much the temperature of the air in the bee cellar that counts as it is the quality, and what ice does to the quality is a heap. In fact, our cellar is constantly in temperature higher than most authorities say is the standard, yet they are perfectly quiet and doing well except when the temperature runs up extremely high or when there is a calm day on which the ventilation is not easy to keep good. And "quiet" in a bee cellar means to the eye and not to the ear, for there is a way—a slight hum— that sounds mighty good to a beekeeper's ear.

You ask if the bees stay in the hives in the cellar. Yes, at least they are supposed to. Of course old bees are constantly dying, and they crawl out of the hive to die. In a cellar containing as many colonies as ours has—say 450—it is estimated there will be about ten or twelve bushels of dead bees by the end of winter. When bees are wintered outside, they have to get out of the hive about every other week for what is called a cleansing flight. That is, they must get out to relieve the bowels, or they will develop dysentery. When they are wintered in a cellar, the flight is not necessary. In a cellar the temperature is high enough they do not have to work to keep the cluster warm. Consequently they do not eat as much honey. When they work, they have to eat. When they eat, they have to have the flight. In general the good colony needs from 35 to 40 pounds of honey from the time the honey flow stops till it begins again—till they can forage again.

March 9, 1915

I am cooking a piece of our pickled meat today. We had not used any because we wanted to find out about it first. When we made the pickle the first time we borrowed Pease's boiler, as it held more than ours. We boiled the pickle and set it aside to cool overnight. Then we put it on the meat. Some time after that we awoke to the fact that the boiler had a copper bottom and a copper rim near the top. Well, we didn't want to poison ourselves, so we sent a sample of the pickle to Professor Loy in Laramie to analyze. In the meantime we did not eat any of the meat. Yesterday we got his letter saying that the meat was perfectly all right. He said he thought he might be able to find at least a trace of copper but had not been able to get the slightest reaction for copper. I think that is one reason why he waited several weeks before answering us. Last year Mr. Nauser sent us a piece of beef that had been in brine for several months. I soaked it out well, changing the water several times, as one would do with salt fish, and roasted it. It was fine, and if I had not salted it any in cooking it would have been almost as good as fresh roast beef. I intend to use a good deal of ours that way. Of course I may have to soak it 24 or even 48 hours in water, changing the water several times, and 12 or 18 hours in milk — skim milk, sour milk, or buttermilk — any one will do.

March 11, 1915

The other night the newlyweds, Mr. and Mrs. Roach, went over to Hoffmans. This time they walked over. John saw them go by here hand in hand, swinging along like youngsters. They didn't see him till they were past, as he was in the barn when they went by. Then they heard him rattle the pump. They turned and spoke, but still held hands. John and I have always gone about hand in hand, when we go over the farm anywhere, or walk to the bee house or bee yard. He has always teased me about what Mr. Roach would say if he noticed us, and I always answered that we were setting him a good example. Well, when he saw the new couple doing the same, he had to agree that the example had not been for nought. I was over yesterday for a while, and we had such a good time. Of course she is as homesick as can be, and of course I know just how she feels. The first three weeks I was out here were the hardest weeks of my life, I know. I didn't want to undo what I had done, but I was realizing for the first time the finality of it, how far I was away from all of you, and what a change had really taken place. I wasn't unhappy, or sorry, or anything like that, but nevertheless I felt like a raw nerve all over. I told her yesterday she would get over it in a little while. I offered her my shoulder to weep on any time she wants it, though I told her I knew his shoulder was the best place — that is, for her.

March 14, 1915

We had a right good Aid meeting at Adkins. Mrs. Reese brought up the question of work, and the Aid was willing to work, but not to buy material and sew it up. Meeting after next we are to have an all-day meeting and sew for Mrs. Brown. The Presbyterian Aid at Powell does this quite frequently. I was surprised and shocked when I heard what the charge was. I heard the ladies say that the Powell Aid charges seventy-five cents for an all-day's work. I thought that each woman would hardly earn seventy-five cents a day when there was a number together, all talking and not working as fast as one or two alone. Then the ladies went on to say that at least six women must come to sew for the seventy-five cents, and as many more as came made no difference in the price. Then I found that the price charged was 75 cents for the whole work, and at least six women must work. Fancy getting the work of six and maybe ten or twelve women all day for seventy-five cents. For instance, Mrs. Buch had the Powell Aid work for her. Her house is large so there was room to have a large cutting table handy all the time. Well, they made nightgowns for the whole family of five, did a lot of mending, and lengthened the hems in half a dozen or more of the girl's dresses — all for 75 cents! If I had a lot of simple sewing to do, I'd have the Aid do it. I wouldn't want them to do anything important, for that kind of work needs careful attention. But plain sewing, such as most underwear, or hemming towels, or mending stockings, or such, they could do all right. Making aprons would be all right, too. John asked me if I wouldn't get them to make the shirts I am going to make for him, but I said those shirts had to be made right, and I didn't trust them to a crowd — I'll make them myself.

We finished putting the foundation yesterday in the 2520 brood frames that needed foundation. Yesterday afternoon we hauled the 252 hives full of new frames into the new shop. It was quite a little work to do it. We didn't think it would take so long, but as 36 hives made a wagon load — with high side-boards — it took longer than one would think. It was quite dark when we got done. Then we had the chores to do. As John had mashed his finger I did the milking last night. I like to milk, really, as it gives you such a comfortable feeling to be surrounded by a lot of cows and horses, all your own. There is such peace and quiet all about, that one can't help feeling like counting his blessings.

There have been so many filings during the past few days.

I think yesterday's paper said there were fourteen during the past week. Land will soon be entirely gone around here. The new twenty-year law has induced people to come, and the hard times have added to that inducement. You see, under the new law, settlers have to make one payment now, amounting to about five percent of the total, and have twenty years to pay off all the price, with no payments after the first until five years have elapsed. It looks good to a man with limited means to be able to make one payment and then have the use of the land five years before having to make any more payments. Then the second payment, after the five years, is a very small one. The next is larger and the next larger, and so on, till all is paid by the end of twenty years. This new regulation will make it possible for men with smaller capital to settle here. Heretofore a man had to have enough ready cash to make his first payment and his second, and to live on for at least two years. Of course in either case a man had to have enough to build some sort of a shack and to fence his land, and get whatever machinery he had to have. Why, Cora, even the piece of land this side of the cemetery has been taken. A family with a number of children has built a tent house on the bluff and is living there, above the ditch, where there is no water. Of course there is water on part of the land, and of course, too, they have to pay only for what is irrigable, but their house is high and dry among the sand and cactus and, I might add, the prairie dogs. I wonder if the "cute little things" won't be holding up their hands all summer at the foolishness of some men for filing on some of the places that are filed on. Or it might be they will be holding up their hands in despair at the knowledge that all their playgrounds are taken and they have no place in which to burrow their homes.

March 19, 1915

Wednesday morning John had the men help him to set out 150 colonies of bees. The warm weather made it impossible to keep the temperature in the bee cellar anything like desirable with so many bees there. With 150 colonies less it is easier to keep cool. Each hive makes quite an appreciable amount of heat. The men set the bees out early in the morning, beginning work at two o'clock and finishing at six. I had breakfast ready for them when they quit. That was a beautifully warm day, and the bees were out in swarms from the colonies outside. They wanted water, and every place where there was water to be found you could scoop up the bees by the handful. They got a fine flight and ought to be in good shape now for this spell of cool weather. We shall not set these colonies back in the cellar again. We would like very much to hold the greater part of the bees in the cellar till about the fifth or maybe the tenth of April, if the weather doesn't get too warm. We are pretty certain to have some bad weather yet and we would rather have the bees inside till all chance of any prolonged cold spells is past. The point is that we have to protect all we set out now. If we can keep them in the cellar till the second week in April, we won't have to go to the trouble of putting straw and boards around each hive. Yesterday morning John and I went through all the hives outside, putting on inner cover boards, seeing if the bees needed more honey for feed, and reducing the entrance to only about half an inch. All this will help to keep them warmer.

We set the incubator the first of the week and it is running all right. The temperature goes down a little at night, so I turn the lamp up at night and turn it back down again in the morning. Otherwise all I do at present is fill the lamp. The lamp for our incubator has a metal chimney with an isinglass insertion to show the flame. Consequently we do not have any glass chimney to clean or to get broken. Our incubator is a Sure Hatch, 1907 model. That is getting pretty old now, but it still does the work all right. It is a hot water machine, 200 egg size. We put in 208 eggs. In a day or so I shall have to begin to put a dish of water on each side of the floor of the incubator and renew the water as fast as it evaporates. The dry air out here is bad on the eggs, and moisture has to be supplied. Several times toward the end of the hatch we sprinkle the eggs with warm water when we take them out to cool them, and during the last

oth rather wet with warm
enew it. When people set
hey usually set the nest as
then when the eggs are
set of water on the ground
rather wet. This moisture
d. We are getting a good
y. Unfortunately, they are
ow.

March 21, 1915

The day was lovely — warm
the time church was over,
owing, and the ride home
was far from the pleasant buggy ride the earlier trip was. We
went to the Baptist church — we had been there before and were
glad to get away that time, and still were more glad today.
We went there this morning for the reason that we have been
promising a long time to go to Kinton's to visit. Now we haven't
yet become hardened to descend upon helpless people after
church without an invitation for dinner, so John conceived the
bright idea of going to church where the Kintons are leading
lights and of exposing ourselves to an invitation home to dinner
and to spend the afternoon. We found today when none of the
Kintons were at church that they have been sick, with chicken
pox. We didn't care to be exposed to that, dinner or no dinner
invitation, so after church, when that happy time finally
arrived, we came home to our kettle of vegetable soup, soup
meat, horseradish, baked apples, and doughnuts.

The Baptist minister is a man who ought to have been
superannuated some time ago. He is as good hearted and good
intentioned as can be, but everlastingly long-winded when he
gets started, and doesn't say much anyway. As soon as this man
begins to preach you can't see his eyes. All you can see is a rim
of red filled with water. As soon as he reaches the firstly he
turns on the tears. He cries all the time, no matter what he

talks about, only when he talks about affecting matters he cries worse. This morning he got to telling about the death of his father, and actually had to stop once till he could get the tears out of his nose and eyes. I can't exactly say I like that sort of preaching. In fact, I believe I would go so far as to state that as soon as he begins to weep, my religious feelings ooze away with the brine. The more he weeps the less devotional I feel. He kept saying in his sermon this morning that he was not sure he was the right man for the place. John said he could tell him the answer to that in a few words.

I wish you knew the Murrays. They are dears. They are more like the people I was used to in Bloomington than most of the folk around here. We have taken quite a shine to each other—all four of us. They have sure been boosting this country. Two of their former neighbors in Missouri and two of Mrs. Murray's brothers have filed on land here within the past couple weeks. Mrs. Murray is so delighted to have her brothers near. Both are unmarried. Cheer up, Cora, maybe there's a chance there. One of them is awfully nice and just about the right age for you. The other is nice too, but he is older and not so good looking.

March 25, 1915

I have been wondering what sort of an April Fool joke I would get on John this year. There is no use making fake candy, for I fooled him on that last year. The other night when I was picking out the nuts for the schnitzbrod I had an idea. I was using English walnuts so I just saved a lot of the whole halves of the shells and some of the nuts, and will fix up a lot of nuts with various things inside. I haven't decided yet what I shall use. Some of them will just have a slip of paper—April Fool. I wish I could fix it so he'd get one of those first. In others I'll put candy or filling of some kind.

The next time I go to Powell I must get a package of Easter egg dye. I like to have a few eggs for the youngsters as well as for ourselves. Last year it was the day before Easter before I realized the fact. We were not going to town again, and there was no chance to get any dye. I began to search my brain for a substitute, and to search the cupboards and closets as well. In the closet in the old house I found a piece of pink mosquito bar. The idea struck me to boil this to see if the color would come out. I did and it did. Then I boiled the eggs in the water I had boiled the netting in and I never had such lovely pink eggs — much prettier than regular dye pink. But there doesn't happen to be any pink netting on hand this year and it will be cheaper to buy a package of dye than to buy mosquito bar.

April 1, 1915

John went to the river yard this morning. When he got back a little while ago he noticed a little sack of English walnuts sitting innocently on the gasoline stove. "O," he said, "when did you get the walnuts?" and dived in. The first one he opened had a roll of cocoanut candy in it. He was got. He was so surprised he was afraid it was cotton or soap or some such thing, and hastily stuck it back in the sack without tasting it at all. Then he started after me, and I am afraid that if I were less strong than I am I would have got a good spanking. As it was, I was able to hold him off till I reached a convenient chair and sat down. Then there wasn't any place to spank. By the time he washed his face and hands and ate a slice or two of bread and butter and a few peaches (about a pint) his faith in humanity was restored and he was willing to find what he could find in the nutshells — even to the one filled with a slip bearing the compliments of the day.

I am making a path leading from the front stoop to the front gate. People have a habit of just tripping across the lawn anywhere, so I decided that maybe if we'd lay out a walk bordered with stones on each side people might take the hint and walk there. At least we think the idea is worth trying. John raked off the manure from the yard the other day and the lawn looks fine. We are right stuck up about it. Maybe when it reaches the cutting stage we won't feel quite so gay as we push a lawnmower over it, but we are willing to risk trying. There isn't a house between here and Powell but one that has a lawn, and most of them have no attempt at one. The Murray's, I am glad to say, brought with them their ideas of a nice yard and want to start a lawn as soon as possible. But most people just take it for granted that this is a bare looking, sandy, cactus-covered country except in the gardens or fields, and don't try to have anything else about the house. It is just as with the bulbs—the tulips and Easter flowers. People just take a spell when they see ours and declare they hadn't any idea such things would grow out here. But they never had the nerve or the faith to try them. They just imagine they won't grow and that is the end. I think the main trouble is that folk get in the habit of thinking they are in a new country and they just accept the lack of flowers and grass and don't try to have anything different. I sort o' think it's true here as anywhere else—you can get any-thing in the world if you just go after it hard enough.

April 2, 1915

Today is such a fine warm day I have been out in the yard and garden most of the morning. Of course it is too early to make garden yet, but we are getting the place ready. I raked up weeds and burned them. John is now scattering manure over the whole garden, and Mr. Pease is going to plow it for us tomorrow or Monday. So we'll get the garden in order and then I can plant the sweet peas and some early lettuce and maybe a few radishes. I got quite a lot of flower seeds, but all of the hardiest and most easily cultivated kinds, such as poppy, phlox, gaillardia, nasturtium, portulaca, and such. I did send for a package of the sweet scented carnations, thinking that maybe I could raise a plant or two to have in the house next winter. I also sent for some hollyhocks that will bloom the first year and ever after. In vegetables we stuck to the plain ones mostly—beans, peas, corn, lettuce, radish, salsify, beets, turnips, though we are going to try popcorn and peanuts. Of course I have the cabbage, celery, kohlrabi, cauliflower and such already up in the house. We are going to plant the musk and water melons down just below the beeyard east of the house. There is a fine, sandy spot of soil there. John will manure the place well, and I believe he means to bring some soil from the river—that soil is pure leaf mold.

How good it was of you, Edith, to send us the box of Easter eggs and rabbits. We have enjoyed them immensely. I was thinking the first of the week I wished we could get some candy eggs for Easter but I don't know whether or not we could have got them out here. Then your box came. The eggs are most awfully good and you sure did remember my fondness for licorice. I am glad to get the sealing wax, too, though John is not so keen on the subject. I have made a stamp H which I shall use on state occasion. Ordinarily the mailman gets almost up the hill before I get to the sealing wax stage and on such occasions there won't be any time for fancy doings.

I must explain about John. Your box came on the first of April. I opened the box and passed the candy, and I noted the sealing wax and also that the sticks were broken into a number of pieces. I didn't have time to pick out the sealing wax before I left to go over to Murray's. As soon as I got back I put the candy in a dish and took out the wax. I fitted the sticks together, and one piece about 3/4 inch long was missing. I hunted and hunted and couldn't find it. When John came in later I noticed he looked rather odd and I immediately inquired the reason. I discovered that while I was gone to Murray's he had come in for a piece of candy. He took the first piece his fingers touched and put it in his mouth. As soon as he chewed he discovered it wasn't candy at all. He thought the stuff was something I had put there to fool him. The matter was made worse by the fact that while I was gone he had been working as hard and as fast as he could to fix the wash machine with a new stand and a bench. After this work to surprise me, he came in and bit into— sealing wax. Well, it was sort o' the unkindest cut of all. Every time since that he has started to eat some of the candy he inquires solicitously if there is any more sealing wax in it. Of course after I got home and we held an explanation fest, and then next morning when I discovered the surprise in the shop, things were all right again.

The neighbors all around us are plowing or working the soil. Mr. Pease plowed and harrowed our garden the other day and yesterday he plowed for grain for us in the field just south and east of the garden, down to the bee yard. We went through the bees again this morning and we are glad to say that there are not as many dead and weak ones as we first thought. There are a plenty, 'tis true, but not as many as it seemed the first time we looked at them. This winter was such an unusual one and this spring so unusual, that on the whole we would have more bees now if we had wintered outdoors. But winters like this are rare.

Our incubator didn't do very well. We haven't much more than a sixty per cent hatch—really about one less than that. There are a few weak chicks that will die, and the sooner the better. I think we'll have eighty-five strong chicks out of the lot. We don't need as many chickens to eat this year as last because we have the beef, and we really don't want to take as many through the winter next year as we did this. We now have just about fifty hens. Thirty is plenty. The most eggs we have got any one day this year is 33. We usually don't get more than two dozen eggs a day. Of course with eggs as low as twelve and a half cents a dozen, we get quite a bit of cash for the eggs. I should hardly say cash, though, for it is usually the case that we have to take out in trade the amount for the eggs. The stores won't run a bill for anybody. But if you take in produce, they will run a bill for what they owe you above the amount immediately taken out. Rather a one-sided procedure, n'est-ce pas?

I had some callers yesterday, Mrs. Jones and Mrs. Collins. Mrs. Collins is a very up-to-date lady and left a visiting card. I was amused when she took it out of her case and cast her eye about the room to see where to lay it. Unfortunately I hadn't instructed Bridget to be standing ready, holding out her "pan." Mrs. C. looked wildly about and finally laid the card on the table. The idea that a card tray might be needed had never entered my head. In fact, when I went calling one day and took my cards along, to use in case anybody might not be at home, John said people wouldn't know what the cards were if I left one. This one that Mrs. C. left yesterday is the first visiting card, except my own, I've seen out here. I told John last night I guess I'd have to invest in a card tray now. He said all right, we'd just got a new 5 and 10 cent store catalogue. He thought that would tease me, but I told him I'd about as lief get one there as anywhere.

April 26, 1915

The Werts have a new automobile. It is a Ford touring car and is a beauty. My, but we'll be glad when we have one, too. Werts were going to finish building their house this year, but decided to get a car instead. Mr. Werts said he believes you can get more fun out of a car than out of a nice house. I told him we might come to the same conclusion if we couldn't afford both next year.

April 27, 1915

John and I both have spring fever today. His really is a spell of aching. Every once in a while, especially when we have a touch of eastern weather, he will ache from the lame leg. His forearms, the calves of the legs, and the muscles of the back are the sore parts. Last night he took a hot bath and then I rubbed him well with Absorbine. This morning we were both lying around, not worth much, and I said, "Do you know what mamma would do to both of us if she were here? She'd give us both a dose of Ague Tonic before we could say Jack Robinson." I really thought a dose wouldn't hurt either of us, so I agreed to take a dose if he would. It wasn't a fair bargain, however, for he doesn't mind the taste at all—in fact, he rather likes the taste of quinine. When I found that out, I told him he couldn't watch me take mine. I wasn't going to have him enjoy taking the medicine and then have the fun of seeing me make a face over mine. So he obediently hid his face in the couch pillow— and then peeped every half second.

May 4, 1915

I had my first experience in "votes for women" yesterday and found out how it feels. The election was that of a school board member and a special tax levy for school purposes. Of course that is mere formality. So, hurrah for equal suffrage. The funny thing was that I came near being voted on as well as voting.

Last fall I started the agitation for a woman on the school board. There are lots of things a woman sees that a whole board of men would be blind to. I don't know just when the time would be ripe for action on the part of the women, but I thought we couldn't begin too early to talk about the matter, even if we didn't do anything for a year or two. Well, I heard last week, to my infinite surprise, that I was going to be a candidate at yesterday's election. I asked who was running me, and how one got run, but no one seemed to know who was back of it. I didn't in the least object to being a member of the school board but I decided one thing: I wouldn't run unless I was practically certain of election, not so much just because it was I, but because I felt that when a woman, any woman, actually made the race, she must be elected for the sake of the principle. In all the discussion of the subject, it was always taken for granted that if any woman's name came up, it should be mine.

There was one very important feature which largely determined the matter of my name's not coming up at this time. This school district is a large one. It includes Garland, Penrose, the Star School, and the Kinne School. The school board consists of three persons, one elected each year to serve for a term of three years. It has come to be an accepted, though unwritten fact, that one of the persons is to represent Garland, one Penrose, and one the Star and Kinne schools together. This election was for the Garland district. We live in the Star-Kinne district. If my name had come up, a lot of literal-minded men would have brought up the unwritten custom and there is a question as to whether we women could have carried the election. Next year the term expires for the member from the Star-Kinne district. By then we will be ready for action. We decided it was better to wait till we were really ready for action and then do something than to try to do something when the times were were not right. Also we learned today how the thing is done, and we'll know how to do it.

The thing that amused me so much today was the fact that the men were so scared that the women were going to do something. The men had everything all fixed. Only one man, L. J. Wood, was nominated. The man who nominated him prefaced the nomination with the statement, "It is customary to have a member to represent *the district in which he lives.*" O, it was fun. I couldn't keep my face straight. When all the women sat still and let the nominations be closed, the men all looked as if they had done a hard day's work. Not all the men, of course, for there were quite a number who think there ought to be a woman on the board, but the men who *think* they run things. Mrs. Jones did start to get up to put up my name, but the men moved so fast she didn't say anything. I am glad she didn't, for we would have had a hard fight on our hands to win at this time, and next time we'll be all ready beforehand. Our woman's club can control the election if we stand together. And so you see, I am in politics. Well, well. Who would have thought it. Of course I wouldn't say it outside the family, but I'll own up to you it sort o' flatters me to have everybody take it for granted that if a woman is to be elected it will be I.

Ye went to church yesterday. The day was Mother's Day. Now I approve very highly of honoring mothers all we can, but it's mighty hard on a person whose mother is 1800 miles away. Of course it made me most awfully homesick. One reason why I went to bed so early last night was that I was so homesick I cried, and John had me go to bed so he could coax me to sleep and make me forget it.

We had a lovely drive yesterday. We went down to the river straight south of Powell, then came on eastward, driving to the river again whenever we could. The only drawback was the gnats — the gnatsty gnats, as Edith called them. We ate part of our lunch as we drove along and then had peaches and cake at the river. It was the middle of the afternoon when we got back. What with the fresh air and the breeze and the sunshine we were both so sleepy we could hardly keep awake.

I must tell you a cute remark John got off the other day. He came in about milking time in the evening to where I was sewing in the bedroom and announced that I hadn't washed the milk bucket that morning. Now Cora will tell you what an elusive thing a milk bucket is, and how easy it is to forget it when you are washing dishes. Still, as I took a rapid mental survey of the kitchen as it was that morning when I did the work, I couldn't remember a milk bucket on the landscape, so I had sense enough not to begin to apologize, but to ask, "Where was it?" John answered, "Down at the barn." Then of course I had him — or I thought I did. "I think you had better get me a long hose," I began, seriously, as if getting the milk bucket washed at long distance was the main issue of my life. "O," he said, as seriously and as earnestly, "Aren't yours long enough?" The implication that I could go down to the barn and get the bucket, as well as the play on meaning, made me roar.

May 11, 1915

We have just been up to the corner to look at the weir which measures the water we get. This year each unit is allowed a certain amount of water—two acre feet for each acre, for the minimum regular charge—one dollar per acre—and all above that used must be paid for at the same rate of 50 cents an acre foot. An acre foot is enough water to cover an acre a foot deep. The amount allowed is about enough for the average farm. The man who wastes water has to pay for the extra he needs. The Reclamation Service has had trouble with people wasting water. Some farmers have the idea that there is an unlimited supply in the river (which is true) and that it doesn't make any difference to anybody how much they let run to waste. But it does make a difference.

This spring the Service put in a weir at each unit to measure the amount of water delivered. The unitholder can tell if he gets as much as he ordered, and the ditch rider can tell how much to charge up to the unit.

May 14, 1915

We went to the river yard yesterday and found things in excellent shape. The colonies are extra strong. There are only about eight dead ones out of 112, and only three or four that are not extra strong. Down there the cottonwoods and willows give an abundance of pollen very early, and this stimulates the bees to rearing brood. Then this year there are scads of dandelions down near the river, and the bees are doubtless getting a little honey from them as well as pollen.

I told you that the Farmers' Union wants to get in fresh fruit in carload lots this summer. John is also thinking of having it work up a co-operative insurance organization and perhaps organize a money-lending society. Insurance here is extremely dear. We have to pay a rate of $3.45 for five years on house and contents and of $3.00 on bee business fixtures, barn, shops, etc. This makes the insurance cost a little more than sixty-five dollars on a little over two thousand dollars worth of property. One of the Colorado Farmers' Unions has a fire and stock insurance company that cuts the rate down half. There is no reason why we shouldn't have one here — if only someone will do the work. Of course it would mean a lot of work, but I guess one couldn't serve his community in a better way than by helping the neighbors get what they need at lower prices.

I had the very great pleasure yesterday of receiving, instead of the usual blue slip, a card from Orange Judd Company which read, "Your contribution 'Homemade Soap' is accepted for Orange Judd Weeklies, but may not be printed for some time. When it is published, a copy of the paper will be sent you, and payment will be made late in the month following date of publication." The card came from Springfield, Mass., though I sent the article to Minneapolis, where the *Northwest Farmstead* is published. Just imagine me with my hands in my vest strutting around. I wonder how much I'll get for the article. It was about two typewritten pages long. Maybe I'll be a writer yet someday, if only on household topics. Maybe I can earn enough to pay the postage on the things that aren't accepted, so I won't lose anything on the whole deal. Anyway, maybe I'll learn how to write and that will be worth something. Every once in awhile I dash off something, let it cool, and fix it up so it sounds all right.

May 17, 1915

John and I were laughing last night about how rich we are getting, or rather, ought to be. We are taking in at present a dollar and seventy-five cents a day for pasturage. The cream and eggs we are selling will make the amount come to three dollars a day, and there is a dollar a day pension. That amounts to four dollars a day. I said last night there is no use of our working when we have an income of four dollars a day!

Well, we are at present on the foundation where the house is to stand, except that we are above it. The house has been jacked up but has not yet been let down entirely on the foundation. We are considerably higher in the world than we were where the house stood before, as the foundation is about two feet high—that is, above the ground. The men finished moving the house while I was cooking dinner, and I felt like the cook on a steamboat. I stayed out of the house most of the morning after the men began to work.

When John's old two-room settler's house is moved, the farm will begin to take on the appearance of a place with some plan, not a higgledy-piggledy scattering of buildings. We are planning each building such a distance from every other building that fire could not sweep from one to the other. We can soon begin to plan the yard as a whole and put out trees where we want them to stay, in the back and side yard as well as the front. Someday we are going to have a scrumptious place. I am glad you saw it last summer in its rawness and its worst condition, so you will be able to appreciate with us the changes as we make them. It's lots of fun to work out a place in a new country. Of course it takes a long time to get things really in shape but it is mighty satisfying to be able to do everything the way you want it.

I saw a hat at church yesterday that is one of the prettiest hats I ever saw. The hat itself was a straw, a fine, silky-like braid. The shape was almost that of a sailor, with a medium brim and a fairly high crown, rather broad also. The color was the stylish one that is half way between gray and tan—champagne or beige, or something like that. The trimming consisted of velvet ribbon about an inch wide simply laid around the crown, not all the way around in the back, but reaching to the edge of the brim on each side of the back and hanging from there with a long loop and end. This ribbon was a dull, Delft blue. The rest of the trimming was a medium sized bunch of foliage and tiny buds at the left front, topped with a rather high-standing rose made of satin ribbon. The rose was a lovely, clear, rather deep pink. The dull color of the hat, the dull blue of the ribbon, the dull green of the foliage all led up to the wonderful clear pink of the beautiful ribbon rose. The hat was very simple, but as artistic a thing in color and form as anything I have ever seen.

I guess you girls know we have a ribbon-flower factory in Powell. The proprietor, Mrs. LeMareschal, had a flower factory in St. Louis. She had to come here for her health, or that of her husband, and brought the establishment with her. Her flowers are shipped all over the United States. She makes the most beautiful ribbon flowers I have ever seen. She has a millinery store too, and it is said her hats are ridiculously low in price, though they are almost always very artistic and pretty.

June 18, 1915

We are getting out circulars for the Farmers' Union — counting on sending a letter to practically every head-of-family on the Flat. That means about 500. At Powell we found we could get the 500 printed for about three dollars. It took our breath away to find we could get it done that cheap, and we immediately told Mr. Peterson to go at it. He will have them ready Monday. We have the envelopes all addressed — Mrs. Hancock, Mrs. Lew Cline, and Mrs. Pease helped one afternoon and Miss Smith helped yesterday.

I went to the flower factory in Powell this morning and got me some flowers for my hat. I got two sprays, which the milliner made up to suit. You ought to see her twist up a bunch of flowers. She will take a little flower, then a leaf, then a bud, and twist them into the most artistic spray. I told her I wanted something in lavendar or purple. She showed me lovely velvet pansies and said that little ribbon rosebuds in shades of pink, and green leaves would go well with them. She twisted up a spray consisting of one yellow and purple pansy, one purple pansy, a bud, half a dozen leaves, and half a dozen wee pink ribbon rosebuds. I liked it so well I told her to make another. I think the two will finish the hat completely. She charged only thirty-five cents a spray. The spray is about eight inches long. She finished the stems with rubber, so the stems can show, as is the style this year. She makes a great many store-decorating flowers. She showed me a big trunk-full ready to ship out. These were sweet peas in vines. She had several great shipping boxes of sweet peas on stems, a new kind imitating the new orchid sweet peas. They were lovely. She also had great red roses, such as stores use in tall vases and jars, and quantities of smilax vines. She was making rambler roses and her work table was loaded with the little roses ready to be put together with the leaves she had also ready. She makes all sorts of flowers and leaves—silk, velvet, ribbon, lawn, plain, waxed, and frosted. She showed me her forms and press. The pieces for the flowers and leaves are cut out with stamps or punches, a dozen or so thicknesses at a time. Then they are pressed into shape, tinted as needed, waxed, and put together. Then the leaves and flowers are put together in sprays. If ever I run out of work and want something to keep my fingers out of mischief, I'll get a job making flowers for her. I imagine it would be pleasant work for an invalid or a convalescent—not that I want to become one of the last mentioned in order to be eligible for a job, however.

June 21, 1915

When we went to church yesterday morning we noticed the Hindoo who is working for Loomis's at work with his companions in the beet field. There have been about 1200 acres of beets put out this spring here. Practically all the hand work is done by imported help. Each man who has twenty acres of beets in gets a "beet family" or several men who put in less acreage go together to hire a family. Sometimes the families are several single men, but more often a real family with a whole raft of children. Most of these people are Hungarians though some are of other Slav tribes. The single men are mostly

Americans and Mexicans. Loomis's have a Hindoo, however. These beet people work on Sunday the same as any other day — that is, most of them do, especially the men. Last Sunday when we went to church the fields were quite muddy, and the Hindoo had taken off his shoes and was working in his socks. John is fond of the limerick about the Hindoo — you know it:

> The poor benighted Hindoo,
> He does the best he kin do;
> He sticks to his task
> To the very last,
> And for pants he makes his skin do.

Now this Hindoo made the rhyme change a little, for when applied to him we decided it would have to read in the last line, "And for shoes he makes his skin do." Loomises have built a little addition to their house — a sort of lean-to at the back. John took a good look at it yesterday and remarked that it was more of a subtraction to the house than an addition.

June 24, 1915

I hope I can be there next fall for the Indiana Club reunion. It is certainly complimentary for some of the old friends to say it wouldn't be worthwhile coming to if I weren't there. Don't have it too early in the fall, for I couldn't get there for two reasons — one is I couldn't leave till the honey was all graded and ready for shipment, as I do that part, and the other is I couldn't go till the honey is sold as we won't have any fortune of ready money by that time, after we settle for the things we are having done this summer.

John has about concluded that he won't go east next winter. He would rather use the money it would take for his trip to help one of his sisters who has not been too well for over a year. We have been quite worried about her. I think it is lovely of him to care so much for his sisters, and you may be sure it argues that a man who is so tender and solicitous about his sisters will be more than so for his wife. We helped this sister a little this past winter and the thought that we cared enough to help was of more benefit to her, I believe, than the medicine she took and the doctor's care. John has always hoped we could get this family out here somewhere on a farm and help them to get settled on it and to make the payments till they could own it themselves.

We wish they lived closer, so we could do something for the youngsters. They are such nice children. If anything should happen to Anna, we might have a chance to get a whole family readymade for us. John is always saying how good it would be for the children to be with me. Ahem.

John laughed at me the other night, and when I found out what I had said I laughed more than he did. We had gone to bed and were stretching out in the most comfortable position. I said something about putting my arm under my pillow, and John asked me if that was a comfortable position for me to lie on my stomach with my arm under the pillow. "Why yes," I answered, "when I want to be comfortable I always put my head under my arm." He began to laugh and I couldn't see what was funny. He asked me again and I said the same thing over. Then how he did laugh, and finally I caught on to what I was saying. When I could talk for laughing, I said, "Did you think I was a chicken?" "No," he answered, "a goose."

Bloomington, Indiana
June 28, 1915

(letter from Cora)

I wonder if Edith has written recently about Edward and the possibility of his coming West. We do so hope he can, but he says he simply can't. He really does need the rest this summer before he finishes law school. My plan is for you to ask him to come to help you. You'll have to be not only tactful, but clever about it as I fear he'll be a little hard to manage. Don't you think you could put it up to him that you need him for the summer and that you'll pay his way for the help he'll be? If he suspected I was paying the fare he wouldn't think for a minute of going. The fare will be about 70 or 75 dollars, but I think you'd better send him 75. Please tend to the matter right away as he really ought to be out there soon. I wonder if it would be better for John or for you to make the offer? If John writes you can write, too, of course. I do so hope you can manage it all right. Please write to Edw. at once and let me know what the arrangement is about the money. I know you are as anxious as I am to have Edw. there—you really are, aren't you? And if he's going to come he might as well go at once. Then Bady can come later and so can I. Do you really think you could stand three of us?

July 1, 1915

The neighborhood had somewhat of a surprise the other day when Ernest Richards appeared "in our midst" with a bride. There was a rumor all spring that he would be married this summer, but he had never said anything to me about it, and I didn't say anything to him, thinking he would tell me when he got ready. The last time he was here a week ago I had it on the tip of my tongue to tease him about the rumor but then concluded it was really none of my affair. The girl is from Indiana. I haven't met her yet, so I don't know whether or not I know her. I know her first name is Cora. I can't think of anyone I know by that name except—well, I'll tell you a story. The other day Laura Reese was in the post office when Richards came in and asked for his mail. He was alone, though it was after she was here. He said, "Is there any mail for Cora Richards?" Laura jumped up, ran home as fast as she could, and cried, "Oh mamma, mamma, her name is Cora. Do you suppose it could be Cora Hennel surprised us all and didn't let us know she was coming?" Well, when they told me about it I assured them it wasn't you, and Mrs. Reese verified my assertions by saying she had met the bride, and it wasn't Cora Hennel.

July 7, 1915

I guess I'll tell you the best news first, though I suspect you already know it, as a letter from Edward has had time to reach you before this does. It is that we had a telegram from

Edward yesterday saying he would come the first of next week. We are as tickled as can be. Poor lad, I'll wager he is as delighted to come as we are to have him. He says if we are willing to run the risk of getting such a poor farm hand as he is, he'll be glad to come. He says to send him the fifty we mentioned. I went to Powell this morning and sent him a New York draft for that amount. Cora, will you please send the fifty to us as soon as convenient? There is no hurry, but we'll need it before you get here. We have been saving fifty dollars to get a telephone put in, and we'll have to pay as soon as the phone is put in. The poles are due to arrive in a few days and will be put up at once, and as soon as they are up the line will be completed. The Powell Telephone Company, which is a cooperative affair, has recently reorganized. The shares of stock are fifty dollars face value. Each telephone number user has to own a share of the stock, and gets his line put in. If the line doesn't cost as much as fifty dollars to install he gets a refund, or has to pay only the actual pro rata cost of his phone, all the phones on one line being charged with an equal share of the building expense of the line.

Our Fourth of July celebration was a glorious success. People thought the program as a whole was simply fine, and the speech was one of the best I ever heard. I was on the program twice, once to read the Declaration of Independence and the other to announce our lecture course.

At noon we had a good time. We invited some Powell people to eat dinner with us, and we and the Werts, the Hancocks, Saxes, and Mrs. Werts' sister, Miss Robinson, all ate together. In the afternoon I spent most of the time in the Club stand. We sold lemonade, crackerjack, ice cream cones, sandwiches, iced tea, and cookies, and had a fine trade. We sold about eighteen gallons of lemonade. I got to Garland before eight o'clock in the morning, and Mrs. Brown and I made the lemonade. I have never made a large quantity at one time, but figured out the proportions and, strange to tell, got them exactly right. For a ten gallon jar we used four dozen lemons, six pounds of sugar, and an ounce and a half of tartaric acid.

We put in ice to take up the space of about a gallon of water, and filled up the jar with water. The lemonade was simply fine. We took in over fifty dollars at the stand, but as the expenses were over thirty we didn't make any fortune.

We had our first mess of green peas today. My, but they are good. I have six rows across the garden, in three sowings a week or so apart. We'll have just loads of peas. I know the girls will be glad, for the peas here are so good. I never had as many as I could eat till I came out here. I want to can some this year. Your way of canning beans, mamma, is what we call out here the government way, for it is the way the government bulletins recommend. People here can corn, peas, beans, and all sorts of things that way. Usually they boil the jars an hour a day for three days, leaving the jars standing in the boiler untouched between boilings. Some vegetables will not keep if boiled only once, even if boiled a comparatively longer time. Peas, I understand, are quite hard to keep. The newest government bulletin, however, recommends boiling peas only once, for I believe three hours. But the peas must first be "blanched," that is, covered with boiling water for a certain time, then with cold, before being put in the cans. Corn is also somewhat difficult to keep unless done just right, but almost everybody here cans peas, corn, beans, and all sorts of vegetables. They are mighty handy in the winter, and much nicer than the bought goods. Some fewer people here use canning compounds, which are only salycilic acid, but the majority can by complete sterilization.

July 8, 1915

John has gone to the Farmers' Union meeting. He is anxious to get the arrangements made for getting in the carload of fruit. We now have estimates for almost a car of fruit, a big car of cement, and about four cars of lumber. We shall also begin to get in coal in carload lots soon — maybe the latter part of this month. I tell you, it takes a hustler like John, who isn't afraid to tell the natives what is good for them, to do the community some good. We usually pay a dollar a crate for a peach box that holds a third of a bushel. This year we'll get them for a dollar and a half a bushel—just about half. The prunes cost $1.35 a crate here last year; we can get them for not more than .85 and maybe less.

Bloomington, Indiana
July 9, 1915

(From Mamma)

Well, Cora is Dean [of women] now (for the summer) and you will have to be Dean when E & E get there   you see E is to get well and will need lots of sleep so remember there are to be no late date nights but have everybody in bed by 9 or 9:30. E is used to going early now and when she comes home and stays up late a couple of nights she is all in so dont let her begin it   besides if they are at the table three times a day together that should do   Dont treat E as company but let it be work what ever he is able to do that will be better than just sitting around and talking about the past and dont make to big a fuss over E or John will not like it. Burn this and dont let E or E see it.

July 12, 1915

I am enclosing a letter we received from Edward. You can see by that he is glad to come. Of course he does not know that Cora has anything to do with the matter and he won't find it out, either. John thought maybe we'd better tell Edw. that we don't expect him to do the work of a hired man and that we got him here on a ruse to get him well. But after this letter came we saw too plainly how anxious he is to work at something. I had an idea, knowing Edw. as I do, that the best way to help him, as it is any deserving person, was to give him a chance to help himself. And his letter makes this very evident. I am so glad you are making it possible, Cora, for you couldn't do anything better for him or for Edith than to help him get well and strong now so he can start in on the final lap of his law work with vigor and courage.

I guess the most important thing to tell you is that Edward arrived all right. My, but we were glad to see him—about as glad, I believe, as he was to get here. We didn't know which train he would come in on yesterday, as we didn't know whether he would come by way of Denver from Omaha or by way of Billings. John met the noon train, which was an hour and a half late, but no Edw. We both went to the afternoon train then, and he came. The train had a long line of freight cars, and had a lot of freight to unload at Garland. Of course the passenger coach was way down the line toward Frannie when the train stopped, and John and I started down that way to see what we could see. It wasn't long till a figure in white jumped off the passenger coach at the end and came running with his hand waving. Well, naturally, we did the same, and we met somewhere between Garland and Frannie. Maybe we didn't have a meeting! We had taken the wagon, as we knew Edw. would have a trunk, and we all three sat on the seat on the way home, Edw. in the middle. He held on to both of us all the way.

After we got home we had supper and then washed the dishes and talked and talked and talked. John got sleepy after a while, so he took his bath and went to bed, but Edw. and I just kept on talking till college hours were up. Today we have been going at it pretty steadily, and I guess we shall keep on doing the same for quite a while.

Tomorrow Edw is going to drive to Powell in the morning for gasoline and coal oil. We don't want him to do any heavy work for a few days. Tomorrow afternoon I'll have him help me clean the living room and get it and the kitchen and bath room ready to have the floor oiled, which he will do in the late afternoon. He is going to learn to milk, too, for he told John a while ago that next Sunday he would milk both cows. We shall give him something to do right along, but nothing strenuous like mixing concrete, for instance, till he has had time to harden a little bit.

We have finally finished doubling up the weak colonies here in the home yard, and find we have 119 out of the 450 we put in the cellar last fall. That's quite a comedown, isn't it? The bees at the river, however, are doing better than they ever have done. Of the 110 there 103 came through the winter and of these we have already made 59 new colonies. The 119 we now have are good and strong and ought to begin doing pretty good work from this time on. In fact, three or four of them have already been doing work in the supers.

Mr. and Mrs. Richards were here to call this afternoon. She is a dear. I gave them a mess of peas and lots of lettuce, and all the bouquets I had on hand. I wish you could see some of my candytuft. I had one bush this morning, before I cut the center out, that was at least a foot and a half across, and a foot high, one perfect bouquet itself of white. My mignonette is blooming and blooming, and so are the nasturtiums and sweet peas. The centaureas are just starting, and one California poppy and one other poppy are in bloom. One calendula is also out.

August 4, 1915

Today is the day Edith arrived. We met her this morning and naturally we have been celebrating ever since. She says she was quite worried about making connections, as the train to Omaha was late and got later as they progressed. About Alliance something happened to the engine and they had to go a good way back to get another engine or get that one fixed.

August 23, 1915

Today is quite an important day here. It is Edith's birthday and the day that Cora arrives. The cream puffs are already made. We intended to use ice cream but it is raining this morning and quite cool, and unless it warms up a good deal by noon we'll wait with the ice cream till another day. We had ice cream yesterday and the day before, anyhow, but of course that didn't do Co any good. We shall have fried chicken and roasting ears for dinner. The chickens are ready killed but not dressed. Bady is now washing up the dishes in the kitchen. It is now nine o'clock and the house is all cleaned and there isn't very much to do before we start to meet Cora. My, but we'll all be glad to see her.

August 23, 1915

Cora arrived this morning as per schedule, but her trunk did not put in its appearance. It is strange that her trunk should not arrive, when Edith's did—especially as Edith's train was late all along and Cora's was on time. We'll go after it again soon, as it might have got left at Frannie.

September 3, 1915

John has gone to Garland to get our new binder, which is to be ready this evening. We did not expect to buy a binder this season, but to rent one to cut our grain and sweet clover. One neighbor rented his out at 35 cents an acre, but decided afterward he would not rent it unless he went along, when he would charge a dollar an acre. As we have about 35 acres of clover and 10 of grain, our bill would have been considerable. We found that we can get one now, use it to cut this crop, and pay for it out of the proceeds. Maybe you will be interested in the price out here—a hundred and fifty-five dollars. That is quite a good deal, but of course when we are starting in to raise sweet clover and grain right along we have to have the binder.

September 6, 1915

Our carload of fruit came in today and so we shall have a couple busy days. Tomorrow morning we shall unload what has been ordered by people around Garland, and the next day we shall unload at Powell. After that we'll have all our own to can. I think we shall have a regular family party at the car, as John and Edward will go to do the handling of the fruit and Cora and I will be cashier and secretary. We have each person's account figured up, what his bill is, what he paid, and what he owes. We think the fruit will be extremely nice, for the grower said in his letter that inasmuch as he did not have as many of the Late Crawfords as we wanted he was sending extra fine Elbertas. The usual count of Elbertas is from 60 to 80 peaches to the crate. He says that many of these will have only forty-five to the crate. They surely ought to be fine.

This car consists of 114 boxes of pears, 243 crates of Italian prunes, and 633 crates of peaches. The grower gets $359.54 for the lot. The freight is $336.50. Forty-five dollars of that is icing charge for the refrigerator car. That looks as if the railroad gets a large share of the total, but the distance from North Yakima, Washington to Wyoming is quite considerable. The weight of the carload was 24,755 lbs. Union members pay 60 cents for the peaches, outsiders 70; members, 77 cents for prunes, others 85; members $1.30 for pears, others, $1.43. The prices in the stores here have been lower this season than ever because the stores are competing with our prices, but even then we make quite a saving. Peaches have been brought down to 80 cents, prunes to $1.40, and pears are $3.00. You will be interested in knowing our margin for expense. We have $100.80 over what the fruit and expressage cost us. Out of this we have to pay our expenses for correspondence, telegrams, etc., in ordering the car, printing, postage, etc. on the circulars we sent out for getting orders, and such other expenses. This amount will go into the Union treasury to be used in other cooperative ventures.

September 16, 1915

By the time this reaches you, you will be everybody together again. My, but I did hate to see the girls go off yesterday. I think I've spent most of my time wiping away the briny tears since the train pulled out. I felt lots worse this time than I did last year when Cora went home in September. I think perhaps the idea of going home myself before long made me worse this year. Last year I had no thought of being able to go myself and didn't think about it as much as this year when you started off. Somehow it always makes me homesick to think of going off on the train. I can think of you all at home, and even of being there with you, with nothing but pleasant thoughts; but just let me think of *starting*, and I am homesick as a baby. Another reason I felt so bad this time was that we were not able to do anything to make you have a nice time while you were here. Actually, half the time I didn't have time to answer your questions, much less say anything myself. And when I think of the way we kept you at work, I get ashamed of myself. I don't know what I would have done to get all that fruit canned if you hadn't been here to help, but when I think of how much work it was. . . . Well, maybe sometime you can come out when we are not at the rush end of a season; and anyway, John insists that when we get so busy again I have got to have a hired girl to look after the housework.

If you were here today, you could imagine you were nearer the city than when you left. The telephone men have been working putting up the line on our house, and putting in the box in the house. They tell us that by tomorrow we can have service. My, but we'll be glad. It will save John miles of travel and will give us much closer connection with the people we care for most — Murrays and Werts and such folk. I wish the phone had been put in when it was promised — last spring — so it could have been in use when you were here. You could have visited with folk over the wire since we couldn't go in the buggy. The house seems awfully still and lonesome; and when I clean it up it just stays clean. Things don't seem natural, somehow.

September 19, 1915

Usually the water is turned off here in October in order to give the Reclamation Service time to get the ditches repaired and in order before the ground is frozen too hard to work in it. Last winter there was so little snow and rain that a good deal of alfalfa died from lack of moisture in the winter. So this year the Reclamation Service is arranging to have the water turned off the 25th of September for about a month, when they will do the repair work, then turn the water on again till late in

November. In this way people can water their fields enough to give moisture to last during the winter.

I am sending Pater this week's Powell *Tribune*. He will be interested in the article about the grain yield on Sedwick's farm. This farm is one of the earliest settled and the grain was no doubt grown on land that had been in alfalfa a couple years. Sweet clover would have done the same good to the soil. You know on this raw land one grain crop can be grown and then some soil-building plant like alfalfa or sweet clover should be grown for a couple years before grain is planted again. This soil needs the humus that a forage plant produces. It pays to build up the soil, especially if, as with the sweet clover, you can grow a more than paying seed crop all the while you are improving the soil. On new land, the procedure is to plant grain the first year and with the grain sow sweet clover. This is done in the spring. This sweet clover will bear seed the next season. At the end of the first season another planting of sweet clover seed should be made to insure a crop the third season. After that the sweet clover will seed itself as long as you want to grow it. After the third crop the land can again be sown to grain, if desired. From now on, since the new alfalfa meal mill has been started at Garland, there will be a market for all the alfalfa grown, for the two mills at Garland and Powell can handle an enormous amount. They pay $6.50 per ton for the hay delivered at the mill. Alfalfa makes three cuttings per season here. The hay can be hauled to the mills in the winter, and when it is cured in the summer it is stacked right out in the fields and hauled to mill from the stack. The dry winters insure two things: the safekeeping of the alfalfa in the open fields and good roads for hauling. After a farm has been built up for a few years with sweet clover or alfalfa, either of which is a paying crop all along, anything may be grown on the land. Sugar beets and potatoes are favorites here.

The honey is done, thanks be. We finished this morning. That is, the cleaning and grading and casing is done. We still have the cases to nail up and sort into the various grades according to the stamp on the box.

I managed yesterday to get through the summer's darning of stockings. It indicates that I am not much of a housekeeper, but it is actually a fact that I have not been able to get at darning stockings since about the middle of the summer.

I didn't tell you in the letter yesterday about the wind storm damaging the sweet clover for the reason that it made us feel too bad to talk much about it. We weren't the only ones that lost. Hutts had ten acres that is almost gone; Peases have about three or four, and I suppose there are others we haven't heard of yet. Hart's most likely was not cut either. The heavy rain we had week before last kept the stalks so green and made the field so wet that the clover could not be cut, both because it was not ready and because the binder could not be run in the field. We thought the stalks were still too green to shatter. John wanted it cut last week, and it would have been, only Mr. Pease had to dig his own potatoes. John says we'd be ahead if we had bought Pease's potatoes and left them in the field. There is one great objection to having another farmer work for you, and that is he always has something that has to be done at home when you need him. If we had had any idea there was danger of shattering by the wind, we would have hired someone else last week to do the cutting. We knew it had to be cut, but didn't think there was any rush. After this we won't wait for anything or anybody when things are ready, even if there doesn't seem to be any reason for hurrying.

The wind didn't strip the seed off the bushes; the seed wasn't that dry. What it did was to rub the stalks against each other so that the stalks rubbed off the seed. Where the bushes are not so close together the seed is unharmed; but where there is a heavy stand, the seed is nearly all rubbed off. And of course you know that we had a wonderful stand. Naturally we feel pretty bad about it, for it is discouraging to work all summer and then lose your returns for labor. We had been counting on paying off some borrowed money and doing some more improving on the place. The fact that the honey crop is only about 2/3 of what it was last year doesn't help out any, either.

I think John is worrying more about me than about the loss itself. He thinks it is a shame for him to bring me out here to have to stand disappointment and hardship. Of course he ought now to worry about me, for I am all right. Of course we won't be able to have an automobile, as we had hoped, or to do much to the house, but goodness knows such things are not essential to one's happiness or even comfort. I reckon Providence won't forget us entirely, though it did look this time as if it lost track of our number.

October 24, 1915

I'm not sure yet just when I'll start east. I'd like to start the end of this week, so as to spend Sunday travelling. In that way I could get home a day or so earlier than by waiting till Monday. I know I could help you somewhat at home, Cora, but since I could not get there this week in time to help you get your Indiana Club* book copy ready for the printer, a day or so more or less next week won't matter a great deal.

October 25, 1915

Here is the day you wanted me to be in B. and I am still in Wyoming. Well, it couldn't be helped this time. It certainly is a good thing I didn't try to start sooner, for I couldn't have done so. Our car of honey is not yet loaded. The substitute car has not yet arrived and I could not leave before the honey was shipped, as there is too much to look after for John to try to do it alone.

---

*A university-centered literary and social club in which the Hennel girls were active and whose history Cora was writing.

Ilove you dear, and it hurts me more than I can tell to be separated from you. But I won't let that spoil my trip, for I know I can't have you now. But I'm thinking of you and of your love for me all the time just the same.

Honeyhill Farm
October 28, 1915

My Sweet Mahme:

That dish washing was not so bad.
Gee!
My mahme has gone to the city.
She is having a grand, good time;
Going out every evening at ten o'clock to dine.
But I'm left behind,
Eating raw oats and calling them fine.
Sure I'm having one Terry-ble Time.

From your boy, Jonny.

822 East Third Street, Bloomington
November 2, 1915

Dear John:

Your letter is a peach. I have read it till I nearly know it by heart, and everybody in the house and everybody that has come to the house has been amused at the Terry-ble Time you are having. I slept with the letter under my pillow last night. It was the best substitute I had for that dear arm that is always waiting for me when I come to bed.

Everything here seems perfectly natural. Mamma insists she can hardly believe now that I have ever been away, as she says the two years I have been gone just disappeared. There are only a few of the Indiana Club people still here that were here when I knew them, but all that are here have been to see me, either to meet me at the train or to come here to the house.

Miss Collins has also been here to see me. I went to the office this afternoon with Cora to help her get some stuff for the Club book, and of course saw a lot of people there — President Bryan, Mr. Cravens, the deans, and a lot of others. They all seemed glad to see me.

I was surprised yesterday when Pater wasn't at the train to meet me, but when I got here I easily saw the reason why. He was in the front yard waiting for me, and was talking to the cab man who had just brought out my trunk and suitcase. He ran to meet me, and began to cry so he couldn't say anything at all. Of course I was in the same state myself, and we both helped each other into the house. After we got into the parlor he held on to me and just hugged me and hugged me, and cried and cried. I didn't know he had aged so until then. He is so glad to see me it is almost pathetic. He follows me around and takes me to see everything on the place. I knew he missed me, but I hadn't any idea it was as bad as it evidently has been.

November 5, 1915

Dear John,

I was tickled at Pater yesterday. I mentioned something about the Still sale at Powell. Pater wanted to know where the place was, and I told him it was 3/4 of a mile from us. He remarked that he supposed that was one of our closest neighbors! I immediately stopped long enough to get a pencil and paper and draw a map of the country for about a mile each way from our corner. He thought it looked like a town.

As soon as we get this Indiana Club book out of the way I can begin to explain to Pater how irrigation is managed. He knows how the ditches are run, and the arrangement of the thing, but doesn't understand how you work it to make the water get to every part of the field. I guess he had the idea I had before I went west — that you just ran the water through the ditches and let it seep through the ground from ditch to ditch. When I began to talk about acre feet he thought I was mistaken, for he said a foot of water over an acre was a tremendous amount of water to use even in a whole year. I explained that the water kept running over the ground and didn't mean that it ever really stood deep on the ground.

Dearest Johnny,

Pater and I took a walk today, the same as we always used to on Sundays. We have been working so steadily on the book that I guess he didn't think I'd take time to go with him, for when Cora told him this morning that he wouldn't have to go walking alone this afternoon, she said he was so tickled he almost jumped out of his chair. I am so glad to go with him. There was a concert this afternoon by the orchestra I should have liked to hear, but I would miss anything to go with Pater. We walked six miles this afternoon.

While I was away several faculty people came to call. One couple stayed till we got back, about six o'clock. Two more faculty people were here this evening, but not to see me, as they are new ones that have come since I left. They got to asking me about the bees, and of course when I got started on that subject I could hardly stop. Cora told me she thought maybe I'd better talk on bees Wednesday when I have to talk before the Association of Collegiate Alumnae. My subject is Women in Wyoming. I told Co I had more first-hand acquaintance with bees, maybe, than with the question of the status of women in Wyoming, but I was just as enthusiastic about Wyoming as I was about bees, and that is saying a good deal.

I have been trying to plan out the things I have to do, and I can't see how I'll find time to get them in in the next month. I want to spend at least a week at Evansville. I want two days at West Franklin and at least half a day with Carrie. Then there is Grossmans, which as you suggested, might be run in as the evening of one day at West Franklin. In Evansville there are ten families I have to call on. Some of these calls can be short, but still they will take time because it is so far between places. Next Friday we have to go to Indianapolis and won't

get back until Monday. I have to spend two or three days at
the dentist's and I do want to see a doctor, too. There is four
or five day's steady work yet on the book, and the reunion itself
will take at least five days.

November 9, 1915

I went to the English Department this morning and had a
pleasant time. As I approached the building I heard someone
upstairs call, "Hello Miss Hennel," and there was Prof. Rice
hanging out of a window calling at me. Afterward, I was
standing in the hall talking to Prof. Stephenson and then I went
to the door of the office where Mr. Hale and Mr. Senour were.
When they looked up I said good morning the same as I
always used to, and it took both of them a little while to realize
I hadn't been doing it every morning. Mr. Hale answered good
morning and started to go on with his work. Then he realized I
had been away and fairly jumped to shake hands. He said he
had seen me talking in the hall to Prof. Stephenson and did not
realize that I was someone strange.

November 12, 1915

It is dear as can be of you to say I might stay two weeks longer
than I had planned. The people here are delighted with the
suggestion. Mamma says to tell you you are all right. I don't
know yet whether I can stay away that long or not, for it is
most awfully hard to stay away from you. I'd give anything right
now to lay my head against your shoulder and feel your arms
around me. I suspect, though, it will be best for me to stay a
while longer, because if I don't I'll hardly get a chance to do
any visiting with the folk here. We will be kept in such a rush
for the Indiana Club reunion, then I'll have to go to Evansville
right after that, then there would be only three or four days
after I got back from Evansville before I'd have to start west.
This way I can spend more time with Pater. Also, I can take a
few days more at Evansville and can spend more time with
Anna and Carrie, which I want very much to do. I know you

will think the time dreadfully long too, but we'll have the rest of the year and maybe several years together before we come east again. I hope next time we both can come. I told Carrie last night in the letter that I'd give anything if you could be there when I am, for you want to see the children so much, as well as the older people. I said you couldn't come after our big loss and that I wouldn't have come myself if my sister had not insisted last summer on giving me this trip east as a Christmas present.

November 17, 1915

There is a committee of the Indiana Club in the parlor now making the final arrangements for the celebration. So far as things are planned, this is what will happen: Edith will come home tomorrow (Thursday) night. Friday night the other people will get here. Friday night there will be a big bonfire over at college and after that a reception at the Student Building. Saturday morning the main crowd will come. At noon the active chapter of the Club will serve a buffet luncheon here at our house to the alumni and visitors. We are counting on about 125 people. In the afternoon is the big football game. Immediately after the game the Club is to have a reception. At eight o'clock that night is the big Club banquet, and after that, there will be the organization of the Club alumni organization. On Sunday there will be visiting and dinner and more visiting, and taking people to trains.

It is pleasant, dear, to be back here where I spent so many happy years, and where I know so many people. But there is one thing certain and that is, since I know the new life with you, I wouldn't want to come back here to stay. Our life and work together is so much pleasanter to me than even this life here was. Good night, dear heart, and God bless you.

The great celebration is about over. Most of the people went away on this afternoon's trains. I can't begin to tell you what a lovely time we have had. It is all so full of meaning and friendship that as you said so many times, it will be a source of pleasure in memory all my life.

I have so many things to tell you, but they are so long I can't write about them all. You have said several times you wanted me to get happy experiences that will be pleasure to me all my life long. That is just exactly what happened. I am sure I will be happier all my life and better because I will be thankful for all these joys.

I wish you could be here to enjoy the Victrola. It certainly is lovely. There is one song that the folk here call my song. I play it whenever I get too lonesome for you. It is called "My Little Gray Home In The West."

When the golden sun sinks in the hills
And the toil of the long day is o'er,
Though the road may be long,
In the lilt of a song
I forget I was weary before.
Far ahead where the blue shadows fall
I shall come to contentment and rest,
And the toil of the day
Will be all passed away
In my little gray home in the West.

There are hands that will welcome me in,
There are lips I am burning to kiss,
There are two eyes that shine just because they are mine,
And a thousand things other men miss.
It's a corner of heaven is there,
Though it's only a tumbledown nest,
But with love ruling there,
Why no place can compare
With my little gray home in the West.

It's true dear. No place can compare with our own dear home, and no one can compare with you.

When I came away I left something in the cellar for you. It is in a small-sized cottolene bucket that when I left was standing on the north shelf just behind the canned beans. Unless Mrs. Pease moved it when she cleaned the cellar, it ought to be right in that spot. I hope you can find it. When you find it, you will see what I will be thinking of on Thanksgiving Day. I can't be with you for your birthday, but I'll be with you just the same throughout the day, for I'll be thinking of you all the day. And now, my dearest, every good wish I can think of I am thinking of for you. I wish you many, many years of joy and love and work, and I hope I may be with you through them.

Evansville, Indiana
November 25, 1915

I stayed last night at Aunt Lena's, in the room we stayed in the first night we were married. Naturally, dearest, I lived that evening and night over again, and I wanted you so I couldn't keep the tears back. I thought of all that happened that night, after we had gone into the room, just we two, and closed the door—a time every girl looks forward to with much happiness and much fear. With you, dearie, I soon lost every vestige of fear and naught but the happiness remained and still remains.

Through all my girlhood dreams I had pictured one thing. It was a vision of myself, with a husband by my side, kneeling together by our bedside in the first night we were together for always, saying our prayers together, and asking His blessing on our new life together. Always I had that picture in my mind, even before I knew who the man was or even that there would be any. I can't tell you what joy it gave me on the night we were first together, or what joy it has given me ever since, to know that this dream came true in so complete a manner.

I have often told you that the time I felt the first real love for you was when you wrote me the letter telling your ideal of a home. It was one, you said, in which you did not wish to be master, but wished to be partner with some one else, who hand in hand with you would look to the Master of all as head of the house. It was your saying this that made me say "There is a Man." I knew when I read that letter that the man who wrote it was saying what I had always held as my deepest religion.

I am giving thanks today, beloved, for all these things I have mentioned, and for a hundred others, all of which can be summed up in the one word—you. God bless us, sweetheart, as He has so richly done in the past, and give us not only the good things themselves but also or perhaps first the power to realize how blessed we are.

With deepest love.

West Franklin, Indiana
November 28, 1915

I wished all day you were here in West Franklin with us. If ever your ears burned it must have been today, for every other word any of us said was John. The folk asked a thousand questions about you, all of which I answered to the best of my ability. I told them how you were and how nice you were and how good, etc., etc., ad infinitum. I even told them it was my belief you were happy.

I came out from Evansville with Lincoln. He took me to his house and everybody came up for a few minutes to see me. I stayed there last night and this morning I stopped a minute at your mother's and at Anna's, and then spent the day at Pacific's. This evening I came back here to Mother Harp's. Anna and her children, Carrie, Trula, and Howard, came to see me. I'll stay here tonight and spend tomorrow with Anna and then Pacific will take me to Grossman's tomorrow evening.

Johnny dear, I wish you could see these blessed children. You never saw a prettier or more attractive lot of youngsters in all your life. I can't tell where to begin to talk about them. I'll have to save most of it till I get home and tell it in person.

Someone told me yesterday that two persons (I don't know who) had a discussion as to which of the three Hendricks brothers was the handsomest. It seems that one of the two voted for Pacific and one voted for you. Poor Lincoln was left out entirely. If I had been there when the argument was on, both Pacific and Lincoln would have been left way back in the race.

December 10, 1915

If the selling price of the comb honey was $1168.74, I suppose we sold enough extracted to bring the total to $1500, did we not? Would the season's expenses be much more than $500, not wanting our own labor? In other words, did we get $1,000 for our work?

Honeyhill Farm
December 14, 1915

(From John)

I suppose this will be the last letter that I can get to you before you leave Bloomington.

The winds that blow over the mountains, the winds that blow over the plains, the winds that blow over the mountains, blow back my Mahme to me, to me. Blow back, blow back, blow back my Mahme to me, to me. Blow back my Mahme to me.

Gee, Mahme, did you know that you are welcome and wanted back here at Honey Hill? Well you are.

> Hurry home Mahme to see;
> How fat old Bill is,
> How many eggs we have,
> Our big wood pile,
> The fine weather we are having.
> The snow on the mountains,
> The bees in the cellar,
> Orfling Annie's fancy yoke,
> Our sawdust pile,
> Our new chimneys,
> Our new buggy bed,
> And to see what you shall see.

And bring a place to pillow your lover boy's weary head. Then you'll be here because I'm here, and we'll be glad because we are here, because we are here, and we'll be here because we are here.

Well, I guess that I'll just fill in by saying that I'm glad the time for your departure this way-ward is at hand. Gee, when my Mahme gets on that train the iron horse will be full of energy, nervous and prancing to start toward home. And just as soon as it gets started it will say: What-a-Mahme, what-a-Mahme, what-a-Mahme. . . .

Well, my Dearie, you have had a fine time visiting your old home and friends and I'm just as glad as can be that you have. I wish I could have been with you for two or three weeks. But I soon will be for several weeks and that will be just as gooder.

Well, bye, bye, my Mahme, be sure to start as soon as you can Tuesday morning. I'll be waiting for you when the train arrives. No, I'll not send a kiss either, I'll wait until the train arrives.

Near Thermopolis, Wyoming
December 24, 1915

Dear Everyone at 822:

We are speeding along through wonderful scenery on one of the finest days I have ever seen. The sky is our usual clear blue and the sun is *really* shining. This road from Cheyenne to Frannie is great. I have never seen such beautiful scenery. Through the Wind River Canyon the railroad follows the bank of the river for 20 miles. There are five tunnels right on a straight. The mountains go up sheer from the road and the river. On the cliffs are lots of cedar trees. With the slight powdering of snow they have on them now they are especially beautiful.

Just before we got to the canyon we stopped at one station where the cedar grows right down to the track. I jumped off the train and asked the porter if I'd have time to get some. He said he'd get it, and got me a bunch. It is bright green, with blue-gray berries half an inch in diameter. It makes such a lovely dining table bouquet and lasts so long. We are soon coming to another canyon, the Sheep Canyon. I am anxious to see if it is as fine as the one we came through.

I had a lovely time in Boulder with Edward.* He certainly knows how to take care of a person.

Christmas Day, 1915

I got home all right as per schedule yesterday. The train was late but we made up nearly all the time before we got to Frannie, so we got to Garland just about on time. John had brought some oysters from Powell, so we had oyster soup for supper. We opened the trunk and got out some candy and that was about all we did. I didn't know I was so tired till I got home. Then I felt as if I didn't want to move any more for a while. We didn't wash the dishes or do much of anything but just visit, and went to bed about eight o'clock.

December 26, 1915

We had a lovely Christmas, together at home. We visited and loafed and worked a little and ate a lot of candy and nuts, and trimmed the Christmas tree and had a general good time. For Christmas dinner we had more oyster soup and fried oysters and also "roysters." You will be interested in the way the oysters are sold here. They are fresh raw oysters, not "Cove oysters." They come in a tin can, not round, but oblong. The price is 50 cents a pint. The can we had was 1½ pints and cost 75 cents. These were as fine oysters as I ever saw. Some of them were three or four inches long.

I wish you could see what I saw when I got here — my Christmas present. John has had the kitchen work table — shelf and all — covered with shiny zinc. The shelf is now fixed so that all you need to do is to pull it up and it stays. This is accomplished by a stick brace with a hinge in the center. The water

---

*Edward Ellis was now a law student at the University of Colorado.

shelf of the sink is also covered. Talk about dandy! You can wash the table just like a dish. Also, he fixed the kitchen sink so the water doesn't stand in it but runs out as it should. He is just too good for words.

December 30, 1915

Two years ago today there was something going on at 822, wasn't there? It doesn't seem as if it is two years since then. We are celebrating the day today all alone. John invited old Mr. Nauser to come up to have dinner with us today, but the day is pretty cold and he did not come. We had a nice chicken dinner, but even that isn't worth driving eighteen miles for in zero weather.

I went to Thompson's this morning for a while, for Grandma Thompson died yesterday of the flu and Mrs. Thompson has it now. Mrs. Lovercheck and I dressed the body, all but the dress waist, which we decided had better wait till tomorrow morning. I combed the hair, but we did not curl it yet. We'll do that tomorrow also. I am so glad I have found out that it isn't such an awful task to take care of a person who has died. I used to think I couldn't do anything like that, but I find the worst part is what you think is the case and not the fact at all. In other words, it is just the idea. I am going there tomorrow morning and will stay all day tomorrow, staying at the house while the funeral goes to the cemetery.

Our blizzard blew itself out yesterday, and this morning there is only a light wind and no snow. It "snew" pretty hard during the night — O, an inch about — but the wind did not blow much of the night. John got up at midnight to see if the coal oil stove was burning all right in the basement, and the thermometer outside registered ten below. We thought it would be pretty cool this morning, but when we looked at seven this morning it was up to two below. It is now four above at 2 p.m. The sun is shining brightly as can be, and from inside the house you would think it was quite warm outside. However, as long as the temperature is within a few degrees of zero, it is a little chilly outside if you stay out long.

COMPANY DINNERS

I never liked blackberries; fresh or canned,
Preserved or jellied, I always passed them by.

Then after I had lived
In arid western country, where all fruit
Had to be shipped in, I went back east
To visit with John's mother, and she served
Blackberry jelly.
I hadn't eaten any for so long,
To my surprise I found it tasted good.
Politely I remarked
I had enjoyed the jelly very much,
And added that blackberries do not grow
Out where we live.
But when she served blackberry jam for tea
I found at once
My old distaste for berries had returned.

Next day I went to dine
And visit with John's sister. I am sure
Her mother must have told her what I said
About the jelly, for we had
Blackberries.
She had a cellar full of fruit,
A dozen kinds and more I dearly love,
And there I sat and ate
Blackberries.

John's brother's wife was next, and when I ate
With her, she opened up both jam and jelly,
Both, of course, .
Blackberry.

Then when I had made the round
Of relatives in Franklin, we drove out
Ten miles into the country, and took dinner
With an old uncle and his family;
And we had
Blackberry pie.

I think I know just how a preacher feels
Who never cared for chicken.

If the baby has red hair, who is to blame? Poor Old Dad

FAMILY AND HOME

2

1916–1921

January 3, 1916

Our cold spell has gone away and today we hare having warmer weather. The sun is shining just the same and there is a good Chinook blowing. Last night when we left Murray's there were banks of clouds along the western and southeastern horizon. Mrs. Brown exclaimed, "Chinook! See the clouds." None of us knew what Chinook clouds looked like, but she assured us they were the real article and sure enough, during the night the wind started in and this morning the thermometer was 17 above instead of 17 below. We'll be likely to have a lovely spell of weather now. I hope it will last, for we are going to have our Club pie supper next Thursday night. The men are going to have a rabbit hunt during the day and the supper is to follow that. The men here usually have the hunt on New Year's Day, but there were so many things to prevent it this year that it was postponed. Usually the men divide into two sides, and the side that kills the most rabbits gets an oyster supper from the losing side. I don't know how they are planning to work the winning and losing teams this year, but I know the Club supper is to take the place of the oyster supper, with chicken and rabbit pie as the main dish.

822 East Third Street
Bloomington, Indiana
January 3, 1916

(From Mamma)

Pater said for you to not do any more of what you did the other day   he said if you did it once more people out there would just expect it of you all the time. I am sorry you had to do that much   don't let it worry you but forget it as it's something that must be done but I think they should have had someone else do it. Why dident they get the nurse. I am glad you took precautions and hope you will not get the grip   for preventative use a few drops of peroxide to gargle and to snuf or rather run through the nose till it comes out in the throat. I know you and John are doing a lot for the community out there and we are glad you can do it but there are some things you must leave to others.

Today is the day we are butchering. I like butchering here for none of it comes in the house, and the women folk don't have anything to do with it. All the men ask for is an occasional pan or kettle of hot water, or knives, or something like that. The work is all done outdoors or in the old house and as far as I am concerned there might not be any butchering going on within a mile. They killed the cow this morning and skinned her, and salted the hide. If the meat cools enough they will cut some of it up this afternoon, but they always wait till the next day to cut the steaks, etc. Then it is so much easier to handle afterwards, either for immediate use or for canning.

We had hasenpfeffer for dinner today. John shot a rabbit this morning. I had not intended to cook it today, but it occurred to me that while the men were working with fresh meat, the smell of which often takes away their appetite, something spicy like hasenpfeffer would taste good.

We are planning to have the hide of the cow we killed today made into a robe for the buggy. We hesitated a little to do it, as the cost will be something like ten dollars all told, freight and all, but it is so seldom one can get such a fine, good hide that we have concluded we can afford it at the present time. We shall send the hide to Mason City, Iowa, where the H.B. Mickle Fur Coat and Robe Co. is located.

When I got home there was awaiting me a bundle of marked papers from the Orange Judd Company, and what do you think? Every one of the articles I had sent in was accepted. I got a check yesterday for $3.80 for the following items: Magnetic Helper—.50, Shoshone Baked Apples—.40, Even Skirts—$1.40, a Clothes Closet Substitute—$1.50. The pay is practically two cents a line, so you see some of the articles were just scraps. Nevertheless they all count up, and a check for $3.80 once in a while is not to be refused.

We have not threshed yet, and we are getting discouraged. So long as this snow stays on the ground and the weather is so cold the threshermen will not start. We want the clover seed threshed, of course, as it has all been contracted for long since, and delivery should have been made before this. But we are more anxious about the grain for several reasons. One is that we depend on the straw for the roof of the barn and it is rather hard on the cattle in blizzards to have only part of a roof above them. Of course when there is no blizzard, just cold weather, the stock here will stay out doors rather than go inside. These nights when the thermometer goes way below, the horses stay outside in preference to going inside. Last week when we had an awful blizzard and our horses were shut inside, other horses that were in the pastures around went calmly on grazing right through the snow and wind. The stock here develops heavy, fuzzy coats in the winter that are a great protection. But still, we prefer to have a barn with a roof on it. The other reason is that as long as the grain is in the stacks in the barn-yard we cannot use the barnyard to run the cattle in, and have to drive them in the pasture as soon as we let them out of the barn. Then too, the chickens are getting more than they need while they can scratch all day in the grain. We hope we can get the threshing done before spring, but goodness only knows now when it will be. There are four threshing outfits on the Flat, but none of them can get here now.

This morning it was 22 below at six o'clock and in all probability lower than that earlier in the morning. This is the worst spell of cold weather either of us has ever been through. To look out you would never think it was that cold, for the sun is shining as bright as can be, the sky is blue as can be, and from indoors it looks lovely. But when you get outside you can notice it. I seem to notice it chiefly by the fact that the air seems so rare — it is hard to get enough to breathe. Of course I have not been out more than a couple minutes at a time. Rolla Roach, just west of Loverchecks, is having a sale today. I'd hate to do a sale today and stand around outside for hours. There seems to be a pretty good crowd in spite of the day. I notice, however, that most of the men came on foot instead of driving.

We did not go to church this morning for two reasons. One was this is one of the days when a rocking chair looks good to me and the other was that it is still cold. Today is the first time since last Monday afternoon that the thermometer has risen as high as zero.

We have been working away at John's speech for the Farmers' Institute and at various other things connected with the Union work. It is likely that the Union will start a mutual fire insurance company soon, so we have been studying up the by-laws of various mutual companies and have written out a set that may do for us. Of course we would want a lawyer to draw up the articles of incorporation. But we want to know just exactly what we are doing, and as the Union means John when it comes to doing anything, we have to know where we are. We have read two books on cooperation from the Orange Judd Company, Poe's "How Farmers Cooperate and Double Profits," and Myrick's "How to Cooperate." We have also been studying the U.S. Comptroller's booklet on how to organize a national bank, and various other booklets and leaflets from the Federal Reserve Commission. Of course we don't intend to do all these things, but we want to have information on all subjects that might come up.

If you were here you could have brick ice cream every day. We do. We had brown and white, chocolate and vanilla, day before yesterday, chocolate yesterday, and pink and white almond and vanilla today. I use a half pound cocoa can as a mold. I fill it half full of one color, set it outside a couple minutes while I flavor the other color and then pour that on top. Then I set the can outside until we want the cream and it is all ready. A half pound cocoa can filled full makes really more than we can eat at one time. It would cut three nice slices. It is better, though, to fill the can only two-thirds full and cut two slices, as they are nicer sized.

The doctor has recommended John's sister Carrie's husband go west for a while. He is the one, you remember, who was so badly hurt in the Howell shops just when I came east. The strain has broken him down and he has what amounts really to nervous prostration. We hope he will come here right away, for we are positive he will get well here. You know how much this climate did for John, how it built you up, Co, when you were just about down and out, and what it did for Edward last summer. It will do the same for Joe. He can get his fare paid by pass, as he works for the L & N, and it was in their employ he was hurt. The railroad doctor has been treating him since he was hurt. If he stays in Indiana I doubt if he will ever get really strong. If he will come out here now and get a good start, I am sure he will get right strong and entirely well. He is such a fine fellow we'll be glad to have him with us.

Well, a number of things have happened since I last wrote you. I guess the most important is that John gave his talk at the Farmers' Institute yesterday and did a mighty good job, too. He took up the history of cooperation, mentioned four successful cooperative associations in this country and told what they had done, especially the Colorado Honey Producers' Association with which we ship our honey, told what could be done with a reorganization of the cooperative creamery here so it could do other things besides make butter, and then told what we needed and could do in the way of mutual insurance and mutual finance. His talk was almost an hour long, with the time he used in explaining the charts we had made showing the work the Union did in 1915, the rates of insurance of the old line and the mutual companies, and the saving possible here on insurance, interest, and coal. He came after Mr. I.D. O'Donnell, who is U.S. Superintendent of Irrigation and a man of national reputation. Mr. O'Donnell spoke for over two hours, and did not stop till about half past four. By that time the farmers ought to have been starting home to do their chores, but a big crowd stayed to hear John's talk. John got many compliments on it, and we are quite satisfied that what he did was worth while.

An agent for the Cheyenne paper came along just at noon today and had dinner here. We did not care for his paper, but he gave us a month's subscription for dinner. I did not want to take anything for his and his horse's meal, but he assured me that he always paid thus for his lodging, saying that if he had not been able to get it here he would have had to go to Garland and pay cash for it. In either case he would have charged it to the company, and the company preferred to pay in subscriptions rather than in cash. We don't care for the paper, for since it comes from Cheyenne it will take two days to get here and by that time the news is stale. But I guess we might as well have it for a month under the circumstances. You remember the Indianapolis woman who said they took the *News* because it just fit her pantry shelves. I haven't measured yet to see if this will fit mine or not, but I guess I can make some use of a month's copies.

We have heard definitely about John's sister and husband, and we are looking for them out the latter part of next week. Carrie wrote she was afraid to have Joe come alone, so she would come with him. We wrote them at once to bring the children, too, so they would all be here. They have always wanted to file here, and we think if he will work for us this summer at regular wages and not draw much of the wages, we can help them file this fall. There is no need for the family to be separated, for the children can go to school here as well as in Indiana, and the state here furnishes books so they won't be at any expense for books for the rest of the term. We can fix up the bedroom in the old house for them to live in and Carrie

and the children can earn their board by the help they can
give. I can turn over practically all the house work to her and
be free to help more with the bees. Little Joe is old enough to
look after the garden, once it is planted, and Mina Lell is big
enough to help wash dishes and do lots of work about the place.
The children can look after the chickens and do lots of running
errands and chores. I really will be glad to have a woman to
help in the house. Carrie is such a good housekeeper and is so
neat about her work that she will be fine.

February 28, 1916

The insurance committee finished the work of organization
yesterday and we were anxious to get the articles of incorporation and by-laws off on this morning's mail to Edward
for his passing on. John had always intended suggesting Edward
as legal advisor when the time came, but Mr. Murray brought
up the matter at the last Union meeting and the Union voted
to have Edw. do the work. They all have a big opinion of him
here from his work last year for us. There isn't a lawyer here
we would have do the work, as one is a bonehead and the
other is in with the interests, and his wife is an insurance agent.
So we worked a good deal of yesterday getting this insurance
business all copied up and writing the business letters that had
to be got out for the Union. We don't like to do such work on
Sunday, but sometimes things just have to be done.

We have been wanting to get a hired man, but did not
know where we could get a good one. The other day while
John was in the Reclamation Service office paying up our fees
for the past season, a young man came in and asked if the
clerk could tell him any place where he could get work. John
liked the looks of the chap and talked to him, and brought him
home with him.

He is a young man about 22 years old. A week before he
came here he was a member of the U.S. heavy artillery on the
Mexican border. His time was out and he decided that he had
enough bullets, so he did not re-enlist. He is now on the

reserve list, according to the new regulations, and can be called back for three years more in case of necessity. He came to Billings hunting work and then came here. We like him very much and think at present that we are fortunate in getting him.

February 28, 1916

This new boy we have seems to improve on acquaintance. He is very nice around the house, always seeing that the coal buckets are filled and the fires are fixed if they need attention. This noon I remarked that I didn't like to have the coal in the basement, as it was heavy to carry up stairs. Usually the men fill the buckets, but this morning I ran out and had to get some. The boy filled both buckets and when he came back he told me that whenever the buckets got empty I should be sure to "holler." His name, by the way, is Vern Newcomb. Of course we may be mistaken in him, for you can't always tell about a new man, but he certainly looks and acts right.

I am sorry that all the additions I can report to our family are large ones. Unfortunately there doesn't seem to be any ground for sending a report of a small addition — at least not at present. But there is plenty of time, yet, I reckon. Anna and Sam waited five years, and others longer. We haven't waited that long, yet.

March 5, 1916

I thought all along that this boy we have was too good to be true, and we have found out now that such is the sad truth. He is one of the nicest persons to have around that we ever had, and is a fine worker. We both took a great liking to him. But — he has epilepsy. He had an attack at Pease's the other morning while he was helping Mr. Pease clean his and our grain. Peases had never seen anything like it and were scared to death. They evidently forgot in their excitement that we had a telephone, for they sent Gladwyn up here for John and sent Rachel to another neighbor to telephone for the doctor. As soon as Gladwyn told John what was the matter, John knew what the trouble was, and of course he would not have sent for a doctor. But Peases were so scared they did so. The boy got over the attack and in less than an hour was back at work and worked all day. After John came home, we talked the matter over and of course we will not keep him. It would be too dangerous — he might get a spell while irrigating, and drown. Besides, we wouldn't want that sort of thing around the place. It would be too hard on one's nervous system either when he had a spell or all the time when you were afraid he might be going to have one. Naturally he said that was the first attack like that he had ever had, and laid it to his nervous shock in Mexican border service. John and I calmly looked over his letters while he was gone, for we wanted to know to whom to send a message if anything did happen while he was still here. We found that he is subject to the attacks and has been for a long time. We also found that he was stationed in Yellowstone Park and lately has been in California, and we think his stories about Mexican border service are fabrications. We advised him that the best thing for him to do was to go back home to Michigan to his own people. He told us that he has one brother who has a dairy farm in Michigan who has wanted him to come and stay there, but that he did not want to go until he could invest a little in the business himself. Since we know this weakness, we told him he'd better go there now. Finally he decided that was best, and allowed us to send a telegram to his brother telling of his condition and asking for transportation. The boy really did not want to have to ask for help in paying railroad fare, and hesitated a long time on that account. He is a decent chap and would rather make his own way if he could. We ought to get an answer from the brother tomorrow or the next day.

March 9, 1916

Carrie and her folk arrived safely this morning. We are glad they are here and all well. Joe stood the trip beautifully. He does not look as bad now as he did when I was there in

November, but I am sure he would not have got well in Indiana if he had stayed there any more than John would have got well there. I am likewise sure he will get well and strong out here. John went to Powell on an errand and took Mina Lell and little Joe with him. Of course the children were delighted to go with him and nothing could have persuaded them to stay home after he invited them to go along.

March 12, 1916

Vern is with us yet, but we hope he will go away tomorrow. In fact, we expect him to do so. He was to go Saturday but we let him stay over Sunday as he could not have done anything in Billings on Sunday. He means to go to Billings and try to get work on a cattle train going east. We telegraphed his people to send him transportation but they did not answer by telegraph but by mail. Their letter did not arrive till Friday, and in it his brother said that his wife had a new baby, and the expenses were so great that he would be in debt himself when he got through with the doctor and the nurse, and that at present he could not send him any help. We were very sorry to find that the brother would not help him, as he is absolutely not able to earn his own living entirely. We hate very much to turn him away for we feel so sorry for him, but we cannot be a charity organization.

The insurance committee finished its work a week or so ago, and appointed nine directors to carry on the work of the newly organized company. The directors met yesterday and now you have the honor of having the president of the Shoshone Farmers' Mutual Protective Association of Wyoming in the family. Mr. Murray is the secretary-treasurer. He is going to do the soliciting for insurance. Several weeks ago the men who were on the committee and a few other men that they got to help made a sort of canvass and got over $60,000 worth of property to be insured when the company would be ready to do business. We are certain that the total will show at least $190,000 when a complete canvass is made. The directors yesterday decided to employ Mr. Folsom, Edward's law school dean, to do the work of passing on the articles of incorporation and by-laws, and making them complete and perfect. Folsom wants $100 to do the work but insures a perfect result. He assures the directors that no law suit can ever be brought successfully against the company. $100 sounds like a lot at the start but the time to do the safe thing is at the start of a corporation.

March 14, 1916

Vern went away yesterday afternoon. We were mighty glad to have him go and yet we all felt about like a funeral when he went, and he most of all. He didn't want to go at all. I guess we treated him a lot better than most of the people he has been with. We really have given him a lot more than he really earned, but we didn't want to turn him out into the world without a dollar or two, when he is so helpless at times. He had a very bad spell here yesterday morning. John saw that it was coming and took him over into his room and set him on the bed and made him stay there till it was over. It was more than an hour from the time we first noticed the symptoms till he was all right again.

March 16, 1916

John and Joe went out this morning to look at land. I think if they can find a place that is worth filing on they will take it. The land is pretty well taken now. There are two pieces withdrawn from entry because they are seeped. They are withdrawn until a ditch can be put through. John thinks maybe they are worth taking as they are so fine in the way the land lies. There is such pretty level land on them and the land lies in such a way that it can be drained when the ditch goes through that way.

John and all the rest of the folk went to church this morning. I stayed at home and loafed. It felt good to do just what you wanted to with no one around to have to talk to if you didn't want to talk. I decided that would be more fun than going to church. When you are alone a good deal you like to go into a crowd; when there's a crowd most of the time you like to be alone occasionally. I had a Woman's Home Companion I hadn't read and had a fine time all alone. This afternoon John and I took a drive. We were going to stop at Richards for a while but no one was home. When we got home, our new neighbors, the Vosses, were here.

Carrie and the folk have about concluded to file. The only piece of land that seems good is the other side of Brown's over toward the hills on the extreme edge of the Project, east of Garland. They don't much like the idea of going way off there to live but of course the better the ground the more the advantage. This piece is quite desirable, if it were not so far on the edge of things. They think at present they will go back east after they have lived here the three years necessary to prove up, and so they think they can stand it to live in an out-of-the-way place for that long. We will rent the ground from them from the beginning. Of course a renter gets the whole first crop for putting the raw land into condition, levelling, etc. After the first year we will pay share rent — one-fourth.

Joe filed this morning. There are 62 acres of irrigable ground and enough more that he does not have to pay anything on to make a total of 79.94 acres. We want to get a good deal of that place under cultivation this spring. We'll plant grain as a first crop, and with it red clover and some alsike clover.

Just east of the piece of land on which the folks filed there is another piece of some seventy acres of irrigable land that is simply fine. We wish one of you would take it. You remember, Co, how Miss Berry is always telling you to invest your money in land. Well, for a small investment here you could get a piece that after the first year will make its own payments and bring in a nice little income too. Of course we would want to rent it from you, or in case we couldn't tend it ourselves would see that the one who did rent it was all right. However, if we rented Joe's piece and yours was right along-side, we'd want it too, for then the two could be worked together, and if Joe lived right there he could see after both for us. Pater could get the prove-up right for you by a seven months' residence, and you would have a farm that would be worth a hundred dollars an acre, for the paying of $57 an acre, the farm practically paying for itself. After the first payment and the fencing and putting up of whatever little house you would want, there would be no payment due for two years, and by that time you would get more than enough from the income to make all the subsequent payments as they came due in the twenty years. You'd better think about it. We'll tell you when we have figured it up just exactly what expense there would be at the start, for filing fees, first payment, fencing, and house. I think you would be very wise to put in your money, Co, and Pater put in your time for seven months, and get a farm out here.

I must tell you about the mirage we saw Saturday evening, one of the best I have ever seen. There had been a fall of snow the day before on the mountains and on the low slopes west of the Flat. Late Saturday evening the sun was shining just right to give the whole western part of the Flat the appearance of a great lake. I think the reflection of the snow and the sun was partly the cause, but we think the mirage was one of the big Shoshone Reservoir. Looking with the naked eye you could see a lake that was immense in size, with the sun shining on the water. We got out the field glass that Joe has, thinking that it would dispell the illusion, and to our surprise we found that it not only did not dispell it but increased our view of it. With the glass we could see the spray dashing up and down and the waves washing on this lake. I could not believe my eyes. Carrie looked first and when she reported that she could see the water dashing, I thought she had a pretty lively imagination. I looked then, very skeptically, and to my great surprise I saw great clouds of spray dash and change form. I could not believe at first that I was seeing right, but confirmed it by watching for quite a while. Later Joe saw the same thing when he looked through the glass.

April 3, 1916

Our cistern is getting so low we do not use water from it for washing. This morning the men got us water from Hugh Smith's cistern. The irrigation water will be turned on in a couple weeks now, and we won't run out, but we wanted to be sure to have enough for kitchen use until the water was turned on.

Have you decided to accept our Thanksgiving invitation?* We hope so. Of course Edith, in Gary, is included, but please don't extend the invitation or the information to anyone else.

April 4, 1916

We are so anxious to have our piano here. Do you suppose it would be possible for us to get it right away? We can keep it in the bedroom this summer or even in the living room by putting the bookcase in the bedroom. Carrie plays, and the children and she and Joe all sing very well. It would be such a comfort to have it, so please let us know what you think about our getting it at once. We'd like to have music in the house this summer and fall, for the other reason, too.

---

*The original copy of the "invitation" does not exist among family papers. It apparently read "Mr. and Mrs. John Hendricks cordially invite you to a birthday party at Honeyhill on or about Thanksgiving."

Today you got the letter we wrote you last Sunday. I think the first thing John said when we woke up this morning was "Today they'll know."

Joe is getting along so nicely that if you saw him now you wouldn't believe he had been so down and out so short a time ago. For the past three weeks now he has worked every day. He gets pretty tired by night, but he always feels fine by morning, and sleeps like a log. He says that since he has been here there was only one morning he did not feel fine. He has had to take his medicine occasionally, the nerve tonic, but that isn't anything to what he had to take in the east. By fall he will have forgot that he was ever sick. We knew he would improve like that, and for this reason we were so anxious for him to come out here. Carrie isn't in love with the country but is perfectly willing to stay when he improves as he is doing, and when there is a chance for them to get ahead here. In Indiana they never would have got ahead, for he couldn't have worked regularly and would soon have lost his job under such circumstances.

822 East Third Street, Bloomington
April 7, 1916

(From Mamma)

Oh, what a lovely surprise you gave us and you can guess how happy we are about it. Cora is as tickeled   she cant keep from grinning as you will see when you get her letter.

I wish you all the good things I can but could not wish you anything better than that your children make you as happy and will be as much comfort to you both as mine have been. I don't believe a day passes that I dont thank the Lord for my children   not in a set prayer at a stated time but a more fervent thanksgiving prayer that comes from the heart. I surely have a lot to be thankfull for to have three girls who have been such a comfort to us and who love us as much as you three do. Even if we are separated I know we all love each other and think of each other as much as if we were together every day. So my prayer for you and John will be that you have as dear and loving children as I have. I am sending John's letter to Edith.

April 9, 1916

We are sorry that you are not thinking of coming out and filing. As for being here in the cold weather, that would not be necessary at all, for you would have seven years' time in which to put in your time on the homestead. If you would be here anywhere from the middle of April to the middle of December, you would most likely not have any severe weather at all. But most likely it wouldn't be necessary for you to stay seven months in any one year. If you merely established residence by living there a month or two in the summer, put up some improvements, even though ever so little, and had the place put under cultivation, there would be little trouble for you to prove up after a year or two. We are sure that if you came out in the summer time, Pater, you would enjoy the climate immensely and would grow ten years younger in six weeks. So don't be afraid of having to run into cold weather, for that can easily be avoided. We are certain the place would be such a good investment for Cora that we hate to have the chance go by. For a couple hundred dollars she could get something that would pay for itself and be worth at least $2,000 in three years' time. The opportunities here for such investments are getting less and less, and in a couple years there will be nothing here at all, except to buy a farm outright. We would not advise you even now to buy a farm, for that would require an investment of at least $2,000 right now for the poorest ones. But when you can get it for an expense of not over four or five hundred for filing, fencing, house, and all improvements, it is different.

April 11, 1916

Your letter came yesterday answering John's letter of Sunday a week ago, Mamma. We didn't think you could answer so soon. Thank you for your letter. It makes both of us have tears in our eyes to read the nice things you say. We knew you would be glad at our surprise, for we are so happy ourselves we hardly know what to do. We are like two kids that have been promised some specially nice toy for Christmas. We can hardly wait till the time comes, but there is no use trying to hurry things, as they have to take their own time. We will most likely get Cora's letter today, and we can hardly wait till that comes.

You can guess that we are glad Carrie is here now. It looks as if when you try to help some one else you help yourself most of all. When we were anxious for them to come on account of Joe's health we did not know about this ourselves. Now that Carrie is here I can put off as much of the work as necessary on her and know it will be done and done right.

April 14, 1916

Well, I have had my first experience at a baby case and learned a lot of things that will come in handy about six months hence. Richards have a little girl, just what they wanted. Yesterday afternoon I was in Garland to go to Club and some one told me that the telephone central was trying to get me. I went to the office and found the call from Mrs. Richards, who wanted me to come at once. I was riding with Werts in their auto, and as soon as they had their business done in Garland Mr. Werts took me to Richards. She had an awful time. You can guess that Ernest was all in when it was over. He braced up again in about a minute, however, and was all right again. Mrs. R. is getting along splendidly now.

Of course it was all no easy work, but I really was glad of a chance to get some first hand experience under good direction. I am very tired now, as we worked steadily from about nine last night till one today, without any rest at all. I am feeling fine otherwise and as soon as I get a night's rest I'll be all right again. I knew it all theoretically, but am glad to get it practically too. The doctors both asked me if this really was the first case I had ever been at, hard or light, and told me I would make a first-class nurse. Ahem!

Cora's letter has at last arrived. So you think Peter and Repeater all right, or else Kate and Duplicate. But just suppose it is Repeater and Duplicate. Then what? You ask if you should tell the Evansville folk about little Johnny. Well, no, we'd rather not yet for a while. This is too long in advance.

We shall be so glad to get the piano. By all means wait till you get to Evansville, for you can see about it so much better in person. We are not in a rush for it, but want it this summer as soon as is convenient.

April 18, 1916

My new corset came yesterday and Carrie fitted it for me this morning, and I now have it on. It certainly feels fine. It needed a couple darts taken at the top of the back. Elsewhere it was all right, as the fitting is controlled by the back, front and side lacings. This will be a great comfort all the time, I am sure. I hated to pay as much as two dollars for a corset, postage and all, but decided it was wise in the long run. The bones in this are flexible and strong but very soft, not like ordinary steels. The bottom of the front buttons with three buttons, the rest hooks with five hooks like an ordinary corset.

April 25, 1916

I had a letter yesterday from the *Farmstead* saying that they have accepted two more articles I sent them last week. These are long ones, too. I told John this morning that first thing we knew I'd be able to get little Johnny's "trousseau" with the money I got from articles. One of these is on the subject of using carrot leaves as foliage with summer flowers. If you never tried it, just plant a few carrots to use as foliage with your sweet peas and other annuals. The article also told how to make bouquets and arrange your flowers. The other article is on the no less important but much less pleasant subject of slop pails and the necessity for using lids on all house vessels. I was driven to write it by several experiences recently where otherwise clean and careful housekeepers never used lids on their chambers at night. I was one place where even in sickness the slop jar was just set in another room after being used, without being covered. People seem to think that because there is no odor at once apparent, there is no need of a lid.

If you happen to run across any remnants of pretty embroidery for baby dresses, I'd like you to get me a piece or two. I don't want many such clothes, but I would like a couple embroidery dresses. I shall make the everyday dresses of plisse, which is like crepe but very much softer and finer, but with as good wearing qualities. You may be sure that the everyday dresses will be as plain as they can be made — just a slipover style with practically no trimming. The petticoats for everyday will be made of baby flannel, fastening only on each shoulder. Baby flannel is softer and finer and also cheaper than outing, washes better, and can be boiled like muslin. A wee baby doesn't need fancy trimmed clothes. All it wants to be as sweet as can be is to be clean. Of course I shall put some little crocheted edges on some of the things, but nothing elaborate.

We got just a hundred chicks out of this incubator. In spite of the fact that the eggs had been left out several times the chicks are as strong and husky as can be. They are a week old now. The weather was so bad we did not put them outside in the brooder till yesterday. We have had fun about these chicks and yet it has been somewhat of a nuisance. We kept them in a big box in the kitchen, and don't you know the little rascals got so used to having us around that when we would go out of the kitchen and leave them alone they would squeal and squeal. They were not hungry or thirsty or cold, they just wanted company. As soon as any one would go into the kitchen they were all right and stopped howling, whether he talked to them or not. The box we had them in was shallow, and if we left them alone they would manage to get out and start in to the other room where we were, yelling bloody murder. As soon as one got to the door where he could see some of us, he would shut up and sing a little tune as sweetly as could be. After we put them down in the brooder in the yard they nearly yelled their heads off the first day. They were not cold, for the sun was as warm as could be and they were nicely protected from any wind. They were just lonesome. Today they have forgot most of it and in a day or so will be all right. Carrie said yesterday that if little chickens were that easily spoiled, no wonder a baby soon learned to get what it wanted by crying for it.

May 18, 1916

We put a new bee yard on Ries's place, about two miles south of here. The place is on waste land that will never be cultivated, so there is no danger of our having to move away if we don't want to. The bee yard will be just at the top of the cliffs, about 1/4 mile this side of the river. There is a cliff nearby that protects it somewhat, in which we can build a bee cellar with very little work if we should want to winter them in a cellar down there. We can pay the rent with honey, an interesting feature. The Ries family came here from Chicago last year. Mrs. Ries is Mrs. Horn's sister. Mr. Ries was so poorly with consumption before they left Chicago that for months he had to live on milk and eggs. Now he eats everything in sight and when we were there the other day he was working in the field with a team and looked as if he never knew what sickness was. They have six little children, and he is not so young any more. We like to help them along a bit and are glad we could find a suitable place on their place. They have been buying honey ever since they came and are very fond of it. They will be glad to trade a bit of their waste land for their supply of honey.

May 19, 1916

We had a bit of bad luck the other day, when our mare lost her colt that was not yet due for two months. Of course we hate to lose the colt but we are so thankful the horse is all right we cannot think much about that. There seems to be so much trouble out here with horses losing their colts. Last year more than fifty per cent of the mares lost the colts, and I don't know how many cases there were where the mare died too. So we felt pretty well when Belle got over this all right.

Belle had got sick down at Nauser's. From the way she acted they thought she had an attack of colic, particularly as she suffered so terribly, and then seemed to get over it all at once. They watched her a while longer but she seemed perfectly all right, and they drove her home the same as usual with a load of bees. The next morning she seemed listless and in more or less pain, though not in any violent pain. John sent Henry, the hired man, for the veterinary for we could not tell what was the matter with Belle and did not want to run any risk. Before Henry got to Powell, Carrie and I, who were here alone with the children, found out for certain what was the matter. We called, and when the doctor found how things were he did not think it necessary to come out, as there was nothing then to do. Carrie and I watched Belle and saw that she got along all right. At first we wished that there was a man here to look after things, but afterward we were rather glad the men were all gone, for they would have been more distressed about it than we were. We knew there was nothing to get excited about and so we took things calmly.

June 4, 1916

We had a peddler for dinner today — at least I suppose one would call him that, though a man who goes about with a stock of goods in a big, two-horse wagon might deserve some more elegant title. He came just at noon as we were finishing dinner and asked if he could get a meal for himself and team. I told him at once he could for himself but that he would have to see John about the team as we are out of hay. They managed to get enough for the team, so he stayed. After dinner he wanted to know what he owed, and of course I would not take anything for the dinner and John did not want anything for the feed, but he insisted that he never did that way. So John told him he could give me some little notion out of his stock if he felt better to do so. John went to the wagon with him, and the man gave him two pairs of silk stockings for me. The stockings are a bright tan in color and I do not have any tan shoes, so I guess I'll have to lay them aside for a while. John said I could wear them for every day and then it wouldn't hurt if the stockings and shoes did not match. After I looked at the stockings I said I appreciated the compliment but doubted if I could ever wear the stockings. They look like about a size 8. I have not tried them on yet, but don't believe I can wear them. I guess I'll just save them if I can't and maybe one of the girls can when they come out this summer.

June 8, 1916

John engaged the doctor yesterday. It is wise to do so early, for then he will take care of you if you need it at any time.
It is always wise to have the urine examined about once a month just to be sure. I am as well as can be, and want to stay that way.

June 15, 1916

I suppose by the time this letter reaches you you will have heard from Edward and know that he will be with us by then. We had a telegram yesterday from him saying that his nerves had given way again and wanting to know if he could come right here. Of course we telegraphed him at once to come right along. John says he thinks the high altitude of Estes Park was too much for Edward when he was worn out with the year's college work. We are glad we are so close that he can come here and we are sure that a few weeks will set him up here the same as it did last year.

Carrie said last night when she heard that Edw. was coming that we would soon be known as running a sanatorium. John said he guessed we'd run a nervatorium. I said I wondered how long it would be before some of you would be saying that we have enough nerve ourself to be able to divide up with anyone who needs a supply. I certainly am glad we are out here in this healthful country where all who need to go to a good place can come. If Edw. is here, maybe we'll have a drawing card for some of the rest of you.

I guess everybody around here knows now that we are expecting sometime this fall. Mrs. Pease acted the other day as if she had known all about it for at least six months and maybe longer. I told John they would all believe they knew about it before we did ourselves. Mrs. Murray wrote me a note the other day to say that the news was out, and that she could hardly wait to tell me the funny things connected with it. Mrs. Pease and Mrs. Young and Mrs. Voss went off together yesterday to spend the day out northwest somewhere, and I am sure that if we had responded to the old saying our ears would have burned all day, for I am certain we furnished the chief topic of conversation for them. It makes me sort o' weary that folk talk so much, but I suppose that is all some folks have to live for. I said to Mrs. Murray yesterday that one might as well see the funny side of it. It's just as cheap and a whole lot more productive of happiness.

June 18, 1916

Edward arrived safely yesterday afternoon. We did not know when he was coming but knew that yesterday afternoon's train was the very first one he could arrive on. About four o'clock the telephone rang. I answered, but central said the party had gone. I asked her if it was Garland that wanted us and she said no, it was Frannie. Then I knew that meant Edw. was at Frannie and would be here as soon as that train got in. Every horse we had was over at the other place and John and I were here alone, so he went over to Hoffman's and borrowed a horse and I drove to Garland, getting there about ten minutes before the train did. Edw. was quite tired out when he arrived, but felt pretty well. He isn't in anything like the shape he was last year, and a couple weeks here will put him in fine trim again. It was the altitude that got him at Estes Park, as John said right off. Edw. said if he had not been so tired when he went there he thought he would have been all right, but the hotel would not let him have a single day to rest up before he started in to work.

June 20, 1916

The bees in the Nauser and Ries yards are simply booming. They never were in such fine shape at this time of year before. If the season is anything at all we ought to have a splendid crop. John said yesterday when we were going through one colony in the Nauser yard that if the season was like the 1911 season that colony would produce $30 worth of honey. There is new honey in the hives now, and we don't usually find that until about two weeks later than this.

June 25, 1916

We went to church this morning, and the sermon was good. It was on the subject of "he that conquereth his own spirit is greater than he that taketh a city." The local militia starts to Cheyenne tomorrow and the sermon was a timely one. It discussed the fact that the greatest heroism that the men of the company, or anyone for that matter, can show is to conquer himself, and mentioned that the greatest enemies the men will meet will be those of individual temptations of various sorts.

I am sorry that the companies were called out, even though none of our immediate folk are concerned. When I think of all that John has suffered I don't want to see anyone else go into the same thing. John belonged to the militia at first but could not pass the examination when the militia was called out. He went to the hospital in Indianapolis and had a slight operation performed and then enlisted in the regular army. Joe's brother, who was in the militia, never got any farther than Camp Alger and died of disease contracted there. So maybe John was lucky anyway not to have stayed with the militia that never got out of the U.S., for even if he did stop a bullet he did not lose his life.

Our beef is practically all gone. There are two cans of the pickled and about six quarts of fresh roasted. We would have used them long since if I had not schemed in every way to save them. I am right stingy about them now, for they have to last us till fall. We have two hams yet, and use a good bit of salmon to help out. I simply do not have meat more than once a day. It isn't necessary, and we can't afford it with the family we have at present. We have been using a good deal of the pickled herring, or spiced herring, which we get from Mont. Wards in buckets. They are fine. The fish are whole, about eight or ten inches long and three inches broad and 3/4 inch thick. They are put up in vinegar brine with all sorts of spices and a few slices of onion and pickles in the top of the bucket. We used a ten pound bucket and are now getting near the bottom of a fifteen pound one. John thinks they are about the best thing he ever ate. He says when we get rich he is going to buy a barrel.

You are right about the McLean's Liniment, Mamma. There isn't anything like it for some purposes. It even beats Absorbine. I hate to use it because it stains so badly, but if one takes care there is no danger. We have been using it for my hip and it helps muchly. You would think I was a race horse or at least an athlete if you saw the way John rubs my hip and back when it gives me trouble. He certainly is good at massage. I have about half a bottle of the McLean's, but I can't get it here. So I wish you would send me a bottle when Cora comes. I also wish you would send me about a pint of grain alcohol. We can not get it here at all, and occasionally we would like to have some to use as a solvent for medicine. Mrs. Van Eman advised me to get some tannin and dissolve it in alcohol, and use it on my breast after a while. Alcohol is often necessary for bathing, too, so if you happen to have a pint on hand you can spare I'll be glad to have it. We can use witch hazel for most uses to which alcohol would ordinarily be put, and it is just as good, but occasionally the alcohol is indispensable.

The men got the hay done by noon today. We are glad,

for it looks a little like rain again this afternoon. John thought there would be about fifteen loads and there were twenty-five — that is, western loads, not eastern loads, loaded on hay racks eight feet broad and sixteen feet long. We'll get another cutting from this patch later on, and we won't have to buy any hay this winter at all.

Pater, you would be interested in the way hay is stacked here from the wagons. In this dry climate no one puts hay in the barn, and in fact not one barn in fifty is made to hold hay. The hay is just stacked in the field or barn lot. With the people who raise hay regularly, a stacker is used. It is simply a large, wooden-toothed affair that lifts up the hay in the air by means of a beam and rope, the rope pulled by a horse. The stacker then drops the hay on the stack. The horse is then backed till the stacking fork lies on the ground again. But for folk who do not have a stacker, and of course we do not, the "Mormon method" is used. When the hay is loaded on the wagons in the field, a rope is laid across the rack so that a loop hangs down the center of one side of the rack, and the two ends hang down on the other side. Then when the wagon comes to the haystack the ends of the rope are slipped through the loop and the hay on the load is thus bound together. A large rope is fastened to this rope, the large rope leading over the stack and out on the other side, where a team of horses is hitched to it. The horses are driven on and the whole load from the wagon rolled up on the stack at once. It can be rolled as far over on the stack as desired, merely by driving the horses farther. That saves practically all the usual pitching from the wagon to the stack. It is interesting to see a great load roll over and up on top of the stack. The stack in our barnlot that the men put up yesterday and today is about 40 × 16 × 20 feet high.

August 3, 1916

Carrie and her people have changed their minds about going back east. We rather thought they'd come to their senses after they thought a bit. There is absolutely nothing for them back there, and when they stopped to think they realized it. Of course it is better for us for them to stay here as we won't lose on what we put into their place as we would if they threw up the filing. Carrie is all right, but I suppose she will be having more or less difficulty every little while to let Joe know what's what. We will get their house built as soon as we can and when they are in their own house they can settle their own problems. Of course we don't want them to stay if they don't want to but they surely see it's the opportunity of their lifetime.

August 4, 1916

The Bygrens have twin girls. They call them Hilda Jean and Hilma June. As Mrs. Bygren says the names they are Hilda Sheen and Hilma Shune. I think the combination quite clever, don't you? Edw. says one should have been June and the other July. They then would have pronounced it Yu-ly, which is about the truth concerning Mr. B. and more girls, when he appears to be even mildly enthusiastic.

August 13, 1916

We all stayed at home all day today, except for a little trip which John and Joe took to the other place to see if the grain was about ready to be cut. It is, and Carrie and the folks will go over there the latter part of this week for a few days. I will be glad to have the families divided again for a while, for it is simpler to have fewer folks about. Sometimes I think one gets tired of eating just from seeing so much to eat. Of course you won't understand from this that I don't want the girls and Edw. to be here because it makes more people. It does me so much good to have them here, especially now, for since none of you can be here in November I am doubly glad to have some of you here now for as long a time as possible. There are so many things I want to talk over that can't all be told in letters, even if we do write every day. It certainly is a great comfort to me to have the girls here this summer.

August 17, 1916

I cut out some more little clothes this morning. I now have the six everyday dresses, three night gowns and one petticoat cut out. We intend to make two nice dresses, one of the embroidery that Edith brought and the other a nice mull trimmed in tatting. That is all the dresses we'll make. Then I think we'll need about six petticoats and with the three night gowns that will be enough. I won't make up any of the embroidery you sent till later when the baby gets to wearing short clothes. We have four bibs made and have two pairs of shoes. There are two dozen diapers already hemmed and I have the goods for another dozen. I want enough clothes so that we won't have to wash a piece every time the child needs something clean, but at the same time I don't want a lot that aren't used right along.

September 11, 1916

Today has been a rather busy day at Honeyhill. Cora and Edith went to Powell to take cream and do some errands. Joe has been cutting grain for Mr. Ries. John went to the Ries yard early this morning and got a load of honey after having Joe help him load up two loads. Carrie washed, and I cooked dinner for the family and the four men who are working here stacking clover. So all in all, all of us haven't had much time to sit about worrying about the war in Europe.

We were amused at Grandma Hoffman the other day. She came over and wanted to know if that was honey that John had brought home in the wagon that day. She said she insisted it was honey because John had it so carefully covered up, but Mr. Hoffman said it could not be honey because John had a whole load and he never heard of a whole load of honey. In fact, he was inclined to think that there wasn't such animal as a whole load of honey! Well, you should have seen her when we told her they had brought home *four* whole loads that one day. She then wanted to go out to the shop to see it. Well, it really is a worthwhile sight to see something like a thousand or 1100 supers all filled with honey, 24 or 28 sections to the super.

Carrie cleaned out our bedroom this morning and the men moved the piano into it at noon. It is cool enough that we will want to put up the heater pretty soon, and we thought we had better get the piano moved while there was plenty of help.

I can't tell you how much good it did for me to have Cora and Edith here this summer. As I told Edith in a letter, it helped me more than I can say. Since you have been here, I feel ready to meet anything that comes along. I know you can't be here when the baby arrives, but your having been here is almost as good. All of you seem closer since you have just been here.

If you were here today you could join us in a peach bee. I want to can as many of ours as possible today. Carrie canned nearly all of hers the day we unloaded the car at Powell. She was alone all day, as we were at Powell and Joe was with us to help unload. She got 42 quarts canned all by herself, doing the peeling and all. We have not so many to can, as we have only six crates of peaches for ourselves.

We had such a nice time at club meeting at Murray's yesterday. They sewed a whole lot for me. I took along what I thought was a lot and it was all finished except the making of the comfort. The women hemmed six squares of canton flannel and eight of cheesecloth, put the hems in five dresses and three petticoats, put the cuffs on the sleeves of three or four dresses, made one little kimona and hemmed two others, and crocheted an edging on the necks and sleeves of two of the kimonas. I think that is a good deal. Mrs. Murray had the napkins (plain white crepe ones) adorned with a blue crepe paper H. She served cocoa and vanilla wafers, and then little blue and white crepe paper baskets filled with candy, and candied popcorn and salted peanuts.

I had told the folk long since I did not want them to give me a shower, but lo and behold, didn't they all give me things yesterday anyhow. They explained that they had talked about it at the meeting at Mrs. Brown's and that the ladies said they were going to give Mrs. H. something anyhow even if she didn't want it, because they wanted to do so. So they brought in the things yesterday. They gave them to me in a big basket all trimmed in blue and white paper with a big bow on the handle. Mrs. Horn made two flannelette night gowns. She always makes two, so as to be prepared for any emergency! Mrs. Hutts also brought a gown, catstitched in blue. Of course these were all white. Mrs. Young, Mrs. Gray, and Mrs. Love all brought little bootees crocheted of wool with silk trimmings. Some were all white, others pink and white. Mrs. Meyers brought the cunningest little pair of shoes — black patent leather lowers and white kid uppers. Mrs. Bygren brought a knitted hood (bought ready made) with a silk veil that fastens up as trimming, being looped up with a silk braid on a button. It is as cunning as can be. Mrs. Hart's was a bib; Mrs. Chas. Peterson's a pair of white stockings. Mrs. Murray gave me the lace she had ordered from the Philippines, and the girl that made it sent some insertion she had made for me "because I was a good friend of Mrs. Murray." Mrs. Van Eman's was a half dollar, with the legend: "to start the baby's bank account." Mrs. Ries did not come but she sent a baby blanket, made of a number of thicknesses of flannelette with the tacking done in such a way as to look like little roses, and a very fancy crocheted edge all around. It must have been a lot of work. The edge and tacking is done in pink. Carrie said she guessed Mrs. Ries wanted to show her appreciation of our cutting their grain. Mrs. Clark gave a little pink cap trimmed in lace and a pair of pink bootees. Mrs. Werts and Mrs. Hancock telephoned during the afternoon that they were all ready to come and that the men were to have been done with the horse at noon so they could use it in the afternoon. It was then four o'clock and the men were still using the horse, so they could not come.

October 1, 1916

If you were here today you could see something I suspect you never saw before—a full-fledged snow storm on the first day of October. It was windy all night and the wind continued part of the day. It has not been extremely cold, but raw and unpleasant outside. About three o'clock this afternoon a snow-storm blew down over the bench from the north and for a while it "snew" so hard we could not see Young's house [a quarter mile away]. The ground was all white, the roads being white ribbons across the landscape. Of course the snow did not stay long on the roads and in the bare places, but where there is grass or weeds the country is still white. I guess when the clouds lift the mountains will be white from top to bottom. We had had the heating stove ready to put up for a week, but as long as it stayed warm we did not put it up. This morning John decided the time had come and they put it in. We are glad now they did, for the heat feels good this afternoon.

October 3, 1916

We now have the total count of what we will have to ship in the car: Fancy, 56 cases; No. 1, 706 cases; No. 2, 322 cases. Total, 1084. With what we sent to B. and what we have sold locally the count is just about 1100 cases, and there will be about 5,000 pounds of extracted.

Next week John is going to do some insurance canvassing. Mr. Murray covered about half the Flat and did not get the rest done before school started, so Mr. Biesemeier, one of the directors, and John have divided the rest of the territory between them and will try to do the canvassing. So many people want the insurance but have not applied for it. The directors would like to have at least $100,000 in effect by the first annual meeting in January. There is about $70,000 in effect now. When that is done he will have time to do some odd jobs around home like making the little bed and the chest for the baby clothes and such things.

I have a job ahead of me this week in letter writing. We want to send out about a hundred letters to clover buying firms.

These will all have to be first copies, so I can write at that any time I have spare minutes. The letter will be only three or four lines long, so it won't take much time to do it all. If we can get in touch with some firms that buy for their own customers, we can get better prices than if we sell to large commission firms that resell to other merchants. We have a directory of industries that the Burlington Railroad puts out. It contains a list of all the business firms along the Burlington route. The firms are listed according to the kind of business they carry on. It is quite a useful volume.

October 9, 1916

The men are baling straw this afternoon to use in shipping out the honey. When the comb honey is packed in the car there must be bales of straw put at each end and otherwise packed in so that any bump there may be will be absorbed by the straw. In this way the honey is protected from the jars in switching, etc.

When we put the honey in the basement last week we took out some special short time insurance on it, as in the mutual company we can not get more than $2,000 on one risk. We already have that much on the house and did not want to risk the honey unprotected. Of course we had to get this special insurance in one of the old line companies and got it from the agent in whose company we were formerly insured. Now what do you suppose? That agent is spreading the tale that John Hendricks has given the mutual company the go-by and has come back to the old-line companies. Isn't that mean? But as John is going to do some insurance canvassing himself soon, and as we are putting out a Union circular this week in which the matter can be made clear, I guess the agent will wish in the end he had kept within hailing distance of the truth.

I must tell you about the scare John had yesterday. He started out to do some insurance canvassing in the morning. About an hour after he left, I got the word that the car of lumber had arrived. I knew it was imperative for him to know about it at once, as he would have to arrange to unload and also to notify people in time who had bills in the car. There were four other folk who got some lumber in this car besides ours and Joe's. I knew the first place John was to stop so I called there and asked them to have him call up home when he got there. Then I stuck closer to the house than a sand burr, waiting for his call. Other calls came, here and elsewhere, but not his. Finally, about two hours later I heard a buggy drive up like fury and in he came on the run. He had been trying and trying to call up and could not get me. Every time he called the *usual people* would butt in. I had told him that if I needed anyone I would call up Mrs. Murray, so he had called her up to see if I had called her. While he was talking to her the same people butted in again. Well, he had visions of me in all sorts of conditions and didn't know whether he'd find me lying on the floor or not when he got here. Poor fellow, he was certainly scared. After he got his breath he said he was going to tell the telephone company manager that he would pay fifty dollars any day the manager would string up an extra wire and put that whole family on one line where they couldn't continually bother everybody else. He did call up the manager, but he was in Billings. Shortly after John got here, Mrs. Murray called up to see if anything was the matter and while she was talking the same ring butted in on us. It certainly is exasperating. I told John I was awfully sorry for him to have such a scare and trip, but he said the one to feel sorry for was Bally. I guess Bally broke the speed record that time. Several people called to John as he passed and wanted to talk to him—about potatoes, I suppose—but he did not hear them or else just waved his hand, and like John Gilpin rode on.

October 17, 1916

I had my first experience yesterday getting ready to vote. I registered. I don't know whether I'll get to vote or not but thought it would be a shame to lose my vote for lack of registering if it would be possible to get there. If the baby doesn't arrive till after Nov. 7 I can vote all right. If it gets here a day or two before, of course I won't get to. Well, when you register, you are given a blank form which you sign. Then the "registrar," as John calls him, asks you how old you are and in what state you were born. He writes this down in a book and the ceremony is over.

John is working at making a crib for the baby. This baby won't have to sleep in bed with us, but will have its own bed from the beginning, to the great comfort of all three of us, as well as the health of the child. I will make a mattress to fit the crib and as it will be just about half the size of the bed we'll get later, the covers and blankets can be used doubled from the start.

October 20, 1916

I know you are all anxious to know when the baby will arrive, and I'd be glad to tell you if I knew. In fact, I'd be rather glad to know myself. It might be in two weeks and may be three or even more. I haven't any way yet of knowing definitely. Mrs. Van Eman told me some ways, but none of them seem to apply, at least not yet. I do know I've been considerably more uncomfortable these past ten days or so, but that doesn't tell much of anything. There isn't anything the matter, so you needn't worry. It's just a case of too much of meself for comfortable locomotion or even lying down. Maybe it'll be twins yet. I have not had any pain — merely discomfort. And so long as I am perfectly well, what more could one ask for.

October 26, 1916

Before this reaches you you will have heard from us. Mrs. Van Eman and Dr. Graham are keeping me company now. John is out in the field just now, changing his irrigation dams.

This morning about three o'clock things began to develop. We waited till about five (even napped in between) and then John hitched up and got Grandpa Hoffman to go for Mrs. Van Eman. I got up when he did and worked around the house getting things into shape. Mrs. Van Eman got here about seven and now has everything ready. She says everything is in fine shape, perfectly normal.

I have just got out thirty coal letters on the typewriter. We were anxious to get them out today. Dr. Graham has been laughing at me. He says I remind him of the old lady who was always knitting, and of whom it was said if she were to be hanged she'd take a few stitches while she was waiting. They laugh at me when I stop writing and take time to wiggle a while.

With love, Ce and J.

3:30 P.M. — All over and everything lovely.

John.

Powell Wyo, 5:10 P.M. OCT 26, 1916

Joseph Hennel 822 East 3 St Bloomington Indiana

Your grand daughter arrived this afternoon three ten everything all right.

John Hendricks

6 A.M., October 27, 1916

Well, it's all over but the shouting and from the way this young lady emits volume as well as sound that part of the performance will be adequately looked after. She made her first remark as soon as her head had arrived, before the rest of her was out in the light o' day, and all the while the doctor was taking care of her she kept up the music. She is the cunningest little maiden. She weighs 8 pounds and is as plump as can be. She was not red at all, but pink as a rosebud, and not a bit wrinkley.

Everything went beautifully. There wasn't any hurry, but better so, for so far as we know there isn't the slightest laceration inside or out. It was just 12 hours from the first indication till it was all over. I woke up at three A.M., or a little after, wet with the water. Pains began about half an hour later. They kept up with from 2½ to 15 minute intervals till noon, when they came more regularly and more severely. About one o'clock I went to bed and things settled down to business. As we told you in the message, it was all over by 3:10.

The doctor was simply fine. He came about 9 A.M. and stayed till it was all over. As soon as the final labor began he helped constantly, and I am sure the reason there is no laceration is largely due to his help. He used only his fingers, no instruments.

Now I must tell you about my lovely surprise. You know I haven't been able to wear my diamond ring for a month or more because my fingers have been so slender. Yesterday morning John asked where it was and said he'd put it on me after a while. After the baby was here, he was sitting beside the bed and slipped a ring on my finger. The doctor was in the room, so I didn't say anything but just looked at it without looking at the ring. After a bit, though, I looked at the ring and it was not the diamond, but a most beautiful enormous topaz, set solitaire style. It must be a whole carat in size. As we were looking for the baby in November he got a November birthstone. I am glad it is, for I always loved a topaz, and don't care at all for the October one, opal. John got Mr. Murray to send for this so I wouldn't know anything about it. He told me he had thought of that when he was only a boy and has waited all these years for the opportunity. The thought and the ring are the most beautiful I've known for a long time.

We all had a fine night's rest—baby, John, Mrs. Van and I—and everything is lovely.

Ce, J and Baby

We are all getting on famously. We sleep at night almost as if we didn't have something new in the house. John looked after the unloading of a car of cement yesterday and was pretty tired so we went to bed at nine. We slept till about three almost without waking. Of course I had a few pains that didn't let me drop right to sleep but nothing enough to make me feel as if I had any ground to make a fuss. When we woke at three we lay and talked a while. The baby fretted about that time, and as hot water didn't seem to satisfy it, Mrs. Van brought it in and let it nurse. We all went to sleep again then and slept till nearly six. After John got up I heard him make the fires and heard Carrie come into the kitchen. Then I went to sleep again and had another good nap. I haven't had a speck of fever and my pulse hasn't skipped or hurried one beat. The doctor was here last night and he says I look fine and that all I have to do is to mind Mrs. Van Eman and be good and take a rest while I have the chance to stay in bed. I am so well and strong I suppose I could be smart and get up in three or four days — and pay up for it for the next five or ten years. No thanks. I'm too closely related to Rip Van Winkle to miss a perfectly good opportunity to loaf.

The neighbors are lovely. There seems to be general rejoicing over the baby and my getting on so nicely. Club met at Young's, almost next door, the day the baby came, and as soon as everything was over Mrs. Murray went down and told them. There were a half dozen or so new members to be put on the list that day, and they sent word that Miss Hendricks headed the list. When the ladies went home they all stopped out in front and talked with Mrs. Van. They said they wanted to come in but would wait a while. Later in the evening Mrs. Young and Grandma Hoffman came and begged to come in just one minute. It seems that the neighbors were a whole lot more worried about me than we were. They thought that because I was over 30 there was no telling what might happen.

The Richards were here a little while last night. She is so nervous, poor girl. She lent us the first little shirts and bands, and they had not been brought up the other morning when we knew we'd need them. So John drove down after the bundle. When she found what he wanted, it startled her so that she nearly fainted, and after he left she had to sit down for half an hour she was so weak.

Mrs. Van surely knows her business all right. She not only puts a good bandage on the abdomen, but also puts one on the breast. You can't imagine what support and comfort that gives. She says she never saw as small a person as I with such a breastwork! She knows what to feed you, too. As I started to be sick early in the morning, I did not eat anything that day, or drink anything except half a cup of strong coffee as medicine at noon. After the baby came they gave me a cup of cocoa. Late that night I ate half a wheat biscuit. Yesterday I had a little milk toast and cocoa for breakfast, a few spoons of soup and crackers for dinner, and a wheat biscuit and milk for supper. This morning I had a piece of toast and two toasted crackers and some hot milk. This sounds like a lot, but I eat only a small amount at a time.

October 29, 1916

It seems strange to stay in bed when you are not sick, and yet somehow it feels nice to lie still and not feel as if you ought to get up.

Mrs. V. and John measured the baby this morning and she is 20 inches long. Mrs. V. says that 18 to 20 inches is the usual size. I guess I told you she weighed 8 pounds. She is perfectly formed everywhere and there is not a spot on her of any kind. She looks like John — at least, we think she does — though I guess you can't tell much what a wee baby looks like. I must tell you about her hair. That was the biggest surprise of all. It is dark red. Mrs. V. says it will be dark brown when its color is settled, but at present it is a most beautiful auburn! Dr. Graham quoted us a song that went, "If the baby has red hair who is to blame? Poor Old Dad!" We told him that was certainly true in this case, for there is no red hair on the Hennel side that I know of. I don't know that I ever thought about what color the baby's hair would be. If I did, it was to take it for granted that she would be a cotton top, same as we were.

I got to sit up in bed yesterday noon and feed myself for dinner. It seemed nice to feed myself again for a change. Today I can sit up a while in bed propped up. Of course I can write lying down as well as sitting up.

November 3, 1916

I must tell you how lovely the carnations are that you girls and Edward sent. They came down on the morning train from Cody on Wednesday and John was in Powell that morning and got them right away. They were as fresh as if they had never been cut. I put them in the green wicker vase and they are such big, stiff-stemmed, upstanding beauties. I wrote Edward yesterday that if I were in the biggest city in the land I couldn't get better nursing or more luxuries than I have had. John got every sort of fruit, oranges, grapes, etc. and nuts, and all sorts of good things. Mrs. Ries sent a box of their good candy, the neighbors brought all sorts of good things, and you all sent me flowers.

November 5, 1916

Behold me up again, sitting at the machine once more. I got up this morning and was up for dinner. Mrs. Van showed me how to bathe the baby this morning and answered about a thousand questions I asked her. She was called to another place yesterday but would not go until today. I certainly hated to have her leave, as she has been so fine to have here.

I must tell you what she said about the baby. This is the sixtieth baby she has brought to people in Wyoming, not to mention all the babies she brought to Ohio folk before she moved here. She says that all told, taking everything into consideration, this is the best baby she ever took care of. What do you think of that? She says that as a rule her babies are good and don't cry much, grow all right, and are easy to take care of, but this baby broke the record. She said I should tell you that. She said she hardly ever had a patient that was less nervous than I was and that I had given the baby a good nervous system, or rather, that the baby didn't seem to have any more nerves than I did. I told her I had tried to forget there were such things as nerves while the baby was on the way, and she said I did a good job of it. That certainly makes me mighty thankful.

November 9, 1916

We have not heard the final election returns yet and are wondering how things turned out. The last we heard was that Wilson was ahead, with only Minnesota and California to hear from. The western states can generally be counted to be for him, as his work for the irrigation projects and for farmers in general has been so good. There has been more done for the farmer during the past four years than in any forty years before. The Democrats have passed all the things the Republicans promised since the Civil War, just about. The Republicans always talked but they never did anything to relieve the farmer's condition. I guess Wilson got a pretty heavy country vote, and especially an irrigation farm vote. Of course the total of such votes is not great, but it helps a little.

The baby is as good as can be. I take care of her myself at night now. She sleeps in her own crib rolled up beside our bed. She nurses at nine, then about one, and again about five in the morning; then she sleeps till about nine. She is the dearest little thing.

November 16, 1916

As to the name, I think we will call her Cecilia, though we have talked some of calling her Barbara. John says Cecilia is too long for everyday use. The Sweetens* and all John's people call me Cecilia, too, so for that side of the house there would not be any distinction between Cecil and Cecilia. So far we call her Baby or Little Girl or some such name as that. It

---

*Carrie, Joe, and their children.

seems strange to call such a wee mite such a long name as Cecilia when you talk to her.

We have been pretty nearly living on rabbits lately so far as meat is concerned. Really, you can hardly tell the rabbit meat here from chicken. It is quite as good. One of Little Joe's chums sent him his rifle, a pretty good 22 rifle, and Joe has been going hunting. Occasionally John gets a rabbit, with a stone or with the rifle, but usually Little Joe gets them. Joe and one of the Vernam boys went hunting Saturday. Joe is new at the business but Ray is an old hand, if he is only 15 years old. Ray shot nine rabbits Saturday. He says they will keep in this cold weather.

November 20, 1916

It feels so good to be able to work again. This morning Carrie got the washing well started and then went to their place to get dinner for the six men who are working there today at the concreting. I'll be glad when I can do all my own housework again. To be sure it is fine to have the help now and during the past couple weeks, but I suspect in a couple weeks from now I'll feel a whole lot better if I can hustle around and get things done myself. I was beginning to be afraid that all the loafing I did the past months was spoiling me for real work, but I guess it won't. My, but I'd hate to be a lady of leisure all the time. It must get awfully tiresome.

November 26, 1916

This seems to be a "joining" time, for the Union has been increasing rapidly in membership. I guess there have been at least twenty-five new members within the past six weeks. At the meeting tomorrow night the Union is going to adopt a new form of organization. Originally it was a local chapter of the Farmer's Education and Cooperative Union of America, but we have not been able to discover any benefit that accrues from belonging to that organization. John has got up a new constitution and by-laws, making the Union a merely local organization, whose purpose is "the uniting in a mutual association the producers and consumers of the Shoshone Project and neighboring communities for the purpose of marketing their products, buying for them any and all supplies that can be bought in wholesale or carlot quantities, promoting new industries, and developing the same into stock companies or other forms of permanent organizations as the producers and consumers may designate."

I was amused at John this afternoon. He remarked that one of the greatest difficulties in raising a girl was that you had to hunt and hunt to find a man who would be good enough for her when she was old enough to marry, whereas if you had a boy almost any girl would be good enough for him! I didn't exactly agree with the latter part of the statement.

November 29, 1916

You ought to see what a smart baby this one is. She already uses two words. Today is the first day that she sprang them on us. One is ga-a and the other is guh-wah. Of course you know what they mean so I won't have to send the dictionary along!

December 4, 1916

I have no doubt that you would all like to see Cecilia and it would be nice to have her visit you at Christmastime with Edw. as delivering officer, but I am reminded of the question Mrs. Murray asked last summer when Edw. suggested that he was going to borrow Max for a whole day: Would Edward provide the refreshments for the baby while he was away from his mother? I am afraid that at the present reckoning baby and I are like Ruth and Naomi. Well, there is a good deal of convenience in such an arrangement after all. I saw an ad in the paper the other day that said: You need an Icy-Hot to keep the baby's milk at the right temperature during the night. I said to myself, says I. No I don't either, praise be.

December 4, 1916

Cora, if you want to see a delicate birdlike appetite (the bird is the ostrich, of course) you ought to be here now and see me. I never was so persistently and consistently hungry in all my life. I suppose the reason is that the baby gets a good part of what I eat. I am simply starved most of the time and generally eat a lunch in the afternoon. I don't eat breakfast till about nine usually, so I can generally manage till dinner time. When we are alone again, and begin to have breakfast at eight and dinner at three, I am quite sure I will eat lunch at twelve and a "piece" (besides an apple) before I go to bed.

We have been corresponding with various seed firms that buy sweet clover seed, and have answers from 18 houses that want to buy in carload lots. I wrote over 150 letters to seed houses all over the middle west. There are three houses that want small lots, too. As soon as the seed is threshed and recleaned we will send samples to the various houses and see what they will offer us for it. We are asking thirteen cents for scarified seed. The scarified seed, with the outer coat slit to speed germination, seems to be so much more in demand now than the natural. Mr. Hardy has a scarifier that John will get and we figure it will cost 50 cents a hundred pounds to scarify the seed. Most likely we can get about a cent and a half a pound for the thus treated seed. The neighbors insist that we will get as much as 300 bushels of seed from our stacks. Well, "Barkis is willin'!" We will be satisfied with 200 bushels, however.

December 10, 1916

John has been properly introduced to O'Henry, and, like the rest of us, he sits and reads with one perpetual grin on his countenance. At the present it is "The Rubaiyat of a Scotch Highball" that is the cause. Thanks ever so much for lending us O'Henry for a while. We'll try to take good care of him while he is visiting here.

John enjoyed the honey you sent very much. He has always said he believed he liked the Indiana honey better than he did this western honey, although the western honey has the more delicate flavor. Well, after he ate some of the Indiana honey now that he knows what the western honey tastes like, he was forced to confess that he likes our honey best! I guess maybe he had forgot just what eastern honey did taste like, and as he acquired his taste for honey on it, thought it was the best, just as a man thinks the foods he had as a boy are better than what he gets after he is grown up.

You know how we joked about going to Denver for the holiday if the farm and the bees made as much as $5,000. Well, since the clover has turned out so well the farm and the bees have done their part, but since the crops are not sold I guess we'll not live up to our part. This would be a good time to go, too, for we got a letter recently asking John to be on the program for the Colorado Honey Producers Association meeting, with a paper on "Some Experiences of 1916." He will write the paper, as they wanted it whether or not he could be there himself. We wrote the manager the other day that we had promised ourselves the trip to Denver if the total of our income was $5,000 but that since the honey was not sold we could not make the trip. We told him that if the honey moved before the holidays we would come. So we may still make the trip, if our good fairies aren't too busy already to hustle up the honey sale.

December 22, 1916

Cecilia took her first trip abroad yesterday afternoon when she made her first appearance at Club, at Mrs. Gray's, the next house toward Powell from Murray's. She and I went alone in the buggy. I had her well wrapped up, as she had on mittens and a knitted wool hood and was wrapped in the two blankets that are alike. She did not get a bit cold either way, although the thermometer registered only twelve above when we started and was probably down to about five when we came home. Mrs. Gray had a wash basket fixed with comforts and pillows for her to lie in, and everybody seemed as much interested in her as in the Christmas presents.

If you had a Christmas as fine as we did, you certainly were happy. This is the best Christmas either of us ever had. Of course the baby comes first in counting our blessings, and added to that are so many more we can hardly enumerate. We are so happy we go around grinning like Cheshire cats all the time.

First I must tell you about the clover seed market. The man who bought up last year's seed here is trying to buy this year's crop too. He started in the fall with gloomy stories of the over-yield everywhere and how the house for which he buys has two carloads left from last year. He began by offering seven cents a pound and then he came up to nine and now he offers ten. Well, John decided that if there was to be a profit we growers might as well have it ourselves, so we got busy. We have written over 200 letters about clover seed, from which we got about 25 replies. Of these, 18 were from houses that want to buy in carlots. The first of last week we sent out samples to about 22 houses. Before the end of the week the telegrams began to come in, and one house in Atchison, Kansas, wants 1200 bushels at twelve cents a pound. We wired them again today that we are not anxious to sell until the whole crop is ready for market, and that we think we ought to get a little better price than that. We really think we'll be able to get 12 ½ or 13 cents a pound. Now every additional cent on our crops means about $180 to us, so you see how much we are making by doing the marketing ourselves instead of selling to a buyer that comes along. If we had wanted to, we could have made five or six hundred dollars ourselves on the deal by buying the seed here at ten and eleven cents and selling it for twelve. But we believe that we will do the community more good and in the long run ourselves too by letting each producer get the returns of his own labor. The amount we will make on just our own crop over what the local buyer offered will buy our automobile and run it a year. (The price of the Ford car we want is listed at $360.00 plus freight and delivery.)

One big plan John has for this clover seed deal is this: Heretofore the farmers institute has had to charge admission to pay the expenses. Now if the Union (which is John) sells the clover seed for the people here, we will charge 1% commission and the money that is made in that way will pay the expenses of the institute and the meetings can be free to everybody. If the Union can do some things like furnishing a free, week-long, institute, the community will begin to wake up to what the Union is doing. Heretofore the institute has been run, as has almost everything else here, by the bankers of Powell. There isn't any reason on earth except the stupidness of the farmers that lets the bankers and business men in Powell run the farmers' affairs.

Well, that is quite an oration on the Union, isn't it! But we are so delighted over the clover seed situation that we believe lots of good things are ahead of us for ourselves and the community too.

December 29, 1916

The coal shortage is beginning to be acute here. There has been practically no coal in either Powell or Garland for about a week. The Union has five cars on the way but the railroad has been unable to get them in. Yesterday we sent a telegram to the secretary of the Public Service Commission of Wyoming, asking him if he could not help us. We got an answer from him within a few hours saying he had wired the C.B. & Q. superintendent at Casper to give us all the relief he could. John then telephoned to the mine at Owl Creek and they promised to get ten cars out for us right away. The only coal that has been in Powell this week is one car of pea coal, hardly better than nothing, for it is from a poor mine as well as being a poor grade. John said if you tried to fire up on that pea coal from Sheridan you would keep warm, for you would get hot under the collar.

John is having about 600 copies printed of a contract form by which the farmers agree to get their next winter's supply of coal in August at the time when the mines give the best prices because it is their slack season. We can get the coal then at about $1.50 per ton less than the price now. He thinks the farmers of the Flat can use about 4,000 tons if we get it this way, and that will do away with the winter shortage the Flat has suffered for the past two winters.

December 31, 1916

1 916 for the last time. Inasmuch as it will be 1917 in about 3½ hours, I guess I won't write many more letters in 1916.

Yesterday it was three years since a very important event took place at 822. These have been three mighty happy years, and the third one was the best and happiest of all. We start out on the fourth with splendid prospects in every way—in our own work and in the community work. Best of all, there are three of us instead of only two.

I was thinking the other day about how my life has been running in three-year periods—3 years in the Evansville high school, three in teaching, three in college, two three's in college teaching, and now three out here until the baby came. It really is interesting. Every important change comes at the end of a three-year period.

We celebrated our wedding anniversary today, as we were busy yesterday. John put on his wedding suit and shirt, and this afternoon I put on my wedding dress. Yes, I can still wear it, or perhaps I should say I can wear it again. I did not know whether or not I could. When John buttoned it, we wondered if it would connect all the way. He fastened the first hook and said, "No. 1 goes." Then he went on, "No. 2 fastens" and so on till "No. 6 is not so easy; No. 7 is harder to fasten; No. 8 is tight, No. 9 is—easy. No. 10 is easier. No. 11 is so loose it will hardly stay shut." The dress was not too tight at all. In fact, it fit just about as a dress-up dress ought to. I kept it on only about three hours because, well because wedding dresses aren't made with the object in mind of giving babies refreshment.

The Sweetens moved to their own place yesterday afternoon. They took over most of their things Saturday and finished yesterday morning and afternoon. So we are alone again. Well, we are mighty glad, and of course they are just as glad to be in their own house. Having two houses here so each of us could spend our evenings alone made it a great deal better, but even then it was not as pleasant as for each family to be alone, and what was true of our wanting to be by ourselves was true of them too. So we are all glad their house is ready and that they are in it.

I had a nice time at Murray's yesterday, where I spent the day. She had asked me so many times to spend the day with her and I have never done so. We got out the East End Club program for the year, and we think it is quite good. We fixed up a program for every meeting and assigned the person who is to give a paper or review a farmers' bulletin or lead the discussion. The topics relate mostly to home keeping and farm work, such as how, when, and what to plant in a garden, what to plant for orchards here, how to do various household tasks, time savers, soups, suffrage, school lunches, cooperation of parents and teachers, musical programs, etc. You can see there is plenty of variety. One meeting is devoted to suggestions for Christmas presents, along the latter part of October. Just before Christmas we have a party at which each person brings a gift for one member. Tomorrow is election of officers. I do not know who will be elected, as Mrs. Murray and I both want to get out of it. I simply won't promise to go regularly with a small baby, for she comes first in considering the weather as fit or unfit for her to go out. Some of the ladies told Mrs. Murray they know I would not be able to come regularly but they wanted me to be president again because I could do more without trying than anyone else could by working her best. I don't agree, but "thank you for the compliment just the same."

I wish you could be here tonight and see what Wyoming moonlight and snow can do to the scenery. You would be sure it was daylight and not moonlight. Now maybe you will think I am stretching it, but it is actually a fact that last night when the men came home from the Union meeting I could see the buggies when they were at Werts and that is three quarters of a mile away. I am not a bit afraid to stay alone while John goes to a meeting when it is moonlight like this. On dark nights it is a little different.

Nordmarks were here today and we had a very nice time. I wish we were where we could see them oftener, for it might be possible for John to get Mr. N. interested in things here and persuade him to throw off his lethargy. He is not an old man — less than fifty — but he could pass for twenty years more than that. He is not very well, but I suspect that worries and not physical illness is at the bottom. Mrs. N. said today that a number of large investments had proved failures. I assume she meant money investments. She said they decided the best thing for them to do was to get into some quiet corner and stay there a few years out of the world. I asked her what he thought of his investment here and she said he thought the money he put in the place here was extremely well invested. I would like to see her often until her baby comes. Of course she is inclined to worry because of losing the first one. She is older than I am and not well built for having children. Her chief drawback, she explained herself, is that "she suffers from the artistic temperament." She feels at home here and told me things she has not told anyone on the Flat. She seemed to feel that I was a kindred spirit. (I hope not in the artistic way!).

The dinner was right nice, if I do say so. We had roast beef, mashed potatoes, gravy, green peas, bread and butter and honey for the first course; asparagus-pimiento salad for the second; baked apples with whipped cream and cake for dessert. I had just removed the first course and was ready to serve the salad course when there was a knock at the door, and there was Walter Fowler, come to ask John about some things he needed to know for his farm. He was just coming in as I came into the dining room with the salad on the tray. I must say the salad did look pretty, the pretty plates, the green of the asparagus, the red of the pimiento, and the white of the dressing. Well, he just stood still when he saw what I had, and I calmly went about putting the plates on the table in front of Mr. and Mrs. N., who of course had not got up. Then Fowler broke out with, "Well, putting on the dog again—as usual!" His eyes were as big as saucers at the sight of the well arranged table and asparagus in January 1. Of course I invited him to sit down and have some (holding on to my plate of salad which would have made a return trip to the kitchen and reappeared as twins if he had accepted) but he declined, saying he had already dined. If there is anything above others I love to do, it is to impress Walter Fowler. It is funny, but every time he appears, almost, Fate seems to be propitious.

January 18, 1917

I must tell you we did big business at Honeyhill yesterday. We closed a deal for the sweet clover seed raised on the Flat, about a $10,000 deal. Mr. Smith of Fromberg is the local agent for the A.A. Berry Seed Co. of Clarinda, Iowa. He bought the seed here last year. Well, the Berry firm wanted the seed pretty badly and they sent in one of their special buyers to help Smith make the deal. Smith and the man were here yesterday and finally offered us 11-3/4 cents and bags, and we accepted. They gave us a check for a thousand dollars to seal the contract, as advance payment. Of course that is on the whole lot, not only our own. We had bids of twelve cents from several firms, but these firms had not agreed to send an inspector in here and pay for the seed when loaded.

John got the farmers who are raising sweet clover seed— about 15 men all told—about $1500 more than they could have got if John had not got to work on the matter and done the dealing with the agent. The fact that we knew the market made the Berry people think we were important enough to send in one of their travelling men, and that is some compliment to us the first season we have done any of this work. If we had had a little more experience we might have held this firm for the extra 1/4 cent. Next year we'll know a little more. But we think we did pretty well for amateurs on such a big deal.

January 20, 1917

We found out something yesterday that is not good news. The woman on one of the places near our Nauser bee yard telephoned yesterday that the water from the river was getting in the yard where the bees are wintered. John had to go right down and see what was doing. He found that there was an ice gorge in the river, or to say more truly, the whole river is full of ice. The channel has been switching from one side to the other, as the current can get by the ice. The bees are packed in clusters of eight to sixteen colonies. There was snow all around the clusters, from what fell in November. The water had crept in on this snow and turned the whole place to ice. There is danger now that more water will come in on top of the ice that is there now, but there is no way to prevent it. We'll simply have to let it go as it will, and, as John says, chalk up the cost to experience. No one would ever have thought that there would be any danger where the bees are, as it is a particularly high place where the river had never touched before. but of course you never can tell what will happen when ice gets in the river and blocks it.

One thing John found out yesterday is how much time a Ford will save us in doing the work in the outyards, or rather, in getting to the yards. With a team it takes two hours at the very best to get to that yard. It took just forty minutes yesterday to make the trip in the borrowed auto. We can save three hours a day easily by going down in an auto. Besides, the trip is the hardest part of the day when we go with the team. We get tireder riding than we do working. So we will certainly be glad to make the trips this year in a car. We hope to have the auto by the time of the Farmers' Institute, the latter part of next month.

We have been interested in an ad that is appearing in the *Farmstead,* showing an attachment for making a Ford car do tractor work. You can use it to draw a heavily loaded wagon, or to plow. We have been thinking of buying another horse to match the mare we have, but have decided to investigate this first. We would have to pay from $150 to $200 to get a horse that would match the one we have, and the harness would cost $15 or $20. This affair costs $195 and the freight. If we can use the Ford to do the plowing, that will certainly be a big advantage.

The little testament from Grandpa for Cecilia came today. It is certainly a treasure. He has written in it "Cecilia Barbara Hendricks from her Great Grand Father, Chas. H. Thuman. November 3d, 1916." In the front is this inscription, which of course he did not write. The book itself bears the date 1843. It is bound in black leather with flower design centerpiece and border pressed in. The edges still show gold, but the one white paper is all yellow. But just think! It is over 70 years since Grandpa got it. Isn't it lovely of him to give Cecilia such as personal gift?

I don't see how you can say I have not mentioned the color of the baby's eyes. I don't remember when I did so, but if I didn't, I sure am surprised. I can't believe there is anything about her I have not talked about. I guess we are normal parents all right, from the amount of conversation this baby furnishes! Well, her eyes are blue, deep, dark blue, blue as blue ever was. Her skin is so fair and her hair red and her eyes so blue we call her our red-white-and-blue girl. I called her that just now and she giggled out loud.

January 30, 1917

There was a woman here a while ago who walked two miles to come here to see if we had any work for her to do. We did not, and if we did have I wouldn't have her to do it. They lived in Hugh Smith's house a little while, just behind Roach's place. The man is rather old and not a very good worker. I suspect he tries hard enough to get work now, but work is scarce for the weather is so cold nothing can be done outside and people don't hire a poor workman at this time of year. She said they are having a hard time now, and I don't doubt it. The woman is, according to the reports of the neighbors, pretty much of a shrew and a no-count person. Reminds you of "po' white trash." But when it is cold and people are likely to be hungry you rather forget such distinctions. They have two boys, about ten and twelve. One of them has spells of some kind. The mother said he fell out of a street car and hurt his head. They live now in the little beet house on the Loomis place, where they lived all summer. Several weeks ago she came here to see if the Union had any coal at Garland, and she smelled so that after she was gone we had to air the house. It was awful. So as I said a while ago, if we did have work I wouldn't want her to do it. Nevertheless I feel sorry for them. We gave her a good piece of meat and some sections of honey. With flour so high I don't wonder that poor folks are short of provisions. It is about all a man like that one can do to get flour and coal these days. I guess the growing boys are hungry as bears, too. Poor folks. Even if they are careless and dirty one can't help feeling sorry for them in this kind of weather.

I must not forget to tell you that John has saved the Telephone Company. There was a meeting yesterday and they adopted his plan. It is to have at least 25 stockholders go security for the debt of the Company until the debt can be paid off, and thus prevent the company from falling into the hands of the Western Electric, which is the Bell Co. The strange thing about this local company is that it is actually earning enough to pay the running expenses, the interest on interest-bearing debt, and almost $400 a year besides. If its business were only handled in a business-like way right now it could pay up its debts in a few years without any more income than it has at present. But there is such a demand for more telephones that it is easily possible to put in 200 new phones this coming season. With that addition, the income will be greatly increased. John's proposal included the stipulation that the men who sign the notes to provide the security should have the say as to the directors for the coming year. That was agreed at the meeting, so John will most likely be a director, as he proposed the plan. With a few level-headed business men to run the company, it will be a paying proposition for the stockholders. As soon as the debts are paid the exchange fee can be lowered (we now pay $1 a month) and still provide enough to pay the running expenses and provide a sinking fund for repairing and replacing the system as it needs it.

February 2, 1917

We have been making house plans. We got the blue prints from the lumber company yesterday made out according to our plan. There are some things we want changed from the way they worked out our plans. The lumber company in Seattle we get our carloads of lumber from will work out the blue prints and figure your lumber bills. They will furnish the blue prints that an architect would charge from $50 to $100 for and charge nothing for the service. If all our bees at the river don't get refrigerated too much, and these here at home come out all right, we will start building in the late spring. We both fairly jig at the prospect of a place big enough to lay down two things without having to put one on top of the other.

February 4, 1917

The paper yesterday said that railroad conditions in the west now are the worst the roads have ever known. Even the great, proud coast-to-coast trains are hours and hours behind schedule. Every snow plow the Northern Pacific has is in use. In some places the snow is drifted twenty feet high in the places where there are fences to keep the snow off the tracks. I am glad none of us have to do any travelling now. One article said that in one place in Nebraska there was a long string of trains, one right after the other, all waiting for the first one in line to break through the drifts so the others could follow. Some were freight trains, some locals, and some the fastest passenger trains. This winter is the worst the oldest inhabitant here has seen and I suppose it is the same throughout the west. The great amount of snow is unusual here. Of course it is a good thing for the fields, especially for the alfalfa and for the orchards, and especially fine for the dryland farmers on the bench and the cattle and sheepmen who range on vacant lands around the Project. This snow will mean lots of pasture next spring.

John has gone to Powell. Mr. Roach is "proving up," and John is one of the witnesses.

February 9, 1917

There have been a number of farms change hands recently. In almost every case the buyers and the sellers both are residents who intend to stay here. They simply want larger farms of different locations. Farms here have been cropped long enough now that people know for what they are suited and the man who wants to raise beets wants a beet farm, one who wants grain a grain farm, one who wants potatoes a potato farm, etc. Heavy soil is suitable for grain, light soil for potatoes and beets. Mr. Buch, who lives opposite the cemetery, sold his place last week. They have two farms, one in his name and one in hers, which adjoin. They have about 120 acres of irrigated land and some 40 or 50 that are above the ditch and cannot be watered. Mr. Buch was a druggist and not a farmer. He happened to be talking to a neighbor, Mr. Scott, recently about selling places in the neighborhood and remarked that he had better not get an offer or he might sell out, too, although he did not intend to or did not expect to get his price. Scott asked him what his price was, and he said $9,000. "I'll take it," Scott said, and immediately wrote out a check for the amount. Buch took it and has been sorry ever since. He doesn't know what he will do as he had no plans whatever. Scott is a man from Nebraska who has been here several years. He made his money raising potatoes in Nebraska and has come here to make more money as this is a better potato country than even the best of the eastern districts.

We are somewhat disappointed in the prices we got for the honey. We got about 30 cents a case less than we had hoped to get and on the No. 2 the price was still less. I do not know what it will all amount to. It is fortunate that the low price is this year when we have such a large crop. That helps out. I suppose we will get something like $2400 for the lot instead of about $2700 as we had hoped.

We asked for the bill from the doctor and from Mrs. Van the other day so we could pay. The usual charge out here for the doctor is $25, but for some reason Dr. Graham told John he did not want to charge full price and that $15 was about right. Just think! Mrs. Van was here just a week and a half at $15 per, which makes $22.50. I think we have come out mighty lucky, for most of the people round about have had such big bills after their babies came. The doctor bill at Richards was $50. Mrs. Roach had to pay $15 a week for her room at the hospital, and the doctor was extra. Then too, since Cecilia gets her food au natural, we have been saving the expense of a lot of costly food. Richards have had to spend dollars and dollars on food for their baby. So we feel we are extremely fortunate to have such a well baby and to get her without a great expense. I hope we will be as fortunate the rest of the times when our family arrives.

I think this baby is going to be a little mischief, all right. Sometimes when she is lying in her bed wide awake, and we talk to her, she will turn her head sideways and not look at us. She will lie just as still as a mouse and not move a muscle of her face. But if we keep on talking to her, she will smile and look as mischievous as can be, but never look at us. It certainly looks cute to see her have her eyes wide open and her face turned away, and then smile at what we say.

I had to laugh at John this afternoon. First I must tell you that often when the baby looks sober, he will say, "Can the baby smile?" Usually she will grin all over her face. Well, what I started to tell was about me. My cold has reached the place where I have to cough. This afternoon I was lying on the couch and got a severe coughing spell. It made me feel sick and I thought I would have to be a "Whay-all." John ran and got me the bucket and then came and sat beside me and held my head. I guess I looked about as forlorn as Hughes did the second day after the election last fall. After a bit John put the most engaging look on his face and said to me, "Can't the baby smile?" Well, of course I laughed and that made me feel lots better, and in a little while I was all right again and didn't have to be a whay-all at all.

March 7, 1917

Ever since Cecilia has been in the living room and big enough to look about, the bookshelves and books have attracted her attention more than anything else. I think she will be literary when she is grown. I hope so. Or maybe it is the colors and gilt that attract her. So perhaps she will be an artist. I think she is like a bird. She seems to talk more when the typewriter makes a noise than at other times. Also when we want her to stop making noise and go to sleep, we just put a cover over her crib and make it dark, the way you put a cover over a canary's cage when it sings too loudly. She does not know what it is to be rocked to sleep. If we take her up and rock her when she is sleepy she will wake wide up and want to play. I guess she does not want to miss the pleasure of being held and rocked.

March 19, 1917

The papers this week have the rates for water this summer. The operation and maintenance charge is sixty cents an acre. That includes two acre-feet of water. That is, one has to pay sixty cents an acre whether he uses the water or not, and if he does use it he can have up to two feet per acre. If he needs more water than that, it costs twenty cents for the third foot and fifty cents a foot for all above three feet. The reason the price is so much higher for the additional above three feet is that three feet is in most cases enough for any land. All above that goes to waste, and more than that is likely to cause trouble for the land lying lower by making it seepy.

Our first advance payment check for the honey came yesterday, after long delay. The check was for $1080, as we had 1080 cases of honey to go in the car. John banked the check this morning and arranged to look after the most pressing of the bills that need to be paid. We will settle up the others when the rest of the money comes in.

The wind today is suitable to the season — March. I suppose, Mamma, if you were here, you would be like the Englishman in the story Buffalo Bill told. They were riding in Colorado, and all of a sudden the breeze sprang up strong enough to blow the Englishman clear off the wagon seat to the side of the road. He picked himself up, and as he climbed back in the seat he said, "I say, now, don't you rather over-do the ventilation a bit in this country?"

John went to the river bee yard a few days ago and discovered that practically all the bees there are dead. As the ice thawed the water got into the hives and of course the bees could not stand that. As we had 170 colonies there the loss is quite considerable. It means that we will have to buy bees by the pound this spring to fill up the empty hives and that will take a couple hundred dollars. It is foolish not to do it, tho, for to let the hives stand empty is poor business. Of course this loss, provided we do not have any more when we set out the bees that are in the cellar, is small compared with what we suffered year before last, still it is more than we care to have.

Since we need to spend the money for bees this spring, we

have been wondering, Co, if you would care to let us keep the use of the $125 we owe you a little while longer. If we paid you back we would have to get the money either for that or for the bees at the local bank, and pay 10% for it. We want to pay you whatever interest you think is right, for since we need the money longer we do not feel we should take it for nothing. Please let us know if you can spare the money a while yet, and if we can have it.

March 26, 1917

I wish you could be here to see the world here when it is all white. You never saw anything more beautiful. I said last night when we were writing to one of John's friends that when you can see a circle with a diameter of a couple hundred miles, it makes a lot of whiteness when it is all white. The snow is beginning to go now and I suspect it won't be long till it is all gone.

Mamma, you are mistaken about people using less honey now. There is a greater demand than ever for extracted honey. In fact, the extracted honey market is way up and the demand unprecedented. As long as the war lasts that will be the case, for a great deal is being shipped to Europe. There is hardly enough now to supply the demand in this country. There was an unusually large crop of extracted honey produced this year, too. As for comb honey, the crop this past season was 40% above the usual amount. The reason the price went down was because of the extremely unusual crop. Compared with the previous season there was 40% more comb honey and 28% more of both kinds and it is apparent that practically all of this enormous crop has been disposed of. Honey is really the cheapest food that one can buy, if actual food value is counted. For instance, half a pound of extracted honey is equal in food value to each of the following: ten eggs, six ounces of cream cheese, 3/4 pound of beefsteak, one pound of codfish, eight oranges, five bananas, half a pound of English walnuts, one quart of milk. So you see when you eat a slice of bread and honey you are eating something that is pretty valuable as a food.

I was so amused at the baby this morning. I thought she was asleep. She had her eyes shut and was quiet as could be. In fact, she had been asleep for about half an hour. As I passed the crib I stopped and kissed her hand. Without opening her eyes she grinned all over her face. I did not say a word or make a sound, but kissed her hand again to see what she would do. This time she opened one eye just the tiniest bit and grinned again. Of course I was so tickled then that I had to laugh and say something to her. When I spoke she opened both eyes and grinned some more. She certainly is the smiliest baby I ever saw. Often when I pass the crib when she is awake, I will smile at her without speaking and she will smile back without making a sound. Then she will go on playing with her fingers as if she had not been interrupted. Her whole face lights up so when she smiles. She looks now as if she ought to be pretty when she is big, but if she doesn't have a pretty face she will be lovely when she smiles.

March 29, 1917

We had some good news yesterday. John had a letter from the Federal Farm Loan Bank in Omaha saying that the instructions they had from Washington were to extend the benefit of the farm loan act to reclamation projects the same as to any farm land. That means 6% money for the farmers here. And that means much quicker development of the community. A man can afford to borrow money at 6% to make improvements on his farm—house, barn, silo, etc. He can't afford to pay 10% or 11%. This money can be borrowed for a term of from 5 to 40 years. The total interest rate and payments on principal would amount to a little more than 8½%. Think of getting the use of a thousand dollars for twenty years for $87 per year, and at the end of the time owe nothing.

April 2, 1917

The old Telephone Company decided to let the company be sold at sheriff's sale to pay the debts, then a dozen or so of the men got together, formed a new company, and bought the property when it was sold. The total indebtedness was about $8,000. Altogether there are thirteen men in the new company. They did not have to put up any cash, for the banks readily lent them what they needed; and so we are now the owners of something like $1150 worth of corporation stock without having to put up a penny. There is no doubt in the world that the company can pay off the total indebtedness in about four or five years at the most, and maybe in less, and then pay a good dividend on the stock. The trouble is that the old company was not managed.

The new company has hired a *competent* manager for $1200 a year. He will spend all his time looking after repairs, new construction work, and anything else like that, and will oversee the central girls, keep the accounts, send out the bills for collecting rents, etc. The old company charged $1.50 a month for rental phones in residences. The new company has reduced the price to $1.25 a month provided the rent is paid quarterly in advance. Otherwise the same rate prevails.

There is not a doubt in the world that with careful and proper management the company will pay a big dividend. So it seems that we are getting something for nothing. I guess, though, John will put in enough work to pay for our share. We have been laughing about the telephone stock and saying that Cecilia could go to college on the returns we get from this stock. If the company pays off all indebtedness inside five years, and the stock then bears 10% dividend (it will probably pay more, from what the old company should have done, properly managed) by the time she is ready for college she will have something over a thousand dollars to go on, not counting any interest on the money.

We were amused at Aunt Lizzie's letter, especially where she says she wishes the Kaiser were in heaven. I guess there are lots of people who wouldn't wish him such a pleasant abode. From the newest news of what is happening in Germany since Russia became a republic, I guess the Kaiser is beginning to find he does not have to die to get to a warmer place than heaven. We do hope that what has happened in Russia will make Germany a republic before the end of the war or soon after.

John was writing to his brother a while ago and got to telling him of all the titles John now possesses. He enumerated the secretary-treasurer of the Shoshone Farmers' Union, and of the Garland Federal Farm Loan Association, secretary of the Project Telephone Company, and president of the Shoshone Farmers' Mutual Insurance Company. Then he added, "Und das hat die Lorelei mit her typewriter gethan." That is what he always says when he talks about what he has been able to do in community work.

If you were here now one of you could sit in the front seat with "pa" and the rest of you and I would "sit in de back seat mit Grandma" when we go to Garland this afternoon. Yes, we got it day before yesterday. John and Glen, our hired man, went to town and Glen drove it home while John brought the horse and buggy back. John had never driven a car and Glen knows a good bit about autos. But when John got to Thompson's half a mile west of here, he found Glen cranking away at the car. It had stopped when he slowed down to cross a high place in the road. He tried to change from high to low gear and had killed his engine in doing it. Then he couldn't get it started again. They came on home and John telephoned to the garage man that he'd better come out and bring it home for us. John walked back to Thompson's, cranked the car, got in, and drove it home, without ever having had his hand on a steering wheel before. He got along so nicely he decided to take another little ride, so of course Cecilia and I put on our bonnets and went with him. We drove down to Richards' and back. John got along famously. He has worked with gasoline engines a good bit, so of course it is nothing new to him to run an engine, but naturally he had to get used to the various pedals and things to push and pull. He still kills his engine occasionally when he changes gear or experiments, but the only way to learn is to try things and see what the changes do. Of course the garage man showed him what was what, but in about three minutes' time, and naturally one doesn't remember all when he gets it that fast. We have a couple of the manuals and are studying them. I am going to run the car as soon as I can get time to do so. After John learns to know everything to do and how, then I will take a turn. I'll have to learn pretty soon, though, for reasons next given.

Yesterday John got a summons to serve on the federal grand jury at Cheyenne for the May term of court. It will be hard for him to get away at that time, and he won't make anything at it, for he will have to hire a man to take his place while he is away, but the trip and the experience will be worth a lot, so we want him to go. The trip takes him through all the pretty part of Wyoming, on the road from Frannie to Denver. We don't know yet what the pay is for the work, but it is probably three dollars a day and mileage at the rate of ten cents a mile. It is almost five hundred miles from here to Cheyenne. Rather a long trip—to travel a thousand miles—to do jury service, isn't it? We have been wondering how they got John's name, and that is one of the things he will find out. It is rather worthwhile to be known at the state capital, isn't it? So far as I know, only one man in this community has ever been called for federal grand jury service.

John is studying the automobile catalogue. I think there are some ten or twelve pages in the Mont Ward catalogue on specialties for Ford cars. It is not a question of what we can get but of what we can't get along without. Of course the car comes equipped but there are such things as mud chains and the like that do not come with the car. We simply must have the rear chains here for the sand and at present for the mud. This spring the roads have simply been awful. It is not usual here to have bad roads in the spring because there is usually not enough moisture in the winter to make a spring thaw except places where seepage water comes up. But this winter we had so much snow that the roads everywhere have been bad. It does not take long to get the new look off a car when one drives on such roads.

We can hardly wait for our tractor to come, not only because we want to see it work, but because we need it. If it does not come soon we are going to be so behind with the farm work we will never catch up. One of the neighbors southeast of here has a tractor of the kind we are going to get, and his works splendidly. He got his about ten days ago. The other day he passed here, when the roads were at their worst, drawing a drill and a cow. The little Ford just walked right along. Yes, the cow was walking — that is when she passed here. Dr. Mills is the owner of the tractor and he has tried out the Mak-a-Tractor and it has done good work plowing. So we think we will have something worthwhile when it gets here.

We will keep as many horses as we have now, with the Ford, but we won't have to get any more. If we did not have this tractor, we would have to get a number of extra horses. Last year we were hiring horses all the time. You can't tend two 80-acre farms with two good horses and two old plugs. We have about 63 acres to plow, harrow, and seed on Joe's place. Two of our horses, the two grays, are not fit for heavy farm work any more. Sweetens use Bill for riding and driving, and we have to have one driving horse here and one extra when three horses are needed for farm work.

I have been to Mrs. Nordmark's, where they have a new little boy. She is the one that by her own confession "suffers from an artistic temperament." She certainly lacks a good deal of practicality, that is evident. They could not get a nurse, and only Mrs. Ries was there with the doctor when the baby came. Well, the next day the doctor managed to get a nurse, a trained nurse, who came while I was there. She was an excellent nurse who knew her business, which was to take care of the mother and baby. But like all trained nurses she did not expect to do anything but the nursing. She would not cook or wash dishes, etc. Well, Mrs. N. got to scrapping with her right away, on the most trivial matters, making the situation as difficult as it could be. The things she did were not because she was sick, but from "temperament." I reckon "temper" would express it better. Well, I heard later that she sent the nurse away the same evening. She did that once before when she was very sick, that time to a kind-hearted neighbor that was trying, very unskillfully, to take care of her. She merely ordered, "Please go away. I do not want you here." In this deal, Mrs. N. has decided she won't have anyone but Mrs. Van Eman. I suppose when Mrs. Van gets there Mrs. N. will find something the matter with her, too. But in the meantime, poor Mrs. Ries is wearing herself out trying to do what she can to take care of her own six children and this newcomer, not to mention Mrs. N.

Some time ago Mrs. N. told me she was afraid Mr. N. would not be interested in the baby and that he would not want it. Well, right now when he is the very busiest, trying to get his grain in, she makes all the extra worry she can by sending the nurse off and leaving all the housework and extra care to him. If she tried, she couldn't find a better way to make him resent the arrival of an heir, for if he doesn't get a crop planted this spring, he will have something else to brood over. She is so anxious to know us, because we are what she considers "high-brows." The more I know her, however, the more I conclude that our acquaintance had better remain yon side of familiarity. Maybe I'd get on her nerves, too, after a while.

Our tractor came a couple days ago. When they started to put it on the auto this morning they found that the factory had sent a radiator for a 1916 Ford instead of for a 1917. We telegraphed to the factory and also to the *Northwest Farmstead,* in which paper we saw the ad. We asked the *Farmstead* to hurry up the factory. As the factory is in St. Paul and the *Farmstead* in Minneapolis, they can get together on the telephone. The *Farmstead* likes to help its customers who answer ads in their paper. John is very much disappointed at the mistake, for we hoped to get at the plowing on Joe's place tomorrow and turn it out. The time is ripe for swift action.

We got our final returns on the honey crop and were amazed to find that this year's expenses of marketing were about six times as large as usual. It generally costs about two and a half to three per cent to market the crop. This year it cost a little more than fifteen per cent. That is outrageous. The main difference came in because the cars both had to be localled to Denver and the freight cost so much. Generally the cars are sent right out from here with a carload rate to destination. This year it was a question of the right amount of each grade in the car to suit purchaser, and the honey had to be shipped to Denver and there rearranged. We are about disgusted and are going to do all we can to market our own crop this coming season. Of course we will list it with the association, but in the meantime we will do all we can to find our own market. It cost us $404.75 in exact figures to market this year's crop. Ordinarily it would have cost about $75 to market the crop through the Association.

John will have to be gone to Cheyenne only about a week. He wrote to the U.S. deputy marshal to find out how long the session of the federal grand jury would be, and received the answer that it never lasted more than a week. So that will make just a nice outing. I am so glad he can go, for it will be a fine trip and a good experience, and will make him feel more like starting in hard on the season's work. A little trip does set one up so. He will start on Friday of week after next — May 11. He has to be in Cheyenne on Monday, May 14.

Well, if I don't stop and give a certain little girl her lunch pretty soon, it will be long past college hours before she and I remain. She is such a darling little daughter. I wish a dozen times every day you could see her. She is so pink and white. Mrs. Murray always insists Cecilia looks as if she had been shined with Sapolio, she is so fair. But I don't even use any soap on her — just plain water.

I don't think there is any question as to whether or not the tractor will work — it certainly does that. One of the men here told John the other day that someone at Cody has one just like the one we have — A Staude Mak-a-Tractor it is — and pulled a six ton load up the hill at Cody with it. That Cody hill is famous for stalling autos and loads. We got two gears for it, one for road hauling and one for tractor work in plowing. The road gear makes the machines run much faster than the plowing gear. The road speed is five miles an hour. I think the plowing speed is less than half that. But even at that, the machine is supposed to plow from five to seven acres a day in a ten hour day. That beats a team or a couple teams all to pieces. The tractor part is easily attached to the Ford. There are three parts that stay on the Ford permanently: one is a force feed oiling system that makes the oiling on the auto like that on high priced autos. Another is a frame of heavy iron that fits on the under-part of the chassis of the Ford, and on which the tractor rear axle works. The third is a radiator that is eleven times as powerful as the usual Ford radiator. The more you reduce the speed the better the radiator has to be to keep the engine properly cooled. These three parts stay on the auto; then there are two hubs with bearings in them, one for each back wheel. Then there are two large eight-inch tire iron wheels connected by a strong steel axle that fits in to work on these bearings. When you have the first three mentioned parts permanently attached, all you do to turn your Ford into a tractor is to take off the hind wheels, fit in the bearing hubs, and bolt the two big tractor wheels with their axle on. It is quite simple.

I wonder what John will have to say when he comes home from Joe's this evening. Usually when he goes over there he comes home disgusted about something he has bumped into. He has got past the stage of saying anything to them, however. He said the other day, "I know I am losing all the time, so I might just as well swallow the loss once for all and say nothing till the three years are past. Then I hope they go back just as fast as they can. It doesn't do any good to say anything." Once in a while, though, he does say something—can't keep from it, and I certainly do not blame him for getting exasperated. For instance, the day after the cow lost her calves, Joe was to stop in Garland at the blacksmith shop and bring along a plow that they needed first thing in the morning. He came blithely along and never thought of it. Well, of course he had to turn around when he got here and go back for the plow. It was just ten o'clock that morning when he and Glen and the team got to work at the day's work. When he got back with the plow he was just as happy as if he had been doing extra well, and began to talk about the surprise of Lell's having three calves. John couldn't stand it and just told him that he wasted more here in fifteen minutes than would pay his wages for half a year. Of course Joe tried to talk back. Every once in a while John gets so disgusted he wishes he had not tried to help them. Of course if we had not, we would have our own house now. But I am not sorry. To be sure if we had it to do over again we would do it in a different way. We would never urge them to come out here, but simply send them money and let them stay there. We could have sent them a good many hundred dollars and never expect it back at all, and be better off in the end than this way.

The thing that hurts John worst is that he counted so much on the pleasure of having his sister and her children near him, and now they don't give him any pleasure at all but all the opposite. Ever since their drunken step father robbed them of their childhood together John has looked forward to being able to be near his sisters and help them. And now when he has tried to make this come true, he gets only more disappointment. He is helping them, though, even if they can't see it. Joe never comes around since they moved to ask John if he can help in any way. But he always wants a horse and saddle any time and all the time. They don't like it a bit because the children have had to walk to school part of the time the past few weeks since we have needed all the horses. But we can't afford to furnish a horse to stand idle all day at the school house just so the children can ride back and forth when the busy season is on. I myself have had to do without a driving horse every spring when the work is heavy and am glad to do without, knowing that the farm and bee work is the important thing. Of course they do have a good distance to walk to school but not any farther than you and I walked, Co, and we were only a year older when we began to go to Howell. I was fifteen and you were eleven, and Joe is fourteen and Mina ten.

Well, enough of an unpleasant subject. I don't want you to think I am grumbling. I am far more content about the situation than John is, for he is always worrying because he helped them with what he says should have come to me. I have a notion, however, that any good deed one does brings its reward some day, some way, so I am content. I don't want you to think I am not or that I am sorry we helped them. But I thought it would not hurt for you to know that everything is not always lovely even if the goose does hang high. I guess we are the goose in this case.

May 8, 1917

We went to a school election yesterday and exercised our right of suffrage. People talk about objecting to women suffrage because it takes the women out of their homes, where they belong. Why, voting here is a regular family affair where both men and women vote. The whole family goes, and it becomes a regular social, where everybody visits and has a nice time. You'd think it was a social afternoon if the refreshments only made their appearance. The men talk and visit with each other and the women do the same, and then they all mix and have a general good time. You get a chance to see all your neighbors and have them see your baby. We have not heard yet who was elected as the polls did not close till five o'clock, though the meeting part was over when we left about four.

May 11, 1917

John started to Cheyenne this morning. He will go as far as Kirby today, and stop over to see the manager of the Owl Creek Coal mine about getting coal for August delivery. The Owl Creek coal is preferred by most people as it is the best coal, with the exception of Fromberg, that is mined around here, where the mine is on a railroad. John will start on from Kirby tomorrow afternoon and get to Cheyenne Sunday morning about six.

May 13, 1917

Our first lot of bees came yesterday. We expected directions with them but there was not a word. I guess the grower thought that anybody who ordered as many as we are ordering would know all about it. Of course we had instructions but would have been glad for some from the particular man from whom these came. The directions in the book we have did not fit entirely and I had to do some tall thinking to figure out just what to do. John got everything ready as best he could, but naturally could not meet situations that we had never met before and did not know what to look for. I figured the best I could and did what I thought was right. Mr. Hardy* happened along last night, after I had the bees all in hives, and I was mighty glad to see him and ask some questions, as he has been getting package bees for several years now. He said the things I did

---

*A. D. Hardy, another beekeeper in the Shoshone Valley.

were exactly right. He looked at the bees and said they were in fine condition. Only two packages out of the 25 had any considerable number of dead bees in them. I am sorry John has to be away right now, for he would enjoy so much taking care of these bees. But I am getting a lot of valuable experience, that's certain, and having to do a lot of original thinking on the matter. If he were here I would probably help what I could, but would have my main attention on something in the house or garden and not put much gray matter on the subject. This way I have to use my brains as well as my fingers.

Cheyenne, Wyoming
May 14, 1917

(From John)

If you were here tonight I guess you could "sleep with a U.S. officer."

I got up this morning at 6:15, went out and had breakfast consisting of wheat cakes and honey and a glass of milk, 20¢. When we have this at home I consume a $1.50 meal, prices a la DeBarron.

Ahem!! Yes, the Governor was glad to see me just a little while ago when I called upon him.

The Grand Jury was organized from 10:00 to 10:30 and was then dismissed to meet at 1:30 this P.M. After dismissal I went out to the State House to see Mr. Floyd, Sec. of the Pub. Utilities Comm. about the tel. business. As I left his office he asked me if I did not want to see the Gov. Of course I did, so that is how the Gov. was glad to see me.

Hoping that my girlies are both fine, I remain,

Your lover, John

May 20, 1917

We are looking for John tomorrow. He was not absolutely certain the Grand Jury would finish up its work by Saturday night, but the attorney thought they could get done. John has enjoyed the work very much. Of course they had a number of very sordid trials, such as white slave cases, but they also had some very interesting ones such as a conspiracy and robbery case involving the stealing of some $150,000 worth of gold ore. I was tickled at John in one case, involving some Mexicans from Powell and some sort of liquor violation. I don't know just what the case is against them, but it must be pretty serious, for in speaking of one of the Mexicans that died recently, after the investigation had started, John remarked that he was a lucky boy to die and get out of it.

I read a poem in the Digest that has amused me immensely. It goes thusly:

> *Betrayed*
>
> The other night
> I went to the theatre
> With a low-brow friend,
> And the orchestra played
> "The Little Brown Jug."
> And he thought
> It was the national anthem
> And stood up,
> And I did, too,
> Darn him.
>
> —Arkansas Gazette

Isn't that rich? The psychology of it is perfect.

May 22, 1917

John is having to stay a good bit longer in Cheyenne than he expected. The attorney told the jury he thought they could get done by Saturday night but then dallied around presenting part of the evidence in one case, and they will not get done until tonight, Tuesday. John can not leave there till late tonight and will get home tomorrow night. He is not anxious to stay this long, but is not surprised, for when he went he hardly expected to get home under two weeks all told.

John got home all right last night. He did not stay till the whole work was over, but got excused. He stayed till the work was done, all but reporting to the court. The attorney had monkeyed around since last Tuesday getting the papers ready in one case so the jury could report and be dismissed. Every day he would tell the jurors they could go home the next morning, and every morning he told them it would be the next. John got tired of waiting and doing nothing, so he just insisted that he had to go home and got excused.

I got a good joke on him I must tell you about. When I emptied his pockets as I hung his coat away, taking out the billfold and checkbook, etc., and putting them in their accustomed places, I pulled out a play bill. The side that was toward me read as follows: "Special attraction. Leo Kendall and Palm Beach Beauties. A Musical Comedy Production. Pretty girls. Special scenery." I was so tickled I could hardly say anything. It was the bill of a vaudeville he went to, an acrobatic performance; but the ad on the bill was so very much absolutely what the funny papers give as the sort of show a man goes to when he is away from home that I teased John a heap about it.

This is enlistment day. I suppose a lot of young men and their mothers and sweethearts are scared to death, and a lot of others are glad. It is too bad that anybody has to go, but since the situation's what it is, the conscription plan is the very best possible way to solve the problem. This registration is merely taking an invoice of the stock there is available. Then the most eligible will be chosen. I was telling Edward the other day in a letter that there are many young men whose physical side is their most highly developed side. They are the ones who ought to go in the first lot of men. Then there are men whose mental side is the more highly developed. They can serve their country in other ways, most likely right here at home, by carrying on business and commerce and agriculture, for these things are as necessary to the success of an army or of a cause as the fighting men themselves.

June 11, 1917

We got your letter Saturday, mamma, saying you were on the way to Gary and that you did not know what was going to take place when you reached there, but that you had your pretty strong suspicions. You said that no doubt Cora had written us saying that she was already there, and telling the purpose of her going. Now if you want to know what being on the anxious seat is, curiosity to the nth degree, you just should be in our shoes. The letter came Saturday, as I said, and no other letter from Edith, Edward, or Cora. Here we have to sit until this afternoon, two whole days, waiting for further information. It takes some weight to keep the lid down under these circumstances. Well, I suppose that whatever was done has been done almost a week, and that we will find out this afternoon what did happen, so we will just have to sit tight till then. Edith wrote only a few days ago that it looked like no Wyoming for her this summer, and she may be the first one here, if certain events have taken place. I have two or three theories about what E and E have done, but theories aren't facts, and facts won't get here till this afternoon. Whatever they did is all right, of course, but what if the mails would be late as they have been and we did not get any letters even today! Well, I guess we'd have to put an extra rock or two on the lid and try not to blow the top off till tomorrow's mail. John is going to Powell this morning and he may be able to get today's letters this morning. That would save a few hours of curiosity from going clear to seed.

June 11, 1917

Well, there were a couple hours clipped off our time of waiting to know what happened last week, for John brought a letter this morning from Edw telling that the wedding took place. He said they were married "about eleven yesterday morning" but inasmuch as he did not date his letter we are not sure when the event took place. I think it is so nice that Rev. Barr performed the ceremony. Edw said "today we are going to Gary and tomorrow we are going home" and "we will go down to Evansville this next week." I am so glad they will get to spend a little time at least in Bloomington and that they will get to go to Evansville. All the folk there will like it so much to have E and E come there and get reacquainted before they come west. I know that when E gets to Colorado I will want to see her so badly I won't know what to do. I wonder if they are planning to come here? I hope they will. As long as you are all so far away in Indiana I know you can't get here till a certain time, but if you live closer I am sure I would be wanting to see you all the time.

If Edith is still there, tell her that after they get back west and the bar exams are over, they had better come here while Edw is deciding where to locate. I will let her practice making bread and doing all sorts of things she will want to practice up on.

I guess you had your hands more than full this year to have a bride and groom to look after, and particularly a trousseau when the commencement rush was on. It is lucky that Cinderella had some nice dresses on hand that could easily be made for the bride. Poor Cinderella. What will you do now that you are the only one to wear the dresses that Mamma makes? Mamma, I guess you will be glad to have only one daughter at home to make things for.

June 19, 1917

We heard this morning that General Pershing and his troops were safely arrived in France. That is good. Also that the King of Greece has abdicated. That will help a little too. We do not get news very fresh now. We do not get a daily paper as they are all so expensive and come three or four days late anyway. The Digest always has the best of the news in it, but of course it is late. Our local weekly paper has a patent inside with very good news items in it, but that, too, is a weekly summary and we get it about a week after the news happens. I was amused at one of the neighbors who calls Pershing "Perishing." I told John that here is where the Perishing had gone to the rescue.

We were so glad to know of Edward's prospects. We had wondered and wondered what it was that he had to be married on, and of course knew he must have something definite in view. I am glad he has such a good chance. Going into a firm at Lamar, Colorado, with someone else who has already worked up a business isn't quite like hanging up a shingle and waiting for clients to appear. It is fine that Edw makes friends so well, and I am sure E will be a valuable asset to him in this respect, as well as in countless others.

June 24, 1917

We were amused at an article we read the other day about who was responsible for the war. It was taken from a Catholic paper and announced that the real person had been found who was responsible for the terrible war. It was — hold your sides — it was *Martin Luther*! The argument was that if he had not taught disrespect for spiritual authority this war would never have started. It goes this way: "The real cause of the horrible world war is a German. An impartial student of history must trace it back to Martin Luther. It was he who overthrew authority, who upset the idea of having a central world court where serious differences between the nations could be settled. The fact that the worst war in the world's history has occurred in the midst of our modern civilization, instead of when the nations were still but a few years from barbarism, must be traced to the reprobate monk of the 16th century. He taught men to have no respect for spiritual authority outside of their own little minds. And the world today is reaping the harvest." Now what do you think of that?

I have been making soap. I cooked a kettle day before yesterday and another yesterday. It is enough to last at least a year, under ordinary circumstances. I am so glad to have the home-made soap. The lot I cooked day before yesterday was perfect. When I took it out, the bottom of the kettle was as clean and dry as if it had been washed and wiped. Each cooking is about forty-five pounds of soap. To make this amount, take three cans of lye costing, say, 25 or 30 cents, 13½ pounds of tallow, worth about 8 cents according to what the butcher shops charge (really worth about 4 cents a pound). But say 8 cents; that would amount to $1.08. Add the price of the fuel, say five cents, and 25 cents for an hour's labor, and the total is $1.68. To be sure, the tallow is not worth 8 cents, even if the butchers do ask that for it. But even so, you can see what a saving one can make in the soap, and it does work so much better than the bought soap.

We had a lot of fun the first day I was cooking the soap. A thunder shower came up and we had a little sprinkle of rain. John got an umbrella and came out and held it over us while I watched the soap. We had a regular picnic doing it. Then there was a splendid rainbow, a double one, both bows perfect. The clouds and the storm were fine. East of us there was heavy rain and beautiful lightning. John always makes astonished remarks when I do anything like cooking soap and talks about a college professor cooking soap! or doing such things! Just to think, he will say, of a college professor out here, cooking soap. Of course the answer is "Ain't we wonderful!"

Edith, your letter came yesterday, the first typed one from Boulder. I enjoyed it immensely. Now that you have some time, don't forget to write. I know how you are enjoying the spare time. You feel as rich as Croesus, don't you? I did. The thing that you will enjoy the most for a while is not having to be at any particular place at a given time. It isn't a question so much of working or not working. You will work just as hard as a housekeeper and have to be on the job 24 hours a day, but you can practically choose your own times for doing things, and that makes all the difference in the world. And you can put on a house dress instead of a shirtwaist and skirt, and wear a breakfast cap till noon if you want to. Again, it isn't a question of being completely dressed (I never could abide a kimona as a steady diet) but it's a matter of wearing what you please.

The Sweetens have given up again, and this seems to be the end, really. We are not trying to persuade them to stay. They want to sell their place and get away as soon as possible. Of course they can not sell the place as they have not proved up, but they can sell the relinquishment. The person who buys will have to put in three years' full time the same as if no one had lived there before, but he will have all the improvements. We have put in about $1500 on the place. Besides that, Joe has done some work, and there is the growing crop now. We think the improvements are worth $2500. There is a good four-room house with concrete basement and cistern, a barn, fence all around the place, 40 acres of oats, ten of it seeded with alfalfa and the rest with sweet clover, a good garden, about half an acre of potatoes and as many beans, 1000 strawberry plants and a few raspberries, and twenty acres of ground all ready to plant. The place is an 80 acre tract, but some 8 or 10 acres are not irrigable. That part makes pasture, however, and inasmuch as it does not have to be paid for, not being under ditch, is just that much to the good. Then there is enough pasture along Bitter Creek that runs along one side of the farm to feed from two to four head of cattle. We think we ought to be able to sell it without much difficulty. All the hard work has been done — the bringing under cultivation of a raw piece of land, grubbing out the sage brush, levelling, making irrigation ditches, dykes, and the other things that make a piece of desert into a farm.

Of course we are very sorry that Sweetens can't be satisfied, as this is the chance of their lives. Carrie has been sick, and she is sure she will die if she stays here, so there is nothing for them to do. Joe is always so grumpy that it is a wonder she hasn't been sick before this. She has been having some bladder trouble, and of course she did suffer very much when that was acute. But most of her sickness is in her mind. John said yesterday that it is an awful thing to say, but there are some families that would be a whole lot better off if the head would die and leave the family alone. The best thing Joe could do for his family is to leave them his life insurance.

I think that one thing that makes them discontented is that they get letters from friends in the east telling that work is so plentiful now and wages so good. But they don't seem to realize that living expenses are equally high and that for a family to depend on a man's wages now puts them in a worse condition than it did a few years ago, even with the higher wages. Joe told John the other day that out here he is working for a dollar a day while in Indiana he could earn three. The fact is, he could not earn three, and the fact also is that he gets a good deal more than a dollar a day. It is true that his wages are not more than about $35 a month, but that is every month in the year, rain or shine, whether he works every day or not. Besides, we furnish them with a cow and her feed, free of charge (just now they have two), we gave them half our chickens, give them all the honey they use (which is about $50 worth a year as they use a great deal more than we do) and are always sending something over every time we go. Back there they never could keep their grocery bills and house payments paid, and I am sure it will be the same when they get back. That is, even if he can work. But I am willing to wager dollars to doughnuts that inside of three months he will be back again in health where he was before he came out here. John says that he gives them two years for Carrie and Little Joe to be supporting the family. Little Joe is just ready for high school. If they stayed here there would be no question of his getting to go. Back there I am sure he will have to go to work as soon as he is old enough to pass the age requirement.

It certainly is a shame that people are so short sighted. Here inside of a little more than another year they could prove up on a place that would be worth three or four thousand dollars. The income from that, even if they did not stay longer, would be enough to make the difference between poverty and comfort the rest of their lives. The thing that hurts John most is having to realize that they simply are not worth helping.

> "It's coming to see that she never did know,
> It's coming to know that she never could know,
> And never could understand."

July 6, 1917

The Club decided yesterday to dispense with refreshments as long as the war lasts and to have each hostess give the amount to the Red Cross fund. There are two hostesses each time, and we decided each should give a dollar as her share. That is really less than the refreshments material would cost, not counting the work, but often it is possible to serve when it is difficult to produce the cash, for we use the things we have that sometimes are difficult to turn into cash. But we thought that each of us could manage to produce a dollar when her turn came. The work necessary to make cake, cream, etc., is worth that much, not to speak of the materials necessary. None of us need the bit of refreshments, and we will have about fifty dollars by the end of the year for this fund. We are also going to make surgical dressings and bandages.

July 10, 1917

Cora, I want you to stay here as long as you can, and I want Papa and Mamma to come too, because I do not count on getting east this fall. We have $2000 tied up in the Sweeten place, and $950 in the comb honey supplies that we will not use this year. When almost $3,000 of your working capital is tied up, it rather limits your spending money for the time being. These are difficult times and we want to pay off all that we have borrowed. As I said the other day, prospects are looking up for a good honey crop and we are hoping to come out a good deal farther ahead than we had anticipated. But even then we will not feel as if we can afford the amount necessary for a trip. When you can't get rates, the fares count up so much. I don't think I ought to go without John, as he has not been back since we came out when we were married, and I am certain we could not possibly count on two trips.

Edith, I note what you say about feeling that a whole lot of valuable training and experience is wasted if you do nothing but keep house. It may be that after one is married a while she loses her sense of values (!) but somehow I feel as if the more training I had the better I am able to keep house and that I need it all. And when you get to be a mother, you certainly do feel that you need every bit of sense you ever might, could, would, or should have or have had. Honestly, though, I agree with you, if by keeping house you mean merely getting two or three meals a day for two people, washing dishes, sweeping, dusting, doing some laundry work, and keeping things generally presentable, I always feel that if I don't do anything but that I am worth mighty little. But if I can get that done in time to get in some time on sewing, or letters, or secretary work, or bee work, or even club work, it is different. Also, when the number of people to be slept and fed increases, there is a difference. You have loads of time on your hands now because you are as yet not tied to anything. Wait till you find some civic work to do, and some social work, if only of the pink tea kind — or perhaps I had better say wait till that work finds you and holds you up so you can't get away — it will be different. I have been through it and I know.

If you are actually looking for something, let me recommend the Red Cross work. There is loads of sewing necessary for that, and bandage making, even if one does not want to knit. Our club is taking up the work. If there isn't a Red Cross unit in Lamar, get busy and put one there. I am sending you a couple pages from the August *Companion* that might interest you. The thing is presented in such a sensible manner. I noticed the other day an appeal to women to enlist, in our local paper.

The state agricultural station at the state university wants a dozen or more women to come to be trained to give canning and drying demonstrations over the state. The station will furnish the training and expenses for travelling, if the women will give their time and talents for a month or two this summer. I dare say there are lots of tasks like that which trained women can do now. I saw a statement the other day by some great English woman that interested me very much. She said that the task before the American women today is to see that the babies are taken care of. She explained that what she meant was that the mothers should be taught how to take care of them, and illustrated her point by the statement that during the last summer in England, while nine men an hour were being killed in the war, twelve babies under three years were dying every hour in England. I don't think you need to worry, Bady, about wasting your talents, not in these days.

July 23, 1917

This is fine bee weather. Prospects are still looking up and we are feeling quite lively over the outlook. We got a letter yesterday from the Association manager saying he had sold a car of extracted honey for September delivery at 15 cents a pound. Just think of fifteen cents a pound in carload lots. Ordinarily 8 cents is a good price in that quantity wholesale.

July 25, 1917

We are interested in hearing about who is drafted. I wonder if Edward's number was called, and if he intends to ask for exemption if it is. John says that if Edward will merely walk into the examining office *without* his glasses on, his examination will stop at the first look on the part of the medical examiner.

Inasmuch as this county has furnished 67 more volunteers than its total quota, no one will have to go on this draft. The whole county is exempt. They talk about the West being in favor of peace and against war, that it elected Wilson to keep us out of war. It did, and it always has been against war and did not talk war the way the eastern states did. But when it came to being ready to go, it was the West that stood up and said here we are. Some of the little western states, little in population, I mean, send half a dozen times as many volunteers as New York, that talked war for two years back. Indiana is another state that acted instead of talking. We saw in one of the papers that the town of Gary had enlisted as many volunteers as the whole state of New Jersey.

July 29, 1917

We took a ride this afternoon to Elk Basin, the new oil field some fifteen or twenty miles northwest of here. The basin is really a basin if there ever was one. It is about 500 feet lower than the surrounding bench and is oblongly circular in shape. (Excuse me, Dr. Hennel, it is elliptical. I remember that much analytics.) It is about a mile across one way and a mile and a half the other. All around are steep and jagged precipices. The wells are down in the basin, on some of the high peaks along the rim, and on top of the bench a quarter of a mile or more from the rim. There is quite a little settlement in the basin. If I remember correctly, the output is about 8,000 barrels a day. The place is very interesting. We did not go down into the basin as the road is so very steep we did not want to tackle it with the machine. We want to take the trip again when you are here, Co, for the place is very interesting. From the rim of the basin it looks like a picture more than a real scene. The place is not far from Silver Tip coal mine, though you branch off from the coal mine road after you get up on top of the bench.

August 3, 1917

We just came back from Powell where we saw Company C off. We intended to go to Powell this afternoon for some printing, fruit circulars, and about one o'clock Mrs. Peterson telephoned that the circulars were done and also that Co. C was leaving. So we all piled in and went to see the boys off. Of course there was a good bit of weeping, but inasmuch as these were all volunteers it wasn't like a farewell when the boys had to go and didn't want to. Just as the boys were all on the train, and the train started to pull out, everybody started to cheer and swing his hat. John was holding Cecilia. He waved his hat and gave a couple of whoops that would have waked a dead Indian forty miles away. I wish you could have seen the baby. She was so surprised she did not know what to do for a second or two, and then she puckered up her face into the awfullest ready-to-howl expression you ever saw. We both had to laugh. I took her right off and she did not cry, but her face certainly was a study for a few minutes. I guess she did not know there was that much noise in her daddy.

August 10, 1917

What is that new song you mention, "Back in Indiana?" We are in the back woods, you must remember, so don't fail to tell us about such affairs, so we may keep at least within hailing distance of what is new.

August 13, 1917

Cora arrived all right on time this morning. John and Cecilia and I were there to greet her. We nearly did not get there in time, though. When we turned the corner at the Hardware Company store, behold, didn't that train come sneaking along the other side of the station. John turned on a little more juice and drove up to the station and turned around. Out we hopped and just as we got to the station Cora got out of the coach. We thought she was there, for both trainmen got off and the second one swung out a straw suitcase. I said to John, "That looks like Cora's," and, sure enough, she followed. My, but we were glad to see her. I ran up to greet her and then we turned to where John and the baby were. She kissed John and then looked at the baby. The baby looked at her and then grinned like a Kewpy. She fell in love with Co at once and could hardly stop looking at Cora even to finish the breakfast she was rudely disturbed in when we arrived at the station. She and Co have been having some good fun this morning.

I certainly did hate to see Tody go away this morning. I did not shed any tears at the station, tho, did I, Co? To be sure, John had to lend me his shoulder after we got home, but that was in the privacy of our own demense. I did not want to be selfish enough to keep you any longer, but when one gets to thinking how long it is until next August, it is rather overwhelming. I know from my own experience how glad you are to see her, Edith. You see, I know from the way I felt the first year and this year. The first year it was because of everything new that none of you knew anything about, and this year it was because of the baby. Now that Cora has learned to know the baby, she can tell the rest of you about her. Until some of you had really seen her I couldn't make you really know her.

I wish you could have been here this morning. Last night a storm blew down and there was quite a bit of rain here. Of course that means snow in the mountains this time of year, on the tall ones. This morning the clouds lifted a while before the day set in rainy and you should have seen the new white snow on the mountains to the west and north. Bear Tooth has a new sprinkling, but the tall mountains over in the Park and the tall ones to the southwest were dazzling. Even Cedar Mountain, the one west of Cody we went around when we went to the Dam, had a new white bonnet. This is probably the end of the season here. As soon as this damp spell clears away we will have frost. Well, we have nothing to complain of, for this is with one exception the longest season John has known in the six he had been here. Yesterday the bees hummed like summer and no doubt put in at least another $50 worth of honey.

The new hospital in Powell is now doing business. The doctor in charge is Dr. J.R.A. Whitlock. I do not know where he came from, but he seems to be a pretty fine man from the looks and actions of him. Powell really needs a hospital, for when houses are so small diseases like typhoid or any contagious disease are hard to handle. If you have only two or three rooms in your house you can't very well keep one room as a sick room and keep the other part of the house shut off. I guess there will be a good many babies make their first appearance at the hospital. In ordinary places I feel rather sorry for a baby that has to give a hospital as its first address, but I don't feel that way here. A baby out here is likely to get a better, quieter start in life in the hospital here than in a house where there are already three or four children in two or three rooms, and the mother certainly gets a few hours a day at least of quiet. There aren't enough Mrs. Van Eman's to go around, either, and unless one gets her or a kindly disposed but inefficient neighbor, there is no alternative but a trained nurse, which means about $20 a week and a maid to wait on her. So in most cases it is simpler for the mother to go to the hospital and have the neighbors or a hired girl look after the rest of the family for a week or ten days.

There is one thing in the new tax bill that will strike up pretty hard and that is the three cent letter postage. It is too bad that one has to count pennies when it comes to so pleasant a thing as letters, but unfortunately such sordid things enter into housekeeping accounts, don't they? It will be hard on all of us, especially here and at Lamar, but I want to suggest that we each write three letters a week instead of the number we are now writing. We can plan between us, Edith, so that excepting for postal delays, we can get a letter to 822 each day of the week. If you write three and I three, that takes care of the six mail days there. Then you can send me the ones you send there and I can do likewise, and each of us will hear at least every other day. I guess we can get along all right that way, don't you think? Maybe if I write half as many as I do now, the letter will be worth reading.

A year ago right now there was something doing in this house, I tell you, for within about a half an hour from now a new voice was heard. It made itself heard, too, right from the start. I don't think there is anything in the world more satisfying than the sound of the voice of a new baby.

There are various reasons why we are glad we are not in Germany, but we did not know about the tire and gasoline one. A new tire here costs $18, which we think plenty. Gasoline is about 25 cents, which we consider ditto. We are looking up the steel-shod tire proposition. We have the literature from a Denver firm that guarantees 5,000 miles without a puncture. The steel shod tire is made of tough leather, steel studded, and cements on an ordinary tire. The price is about 2/3 of a rubber tire. Our tires are all good yet, but by the time they begin to wear we want to get these protectors.

Since yesterday John and I both have had a smile that won't come off, and we have hardly been able to walk straight. The reason is that John closed up the clover seed deal for the Union yesterday. We had been hoping all along that we would be able to hold the price up to ten dollars a bushel, or 16-2/3 cents a pound. We were in communication with some eight houses, four of whom had sent their men in to see John. We knew that when the market hunts us up instead of our hunting the market, there was hope, but even at that we were not over-sanguine. Buyers have been getting it here for from 15 to 15-3/4. Day before yesterday John had a long distance call from somewhere in Montana from the Northrup-King representative saying he would be here yesterday to deal. So John sent telegrams to six other houses telling them if they wanted the 1500 bushels to wire at once what they would pay. We got answers from all of them, either with offers or statements that their representatives would get into communication with us at once.

The best offer we got was 16¼ from the Albert Dickinson Co., Minneapolis, whose agent had been here shortly before.

They were buying seed at Lovell at 15½. If they offered that, John thought we might possibly get the 16-2/3 he wanted. When he began to talk business with the Northrup-King man he quoted him the price he had given him the day before over the telephone — 18 cents. The man had then offered 16. John thought he could hold out a while for 18. Before more than a few words had been passed the agent said he would pay seventeen. Of course John jumped over himself, but he kept still and went on talking, and did not say yea or nay. They came in to dinner then (John had met them — there were two of them — at the train and brought them home). As they ate John asked questions about their furnishing bags, paying an advance, sending a man here to inspect, accept, and pay for the seed as loaded, etc., and at the end of the meal he told the man that if the firm would do these things, he guessed the deal was on. Just think, 17 cents, $10.20 a bushel. Last year we got 11-3/4¢ and thought that was fine. Of course all prices have gone up and this raise is about normal, but we were afraid the clover seed might not keep pace with grain, etc. The argument John put up for the 18 cent price was that unless clover seed kept pace with other farm produce we would have to quit raising it here and grow something else. Our seed seems to be unusually good this year, same as everybody's else. We will get anywhere from 150 to 200 bushels. We are hoping now that the price is up so well that we will come near the 200 bushel mark but we are not sure. We will thresh next week and then we will know where we are.

November 7, 1917

Mamma, you have asked several times what the big potato growers do with their potatoes. Some of them have cellars, or rather, pits, or as they are called here, "caves," made with concrete walls and earth roofs. They put a good many in these and keep them until spring. But the main bulk of potatoes grown here is sold right from the field. They are piled and covered with straw and earth until they are hauled to the cars.

Sometimes the growers misfigure the weather, as they did last week, and then they lose a whole lot. For instance, Mr. Hutts lost about 600 bushels, out of about 1800 bushels; Mr. Biesemeier lost 100 out of 300; and on the Werts place about a thousand bushels got frosted so as to be practically useless. A frosted potato is worth less than nothing, for it can't even be used for stock feed and has to be hauled out or left in the field. Most of the potatoes lost here were dug and either not covered deep enough or left in open shed. The men who have lost them all say they can only blame themselves. Very few were lost here that were still in the ground. At Billings, however, it was cold enough to freeze those not dug. Potato growers here might just as well take it for granted that we always have a very cold spell in October, and prepare for it.

We went to Powell today and invested in a gasoline lamp. My, but it does make a light. We got an "Air-O-Light," Coleman Lamp Co., Wichita Kansas. The price on these lamps, like everything else, has gone up. This comes with a white shade, but we wanted a green one, which is a much better shade but more expensive. We also got a wire protector which keeps the mantles from being exposed. The price all told was $12.35, which we think plenty. We could have ordered one a little cheaper, but this one has a five year guarantee and it pays to pay a little more in the beginning and have something good, especially when the cost is big anyhow. We got this from Jos. Rosenberg at the Monarch Hdwe. Co. He started in here a few years ago selling gasoline lamps and now has one of the biggest hdwe stores in Powell. We have the nice Rayo lamp from Grandpa, but it eats up so much coal oil that it is quite expensive. It has to be filled every day from now on until spring, and uses almost a quart of oil at a filling. So you see that counts up. This gasoline lamp holds ½ gallon and will burn from 20 to 25 hours on this quantity. Coal oil costs 15 cents and gasoline 25, so you see there is a decided difference, not to mention having a light that is about ten times as good and white, like a gas mantle light, instead of red. Then too, this lamp has to be filled only about twice in three weeks and there are no chimneys to clean. That makes quite an item, if one's time is worth anything.

I don't see how I waited this long to whoop for joy at the very prospect of your coming closer, E. and E. I told John it costs only $3.60 to go to Worland by train, and he immediately said it did not cost that much to go by Ford. Edw., John says that if you have an opening there, take it. He says Worland is a booming town and that it is fine oil country, and that it ought to offer good prospects for a lawyer. O my O me, we would be so tickled we couldn't walk straight if you came close enough for us to get together when we wanted to or needed to. Of course you would want to know what you were getting into before you went and that it would pan out all right, but I assure you it would be worth a whole lot to us to have you close by.

The clover seed turned out pretty well, but not as much as it might have. We got just the same amount that Murrays did — 161 bushels. We have about 1/3 more acreage, but the watering was not properly done. John says he is going to do his best to look after the watering himself next year. It means so much on the crop. Of course 161 bushels is not at all bad. This will clean out from 15 to 20% in the recleaning but even then at $10.20 a bushel the result will be enough to make some difference in one's bank balance — at least over night.

I was amused at what Mrs. Murray said the morning she went away to visit relatives in Missouri and yet I felt like saying amen. She said she was so glad she was going somewhere for a while where she wouldn't have to think a thing about cooking or what they would have for dinner or even if they had any. She didn't care what the folks they visited gave them to eat, or even if they didn't get a meal once in a while, or if it was only bread and butter — she did not have to plan it and cook it and serve it and clean up afterward.

From the recent news, the submarine menace isn't much of a menace anymore. It seems that one week recently there was only one ship of any size at all destroyed and only half a dozen all told. There were less in the whole week than in each day at the beginning of the peril. I guess Germany is getting to the point where she is losing out all around. Well, the sooner the better, for her sake as well as ours. Just so she is completely beaten so she will have to give up entirely.

Cecilia has taken a notion today that she does not want to sleep in the day time. She would not take a nap this morning or this afternoon. She is as frisky as a little colt all day. I put her in the box in the yard but she climbed right up and surveyed the landscape. This afternoon the same. Yesterday the telephone rang and she began to say "Ahhh-h-h." Then she shook her head no and said "papa." Which means that when the telephone rings she should not talk but let papa talk. I don't see how under the sun I am going to train her when I get so tickled at the things she does that I have to laugh. I can't see that it does much good to spank her when you are so tickled that you laugh at what she is doing. For instance, she has discovered that there is something under her nursery chair that will make the loveliest rattle if you shake it against the sides of the chair. Of course I don't want her to do that, and have scolded her and said no, no, a hundred times. I have slapped her hands till she cried and of course I cried too. Yesterday she was sitting on the chair and got to playing with the little pot. I told her no and slapped her hand. She would shake her head and maybe say no-no-no, and go right ahead just the same. After I slapped her hand right hard she held up for my inspection a toy she happened to have, and when I was looking at that she sneaked her other hand down inside with the most angelic expression on her face, and rattled to beat the band. Naturally I was so tickled I couldn't keep from whooping. Now please tell me what is a poor mother to do under such circumstances.

(From Mamma)

So my big girl is worrying how to train her little girl who is just too sweet to spank and cute enough to make her mother laugh when she does not want to. Well my dear just dont worry about training her at all since she has such a good beginning as to sweet temper and brightness and good nature and good nerves. Why there is no use at all to worry because little girls change so much and will do a thing one day or perhaps one week and then forget all about it and do something else. why you girls did a lot of things that you would hardly believe one of you would draw up one eye in an ugly way   it worried me a lot but in a little while it was forgotten (I don't remember which one it was that did it.) To be sure there comes a time in the life of almost every child when they ask for a whipping but its not often   I imagine you did not get even many slaps and where are three finer girls in one family even if I do say so Well as I was saying the easyest way to cure something you dont like a baby to do is to attract her attention to something else at the time.

I do think its so nice for you to have someone to tell all about the babys cute ways because we do enjoy it so much and I would give a lot if I could have kept a record of what you children did   some of the things were so cute and as we are filing all the letters it will be a surprise even to you in a year to read them over. Why some of the cute things Edith said we wanted to remember and yet we have forgotten   Do you know a baby with generations of fine ancestors has an inheritance that is worth a lot and Cecilia surely has that. How I would love to see her.

December 2, 1917

We got our honey all off all right Friday. We were glad to have it go and particularly to have it go where it did. The government has put an embargo on honey export as there are other things more important now for export. The embargo went into effect Dec. 1 so Friday was the last day we could ship ours and have it go abroad. I will copy here the article the Powell *Leader* had this week:

> The Shoshone Project has done its full part always in helping the government to carry on the war, and now it is to have a part in helping the Allies. A carload of extracted honey from the Shoshone Apiaries of John Hendricks was shipped this week for export to the Allies. The shipment goes out under government orders which are as rigid and limited as military regulations. The honey is packed in wooden crates, two sixty-pound cans to the case. For export shipment each case must be strapped with an iron band at each end. The extra labor involved in putting on these strapping irons is no inconsiderable amount.
>
> It is to be hoped that the ship that takes this honey across the ocean will escape the subs so that the Project may have a definite part in helping to sweeten life a little for the Allies.
>
> In an interview, Mr. Hendricks said, "It is a source of much pleasure to a man who is disabled for service in this war from a wound received in Cuba in '97 to know that even if he can not go into active service he can help in a direct way. Sugar is very scarce in Europe and the production of honey has been interrupted so much there that the supply is small. Sweets of some sort are practically necessary for military rations, and there is nothing better nor richer in food value than honey. When you think that a pound of honey has as many calories as twenty eggs or a pound and a half of beefsteak you can see at once that honey is as valuable a food as it is a good one."

December 20, 1917

We had our Christmas party at Club today. There was so much business on hand that we did not get to do much in the way of celebrating except to get our gifts distributed. Each of us took a gift, price limit a quarter. The main business this afternoon was getting ready for the election of officers at the next meeting and organizing a Red Cross branch. It seems that legally we can't do Red Cross work unless we officially take out a branch charter. We proceeded to start the red tape to winding this afternoon. As for the election of officers, I fixed it so that there won't be any difficulty in my getting out of being president for next year. I proposed that we have a nominating committee to propose at least two persons for each office, and then accept any nominations from the floor at the meeting. If the whole thing is left till the meeting, someone moves that the same officers be kept and it is carried unanimously. Then if we refuse to accept, nobody has thought of anyone for any office and the whole thing is done in a slap-dash haphazard way. With a committee, at least three women have thought about the matter for the length of the committee meeting. You may be sure I had my committee carefully picked out before and had consulted Mrs. Murray about it, but I did a beautiful piece of acting and carefully surveyed the members before and while announcing the committee. I put Mrs. Murray on to make sure that neither she nor I would be on the list proposed.

Sunday before Christmas, 1917

We went to a picture show again yesterday. I told you that every Saturday afternoon the merchants give a picture show, admission to which is secured by tickets they give. What it means is that the merchants pay the movie house a certain amount. All you do is ask for as many tickets as you want and the merchant hands them out. One man said, "You might as well take a lot. It costs me just the same whether the tickets are used or not."

Christmas Day, 1917

You couldn't imagine more ideal Christmas weather than we had today and last night. The moon was so bright and the stars so clear and shining, and the new snow on the ground so typical of the season. I said to John last night that it was a shame to stay inside, but as the temperature was about six below, we did not poke our noses out more than to appreciate the loveliness of the night. During the night it turned warmer and this morning it was ten above. A fog hung low and the cold air turned every bush to a bejewelled Christmas tree. During the morning the mist cleared away and the sun came out. You can imagine how pretty everything was. The frostiness stayed on the trees all afternoon in spite of the fact that it got almost up to 30 during the day. Tonight the moon is clear and bright and the night is like last night. The scenery has been just what you read about in stories or see on post cards typifying Christmas.

How I do wish you could have been here to see Cecilia. She simply couldn't lay down that pink baby all morning. She hugged it and sang to it and squealed over it and put it to bed and took it out, and did everything you could think of. We departed from the usual rule of nothing between meals for her today, for what is Christmas for, anyway. We ate all day ourselves. She ate some candy, and a couple pretzels and several of the cakes. She takes after her grandpa and her daddy, that is sure, when it comes to a sweet tooth. We laughed and laughed and were so tickled we couldn't do anything but hug her a number of times. When she saw the coon jigger she simply shouted. She watched it a while and was so tickled and excited she began to cry for a minute. Then she stopped and laughed again, and since then she can't see the coon jig enough.

I am not going to try to tell you tonight how much we like all the things you sent us, nor to tell you about the gifts we got from others. It is getting near bedtime, but we simply couldn't let the day go by without writing you a few lines. We have thought of you all very much today and wished we could all be together, especially on account of the baby; it seems selfish to keep her all to ourselves when we know how much pleasure she is and would be to you all.

I will tell you about one nice present we got in the mail today. It is the returns on the honey, and is a check for $3,238.88. Three thousand two hundred thirty-eight dollars and eighty-eight cents is about as much of a check as either of us ever got at one time. We are rich tonight. Tomorrow we will not be so rich, for John is going to town and, as he puts it, stop a lot of interest. We are planning to pay off a good deal with these returns. One thing we will pay off is the money that

John borrowed to get his start in beekeeping out here, five years ago. That amounts to $900.

We got the car of clover seed off our hands yesterday and certainly are relieved. The Union has a meeting tomorrow night and at that meeting John will hand over the reins to — well, most likely to nobody. But he won't have it. What he thinks is the only thing to be done is to organize a stock company and then have definite contracts with members. If that is done, he is willing to be a director, but will not be manager. But it is likely that nothing like that will come out. There was a committee meeting here a short time ago to talk over the stock company proposition and of the four men on the committee, John was the only one who thought a capital of at least $5000 was the minimum. One man suggested one thousand and another put the maximum at $2000. With men of such small comprehension it is useless to try to do anything.

I know you will all laugh at me when I tell you I am still president of the East End Club. I thought sure I had things fixed so someone else would be elected, but the pesky nominating committee never got together and instead of sending in their lists as they had promised, they did not, and so although we got a majority of the committee over the phone and got their nominations, we had only one suggestion for president, though we had plenty of names for the other offices. We had organized our Red Cross Branch just then, and had given Mrs. Brown, the woman whose name we had recommended for president, such a heavy place in the sewing work that she could not do both that and the Club presidency. Then all the women with one accord insisted that they did not want any change, that I had been it since the beginning and they didn't want anyone else, etc., etc. Of course I appreciate the compliment, but I did not want the office nevertheless. The Club has been doing Red Cross work for almost six months now. Our branch started in with 53 members, which is pretty good.

We are so tickled and delighted and everything else that is happy about the possibility of your coming to Worland, E and E, that I have been able to think of little else since your letter came yesterday. It seems too good to be true to have you that close. We are sure that you are doing the right thing in making the move, and that you will be a whole lot farther ahead in a few years than if you stayed where you are. Of course you will have to sail pretty close to the wind for a year or two, most likely, but who doesn't when they are starting out on something worth while. We certainly played pretty close the first couple years we were here, and even yet our bank account sometimes and often looks like a snowbank in July. But when you are getting somewhere, what does it matter.

We have been inventorying our affairs and making plans for the coming year, and we find that at a low estimate we have assets to the amount of over $23,000. That is not counting any possible striking oil, or anything of that sort, but just a plain, simple counting up of what we actually possess. Yet we are by no means out of the woods when it comes to needing money, and our running expenses every year make us borrow in order to have the cash when we need it. Of course that is the trouble with a business like this where the income comes in about once a year on each crop. But when we have a business that amounts to at least five thousand dollars, why should we hesitate to borrow on it? Six years ago when John first came here and wanted to borrow a thousand dollars to get a start in bees here on a larger scale, he had to mortgage everything he had to get it. Now the bank is glad to lend him anything he wants on merely our personal note for short time loans.

I am telling you all this merely to show you that in our case it took about four years for us to get to the point where we can feel we are doing something. Even yet we haven't been able to get the things we would like to have — to finish our house, for instance, or to get a lot of things that would be comforts and luxuries.

January 25, 1918

We had a fine treat last night. Murrays have just got a new No. 17 Victrola and invited us over to hear the music. They have about 48 records that were sent with the machine, from which they are to select what they want. They wanted us to come while they had all the records so we could hear the whole lot. We enjoyed them all, but the ones we like best are the old ones we know. This Victrola was ordered through a local dealer but was shipped from Sheridan, where I suppose there is a branch house. The local dealer does not carry this good a Victrola. They are paying $275 for this, without a single record. I wish you would tell me what size yours is and what it cost you and whether or not you got records with it. Of course prices have gone up, but $275 seems pretty steep. So far as I can tell this one is just about like yours.

January 27, 1918

We are reading H.G. Wells' new book, "The Soul of a Bishop." The librarian at Cody sent it the other day, together with Beatrice Forbes-Robertson Hale's "What Women Want." I remember hearing Mrs. Hale some years ago, and like her. I have just started the book, but it is good. It is a summary of feminism, of course. Wells' book did not have the pages cut, so it evidently had just reached the library. My, but it is a luxury to sit down with a book and get to cut the pages. I always feel so rich when I can do that. We have got so now we do not specify what we want when we return a book or books to the county library in Cody, but merely say "More." I am glad the librarian has such a good opinion of the kind of things we care to read to send us things like the Wells first.

Sunday, February 3, 1918

Today has been another fine winter day. We went to church this morning and the service was fine. The sermon was simple but very good, and the special music was by a woman who is visiting here. She has a real voice and sang that beautiful thing, "The Voice of One Crying in the Wilderness." I suppose one ought to go to church, as you say, Pater, to say his own devotions irrespective of what anyone else says or does, but it frequently happens that what one hears as a sermon is so trivial that one is prone to think of light instead of serious things. I would not go the end Wells does in his "The Soul of a Bishop" and say that there should be no religious organizations, but it is true that church services are not always edifying. The bishop comes to the conclusion that the Church of England is a dead shell, and according to a good many of the things produced as evidence—such as services, rituals, the lives of a number of the church leaders, the free thinking of the younger generation—it must be. But when the bishop gets this far, he feels that he has to go the whole way and get out. Then of course if he starts another church he will merely be adding confusion by starting another of the long list of denominations, so he concludes there must be absolutely no organization whatever, and that every person shall be entirely free and untrammelled. Of course if he must get out of what existing organization there is, his argument the rest of the way is logical; but it seems to me there is a flaw somewhere. Human beings are gregarious in religious instincts as well as in social, and a purely individual religion would get only a very few rare spirits anywhere. It is on a par with Ellen Key's theory of individual freedom socially—she acknowledges that her theory applies only to *exceptional* women. Evidently she and Wells both are blind to the fact that there are so many others of us who can hardly classify in that class. How Wells can overlook that and be the socialist he has always been is queer.

Thursday, February 14, 1918

I guess you in Bloomington think that with both of us, Edith and I, together it is worse than when we are apart, for we have missed a couple days in writing to you. Edward wanted to go back to Basin and Greybull to look over the law situation there, after deciding against Worland, and so Edith is here.

About nine o'clock last night the telephone rang, and it was Edw. from Greybull to tell Edith that he would stay there the rest of the week. Now if you think there is any question about the fairies knowing where E and E are, just listen! When Edw. got there, of course he went to see the lawyers to get a line on them and on the business the town affords. When he and E came through the town the other day Edw. skipped off the train while it stopped and talked to a man on the platform, who luckily happened to be the town marshal. The latter told Edw. that there were two lawyers in the place, one a good one and one not much. (Edw. found yesterday that the not much one had failed in the bar exams the first time and was trying them again yesterday.) The man he saw yesterday was the lawyer the marshal said was the good one. This man told Edw. that he is rushed with work, the term of court coming on soon, and that if Edw. would stay the rest of the week and help him out he would guarantee Edw. at least his expenses for this trip. It will give Edw. a chance to look the place and the man over and find out what kind of work there is from actual experience. The lawyer there wants Edw. to come there and work in connection with him. Each is to have his own clients and do his own work, but they will work together. In this way there will be no partnership and each man gets what he earns, but they will not be working against each other. There is to be an office vacant soon in the same suite with him that Edw. can get and they could use each other's libraries, etc. Edw. says this lawyer is not insisting that Edw. locate there, but is telling him it is a good chance.

Friday, February 15, 1918

We were muchly surprised last night to have Edw. call up from Frannie and say he was on the way here and for us to meet him. When he got here he told us that the Greybull lawyer, Mr. Marshall, had given him an extremely difficult piece of work to do that morning, and that with his usual luck Edw. had happened on the very thing needed to make out the brief and had turned it out complete in a very few hours. The man read it through, then read it through again; then he offered Edw. a partnership. He gave Edw. his books to look over and let him see exactly what he had taken in. Edw. examined the record especially for the past few weeks and found that in that time the money taken in over the counter amounted to $600. This does not include any fees for suits or anything like that, but merely fees of various sorts such as notary, legal advice, drawing deeds and wills, and such. Edw figures that 1/3 interest will mean about $250 a month. The one day Edw was there the man took in about $25 in over-the-counter fees. Marshall is a man of about 45 who was formerly located in Billings. He was an attorney for the Burlington.

Greybull is a new town, or at least a town that has newly grown up. There are three oil refineries there and there is a payroll in the town of something like forty or fifty thousand dollars. The town has about 2500 or 3000 inhabitants. The place is about forty miles closer to us than Worland, and is about 60 miles from here. By train it is about as close as Indpls to you, and by Ford-way, as John says, it is only about 60 miles. The train that leaves here a little after nine gets there about twelve, so we can leave here after breakfast and get there before dinner.

March 10, 1918, Sunday

I wish you all could have been here the other night to see the Northern Lights display we saw. It is the most wonderful one I have ever seen. The main part of the display was in the east, not in the north. I think the reason was that there was a bank of clouds in the north, and the light was reflected around this cloud bank to the clear east. The whole east looked as if there were a great fire somewhere, only the light was a pink-red instead of a brick-red, and it was high up and did not come to the horizon. Part of the time this red glow was massed solid across the east. Then fingers of light stretched up from it, some of them pale and some of them deep red. Across the whole north there was a queer yellow-white light against which the clouds stood out in relief. After a while the clouds massed near the horizon and the fingers of light stretched up from them toward the zenith. Across the west a great, long plume of white light stretched about half way between horizon and zenith, and in the south was another like it. It seems queer to me to see the light so far away from the north. It is as if a huge feather of light had been wafted away from the main body and was floating off on the atmosphere. The bright red in the east lasted for about an hour. Then the light travelled north, as the clouds there banked lower on the horizon, and the red color, though not as bright nor as far spread, appeared in the northeast. The rays shooting up from the north grew brighter, too, and as long as we watched them still shot up skyward. I do not know how long the whole affair lasted, as we did not watch it more than about an hour and a half.

Sunday, March 31, 1918

It is half past eight by the clock and half past nine by the watch, which means that the watch has been set up for the new time that begins tomorrow, and the clock has not. I will set it up when I get ready to go to bed. We were talking at supper about the new time and saying that the best article we saw on the subject quoted in this week's Digest, says that the new time won't make much difference with farmers as they go by the sun anyway rather than by the clock, and that it would mean most to city people and especially those who work in factories, etc., where the hours are long. Jack [the current hired man] then said, "As I see it, the object is to give such people as these more daylight at night." I told him I thought he had it exactly right, and that I had never heard a better Irish bull. Which tickled him immensely, for he is nothing if not Irish. He was born in Ireland, and as his father was never naturalized here Jack is still a British subject.

Carrie* was telling me yesterday that Mrs. Wallace has constantly been stirring up such a mess at the Red Cross that

---

*The Sweetens had not left after all.

things are going badly. Mrs. Wallace has got them to the point now of having another election of officers, insisting that officers have never been properly elected. Mrs. Wallace has always been a strong pro-German in the war, and when it first began you did not dare say a word to her about the matter or she would get on a regular tear in favor of Germany. Since the U.S. has been in the affair she hasn't talked like that, but it appears to me that at the present instance she is one who ought to be indicted for giving aid and comfort to the enemy, for anyone who hinders the progress of the Red Cross and makes people dissatisfied with it is surely in that category.

Walter Fowler is home for the summer. He has a six month's leave of absence from the bank, according to the Powell paper, to run the farm. Well, I am sure he is needed on the farm, for Mrs. Wallace has enough to do to do the cooking for such a bunch of men, not to mention looking after things and besides she always insists on taking the place of a man in haying time. I am glad Walter is here, for it is a pleasure to have some one in the neighborhood in conversing with whom you can use all the brains you have. There are so many people (everywhere, I suppose) with whom you can carry on a profound conversation without ruffling the cortex of your brain. We have wondered if Walter's being here is in any way connected with the order not to draft men who are "actively, constructively, and exclusively engaged in agriculture." I'd hate to think he would dodge, but one can't help wondering. Mrs. W. has expressed herself so decidedly against his even considering military service that it makes one wonder twice.

Wednesday, April 9, 1918

We had our Red Cross scrap meeting yesterday. Yes'm, scrap. No scraps or remnants or relief bundles, or the like, but fuss, racket, quarrel, fight, whatever you want to call it. Only be ladylike, if you want to emulate Mrs. Wallace, even if you do call another "lady" a liar. Honest, you never saw such a little-kid-fuss-at-recess procedure in your life. So far as I can make out, the main part of the whole business is that some folks naturally can't get or keep things straight, and a few others won't, and so there is a mix. Mrs. Reese is chairman, and she says if she is, she is, and is going to be; Mrs. Wallace is secretary and is trying to run the chairman, who won't be run. So there you are.

Mrs. Reese did make an appointment or two that was not according to Hoyle, but all that was needed was for the executive board to take formal action on her appointment. But no, Mrs. Wallace had to have things done just so. Then Mrs. Kilgore got mixed up in it somehow, it being said that she said the election had not been properly carried on, etc., etc. After things got wound up a while, Mrs. W. got up and said that she never had done anything that was not ladylike and never intended to, that she always comported herself like a perfect lady in speech and action at all times and with everybody, etc., etc., etc. A little later on when Mrs. Reese was saying something, Mrs. W. broke right out with the statement that if Mrs. R. would adhere to the truth when she was talking, things would get along better. Naturally the atmosphere was rather electric for a minute.

When things were all talked out, I made a speech. Yes sir, I did. I told them that when this mix-up started, the thing that suggested itself to me was the speech of Lady Macbeth when Macbeth saw Banquo's ghost and had a seizure. Lady Macbeth, you remember, told the guests who were present at the banquet to "stand not upon the order of your going but go at once." I went on to elaborate on the theme that now when the ghost of Prussianism is stalking over this land it is not any time for us to be arguing about who does this and who does that, but that we should "stand not upon the order of our doing but do at once." Then I told them the story about the farmer whom some one asked if they had a hard school to teach. He answered, "O yes, we've got a mighty hard school to teach. It is an awfully hard school to teach, but we've got a teacher now. She can manage 'em all right. Why one day last week she didn't teach a single class all day. She just kept order. But she keeps order, all right." I said that when our boys across the water need things, this isn't the time for us to be sitting around keeping order. Then I spoke of the work that has been done by this branch, really remarkable in amount in the three months we have been organized — several hundred sling bandages, over 70 pajama garments, 75 knitted articles — socks, sweaters, scarfs, etc., and some miscellaneous items. I told them that since I had not been well enough to do much myself I could talk about the work without boasting and that the thing for all of us to do was to keep on working and *quit talking*. They gave me a big applause when I stopped and one of the Powell committee told me she was so glad I made the speech, for she thought that after that the people would just have to go to work.

Sunday, April 14, 1918

Cecilia now owns a "baby" bond and eight thrift stamps. I took her bank account to the bank yesterday and had it and her savings bank turned into the above-mentioned. We will keep getting thrift stamps with the contents of her little bank. We ourselves have invested in five one-hundred dollar third liberty bonds. Of course we had to borrow the money, but it sure is the time to lend our credit to the nation now. We can pay off the money when our crop returns come in next fall.

Sunday, April 28, 1918

Thanks for the hot cross bun recipe, Edith. I shall try them some time. I am using very little white flour now but I do use some of it occasionally for dessert purposes. We use corn bread for dinner every day, and after this I am going to bake rye bread for a while at least. We have about 50 pounds of the rye on hand. We want to try to heed as much as possible the request of the Food Administration to refrain from using wheat until the new crop is in. We have a sack of graham flour on hand, and about six or seven pounds of white flour, and I would like to make this much wheat flour last us until the new crop comes. I saw a notice that that would not be until September, but surely the new crop flour will be on the market long before September.

Thursday, May 9, 1918

I have not told you about some excitement we have been having here because I wanted to get the whole tale before starting to tell you about it. Last week the boys in the Garland high school wanted to burn the German books there. They had not been using them for two years because as soon as the mix-up with Germany began, Mr. Richards quit teaching German in the high school. The boys asked Mrs. Richards if they could burn the books, and she told them that the books belong to the school board, as this state furnishes the books free of charge to pupils. She told them if they got permission from the school board they would all have a celebration together burning the books. Of course Mr. Richards agreed, but three of the big boys — two of them the bad boys of the school — would not wait to hear from the school board but went to the library at the next recess, got the books, took them out on the fire escape, and there set them on fire, and threw the burning books down among the primary children on the playground. Of course Mr. Richards could not stand for anything like that, and he told the boys he would have to expel them until they made things right with the school board.

Of course the boys told things wrong, and that night a gang of fellows decided they would burn the books anyway. They went to the member of the school board in Garland and asked him about the matter. He told them that the boys had been expelled not for burning the books but for refusing to obey the orders they had been given, and that the teacher had to maintain discipline. But they decided that they would not only burn the books but would make Mr. Richards do it himself. Two auto loads of them went out to Richards', seven men in all. One man went to the front gate and called Ernest out, saying they wanted to talk to him. The other six hid behind the cars so he could not see them. Of course Ernest came out when someone called to him, and when he got out the others jumped out and grabbed him. They told him he would have to go to Garland with them and burn the books. He told them that when he signed his contract as principal he had promised to preserve the property of the school, and that he had no right to destroy it. Then they drove him to Garland.

A big crowd was there, for the news had been spread that Garland was going to burn a lot of German books that night. Practically no one knew, though, that the men had mobbed Richards and brought him there by force or of course they would not have been willing to go ahead with such procedure. They tried to make Richards burn the books, but he refused, again saying he was obliged to protect school property and not to destroy it. They kept him there until they had burned a lot of books and then took him back home. He was coatless and hatless all the time. The gang had a rope with them, too. One of the boys said that they thought they might have to tie him to take him, but someone said the other day that all it would have required was a little bad whiskey and they might have used the rope otherwise.

When the two autos drove up to Richards' it was just getting dark, and Mrs. Richards was lying on the bed where she had just put the baby to bed, and was half asleep. She said later she thought it was Murrays and we, but when no one came in she decided it must be merely some one to see Ernest, and she dozed off again. Now why Ernest did not cry out and call for Mrs. R. when the men grabbed him, I am sure I don't know, unless it was that he did not want to scare her. When he got back home, Mrs. R. was asleep, and she thought he had not been away.

Mr. Richards had a nervous breakdown that night, after the mob took him back home, and Mrs. Richards had one the next morning and one the following morning. She was about worn out from the year's work anyway, and this was more than the last straw. At first they thought they would sell out and leave the community but since a lot of us have stood by them, they feel better. Ernest intends to have the whole seven of the men arrested, either for mob violence or, if that won't hold, for assault. The gang is scared to death now, and a little legal procedure against them will shut them up completely. Of course we all feel so badly about the affair, for Richards has been loyal as can be always, even taking German out of the schools a year before most of the schools thought of doing so.

May 11, 1918

Perhaps you would like to know what has happened since my last letter, in the Richards' case. Nothing particular has taken place, but some expression of opinion has been put out. The Powell *Leader* had a nice article telling the facts exactly straight, giving the names of the mob, and then closing with a paragraph saying that the mob had done what it had in a spirit of supposed patriotism, but that it was sorry patriotism to mob a man who was doing his duty, take him away from his own home, and try to make him do something wrong. It closed by saying that such was no liberty or freedom at all, and certainly not the kind we were fighting this war for. There was also a statement in the paper from the school board, signed, saying that they were not in sympathy with the way the mob had treated Prof. Richards. The county superintendent was down yesterday at Richards' (John met her there) and she is backing Ernest in every way, is opposed to letting the boys graduate who were expelled, until they make things right with the school board as they were instructed to do, and says that Ernest shall pass on the grades of all the pupils in the high school, just the same as if the examinations had been held.

May 28, 1918

We are doing our bee cellar over. It had only a dirt floor and straw walls and roof, with earth over the straw. We could not keep the temperature steady nor keep the cellar properly moist with this arrangement. We are digging it a few feet deeper and concreting the floor and walls, and are also making it larger. Above the cellar we are building an extracting house, with steam heating arrangement for keeping the honey at the proper temperature for extracting (about 100 degrees). One room will be built for a heating room, another for an extracting room, and in the basement will be a large tank for a honey storage tank. The extracting room will also be on a level with a wagon box so the honey will not have to be lifted up or down at all. It will be put from the wagon or truck on a hand truck that will carry it into the heating room, then into the extracting room. From the extractor it will run downstairs into the storage tank to cool and clear and settle. Then it will be weighed out into the cans, and from there can be loaded on the wagon from another platform that is also wagonbed height. This arrangement will eliminate all the heavy lifting, and the steam arrangement will make it possible to extract the honey always at the proper temperature for the best results. Extracted honey work is very heavy for John. That is why we always raised the comb honey. But now that the market wants the extracted, and probably always will after this demand is created, we want to produce what the market wants, and we have to be prepared for it. Comb honey is lighter work in production, but extracted is easier work, for you do not have to watch the bees so closely. You can control swarming and keep them at work so much more easily when they are working on the big sheets of extracted than the small sections of comb. Then too, the finish does not count. In comb honey, the clear, pure white finish is 3/4 of the problem of production, and the problem of having the bees finish up entirely every section in the super is the other half. With extracted, finish does not count very much and the problem is so much simpler.

Sunday, June 2, 1918

John has gone to Billings to buy a tractor to use in running the clover huller we bought last week. One firm in Billings has a $3000 one they are offering for about $1800, used. It is a good big one — a 30-60 International Harvester — which I believe means you could pull as many plows with it as 30 horses could pull, and could run as large a thresh machine as 60 horses could run.

We had such a fine view today, just before we got to Cowley to take John to the train. Cowley is in the Big Horn

Valley, east of here. There is a long hill, perhaps a mile in length, between Cowley and the top of the ridge. Before you get to the edge of the ridge, you travel for miles along regular sage brush country, sandy as can be, up and down, up and down over small hills. Then all of a sudden you come to the edge and can see the whole valley there before you. Straight ahead to the north is Cowley, the railroad station and several rather large manufacturing plants (a refinery and a carbon plant, I think) about a mile away, almost down below you. About a mile farther on is the town, showing white and a few red brick buildings among a lot of trees. Straight ahead to the left, and about five or six miles away, is the new town of Deaver, practically all white, the government compound showing up very plainly. Away off to the left you can see a scattered oil well derrick or two and rough hills and rocky, mountainous looking crags. Directly to your right is the town of Lovell, the huge red brick beet sugar factory standing out plainly in the foreground. The town is quite large, and very attractive looking. The whole valley is green with trees and growing crops, alfalfa, clover, and grain. Far away across the valley, sometimes closer, perhaps ten or twelve miles, and sometimes farther, perhaps twenty, are the foothills and then the high ranges of the Big Horn Mountains. John stopped the car and we all looked at the valley and the mountains for a good bit before we started on the long downslope to Cowley.

We went through Byron on the way down and passed a house where there were three large lilac bushes in the front yard, in full bloom, two white and a purple. I got so excited I nearly jumped out of the car. The sight of them made me homesick. It is queer, but a flower like those we have at home in Indiana will make me homesick in a minute, far more than anything else. I decided at once that when we came back I would get some of the lilacs. I had Jack stop the car when we got there, and even if it was Sunday I walked in and asked if they would sell some of the lilacs. I paid a quarter for a large bunch. My, but it is good to have them. The whole room smells from them. I sent a couple sprays to Carrie this evening and have a bunch ready to send to you in the morning, Edith. These are the first lilacs I have had since I have been here, except some that came from 822 and were not very fresh when they arrived.

June 4, 1918

John came back from Billings this noon. It was well worth his while to go, for he bought the tractor we were talking of. He did not get the price reduced any ($1850) but the company threw in the four-bottom gang plow we need, and as that listed at $100 we made a good bargain. With this tractor and a four-share plow, our plowing won't look so large a job as with horses. Since we have it, we will plow up a lot of clover land next spring and plant grain. The land has been in clover long enough that it is now built up splendidly and ought to yield a fine crop of grain. We would have put in a lot of wheat this spring if we had had a means of plowing.

Sunday, June 12, 1918

We had a wedding announcement the other day saying that Bessie Mather was married to Walter Fowler on Monday, June 10th, in Billings. I called up Mrs. Wallace and expressed good wishes, and said we want to call as soon as they get back, which will be in about a week.

Walter certainly is an interesting man and deserves a worthy companion. We will have them over to dinner some time soon, but I think I shall wait till there are a few new vegetables on hand, and perhaps strawberries. With green peas, head lettuce, and strawberries one can present a much more "fahncy" table.

If you are certain you are not going to teach this summer, Co, then I know what you are going to do. You are going to be nurse girl to the liveliest little rascal that ever moved, and get some exercise trying to keep up with her, while her poor mother gets a chance to do some of the things that need to be done on a farm and a bee ranch. Edith has told you how almost impossible it is to try to do anything when you have to keep one eye on a skipper. Just come right along as soon as school is over, and when you get worn out trying to go as fast as Cecilia does, you can go down to Greybull a while and recuperate. Then you can come back here again.

We took a trip to Lovell, Kane, and Cowley this week to see about sweet clover and whether or not there was enough to make it worth while to take our huller in that territory. Well, we certainly found loads and loads of it, so much that if the grasshoppers don't eat it all so that no seed sets, we will have work for a month or two after we get the threshing done here on the Flat. John is enthusiastic over the prospect, and is already counting up so much money that I tell him I can't count that much and that he ought to have married the sister that majored in higher mathematics.

In several sections near Kane, Cowley, and Lovell the grasshoppers are very bad. The beets and sweet clover seem to be suffering the most. In some places the clover has been so late in blooming that bees have been starving, at a time of year when they are usually bringing in lots of honey. One man told us that lots of colonies had died for lack of food. The hoppers have kept the clover eaten down so that it did not bloom until recently. The farmers are using paris green, and that helps, but does not seem to check the trouble as there are such quantities of the insects. One man told us that he has used fifty dollars worth of the poison, and would have to get at least half that much more. He showed us where the hoppers were dying by the handful, but still the place seemed full of live ones. The hoppers always go into the shade to die, he says.

We found the roads good from here to Penrose, and thence to Lovell. The roads from Lovell to Kane are fine. We drove to the bridge across the river below Kane and stopped for dinner. We built a little fire and roasted wieners, and had bread and butter, and cheese, and noodles and onion creamed together, and jelly, and milk for the baby.

After dinner we started to Cowley, and then our troubles began. We soon struck a place where the river had been in the flood a couple weeks ago. The river had washed out of the usual bed and started a channel about a mile lower down. There were three bad places all in a row. The first two still had water in them, and we managed to get through; but the third one was dried just enough to make the mud as stiff as heavy glue. The wheels sank down until the front wheels were solid and the axle touched. Here we got stuck and John had to hunt some one to pull us out. He had to go to three houses before he could get a man and team, as most of the men were working on the ditches that had washed out. After about an hour he came back and we got out. We wondered what the man would charge and were surprised to find that he did not want anything. Finally he said if we did not think a dollar was too much. . . . John told him he would just as lief give him two, but the man assured us that if he had a dollar he would go home happy. We assured him that we would go ahead happy, so we all did.

About a mile farther on the roads parted. There were two ways to Cowley: one through Crooked Creek, about three or four miles farther around, and one more direct; but the direct road has a bad canyon in it and we decided to take the good road even if it was a little farther. After we had gone four miles from the crossroad, we were told that a bridge was out so that it was impassable. There was nothing to do but to take the canyon road, so back we went, having driven eight miles with nothing to show for it but a chance to see Crooked Creek country. This lies at the very foot of the Big Horn Mountains and is really interesting — that is, for any one who is driving through. But to live there — O no. The farms are ranged along the creek, only one farm wide most of the way, with no telephone lines, no mail nearer than Cowley or Kane, miles and miles away, and no neighbors nearer than a half a mile to a mile. No thanks.

A storm had been gathering for some time, and just before we got to the canyon it struck us. But after we put up the curtains and got in the car, we did not have any trouble keeping comfortable during the few minutes that it rained. John walked down into the canyon and up the other side and inspected the road. We tightened the brakes and saw that the car was all right in every way, and then started in. We all rode down to the bottom, and then I got out to be ready to put a stone behind the wheel when it was necessary in case we stopped before we got to the top. It was. I never saw such a hill. John says it is 150 feet long and 100 feet high. Honestly, it goes right straight up. A 45 degree angle looks like a level road compared with that. Well, we got along pretty well and by having one of us run the car and the other push and then block with a rock, we made pretty good progress till we were about half way up. Then we stopped. Believe it or not, it is a fact that although we had over six gallons of gasoline in the tank, the car was standing at such an angle that the gasoline could not feed into the carburetor. When that happened, of course there we were. It was 2½ miles to the nearest farm house but there was nothing to do but for John to walk there after help, leaving Cecilia and me to watch the car. I piled a lot of rocks behind the wheels so that it could not possibly roll back, and then there was nothing more to do but to wait till he came back. It took nearly two hours until he came with a man and team and wagon, and that was making excellent time.

When we had crossed the gully in the bottom of the canyon, it was perfectly dry, for I walked across it. Just about the time John started off for help, which was half or three quarters of an hour after we had crossed the bottom of the canyon, I thought I heard water running; but I assured myself that it could not be, for there was not water anywhere. However, I began to investigate and discovered that there was water running through the gully in the canyon over which I had walked a short time before. The water soon was about three feet deep and spread out across the road for over thirty feet. I then realized that the water was coming down from the mountains where the rain had evidently been pretty heavy. I watched the water come up and then begin to go down. It was my first experience with the mountain streams, but before we got through we knew a lot more about such streams.

When John and Mr. Davis got back, Cecilia and I were certainly glad to see them. It was then about eight o'clock. While John was gone, Cecilia kept asking for a drink, but there was no water to give her except that in the stream, which was about two thirds mud. I gave her some bread and jelly and that helped distract her attention but did not satisfy her thirst.

It did not take long to pull the car up the hill with the team, and we started off, though Mr. Davis and John spoke then of another place ahead where we would most likely need help through a place called Copenhagen Wash, another gully. We concluded to go ahead with the car, however, and then if we needed help to wait there till the wagon came along.

Copenhagen Wash is another dry gully generally, except for a very small stream of seepage water that runs down it — so small that when John went for help he stepped across it dry shod. When he and Mr. Davis came back with the wagon, coming to get us up the hill, the storm water was running down and was about two feet deep. When we got back, on our way out, the banks showed that the water had gone down considerably and so we concluded it would be safe to cross, with the wagon pulling the car.

Mr. Davis drove into the water and the car started after him, with us in it, John steering. The tow line was long enough that he got well into the stream before the car got in. When the horses got into the channel, one of them was washed off its feet and the other one lost its footing once but managed to get up again. Evidently the flood had washed the gully out so that the center was very deep, because the banks showed that the water had already gone down about two feet. When we saw that the horses were down, we knew we could not dare go in with the car. Mr. Davis yelled, "Cut the rope!" and John managed to get out, get his knife out, and cut the tow rope just in time before the car was pulled into the channel, and also in time for Mr. Davis to succeed in getting the horses where they could regain their footing and then get out. If the car had been pulled into the stream, it is possible that we would have been in a pretty serious position. After Mr. Davis got across, John carried the baby and me out of the car to the bank, and then we got a cushion out of the auto and a blanket and prepared to "set a while." We waited an hour and then decided that the water was running down so slowly that we might as well give up trying to get the car through that night, as it was then about nine o'clock. So Mr. Davis came back to get us on his wagon. The water had gone down at least a foot while we were watching it, but as he came through it was still deep enough to float the wagon rack off the bolsters, and of course we could not go across with ourselves and the baby that way. So we sat and waited another hour, meanwhile finishing the remains of the bread and butter and cheese and jelly we had left from dinner. After another hour the water was run down so that we could drive through without having the water come up into the wagon bed.

Mr. Davis took us home with him and we stayed there all night. They are lovely people, a young couple with two small children. We really enjoyed ourselves very much. The next morning John and Mr. Davis went after the car, and by that time the water had run down so they could pull the car through the "wash" and up to the house. It is evident that there must have been a cloudburst near the foot of the Pryor range for enough water to flow down a dry "wash" in an hour's time to make a stream over thirty feet wide and over seven feet deep. The place where we had the trouble is about ten miles from the foot of the range. You can imagine how fast the water ran if it came down ten miles through a dry canyon in about an hour or an hour and a half.

We did not have any more real difficulty after that, though we found some more washed-up roads. We are all thankful we are home again, safe and sound. John says the experience is like going into war—you are glad for the experience but don't care to repeat it. We did not realize at the time at Copenhagen Wash that we were in a pretty serious place, but since we have thought it over we have not felt quite so comfortable about it. However, it is all over and we are all right.

July 20, 1918

We had some sad news yesterday — a wire from John's brother that their mother died yesterday morning. Carrie feels awfully bad, of course. We are so glad she made the trip last spring when she did, for it is so much better for her to have gone then than now. None of us will go now. We couldn't do anything, and the fare is so high.

August 4, 1918

You will be interested, Edith, in knowing that we have something now that is complete annihilation to Cimex Lectularius. It is an insect powder that the Raleigh medicine firm puts out. I have used it for several years for flies, and it is fine for that. We found out it was good for this from a family that recently moved into a house that was alive with the pest. In a few months' time there wasn't one, and we are fast approaching that happy place ourselves. I do not think I have mentioned in the letters that we discovered a few weeks ago that we had a visitation of bedbugs. I was horrified. Mamma, I guess you know what a faint, sick-at-the-stomach feeling a housekeeper has when she discovers such a condition. It was about the time we had the concrete workmen here, and I supposed one of them had brought the one I saw crawling on the couch. But when we found there were some in my bed, I knew they were not responsible. I mentioned it to Joe one day, thinking I would caution them to be careful and not carry any home from here, and, to my astonishment, he said that their house is full of them. Then of course I knew where they came from. I told John that it was no disgrace to have some one give you some, but it was to keep them and that I would bet anything he wanted that it would be a mighty short time before we were rid of them. We went at them right away, and have kept at it ever since, and now we have to hunt mighty hard to find one. I have not seen any for quite a while. I told Carrie about the powder and she got some too, so maybe the source of supply will be destroyed.

We hope to begin extracting tomorrow. We wanted to do so today, but they had to work at the engine and binder today.

The merchants in town want honey, and so do lots of people who get large cans direct from us. People have been coming in a stream lately wanting honey. Sugar is at a premium, and almost impossible to get; and now it seems that the grocers can't get syrups of any kind any more—Karo, etc. So they want honey. One of them said last night they certainly needed a little sweetening mighty bad at the present time.

August 11, 1918

Yesterday when the mail came I was very much disappointed not to get any word from Cora about her plans for traveling. We concluded that the mail must have been hung up somewhere, for she surely would have written here and to Greybull to tell each of us about her plans. We concluded we would meet the train tomorrow anyway. This morning John went past the mail box and happened to notice some mail there. There were three letters that had been overlooked when he got the mail yesterday—one from Co saying she would be here tomorrow. We rather thought that she would come here first but did not take any credit to ourselves for the attraction, it being a certain young lady. Next year the tables will probably be reversed in favor of the younger member at Greybull, who by that time will be beginning to say things and show desires. We are so glad Co is coming west that we can hardly contain ourselves.

August 27, 1918

Pater, did you ever try mixing your butter and honey together before putting it on the bread? John always takes what butter and honey he wants, mixes them well together on his plate, and then puts it on his bread instead of spreading the butter and then the honey. He likes it so much better that way. Another good combination is honey and peanut butter. Take about equal quantities, stir well together, and try it on pancakes or on some of the dark breads—rye, for instance. For pancakes we always thin the honey, as it seems so much better that way.

I put what honey we will use for the meal in a bowl, add hot water (about half as much) and stir. Let it stand in a warm place till ready to serve, but do not let it boil. Don't skimp on honey. There is all of that you can use and you might as well have it.

Tuesday, September 23, 1918

This is the morning that you start in again at school, Co. We have been talking about you as the men have been eating breakfast. I have been frying pancakes for them and still have some on the stove. Mr. Carr, the hired man, started the talk by speaking of the fact that you were at it again this morning, wondering if "Aunt Grandma" were now going to school. We were speaking of you last night at the supper table, and I read the parts of your Billings letter telling how the train nearly kept you here and also how you wished you could give us your presence. Mr. Carr remarked that he believed you really did not want to go away, and that he thought we were just as anxious to have you stay. He said that he was ready to state frankly for himself that he did not want you to go.

Tuesday, October 1, 1918

So, when the mail came in last night I was so busy that I could not look at it, though I noticed there was quite a bunch of it. But then the Hired Man would give me no rest and constantly inquired if there was any news from the Hired Girl, so I stopped and went in and got my letters — one from you and one from Edith. I read them, in part, to everyone, and then read them again to myself. Later in the evening, I was looking through the mail again, and didn't I find another letter from you. Two of yours had come at the same time. You should have heard the H.M. He assured me that there were many things he could forgive, but that he could not forgive me for overlooking one of your letters. This morning he was talking about your letters again and he said I should tell you that all that side stuff about college, etc., is all right in its place, but that it does not interest us. What we want to know is: WHEN ARE YOU COMING BACK? He talked on for a while and then said that the H.G. would sure think he was absolutely crazy to talk like that. He wanted to know last night if I didn't think you might be able to come out here for Christmas!!!

Mr. Carr is about the finest man we have ever run across, and we feel lucky to have him interested in our work enough to want to stay here and work with us. It is such a rare find to locate a man who has real brains. Most of the hired men are pretty short on that useful commodity. Since we have branched out into several lines of work, — the bee business, the farm, and the clover huller — John has been looking for several years for someone who would help out with the bees and perhaps eventually take over the actual work with them, leaving John's time free to manage the other part of the business. He is a college graduate, a very expert chemist who earned over $7,000 a year in New York until his health broke and he had to come west.

Mr. Carr's father got his civil engineer training at the University of Dublin, which Mr. C. says was then the best college for that in the world, except one in Germany. When he came back to the U.S. he needed one more bit of work, and took a year of post grad at Cornell. He was one of the oldest grads of Cornell for a long time and when he died the alumni club sent a beautiful wreath. If I remember correctly, the year of his post grad work was 1858. I have not asked Mr. C. yet about his own college, as it has not come handy. I do not remember myself whether it was Boston Tech or Mass. Inst. of Tech.

I think when you write, Co, it might be nice for you to say howdy direct to the H.M. I was joshing him last night about Edith's statement of his having to look at the sunset all alone, now, and he said it certainly was lonesome.

I do not think there is any question about Mr. Carr's trying to get into service. The two days they unloaded the apple and grape car the weather was bad—rainy, wet, and very muddy. He had wet feet most of the time, though he changed his stockings and shoes several times. Of course he was sick the next day but would not give up. He announced the other day

that any and all questions as to how he feels are entirely deleted
henceforth and forever afterward. Nevertheless he realizes that
he is not yet strong enough to go bagging for Germans. He
told me the other evening that when he was at Garland that
afternoon one of the boys was talking about going to Billings to
enlist and he said he simply got up and left. He could not bear
to hear talk about it when he could not get in himself. And he
had tears in his eyes when he told me about it. He said that by
the time the war is over he guesses he will be well and strong,
and then there won't be any chance.

Sunday, November 3, 1918

Mr. Carr said last night that the sunset was perfectly
beautiful, but that he wouldn't for the world think of Miss
Hennel while he looked at it. He says every once in a while
that anyone who would choose to stay in B, when she had a
standing offer of $5 a week to take care of this baby is hopeless
and does not deserve any sympathy.

I think the reason Mr. Carr feels so badly about his
classification is that this is final. Every time he tried before he
always felt that there were other chances. Now that he has been
drafted and turned down so flat, it is all over. When you were
here he was still hoping. Now he has given up all hope. To be
sure, he feels that the work we are doing here is worth while,
and that helps him a lot. Then too, he and John get along so
well that they both have a ripping circus all the time, just being
with each other. I never saw two men fall in love with each
other the way they have. Each one takes me aside and tells me
how fine the other is and how much he thinks of him. It is
quite funny for me.

Friday, November 11, 1918

We are anxious to hear what the peace terms are. It is
almost unbelievable that the fighting has really stopped. I
hope it is for good and all. We have heard that the Hohen-
zollern's have abdicated. Of course that had to take place. If

the Kaiser has deserted his people, I wonder if the Kaiser's Gott has left too. I do hope that the terms will be severe enough. I can hardly believe it is possible that the war really is over this fall. Everybody was ready for another year. Just think, it took the U.S. only one real campaign to put an end to the war. But when the top of the hill is almost reached it takes only a little push to get over the top. And the Allies certainly did a lot of hard pulling in the past four years. We have heard that Bryan is to be put on the peace commission. I do hope not. The men are almost rabid on the subject. If such a thing happens I am sure they will feel like biting somebody. Even so calm a man as Mr. Murray told me the other day he nearly fainted when he saw the announcement of the possibility.

We had a Billings paper the other day which had a news item saying that the nice couple we stayed all night with near Cowley when we were caught in the mountain storm both died of the flu, leaving two small children. We have felt quite badly about it, as we liked them so much. There are a boy of about three and a half and a girl less than two. Then there is the fourteen year old brother of the man, an orphan, whom the man was taking care of. The couple were both quite young, and such fine people. I do not think either one was 25 years old. The paper account said the children would find no difficulty in getting a good home, so I suppose the Mormon relatives of the Davis's will take care of them.

Sunday, November 17, 1918

This will be a busy week with us. The honey will be loaded out tomorrow and Tuesday. Ours and Hardy's goes in the same car, as the freight rules now demand maximum shipments. There will be 568 cases in this car. As each weighs 120 net, you can figure for yourself what the amount of honey shipped will be. And as we are getting 24 cents a pound f.o.b. here you can also figure out what the value of the car will be. I guess I never told you just how our honey crop did turn out. We produced 35,000 pounds. Of this we will ship about 28,500 pounds, as we have shipped a number of cans and cases on small orders. The rest, or about 6500 pounds, we will dispose of locally. We sold about 1000 pounds early in the season at 20 cents. The rest we have charged 25 cents for on local sales. There will be a couple thousand pounds that will be slightly discolored from having to be heated (this is the cappings that were cut off when the frames were extracted). The price on this will be about 20 cents. All told, the crop will bring in about $8500.

Wednesday, November 20, 1918

Mr. O'Brien, the representative from Northrup King and Company, is with us now, and will be here a few more days. The funny part about it is that he can't enter Powell. The council has passed an ordinance recently that anyone who comes from farther than the limits of the Project can't enter the town until after he has been here five days because of the flu epidemic. Just where he is to go these five days is not apparent, although any house he enters will be quarantined while he is in it the five days. That is, any house in the city limits. Of course the council has no jurisdiction over anything but the city limits. Mr. O'B went to Lovell and Greybull Wednesday last and came back on Friday. John and Mr. O'B went to Powell yesterday to load out the car of seed, and the train conductor (Old Lady Rogers, as the train men all call him) told the town marshal O'B had got off the train at Garland the night before. The marshal hunted O'B up at the car and wanted to take him before the mayor for violating a city ordinance. That meant the fine of $100.00. O'B finally got the marshal to let him get out of town. So he took the car and came out here, and John had to go on alone with the seed loading. O'B can't go to Powell tomorrow either, to finish up the car, but John will attend to it all.

Edith, you say you think you might get into trouble for food hoarding if anyone looked into your cellar. Well, if they got you, I guess they would come after us, too. Howsomever, as the gov't requests us to save all the food we can, and as we observed directions and raised it ourselves as well as canned it,

I guess we would get a ribbon instead of a rope. It looks in our basement as if, as Mr. Carr says, the wolf would put off his visit here for at least two days. We have canned peas, beans, corn, carrots, asparagus, greens, and tomatoes, besides meat and soup. There are fresh salsify, parsnips, turnips, cabbage, potatoes, onions, squash, and sauerkraut, and dried navy and pinto beans, and corn. We have plenty of pickles, pickled beets, chili sauce, and chow chow, and preserves and jelly of various sorts, besides a quantity of grape and black currant juice. In fruits we have a lot of fresh apples, and canned pears, peaches, apples, prunes, green gages, and three kinds of plums, and black currants. I will can a lot more of the beef they are killing today, so we surely won't get hungry for a while at least.

Thanksgiving Night
November 28, 1918

We had a Thanksgiving dinner and the men seemed to enjoy it very much. The meat was a roast beef heart, and it certainly was good, with plenty of dressing and brown gravy. We had mashed potatoes, peas, and cabbage-pimiento salad. The dessert was mince pie.

Even though we did not formally celebrate today, we all felt mighty thankful all the time, for one certainly has reason for being thankful now. I venture the statement that nine-tenths of the people in the world—that is, the U.S. and western Europe, would give as their first reason for being thankful that the war is ended, and that certainly is a mighty big reason for being thankful. Then after that there are some private and personal reasons why we are thankful that would take a book to enumerate. But chief and foremost is that we are all well. And another chief and foremost is that we have the baby. We never get done being thankful for that, and I hope we never will.

Cora, it is my opinion that Mr. Carr will not begin writing. He is always talking about when you will be here again, and every day asks what the news is from the H.G. or A.G. But I am quite sure he does not intend to open any correspondence on his own hook. I read him what you said about our having slighted you in re your having complimented him on his looks. He said to tell you that I always read the letters to him and John at supper and that often they are too tired to realize the fine points. He thanks you for the compliment just the same.

He was invited to Garland last night to a dinner party. The two Merring girls who are the telephone girls at Garland gave it. He and two "lady" school teachers were the guests. I can imagine how he kept those four girls amused all evening, can't you? When he started to get ready, all of his clothes but one pair of trousers were sticky with honey, and all of his shirts were dirty except one that had the whole back torn from a barbwire snag. His trousers also had a snag in them. I mended the shirt and the trousers, and then he brought me his coat, which had only one button on it, and that up where it did not do any good. He told me to give you the picture of the hired man waiting to go to a party till the boss's wife mended his one shirt and his one pair of trousers, and sewed a button on his one coat. I don't know when anything tickled me so much as to think of such a situation for a man who had two dress suits always and who never ate dinner in his own home without dressing for it. You remember he said his father would not let them come to the table unless they dressed for dinner each evening.

We will finish threshing this afternoon, and I may say without being in fear of extravagance of expression that I am glad. The bee cellar is finished, the bees are in and when the threshing is done, we really ought not to have many more dinners for a lot of men. I am now ready to take the train any day for Greybull, though I would appreciate a few days more to finish up a lot of sewing I have started. I am leaving the hand work to do at Greybull, as we can make buttonholes while we sit and talk, and after you begin to feel good, Edith.

If you could only see this big girl here you would know in a minute she is Edith's child. I am sure, mamma, that you would be sure she was yours, for she is the very image of Edith's baby picture. She weighs nine pounds and is as fat a youngster as you ever want to see — just fat enough to be pretty and not sloppy. Edith is getting along fine as could be. The baby has a cold. Edith has had a cold the past few days and the baby had it when she arrived. But we do not think there will be any complications, for she is getting along nicely now. She cried a good deal during the night and began again about half past ten this morning. Finally the nurse gave her a bottle of warm water and she hung on to it and drank every drop. She is sleeping now. She was born hungry, it seems, for when she was only a couple hours old — about four — she grabbed the spoon the nurse was feeding her from and held it in her mouth.

Edith began to get sick about six yesterday (Sunday) morning. We called the nurse and she came about nine. The doctor was in and out a number of times. Edith began to get pretty sick about two o'clock and went to bed, and the baby came at 7:30 in the evening. But everything went perfectly and the very slowness was, of course, a help toward making recovery sure and quick.

More anon. There is too much to do to write longer. Edith Rhoda almost came on our wedding anniversary.

No, I don't think any of us will stay up tonight just to see the new year come in. We have the most important new arrival already, and we will all be glad if she sleeps and lets everybody else do likewise.

Five years yesterday! I can't believe it. With John away in Denver, and the day after the night before celebration here, it wasn't exactly an ideal anniversary, but we were all so glad that the two Edith's were alive and all right that we didn't have time to care about anything else. And what more could any one wish for than that.

Saturday morning, January 18, 1919

Now for the answer to the great question as to whether or not we are coming east. From what you say in your last letters, the situation is worse than ever. All the medical warnings say that March is the worst month always for flu, grippe, and pneumonia. So taking it all together, we have concluded that we ought to be thankful we are all alive and well and not run any risks of making things otherwise. So if you will solemnly promise that all three of you, Pater, Mamma, and Cora — Grandpa, Grandma, and Aunt Grandma — will come to Wyoming this summer of 1919 and get acquainted with Cecilia Barbara and Edith Rhoda, we will agree to wait till then to see you.

The flu situation here is all right. There are practically no serious cases. I think that all told there have not been a dozen deaths on the Project. The Cody schools have been running six weeks now and not one single case has developed in the schools. The Powell schools will start Monday and the Garland school has been running several weeks. Of course Powell quarantined closely from the start and that is perhaps what has prevented a real epidemic. I noticed in yesterday's paper that the county health officer has forbidden any dances for an indefinite time yet, saying that dances have proved to be the most prolific source of contagion. But practically everything else is out from the ban — schools, churches, movies, public gatherings of all sorts. For a while Powell forbade the holding of private parties except of just a few, such as entertaining your relatives at dinner, and even then only when the crowd was very small. The marshal went after one party here where 25 or so were present, but the group got word before the marshal arrived, and dispersed.

Maybe you would be interested in a general account of the year's business. We have certainly had a good business year. Our bees produced about $8,000. Our part of the seed that was produced on Joe's place and what was raised on our own place brought a little better than $2,000. Our commission on two cars of clover seed was $649.50. What we made on handling fruit is about enough to give us a thousand dollars on the seed and fruit commissions. Our share of the potatoes that Joe raised on this place amounted to about $250. The volume of business, counting the fruit and seed that we handled, totaled about $40,000. The value of the two cars of seed was a little more than $23,000. The three cars of fruit and seed that we handled totaled about $40,000 and the value of the two cars of seed was a little more than $7,000. The honey and our own seed will bring the volume to something over $40,000.

For the running expenses to finance the year's business, we had to borrow $3800 at various times during the summer, from the bank. This we paid off during the past two weeks. We have not put our labor bills all together yet, but we think we must have paid out something like $3,000 for labor this year. When you look this all over, you won't have to receive any other proof of the fact that sometimes we were too busy to write letters.

So I am afraid we will have to be at home this year when the income tax man appears. If the bee cellar proves a success so that the bees come out all right in the spring, by this time next year we will be in our new house.

Mr. Carr went to Byron yesterday for the final load of gasoline to fill our underground tank and when he got back he announced that he had contracted for the entire output of gasoline of the little refinery there for the coming year at 18 cents a gallon. The ordinary price of gasoline here now is 26 and 27 cents. People have been going for miles to the refinery to get the 18 cent gasoline, some of them coming from Greybull.

There is no question whatever that it is a good buy to contract the gas, as the profit will be large, selling it lower than the Standard Oil sells it to the dealers in the neighboring places, and this refinery is so small that it is not big enough to draw the fire of the Standard Oil or any other big company, at least for a year. Mr. Carr plans to sell the gasoline in Powell, Garland, Cowley, Lovell, and Deaver, and maybe Frannie. Of course he offered John a half interest in his "company," and I rather think we will go into it. It sure looks good. Gasoline always goes up during the summer here, and the price is seldom less than 30 cents during the heavy using season — about May to October.

Monday morning, February 3, 1919

Co, Mr. Carr says he is deeply disappointed that any one who has been here in the big West as much as you have should have qualms about an oil venture. Did you think that we would contract for 500 gallons of oil a day and then just sit and wait till some one came around each day to buy it? You don't compliment us much, if you thought that. Let us assure you that before we sign a contract to buy oil we will have arranged for contracts to *sell* the oil, to an equal amount per day, to dealers in some four towns round about.

Wednesday, February 8, 1919

John and Mr. Carr went to Billings Monday afternoon on about an hour's notice. Mr. Carr went to the oil well and happened to meet the manager from Denver, who happened to be there. They had been waiting for two weeks till his arrival in order to arrange the oil deal. The man was going to Billings that afternoon, so Mr. Carr hurried home and then he and John hustled off to Billings, too. They were on the same train with the man and had plenty of time in the Pullman and in the diner to talk over the deal, and make all arrangements. They got everything just the way they want it.

They have all the territory around here and may get southern Montana. The oil company is increasing its refinery capacity to 500 barrels a day with a larger capacity yet to be established, and we want to handle it all. No contract is to be signed (by us) with the company until we have time to contract the oil to dealers in all this territory—Frannie to Greybull and Frannie to Cody. We think we will be ready by the middle of this month to know just what we can sell each day, and will then be ready to sign a definite contract.

I can see and hear you all laughing at our big plans, but just you wait a little while. One of the first things Mr. Carr said about John when he got to knowing him was that if John did not have that lame leg he would have died a millionaire. When John and Mr. Carr get their heads together, there is some mighty good business planned, I can tell you. John is always saying that his business has increased so since I came here. His net earnings this year are three times what his gross earnings were the year I came. I told him the other day that if two of us could do that, three could do proportionately as well, and maybe better.

February 16, 1919

So, there is the best story out now about Mr. Carr that anyone could imagine. He heard it in Garland this afternoon. Mrs. Collins, the wife of the store man, told him that Mrs. Dabbs, the wife of the banker, told her that Mr. Carr is a millionaire's son from New York who is being paid $10,000 a year to *stay away from home.* Mr. Carr is so tickled he can hardly talk straight about it, and assured Mrs. Collins that he would be glad to pay her to keep telling the story. You can imagine what discussion there must have been in a place like Garland over a man who begins to do things as he is beginning. After the oil deal became known—and all they knew was what Mr. Carr had himself told them—the news was out that he had *bought* the Byron oil field. He said when he told me about it that he guessed the next thing he would buy would be the railroad from Frannie to Cody.

Mr. Carr has had ever so many offers of capital for the oil business. Mr. Longley of the hardware company in Powell, unsolicited, offered him working capital as soon as he heard of the deal. Longley has made scads of money in all sorts of ways (all legitimate) since he came here. Dr. Humphrey, the dentist, also inquired if Mr. Carr did not want some working capital. The other day Mr. Lewis, who is known here as "The Potato Man" as he marketed practically all the potatoes shipped out from here last fall, was talking to Mr. Carr and offered him any amount he could use, up to $25,000. The same day the store keeper at Byron told him he intended to sell his store there and would have about $20,000 he would like to put at Mr. Carr's disposal if he wanted to use it for carrying on the oil business. About all one can remark is "Now what do you think of that?" It is a compliment to Mr. Carr, as well as to the business for these men do not know anything about him except from what they have seen here.

The oil situation changes almost from day to day, and new openings occur that Mr. Carr wants to work out before making a definite venture. Just now there is talk of buying the crude oil and refining it as well as selling the refined gasoline. That is most likely the trend things will take, as the refiner, Mr. Larson, who is an elderly man with 20 years' experience at gasoline refining, has taken a fancy to Mr. Carr and wants him to go in with him to refine as well as sell. No, Co, we don't know anything more about him than we have told you. He did give the manager of the oil company a lot of references when he first got into business with them. But the business men in Powell have no way of knowing anything about him except what he has told here himself.

Co, we haven't any suggestions as to the apparent mystery. John says he has always taken him for what he represented himself to be. As for me, I am frank to state that somehow it doesn't worry me. I can't seem to get myself excited over it. We say he is all right.

Monday, May 5, 1919

I have two pieces of news that I think will interest you. One is pleasant, the other is not, from my point of view.

I'll get the unpleasant one out of the way first — and briefly. I am writing this in bed. Yesterday morning I began to suffer indigestion pains in my stomach. Simple remedies did not help so I called Dr. Graham in the afternoon and it kept getting worse, so much so I felt I could not stand the pain. He gave me a hypodermic, which stopped the pain but made me feel as if I were made of lead or something heavier. Then I began to be sick at my stomach. I could not raise my head or even speak without having to be a whay-all. By eleven last night I got so I could keep some medicine inside where it belonged. I slept pretty well during the night but am so weak today I have stayed in bed. Carrie took Cecilia home to spend the night and this morning she came here and got dinner for the men. Mrs. Lovercheck called up Carrie to ask how I was this morning and also to ask if there were men for dinner. When she found out there were she sent up a pie. Wasn't that nice. I am lots better now and will be all right when I get rested up. I haven't any idea what made me sick. John says it is from running a boarding house. Well, fortunately, that ought to stop soon, which introduces the other.

Mr. Carr is married. He sneaked off to Billings a week ago "on business," met his life-long sweetheart and traded his bachelorhood for the titles of husband and father, acquiring a family as well as a wife. She was a widow (sod) with a seven year old son. She was a New York girl but has lived in St. Louis for two years with her sister. Her first husband has been dead at least that long. Mr. Carr says he has been waiting for years for her.

Co, you remember when Mr. Carr told you that he had always thought that if ever he married it would be a Protestant girl before he had time to think much about it? Well, he must have had this girl in mind then. They were sweethearts when they were growing up. They had a sort of scrap once and broke off. She married another man. Mr. Carr says he always knew that if her husband died he would marry her himself some day. Some time ago she and her mother and sister came west on a trip as far as the coast. She and Mr. Carr have been corresponding off and on since her husband's death. When the party started back they came through Montana. She decided to stop at Billings and call Mr. Carr by telephone. Of course he at once went up to see them. He began to urge her to promise to marry him in the fall. She suddenly said she would marry him, but right now or never. So he took her up, considering that he had waited long enough.

Wednesday, May 7, 1919

What did I put on my Prince Henry for?
Mr. Carr said yesterday he would bring the folk out here this morning for us to meet. I thought then that her mother and sister were here too, and expected them all out here for dinner today. Although I was pretty wobbly I got up betimes this morning, cleaned the house within an inch of its life, washed the kitchen window curtain, put embroidered pillow cases on the pillows, the monogram bolster slip on the baby's crib pillow, and got a bouquet of dandelions for the table, which I even washed and polished. I shined the silver and the bread tray and the silver candlesticks, and if we had had one, I suppose I would have "polished the knocker on the big front door." I was all ready, when Mr. Carr telephoned from Powell about something John wanted from town and said they would be right out. Well, it was nearly an hour before they came, and when they did appear, it was only he and the bride, and they stayed

about ten minutes, as he had to go on down to the oil wells. So here is my nice clean house. Well, it is fortunate that once in a while I have an occasion that compels me to shine things up.

When they got here, Mr. Carr actually knocked at the door before they came in, and when I appeared he began to sing, "Here comes the bride!" She is a dear. She is very tall and slender and very dark, with large dark eyes. She wore a midnight blue coat suit, with a georgette waist, cut rather low, and embroidered in the front and trimmed with ribbon. I think the waist was tan with blue trimming. She did not take off her suit coat. She had on low pointed slippers with French heels, and very lacy silk stockings. She carried a top coat, a tweed mixture in a shade of tan. Her hat was a large one with braid crown and georgette brim, trimmed on the edge with ball trimming that was black. Mr. Carr says they are coming again, and again, and again, then some more and lots of times besides. He counts this his home. He was telling her this morning that this had been home to him for a long time, the only home he had, and that it would continue to be home to him "until Grace made a home for him." He said this last to me. When I told John about it, he remarked, "Saved by Grace, as the Methodists say." As to who was saved, John did not state. I rather think it is meself that was saved, for praise be, they have rented them a house in Powell and are going to housekeeping. If Mr. Carr goes away, we will advise him that the truck driver should be paid a flat wage, and board himself. The reason for keeping the truck driver here was that he should be where Mr. Carr was. The prospects of losing two boarders are too good to be true. It isn't just the cooking and dish washing — it is the washing and cleaning, for the washing and taking care of an extra bed counts up considerably.

Mrs. Carr. said that when they drove up to this place this morning, he announced in a very melodramatic, but earnest manner, "Here is Honeyhill Farm, the place that made your husband a well man." She says he can't get done talking about how much good it did him to be here and how well he has got since he has been here. Mr. Carr says he can't understand why they were so foolish as (1) to want to keep their marriage secret and to stay away from each other, and (2) to think they *could* keep it from becoming known if they wanted it kept quiet.

I ordered a pattern yesterday for — guess what? Coveralls! Can you imagine me in such attire? Well, we have concluded that it is very much easier and pleasanter for both of us if I get Helen Young to do the house work and help John with his work, and thus do away with the necessity of hired man help. Helen can do all the necessary work in about six hours, and it won't cost more than about a dollar a day. A man's wages are at least two and a half times that, besides making all the extra work of bedding, etc., and clothes washing, and three meals. If I do outside work I need suitable clothes. Heretofore I have worn bloomers in the bee work and a dress over them, but that is a nuisance. It is such a bother to have a lap. The first frame of honey you pick up leaks honey all over your lap and then you are sticky the rest of the time. So I have concluded I won't have any lap. I looked at some coveralls at Powell yesterday. They were four dollars a suit and made of khaki that would fade the first time it is washed. The ones from the mail order catalogues are about the same. So I will get some galatea and make me a couple suits. I can make them for about $2.25 each, and have suits that won't fade.

We continue to enjoy having Edith and the baby here. Edith Rhoda is growing and changing so that Ted will hardly know her when he gets back from St. Louis and Bloomington. Since he went away she has begun to coo and talk so much and has learned to hold things and reach for them. It is so nice to have a little baby around. Cecilia is not a little baby any more, but a big girl. I have told Edith that since E.R. is here I want more than ever to have a little baby again. One forgets so much about a baby. I had forgot entirely the time when Cecilia was at this stage. I do hope we can have another baby of our own before so very long.

Sunday, May 25, 1919

We took quite a trip today, in search of material to botanize. We drove past Ralston and over the prairie west of there, taking the road that runs about two miles south of the Blockner sheep camp there on the bench. I had never been over that road before. We drove some eight or ten miles past Ralston, or about 20 miles from home. We started about a quarter of eleven and were back home about half past two in spite of a blowout, two punctures, and a loose radius rod.

We did not find as many flowers as usual because this has been such a dry winter and spring. You will know how different it is from last year when I tell you that last year Sylvan Pass, in the Park, was still drifted with snow so as to be impassable the first of August, while this year it is clear the first of May. Naturally the dry winter and spring kept the wild flowers from growing and what we did find are rather small. We found some half dozen kinds, nearly all of them of the aster or sweet pea type. We found white and yellow asters, and blue, yellow, white, and pink ones of the pea shaped blossoms. These varied in size from a quarter of an inch to an inch or more in size of blossom, the foliage and size of the plant varying even more. Some of the small ones were only a couple inches above the ground, while some of the tall ones were over a foot. The blue peas are so pretty. They grow in patches sometimes a foot across and are one mass of blossoms with blue upper and purple lower parts. Due to the lack of moisture the plants and blossoms are rather small this year—only about half an inch for the blossoms.

Monday, June 9, 1919

When Pater arrived, of course Cecilia did not know him and was pretty shy. She sat on his lap all the way home but did not say a word, nor did she until about the middle of the meal, when she spoke to Edith. Several hours later, about the middle of the afternoon, after she had walked about the yard several times with Grandpa and me, she suddenly inquired, "Where is Grandpa?" I told her he was walking about the yard. She said, "I need to help him." Off she went to find him, and from that time on they have been inseparable.

Pater is having the time of his life. He can't get done telling how much he enjoyed the trip and what fine people he met on the way. He says it is easier to make the trip out here than from Bloomington to Evansville and back. He said he was not nearly as tired from this trip as from the last E trip, and that he was rested when he got here. Ted did a good job escorting him. Pater tipped the porter till he stood around watching Pater's every move, and Pater enjoyed it even more than the porter did.

This morning Pater noticed John's surveying outfit that we use for running ditches, etc., here on the farm. Pater got it out and had a great time with it, renewing the days of his youth. He keeps saying every little while that it is grand to be where you can *see* somewhere. He does enjoy the view. It has been cloudy most of the time on the mountains, so he has really not got a real view yet. But of course it is lots farther than he is used to seeing.

Yesterday morning Pater got up before the rest of us did — as it was Sunday we slept late. He said his heart was bothering him. He was afraid of the altitude and wanted a doctor. He insisted he did not want the medicine, but he wanted to know if the altitude was high enough to send him home, and also because if anything happened he did not want a coroner. We could not get the doctor then as he was out on a case. John and the baby and I went to church and on the way home we hunted up the doctor and asked him to come, saying we thought Pater needed reassurance more than anything else. Dr. Graham soon put in his appearance and he and Pater had a nice visit. The doctor told him he had a mighty good heart for his age and that there wasn't a thing wrong with him organically. He asked Pater what he was taking, recommended a better preparation in tablet form with all the necessary ingredients in one tablet, and assured Pater that he was as safe here as anywhere in the U.S.

Tomorrow is Good Roads Day. The whole county is divided into sections with a captain for each district. John is it here. He has the road from Bygren's corner to the railroad track (1½ miles) and from our corner a mile west. There are nine men in his gang. They will fix all the bad places in the road, put in several culverts that are needed, repair one that is broken, take out a bad place that is caving in and fill it up, and make waste water ditches all along to keep the water from getting into the road again. The women and children will come here at noon for a picnic dinner. They will each bring something. We will have baked hash, potato salad, beets, pickles, bread and butter, ice cream and cake. I will make all the hash and we will also make about two gallons of ice cream, maybe three, and the iced tea and coffee for the crowd. That will keep me pretty busy tomorrow, and I guess the women will stay all afternoon.

Wednesday, June 18, 1919

We are working on the car and it is in about fifty pieces now, or fifty thousand, maybe, counting all the bolts and bolt heads and washers. I am appointed chief wash master and am cleaning it all up, piece by piece, while John does the mechanical work. When it is all clean we will paint it and put a new top on it, likewise four new fenders. Pater remarked the other day that the car looked pretty worn and old, and John said the reason was hired men. The man we had summer before last bent every fender on the car, and a good many other parts, too. A hired man always shows off with a car, and the owner stands the damage.

Tuesday, June 24, 1919

Mr. Carr was here yesterday with his face all bandaged up, unable to talk a word and having to write all he wanted to say. He had just come back from Billings and was on the way there again — on last night's train. The X-ray showed T.B. in his jaw bone. He was operated on today for the removal of the infected part. He says the operation was not considered severe and ought not take more than 30 minutes. He has not been allowed to smoke for days, or to eat and drink except through a straw — which naturally meant a liquid diet. While he is in the hospital he will have to live on milk and raw eggs, so he came out to get some fresh eggs. Mrs. Carr does not know it is T.B. and he would not tell her for anything as it would scare her to death. He said she would be afraid it was a return of the old trouble. He assured us long ago that the old trouble was not T.B., you remember, but what he said yesterday, as I just quoted, sounds odd. The thing I am afraid of is that even if this place is cured up all right the T.B. will break out somewhere else. We are very much afraid he will not live many years.

July 1, 1919

When we told Pater good bye at the station Cecilia wanted to get on the train with him. As the train pulled out she began to cry — she wasn't the only one, either. As we got in the auto she kept on crying and saying she wanted to go on the train with Grandpa. We asked her what she wanted to get on the train for, and she said she wanted to go home with Grandpa and see Aunt Grandma. She cried a good part of the way home. She did not want Grandpa to go home, in which she is exactly like her father and mother. I don't know which of us is more disappointed, John or myself. Pater was here so short a time before he went to Greybull and so few days after he got back that we did not get to show him nearly all the things we wanted to, on our place and elsewhere. Just think, Pater, you did not get to look inside a bee hive.

July 13, 1919

Edith and Ted are with us. Edw did not really intend to stay so long when he came, but things have happened that made him do so, and will make Edith stay a few days longer while Ted goes back to Greybull tomorrow and back here the next day. The things that have happened make a long and a very sad story.

The beginning and the end of the story is that Mr. Carr has disappeared. He has been going to Billings for treatment since this last T.B. broke out. On July 3 he telephoned to Edw in the late afternoon that he wanted very much to see him on business that night, so they arranged a meeting, with some of the other men, for 9:30. Ted and E drove right up and got here about 9:30, and Ted drove right to Powell. Shortly after, Mrs. Carr called up here to say that Mr. Carr had got so much worse he had gone to Billings on the nine p.m. train. Of course Ted was sore at having made the trip for nothing. A day or two later Mrs. Carr got a note from Mr. C. from Billings saying that he was feeling better, after the treatment, and was starting for Denver to see a certain man on business. He said if he were delayed he would telegraph or write. No one heard from him since then.

The first anybody knew anything was wrong was when his check which he had given Fred to pay for gasoline at the wells was turned down by the bank for insufficient funds. Then a day or two later there came a telegram from the Denver man asking where Mr. Carr was and when he would be in Denver. Upon inquiry at Billings, it was found from the specialist that on July 4, the date of the note Mr. Carr had written to Mrs. Carr, Mr. C had asked the specialist to tell him frankly and finally just how he was, and the specialist told him it was only a question of a short time till the T.B. got into the glands, and when it did he was finished, for a hemorrhage would inevitably follow and he would go off like a flash. At first we were all afraid that Mr. Carr had gone out of his mind when he found that out. He had been so worried for weeks that he was half crazy, and the pain was so severe that for days at a time the doctor kept him under an opiate, not enough to keep him unconscious, but to kill the pain. At one time about two weeks ago he had used so much of the opiates that his whole right side was partly paralyzed, and he could hardly use his hand.

The last three days he was here, June 30 to July 2, he was doped all the time to make the pain at all endurable.

We were afraid that he had killed himself, as he had told both Ted and Mrs. Carr during the past few weeks that if he really had T.B. he would do so. Then it developed that he had collected for the gasoline that was sold and had not turned the money in at the bank but had given checks to the oil company, to Mrs. Carr, and to others, that had nothing in the bank to meet them. It is evident that he had several hundred dollars with him when he went away. He owes money in various places, and the assets are only about one-fourth of the liabilities. We helped him to get started in the gasoline business and he owes us a good bit. But none of this, except a small amount to the oil company, was pressing, as the notes were not due — some of them have months to run yet.

On comparing notes with various persons — Mr. Lewis and the other business men, and with us, Ted has found that Carr's stories did not match at all, and that he told Mrs. Carr things that were not true. One story he has told continually since he was married is that Mrs. Carr has money. She told Ted she does not have anything, and in fact, Ted and Mr. Lewis had to help her get out of town to go to her sister in Billings. Mr. Carr had not left her enough money to take care of her while he was away. Of course she expected him back in a day or two and did not think of asking for the money to pay the hotel and restaurant while he was away. We do not know what to make of it at all. Edw thinks that Mr. Carr is just plain crooked and has skipped out. But if he did that, why under the sun didn't he get enough money to make the skipping worth while? He had so many friends in Powell that he could have worked for any sum almost, and for him to go with a few hundred dollars does not seem worth while. Another thing that makes Ted think he is a fraud is that in his will, which he made several weeks ago, when he first knew he was really sick, he mentioned a man in Denver, saying he was vice-president of a certain bank, and an old friend of his father's and of his, and one who could tell about him. He also said he had a safety box at this bank containing some jewels. After Mr. Carr disappeared Edw got into communication with this bank and there is no man connected with it, or ever was, by the name Mr. Carr gave, and there is no safety box in his name. In the will he also mentioned the interest he has in his father's estate, naming the bank in New York that had charge of the estate. Edw wrote there, but has not heard. We found among his papers the name of the sister he talked so much about, and wrote to her husband; but we think maybe that name was a fake. He did not leave a single letter from any of his people.

Another thing that looks bad is that he told us that Mrs. Carr was his boyhood sweetheart. She admitted to Edw the other day that she never knew him until 1913, when she met him in St. Louis, and that he has made her say that she knew his family, when she really did not. She says she has fought against telling that ever since they were married but that he insisted it was necessary for her to say she did know his people. She says that they have been writing for several years and that he had persuaded her to come to Billings this spring to marry him. Of course on all these matters we have only her word, but the poor girl seems so absolutely honest in what she says that one can hardly doubt her, especially as so many of Mr. Carr's other stories do not jibe. We do not know what to think. We know that Mr. Carr has told lies by the wholesale in the past couple months, since he left here—left our house, and that some of the things he told us since then and before are not true. And yet we can not bring ourselves to think that he is really a crook. We still have enough faith in him, in spite of all the present appearance of things, to think that if he is alive we will hear from him or of him some day in explanation or regret for what he has done. Maybe we are plain crazy ourselves, but we can't help thinking so. John said today that if it were certain that Mr. Carr was a plain confidence man, he would be just as sore as could be, but that he did not think so, and that the business that Mr. Carr started here was a real business and worth helping any man, and especially a man who has been down and out because of health and who was working so hard to get back into business. For no matter what Mr. Carr has said or done recently, he is and was a worker.

If it is true that Mr. Carr deliberately planned to run away, we think it came only in the past few weeks since his health has failed entirely. He may have thought that he would not live long enough to straighten out all his financial matters anyway, and so he might as well drop out now with enough money to last him the rest of his short existence.

The creditors have begun making attachments, and after much consideration Edw has about concluded that the best thing to do is to throw the estate into involuntary bankruptcy. That won't cost as much as a dozen attachment suits and will settle the whole matter once and for all.

Well, it is all a sorry business, and I don't know which I feel sorrier for, Mrs. Carr or Mr. Carr himself, or ourselves for losing some money. We feel, though, that the loss of the money is far less than the loss of our faith in him, as he seemed such a really fine person. We haven't entirely lost faith in him, for as I said above, we think there will be more to the story some time, but I guess we are the only ones who think that. There is undoubtedly something wrong about him, for your checking up of his and his brother's and father's names did not come out right. Ever since then John has said that there was something wrong somewhere, but the business Mr. Carr was carrying on here seemed in itself sufficient security for the advances we made him.

Wednesday, July 16, 1919

Edw had to go to Cody to start an attachment suit for John against Mr. Carr's property. The oil company to which Mr. Carr owes some $1500 or $2000 is starting something too, and we want to get in also for there is no reason why we should not get a whack at the division when it comes, even if the assets come out only 20 or 25 cents on the dollar.

We had a visit this morning from the sheriff and an attorney from Lovell, Mr. Little. They came to attach whatever property there was here of Mr. Carr's and said he had said he had a ¼ interest in our bees, and also that the truck here was his. John advised the sheriff that Mr. Carr had an offer to work for us this year in the bees and to get a share in the increase he worked up, but that the bees here are no one's but our own, and likewise the truck. He said Mr. Carr had a truck but that it was not this one. He also told the sheriff that we had backed Mr. Carr to start him in business by helping him to get some money at the bank, and the sheriff laughed and remarked that if we were stung like that it was a cinch he wasn't going to bother us any further.

Thursday, July 24, 1919

We went to the movies last night and saw "Little Women." It was quite good. It was all done sweetly and sensibly and not a bit was overdone. The scenes were all taken in the proper village in Mass. and the scene showing Emerson was taken by special permission in the Emerson house. Beth's death was done without any maudlin, melodramatic, sentimental nonsense. Laurie was as dear as the book says, the girls were fun. Everybody roared when Jo called her mother aside from a family party to tell her that John Brooke was proposing to Meg, and then later when Jo, on finding the two lovers in the deserted living room, shouted to the party out at tea under the orchard trees, "O come quick, everybody. It's important. John Brooke is kissing Meg and she acts as if she likes it." Finally the mother makes her understand that when she stumbles on such an affair the thing for her to do is to go away and leave the two lovers together. We enjoyed the whole picture — six reels — very much.

The Murrays are going to Billings for the circus. Of course I am not the mother of two sons, but I confess I would not make a trip to Billings in an auto for the sole purpose of attending a circus. They have been laughing so at Max. His reason for wanting to go is to see the "ephelant." Miss Jenkins was down at Murray's and said she would like very much to go to see one animal she had read about and had seen pictures of but had never seen herself. They asked her what it was, and she explained it was the "geograph." Helen told me about it, and went on to explain that what Miss Jenkins meant was the ji-raffe. I was very much amused, for it seemed to me just about as bad for Helen to call it the jī-raffe as for Miss J. to call it the geograph.

This is the day on which we began the extracting for the season 1919. It is about the earliest start we have ever got. If we can keep at the comb honey in like fashion and have it cleaned, graded and cased as we go along, there won't be such an awful rush at the end of the season.

We have so many trains on our little jerkwater line now that you'd think we were on a real railroad, instead of on Rogers' Limited Division. Yesterday there was a special passenger train along about an hour before the regular morning train, composed of four Pullmans, a baggage car, and a coach. The Park train that goes to Cody about five in the morning and back to Billings about nine at night usually has at least four coaches. Yesterday there was a special freight train as well as an extra passenger, so there were five chances of getting to Frannie yesterday. Not that anyone would want to go to Frannie to stay, but often it is interesting to *get* there.

Mr. Norton told John the other day that it now seems that Carr was a regular crook, and then, laughing, he remarked, "I was glad to turn him over to you when I did last fall." We do not know whether he meant that he suspected anything at the time, but rather think not, as he and Carr were such good friends all winter.

As to the lady called Mrs. Carr, perhaps we had better do what the man in Billings did. When Ted was talking to Mrs. Carr, the telephone rang, and he answered it. The man at the other end wanted to talk to Grace. Edw asked if he wanted to talk to Mrs. Carr. "I don't know anything about any Mrs. Carr," came the answer, "I want to talk to that woman they call

Grace." So maybe we had better speak of her by that appellation. Do you remember how we joked when she first appeared about being saved by Grace? Well, I guess we will have to hunt up some other slogan now.

Thursday, August 21, 1919

If you had been here yesterday you would have seen the queerest weather we ever had. There are big forest fires somewhere and the air is thick with smoke. Yesterday it was so bad that we did not catch a glimpse of the sun all day. It surely must have been somewhat cloudy otherwise, as there seemed to be a coolness in the air that was suggestive of rain, although there was not a sign of it. The air was a queer green color all day, like twilight. The color on the grass and trees was like that of late evening just before dark. The crickets sang all day and the bees did not fly or hum at all. I never saw anything like it. The smoke was so low and so close that we could not see more than about 3/4 miles to the south. Today the sun showed about the middle of the morning. It looked like a ball of fire, a queer red color. It got brighter in an hour or so, and one could not then look at it directly; while it was dim one could see very plainly the large sun spot the papers have been talking about. Today the smoke seems worse than yesterday, even though the sun shows somewhat and it is much warmer. We can not see the hills to the south at all, even in outline. The whole place looks as if it were in a heavy fog that is thin close at hand and thick a little distance away. Both yesterday and today there was a smoke odor in the air, enough to make one notice it when breathing and to make one's eyes hurt. We do not know just where the fires are. Last week there was one between here and the Park. We heard that it has broken out again and also that there is one on the other side of the Park, in Idaho. Last week there was a call for helpers from Powell to fight the fire. In 1911 there were such heavy fires in Montana and Idaho that the air was heavy here for a long time. That year there were such early frosts that the grain did not ripen. It was laid to the cloudy atmosphere caused by the smoke. After days of cloudiness there were heavy rains, followed by frost. These smoky days are hard on us because the bees do not work, and every day now is worth between a hundred and two hundred dollars to us in the honey the bees bring in.

Wednesday, August 30, 1919

While Edw was at Billings to go to the dentist he found out some more things about the Carr case. The two most important things are both exceedingly unpleasant. One is that he and Mrs. Carr were never married. Edw had suspected it earlier but this time he went over the marriage license returns in the court house, both the issuing of the licenses and the returns of the officiating minister or justice, and found nothing at all. Mrs. Carr had given him the date of the supposed wedding and on different occasions had given it on different dates. That was rather suspicious to start with. Then she had told him at one time that a clergyman married them and not a priest, and at another time said it was a justice of the peace. Edw saw the justice and found he knew nothing of them. Edw went through the court house records for about two months each way of the supposed dates and found nothing. So it is rather evident that there was no marriage, and that either or both of them could easily be hailed before a federal court on a white slavery charge. The other thing Edward found out is that the report supposed to come from the Billings doctor to the effect that Mr. C. had T.B. in the last stages is not true, and that there is a mistake somewhere. The doctor told Ted that Mr. C. did not have T.B. and never did have it. When he first came to this part of the country he had asthma, and that was what caused the throat trouble. The trouble now is an entirely different thing. It is trench mouth, caused by, and the indication of, a very virulent venereal disease. The doctor said that three treatments would have relieved and perhaps cured the mouth part of the disease. Of course the disease itself is almost incurable except after long, long treatment, and then there is always a question for years. So the reason that Mr. C. left these parts was not that he was about to die. We do not yet know just what the reason is. It is evident that there was some urgent reason, because he would not have left a paying business without making something out of it by selling either the business or the truck and car he had, or both, and he would not have gone without getting a real amount of money if his intention had been to beat folks in general. Then too, he must have gone in a hurry or he would not have left on the nine o'clock train after making arrangements with Edw over the telephone for a meeting in Powell at 9:30 that evening. Well, it is all a nasty affair and it seems that the farther it goes the nastier it gets. We are mighty thankful that he got away from here before the disease broke out.

September 22, 1919

John heard in Powell this morning that it was being told there that Mr. Carr committed suicide in Denver. Art Owens told John, saying he heard it at the barber shop. I would like to know how much there is in the rumor and where it started.

Sunday, October 12, 1919

When we ate dinner today we wondered if we would be eating dinner at Grandpa's house two weeks from today. I am going to try to make it, but you must not be disappointed if we do not get there until the middle of the next week. John says I should get started as soon as possible, and I am doing everything possible to carry out his instructions. I will even let go some of the sewing—in fact, practically all of it—that I planned to do before starting. Maybe I won't be so tired or rushed after I get there to do what absolutely needs to be done. So today I packed up the goods and the patterns I intend using, and will bring them along.

October 16, 1919

We will go over the N.P. from Billings to Chicago, reaching Chicago at 9:10 Friday night. We can get a Big Four train out of Chicago for Indpls at 11:30, reaching Indpls at 4:50 Saturday morning. The I.C. train leaves Indpls at 6:40, so we ought to get to Bloomington at about 8 o'clock Saturday morning. It makes me jump up and down on my chair just to think of it. If we are sleepy we can go to bed early Saturday night, maybe, for I won't want to go anywhere that first night, and maybe by evening we can have enough talked out to let the rest wait till the next morning. *Edith, are you going along?*

October 17, 1919

Edw called yesterday afternoon to say that Edith and E.R. would go east with us, so we arranged to meet on the train at Frannie next Wednesday afternoon. We will leave Billings as scheduled in my yesterday letter. I am going to get this girl of mine to Bloomington for her birthday, so you may expect us about as planned.

December 22, 1919

We got home all right, and on time, the only time we were on time after Chicago, or Bloomington, for that matter. We came home and when we got here found we were to go right over to Sweeten's for dinner. We went and had a fine dinner but did not stay long because John wanted to go to the bank that afternoon.

We got a check yesterday on our shipment of honey, for $6,000. The complete returns are not in yet, so Mr. Rauchfuss sent us only the main part of the amount. John had already got about $1300 in advance payment and Mr. R. says there is still about $600 to come after the settlement is complete. Not bad for the comb honey crop, is it? We still have on hand two or three thousand dollars worth of extracted honey. This six thousand dollar check was the largest we have ever received for honey — or for anything else for that matter.

Let me say again that we did indeed receive the check that you sent at Christmas for records. I am sure I have mentioned it several times, but want to say it again. Since the Red Seal records are cut in price we can get several for the amount you sent.

We are hoping our machine will come soon. We are like two kids waiting for a new toy and can hardly wait till it gets here.

Cecilia and I spent the afternoon at Pease's yesterday. When we got home I wondered why John had a continuous smile but did not understand till we got into the house. In the kitchen I saw a box that evidently had held records and then I knew that the records had come. When I went into the living room, there was the talking machine as well as the records. Wasn't it fine that they came at the same time. You can guess that there has been music in the air ever since. We like this machine immensely. I think I never heard one, not even a Victrola, that played so smoothly. There is absolutely no grinding and scratching.

Of the records we ordered positively 25 Red Seal and got 17 of them, 33 Victor and got 18, and 6 Columbia and got 2. Then in the tentative order—ones that can be returned—there were 43 Red Seal, of which 26 came, and 102 Victor, of which 48 came. The whole lot has 111 in it, and we will probably keep about half of them. Nearly all of them are standard things, but you know how it is—some things one likes and some things one doesn't. For instance, we have "The Last Rose of Summer" by Tettrazzini. As soon as she began to sing, Cecilia began to wrinkle up her face, and finally, when she could stand it no longer, she said, "O mamma, she sings too loud. It hurts me." We agreed with her. It was so shrill that one winced. Have you ever heard Mme. Shuman-Heink sing "His Lullaby," from Carrie Jacobs-Bond? "You cried in your sleep for your mother dear?" I don't care for her voice at all in that. I may be lacking in artistic appreciation, but Caruso is another voice I care very little for. I would rather hear Evan Williams any time. We have several of Caruso's and the "Home to Our Mountains" by Caruso-Schuman-Heinck. (I am enclosing the whole list of the records we got.)

Tuesday, February 10, 1920

John has been making house plans for some time and we have now finished them to about what we want. We think we have about as nifty a scheme as can be found. We are going over to Horn's tonight to get him to help finish figuring the lumber we need, and then John will be ready to see how much it will cost for the lumber. Lumber is up almost out of sight, but there isn't any sign of its coming down for several years, and we don't want to wait that long.

Thursday, February 26, 1920

I am enclosing herewith the plans we have finally decided on for the house. You may think that the upstairs gives us too much room, but inasmuch as it won't cost much to finish it that way we thought we might as well do it while we are building. The downstairs is what we want as it is. There will be a basement under the whole house. The east end of the front part of the basement will be partitioned off and lighted for a wash room, with hot and cold water right there. The west end of the north part will be the coal room, another part will be the furnace room, and another partitioned off and fitted throughout with shelves that will be the canned goods storage department. We will not put a bathroom upstairs as one will be all we will need, but we will put a toilet upstairs as it will be so convenient. Of course there will be one downstairs, too. We will have triple windows in the west end of the living room and the north end of the dining room. There will be a north window and east windows in the kitchen. With the built-in china closet, which will have drawers for linen and, below, a cupboard for kitchen utensils, and the built-in kitchen cupboard with tilting flour bin, etc., I think I will have plenty of space to put things away in the kitchen. John thinks we are planning too much closet space upstairs if we have all the room under the rafters made into closets, as that will give two large ones to each room, but I am sort o' skeptical about too much closet space. I don't believe there is any such animal.

Wednesday, May 26, 1920

Well, we have ordered our house. We got bids from the Contractors' Lumber Company at Seattle, Wash., from Gordon-Van Tine at Davenport, Iowa, from a so-called Farmers' Lumber Co. at Omaha, and from Longley Templeton at Powell. We ordered from the Contractors at Seattle. We have got lumber from them many times in car lots, and have always found it better than anything we can get locally. The Contractors and the Gordon-Van Tine bills were pretty close together — only a hundred or so dollars difference. The Farmers' Co. and the Longley bids were pretty close together — only a hundred or so dollars difference. But between the two sets of bids was a difference of just about a thousand dollars, or almost enough to pay the carpenters. Naturally we took the lowest bid, knowing from experience that the lumber from that firm is more than satisfactory. Then too, they made our blue prints and specifications, and the charge for that work — something like $30 — will be rebated if we buy the house material from them. The price of the lumber will be somewhere around four thousand dollars. John sent them a check for that amount the other night. So far, that is the largest check we have written. We have received larger ones, but not written larger ones.

Sunday, May 30, 1920

We went to the Memorial Day services in Powell this morning. The first part was held at the Lyric Theatre and the last part at the cemetery. The American Legion had charge. They had invited all soldiers of any war to meet with them and march with them, so John went. There were two

Civil War men, two Spanish War men, and perhaps forty or fifty World War men. The commander of the post had asked some one he knew to speak for each group. Old Grandpa Loomis spoke for the Civil War veterans; Mr. Wiggins for the Spanish War men, and Mr. Callahan for the World War men. Mr. Loomis gave some reminiscences about the attitude of the northern and southern men then and now, and spoke of pensions; Mr. Wiggins made a very good speech on the subject that the men of the U.S. are always ready to do anything that needs to be done — to meet any situation that arises; and Mr. Callahan — well, I wish you could have heard him. He is a young fellow, not more than 22 or 23. He lost his wife in the flu last year, and has a very small child. He was in the worst fighting in France.

Well, he said that what he wanted to tell about was a memorial service that he attended in France. His regiment had been 12 days at the front. During that 12 days fighting they were so busy that they did not get to take care of their own dead. Then when they retreated for a short rest, the dead were buried and the chaplain suggested that they hold a short memorial service. They did not have much of a band, as their band men had been made stretcher bearers and a good many of them were among the dead, and then besides, the band had been divided among three groups so that each would have a little music. But he said they had a few pieces, and the band played. Then the chaplain made a short talk in which he reminded the men that the real heroes were the ones who were not present to know it. Callahan said they had been so praised by dispatches that they had begun to think they really were some folks. But when the chaplain reminded them of the others who would never go back, he said he made a vow then and there that he, for one, would never forget them and that there would henceforth be one day in the year that for him would be a little holier and full of meaning than any other. He said there were perhaps 500 little wooden crosses where they stood, and countless graves without markers, as the battle had gone forth and back across that place.

He spoke in a very simple way, with no gestures, no oratory, but with such earnestness that he had to stop a time or two to control his own voice, without any wishy-washy effect, and by the time he was through, stopping shortly with a statement that he thanked God he was one who was permitted to come back, and that he adjured the audience to remember always, with great joy and not sorrow, those who were not able to come back. Well, by that time it was a pretty solemn moment for every one who was there. I never heard a man speak with such simplicity and earnestness of a real experience. After the services were over (they included music by the band and several vocal selections, one a bass solo with chorus accompaniment of "Tenting Tonight," perfectly beautiful, and a male quartette about comrades of the old brigade) we went to the cemetery where the graves of soldiers — some half dozen, I think — of the Civil and this war were decorated, with the proper accompaniment of band music, prayer, service reading, firing a salute, and taps.

June 24, 1920

Well, our party last night went off very well. And such a crowd — about 125 people. The Van Emans sure have a lot of friends, none of whom want them to move away. No one made any disturbance except Mrs. Pease, and for some unaccountable reason she has been trying to queer things from the start. She never liked Mrs. Van Eman (goodness only knows why) and evidently thought she could run the community. The past few days she has been knocking because, as she herself said, the party wasn't being given at her new house, which is as nice as anybody's. Can you imagine it? So far as I can figure, her whole grievance is because she was not put on the original committee of three to look after the reception. When I was asked to appoint a committee to look after it, I named Mrs. Murray, Mrs. Jones, and Mrs. Low. Or rather, Mrs. Brown and I did, as she named Mrs. Jones and I the other two. She and I are the remaining officers of the quasi-defunct East End

Club which merged into the Red Cross during the war. As no new members have been taken in during the past two years, Mrs. Hart thought that by having the East End Club give the reception we would get all Mrs. Van Eman's old friends.

When I made Mrs. Murray chairman of the committee, she was joshing me over the telephone about being slick enough to get out of the work myself by putting her on. We thought it was a good joke, but evidently some of the neighbors were rubbering and told Mrs. Pease that Mrs. Murray and Mrs. Hendricks were quarreling over the telephone as to which one should have the honor of doing the work. Well, Mrs. Pease got her limber tongue to going, and you can guess how much it wagged. Hart's new house is a perfect beauty. Inside it is beautifully arranged, and all finished in lovely browns and tans, walls and woodwork. It is two stories, with front, back and side porches, the side porch being a regular pergola. Pease's house is an old house made over, and while it really is very nice for a made over house, it isn't anything like Hart's. The house they started with was a straight up-and-down box house of two stories, and naturally they were rather handicapped by having to use the main part of it as it was. Well, now for the joke. Mrs. Pease told Mrs. Hart — right to her face, mind you — that her house (Mrs. Pease's) would be in style long after Hart's was out of style because Hart's was built after a bungalow style and the bungalow style was already passing out and was already not considered the very best style. How's that for nerve — and taste? Well, maybe you are tired of neighborhood gossip, but the whole affair has made me grin and snicker for so long that I couldn't keep it to myself, and of course there isn't anybody out here I would talk to about it.

Monday, July 5, 1920

Our house is here. The car of lumber and mill work — it is all packed in one car, loaded to the roof — got here Saturday. It took just a few days to get here from Seattle. We have had fruit cars on the way eight days coming only from north

Yakima. We did not look for this lumber for about a week yet, but here it is, all ready to be unloaded. It seems nice to have it really here and to know that the house is now an actuality. We are piling the dimension stuff and ordinary lumber along the north side of the house, where it will be handy for building, and putting the mill work in the shop. John will take out a lot more insurance on the shop as long as the lumber is in there. We'd be clear up against it if anything should happen to the shop while the lumber is in there, unless it were well insured.

Thursday, July 8, 1920

Mamma, you are mistaken about our having been invited to Pease's the day I first reached here. We were at Werts'. But you are right in saying that Mrs. Pease was good to me when I came out here, and I have never forgot it. I have remembered it specially, and have tried to pass it on to others in every way I could, especially to new arrivals, and have also paid it back to Pease's in a dozen ways. I really liked Mrs. Pease when I first came here, until I learned to know her. After they came back here after having lived a year in Iowa, I really was glad they moved on their other place and did not come next door. She is such a terrible gossip, and I can't stand that, whether the talk is about me, or someone else. She always knows everything that happens, usually before it happens, and knows about everybody's business better than they do. I remember she began to talk about Mrs. E.D. Richards soon after she got here. Mrs. R. was in very poor health when she got here, and immediately improved, and began to gain weight. Of course Mrs. Pease laid it to something else, and started talking. Now it happens that Mrs. R. is specially fond of tomatoes, and one day at some meeting she mentioned the fact, spoke of how late the season is here, and how she missed them, having been used to fresh tomatoes in Indiana for months during each summer. Well, Mrs. Pease reported that Mrs. Richards was craving tomatoes, and that anybody who craved something had to have something the matter with her, and that a baby would be sure to appear soon. Now mind you, this was just a short while after Mrs. R. got here and long before she herself knew that Mary Elizabeth was coming. Now you know it isn't pleasant for a new bride to know she is being talked about like that.

I did not know it till later—in fact, not till after we knew Cecilia was coming—but I found out that Pease's were talking about us too, and evidently had for a long time. I found that what they were saying was that John could never have any children. Mr. Pease had seen him undressed, and he knew from his own eyes that John had been shot in such a way that it would be impossible for him ever to have any children. That was the story that they spread through the neighborhood. John says that if Mr. Pease ever saw him undressed, he didn't know when it was, and that no one had ever heard him say anything about the matter himself. After we knew we were going to have a baby, I had several of the neighbors josh me, saying they had always thought I was a nice woman, and since Mrs. Pease said that John never could have any children, whose was this one going to be? Now anybody who thinks that is funny had better have it happen to her, and she will have another think about the matter.

Then one day several months after I knew Cecilia was coming, one day I felt so miserable that I could not keep my corset on. During the morning Mr. Pease came up. I could not go into retreat while he was here, for I had to do my work and get dinner for the men, and goodness only knew how long he would stay. I went about my business, taking it for granted that any man with any decency or courtesy would pay no attention to me and tend to his own business. He went home, and soon after Mrs. P. came up post-haste, on a made-up errand, and about the first thing she did was to ask me right out in so many words if I wasn't going to have a baby. By that time I was feeling better and was properly dressed again, and she couldn't tell! Of course there wasn't any use in my trying to lie about it, for it was only a matter of time, and I was too polite to tell her it wasn't any of her business. Then she said, "Well, Charlie said that Mrs. Hendricks needn't try to hide it any longer.

There was something up with her and anybody could see it."
Now I hadn't been trying to hide anything, but I thought it was
my affair and no one's else, and hadn't thought it necessary to
put up a signboard at the cross roads announcing it. But she
was sore because I hadn't hurried to tell her before anyone else
knew it. Well, that's enough of an unpleasant subject. I haven't
gossiped so much for ages as in this letter.

Tuesday, July 13, 1920

We got season tickets and have been going to Chautauqua
each evening, but not in the afternoons. The program
has been very good. There was a Bohemian band of 19 pieces
that was splendid. The leader used to be a trombone soloist
with Sousa's and Innes's bands. They played real music. They
did several descriptive pieces that were fine — "The Forge in the
Forest," and "Custer's Last Battle." In the former they had two
large anvils, and during the anvil part of the piece they turned
out all the lights, and having the anvils and hammers connected
to the electric lights, produced flashes of light each time the
hammers touched the anvils. The effect was exactly that of a
blacksmith working at his forge and anvil. The two men who
handled the hammers were perfect. The two hammers hit as
one every time. In "Custer's Last Battle" the music portrayed
the U.S. Cavalry marching and songs, and the Indian marching
and songs, and each was perfect. Then came the battle, with
real pistol shots at intervals, then the Indian celebration, and
the funeral music for the burial of Custer. Then came reinforce-
ments to the cavalry, and the routing of the Indians. The piece
ended with patriotic songs, last of all "The Star Spangled
Banner." As one encore the band played one of those trick
pieces where the leader seems to pull the notes from the various
instruments, though this leader did not move from his place.
But you know the effect — a piece full of rests, followed by little
solo parts — a single boom from a drum, a we-e-e from a fife,
or a whang from a trombone. The leader would beat the time
during the rest, very inconspicuously, and then suddenly he

would lean toward one of the men and, pointing his finger at him suddenly, make a lightning motion. At exactly the same instant would come the response from the instrument. Or when the response was to be from the drum and cymbals, several times repeated, he would wave his arms wildly up and down in the exact time that the booms had. The audience simply roared, and the players themselves were tickled all the way through.

I could talk on for pages on the good things we heard and saw, but it wouldn't mean much to you, so I guess there is no use. The program this year was really fine. Last year's was punk. The company putting on the chautauqua here this year is the Standard System. I think it is the same company as last year. Powell managed the chautauqua through the Chamber of Commerce, which guaranteed the financial end—$1400, I think. There has been such a large attendance that the local people will surely come out away ahead.

July 16, 1920

We are now living jacked up all the time. We expect to move this old house to the side of the yard tomorrow or Monday, whenever the man comes who is to do the job. In the meantime we have jacks under the house ready for it to be moved.

You ought to see Edith Rhoda and Cecilia play together. When they disagree you ought to hear the rumpus! Edith and I just let them scrap it out unless the noise gets too great.

Monday afternoon, July 19, 1920

If this letter is rather addled, don't be surprised. I am and the whole house is. In fact, it is moving about so that I feel as if I were on a fast train or an ocean steamer. You see we are moving today. The house is now almost on the new part of the basement. If I want to see what is in the basement we have been using, all I need to do is look out of the north window in the dining room, and I can see what is there. I looked out the front door a minute ago and remarked to John that we were getting along. He answered that we were almost back where we started. You see when the house was first built, it was without a basement. The next summer we made the basement, right behind where the house stood, and rolled the house back on the basement. Now we have rolled it front again and will soon be in the same place it was at first. So you see, "Merrily we roll along."

Mamma, you need not worry about my being special friends with anybody. Edith and I have talked it over, and agreed frequently that one special reason we are so glad to be near each other is that neither of us cares to be particular friends with any of the people we know. Of course we enjoy seeing them, but there isn't anyone we admire enough to make a confidante. Fortunately each of us has a husband that is friend and chum and partner, and we don't need anyone else, except to see each other (Edith and I, I mean) every little while. I was so glad to have Edith come the other day, as I was right home-sick for her, and had been wanting to go to Greybull to see her, but there just wasn't any chance to get away.

August 6, 1920

So, if I were you I would certainly not be bothered with sweated clothes as long as there was a drug store handy. Get yourself a small size bottle of Odorono—I think the advertised price is 35 cents. Use it according to directions and you won't have any trouble with sweated arms, nor will you need dress shields. I have been using it, and find it is splendid. It can't possibly hurt you if you use it as directed. You see, the reason why the underarm sweat is so much worse is that it does not have a chance to evaporate, as on the rest of the body, because the arm is held so close to the body that the air can't circulate enough to evaporate the perspiration. Being held there, it smells strong. I find that after starting with the Odorono, and using it alternate nights for about three times, after that I do not need to use it more than about once a week, and you can count on it that my work is such as to make me sweat gallons. Even with a gasoline stove, kitchen work is hot—hot dishwater, hot vessels to handle, and a hot room to work in. If I were you I would certainly invest 35 cents. The stuff can't hurt you; and your middys won't have to be washed out under the arms after you play tennis.

August 31, 1920

I must tell you we had a call yesterday from Walter and Mrs. Fowler and their 7-month-old son, Allan. They were on their way back to Billings after a trip through the Park. She looks badly. The baby is a cunning youngster. Fowler looks about the same as usual, but was dressed in one of those gold-brick sales-man kind of shepherd check suits. I'd tie up any man of mine that bought one of those suits. What tickled us about the visit was that when they drove in they asked Ralph, who happened to be in the yard, if *Mrs.* Hendricks was here. For months before they moved away, whenever Walter came over to transact any business, he came here to the house and did it with me, and never bothered to hunt John up, even after I had told him where John was. John says he hasn't the nerve to look a patriotic man in the face. I guess that Walter has sense enough to know how John would consider Walter's actions during the war. It's too bad, for Walter used to be such a lovable chap. He has changed a lot, and the last time we really visited with them, when they were first married, he swore nearly every time he opened his mouth, and used a lot of rough language. They were driving a peachy looking car yesterday, an Oakland sedan, a six-cylinder affair, with room enough in the back part inside to make a bed. When they drove in, Edith, I thought it was you. I wish it was.

Sunday, September 26, 1920

Mr. Horn expects to begin work on the house about Friday of this week. He says the carpenters will bring their own dinners, because I have as much to do right now as I care for. Besides, next week Joe will dig his potatoes, which will take at least two days, and Carrie wants to feed the men here. It is too far to take them over to her house for dinner and supper, and too hard for her to cook over there and try to bring the meal over here. I look forward with no pleasure to the ordeal, since they will have twelve men and we have three more, or fifteen, to get dinner and supper for. I think it is nonsense for farmers to stay to supper. They all have chores to do, and they had better get home and do them and eat supper at home. It is too hard on a woman to cook dinner and supper both for such crews. There is no reason why everybody shouldn't do that way, and then nobody would need to feel queer about it. Of course where there are men batching, they could be invited to supper. But married men ought to go home and eat super with their families.

Thursday, September 30, 1920

We are having real Indian summer now—cool nights, with frost, or even ice, and warm, sunny days. The sky is clear and blue as can be, and the landscape is beautiful. In the morning the eastern mountains are hazy purple, and the western ones pink. In the evening the western ranges are purple and misty and the eastern ones rosy red, with every detail standing out boldly.

The farmers here are feeling the effect of the drop in prices. It seems too bad that farm produce should always be the first thing to drop. Potatoes are now way down—about $1.10 a hundred. Carrie is just sick about it as they had counted on their potato crop to get a Ford for Little Joe to go to high school at Powell. Wheat is down to about $1.55. I guess practically everything is due for a tumble. I wonder if honey prices will go down too. The market is rather dull just now, but it is really pretty early for extracted to move. There is one good thing about extracted honey—you don't have to worry about its deteriorating if it doesn't sell at once, the way comb honey is likely to. If the extracted granulates no harm is done but if the comb honey granulates it is done for.

People around here feel pretty blue over the prospect for farm crop prices. Personally I think that nothing will do much anywhere till after the election. Both parties are holding business at a standstill in order to prove that is is the other party's fault that things are in such a bad shape. No matter which side gets in, things will immediately begin to move to prove that it was not the fault of the party that gets in. The Republicans hold big business capital and are holding it as tight as can be now, so that they can loosen up with a rush if they get into power and thus prove (?) that it was the fault of the Democrats that things were tight. Well, there isn't a great deal of choice between the parties this year—as Meredith Nicholson makes "Smith" say in his article in the October *Atlantic*, "Well, either way, the people lose." By the way, there is a splendid article by ex-president Charles Eliot of Harvard in that *Atlantic* on "The Voter's Choice in the Coming Election." The article by Nicholson is good, too. And in the Oct. 2 issue of the *Literary Digest*, page 36, there is a very interesting article on "What religion is to the nominees." The more I study the two men, the more I must conclude that Cox is a real man, and that Harding is about the biggest policy shark that you could find in the U.S. The Republicans surely made a success of finding a fine figurehead for their party—one who can always say the diplomatic thing, that will suit everybody that hears it or hears of it. The political bosses can pull the string and he jumps with every pull, but in such a graceful manner that no one can tell he is only a mannikin except by studying him. I wonder if he ever had an original thought? Cox makes me think of somebody who is likely to make breaks and mistakes, but what he does, *he* does, not the manager behind the scenes. I am really afraid that we will vote for Cox this fall.

John Hendricks, January 1899

The house at 822 East Third St.
Bloomington, Indiana

John and Cecilia Hendricks
on their wedding day,
December 30, 1913

Cecilia, Edith, and Cora Hennel, c. 1913

A typical homesteader's house in the Shoshone Valley

John Hendricks,
the beekeeper

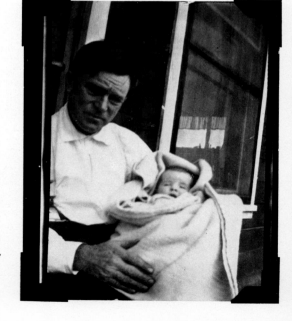

John and his first
child, Cecilia, 1916

Cecilia chases a calf away from a
newly planted tree in front of
the Hendrickses' first home

A meeting of the East End Club,
Garland, Wyoming, C. 1917

*Portrait, 1919. The sisters:
Cecilia Hendricks, Cora Hennel,
Edith Ellis. The children:
Cecilia Hendricks, Edith Rhoda
Ellis*

Joseph, Cora, and Anna Hennel, c. 1920

John and Jules, 1922

Label for honey cans

Cecilia H. Hendricks

Democratic Candidate

for

STATE SUPERINTENDENT OF PUBLIC INSTRUCTION

Campaign circular, 1922

The new house at Honeyhill, c. 1926

The home beeyard, 1926

John Hendricks
by the new shop

John Hendricks with a load of honey

The Hendricks family, 1928

The front yard at Honeyhill, c. 1929

The Hendricks family, 1929

Jules, Cecilia, Anne, Cecilia, & Cora in Bloomington, 1932

Abraham Hendricks, Anna Hendricks Long, John Hendricks, & Pacific Hendricks, Thanksgiving, 1933

Cecilia H. Hendricks, 1931

Heart Mountain

Cecilia Hendricks, June 1961

I wish you could see how our house is growing — like a beanstalk. The frame work is all up now, including the rafters. Both downstairs and upstairs sub-floors are laid. There will be paper over these floors, then lath, and then the finishing floors. Surely this ought to make warm floors, with the air space between that the lath make. The partitions upstairs are all in, and nearly all of those downstairs. The carpenters have most of the siding on the house. There will be a layer of heavy building paper over this, and then the weatherboarding, so it ought to be warm in this respect, too. They will begin lathing and roofing next Monday. The electric wiring and plumbing will also be done then. The mason has the chimneys about half done now, and will finish in about two days more. He will put in the fireplace, too, and the tile for the hearth and facing. The tile is a plain, dark red, smooth finished, but not shiny (matte) tile, 6 × 3 inches in size. I think they are very pretty, and they are as simple as anything one could get. The simpler the prettier, I think, for a tile fireplace. The grate itself is complete, like your Franklin stove, except that it sits back into the chimney and does not have the back polished.

We are sending you enclosed a couple of invitations. Mamma, now you can get excited, as you started to do a couple weeks ago. This time it's really so, I am very thankful to state.

[A small envelope was enclosed, addressed "For All the Family." In it a calling card read: "You are hereby invited to visit our new house any time after January 1 and its new inhabitant any time after June 1."]

Ted came up last night to have a meeting of the officers of the investment company that Carr had a lot of stock in. Ted has wanted for some time to get the matter settled up, so he could get his attorney fees and cash for his one share of stock, and so we could get something out of the shares that we got from Carr. He got everything in shape last night, and we will be able to get something out of the shares at last. In order to settle the whole business Ted offered, with John's ready consent, to arbitrate the suit the Allen Oil Company made against Carr's shares of stock, so we will divide with them. They really lost more on Carr than we did, and it will be cheaper and easier for us to compromise now than to let them go ahead suing and suing and carry the matter on through other courts, for they would appeal if they lost in the lower court. Anyway, getting even something is better than nothing.

On the train to Greybull
November 3, 1920

We are on our way to Greybull as per schedule. I am anxious to see E and find out all the news about you all after her visit home. I telephoned her yesterday and asked her if she had been home long enough to have company and she assured me she had. I told her I wanted to give her time enough to get acquainted with Ted again and she said she had. So we put a "clo" or two in our suitcase and a quart each of milk and cream and a couple dressed chickens in our bag, and started this morning.

I am sorry but not surprised at the result of the election yesterday. How did you enjoy your first experience at the polls? I wonder if there are still people who object to the vote for women because it interferes with their domestic or charitable duties. Yesterday I voted, and I also baked bread and rolls, cooked beans and roasted two chickens so John would have something to eat while I was gone. I cooked meat and gravy and made cabbage slaw and took them to Garland for the Ladies Aid dinner. I put new collar and cuffs on Cecilia's coat of that lovely plush you sent, and partly made a wool dress for her, enough so Edith could put some embroidery on it. I did some typewriting and got a meal or two, sandwiched in, and packed our suitcase and bag for this morning. So if anyone says voting interferes, I say it doesn't.

We are so glad you are glad over our news. Yes, the order is the same as before — for twin boys, but we will be just as satisfied with girls. John says all right, Co, you can have his share in whatever comes, except the right to name if it it's a boy. He named it 22 years ago at San Juan, after — to him — the greatest hero there.

Greybull, Wyoming, November 3, 1920

Edith and I have talked such a streak ever since we have been together that we haven't had time for much else. It has been almost like getting to be back at 822 to be here with Edith since she is just back from being with you. I can't say that it takes away the desire to come for myself, but since that seems to be impossible this year, why this is the next best thing.

November 9, 1920

Cecilia and I got home last night in about the worst blizzard we have had this season. When we left Greybull it was snowing. The storm let up for a while but we ran into it again about Kane and from there on it got worse all the time. It was simply awful at Frannie. You know you have to walk about a mile from the Pullman to the station. The snow was almost blinding, and the usual forty mile an hour wind at Frannie was at least double that speed. It was all we could do to walk, what with the wind and the snow and the loose cinders in the path with loose soft snow on them. When we got on the train to come the rest of the way, the wind was so strong that the coaches swayed sideways as much when they were standing still as when they were running. John met us all right with heavy coats and plenty of robes, and we got home all right. It was pretty chilly as long as we were facing west, as the wind was from the straight north, and hit us in the right ear. But after we turned south it was not so bad. It really was not so cold except for the harshness of the wind. However, our radiator was frozen up enough that the water would not run out when we got here, and John had to leave the engine running a while to get it thawed out.

We certainly had a nice time at your house, E and E, and are so glad we could make the visit. The various things that happened will be pleasure again when I think them over here at home. I certainly enjoyed the salads we had while I was there, which was at least twice a day, and sometimes I ate salad for breakfast! You had all the things I like best — white or red grapes, celery, head lettuce, and pork chops!

Cecilia has been coughing a good bit since we are back. I think maybe facing the wind at Frannie made her cough worse, but it may be just the general storminess we had met all along the way. We are a little bit alarmed for fear it might be whooping cough showing up, as I told you she was exposed about three weeks ago.

November 18, 1920

Cecilia sure has a nasty case of the whooping cough. She coughs hard when she does cough, but does not cough often during the day. When she lies down she seems to be worse, and always has a bad coughing time about half an hour or an hour after she goes to bed. I think I shall see to it that milk is all she eats for supper. Edith, I sure hope E.R. won't show any signs of whooping cough.

Sunday, November 21, 1920

Edith, I am sorry as can be to hear that Edith Rhoda has been coughing, and that she was exposed to the diptheria last Sunday. A double dose like that is more than anyone would want to expose a child to. I am sending you in this mail some of the Luyties' Whooping Cough medicine, a new bottle of which came in yesterday's mail. Be sure to use it, as I am sure it will help, and it certainly can't do any harm. Please keep us advised as to Edith Rhoda, as I am more anxious about her than I can say. No matter how much I wanted to see you, I never would have made the visit if I had thought that Cecilia would take the whooping cough while we were there. If I had only waited till the time I originally planned, she would have started with it before we could have gone. And now see what I did! It makes me sick.

It doesn't seem to me that there used to be so much childhood disease sickness when we were growing up. If there was, I don't remember it. Now every year the country around here is full of it. Right now around here—Garland and Powell—there are mumps, whooping cough, scarlet fever, and chicken pox. Sometimes I think the only thing to do when one has children is just to stay at home and go nowhere. But in your case and mine that wouldn't do any good after all, for the Bygren children brought the whooping cough here and we took it to you.

The plasterer has about half a day's work and the first coat will be on everywhere. Then he puts on the smoothing coat, though we will not have the "skim" effect but just the sanded effect, which is not rough and yet not slickly smooth.

I think the whole house is so nice I can hardly wait for you to see it. Do you remember how you were wishing when you came up the road the first time that the Roach house would turn out to be ours, as it was finished and ours was not so complete looking? Just wait till you see the new house, and you will agree that it was worth waiting for. We are surely glad we can get it, and feel like Thanksgiving every time we look at it.

I must tell you something funny. I have laughed until I don't know what to do about it. Talk about literary criticism! When Mrs. Richards was here the other day, we were talking about O'Henry, which both Mr. and Mrs. Richards enjoy very much. Mrs. Richards said that one day she happened to mention something about O'Henry to Mrs. Murray and Mrs. M. immediately stiffened her back and announced that she would not allow a set or a volume of O'Henry to be in her house. Of course Mrs. R. was interested and asked why. And the answer was this: "Because O'Henry is so nasty." She thought no decent person should ever be caught looking into a volume! I racked my brains and racked them to remember a single story that might have this criticism attached to it, and though I have read about all there are, I couldn't think of one. I finally asked Mrs. Richards if she could cite an example, and she said that all she could suggest was that Mrs. Murray must have referred to some of the stories in which girls trade their virtue for fine clothes and high life. "But," went on Mrs. Richards, "That is life, that isn't anything nasty." And as we went on to say, O'Henry always leaves the reader with the idea that the choice was a decidedly poor one. And he never does go into sordid or nasty details. Isn't that rich? And to think, Cora, that a modest young lady like you would give such a set of books to an innocent che-ild as a christening gift! My, My! And to think further that the supposedly decent parents of the aforesaid che-ild have read and re-read the volumes, lent them to the neighbors, and can hardly wait till the child is old enough to enjoy them herself! It's a funny world we live in, for sure. However, when you remember that the Murrays would never let their 20-year-old niece Naomi go to a movie without knowing the subject of the picture, for fear it might be something that a young girl should not see, you aren't so surprised.

Tuesday, November 30, 1920

Go, you are clear off on your guess as to name. I did not mean to suggest that you could guess it, even if my statement did imply that, for I doubt if you ever heard of the man John admired so much. He came from an old famous military family, which is still well known in American military affairs.

The man in particular that John admired in the Spanish War was in the quartermaster service. His unit was the only one that was properly taken care of in regard to supplies, and not only that, but the work was done in advance so that when the actual fighting began, he asked permission to get into that. He was allowed to do so by the commanding officer. When he got near the top of the hill (San Juan) his men found a wounded Spanish officer and for some reason or other, probably because he was still trying to fight, the men were about to kill the Spaniard. But Ord wouldn't let them kill a wounded man, even if was a Spaniard — that was before the time of the Germans — and the men desisted. I suppose they searched him, or at least would have been expected to, but it appears that they did not get the Spaniard's revolver away, for just as soon as Ord started on, the Spaniard shot him in the back and killed him. John thought that being killed after one had saved a life was about as near a hero's death as one could imagine, and that, with Ord's particular ability in doing his own work, made John admire him very much. His full name was Julius G. Ord—G, not C. It wasn't Julius Caesar.

December 16, 1920

Dear Pater,

The letter with the check has arrived. We can't begin to tell you how pleased we are with your gift. The check itself is such a big one that it fairly took our breath away. We are even more touched, though, at your remembering us.

We have been discussing what we will do with the money. John suggested that we use enough of it to furnish one bedroom. We will get a good bed and spring and mattress, and a chair or two and a rug, and maybe a dresser or chiffonier. Then if we have any left we will get a rocker or two for the living room. Fortunately, furniture prices are dropping so that the hundred dollars will buy a whole lot now. We had a catalogue the other day in which a lot of items of furniture had the price cut almost in two. We think we will wait a little longer before ordering as prices are still dropping. When a factory like Showers has to shut down because it is overstocked, you know prices will be dropped to help move the stock on hand quickly.

Cecilia is as delighted as her parents over your gift and has talked a great deal about it. When I opened the letter (I knew from your handwriting on the envelope it was something special) I was so touched I couldn't keep back some tears. John lent me his shoulder for a minute. Cecilia does not like for me to cry and she immediately began to ask what was the matter with mamma. We explained to her. Many times since she has said, "Aren't we glad our dear Grandpa is so good to us? He likes us so much it made mamma cry when she got the letter. We love Grandpa, don't we, mamma?"

Lovingly yours,

A week from tomorrow is Christmas. My, how the time does fly. I guess the men who are working in the house wish it were about ten days yet, for they have made up their minds that they will have the downstairs done in time for us to be in by Christmas, and they are nearly breaking their necks to do so. Most of the built-in work is done now, except the book case and colonnade in the living room. The buffet in the dining room, the paneling there, and the kitchen cabinets in the kitchen are done. The kitchen floor is laid and scraped, ready for the finishing. The men are laying the oak floor in the living room, hall, and office this afternoon. My, but the house looks prettier to me every time I step in it and see something more done. Little did I ever think that I would have such a house for our very own. John says it is too fine for him, and that he guesses he will have to stay in the old house, as he never has had such a fine place to live in. I told him I guessed anybody that worked hard enough to get such a house deserved to live in it. I wish you could see the dining room. It is panelled about five feet high with the fir paneling, and fir has such a lovely grain. It gives the room such a rich look and is so different from the rest of the house, that when you sit in the living room and look into the dining room the house does not seem at all monotonous the way some houses do. The kitchen is such a lovely room, too, large and well arranged. All the working part is at one end, so that in reality as far as work is concerned, the kitchen is small and convenient and compact. But at the other side is a lot of space where the babies can play and have their things, and you know a child will never play in a room by itself but wants to be in the room where its mother is. And somehow it seems that I have to spend a good deal of time in the kitchen.

Sunday, December 26, 1920

We had the best Christmas we have ever had. We talked about it yesterday and remarked that each Christmas is better than the one before, though each one when it is here seems everything that one could desire. We stayed at home all day, as one should on Christmas, and just had a good time together.

Christmas morning Cecilia woke about an hour earlier than usual, as was to be expected. One of the stories in her reader is about a little girl who spent Christmas with her cousin Dora at the lighthouse. The evening before Christmas they discuss how Santa Claus will get there, and Dora assures May that he always does. Next morning when they find the toys, May exclaims, "He came, Dora, he came!" Well, when Cecilia woke up yesterday morning, she grunted once and then was wide awake. "Mamma," she cried, "he came, he came. I know he did, because I heard the prancing and pawing of the reindeer on the roof during the night." Strange to say, she did not want to get up, but just to crawl over in our bed and stay with us.

Some time ago I said something about how nice it would be if we would have a little baby. She took up the idea at once, though she did not say much. About a week or ten days after that she came to me and said, "Mamma, do you think God has any little babies now?" I told her I thought maybe he did. She wanted to know if I thought he would let us have one, and I told her I thought so. She pondered a minute, and said, "Well, we'll have to write Him a letter and ask for one." I explained that we did not write letters to God, but talked to him in our prayers. Several days after that she crawled into my bed one morning before I got up, and began to talk again about a baby. She said, "Wouldn't it be nice if we had a baby—a little girl, just like me?" I made some answer, and she was still for a while, evidently thinking. Then she said, "No, it would be nicer if we had a boy. We have one girl. I think we ought to have a little baby boy." And ever since, she has talked about the boy we are going to have. Now I have really never told her that we were expecting a baby, but merely answered questions as she asked them, and have never said positively that we would not have a baby. Well, all this leads to what she said yesterday morning. After she had been in our bed a while, John decided it was time for him to get up, so we said our prayers. As she always does when she happens to be in bed with us or awake in her bed when we say our prayers, she folded her hands and kept still as a mouse. After we were done, she said, "O, you forgot to tell God to send us the little boy baby." So we all had to fold our hands again and add a postscript to our matins.

Well, to resume my interrupted account of Christmas morning. You demanded a complete account of how Cecilia acted, mamma, so I am talking thus at length to answer your inquiry. After John got up, Cecilia decided that she wanted to do so also. She went out into the living room, and I heard her say (I was not up yet) "Well, there is my train. There is the doll house. Well, there is the doll. Well, there is the tree. Well, there are the packages." Then John gave her her stocking, which had candy, nuts, and an orange in it, as she had wondered about the day before. Then she got excited. She fairly flew back into the bedroom and shouted, "Mamma, mamma, there *is* an orange in it. There *is* an orange in it!" And from then on till the last bundle was opened, after we had all got up and dressed, she was never still a second.

Thursday, December 30, 1920

We are moving. We really expect to get most of it done tomorrow, but started a few things today. I put up curtains in the dining room, bedroom, and kitchen — which rooms were done, and put up the pictures in the living room. My how different a room looks with a few pictures in it. Our wood-work is all brown, so I am very glad I was sensible enough when I was collecting pictures, framed, to get all brown ones, or be lucky enough to have that kind given me as presents. The pictures are all brown except the two water colors by Florence Ellis, one that Ted gave me for a wedding present, and the other that Florence herself gave me, and they are framed in gold. The two gold pictures are just enough to relieve the monotony of the all-brown ones. You ought to see how suitable the big pictures of "The Hanging of the Crane" that John's brother gave us for a wedding present, looks over our new mantel.

I wish you were here this morning to behold us in all the pleasure of our new house. We are in, although not entirely settled. I do not have all the closets arranged yet, nor all the clothes moved over, but the main part of the downstairs is all done, including the curtains. My, it does look nice, at least to us, and we feel as if we will split if some of you don't come soon to see us. We went to sleep in the new house last night, and woke up in the new year here. We thought it was very nice to start the new year in the new house.

We are using the gasoline stove now for cooking, and will for several days till we can get the range fixed up as we want it. It seems to me that about half the dirt in a kitchen comes from the ashes in the range, so we will have the range fixed so that instead of having to take out the ashes in the ashpan in the usual way, they will shoot down into the basement. John will use a piece of soil pipe, which is an iron pipe four inches in diameter. This will be fitted into an opening of the same size in the bottom of the ash compartment of the range, with a lid to cover the opening except when ashes are to be emptied. In the basement will be some sort of fireproof receptacle to receive the ashes. In this way we won't have any ashes at all in the house. Furnace, fireplace, and kitchen range ashes will all be in the basement and can all be taken care of from there at once. When Mr. Larsen made the fireplace, he got a lid from an old stove and fitted that into the concrete floor of the fireplace. To empty the ashes you just lift up the lid and push them down the hole. Edith, we haven't yet installed your suggestion about coal for the range, but who knows what inventions will arrive in the course of the next few years. (Edith suggested that since we disposed of the ashes so easily we ought to arrange a chute from above through which the coal could be scooted into the stove without our having to handle it.)

John and Mr. Voss put in the automatic control for the furnace yesterday. You know how the thing works—when the temperature gets to whatever point you set the thermometer (68, we set it) the furnace automatically closes or opens. That is, when the thermometer gets to two degrees lower, or 66, the draft is opened and the check is closed, and when the heat is 70 the draft is automatically closed and the check is opened. It sounds almost uncanny to hear that thing working in the basement when no one is down there. We have a clock attachment, too, so that we can have the heat shut off at night, and it will automatically open up the draft and start the furnace at whatever hour we set it for in the morning. So far as I know we are the only ones around here who invested in the automatic device. It costs about $25 or $30 but is surely worth it. With this arrangement, John has to look at the furnace about twice a day, and the heat is uniform all day long, all over the house.

Tuesday, January 11, 1921

John just got back from Byron where he went to get the flour made from the wheat we took down some weeks ago. We bought 20 bushels of hard wheat at a dollar a bushel and took it to the little mill at Byron to have it ground. The mill gives you 31 pounds of flour and 12 of bran (which is bran and ship-stuff mixed) for each 100 pounds of wheat you take down. At this rate the flour is a great deal cheaper than what we can buy in the stores. Besides, we think it is better. What with 11 sacks of flour (48-pound sacks) and the supply of canned stuff and smoked meat in the basement, and the fresh eggs and milk every day, we could go a long time without ever seeing the inside of a store.

Monday, January 16, 1921

We drafted a letter last night to send to our representatives in Congress, and John is taking it around today for the other beekeepers to sign. Mr. Rauchfuss wrote us recently that honey from Central America, a good table honey, is being laid down in New Orleans at 7 cents a pound. To compete with that price, at this distance from wholesale markets, we would get about five cents a pound net for our extracted honey. Mr. Rauchfuss suggested that we write to our men in the Senate and House and urge them to see that a tariff was put on foreign honey.

Sunday, February 6, 1921

If you had done as much typing as I have yesterday and today I am sure you wouldn't expect me to write more than howdy and goodbye in this letter. You see, some ignoramus—or someone who wants a sinecure—has introduced a bill into the state legislature providing for a state apiary inspector whose salary should be paid by beekeepers to the tune of fifty cents a colony per year tax. Naturally we professional beekeepers don't care to pay out everything we earn for nothing in return, so we have been working for three or four days to do all we could to oppose the bill. We prefer that *no* state inspector bill be passed as the present county inspector bill gives us all the protection we need, or at least has done so here in Park County, but in case we can't kill the bill outright we want a real bill passed. The proposed bill #121 makes the position of state inspector entirely detached from any other office in the state. All states that have good inspection bills make the state entomologist or some other similar official state apiary inspector with a small increase in salary or no increase at all. There is absolutely no need of an expense to this state of $10,000 a year and to the beekeepers of 50 cents per colony for no better service than we are now getting.

I have talked and thought and typed bee legislation till I can think of hardly anything else. I know I have typed—counting carbons—at least a hundred pages in the past two days. I spent at least four hours at the machine today. However, in our new office it is a pleasure to work. You ought to see how svelte everything is. It is almost done now, except putting together the big office chair that you gave us when we were home.

John heard this morning that the state apiary inspector bill had been killed, presumably in committee.

Co, I can't say that I like the name Julius as well as I do a good many other names, but it had never occurred to me as being Jewish. The original Julius O. certainly wasn't a Jew, and there couldn't be any greater distinction than that between Jew and Roman. Now the names Isaac and Jacob and Levi would sound Jewish, and yet, strange to remark, of all the Jacobs I know none of them is a Jew, and I know a number of Ikes who would be ready to fight if you suggested they were Jews. Likewise Levi. I know four out here and not a Jew among them. As I said, I don't especially care for the name Julius, but John does, and he cares especially for the man whose name it was. After all, why anyone of us likes or dislikes a particular name is such a queer matter that one can hardly do any figuring on that basis. For instance, Edith and I like the name Anne, and you and Ted don't. You remember that Edith wanted to name Edith Rhoda Anne for her two grandmothers, and you and Ted wouldn't hear to it? Why do Edith and I like Anne and you and Ted not? John never liked very much the name Cecilia; and I have always liked it. Yet he did not object to my naming our first baby that name. Talking again of Anne, if our new baby is a girl, I have thought of calling her Anne Caroline, for her two grandmothers. But probably the rest of the family won't like that name at all. I have always admired our Bloomington neighbor Mrs. Johnston for the names she gave her daughters — Mary, Katherine, Anne, and Elizabeth, four as pretty names as are in the list. But of course if they had been called Mamie, Katie, Annie, and Lizzie, the names would not be so pretty. Coming back to where I started, I am sorry you don't like the name Julius, but it seems to me that when a man has waited 23 years to get to name his son (if he gets to now!) he ought to be able to use the name he has picked out all this time, anything short of Abimelach or Jedediah or Pete. So if the new baby is a boy, I am afraid he will be called Julius Ord. If it is two boys, it will be Julius Ord and John Hennel. If it is a girl —

well, the matter is not all settled, and suggestions are invited. And especially if it is two girls.

Friday, March 11, 1921

We had a good meeting of our revived E.E.E.* Club at Bygren's yesterday. There were not so many people there, but we had a fine meeting. Our subject for the afternoon was lawns and gardens, anything except vegetables. We will take up vegetables next time. I took with me the sister of Mrs. Osborne (the folks living on the Roach place). The sister, Mrs. Teeples, homesteaded at the south end of Pryor Mountains in *1896*, and has lived in this country ever since. She now lives near Bridger. Her mother, aged 81, has just finished the residence on a claim near the *top* of Pryor Mountains, and Mrs. Teeples went there each summer with her mother during the necessary residence. One somehow just naturally has the idea that the Mormons always grew in this country — sort o' like the sage brush. It sounds queer to hear her talk about things "before the Mormons moved into the Big Horn Valley." She told the women yesterday that they didn't know what pioneering was. She said that when she came to Wyoming 25 years ago, she was 3½ miles from the nearest neighbor, and that there were only three women in the entire community. She said they would go miles and miles to get to a meeting such as the one we had yesterday. She said they often went 15 miles to church, and then the crowd consisted mostly of the ones they took along or gathered up on the way. When they first started the town of Lovell, the Mormons and a community protestant church both had services in the school house, the only available building. She said the Mormons, being more numerous, used the large room, and the Protestants used the ell part. She said "We sang our loudest, but they were larger in number and could usually drown us out."

Cora, in the March 12 issue of the *Digest*, there is an article on plays, in which is this statement: "The plays of Eugene O'Neill are, in my judgment, the most original and significant

---

*East End Extension.

things that have been done, in dramatic form, on this side of the Atlantic; and George Cram Cook, an adept of the same school, has recently shown that his earnestness is not unseconded by talent." Do you know anything about O'Neill? His work is evidently quite recent, as his name is new to me. "Beyond the Horizon" is mentioned as being "written with stern sobriety, yet with deep poetic feeling; and the way in which the love of the brothers survives the disaster that befalls them seems to me one of the most touching things in drama." As this criticism was written by no less a critic than Mr. William Archer, it carries great weight. Read the article for yourself—it is called "New York 'Side Shows' " and speaks of "little theatre" plays.

Tuesday, March 22, 1921

No mamma, I do not intend to send Cecilia to school for several years yet, unless things turn out differently than they are now. I know one neighbor who did not intend to send her second little girl until she was seven or eight, and twins happened along when she was six, so that the mother in self defense had to send the youngster to school so she would have time to take care of the rest of the family! However, until there is a real primary teacher at Garland or Star School, or at least the semblance of one, I shall teach Cecilia at home, even if we have to do without things cooked and live on Post Toasties to do so. The primary teacher at Garland is the nicest old grandma you ever saw—she really has a whole caboodle of grand-children. She had not taught for about half a century and then started in again. Her ideas of teaching are as old-fashioned as can be, and the trouble is they are bad old fashion. For instance, she has picked up somewhere one of those awful litho-graphed marriage certificates, given by old Justice of the Peace Adams to a young couple he married years ago at Garland. It has clasped hands and awful looking angels and blue roses and every other awful thing one can imagine. Now she has that pasted up in her primary room as a sample of art. I don't care to have my children instructed in the principles of art in that way. Carrie visited her room one day when she got a class up at the blackboard and let them stay there until recess — more than an hour later. The children don't learn a thing except perhaps a little reading, and Cecilia will probably be able to read long before she goes to school, or is of school age. I intend to get the regular state outline and see that Cecilia gets what the school program calls for — and then I will teach her the things a youngster ought to know. I don't want her rushed so fast. The main trouble with the grades hereabout — Garland, Powell, and the country schools — is that they are always letting children take two grades in one year, and the poor youngsters don't know anything of either grade.

Wednesday, May 11, 1921

You will be interested in hearing that the Garland bank is closed. John has not heard the details. He said he has an idea that the trouble is bad loans rather than insolvency. However, if one had his checking account all in a bank that closed up, it would be rather inconvenient not to be able to write any checks or get any money. When John heard about the bank, he came into the house and said, "My, I wish we hadn't built a house and had the money on hand that we used to build with." Of course I wanted to know what he would do with it, and he said buy a bank. Well, it would be nice to own a bank, but one couldn't very well live in it, especially if it were located in Garland, so I guess it's about as well that we built the house. It would be nice, though, to have enough ready money on hand now to buy that bank at Garland. I imagine it could be bought at a pretty good rate now.

Friday, May 13, 1921

We have heard some more things about the bank at Garland. Mr. Sanders, the Garland merchant, told John the other day that the trouble was "gross mismanagement of funds," and that they thought by the end of this year the bank would be able to pay out 90 cents on the dollar. Mr. Werts told Joe this morning that Dabbs, the bank manager, had lent *himself* $12,000. He didn't say what Dabbs was supposed to have done with the money; but Dabbs has been buying farms during the past two years, and most likely that is where the money went. Mr. Sanders said that Harry Collins, who is president of the bank, was almost a raving maniac the other day when the facts came out about the management of the bank and he found what the actual conditions were. Well, if he was president, it looks as if he ought to have known before things happened what was going on.

May 26, 1921

Our garden is coming nicely now. Things are growing fast since it has turned warmer. I am so glad John is interested and knows how to make and take care of a garden. I haven't done anything to this one except look after the seed and tell him where to plant things. I didn't even plant much of the seed. I hear so many women say their husbands don't know how to do anything in a garden. So many have told me the past week that their gardens aren't plowed yet. I think that is a mistake. Of course it is important for a man to get his crop in, but when one considers how much of one's living can come out of a garden, it is a mistake to let the garden go until everything else about the farm is done. If I had to buy the vegetables—or their substitutes—that we raise and can every year, I am sure it would cost a whole lot. One can keep grocery bills away down by having a good garden. I know one family around here that has five children and the two parents, and last year they had to buy everything they ate, except potatoes, and, I believe, tomatoes. The two oldest boys are 14 and 12 years old, too, plenty big enough to do most of the work in a garden. One day's work at the start from the man and them would be enough to put the ground in shape, and important as every day is early in the spring on a farm, one day sooner or later in putting in a big field of grain wouldn't make a great deal of difference. John has our garden laid out so that he can do all the work between rows with the horse cultivator and in the rows with the Planet

Jr., and that means a saving in labor. One evening after supper and one morning before breakfast, and he goes through the whole garden with the Planet, Jr. I couldn't do it, but a man can, without feeling it is very hard work.

Wednesday, June 1, 1921

The Garland bank failure is still town talk. Mrs. Lovercheck told me yesterday that poor Mrs. Dabbs didn't know a thing about it, nor would he tell her anything even after she found out something was wrong. The first she knew was when she went down town and saw the notice on the bank, and had to get her information on the street. Even then he would not tell her anything about what was really the matter. Mrs. L. and Mrs. Dabbs broke down under the strain and they had to have a doctor with her the whole next night. We have heard that Dabbs was arrested on the charge of having accepted deposits after he knew the bank was insolvent, but that no one thought he could be convicted on that charge. Mrs. L. told me yesterday that it was said Dabbs kept "dummy" notes in his files. After he lent the money to himself, he would, for instance, have in his files a note to someone else, some substantial farmer around here, so that when the examiner came around there was nothing apparently wrong. Of course if they can prove that, I guess Brother Dabbs will have some explaining to do.

Friday, June 3, 1921

The nurse, Mrs. Ingram, called me up last night and wanted to know if it would be safe for her to go to a picnic on Heart Mountain today. I told her I thought it would, as we did not expect to have our party till Sunday. When I told her that we nearly sent for her last Sunday night, she said we would most likely need her next Monday or Tuesday. However, I still hold out for Sunday, and you be likely to hear that Julius will arrive Sunday night or early Monday morning. I have been feeling so well today, better than for a long time. I don't have the trouble with heartburn or the pressure on my stomach, so I am sure the end is nearly here. I am sure I will get along all right, now that I have about got rid of this pesky cold.

Powell Wyo 355P June 4 1921

Joseph Hennel—822 East 3 St Bloomington Ind
Julius Ord arrived safely Cecilia is doing fine
John Hendricks

Tuesday, June 7, 1921

I thought maybe you would like to see my hand again. I wish you could all see your new relative. He has the blackest hair and, as yet, dark blue eyes. The nurse says he will bleach out and that by the time he is toddling he will be a cotton top. He has a nice big head, which is not shaped at all like Cecilia's, it seems to me, as it is narrower across the forehead, and longer. It may be a different shape in a few days, more like hers. But he does not look at all like her, but like John's youngest brother's boy.

I think we got along fine for the whole performance. Naturally, it wasn't much of a picnic for me all day Saturday, but it might have been worse. I was sick at my stomach and was a "whay-all" in the bathroom about a quarter of three. Then they put me back to bed—I had been lying down for a couple hours—and the baby arrived at 3:15. For the next 18 hours I was perhaps more miserable than I had been. I indulged in a nervous chill that nearly shook me to pieces, and had pains right along. I was also nauseated most of the time. The worst of all, tho, was a pain between my shoulders, like a sharp tooth ache. It was fierce. By bathing the spot with chloroform several times during the night I got about two hours rest. During Sunday morning things eased up a little and I felt pretty fair Sunday afternoon. But that evening I had another nervous chill, tho it is hardly right to call it a chill as it was really a "hot." When Dr. Graham came Sunday evening he left something to make me sleep so I got a pretty good rest Sunday night and have been all right since. I think one trouble was we had so much company Sunday. Dr. Graham ordered no visitors, so the people who have come since have been shown the baby and invited to come again.

I haven't had a bit of fever, even today, when the milk came in full flow, and the baby has been nursing regularly for 36 hours now. I don't feel so much as if a steam roller had gone over me any more, tho I suspect I shall be glad to be still for a while. I am sure we are going to get along splendidly. Carrie is a fine nurse.

Friday, June 10, 1921

Our new baby is almost six days old, or will be this afternoon. It doesn't seem that I have been lying here that long already. I am glad it is, however, for now the worst is all over and I am feeling like a different person. The baby is doing splendidly and is good as can be. He sleeps most of the time, as a baby should. He nurses only about every four hours, instead of 2½ or 3, because he sleeps so much, and of course we won't wake him up for that. From the looks of me I would have enough to feed twins. John says the baby ought to thrive, as such breastworks ought to be a strong fortification to any child.

Cecilia is beginning to be herself again. The excitement and the baby and my being in bed were too much for her. She did not get to bed at night until about two hours after her bedtime and was always waked up an hour or so too early in the morning. She is taking a good sleep this morning, as it is nearly eight and she is still asleep. She is proud as can be of the baby, tho she still insists his name is Max. If he had been twins it would have been Max & Bruce, like the two Murray boys. However, she calls him Julius when she speaks of him.

Tuesday, June 21, 1921

What do you think I did this morning? I went to Powell, Julius and I both. Several folk who spoke to us thought I was pretty spry to get away from home before the baby was three weeks old, but it seems to me that I stayed at home quite a while. Maybe it was because I did not get away for some weeks beforehand that it seems long. I enjoyed the ride very much, and since John has overhauled the car it rides so smoothly and so quietly. You would think you were riding in a big car and not in a Ford. When we get the new top on it, it will be like a new car. In fact, since it has been painted, Cecilia calls it our new car.

Folk here sure do a lot of visiting when there is a new baby. Almost everybody has been to see us now. I was amused at the nurse, Mrs. Ingram. She said she never saw such a country for people to visit where there was a new baby. She said this was the first place she ever saw where the men went to call on a woman when she was confined! Well, it isn't quite as bad as it sounds, and yet I was really embarrassed a couple of times when I was in bed to have a neighbor woman bring her husband into my bedroom to see the new baby. Of course it was our fault for having the crib in the bedroom and the baby in the crib. But nevertheless I felt queer to have a more-or-less strange man walk into the room where I was in bed. You needn't worry, mamma, about our spoiling the baby to show him to visitors. When someone wants to see him, we just steer the person to the crib, with the statement, "Of course the baby is asleep, as usual." And I never offer to take him up, unless he is awake and it is time to do so. In fact, I had one man say recently when I said the baby was asleep, "Well, often they look better when they are asleep than when they are awake." How's that for candor? However, he said it *before* he saw Julius.

Some time ago I wrote to the county library to see if they had "The Americanization of Edward Bok." I told the librarian that if they didn't they ought to get it as it was a book every library ought to have. She wrote back that they did not have it but would try to get it. Yesterday she sent it to me. It certainly is interesting. If you want to read something more interesting than fiction, get this book. Bok came to this country with his parents, from Holland, when he was six years old, and when he started to school at once after arriving, did not know a word of English. During the years he was growing up he became acquainted with scores of famous men — Grant, Hayes, Sherman, Longfellow, Emerson, Holmes, Phillips, etc., and he tells in the book about meeting them and knowing them. I want to read instead of getting my work done. While I was hulling peas this noon John read me a chapter describing a visit at Eugene Field's house, when James W. Riley, Opie Read, and various other literary and dramatic lights were present, and the practical jokes Field played on those present. Incidentally, Bok shows how a lad with determination can get somewhere.

Sunday, July 17, 1921

I am sure you will all be glad to hear that Murray's have the baby girl they have wanted so long. She is a cunning little thing, very unlike the boys. Friday Mrs. Murray cooked dinner for the men who were putting up hay. She felt queer a time or two during the morning but not much different than she had been feeling for about six weeks. She finished up the dinner and had it ready to put on the table, when she began to feel rather badly. She told Mr. Murray that if he would put dinner on the table she would lie down a little while. By two o'clock or a few minutes after, it was all over and the baby had arrived! None of them could believe it, for Mrs. M. had never got by in less than sixteen hours before. Carrie was rather dreading the affair, for she had such a hard time at Lovercheck's and at Richards', and a long time here. Carrie was there only about twenty minutes and the doctor about ten minutes before the baby arrived.

Friday afternoon's mail brought a note from Ted saying Edith would be up on that evening's train. She and E.R. came all right, and next morning Edith and John and Cecilia met the train and got Cora. I stayed at home to make a fire so it would be warm in the house when they got here. It is rather chilly in the early morning and I was afraid Co might get cool riding home from Garland. You can imagine how we talked all day Saturday. Cora's trunk came on the noon train Saturday. They went over in the afternoon and got it, and she unpacked it on the back porch and then took it and her things upstairs — that is, what was left after she had given all of us the things you had sent us. Saturday evening Co and E and the children were out in the yard and suddenly we heard them shout, "There is Ted," and sure enough in he drove. So you see we had a regular reunion over Sunday. This morning they all went to Greybull. Cora did not care much to go away so soon after she got here, but there really was no use in her paying railroad fare from here to Greybull when she had a chance to ride down in the car.

We have had an aeroplane in the neighborhood. It has been at Greybull, Edith said, and Saturday afternoon came to Powell, sailing almost over our house. It was the first one John had ever seen in flight, and I am glad he got to see it. It stayed at Powell till Sunday afternoon and then went to Cody. The pilot takes people up for a ride at $10 for about ten minutes.

Cora says that when people ask about our baby she says his name is J.O. Hendricks. When they want to know what the J.O. stands for she says she tells them "Just Ord-inary." However, since she has seen the young gentleman I am inclined to think she has changed her opinion.

Friday night I had to attend the meeting of the School Board as the chairman of the committee from the E.E.E. Club. Talk about a cordial reception! We were just a little bit leery as to what the members of the School Board would do and say when we appeared, but we found they simply fell on our necks. In fact, after we had said our little say, one of them (Mr. Graham) announced that he wanted to ask us a few questions, which he proceeded to do, and we answered them. Also, he suggested that this committee from the women's club should be continued, and should meet with the Board and the teachers just before school starts to talk over a number of things connected with the schools. So we were not only received, but given a long lease on life! Of course when we withdrew we thanked the Board for hearing us, and were thanked for coming and assured that anything we had to say at any time would be gladly heard. My own opinion, from this experience, is that the Board is glad to find out a few things and ready to correct things when brought to its attention, but that, man-like, they know very little of what is really going on. Well, if they invite us to meet with them and the teachers, maybe we can open their eyes to a number of things.

August 9, 1921

We have found out from authority that our baby's name is Jules and not Julius. We wrote to the "Army and Navy Register" to find out, and had a lovely letter from them yesterday. They gave us the correct name—Jules Garesche Ord. We think that Jules Garesche Ord Hendricks would be a little too much of a muchness, as Pater would say, so we will omit the Garesche. The letter said that there are relatives of Lieut. Ord in Washington, and the editor had taken the liberty of sending our letter to them, realizing that they would appreciate the manner in which we had honored the memory of this officer. He also stated that he regarded the incident of enough interest to warrant its mention in the "Register," which is the United States Military Gazette. It's too bad we didn't find out before the baby came, but we would have felt foolish writing when we didn't know whether the baby would be a girl or a boy. However, we know now, and the baby's name is Jules. Personally, I like that better than Julius. John says the men called Lieut. Ord Julius, and he always took it for granted that it was the proper name. Lieut. Ord was the son of Brig-General Edward O.C. Ord, who served in the Seminole, Mexican, and Civil Wars.

September 6, 1921

The honey crop is pretty fair. We had only about 135 colonies of bees this year, so we couldn't have a very large amount. John thinks we will have between 25,000 and 30,000 pounds. The season is practically ended now, as it has been cool since the storm Saturday afternoon.

Joe and Mina Lell are in Powell, going to school. Joe has a janitor job at a bank that pays him $8 a month and has a shoe shining chair at the barber shop that is supposed to bring in about $15 or $20 a month. He has a job in sight at the print shop that pays about $20, I believe. If he gets that he will drop the shoe shining. They have two rooms, practically furnished, for which they pay $12 a month. They do their own cooking. They had to furnish one bed and some beddings, and a few cooking utensils.

Friday, September 23, 1921

Potatoes are not worth much this year. They cost a lot for the fellow that buys them, but the man that raises them does not make much. He sells a carload for about what a householder has to pay for a few to put in his cellar for winter use. The local buyers are paying $1.25 a hundred on board track here. That is about 80 cents a bushel, and that is *only* for the very best No. 1 potatoes, which means absolutely smooth, large, regular shaped potatoes.

We are marketing our potatoes this year through the Minnesota Potato Exchange, a cooperative exchange with headquarters at Minneapolis. John is sure that marketing in this way we will get at least 25% more than the people who sell through the local commission firms. Marketing through the cooperative exchange we pay merely for the cost of marketing and get the highest market price, whatever that is, and not what some commission firm wants to pay. Last year the local firms merely shipped car after car — or said they did — to crowded markets like Kansas City, without having the potatoes sold. The potatoes stood there on the track till they went bad, and the producer stood the loss. It has been more than suspected that some of the potatoes that were shipped from here were really sold in Montana and other places en route, and *reported* to have gone bad on the track at K.C. In that case the commission firms made the money and the farmer stood the loss. But in any case the farmer stood the loss.

We are so hoping that the potatoes in our place will be good this year and bring a good price, so that the Sweetens will have enough to settle up what little they owe and go back. John asked me the other day if I would be willing to lose a few hundred more on them just to get them away from here. I assured him I would for if they went away we could rent our farm to some real farmer and get some rent for it, and could sell off our six horses and a thousand dollars' worth of equipment, get the use of that money and devote our time entirely to the bee business. We are hoping very much that they will get away from here and go where little Joe goes to college, wherever that may be, and yet we feel that little Joe will have so much more of a chance to get a real start if he goes alone. As John said yesterday, how can Joe, Jr., get a really unbiased view of life and things in general as long as he is at home.

September 27, 1921

I am enclosing the copy of the ad we are using for the December number of the *Pictorial*. If it fails, we will be done with magazine advertising. We have had about 75 or 80 inquiries from the *Companion* ad, but so far only two orders. However, the inquiries are still coming in. If it takes people that long to answer the ad (nearly two months) no telling how long it will take them really to make up their minds to order. We have had a run of inquiries from Sutter Creek, Cal., until we have got suspicious and are not answering them any more, as it takes six cents postage to send out a sample and letter, not to mention the cost of the bottle, mailing tube, and stationery. We thought the inquiries were from young girls, all of them Mexican from their names, or Italians, and we have now concluded that they are school youngsters. One letter we got today from there said please send me a bott*el* of honey. Another said send me a sample, please send me two if you can so I can give one to my friend. The first letters we had from there had a list like this:

> soap
> powder
> salve
> perfume
> shampoo
> ~~honey~~

then the honey was crossed out and the letter read please send me free samples of − − −. Of course we were very much amused. We sent samples to the first four or five we got from there, but have stopped now, because it is not our aim to furnish a lot of school youngsters with "bottels" of honey to suck at school.

Friday, September 30, 1921

I had a new experience last night, one that I don't hanker after very soon again, if ever. Mrs. Osborne's daughter, Mrs. Miller, and husband and family are moving here. The daughter and her five children came last week, and the husband is due now. He brought an immigrant car to Billings, and is driving his stock down from there. Mrs. Miller was expecting a new baby in about two weeks. Last night about eight o'clock Mrs. Osborne sent word for me to call the doctor as soon as I could as they needed him. In a few minutes she sent for me to come over. We could not get the doctor from here as our telephone line is out, so they had to send one of the boys to Gillison's to call the doctor. I went over as soon as I could, and in about 15 minutes after I got there the baby arrived. But it did not breathe and its lips and nose were so purple they were almost black. Mrs. Osborne didn't seem to know what to do, but exclaim, so there wasn't anything for me to do but start to work on the baby. I caught hold of it and began to work it to try to make it breathe. Finally it gave a rattling gasp, and in about a minute and a half another. I laid it down long enough to get a pan of hot water and dipped it in that, and then had Mrs. O get some cold water and we soused it with that. We pumped its arms up and down, blew in its mouth, and worked its chest to make the ribs move in and out. We did these things over and over again, and about once in two or three minutes the baby would give another rattling gasp. It was hard to do because neither of us wanted to try to tie the cord and we couldn't move the baby very far, but we kept it up, I working the baby and Mrs. Osborne heating clothes and putting them around it, and finally it began to breathe more frequently, and by the time the doctor came, at least an hour after the baby was born, it was breathing more regularly but pretty weakly and gaspy. Its heart, however, had been strong all the time, and as long as its heart was beating I kept working at it. When the doctor came he took care of the baby, and then we rolled it in a hot sheet and I baked it (and myself, Edith, so you see I paid up for what you did when Jules came) at the stove for another hour before anything else was done to it. The doctor thought it was all right then, but it never did cry. I came home about half past eleven, and I was glad to go to bed, for my back and arms were pretty tired. Just try standing in one position, bending over a bed, and working your arms with a weight on your hands, for an hour, and see if you aren't aware of where the muscles begin and end. However, I was very glad I was there, because one person alone could not have saved the baby. This morning the baby took a spell of gasping and when it would gasp it would stiffen out its arms and legs until Mrs. Osborne was afraid it was taking spasms, so she wanted the doctor to come. He was just starting on another call when I talked to him and said it would be some time before he could get there. It is now almost four hours since I called and he hasn't got there yet. I think the trouble with the baby is mucous in the throat and bronchial tubes. Its lungs seem clear enough when one listens to them, but all the same I should want the doctor to make sure it wasn't taking pneumonia.

Osborne's cow is dry now, and they have no milk except the quart a day (for 6 adults and 9 children, all the children under twelve years) they get from us. This morning I made some cocoa for Mrs. Miller and sent it and a bucket of cream over. Mrs. O. told me when I was there that her daughter said that was the first time anybody had ever sent her anything when she had a baby—and this is her sixth. Think of it! She said where they lived in North Dakota their neighbors were nearly all Russians, and no neighborly neighbors at all.

Monday, October 3, 1921

I am sorry to say that the new Miller baby across the road died early Saturday morning. It never did breathe correctly and they did not have much hope of its living at any time. If it had to go, it is better that it did not live any longer than it did. I was not there when it died, but was over Saturday morning for a while, then came home and made the dress and petticoat to use for shroud, and stayed at the house with Mrs. Miller while they had the funeral Saturday afternoon. It is always sad to have a child die, but I couldn't help thinking that if it wouldn't have had any better care than the ones already there have, it is better off where it is. It makes your heart sick to hear the way those children talk—little tads six years old use language that would make your hair stand on end. They are so rough, too, their only way of playing being to knock each other down and roll over each other. I simply won't let Cecilia be with them at all unless it just can't be avoided, and then I am Johnny on the spot myself. Mrs. Osborne seems very nice, and she is clean as it is possible for a person with as much to do as she has. Her house always looks nice, even with the mob she has. But oh, my, the things she has to do with—or do without, rather. The night the baby was born, I went to the kitchen to wash my hands with antiseptic before I should touch anything, and there absolutely wasn't a thing in the kitchen or pantry except one dirty washbasin, tin, with two rag-mended holes, the basin about the size of a good sized soup bowl. The dishpan had dirty water and dishes in it, and a large bread pan had unwiped dishes. On the stove was a kettle with food in it, and that was absolutely every utensil in the kitchen or pantry, except tin buckets and a wooden chopping bowl. And finally I had to use that tin basin to revive that new baby. Just think of cooking for a family of 16 with no more kettles than that, and a few skillets. I suspect they cook nearly everything in skillets, as there were about four of them. But I guess some of them haven't had water all over their bodies since the last time they went in swimming. I saw Mrs. O. change her baby when it was terribly soiled, and she merely took one corner of the diaper and wiped him with it and then put on a clean (?) diaper. No, it was merely a *dry* one, dry again for the nth time. Poor people. I get ashamed of myself for not keeping things cleaner than I do when I think of what I have to do with compared with what they have. I tell you, it was like getting to heaven to come to a real bathroom and really wash after being there and helping take care of that new baby. Cleanliness is next to godliness, all right.

October 7, 1921

The potato market went down last week and the price f.o.b. here went as low as 90 cents a hundred. It is picking up again now. Today's Powell paper in speaking of the potato situation said, "It (the drop in price) could hardly be otherwise with more than seventeen hundred carloads of potatoes on American markets every day of last week. There is a market in the fall in this country for about 600 carloads of potatoes (per day); more than that creates a surplus."

October 10, 1921

Joe got done digging potatoes Saturday. He has just 30 bushels less than 3,000 bushels. Maybe the members of the family who are not even mathematicians can figure from that how many potatoes there are in our shop at present.

Friday, October 21, 1921

We shipped out a car of potatoes yesterday — one car. We were anxious to get one car sold soon, as Joe needs the proceeds to settle some bills he has coming due. The buyers here now are paying 85 cents a hundred — or a little over 50 cents a bushel. The freight rate to Illinois, for instance, is a dollar a hundred, or a cent a pound. That means that buyers can get potatoes here for 50 cents a bushel, ship them to Illinois for 60 cents, or a total of $1.10, and get about $2.25 a bushel for them.

Tuesday, October 25, 1921

We are to have a meeting tonight. There are some men in the community anxious to meet the farmers. One of them is a marketing expert who has been investigating market conditions for some years for the Farmers' Union, Equity, Grange, and the Non-Partisan League. It was his work that got the sugar beet producers an adjustment of $1.50 per ton more a couple years ago when sugar was so high and beets paid so little. He was sent to Washington during the war to confer with Hoover on marketing farm produce. The other man is the state organizer for the Non-Partisan League. We have been interested for several years in the work of the League in North Dakota and are glad to meet the man who is starting the work in this state. Women as well as men are invited and can become members. As there will probably be some women here tonight I will have to dust and I fixed up a bouquet of pine, juniper with blue berries, and red wild rose haws for on the library table. I put the bouquet in the green wicker vase and it looks quite festive. We got the juniper, pine, rose haws, and some cedar when we went to the mountains last week.

Just at present Cecilia is sojourning—no, the proper word is languishing, isn't it?—in bed. She got her feet wet and of course I made the punishment fit the crime and sent her to bed till her shoes dried. She explained that she wanted to see how deep the water was on the lawn, and it was deep enough to drown her shoes. I told her that the next time she wanted to find out how deep water was she should use a stick.

Friday, November 25, 1921

Murrays, Richards, Harts, and Hendricks had Thanksgiving dinner together at Hart's, and had a very nice time. Mrs. Hart suggested that we all get together for the day and we were all enthusiastic about it. Each of us took part of the dinner and in that way it was easier than if each of us got a dinner at home. I roasted three chickens and made a honey cake. Mrs. Murray made fruit salad for dessert and took butter and a vegetable. Mrs. Richards made the salad and took another vegetable, and Mrs. Hart furnished bread and potatoes. Each of us found something else to take along. Of course Mrs. Murray took a lot of things more than she was supposed to. Cooking is her chief delight and she is not happy unless there are at least two or three things for dessert. She even took along a kettle of lard and some doughnut dough so she could fry *hot* doughnuts for dinner, in addition to the many things already planned. We had such a nice time we decided we would have to get together each year for Thanksgiving.

November 29, 1921

We were threshing and now we aren't. It was too wet Saturday afternoon to go on, so they stopped, expecting, we thought, to start again Monday morning. But Joe took a notion to haul coal from the mine Monday, so there was nothing doing in the threshing line. They were to begin early this morning, but no one showed up, so finally John called Joe and he said he guessed they wouldn't thresh today, but would try tomorrow if it didn't thaw too much today. Well, I am entertaining the Club at an all-day meeting here Thursday, and I just had a picture of a lot of women here for dinner, each bringing one article of food for a buffet dinner, and then our cooking for a lot of threshing men and having to set the table. I considered how Joe had monkeyed around all fall threshing, and I riz right up in my dignity or anger, one or the "tother," and issued an ultimatum that there would be no threshing at Honeyhill on Thursday of this week. When I plan something once a year I am not going to have it spoiled by other folks' dilatoriness. John delivered the message all right, so I guess we won't thresh on Thursday. A while ago the machine men came and are moving the machine to another job.

Friday, December 2, 1921

Well, we had our club meeting here yesterday and had a great time. I wish you could all have been here for dinner, for it is almost like Christmas to have so many bundles to open, all of them containing something to eat. And of course you never know what you will have for dinner until the last package is opened. I cooked a kettle of vegetable soup and made a cake. We had buns, several kinds of meat sandwiches, baked beans, green beans, macaroni and cheese, buttered squash, boiled pickled pork, sweet pickled pears, three kinds of cake, mince, apple, and pumpkin pie, and fruit jello. And of course we made coffee. There were about twenty women and fifteen children, and there was more than plenty for everybody. You should have seen the children eat their dinner. We put down some rugs in the kitchen and let them sit on the rugs on the floor. It was quite cunning to see two long rows of youngsters, all eating.

Wednesday, December 7, 1921

We threshed 340 bushels of wheat and about 215 of oats yesterday. But as wheat is only 63 cents a bushel now, numbers don't count much, although the more bushels the more dollars. It takes more than a bushel to figure a dollar now.

John took about 30 bushels of wheat to the mill at Byron yesterday, so we will at least have flour for this winter without having to sell the grain at such a low price.

Monday, December 12, 1921

There is quite a bit of excitement in the community at present over traces of oil that were found here recently. The U.S.R.S. ditcher is working about 2½ miles north of here, and last week in digging the trench they found traces of oil-bearing soil, and actual oil in the soil they threw out. I have not heard what has happened but I suppose a company will be formed, as usual. Maybe we will all be millionaires yet.

If you were here now you could hear the grand concert of new music. John declared the other day that it was time to make an appropriation for music, so we picked out a lot of records we have wanted and sent to Sheridan for the list. We asked for 25, I think. The ones we will keep are "Anitra's Dance," and "The Hall of the Mountain King" from "Peer Gynt." "Heilage Nacht" by Schumann-Heinck; violin solo "Melody in A Sharp Major" by Kreisler, the music by our new Budget Master, Gen. Chas. G. Dawes; "Listen to the Mocking Bird" by Alma Gluck, with the bird voices by Kellogg; "Silent Night" by the Neapolitan Trio, and on the other side "Medley of Christmas Hymns." "Souvenir," violin solo by Kreisler; "Last Rose of Summer" and "Believe Me If All Those Endearing Young Charms," violin by Samuel Gardner, with orchestra; "Messe Solennelle–Domine Deus" (Praise forever to God the Father) by Caruso. There were some of the ones we did not get that we want, for instance the bugle calls of the U.S. Army, but I suppose we will have to wait another year and try again. My, how we do enjoy this music! We don't need to get each other anything else for Christmas now. We now have just exactly 90 records, besides some Hawaiian pieces—"Hawaiian stuff," John just called it. Of course we play it occasionally for visitors, but it is mighty seldom it gets played when we are alone. There are very few of the 90 pieces, however, that don't get their turn. I have an idea that there isn't a week that we don't play every piece we have. We always play all the hymns every Sunday before we play anything else, so whether we get to church or not we have a service, at least.

December 22, 1921

You would laugh to see Jules. He is sitting in the little rocking chair playing with himself. Each time I look at him he grins and his eyes sparkle like diamonds. He has the brightest eyes I ever did see. He loves to rock himself in the little chair. I never leave him alone in the high chair for fear he might tip it over with his rocking, as he always rocks when he sits up, no matter where he sits — high chair, crib, or rocker. He is talking to himself, and when I turned around to him just now and asked what he said, he chuckled and then laughed out loud. He likes to go to sleep with his crib near the mirror door in the bedroom so he can watch the baby in the mirror. When he wakes up he will lie there and talk to the baby in the mirror and smile. When he woke up this noon I held him so he could see both the door mirror and the one on the dresser. We smiled at the baby in the door a while, then turned and saw the one in the dresser mirror. He looked there, then back at the door, and seemed puzzled. He looked from one to the other, and then looked at me in the most inquiring fashion. Then he put his arms toward my neck and laid his head against me. I guess he wanted to find out which was the real mamma.

Monday morning, December 26, 1921

Christmas Day — or as Cecilia calls it, The First Christmas Day, because she thinks every day this week will be another Christmas day — has been and gone. I can't begin to tell you what a lovely day we had. It seems that each year the day is better and means more to us. Our tree is lovely; it is so nice to be in the house where we have room to put the tree and other decorations; and we had the grandest opening you ever heard of. When John had opened all the packages and the floor was covered with wrappings and boxes and every place available and the floor, too, were filled with gifts, John remarked, "My, what a Christmas I've married into!"

December 31, 1921

Well, I am not too big yet — or now — to wear my wedding dress. I put it on last night to celebrate the anniversary. John can no longer get into his wedding suit, however, so he could not appear as he did eight years ago. When I appeared in my dress John got up and put a record on the 'trola. What do you think the lemon put on? "The Last Rose of Summer!" Of course he immediately made up for it by playing "Believe Me If All Those Endearing Young Charms."

It isn't often in one's life that one gets to vote for the whole family.

3

1922–1926

The beekeepers of the state are to have a meeting in Thermopolis on the 19-20 of this month to form a state organization. The Bighorn Basin Association, which means John, is pushing the matter, so of course we had all the correspondence to do. Yesterday we got out over a hundred mimeographed letters to send out, and a number of typed ones. We spent the whole day in office work for the beekeepers and the waterusers' associations.

John was elected secretary of the waterusers' association last week at their annual meeting. The waterusers' association is composed of all unit holders on the Project. Right now is an important time, as the next business is the formation of an irrigation district, an organization of all the waterusers incorporated under the laws of the state. If we organize into an irrigation district under the laws of the state, we can then get federal farm loan money and save about 5% or 6% a year, which we are not eligible to get now, since the government holds the first lien on our lands until all payments are made.

Walter Fowler has been here for a week or so, looking after some business and being here to attend the waterusers' meeting in order to oppose the formation of the irrigation district. There is a small but very militant minority that is opposed to the formation of the legal organization of farmers here. Fowler and Mrs. Wallace, as usual, are with the wrong side. Fowler did not say anything at the meeting against a district but Mrs. Wallace made a regular spectacle of herself. It seemed the plan of the opposition was simply to block anything that was being done. They did not try to make any motions of their own, but merely worked by waiting till a motion was made, and then moved an amendment that would nullify the object. They were too small in numbers to accomplish anything when a matter came to vote, but by their tactics they could waste a lot of time in debate and keep much business from being put through. Mrs. Wallace got up to speak against an irrigation district and talked and talked and talked and talked and talked and talked, saying absolutely nothing. The chair called her several times for being off the subject but she talked on, and would not stop. John and Mr. Murray said it got really embarrassing for the chair and the meeting. The chair ruled her out of order and still she talked on. Finally the chair simply recognized someone else, and she kept on talking for several minutes after some one else had the floor. The men said that if she had tried to do all she could for the majority and against the minority she was with, she couldn't have done anything better. Women who are unit holders have the same vote and powers in the meeting that men do, and if they have anything to say are listened to with the same respect. But Mrs. Wallace kept saying very few words, always adding "Of course I am only a woman" until the men got sick and tired of it. I guess you would have to hunt far and wide to find any people anywhere who have less respect from the community than she and Fowler.

February 28, 1922

By the way, Co, have you been able to look about for any work for young Joe Sweeten next fall? I hope you can get him a good job to earn his board and perhaps his room if he enters Indiana University. Joe and I both have had letters from Mr. Cravens about work for Joe. Joe is learning sign and window painting and lettering and I thought maybe he could get some work at that. You couldn't get a finer lad anywhere. He is bright as a pin, able to stand on his feet and talk to anybody, and is as good a boy as you can find in seven states. Joe thinks now he wants an M.D. eventually, but is not absolutely sure. One thing he does know, and that is he has his heart set on going to Harvard. But since he has to earn his way, or most of it, he thinks very wisely he had better start in at a less expensive college and land at Harvard later on.

Edith, your account of the ladies club luncheon was interesting. I wish I could have seen the table. Yes, one holds one's breath at a tablecloth eight yards long—especially when one thinks of ironing it. How would one ever keep it moist for the entire length! I am glad to know there are places yet where real flowers adorn the table, not to mention such things as sprengerie and baskets suspended above the center of the table, and candlesticks. I suppose if I moved in select circles in Powell I would occasionally see real flowers, for I read in the paper recently of a bridge luncheon one of the U.S.R.S. wives gave that had real flowers both as decorations and favors. But the more I meet the select the less inclined I am to take the bother to get in their charmed circle or to go to the bother of entertaining in return. Isn't it a shame how lazy we get and how little we care for other people, and prefer our own society? Living on the farm we can pay less attention to others than if we lived in town, and be just as happy, or more so.

Did you read the poem in the last *Digest* on "Montana Wives"? It is rich. The author, I understand, lives in Billings, and was the one who won the prize offered for the best poem by *The Nation*, some time ago, and the prize poem was quoted in the *Digest* a couple of weeks ago. This one is on somewhat the same subject:

MONTANA WIVES
Horizons
by Gwendolyn Haste

I had to laugh. For when she said it we were sitting by the door,
And straight down was the Fork
Twisting and turning and gleaming in the sun.
And then your eyes carried across to the purple bench beyond
    the river
With the Beartooth Mountains fairly screaming with light and
    blue and snow,

And fold and turn of rimrock and prairie as far as your eye could go.
And she says: "Dear Laura, sometimes I feel so sorry for you,
Shut away from everything — eating out your heart with loneliness.
When I think of my own full life I wish that you could share it.
Just pray for happier days to come and bear it."

She goes back to Billings to her white stucco house,
And looks through white curtains at another white stucco house,
And a brick house,
And a yellow frame house,
And six trimmed poplar trees,
And little squares of shaved grass.

Oh, dear, she stared at me like I was daft.
I couldn't help it! I just laughed and laughed!

Isn't that rich? Especially the enumeration of the scenery in
Billings. Of course it is true that if one gets out on the streets
in Billings one can see some pretty good scenery, but I suppose
the suggestion is that the Billings lady just looks out between
her white net curtains.

April 11, 1922

Children, we'll be an author yet. I sent my lines on "Wyoming
Sunset" that I showed you last summer to a magazine of
poetry called *The Lyric West*, and yesterday received the following
note: "We are keeping your poem 'Wyoming Sunset' for use in
a summer number of *The Lyric West*. We pay $5.00 a page on
publication." I had never heard of *The Lyric West* until I saw a
poem quoted from it in the *Literary Digest* poetry page, but I

guess if the *Digest* recognizes it it must be all right. The next
question to guess on is how much poetry is a page! If they print
several columns of fine print on a page my lines won't pay
enough for railroad fare to Frannie and back; but if they print
verse the usual way, maybe I can fill a page. Now if the *Digest*
will only copy, I will be completely satisfied. You may remember
the poem—

WYOMING SUNSET

The western sky is periwinkle blue,
The sun just dipped the gold horizon line.
Thin strands of cloud, like golden eiderdown
Ray upward over the McCullough Peaks.
Blue-black the forests stand on Rattlesnake;
In front, Heart Mountain's triple-crowned brow,
And four score miles behind, tall Sylvan's peak.
Deep drifted snow fields on low Pat O'Hair
Show mile on mile of undulating white.
On Bear Tooth range each snow-enamelled fang
Is rimmed with glowing edge of virgin gold;
Soft velvet patches, purples pansy dyed,
Float wanton through the periwinkle blue.

The artist hand with skill enough to paint
That western sky should win eternal fame.

Against the eastern sky the Big Horns rear
A hundred miles of gullied precipice,
One stark, unbroken, canyon-pierced range.
Along the base, a clinging valley mist,
Along the top, a swelling summit cloud,
Between, sheer rock, nude or black forest clad,
Great fields of snow, and still more fields of snow.
And all—low lying mist, sheer rising rock,
Far reaching snow-fields, undulating cloud—
All, all incarnadine. Barbaric, deep,
Red mist, red rock, red snow, red cumulus.
The pulsing color glows, effulgent, clear,
With radiance unearthly, magic, weird.

No human hand could paint that eastern sky.

I am anticipating the scare of my life. The doctor says the neuralgia in my back and shoulders is most likely due to my bad teeth, and we are contemplating going to Billings soon and having them all taken out. I have 13 of my own teeth, and only two of them are alive. One of the two is good, I think, and I am not sure about the other. Probably they will both have to come out and I guess if I lose all but one or two they might as well be out of the way too. It scares me stiff to think of the ordeal but I guess if one has had two babies and lots of other aches and pains, she ought to be able to stand getting a few teeth pulled, especially if she can be given gas or ether while it is being done. There is one thing certain. I do not want to go around for a year or two the way nearly all the women here are doing, without any teeth in my mouth. So many around here have had their teeth pulled and then wait six months or a year before getting false ones. I may not be vain enough in some ways, but "be gorry" I am not going around looking any more like an *elte hexe* than I have to.

Billings, Montana
Sunday, April 16, 1922

We are in Billings at the Gage, as you can see from this stationery. John left home Friday afternoon for Sheridan for a freight rate hearing with the main freight men of the C.B.&Q., and Jules and I started yesterday afternoon. I did not expect John here until some time today, as we did not think he could get away from Sheridan until last night. However, they took up the honey tariff first thing yesterday morning at the hearing, and it was all over before John got there. He did not accomplish anything by going, but the two representatives of the Wyoming State Beekeepers Association gave John the credit for having started the work for lower freight rates in such as way that they could finish it up and get the rates we wanted.

So Ted wrote you an April Fool letter telling you that they are going to have a boy too, same as we have. I knew you would be delighted. I surely was. It is so much nicer to have two children, and it is so much better for the youngsters. I don't wonder that you didn't know whether or not to believe Ted's letter after the tale he told you last year that they had ordered one, too, when we had and that theirs would arrive about the same time Jules did. Maybe they did order one then, and the delivery was delayed—parcel post packages are usually slower than first class mail—but if Ted is expecting a boy you'd better not tell him that I said anything about its not being first class mail—or a first class male.

Thursday, April 20, 1922

I will again take my trusty "typy" in hand and try to write you a few lines. I do not know just how much I will accomplish, as I am still pretty shaky, and the neuralgia pain in my neck has been simply terrific since last night. For 48 hours after the teeth were out I had real pain, like toothache. Dr. Allen finally gave me something to quiet it and I have taken several tablets, but try to avoid doping as much as possible. The hot water bottle or a hot salt bag help a good deal at times. I think the worst is over now so far as my mouth is concerned and do not expect much more pain there, though of course there is pretty much soreness.

When Dr. Allen first looked at my teeth, he said, "O, you don't want all of those pulled. Why, they are pretty good teeth. They can be fixed up all right." I insisted that most of them were dead, and he tried them out with an electric spark. I really thought that only 2 of the 13 were alive but we found that four were all right, so far as containing nerves was concerned. However, one of them was too bad to keep, and the other three were all on one side of the mouth and of no value therefore for guying a plate, so he finally agreed it would be best just to make a clean sweep and have it all over with. So he said he would give me gas and take out the four wisdom teeth and three of the others, leaving the six front ones to be taken out with local anaesthetic, because the front ones would have to be drawn carefully so as to leave the gums in fine condition for a plate; otherwise the plate would never fit well. So he gave me the gas, and when I came to after it, I discovered to my sorrow that the teeth pulled so hard he was able to take out only two teeth while I was under. A third one had broken off when he took hold of it. So that left ten teeth and a snag to take out. I was almost too dopey from the gas to care much what was going on, so he went right ahead and put in the local anesthesia. By the time he had that in all around my jaw I didn't care what he did. I guess he could have taken off my head and I wouldn't have taken the trouble to object. He loosened each tooth very carefully first so there was no jerk whatever. He had to pull with all his might to get out several of the teeth, but he never jerked me once. My front teeth were about half a mile long, and crooked under the gums, so you see it was no easy matter to get them out. The wisdom teeth, the only jaw teeth I had, were either double-rooted, or the root twisted. Seven of the thirteen had abcesses at the roots, so you see it is certainly a good thing I got rid of them. Dr. Allen himself was surprised to find how many of them really were bad, for they did not show up that way from examination at the top, even if the tops were decayed.

The dentist says it will take about six or eight weeks for the gums to heal up enough for me to get a temporary set. So I will go back to Billings in about that time and have a lower set made. He says I need new uppers too, but I think since I am getting the lower ones so soon, I will keep my old upper plate and then about a year or so, when the gums are really permanently shrunk, get both new sets.

The entire bill, for the gas and all the extracting of thirteen teeth, was only ten dollars. I was certainly surprised. I don't know what he would charge for pulling a single tooth, nor what the dentist here would charge for pulling a lot, but the dentist in Powell charges from $1.50 to $2.50 for a single extraction.

Powell is quite a city now with its new street electric lights. There are street lights all down the main street for blocks. If you were here at our house at night now you could see an interesting natural phenomenon. Ordinarily we can see the row of lights from the upstairs windows, very plainly and clearly — almost five miles away. But part of the time we can see them from the downstairs. Isn't that queer and interesting? Last night, for instance, we could not see the lights at all, just the glow they made, all evening until we went to bed. But during the night I looked out when I was awake and I could see them, part of the line very plainly and the other end, evidently where the level is a little lower, only faintly. Later on I looked out again and could see every one very clearly. It is a matter of nightly interest to us now to see whether or not we can see the electric street lights of Powell. There does not have to be much mirage condition, only about ten feet difference in the bending of the light rays in the different layers of the atmosphere, to make all the light visible to us.

I am glad to announce that I am at last beginning to feel like something, and that work is a pleasure. If I keep on improving like this I will soon be able to take in washing, in addition to my own housework. I certainly am glad the old teeth are out. My mouth is still somewhat sore but does not pain the way it did.

I heard another good mirage story the other evening. Mr. Good said he and Mr. Rickard were at the gravel pit, about half a mile from Rickard's house. They happened to look toward the house, and saw a whole crowd of children, all about the same size, playing in the field next to the barn. Mr. Good said to Mr. Rickard, "Your little girl is having a party this afternoon, I see. I did not know there were so many girls in the neighborhood, all so nearly the same size." They were all just about the same size, about four feet tall. "No," said Mr. Rickard, "I don't know anything about it if Vera is having a

party, but she evidently is, from the looks of that crowd of girls."
The girls played around, skipping here and there, but the men
wondered why they played in the plowed field when they could
play in the nice lawn by the house. Suddenly the whole crowd
of white-clad objects rushed with one accord to the barn, and
the men discovered that they were white chickens, all scared
into cover at one time by a hawk.

Friday, April 28, 1922

You never can tell. Yesterday I was planning to keep my
house clean and be a real housekeeper for a change, and
today I am not paying any more attention to the house than if
it wasn't, but am planning to rush up some sewing and pack
my trunk for Indiana. Your letter yesterday was too much for
us, mamma, and we capitulated at once. As soon as I read it to
John and he knew how much you wanted us to come, he said I
should go and he would get along all right for a few weeks. I
do want you all to see these babies before they grow up, and so
we will come.

However, I do not think I shall wait to get my new teeth
before I start. Would you be shocked to have me come without
any teeth in the lower jaw, and get the plate in Bloomington? I
couldn't get a plate fitted for another week or two yet, and if I
waited for that it would be too late for me to take the trip and
get back by the time I must be back here. So John suggested
going as is, and getting the teeth in Bloomington.

Bloomington, Indiana
May 25, 1922

My Precious Sweetheart:
Ten years ago, on Memorial Day, I began to love you. I
have told you about it before, but I want to tell you again
on this anniverary how I went to church, and when I saw the
Spanish War veterans march in, all of them well and strong,
none of them having seen any service, I thought of the letter I
had received from you just a few days before. The words came

into my mind: That letter is from a *real* hero. The thought of all you had suffered wrought me up so I could not stay in church for the service. I had to get out by myself. I started homeward, and as I walked slowly through the campus, thinking of you and trying to regain some sort of composure before I reached home, I began to realize that I had set you apart from and above all the other men I knew.

In the ten years since then, dear, you have risen higher and higher as I have learned to know you better and better. The better I have known you the surer I am that you are a real hero, and the more I honor and respect you. In the Phi Beta Kappa address tonight Dr. Woodburn defined a patriot as one who stood always for the highest ideals of the nation, whether he ran with the crowd in so doing or stood alone against the majority of public opinion. You are a true patriot in that way as well as in offering your life when that was needed by our country.

For ten years now I have loved you. They have been the happiest years of my life, each one better than the one before. I pray, my beloved, that this decade is only the beginning of our life together.

It is good to be back here in this old familiar place. But behind and above it all is the joy of realizing that you love me and that with you is my life and my home. Good night, dear heart, and God bless you.

Honeyhill Farm
May 30, 1922

My Precious Lovely Sweetheart:

Today is decoration day. I am mighty glad that you attended the memorial service ten years ago today and then didn't. It was the most fortunate thing that ever occured for me. The ten years since that day have brought me the richest, fullest, sweetest and most contented life possible, and has made for me a perfect home with the sweetest, most lovely and interesting family anyone could have. My! what fortune to have such a family and home to work for!

Perhaps this anniversary is a good time to rededicate myself to you and our children. I love you and them. My life is for you and them. You and they make it possible for me to accomplish far more than I could accomplish otherwise. All my life and abilities are devoted to you whom I love. May I be able to give you and them full opportunity to develop and use all your powers!

Your lover,
John Hendricks

Wednesday, June 21, 1922

Dear Everyone at 822:

Do you remember those forget-me-not cards that were on every card stand fifteen years ago with a verse that read something like this:

> I've just got home from the nicest of trips,
>> And found everything all right,
> I had a nice journey, and thank you and yours
>> For making my visit so bright.

"Them's my sentiments" at the present time. I surely had a lovely time. I shall always remember this visit particularly. I can't tell you how much we appreciate your making it possible for me to have the trip home. It will always be one of the happy memories I have of 822. I did so much want you to see Jules, and many and many a time we spoke of how much we wished we could take him to see you. But as long as financial conditions with us were so close we did not feel we could do it. We are so happy now that you have all seen him, because when we tell you things about him now, it will mean something to you.

[While Cecilia was in Indiana in May and June the Non-Partisan League in Powell began to push her nomination for State Superintendent of Public Instruction and asked if she would allow her name to be presented to the state Democratic Convention in July. Cecilia's interest was sparked by the idea, and she agreed to the nomination.

In a letter written in September 1922, to Mrs. F.E. Schilling in Cheyenne, Wyoming, who had offered to support her candidacy, Cecilia said:

"I should like to tell you that I did not seek the nomination for state superintendent. When I was in the East last spring, some of the state leaders asked if my name might not be brought up. At first I did not see how we could consider it, for our work is here on the farm, our children are still small, and we have our own business to look after. If I should be elected, I should have to be in Cheyenne most of the year. Mr. Hendricks would have to be here most of the time, and our home would be divided. One or the other of us would have to be away from the children and lose the pleasure of their company. The expense of running two homes would be great. But when we thought about the matter, we remembered that if there was one thing more than another that I learned in Indiana University it was that when one received an education it was for the use of society at large and not a private possession to be used solely for personal ends. If I can be of service to the people and particularly the children of this state by putting my education and training to work for them, I ought to do so, even at a personal sacrifice. For this reason I decided to be a candidate."]

Maybe you will be interested in knowing how the Non-Partisan League political affairs will be run. The League is not a political party in the sense that it puts out a ticket the way the other parties do. In this state, the farmers will get together — that is, the delegates from each county — about the middle of July, and decide whom they want as candidates for each state office. Then these persons will be run on the Democratic ticket against other Democratic candidates in the primary. Those who win in the primary will appear on the Democratic ticket at the regular fall election. The Democratic state organization has agreed to accept without protest any "real-dirt" farmer that the League wants put up for Governor. The object of the League is to have people in office who know a little more about the country and its problems than to think that the country is the place you go on the 4th of July to have a picnic.

June 23, 1922

I found another honor (?) awaiting me on my return. John announced that I had been elected secretary of the local chautauqua association. They wanted him to be it, and he pushed me instead. The chautauqua is to be held the week of July 16 and costs two dollars for an adult ticket. That is certainly cheap enough. Last year it was free. I hope that scheme can be worked out again, after this year, to be permanent. Last year the Chamber of Commerce got a lot of business men and farmers to pledge five or ten dollars each, until they had enough to pay for the chautauqua. Then they invited the whole community to attend free. Of course that means big crowds and not such good chance to hear everything said, but the spirit of the meetings was great, and what we missed of what the speakers said we made up in the effect of the speaker of the enthusiasm of the audience. The very people who most need the entertainment and instruction of a chautauqua are oftenest the ones who can't afford to buy tickets, particularly people with large families.

July 15, 1922

Pater, and probably the rest of you too, you will be interested in the telegram I just received [congratulating me on being the unanimous choice of the state convention] in Douglas.

So you see you may yet get to visit us in Cheyenne. John says they ought to give him a job, too, so we could both work there! He is tickled as can be, and insists that he has always said he would be known as Mr. Cecilia H. Hendricks. It appears that for a few months, anyway, he may be known as the husband of Mrs. Cecilia H. Hendricks.

(Postscript on a letter written by Edith)
Dear Co:

You may wonder why I have never mentioned Cecil's candidacy for State Supt. Really, I think it is the most ridiculous thing that John has yet struck upon. Mrs. Morton, who now has the job, is a peach, and I would certainly think that Cecil would have sense enough not to be pushed into a job that she could not handle. Just what she would do, with a baby, having to travel a lot of the time, is beyond me. It would not be so bad if Ce were not the Non-Partisan League candidate, but you know the reputation of the League among respectable folks. John has the biggest bunch of fool radical ideas, that I would hate to see Ce get the job, for John would put them all in force. It would really be awful. You ought to hear Ted's idea about it—or rather, perhaps your delicate ears would not stand his thoughts on the subject. It is really very embarrassing to us, as you remember Mrs. Morton was our guest during the convention here last fall and has been working hard for Ted along various lines, and now to have Ce come out and give her the expense of making a campaign, when there was no one else out is rather putting us in a queer position.

Nuf sed.,

Edith

Monday, July 17, 1922

Max Addleman, the local man who was at the convention, came home last night, and was here to supper. Of course he told us all about what had happened, and we all asked a lot of questions. Some of the things that were done at the progressive convention did not suit us at all, and I may decide yet not to run, but in the meantime we are having lots of excitement and fun about the whole affair. There were two conventions at Douglas on succeeding days. On one day the farmers who were delegates from the various counties met and decided on their candidates. The next day the progressives met, with the state Democratic committee present, and the farmer delegates also present. The progressives insisted on nominating a Powell man named Kindler for governor. We do not have any use for him at all, and do not think he is qualified for the office. So we are holding off on my deciding until we find out a few more things about him and just what the Democratic committee think of him and his candidacy. If the Democrats put up a good man for governor, I will run. But I don't care to be on a ticket with a man who is not fit to be governor. The farmer delegates, the progressives, and the Democratic committee all backed my name, it seems, and so far as I have found out, there would not be anyone against me in the Democratic primary. Politics is certainly interesting. In some ways I love it, and in others I hate it.

Friday, July 21, 1922

I am not sure yet if I will be in politics or not. For governor a man who lives here was nominated, and he is the worst possible person in the whole state for governor. We know his pedigree and it is simply awful. He is not honest, which of course is the worst thing about him, and in addition he is the sort of man who will never work with anyone and would always be fighting everything anybody else did if he hadn't suggested it himself. He got the nomination by being on hand at the convention and making a fiery speech at an opportune moment, a speech that he makes at every meeting he goes to and has letter perfect. If the people there had had the opportunity to hear him speak more than once, they would have known better, for he has only the one speech. "He has one song in meetin'." That is all he knows. Naturally he had that one song down so pat he made a good impression. But why any convention should not have looked up the pedigree of a candidate beforehand is ununderstandable. Well, to make a long story short, I notified the state Democratic chairman that I would not run if that man's name stayed on, but that if some honest man were nominated I would be glad to run. He wired back immediately that he would make every effort to overcome the difficulty and that in the meantime it was imperative for me to send my filing paper to Cheyenne, as tomorrow is the last day for filing for state office. He promised not to file the paper unless I gave him permission after the obstacle I objected to was removed. John wrote to some of the labor leaders in Cheyenne protesting to them, and they and the Democratic chairman, Mr. O'Mahoney, got together and are doing something. I will probably get a wire this afternoon or tomorrow morning telling me what has been done. Until then I will not know whether or not I will be a candidate.

Cora, you remember how you have always looked forward to each train journey in the hope that something interesting would happen? Well, you never can tell when it is happening. When our local delegate to the state convention returned, he said that Mr. O'Mahoney, the state Democratic Vice Chairman, buttonholed him on his arrival, and wanted to know if there wasn't a lady named Mrs. Hendricks in this part of the country who was eligible for state superintendent. Mr. Addleman said there was, and he had her credentials with him. Mr. O'Mahoney said he was glad of it, as they simply had to get her to be their candidate for state sup't. He said he had met her on the train some time ago and seemed to approve very highly of her. When Mr. Addleman told me about it, I did not remember meeting anybody by the name of O'Mahoney on the train. (That name, by the way, is pronounced O Mah'-ny, and not O Ma Hon'-ey, as it is spelled.) Since then I have received a letter from Mr. O'Mahoney, saying that he was the man whom I met on the train when I came home from Greybull last fall. I had a very pleasant journey with him, and he helped me at Frannie and at Garland with my baggage and babies. He did not mention his name, and of course I did not inquire for it, but I happened to speak of John in the course of the conversation, and he got my name. And now he turns out to be the Democratic state vice chairman, and from seeing me on the train approved sufficiently of me, when my credentials were all right, to want me to run on his party ticket. He is a most delightful person to talk with, and he is evidently a good politician if he thus remembers each person he meets. So you see Co, "Life brightens, romance revives, chivalry is not dead." Just keep on traveling and you will have an interesting experience too.

July 24, 1922

"Everybody's doin' it, doin' it, doin' it.
Everybody's doin' it now."

Even father. Ted* and I aren't the only members of the family in politics this year. John has got on the bandwagon too. Some of the leading men here have urged him to come out for representative from this county to the State Legislature, and we finally decided that he would. So we promptly filed, and thought about it afterward. Some of the leading Democrats are very anxious to have John make the race, so I guess we will have some fun out of it even if John should lose out in the primary. There are three Democrats that we know of who have filed in this county for representative, so one of them will have to be dropped out.

A Democrat from Cheyenne has come out on the ticket for governor. When we reported that the man from here who was nominated for governor was absolutely no good, and not honest, the leaders all over the state of the various branches of the party — farmer, progressive, and straight Democratic — got their heads together and got a man named William B. Ross, a lawyer from Cheyenne, to run. So far as we can learn, he is a fine man, a progressive, honest, a man who has never been allied with the big interests or corporations. He ran in the primary four years ago and was defeated. Someone told us that later the leaders of the party were sorry he did not win in the primary, as they regarded him as a better man than the one who did.

Mr. O'Mahoney called me long distance from Cheyenne Saturday noon and we had quite a long conversation. I learned that people from here had kept the wires and mails busy,

---

*Ted was running in the primary for Big Horn County's office of County and Prosecuting Attorney against F.A. Little and H.H. Black.

objecting to the man who was nominated for governor, and that we were not the only ones who objected to him. He said the leaders of the various branches of the party, and especially the ones who had led in nominating this man; were very much alarmed over the situation. Well, the result was that Mr. Ross is out for governor, and we consider that he is fine and will strengthen the whole ticket.

Friday, July 28, 1922

We had a very nice time at the Farm Bureau picnic yesterday. We went in the morning, and got there about eleven. We sat around and talked till noon, and then the Harts, J.L. and Leo Werts, Browns, Lewises, and we had dinner together. When we all got our baskets unpacked, you can imagine what a spread there was. I don't know if I can remember it all or not, but we had fried chicken, roast chicken and dressing, potato salad, salmon salad, several baked beans, meat and peanut butter sandwiches, pickles of various sorts, sweet, mustard, and beet, devilled eggs, and goodness knows how many kinds of cake. I remember angel food, chocolate layer, chocolate marble loaf, spice loaf with White Mountain icing, spice layer with caramel. Yum, yum. I wish you could have been there. The Farm Bureau furnished free lemonade and coffee, so you see we had quite a spread. The picnic was in a grove of trees east of Cody. In the afternoon there was a program — some readings and singing, and two main addresses — one by Mr. Oliver Hower, president of the State Farm Bureau, and the other by Mr. O'Mahoney, state Democratic vice chairman. There was a third short speech by the Republican representative from Cody. We felt quite puffed up at knowing both the main speakers so well, and at having them look for us and talk to us a long time.

There was a Democratic banquet and meeting in Cody last night, so John went to that, and I drove the car home. It is the first time I have driven quite that far all at one time. We came along swimmingly and did not have a bit of trouble all the way. I should have liked to go to the banquet last night but felt that it was more important for John to be there, and we did not like to take the children out so late as we would have had to if we had both gone. John said I was inquired for, so you see my existence is known.

The politicking business gets more interesting every day. I knew that the state school superintendent was on various land boards, but I know now that she is a very important personage aside from her relationship to the schools. Practically all the wealth of the state in undeveloped oil lands and other mineral lands, that belongs to the state, is now being sought by corporations, especially the Standard Oil. During the next two years great leases will most likely be granted, and these land boards, one of them composed of the governor, the secretary of state, and the state superintendent, and another composed of these three and two other state officers — auditor and treasurer — have complete control of these leases, etc. So you see that the state sup't occupies a very influential position, and can see to it that the state gets full value for its valuable concessions, if she so desires, as on the one most important board she has one vote of three. Now that I know what importance is attached to the office in the membership in land boards I am really anxious to get in, for it is possible to do a great service to the state in the next couple years by standing like a rock for full compensation to the state for all leases. There is no reason why Wyoming should be a second Pennsylvania, and that is what will happen now unless someone is on the job who isn't bribable.

Well, I must go to the depot at Garland to see Mr. O'Mahoney for a few minutes as he goes through on the train, and it is about time to get ready, so I must stop for this spasm. Are you getting tired of politics? Just say the word, and I'll talk about more domestic subjects such as cherries that won't stay canned and rhubarb that must be canned.

We went to church yesterday (don't faint!) and heard the new minister, Roy Walter. He is such a kid in looks, slight in frame, and not so very tall, but he can deliver the goods when it comes to preaching a sermon. It has been a long time since I heard such a sermon out in this state. Our man can certainly use words, and he uses them with exactment, too. There is one thing to be said for Presbyterian ministers and that is they do have a good deal of education. So many of the Methodist ministers you hear in small places couldn't speak grammatically to save their lives, but most Presbyterians have had enough education to attend to that. We are planning to call on the new minister and his bride tonight and to invite them to dinner this week some evening.

August 1, 1922

We have been canning beans—17 quarts today—all canned with meat. We like them that way so much more than plain. I have long been wanting some of the spring glass top jars so I would not have to monkey with these old Mason jars that take so much time and effort to get sealed. Today John told me that while I was east he had ordered 15 dozen Lightning jars. My, that is a nice surprise! He brought me a dozen of the Kerr lids today to try. What with them and the new spring top jars that are to arrive in a few days, I will have a picnic with the rest of my canning. I wish I had got the Kerr lids sooner. I had so much trouble with the cherries opening, and had enough spoil to pay for several dozen lids. My Mason lids are old and do not fit well any more, and the edges are getting so soft they will not stay put. I think that is the main trouble.

Tuesday, August 8, 1922

The weather still remains rather bad for honey producing. We do not know if the main trouble is weather or grasshoppers. It has been poor ever since the fourth of July and we do not expect more than about half a good crop. In most places it is worse than here. Around Lovell only about a third of a crop is in sight, and some small beekeepers will not get anything. We think that the grasshoppers are partly the trouble here, and that the weather has been such that the plants do not secrete the usual amount of nectar. At Lovell they have done so much damage that in places there is nothing green at all. In some places in Big Horn County there will be no second cutting of hay at all because the grasshoppers have eaten up the alfalfa. Mr. Rauchfuss was telling us the other day that when he went from Cowley to Lovell three weeks ago the air was thick with grasshoppers and there was not a sweet clover blossom along the way because the hoppers had eaten it all up. Last week he went over the same route and there was hardly a grasshopper to be seen. The hoppers had got some disease that cleaned them all up. This disease is terribly contagious, and if it starts there is an end of the hoppers. In some places it is being cultivated, and if the germs of the disease are spread early enough in the spring the crop for that year can be saved, and the hopper menace for the following year done away with. But if the hoppers live long enough to lay eggs, while we may kill them off this year we will have a new crop next year. Mr. Rauchfuss says there are two kinds of disease. In one, the hopper holds on to the stems of the plants and dies there, so that the plants (alfalfa, for instance) can not be used for food. In the other disease, the hoppers drop to the ground when they are sick and die on the ground, and the plants are not rendered useless. The variety of disease that is cultivated is the second kind. One thing the legislature of this state must do before next spring is to provide means of combatting the hoppers, or there will be no crops anywhere in the state. We never had any hoppers here until last year, in numbers sufficient to do damage, but this year they have caused serious loss. Hundreds of bushels of grain have been cut off and are lying on the ground, and in some cases whole fields of grain have been destroyed.

Pater, you will be interested in the fact that I have received a number of letters from Democrats in answer to the letter I sent out [to state committeemen and county chairmen urging support of Mr. Ross and detailing Mr. Kindler's lack of qualification], a copy of which I sent you. The men seem very glad to have the information I gave in that letter. One man answered that he was having the letter published in the Laramie paper and would see to it that all persons in his county became acquainted with its contents. Perhaps the most interesting result was a phone call from Casper saying my letter had been turned over to the man who was calling, Mr. Vogel of the Casper *Free Press*, who is apparently the leader of the progressives there. He wanted to know more fully what my objections to Kindler were and what basis I had for our opposition to him. We talked a long time — twenty minutes, at least — and he asked me if I would get him a letter on the next morning train containing full information, as he had called a meeting for Sunday night in which the progressives at Casper would decide which candidate they would back in the primary. We wrote him a full discussion of the matter and got it on the next morning train.

Another answer I received to the letter I sent out is more amusing than anything else. It is anonymous and comes from Torrington. It is signed "Friends and Ex-pupils of Mr. Kindler." In it the writer or writers say all manner of mean and ugly things about Mr. Ross and assume that he hoodwinked me into supporting him. They assure me that I owe my nomination in large part to Mr. Kindler. "Because he was at the convention at Douglas and I wasn't." Great argument, isn't it, when one happens to know it hasn't any basis in fact anyway. They assured me that my letter would prove a boomerang which would cause my own defeat. I was very much amused at the whole thing. In the first place, an anonymous letter never is worth anything for giving a true statement of the conditions. And in the second place, when part of it is not true, one naturally assumes that the rest is of like calibre. O yes, they said I had already lost the support of that entire community.

The primary is tomorrow, so today will be the last main day for the candidates for the primary. Ted, we wish you the greatest of success tomorrow. I really think John will be nominated all right, but of course one can't tell till it is over.

Thursday morning, August 24, 1922

Hurrah! I just got the news at Garland that Ross was nominated for governor, beating Kindler by five or six hundred. We are delighted. It looked for a while yesterday as if Kindler were going to win, as he was in the lead all day until about nine last night. But this morning the rest of the state has been heard from and Ross wins. You will be glad to know that John got more votes than any other of the candidates for representative. So there is no question of his being nominated. I don't know about any other candidates as yet. I was of course nominated, having no opposition.

Friday, August 25, 1922

We got some good news in a gov't honey bulletin the other day. It said that due to the short crop everywhere, prices were going up, and extracted is already about 50% higher than it was a few weeks ago. It said that in carlots it was being sold (for the quality we raise here) at 12 and 12½ cents a pound. If we can get as much as eleven cents a pound for a carload we will sell a whole car as soon as we can, and get in some money — and get rid of the money overnight, as usual. But at least we can pay up all we owe that needs to be paid for this season. We will go on with the direct selling to some extent, as that is the final solution, but wouldn't try to sell all our crop this season in that way. It looks now as though we ought to have at least 40,000 pounds. A few weeks ago we were afraid we would not have more than about 30,000, but things picked up a little better the past two weeks and the bees have been working pretty well most of the time.

I am sorry Ted did not win out, unless he did not care much about it. There was a man here from Kane the other day, and of course we talked up Ted to him. He said he had heard there was some dissatisfaction with Little because he was too easy on the bootleggers but he did not seem to know much about it, or else was not talking. We told him what Ted stood for, and he assured us he would vote for Ted in the primary.

There is no question that John is nominated. There were three out for the two places of representative on the Democratic ticket. Yesterday the count stood as follows: Hendricks — 248, Ide — 212, McGuffey — 210, with three small precincts yet to hear from. So it is a question as to whether Ide or McGuffey will win out, but John was certain, as the precincts to be heard from have too small a vote to change John's lead of 36 votes. We felt quite good about John's showing because Kindler and his brothers and brother-in-law worked just as hard against John as John did against Kindler. In fact, they spread a rumor that John had withdrawn, but it evidently was put out too late to do any good, for folks voted for John just the same. Mr. Baird, the newspaper editor in Powell, is Kindler's brother-in-law, and of course worked for Kindler, though he is too much of a middle-of-the-roader to take much of a stand against anybody. Baird told me yesterday that since I was now the only state candidate in this county he thought the county ought to get behind me solidly and give me the entire vote of the county.

Mrs. Morton was the one on the Republican side who won out in the nomination. That will make it easier for me, because I hear repeatedly that the school people are sick and tired of her and want a change. Everywhere I go I hear that she is a lovely society lady, but doesn't know beans about how to run schools. Everybody says she is charming to meet, but that her forte is banquets and public meetings where she can shine, and that she doesn't believe in letting her office interfere with her social duties and interests. Since I have heard that from so many sources, I am beginning to think there is a good deal of chance of anyone with some qualifications really being elected. So there may be a chance yet that you can all come to visit us at Cheyenne.

Hurrah! We are going to have electricity pronto. We are the proud possessors of a large private plant. Mr. Roach, who is a member of the Powell school board, stopped in this morning and wanted to see John. He said he wanted to give John a Christmas present if he would accept it with the string that was tied to it, and explained that since the high school at Powell now has city lights, it no longer needs its private plant. The plant was in the way and they wanted to get rid of it, and he thought John might buy it. John bought it for $150. John was glad to discuss the matter, provided the price of honey went up so we could pay for the plant. Mr. Roach assured us that they would wait until the price did go up. So it seems that John can have the plant now and pay for it whenever he gets ready — they will take his note for the amount and give him all the time he wants to pay up. Quite a compliment to John, methinks. My, won't it be nice to have electricity! I do not know just how large this plant is, but it is much bigger than we would have been able to afford if we had bought one new. It should be all right for an electric iron. Won't I be glad!

Well, I made my debut in local politics last night when we went to the dinner for Senator Kendrick. We went first to the Wyoming Hotel, where the bunch gathered. We got there ten or fifteen minutes before it was time to go to the cafe, and just before we started, Senator Kendrick came and spoke to John and was introduced to me. When we all started out to go to the cafe, he came and walked with us all the way down the street. After we got there, we found the dinner was to be at one long table, the full length of the room. When it was time to sit down, Mr. Kendrick asked us to come along, and the local man in charge, after we hesitated, thinking we might be told where to sit, told us to take seats along that side of the table. So Senator Kendrick waited for John and me, and I had the pleasure of sitting between him and John at the banquet. I had never met him, but had seen him before and always liked him. He is such a comfortable person to be with. I enjoyed the dinner very much. We had a very nice dinner, without any style in serving whatever.

September 11, 1922

The electric plant we bought from the high school has been used only about a year and a half. When the school changed over to the city lights they put in all new bulbs of a different kind, so we get all the bulbs from the old plant and ought to have enough to last us a long time. The school board paid $400 for it, so the retail price would have been about $600, and we got it for $150. Electric light plants are a drug on the market in Powell now, since the city current has come in. The electrician told John he has seven listed with him for sale. If times would improve a little, farmers could afford them, but they can't very well. We wouldn't have considered it ourselves if the school board hadn't offered to give us until we were ready to pay for it. The electrician says that running the engine about two hours a week ought to keep the batteries sufficiently charged. He says it should take about a gallon of gasoline a week. One surely ought to be able to pay that much for lights, oughtn't one.

Friday, September 15, 1922

Cecilia announced yesterday that she was a big girl now, and she was not afraid of the dark any more and never would be. I am inclined to think the reason she has grown up so is that by pressing a button as she progresses through the house, she disposes of the dark and there isn't any any more. It certainly is nice to be able to do that. We have a 100 candle power light in the living room, and it lights up the whole room as it never was before. There are certain disadvantages, however, attached to bright lights. Every fly speck—and there are millions of them—on the windows and doors shows up perfectly. The electriciain got the work on the lighting plant done yesterday and they also got the engine in perfect running order, so we are all lit up now. I was surprised that the bill for the work was no more than it was. The electrician finished all the fixtures and cords and did the work, putting up 15 lights. His bill for labor and all was only $25, so he did not get more than about $10 for nearly two days' work.

Honeyhill Farm
September 18, 1922

Mr. William B. Ross
Cheyenne, Wyoming.

Dear Mr. Ross:

I should very much have liked to meet you at the meeting in Casper a few weeks ago, but I knew nothing of the meeting until the day it was held. Everybody here is exceedingly well pleased with the results of the meeting and the platform that was written there.

I understand that you are to be here some time before the election. I want to assure you that we will be more than delighted to do anything we can to help you while you are here or to prepare for your coming. We should like very much to have you make our home your headquarters, if you can. When Senator Kendrick was here recently, he said the main trouble with campaigning was that one never got a chance to rest or sleep, and was fed all the time. We will let you sleep all you want to, and give you anything you want to eat — if it is only bread and milk.

I hardly know what to tell you in response to your request for points I wish made on my behalf. I am enclosing herewith a brief statement of my training for the work of state superintendent. We thought that the fact that Mr. Hendricks and I are both on the same ticket might get us some publicity. It is a somewhat unusual situation.

I might say that in regard to the policy I should hold in conducting the office of state superintendent, I should practice the greatest economy consistent with the proper growth and development of the schools. I should try to see to it that the schools secured and used every penny of available funds each year, but that every safeguard were used to protect the permanent school fund and to increase it. That is, I should feel that the future was just as important as the present and that with wise foresight now, the schools of this state would forever be provided for. I should work for greater uniformity in the course of study at least within counties, so that children who go from one little district school to another in the same district would not have to change texts and courses and even subjects, as is the case most of the time now. So far as present members of boards or office force are concerned, I should not want to sweep the place clean but regard each case entirely on the ability of the individual to do the work in the most efficient manner. I should, however, feel myself free to secure the very best possible ability for each part of the work after I became well enough acquainted to know just what was needed and what the possibilities were. I have always been a pretty hard worker myself, so far as not loafing on the job is concerned, and I should require the same of any one in my office.

Senator Kendrick urged me to get out over the state and make a campaign. I intend to do what I can, but it is impossible for me to travel very far, because this time of year is the one when farm finances are at their lowest. You know, of course, that low prices, short crops, and high freight rates cut down a farmer's profits until not much more than enough comes clear to pay interest charges. Traveling is so expensive that I can not see my way clear at all to doing much of it. Mr. Hendricks is planning to campaign the whole county, however, as with the car he can do that at no very great cash outlay.

I am more sorry than I can say to know that my letter to the county chairmen and state committeemen caused you any trouble. I wrote to these persons at your suggestion and with the hope of helping your candidacy. Every statement I made was fact.

I assure you that we had no desire to antagonize anyone either before or since the primary, and that since the primary we have not said or written a word, because the fight was over. We hated like fury to have to write some of the letters we did, but we felt that it was our duty to the state to prevent the calamity that would result if the person named were to become its chief officer. We believe that a great commonwealth is entitled to have as its head a man like yourself, who is above reproach, either in character or in business connections. We have been told that we would kill ourselves politically by standing so openly for what we thought was right. Our position is and always has been that if we can not take our morals with us into politics, then we will be perfectly happy to stay at home and out. I can not see any reason whatever for women in politics if in their official positions they would have to associate with persons whom they could not meet in any other way without being talked about. If the state needs the help of its women — and I believe with all my heart that it does — then the state must see to it that its officers, both men and women, are its best and not its worst citizens.

I hope that your campaign is coming along swimmingly and that your success will be record making. Mr. Hendricks and I are looking forward with much pleasure to meeting you and learning to know you better while you are in Park County.

Very truly yours,
C.H.H.

Honeyhill Farm
September 20, 1922

Mr. Joseph C. O'Mahoney,
Cheyenne, Wyoming.

Dear Mr. O'Mahoney:

Your letter of the 16th to Mr. Hendricks has arrived. I am having a picture made and will send you a print as soon as Mr. Lucier can get one ready. I did not have anything suitable for advertising use.

The meeting of the Federation of Women's Clubs will be at Torrington early in October. The State Teachers' Association has its annual meeting in Cheyenne about the same time. I do not have the exact dates. I should like very much to attend both of these meetings, but as Torrington is so very far away I do not see at present how I can make that trip. It would be very expensive in both time and money, requiring one to stop over night at Casper both ways, and adding hotel expense there to the railroad fare. I know that women's clubs are Mrs. Morton's stronghold and for this reason can see the advantage of appearing there. On the other hand, it would most likely be a futile trip for that very fact. I understand that it was through women's clubs that Mrs. Morton was elected four years ago. Having elected her then, they would not be likely to change their position *as a body* now, no matter what their individual opinions might be.

You are quite right in assuming that I do not have much money to spend in a campaign. In fact, just now I do not have any. As I said to Mr. Ross the other day, this is the time of year when a farm bank account is at its lowest, and what with short crop, low prices, and high freight rates, not much more remains than enough to pay interest charges. We have an interest payment to meet next month, and that is occupying our chief attention right now. I should like to know if the central committee has any funds that I might get the use of, with the understanding that I should repay the amount later when we are able, whether or not I am elected. I am perfectly willing to put some money into the campaign, whether or not I am elected, but I am sorry to say that we do not have it now, and no immediate prospects for sales in quantity enough to provide printing of circulars unless I can get some money from the committee with which to do it.

In regard to the circulars, I wish very much I might get out something on the order of what Mr. Ross used in the primary campaign. If you have any figures on the cost of these, I should be glad to have the information. I note that Mr. Ross's circulars bear the union label. I think that is very important. I am working on a platform and will send it to you for your criticism before I make any use of it.

I have heard that there has been some discussion of the possibility of merging the positions of state superintendent and commissioner of education. You might spread the information, if you need to, that my training has been such that I could do the work of both offices. In fact, I can not see why most of the work of the commissioner's office is not merely clerical.

Very truly yours,
C.H.H.

I wish you could be here to see Edith and the new baby. Edith is getting along beautifully. She has not been the least bit nervous and has progressed exactly according to Hoyle, and she is stronger now than she was at the end of two weeks when Edith R. was born. Janet Cora has loads of long black hair. It is hard to tell whom she does resemble; however, she is cunning and will be quite pretty, I think. She is large, for her whole eight pounds is all baby and not fat. I rather think she is taller than E.R. was even if she doesn't weigh as much. Mrs. Hamilton has come over every morning to bathe the baby, for which I am duly thankful. What with Jules and E.R. and Edith to take care of, I do not have much spare time.

I have been getting away a little to go to political meetings. I went to Basin and made a speech last night. The men who are candidates for congressmen and secretary of state were there and spoke in a theatre. I did not talk more than about ten minutes. The candidate for Congress is named Rose. One of the things I spoke of was that it didn't make any difference what party one belongs to, the main thing is for one to use his brains and decide on men and issues. I said names didn't count in this election, and then said, "It doesn't make any difference whether you are down on the books as a republican or a democrat. The thing to do is to think for yourself. A rose by any other name, you know. . ." and then I turned to Mr. Rose and, pointing him out, I said "would be just as good a man to vote for." It got quite a laugh.

Well, it is after eleven, and I haven't had more than a few hours sleep for three nights past, so I had better remain. Ted is going to take a turn at caring for Edith and the baby tonight so I can get a night's sleep. Jules has cut two double teeth since we have been here.

I came down here yesterday on the train to be with Mrs. Antoinette Funk of Washington, D.C. She gave a talk here last night in the interests of Senator Kendrick. She is a really fine speaker. I saw an article recently which listed her as the best woman speaker in the U.S. She talked for about an hour and a half last night. I spoke for perhaps ten minutes. She is here in the interest of returning Senator Kendrick to the Senate. So far as I can figure out, she must be in the employ of the national Democratic committee, as she has been in every state where there has or is being a campaign to elect a progressive and defeat a standpatter.

The women's club here gave a reception yesterday afternoon for Mrs. Funk and me. It was the usual pink tea affair, rather a waste of time, I thought. Mrs. Funk expressed herself very decidedly the same after it was over. Of course we got to meet a lot of women, but we couldn't talk politics at all, nothing but weather and such inanities.

I am glad to say that Mrs. Funk corroborates John's and my belief that my trying to campaign the state would be a waste of time and money. I am of the opinion that one does not get many votes by speaking to crowds. Mrs. Funk says ordinary campaigning does very little good, and that the same money spent on letters, circulars, and postage brings in much greater results. As she said, the only advantage in going around at all is for the various candidates to meet each other and to get a little advertising that will let people know what they are running for. But as far as getting votes is concerned it isn't worth much.

Yesterday at the reception a woman played the violin. Jules loves violin music on the 'trola but I do not think he ever saw one played. He stationed himself in the middle of the floor right in front of the player, still as a statue at first, and looked up at her in the cunning way he has. Then he swayed a little with the music and acted as if he were charmed. People were as interested in him as in the music.

Monday, October 16, 1922

I will try to get this out before the mailman appears. It certainly is shiftless to wait till the time arrives for the mailman to come before starting to write, but somehow it seems that there are about two tasks for every minute until now, and plenty that could be done right now. I washed this morning and helped Carrie cook for eleven men and helped John off for a week's campaigning, so you see I did not waste much time. We were out of gasoline, so John took the truck and went to Powell to get some. He came back about nine o'clock with Mr. Edley and announced that they wanted to start immediately. He asked me to pack his bag and pack them a lunch, and then I had to see about a number of things that he had intended to tell me about but thought he would be here to look after — shipping some honey, running the electric light engine, etc., etc. Fortunately my washing goes right on whether I stand there or not, so I got it done before noon in spite of a dozen interruptions.

John and Mr. Edley are going to Meeteetsee first, and will do the territory between here and there on the way. They went by way of Penrose, then across the desert to the county line, up that, and on following the settlements to Meeteetsee. They expect to stop in Meeteetsee several nights, going to outlying farms from there, then on to Cody and back here by next Saturday night. Mr. Edley knows most of the people over that way, and is such a fine man. It will be worth John's time to meet all the people over the country and let them know who he is, whether or not he is elected.

Edith, I am glad you think the reading matter on my circulars makes up for the picture. The picture certainly is one that no one could be persuaded to vote for me because of my looks. It reminds me always of the country fellow who first saw a hippopotamus at the zoo. He looked for a long time in wondering silence, and then remarked, "My, ain't it plain!"

We finished up the invitations for Cecilia's party a little while ago and have those that are to be mailed all ready to go. I am having only a small party this year, six youngsters, most of them six years old. One is a little younger, and Max is a little older, but most are just six. There are a couple others I should like to ask, but if I start into other ages I will have to ask some I don't care to. Then, too, it is so much easier to plan a little party than a large one. If there are only six and Cecilia and two or three mothers it won't be much work. I think I shall use animal crackers and graham crackers for the refreshments, with fruit salad. I will ice the grahams and stand the animals up on them. The place cards will be paper Noah's arks, double, so the animals can be set inside. Of course there will be one birthday cake with the proper candles, but the animal crax will be most plentiful. Children always like them so much. We will use the Noah's ark you sent last Christmas for a table decoration.

What with politicking and birthday parties, I haven't had much time for letters. We went to a meeting Tuesday night and one Wednesday night, and yesterday was the party, so you see my spare time has been pretty well filled.

Tuesday night Senator Kendrick and Mr. Ross, the next governor of Wyoming (n'est-ce pas, Ted?) were the speakers, together with Mr. Louke of Sheridan, who is the Democratic candidate for state treasurer. So you see there was quite an assemblage of dignitaries on the platform (ahem). I had the honor of sitting between Senator Kendrick and Mr. Ross, and of being the only woman on the platform — not political platform, but stage. I was glad to meet Ross as I had been wanting to talk with him for some time. He and I had a talk at the hotel before the meeting and then walked from the hotel to the theatre together. I also had a talk with Senator Kendrick, and I think he and John walked together from the hotel to the theatre. Mr. Ross made a very good speech, and so did Mr. Kendrick. Mr.

Kendrick is a very mild speaking man, and absolutely refuses to say anything ugly about the opposition. He simply tells what he did in Congress and why, and then ends by saying that if he is returned to the Senate, he will hold the same views and do the same kind of work in the same way, and it is up to the people of this state to say what they want. If they want him again, all right; if not, all right.

Wednesday night we went to another meeting, a Republican one. The main speakers were Mrs. Morton and Mr. Winters, who is the candidate for the place Mondell is trying to leave vacant. A local candidate, Ewart of Cody, also made a short speech. Mrs. Morton spoke only about ten minutes and did not say nearly as much as I hoped she would. I was very anxious to hear her speak and to see her, as she had been so highly praised to me both as a woman and as a speaker. She makes a lovely appearance on the stage and has a lovely presence. I was very much disappointed in her speech, however, both because she did not really say anything and because she spoke in such a nice ladylike pink tea manner that people had difficulty in hearing and understanding her. Her voice was rather high and not at all full or strong. All she did in her speech was to review the various departments of the school system of the state, and say that each was doing this or that kind of work. Of course in a way she deserves credit for having some of these bureaus in operation, but most of them are merely routine procedure. People were anxious to have her state her policies in regard to educational matters and not merely enumerate departments. She merely said that she would appreciate any support the people present might give her or the Republican party in general. I am fully aware of the fact that pride goeth before a fall, but if I can't make a better speech than that, I certainly overrate myself tremendously. When I speak here next week I am going to make a real speech, and say something on the subject that people can carry home with them.

We had a fine time at the birthday party. Mrs. Reed came with Donald and she played with the children when they played in the yard, such games as Drop the Hdkf, and Here Come

Three Dukes A-Riding, etc. The first thing the children did was play with the lovely bird game Ted sent Cecilia. There were just enough to have a card each, and they drew the heads of the birds and tried to get the card filled first. Such excitement and such a good time as they had. I don't know how many times they played it over and over. Then they played on the lawn a while, and then came in and we made clowns, or really, jumping jacks. We cut the bodies and arms and legs from cardboard, let each youngster color his own and then fastened them together with string so the arms and legs move. They had lots of fun with them. Then the youngsters played outdoors a while again, while we set the table. We had a strip of crepe paper down the center, and on this the Noah's Ark you sent Cecilia last Christmas. Around this on the crepe paper were the animals that belong to the ark. Then on the table, around the edge of the crepe paper, were set graham crackers that had been iced and had an animal cracker standing on each graham cracker. So you see we had a procession of animals all around the table. The place cards were similar graham crax with two animals on them, and a slip of paper with the child's name. We served fruit salad and let them eat all the graham crax they wanted. Of course there was a pink-iced birthday cake with six candles on it. I had made crepe paper caps, geranium red trimmed in orange (!), tall ones like a witch's peaked cap, and when it was time to come to the table we gave each child one of these and they marched in, wearing the caps, and wore them while they ate. It all looked very festive.

When they went home, each one took along his red cap and his jumping jack, and a couple of animal-graham crackers. The success of a party to a child is what he gets to take home with him, I have discovered, and planned accordingly.

By the time this letter reaches Bloomington, we will be about at the end of the campaign here. Well, I wonder if our address will be Honeyhill or Cheyenne after January 1. I wonder how long it will take to find out if we are elected. In the primaries, when the vote was close, it was at least a week before we knew for certain. So if you do not get a telegram right away, folks at 822, you will know it is because we do not know ourselves what the outcome is. As soon as we are certain we will certainly let you know.

I was quite flattered last Thursday night when I spoke at Powell. It was a terrible night—a regular blizzard was blowing and it was quite cold. In spite of this the theatre was pretty well filled and most of the crowd was grown-ups. I spoke for about twenty minutes, I guess, maybe a little more. I could tell that the audience was listening and responding to what I had to say. A speaker soon knows whether or not his audience is with him. When I finished I wish you could have heard the applause. John said it is the most, and the most spontaneous, applause that any speaker, big guns included, has got here this fall with the possible exception of Senator Kendrick.

Well, this is the day we save the country, or at least the county and the state. It isn't often in one's life that one gets to vote for the whole family. Yes, we really voted for each other. I really think John will be elected, but I do not expect to be myself. I believe, however, if I had got out and campaigned a little over the state where the teachers could have heard me, expressing certain views on certification of teachers, I could have beat Mrs. Morton, women's clubs or no.

We sent a telegram to you this morning, Pater, saying "Indications are that both will get to stay at home." Since then we have not had any further word, so we still know no more. However, the local chairman thought that enough of the county had been heard from to elect both Republican representatives and that while Ross was ahead in the race for governor, the rest of the ticket would probably be Republican. Well, I hope that Ross gets the governorship, though as a matter of fact it would be rather hard for one lone Democrat to put into effect the legislation he wants if the rest of the officers and the legislature are Republican. Senator Kendrick was ahead in the race for Senator in the returns that had come in.

I really did not expect to be elected myself, because I knew if the Democrats won in the state they would do so by only a small majority, and I figured that most likely Mrs. Morton, being in office, would run enough ahead of her ticket to beat an unknown person like me. I hope, however, that she will increase her efficiency still more in the next four years and get standard courses of study and texts and a better certification system for teachers. Of course it is nice for teachers not to have to take examinations, but to get certificates on their college records, but I think that can be carried too far.

Well, I must stop writing and see that Jules gets a nap. He is so cross and sleepy. I will tell you more political news when we get it, but in the meantime you will know that we both are very much relieved that we can stay at home and attend to our own "bizness." Neither of us feels the least bit badly about being defeated, for we did not consider it a personal matter at all. We simply were called on to offer our services, we did, they were thought not necessary, and we are glad. That is the story. Of course it would be nice to be elected, but the price one would have to pay is really too much. So we are as glad as can be. Cecilia is delighted. You never saw a youngster more tickled. "Now we can spend Christmas at home, goody, goody." When John got the news he came to where I was, put his arms around me and said, "Now we won't have to get a radio set to talk with each other. I am glad." And you may be sure that I was as glad myself.

November 10, 1922

I guess it is conceded now that Ross is elected governor, for which let us all be duly thankful that the Union Pacific did not get its hold on the state any tighter than it already has. Hay, of course, was a Union Pacific man out and out.

I am delighted that you will get to go home, Edith, and especially that you can go while Janet is so wee. I think that a little baby is so cunning, and as you say, the folk at 822 have not got to see the children when they were tiny, except Co, who saw Jules a day or two last summer when he was still less than six months old. It really is lots easier to travel with a tiny baby than one a year old, for the small child stays where it is put, besides having its food at the proper temperature always without any bother to the mother. Another advantage for the mother is that she can go visiting while she is starved and can eat the company meals she gets everywhere without getting too much.

There are lots of farmers here who are finding it impossible to make ends meet, since the potato market went to pieces so. Ted may not believe it, but Mr. Mondell said that the farmers here did not deserve any sympathy, because they shouldn't have planted so many potatoes and that they had no one but themselves to blame for their bad financial situation. Naturally that did not make him many votes on the Project. Well, what I started out to tell you is a story that is being told of a man who has — or had — a farm near Powell. He had borrowed from the First National Bank, and found himself unable to meet the notes when they came due. He called up the president of the bank and asked him if he wanted the gates left open or shut. The president said, "Wait a minute. I want to talk to you about the deal." The farmer is reported to have answered, "Never mind. I am in a hurry to catch the train to get away from here. The farm is here. Help yourself. I just wanted to know if you want the gates open or shut." There have been a few mortgage foreclosures, but most of the cases are those in which the farmer just picks up and goes away, to find day labor work to support his family. Nearly all the farmers are having to do something else to support themselves this year. A great many are working for the government in the Willwood extension of the Project, or in Elk Basin, or anywhere and at anything they can find work. One man who lives near here loaded up his wife and four children in an open old Overland and started out only a few weeks ago for Missouri to see if he couldn't get work in the town where they used to live. I wonder if they got over the mountains before the snow storms broke.

P.S. Dear Cora:

Let me suggest that when Ted comes, you avoid the subject of politics if you want to have a good time, for Ted would lose all hope in you as he has in me if he finds out you voted for any Democrats. Of course he may not be as down on Indiana Democrats as he is on Wyoming ones, but he certainly is sore at Wyoming Democrats. He wrote me a special letter the other day to say he really voted for me, but that I was the only Democrat his family voted for. He went on to say that my being a candidate made it embarrassing for him, but as he had announced his intention to run before he had any indication that I intended to run, he could not change his plans. He admitted that he did not think my running hurt him, but he had to keep his skirts clear from a party standpoint. He admitted that Ross is a much better man than Hay and that Hay would have been more satisfactory to the machine politician, but says he could not see his way clear to vote for Ross, although Hay was a bitter pill to swallow.

Of course I wrote Ted to thank him for voting for me, and told him that I hoped he himself would agree that I really could not have refused the honor of being on the state ticket for the sole reason that my brother-in-law was a Republican. Personally, I think all this one-partyism is bosh, and I'd like to see anybody try to make me vote for someone I thought no good just because he happened to belong to my party. I am really very sorry to see Ted so tied down that he can't vote for the people he knows are the best candidates.

Of course you will not say anything about this to Ted or Edith, but I thought you would be interested in the fact that Ted thought my being a candidate on the opposite ticket made it embarrassing for him. I assure you his being a candidate on the opposite ticket did not bother me. In fact, I worked for him whenever I met anybody from his county. But he explained to me frequently that he could not do that for me.

Joe is working at Elk Basin, and Carrie moved there yesterday. He gets four dollars a day. If he has a permanent job, and holds out and can do the work, he will stay there, as he can make more clear money that way than by farming now. One couldn't make four dollars a day on the best farm on the Flat run by the best farmer in these times. John worked all the day before Carrie moved taking things to various places for her. She lent her piano to Richards. The canned fruit was all brought over here and put in our basement, and their supply of flour John stored upstairs here. Carrie tried to get someone to live in her house while they are gone, so she would not have to move everything, but she could not find anybody who would take it even for no rent, and she was afraid to leave anything of value in the house. They do not know how long they will be in Elk Basin, but I do not think Joe will farm next year if he can keep a job there. We have had several persons who want our place next year if they can get it. One of the neighbors got a return on a car of potatoes the other day, and got $61 for the entire car. Murrays shipped two cars. On one they got a return of about $85, and the freight on the car amounted to over three hundred dollars. So out of about $400 that the car of potatoes brought, the railroad company got over three hundred and the producer got less than a hundred. This was $30 less than enough to pay the help they had to have when they dug that car of potatoes. On the next car they got about $30 more than enough to pay their help, so on the two cars they got just about enough money to pay for the hired help they had to have in harvesting, not to speak of their own work then and all season, and any allowance for rent, seed, and water. The more potatoes one has this year the worse off he is.

We finished up the business of our Wyoming Beekeepers convention last night but do not leave Thermopolis until the noon train north today. We will get to Greybull about 2:30 and stay until Monday afternoon at the same time. It will be so fine to get to visit Edith for a Thanksgiving reunion of us here in Wyoming, and then to have her spend Christmas with you.

Honeyhill Farm
Powell, Wyoming
November 29, 1922

Mr. Joseph C. O'Mahoney, Vice-Chairman
State Democratic Committee,
Cheyenne, Wyoming.

Dear Mr. O'Mahoney:

Your letter regarding my expenses for the campaign was awaiting me at Thermopolis when I arrived there. I have not been able to answer sooner because of being kept pretty busy while we were away from home. We were both on the program for the State Beekeepers Convention, and were both chairmen and members of various committees, all of which kept us fully occupied all day and most of the night during the time we were at Thermopolis, for the greater part of four days.

I shall be very glad to send in $50 to the State Democratic Committee, as soon as we succeed in selling enough of our crop to have that amount available. I feel that is a small enough amount at best, and wish very much I were able to send more or at least to remit promptly but at present all I can do is wish. I am sorry that I could not spend the money in the campaign that it is reported my opponent had spent for her, for I really believe that if I had been able to cover the state the way she did the vote might have been quite different.

So far as I am concerned personally, I am really greatly relieved at not being elected, as my children are still so small it is a joy to be able to stay at home and look after them. But I was willing to sacrifice my personal affairs if I could be of any help to the Democratic party and the state. Perhaps four years from now I may be able to put in the time and money necessary to secure victory, if the party again needs me at that time.

Assuring you that I shall send in the amount stated at the earliest possible moment, I am

Very truly yours,

C.H.H.

December 3, 1922

I certainly put in lots of time thinking of you all today. You are at 822 now, and the folk all have a chance to see what a sweet cunning rascal Janet is and how Ruddy is just as cute as ever. I do wish we could all be together for a day or so, just so we could all hear the exclamations of the fond grandparents and aunt over the kindergarten — as well as to talk about a thousand other things. However, our visit last summer is still fresh in mind, and now that you are there, Edith, I think over again of the many things we did and how much joy we had in just being together. We will never forget the richness you put into our lives, Pater, by making that visit possible, and the memories of it are dearer every day.

We had such a good time today, when our crowd all had dinner here together. There were 22 of us all told, so we had quite a crowd. We had roast pork, a whole shoulder — the best you ever tasted, Swiss steak, which we would have called slow steak, mashed potatoes, corn, baked squash, brown, white, and raisin bread, parsnips, two kinds of pickles, pineapple-citron preserves, raspberry pie, and white cake and Devil's food.

Mrs. Hart said that Thanksgiving night her twelve year old boy came downstairs to her bedroom about an hour after they had all gone to bed, and wanted to stay there or have one of the other boys sleep with him. He expressed himself as being terribly worried. He felt as if he were going to die and was afraid to be alone. She had him take a dose of soda and go back to bed, and the next morning and ever since he has felt pretty foolish about the incident. I wonder how many of the crowd today will have to have company this evening!

I have been reading Hutchison's "This Freedom." Hutchison makes out a very good case for children who do not have a good home, but so far as I can see it, I do not agree that the reason why the home was not what it should have been was because the mother was in business. The reason was that she had wrong ideas of the things children should be taught. Faith was entirely missing in their education. They were to be brought up entirely on experience. Another wrong theory was that they were never to see either parent except when the parent was at his best and ready to play with the children. Life is more than play, and no mother can turn over to anybody else all the serious phases of a child's life and keep only the play part for herself. But I can't see that the mother's being in business was responsible either for these theories of hers or for the failures the children made of their lives. And the thing I do not agree with at all is the case that is made out against this mother for the failures of her children, when for exactly the same failure (suicide in one case) this mother's mother is not at all regarded as being to blame, but is merely to be pitied. In both cases the parents failed, but when one mother was in business she was to blame, of course, while in the other case, the mother who had given up her whole life just to stay at home and be a drudge was not to blame, O no.

I wish you could have been here Christmas Day to see the children, and especially Jules. Of course one expects a child of Cecilia's age to have lots of excitement and fun, but you would never, *never* believe that a child of 18 months would carry on the way Jules did. He did not walk straight once all day. Either he ran or he walked in circles. He shouted and yelled and squealed and made every sort of noise the human being is capable of. He played with everything there was, and knew absolutely that it was an unusual occasion, the most important one he has ever lived through. Part of the time we just sat and looked at him, and laughed till we nearly cried.

Honeyhill Farm
Powell, Wyoming.
December 26, 1922

Mr. J. S. Longwell,
Project Manager,
Powell, Wyoming.

Dear Mr. Longwell:

Replying to your notice of the 15th inst. concerning payment of building charges, I regret that it is necessary for me to state that I am unable to meet any of my charges, whether building or O & M, because of poor crop returns this season.

Grasshoppers destroyed about ten acres of oats and new alfalfa. We had prospects for a splendid crop of sweet clover seed, but the storm that occurred during the Project Fair week caught our seed crop when it was almost ready to harvest and blew off all the seed that was in the manner of ripe. I believe the entire fifteen acres will be a total loss. We did harvest most of the straw, but I do not believe it will yield seed enough that any threshing man will do the job. The potato crop is yet unmarketed and present market price gives no basis for hoping that the potato crop will pay production expense.

The thing that I was counting on most for means of paying these charges was the honey crop. But the past season was a poor honey season, the crop being not more than 2/3 an average normal crop. The honey market is so dull that I have been unable to move to date anything more than a small fraction of my crop.

When I gave Mr. Johnson my crop report, I gave him the full acreage of oats, whereas I should have deducted the number of acres that grasshoppers injured to such an extenet that it was not worth harvesting.

Very truly yours,
J.H.

JH:C

The Waterusers Association wants Mr. Murray to go to Washington, D.C. to represent their case before the Reclamation Service. Murray would be the best man on the Project to go, as he is so good at speaking and is so gentle and mild in his manner that he always gets an audience because his remarks are so logical and sound. He does not give the impression of being partisan, but yet proves every statement he makes and is incontrovertible. He is Scotch in his holding to his point and never letting the other fellow forget his argument. We were amused yesterday at Mrs. Murray's telling how his only suit is just about to wear out. She said he was afraid the seat would come through. I said he had better see that he got only on a standing committee, and she said that was what he said, but he had added that he was afraid if he sat on his pants all the way to Washington he would have to get on a sitting committee and stay seated after he got there. Mr. Murray has never had a new suit since they came here, eight years ago, and his old one is truly done for. So I suspect he will have to get a new suit before he starts on this trip.

John has gone to Powell this afternoon as he and Mr. Hardy and Mr. Graham have arranged with the state senator and representative from here to see them about the bee law the state beekeepers' association wants the coming legislature to pass. He also intends to go to the office of the county agriculturist and help in the work of filling out questionnaires that will give information on the present conditions of the farmers here. Mr. Wright, the agriculturalist, who is a federal man, has been called to Washington to report on the conditions on this project, and the men are anxious for him to have plenty of facts when he gets there. We have now some real hopes of promises from the heads of the Reclamation Service in Washington they will do something for the settlers here. At the present time, and for several years back, the payments due the government have been more per acre than the total value of the crops raised per acre. This means that if a settler pays his government charges he hasn't anything to live on, not to mention paying local taxes.

Of course what the settlers have had to do is to pay local taxes and let their payments to the government slide. There is a penalty attached, of course, a high interest rate, for overdue payments, but people have had no choice in the matter. The penalties have been out of reason, some of them as high as one per cent a month, or 12% a year, so that in a few years a man's bill gets pretty high. The Service has been asked to take off the penalties except a fair interest rate, and to give more time for the payment, so people here can live until this low price era is over.

Take ourselves, for instance. Of course we have not had a real farmer taking care of our place in the past few years, but we have not got enough from the place in the past few years to pay the water charges, not to mention taxes and building charges. In fact, we have not got as much as a hundred dollars from the farm in the past two years, except from the pasture, which has kept our two cows in the summer. Joe now has two carloads of the finest potatoes grown stored in our bee cellar, with absolutely no market, and the probabilities are that the potatoes will be hauled out on the field for fertilizer in the spring, the same as we hauled out load after load last spring. When a man produces really fine crops and can not sell them, then it surely is not his fault if he can't make payments. Almost every farmer here has a cellar full of potatoes and absolutely no market. Most of the people who shipped last fall did not get enough out of their net proceeds to pay for the help in digging. When the gross proceeds on a car of potatoes are $400 and the railroad gets $345 for freight, you can easily see where the farmer comes out. In fact, he doesn't come out. One of our neighbors said the other day that her menfolk farmed in the summer for occupation and ran a hay baler in the winter time to get enough money to pay for the farming in the summer time.

Cecilia is interested now in learning to count by fives and tens. She has got so now she can read in any easy book and really reads well. John has suggested that if she is up with the primary class in school we might let her go to school the last month or six weeks this spring after the weather is nice and settled and warm. It wouldn't be a bad plan, for then she could start in next year in the second grade without any difficulty. I am sure she can read now as well as any of the first graders and can do everything else as well as they can except perhaps write. I have the course of study and although I have been attempting to follow it, I found when I studied it that she was up on almost everything in it. I think it must be a pretty good course of study, for all the things in it that are given as the essentials are things she has picked up for herself this year. If the first grade course of study contains the things that a normal child naturally is interested in from six to seven years, it must be all right. This is the course of study that the state school superintendent's department was forced to get out at the request of various parts of the state, especially at the request of the superintendents of this and the three surrounding or adjacent counties. The state department does not have a required course of study, but finally got out this course which they *recommend.* You can bet if I had been elected I would see to it that the teachers were *required* to have some definite plan and not just to wander anywhere so that every school was different from every other in what the children studied and where they were at any time in the year. Most of the country teachers are young teachers who don't know how to make a course of study and need some standard plan to follow.

Did I tell you that the state school inspector had visited the rural schools here recently and had stated that our Star School was the best conducted rural school he had *ever seen anywhere?* It was given its shield for being a standard school and the inspector gave the teachers and pupils exceeding praise. Of course those who have been working to make it a good school feel quite good about it.

Although the whole Garland, Powell, and Star districts have been all put in together, the Powell school board turned over the general direction of the Star School to a committee of three men from the Star District. Technically they are an advisory committee from that district but really they have the direction of the school and the Powell board carries out whatever they ask for or recommend.

Friday, January 12, 1923

We had the pleasure of going to a sale yesterday, a real mark-down sale. One of the hardware companies here is having a big sale, and of course we went to see what they had. We got several things, chief among which I prize an electric iron. We had been intending to get one soon from a mail order house, but the store here was selling their seven dollar irons for $4.98, so we got one. It is a Western Electric Co. iron, for a 30-32 volt system such as ours. I ironed with it this morning and got done in about half an hour less time than if I had heated the irons on the stove. The advantage of an electric iron is that when you set it down for a minute it gets hotter, while an ordinary iron cools off. Then you save all the time of changing irons, and what counts for more, the time you lose when your iron is not just at the right temperature, and a stove heated iron is at the right temperature so little of the time because it is cooling off so fast.

February 5, 1923

John is going to Garland with some honey shipments and will mail these letters this morning. I am glad to say that the last lot of advertising we did has brought in a steady stream of orders. If we could only get an equitable rate on the Burlington for a carload shipment we might be able to sell a carload, for we have had an inquiry and at present we are the only honey producer in this part of Wyoming who can fill the order as it calls for 60, 10, and 5-pound containers. The Burlington has refused to lower the rate on carlot shipments of extracted honey the same as other western roads have done. Montmorency, the general freight agent of the Burlington, promised the reduced rate at a freight hearing in Sheridan last spring but went back on his promise later. All the other western roads give a rate of $1.35½ to all eastern and southern points. The Burlington charges about a dollar a hundred more. We and all the other beekeepers have been working at the matter for over a year but as yet do not have any assurance that the discrimination will be taken away. Montmorency wrote us that the Burlington had not been able to make satisfactory division arrangements with the eastern connections and that is why they can not give the regular rate. It seems queer that the U.P. and all the other roads can make arrangements with the eastern connections and the C.B. & Q. cannot. In fact, we had a letter from one eastern road that is a C.B. & Q. connection saying the Burlington had made no effort to get connecting rates. So there is evidently a nigger in the woodpile somewhere and at present we are trying to find out where and who he is.

February 6, 1923

No, Co, I hope you do not find any necessity for making a trip out here to help celebrate my birthday. I think you have tripped about enough for a few months to celebrate birthdays. We will excuse you from further attendance until in August when we hope you will be present for Edith's birthday, and for the birthday party that is to take place at Honeyhill about a week before Edith's birthday. We have not decided yet whether it will be in honor of John, Jr., or Cecilia's long desired sister. What would you advise? It would be so nice for Jules to have a brother only a little more than two years younger, as they could be almost like twins as they were growing up. But on the other hand, Cecilia does want a sister so badly. However, it would be so much easier to name a boy than a girl, so I guess I will vote for a brother. Please send your suggestions for girls' names, however, so we can be prepared for any emergency. I do not think you need to count on twins this time, for my proportions at this date do not warrant such hopes. At this stage before Jules arrived I had already such elephantine proportions that the whole neighborhood knew all about it and this time not even my snoopiest enemy knows it as yet — at least so far as I know anything about.

The mail carrier brought the box of valentines yesterday. I certainly wish you could have been here, Co, to hear the excitement. Such an exclamation party you never heard. I really don't know which was more delighted, Cecilia or her mother. Of course there couldn't be anything else done until we sat down and made some of the valentines. I had about a million things to do — I had washed in the morning and the separator wasn't even washed! — but we sat down and made valentines for several hours. We had the most fun!

Friday, February 16, 1923

John got the freight shipment Wednesday morning which turned out to be the barrel with the set of dishes. The barrel had evidently been shipped in a leaky car or else left standing somewhere outdoors where it was raining, for the straw in the barrel was all wet and frozen together. The paper that was around each dish was frozen to the dish. We unpacked the dishes from the straw and took off what paper we could, and then just set them all together on the dining table for them to thaw out completely before we began to handle them. We were afraid they might crack if we tried to wash them while they were so cold.

Since the dishes have been on the table it has been just like an art display. Every little while some of us or all of us would go into the dining room and look and admire. Cecilia has been wild about them, and even Jules would run in and shout "dish, dish!" I wish you could have been here for the grand opening, Pater. I know you would have laughed. Both children ran circles around the barrel and then watched like hawks for each piece that John pulled out, and shouted about it. Cecilia kept exclaiming at each piece, "O, isn't it beautiful!" Jules could hardly be held from wanting to touch them, but we kept him in his high chair after we began to unpack, and thus managed to make safety first prevail. While we were unpacking, Cecilia exclaimed, "O, they are so beautiful I just love them!" John said to her, "You'd better love Grandpa who sent them to us." "O," she cried, "I do love him, and I love Aunt Cora and Grandma too, for they are all sending us something nice all the time."

We want to thank you very much for this lovely gift. It will be such a joy to us forever, and we will always have pleasure in the use of the dishes, both because of their own beauty and usefulness, and also especially because every time we use them we will think of your love for us and our love for you. We wish we could repay you in some way, but we do not know of any way except by loving you all the time.

February 22, 1923

John is going to Basin on this morning's train. There is to be a meeting there of the directors of the state beekeepers association. They have a lot of dope on freight rates and think they can put the $1.35 rate across now. The president, Mr. Hamm, has been at Cheyenne getting the new bill about bees passed — the one we have worked over so many times — and while he was there he had conferences with a lot of railroad representatives and freight men and the public service commission, and in the meantime John has got a lot of new stuff on the Burlington proving that Montmorency's statements that he had been working to get the rate but can't make arrangements with their eastern connections are false. Every eastern connection has written us that the Q had no dealings with them on the matter!

Mr. Murray got back Monday from his trip to Washington, D.C. He was able to do a great deal in getting relief for the settlers here. Mondell, Warren, and Kendrick all worked with him heartily. When Murray first got there, Mondell promised to get through the House any bill Murray and his co-workers from other projects could get through the House committee on the subject. He frankly assured Mr. Murray that he did not think they could get any bill recommended by the House committee. But Murray set his teeth and rolled up his sleeves, and the bill was reported favorably out of committee before Murray left Washington. It was passed by the House last Monday and by the Senate yesterday, so Murray feels that his trip was worth making, and so do we all. He is a wonder when it comes to logical arrangement and presentation of argument, and he always sticks absolutely to the truth and never has to take anything back on cross examination. He was away nearly six weeks, and of course had a great trip.

Tuesday, March 20, 1923

I am sure you will be glad to hear that the equitable freight rate has been granted and we can now ship our honey at the same rate that growers on other lines than the C. B. & Q. can. We had letters yesterday from the New York Central, the Pennsylvania System, and the chairman of the central freight commission in Chicago. The new rate will be published in the next tariff issued. Mr. Hower called up from Basin this morning to say that he had just had a telegram saying that the rate would be in effect April 15. So we will now probably be able to ship a car of honey, for since sugar has gone up the honey market has stiffened and there is more demand for it. I am sure you will be interested in a statement the secretary of the Wyoming Beekeepers' Association wrote John the other day about getting the freight rate:

> I have received various communications from numerous sources advising the revision of the freight tariffs. Well, it now looks as though this particular battle in the war has been won. It is up to us now to look for new worlds to conquer.
>
> It seems to me that the credit for delivering the coup de grace to the Burlington in this fight belongs in a very peculiar sense to you. It was a master stroke on your part to write the Burlington's 'eastern connections'.

I think I told you that the Burlington promised the equal rate a year ago in April but later refused to publish it, even after having once sent a telegram to one of the station agents saying it was in effect. The reason they finally gave was that they could not make satisfactory division arrangements with their eastern connections. John conceived of the plan of writing their eastern connections and found out that they did not know anything about the matter at all. They wrote us that they were taking up the matter with the Burlington, and of course when the Q found it was in a hole, all it could do was give in. As long as the Q was dealing with a bunch of farmers, it thought it could be saucy as it pleased. The Q in this case used exactly the same plan that the Republican State Committee in this state did last fall — banked on the ignorance of the people. But fortunately in both cases the people weren't quite as ivory-topped as expected.

Co, I take the *Woman's Home Companion*, and have ever since I have been married. I like it very much but I wouldn't give a whoop for the *Ladies Home Journal*. I think the *Companion* is the most sensible and helpful of any of the woman's magazines. I read every bit of it every month and always find something useful in my housekeeping, if only to find that I am doing my work the way Miss Bradley (Miss Farmer's niece and successor) says it should be done! No, of course I'm not stuck up. I'm merely telling the truth! Really, though, there have been a number of articles telling how to make a kitchen efficient, what your pantry should be stocked with for everyday use, and the like, and I was surprised to find that with only a minor exception or two I filled the bill. So of course you can readily see that I think Miss Bradley is very sensible. The stories are nearly always good, and usually clever and refreshing. Then too, the longer fiction is by people who write worth-while stuff, and there is very little "society" fiction. All in all, I wouldn't be without the *Companion*, but wouldn't pay five cents a year for the *Journal*. I like the *Companion* fashions better than any other, not excepting *McCall's* and the *Delineator*, and the *Pictorial*.

John got a letter from the Governor yesterday and his commission as a member of the State Board of Agriculture. I
have been teasing him ever since and asking if he intended to
have his diploma framed. The commission is a great big parch-
ment about the size of a high school diploma, with "State of
Wyoming, To All To Whom These Presents Shall Come,
Greeting, Know ye," and so forth, and the big gold seal attached
to the lower left hand corner, the signatures of the governor
and secretary of state — all it lacks to be a real diploma is a
piece of ribbon fastened to the seal. We did not have any idea
it would be such a formal affair. Governor Ross wrote a very
nice letter of appointment. Policy and good politics? Sure. If I
had been elected I would be doing the same stunt myself.
However, it is pleasant for a change to get it instead of handing
it out; the duck likes it, you know.

John had a busy time at Cheyenne as he had so many things
to look after, beside the work of the Board itself. He seemed
to be the only Board member who had planned anything,
for he was the only one who introduced any motions not per-
taining to the actual routine work of the Board. Evidently the
other members thought his ideas were cushions, for they sat
down on everything he proposed doing. There were several
matters he was very anxious to get started, but the Board did
not care to take them up right now. John told them he had
hoped they would share with him the honor of accomplishing
these necessary things, but that since they declined, he would
have to go ahead and get all the honor himself.

John had a lovely letter the other day from Senator Kendrick
congratulating the state of Wyoming on having John as one
of the commissioners on the Agricultural Board. The Senator certainly knows how to write a nice letter. And as I said

before, of course the duck likes it. Senator Kendrick is always right there ahead of time when it comes to doing the courteous thing. You remember the piece about St. Valentine? "He did the little kindnesses that most despise or shun; he never did the greater good and left the less undone." Kendrick certainly does the greater good, but he never leaves the less undone. Which makes me believe he is a real man, for he never seems to do it just for the sake of being nice, but always manages to have his letter or word convey the impression that he really means it.

April 30, 1923

We are feeling pretty good about the way the bees have come through the winter. Last year we tried the Kansas Experiment Station plan of wintering and found it the best scheme we had ever got hold of. It is a doubling up plan. In the fall, you put two hives together, one on top of the other, and leave them that way for the winter. Of course you lose the queen from one hive, but if the bees winter well, the queen that is left raises enough bees by the time the honey flow starts to make two good hives again, and you then divide them and give one of the hives another queen.

Well, John went over the yards the other day and he found that out of the 264 double hives he packaged away last fall there is *one* dead hive and perhaps a dozen or so that do not seem very strong. Think of it! Heretofore, with any system we have tried, indoor or out, we never got by with less than from 20 to 30% loss in the winter. Each spring we have had to spend from one to two thousand dollars to buy more bees from the south to replace the ones that winter killed. John says if we had known of this plan ten years ago we would have saved at least $10,000. Now if the grasshoppers and the clover thrip don't ruin the alfalfa and clover, we ought to begin to make some money, provided of course we can sell what we produce! However, we got such a good start on the direct marketing that in another year we ought to be independent of the carload buyers. It means lots of work, but it certainly pays. John said the other day that if I hadn't been able to play a typewriter, we would never have got this far, and he would not be on the State Agricultural Board. I told him I had always been sorry I could not play the piano for him, but that probably it was better to be able to play the "typy" than the piano since I was not one of the fortunate mortals, like Edith, who can do both.

Tuesday, May 15, 1923

I was so glad to get your letter, Co, telling about your Logansport trip. It is fine that you can make such a good speech, so that people are delighted when you talk. Of course we all know that ourselves, but others don't, and we are all glad when they find it out. It certainly gives one a bit of pleasure to know that she can meet any situation that comes up. I was afraid that I had been hibernating so much that I had lost my old-time ability to hornswaggle an audience into thinking that I knew something, but I found out last fall when I went out politicking that I could still make folks believe I was a speaker. On several occasions there were persons in the audience who were really somebody, and of course it was their interest that I watched most closely. It was interesting, too, to see them sit back in their seats when I started to talk, as if they thought — well, she is a woman and of course I will listen politely. Then I could see them sit up straighter and straighter, and really pay attention to what I was saying. After the meeting was over, I could tell from the way they spoke and what they said that they meant it when they congratulated me. I generally had to make up my speeches in between times and on the way to the meetings, too, for I had various other things to occupy my attention most of the time. So I am sure that you can make a speech at any time, Co, on any occasion, with any or no notice.

I wish you could have had some of the fish we had for supper Saturday night. It was fresh fish, with a vengeance. When John did the chores, he discovered that a trout about a foot long had come down the irrigation ditch and decided to stay in the little pool that has washed out where the ditch turns east at the pump in the barnyard. It was a rainbow trout, I think. He brought it up and dressed it and he and Cecilia decided they wanted it right away. So just as soon as he brought it into the house, I started to cut it in pieces to fry. The fish hadn't been killed ten minutes, I guess, and when I stuck my knife into it along the back bone and started to cut, there was enough reflex action left for it to object strenuously. I yelled and dropped it, and it wiggled in the pan. John came into the kitchen and finished cutting it up for me. It is absolutely ridiculous what a shock that wiggling gave me, for it made me cry, and I laughed at myself for crying and cried while I was laughing. John didn't know what to make of me for a minute, and then he saw that I hadn't lost my sense of humor and that I would be all right in a minute or two, so he patted me on the shoulder and told me to cheer up. I guess I am somewhat nervous these days, and some crazy little incident will set off the fireworks for a minute or two.

May 24, 1923

I must tell you a compliment I got the other day from Cecilia. We were talking about our next baby, merely in general. She does not know anything definite yet, as I thought I would wait till school was out before I said very much to her, as one never knows how much a child will repeat without meaning to tell things. But suddenly she said, "Well, I think we are going to have a baby before long." Of course I wanted to know just why she thought so, as I was curious to find out what she did think. Finally she said, "I am positive we will have a new baby, because you are so sweet and smiling all the time."

Saturday, May 26, 1923

I wish you could all have been with us yesterday at the picnic dinner at the last day of school at Star. Talk about things to eat — if there is anything that is that wasn't on the table, it is because it doesn't grow or isn't made, that's all. One couldn't help wishing she had as many stomachs as a cow, or could store up food the way the camel does water.

I am pleased to state we now have a girl to stay with us all the time. She came last night. Her name is Norma Myers and she is a high school girl from Powell. Mrs. Osborne told us about her last summer, and when we couldn't get anybody else this time we got her. I think she is about 18, and is a good big girl. Mrs. Osborne says she has been cooking since she was 13 years old and can do anything about the house. She is a neat looking girl and her mother is always as neat as a pin. Their house looks nice, so I guess she knows how to do things. It will certainly be nice to have our house looked after. John does enjoy having a clean, neat house to sit down in after his work outside is finished, and when I had everything to do I couldn't always keep the house looking the way I wanted it to. The outside yard work in the bees will soon start and then of course I can put in my time to advantage helping John, and he will need help, for we have more bees this year than we have ever had.

Time out for the worst hail storm we have ever had out here—John says the worst one he has ever seen anywhere. We do not often have this sort of storm here. There was a heavy cloud to the south the latter part of the morning and all during noon. About one o'clock it began to break and drift this way. There were huge flying clouds that swung from the high clouds to the ground, and then the whole thing moved this way. Talk about hail! The ground was white when the first shower was over, which, strange to say, came from the northwest. Then there was a short lull, and another shower came, this time from the southwest. Between them they certainly knocked things. You could scoop up the hail with a shovel from the porches and alongside buildings. The fields looked as if it had snowed, for everything was white. The lawn was covered with hailstones and with leaves from the trees. During the storm the leaves flew from the trees as in the fall. My squashes, that stood up so straight and high this morning when I hoed them, are flat on the ground and I suspect nothing but stems. It is too wet to get out to see. The corn looks stripped. I have an idea that this will set the garden back for a week or so in maturing. We are wondering what it did to the beets in the fields, for it surely must have stripped the leaves. There is one thing certain— I won't work in the garden this afternoon, for it rained until everything is soaked. I wonder what the hail did to the strawberries. The storm was really beautiful to look at, for while the heavy black cloud was all over the south and most of the west, and it was hailing like everything here, over to the north and east the sun was shining as brightly as ever on the Pryor and Big Horn Mountains. Then later when the storm had passed here and the sky to the south was blue again, the clouds were between here and the mountains to the north and east and we could see the flying movement of them there.

June 24, 1923

The hailstorm the other day certainly made our garden look sick. The corn is entirely stripped and just the midribs are standing up. But I suppose it will grow again from the centers where they are not entirely killed. The lettuce was just heading, and the tops were beaten off to within a few inches of the ground. The peas were badly battered but I think they will recover. The tomato plants were just showing buds, and the tops were beaten off them, so they will have to start all over again, if indeed they survive. But it was the strawberry patch that was the sorriest sight you ever saw. The leaves were beaten off, so many of them that the next day the patch smelled like a hayfield curing. The green berries were knocked off, and I picked up all that were of any size, hoping perhaps I could save them. I picked up over two gallons of large berries that were still green or just showing a slight bit of color. I have them in a crate and they are ripening, so I think maybe I can make jam of them. They will not be as good as plant-ripened berries, but they will be as good as the early shipped berries and won't be an entire waste. I guess we lost at least half our crop from the hail.

July 3, 1923

We had some good news the other day. The honey market has picked up, and Mr. Hardy has sold a car at 8½, the price at which we have been holding ours for. Mr. Hardy was here the other night and said that he had a chance to sell another car at that price and wanted to know if we would let ours go with his. He does not have enough for a second car and we do not have a whole carload left, but together we can make up the car. So our honey will probably move in the course of a week or two. We will be very glad, for this will give us a chance to get some money on hand, to pay off some of what we owe at the bank, and to have enough to keep us running until the new crop begins to move. We have been selling some all the time, in small lot shipments, chiefly to postmasters, enough to keep our running expenses provided for. We have paid up all interest as it came due and have paid off about at the rate of a hundred dollars a month besides having enough to run on, so you see we have sold quite a lot of honey from our campaign of letter soliciting. But of course it will be very handy to get rid of a lot at once — about 30,000 pounds — and get a little money ahead.

July 25, 1923

Mrs. Murray has invited Cecilia to go with them today to Cody to see the Mrs. Harry Payne Whitney art exhibit in the library building and then to go to the Farm Bureau picnic which is held in a grove a few miles this side of Cody. I am sure Cecilia will have a fine time. I should like to go to both myself if I were as usual, but right now it is too much trouble to attempt such a jaunt. I do hope I can get to see the art exhibit, however, for that is worth seeing. It has been shown only in three places heretofore — New York, Paris, and Chicago. A number of west coast cities wanted the exhibit, but since Mrs. Whitney is making the Buffalo Bill statue for Cody, she decided to put the exhibit there this summer, and it will be there until the tourist season is over.

John heard this morning that President Harding died last night at San Francisco from pneumonia following ptomaine poisoning. Too bad. That will make political things buzz for quite a while, won't it. It makes it rather certain that the Republicans will now have a pretty progressive man as their next presidential candidate and makes La Follette's stock go way up.

I weeded in the garden this morning, and picked corn and beans, so I am rather glad this afternoon to have a sitting down job. I have been working at some overalls of John's that needed the bibs altered, and want to make the two plisse dresses I have cut out. Bending over and stooping down are not the easiest positions for me at the present reckoning. My curves curve the wrong way for that sort of posture.

Our chautauqua begins next Saturday, the 11th, and lasts six days. I am not counting on being among those present this time. Do you know the story of the man in Texas who heard for the first time somebody talking about a chautauqua, and after asking for information on the subject, remarked that he did not see the necessity of bringing in people from outside, for there were plenty of she-talkers in the community to keep going for six days. Well, we may have a she-talker of our own about that time, if it's not a boy. I have everything all ready now for the birthday party, except washing one old blanket to wrap the baby bunting in. I expect to wash that tomorrow with the other clothes.

Cecilia's new bed came yesterday and she talked all day about sleeping in it in her own room upstairs last night. She could hardly wait till the bed was put together and the beddings arranged. She had to have both daddy and me come upstairs to tell her goodnight and to see her in her new bed. She was proud as a peacock. And in about half an hour she was downstairs perfectly willing to sleep near us again. The window rattled — there was a storm coming up — and a moth flew about the room, and she was so lonesome she did not want to stay there alone. She explained that when a person was used to sleeping in a room with other people it did seem awfully lonesome all by herself. I have an idea she felt about as big as a mosquito in that big bed in the big room, all alone. So she concluded she would not try to sleep in her new bed until Aunt Cora is here to sleep with her.

Garland Wyo 205 p Aug 12 1923

Joseph Hennel — 822 East 3 St Bloomington Ind
Cora and niece arrived this morning   Cecil doing fine
John Hendricks

Sunday morning, August 19, 1923

Dear Pater and Mamma,

It has been some time since you had a letter from me, myself, hasn't it? I am so glad Cora has been here to do the writing this past week. With her and Carrie and Norma here, I didn't have to worry about anything.

A week ago right now we were in the midst of the party. I am so glad it is all over and that the baby and I are both all right. I got along so much better this time than with Jules, although Anne was several hours longer in coming than Jules was. The doctor gave me ether at the last. The head was here before they gave me enough ether to put me clear under, but Carrie says the shoulders were larger than the head and that it was quite a long time before the shoulders came, so that it was a good thing I was spared that suffering. I think that helped a lot, for I did not have any of those pesky chills afterward this time. I shook from about eight in the morning until after twelve, all the while the party was on, but not as hard as after Jules came. Since then I have had only one slight indication of a chill, and that was during the night Friday night. I woke up chilling and starting to shake, but John immediately covered me warmly and in less than fifteen minutes I was asleep again all right. I am thankful I am so strong and expect to be able to get up this time by the tenth day.

Anne evidently weighed more than the doctor thought, for when Carrie weighed her this morning she weighed 8½ pounds *net*, and she couldn't have gained 3/4 pound in the first week. I wish you could see what a fine baby she is, with as much black hair as Edith Rhoda when she arrived. John calls her Royal Anne.

Wednesday, August 22, 1923

As you see, I am back in the office again. However, using the machine is not necessarily a proof of that, for this morning before I got up John wanted a letter written, so I had him bring the machine to bed and sat up in bed and typed the letter.

Of course you know by now that we named the baby Anne Carolyn for her two grandmothers. John has a sister named Anna, as well as one named Carrie, so the name is a regular family one. We will call the baby Anne. I have said all along that she looks like Grandma Thuman, which means that she looks like her Grandma Anna, and like her mother, for it has always been said that you looked like your mother, Mamma, and that I look like you.

Norma just remarked that she never saw a father and son as much attached to each other as Jules and John. She added that it would be a help in making Jules grow up to be a fine man to have him think as much of his daddy as he does and his daddy think as much of him. Jules will never admit that he is anybody's else baby or boy but daddy's. He says he loves mother, but he is always daddy's boy.

Our school will start a week from Monday. Cecilia wants to go, of course, but she is not very anxious for school to start, and I rather sympathize with her. I hate for her to start again. She still seems quite a baby to me, even if she will be seven years old this fall. She is quite excited about going to Elk Basin to stay with Aunt Carrie for the next few days, and the trip is as large to her as if it were a railroad journey.

What would you call me if I told you that I have lifted over two tons this morning? Figure it out for yourself. I filled 110 ten pound pails with honey, and in filling and putting the cans away in cases I had to lift each can four times and wheel them (12 cans at a time) about forty feet in the wheelbarrow. Four times ten times 110 makes quite an amount all in one figure but taken ten pounds at a time is not heavy. John is extracting, and I am trying to keep the tanks empty ahead of him so he does not have to stop extracting to draw off. Norma washes the cans and I do the drawing off. As we wash the cans by putting them over a jet of live steam, the washing is very easy to do. The cans get very hot and will dry in a jiffy when they are so hot.

If you saw the way I eat, Mamma, I am sure you would not worry about my needing any tonic. I am the working man of the family now, from the way I am hungry all the time. I always am hungry while I am nursing a baby. As for the wine or liquor, a piece of bread and honey does me as much good and as quickly, for honey, you know, is immediately absorbed and does not need digesting, since the bees have already done that. Like water, it is immediately taken into the blood, without the need of any action on the part of the digestive juices. I remember when Cecilia was born, that just as soon as the baby and I were both taken care of, the doctor said to me, "Now you can have a little whiskey in some water for a stimulant." I asked him if it was necessary, saying I did not care for it. He replied, "O, no, not necessary. A cup of cocoa will do as much good and have no after effects." So of course I informed him that I preferred the cocoa, which Mrs. Van Eman forthwith prepared and gave to me, and I went to sleep. So you need not worry about not having sent some of your cordial. You and Pater use it, if it does you good. I don't need it.

Friday, October 5, 1923

Edith, why don't you get the Bighorn County correspondent position to the Cheyenne *Tribune*? I got it for Powell and find that I can make a little money at it. It does not take more than half or three quarters of an hour each week to type the news items, and so far I am earning about 75 cents to a dollar a week. In the course of a year, forty or fifty dollars will come in handy. Then, too, you get your own paper at half price, which makes it cost you only $3.50 a year, so you earn $3.50 that way. I am frank to state that I usually take the Powell *Tribune* when it comes out each week and hash into brief form the news. You wouldn't have to depend on that, however, for Ted gets about enough to know most of the important things that are happening. You are supposed to clip your stuff and send it in once a month. You are paid at the rate of ten cents an inch. It is surprising how many inches a typed page will make. I figure that even if I don't earn enough to keep the wolf from the door in this manner, I may be able to get a few magazines that we otherwise would feel we could scarcely afford; and every little bit helps in a short crop year.

Wednesday, November 14, 1923

Edith, you can count on us for turkey for dinner the Sunday after Thanksgiving. We will bring the turkey along when we go down to Thermopolis on Thanksgiving Day, and trade it for the loan of your black lace dress. We are to have a banquet on Thanksgiving night, and I would like to wear the dress and my new pearls that Mamma and Pater sent for Anne's birthday. Our new state apiarist, Mr. Corkins, who is professor of entomology at the University of Wyoming, will be there, as he is arranging the convention. There will be various beekeepers and county agents, and their wives, from all over Wyoming. The state apiarist of Utah will also be there, and the director of markets for Colorado, as well as the manager of the Colorado Honey Producers Association. Our own State Commissioner of Agriculture Faville will be there, and the managing editor of the Wyoming *Stockman Farmer.* Dr. Nelson, former president of Wyoming U., will give the main speech at the banquet, and another noted person who will attend the meeting is Dr. Phillips, of Washington, D.C., head of the government entomology bureau. So you see there will be quite a gathering, and I should like to appear as little like a hick as possible. For this reason I crave the lace dress to wear that evening, as I am on the entertainment committee. When one travels with three children, two of them babies, she can't take much of a wardrobe for herself, but I think I shall manage to take along at least one extra dress, my blue silk with the tango georgette inserts, besides my blue serge, which I shall wear. When I told John I was going to borrow Edith's lace dress and wear the new pearls, he said, "Yes, and the folks will think that I can afford to buy you such an expensive looking outfit." I assured him that he needn't worry, for nothing succeeds like success, and the folk would think he was a very successful man if his wife wore lace and pearls.

November 18, 1923

Have you seen Douglas Fairbanks in "Robin Hood"? It is certainly worth seeing. The price here was 50 cents, and it was worth it. The ordinary shows are 35 cents, and this one was worth about three ordinary ones. Mary Pickford in "Daddy Longlegs" comes soon, and I should like to see that too. We enjoyed "Penrod and Sam" so much two weeks ago when it was shown here. The local theatre gets all the best things, I am glad to say.

November 20, 1923

John is at work tearing down the ice house. We have always had trouble in getting ice to keep longer than till about September. He is planning to build an ice house inside the big shop, in the northeast corner of the original part of the shop. He thinks if he puts the icehouse there, with the double roof and walls, and then the roof and walls of the shop too, the ice will keep all the year around. He is knocking out enough of the concrete floor to make a drainage get-away. He will use the lumber from the ice house and the old coal shed to make the new ice house.

Well, our convention sessions are over and we had a great time. We began Thursday night and ran morning, afternoon and night yesterday and morning and afternoon today. They tried their best to elect John as secretary-treasurer, but he absolutely refused. They wanted to elect me, but of course I wouldn't consider it, for which of us was secretary wouldn't make any difference in the wash. We already have as much on hand as we can do.

We had a fine program. As I told you, Dr. Phillips of Washington, D.C. was here, and Dr. Crane, president of Wyoming U. and both of them are splendid. I talked quite a lot with both of them and enjoyed it very much. We had a nice banquet last night, at which I wore Edith's black lace dress and the lovely pearls.

I was chairman of the constitution and by-laws committee — we had never got that done at previous meetings — and of the resolutions committee, both of which took the biggest reports and the most work of any committee. We had so much program that the committee had to meet at odd times, and what with the three children to look after — there was no one I could get but the girl clerk when she wasn't busy — I had to put in a pretty strenuous few days. This afternoon after I had finished the reports for the committees I was on, the members presented me with two huge bags of candy, for the children and me, as they said, a small expression of their appreciation for the work I did. Wasn't that lovely? I knew they had taken up a ten cent collection but of course I didn't know what it was for, as they planned it while John and I were both out of the room. I was the only woman here. Several men planned to bring their wives but the children got sick and the women did not come.

I enjoyed so much working with Prof. Corkins, who is head of the Entomology Department and State Apiary Inspector. He is the dearest kid, about 25, I should guess, but younger looking. He has a wife and a son the same age as Jules.

The State Association has done fine work in the two years it has existed and it was John who really organized it. The biggest thing we have done is to get a department of entomology with a real scientist (Prof. Corkins) established at the University. Instead of working just for an apiary department, this association did the bigger thing of asking for the entomology department, which takes care of all branches of agriculture. So you see we are not selfish.

Sunday, December 30, 1923

Going down! The thermometer went to twenty below last night and will probably go to 25 below tonight. Yesterday and the day before were blizzardy with heavy wind. Today was pretty cold all day, as the temperature did not come up much above ten below all day.

We had invited Bygrens, Loverchecks, and Horns to dinner last night, but when the storm stayed so bad and the temperature kept dropping, we called them up and offered to put it off till noon today. Horns and Loverchecks all came, but only one, Ruth, came of the Bygrens.

We also invited the sheep man, who has a flock of 1500 sheep on the lower part of our farm, so altogether there were nineteen of us. We served roast veal, mashed potatoes, lima beans, escalloped corn, sauerkraut, pickled beets, bread and butter, honey, ice cream, cake, and coffee. Everybody seemed to enjoy the meal, and as most of them went back twice for the main course and for dessert, I think they liked what they had to eat. We made a two-gallon freezer of ice cream and as they did not eat it all for dinner, we had them help themselves to another round before they went home, so it was all eaten but about a quart, which I sent to Youngs when George came for the milk this evening.

Well, the rest of the family is asleep, and I must go too. We wish you all a most happy new year, with everything that you can possibly desire coming your way.

Thursday, January 31, 1924

Mildred Lovercheck died last night about nine o'clock, and Mr. L. was so worried about Mrs. L. he wanted to get her to a quiet place, so they stayed here last night, along with Mary and Grandpa. Mildred took sick two weeks ago last Sunday. The doctor said appendicitis so they took her to the hospital at Powell. She got along splendidly for nearly two weeks, then she got worse and they found an internal abscess. She rallied after that and then went up and down, sinking in the afternoon and rallying in the evening but constantly getting worse. Mrs. L. said she seemed to die by inches. She was paralyzed for several days but was conscious until a short time before she died, and went so gradually they could hardly tell when she was gone. The whole community is sad, for she was a general favorite and as good a girl as ever was.

Saturday, February 16, 1924

It seems to me I have been more occupied the past few weeks than ever before. I don't know that I do any more than usual but it seems to take me all the time to do it. I must have spring fever or something like that, for by the time I get done what has to be done I am too tired and stupid to do much else. Usually I can write letters in the evening but the past week or two I couldn't even do that. I suspect the real reason is that Anne is beginning to get the best of me, and that what extra strength I have she gets. Fortunately she is now old enough to begin to feed some cow's milk, so I hope to save my strength by feeding her that way about one time a day from now on. I gave her some day before yesterday, and she held on to the glass for dear life and drank about a quarter of a glass before she would stop. If she will keep on doing that I will be all right soon, for in another couple months I can wean her entirely. Cecilia was weaned entirely when she was ten months, but Jules was eleven months when he stopped nursing.

I made a speech at the high school yesterday and was advised that it was very good. The occasion was university day. One day each year, usually in February, is set aside as university day, at the request of the state university. President Crane sent out a letter to every high school, to be read by one of the students as part of the program. Another student told about debating at the state university; another about the record of the Powell high school here; another read an article on the future of the university. One of the teachers, Mr. Crawford, a grad of the university, told about the new gym and other new buildings, and of the university and of the improvements since he was a student there. There was some singing of patriotic and state songs. My speech closed the program. I talked for fifteen or twenty minutes on the subject of "Why Go to College." I told the students they should go to college for three reasons: for success in what occupation they enter, for friends, and for the training that will make them good company for themselves. Under the second topic I included matchmaking and told Brother John Craven's story about the state university being the state match factory, and the one about the trustee who objected to making I.U. coeducational because it would be so dangerous to send girls to school with so many boys. You remember how he was converted by the other trustee who asked him if he ever expected his daughters to marry and if so, what sort of men. I told them they would meet fine people at college. I asked them how they would like now to pick out a coat they would wear for the rest of their lives, and suggested that their mental styles would change as well as their clothing styles, and that a misfit in a life companion was even worse than a misfit in clothing. The reason why I took advantage of the opportunity to say such things was the large number of marriages last spring of high school boys and girls. I thought it wouldn't hurt to suggest to them that they would be better off by waiting a few years to pick out their life partners. Of course I told as many jokes and funny stories as I knew that fitted the various points, and managed to hold the attention of the youngsters pretty well, even though it was past time for school to be dismissed, and they were getting restless.

Sunday, February 17, 1924

I must tell you that I am going to have another new dress besides the lovely serge you sent me, mamma. I saw a dress in the Mont Ward Jan-Feb sale catalogue that interested me particularly. In fact, it is the only dress I have seen in a cat for months that I really wanted and I was crazy as a youngster about this one. It has a blouse part of Spanish lace and a skirt part of charmeuse. There is a flower bouquet at the belt. I figured that the dress would be nice for evening wear, and yet with the charmeuse skirt would not be too fancy for afternoon wear. I ordered mine in black, and I do hope they won't be sold out when my order arrives. As the dress cost the immense sum of $3.98 you see I will probably not cause a bank failure in Powell on account of my extravagance.

February 29, 1924

Mrs. Lovercheck was very much amused at a woman who sat behind her in the court room at Cody for the Carey trial. Mrs. Lovercheck took a little vacation — from Monday to Friday — and went to Cody while Mr. L. was on the jury, and as she had never been in a court before, she was very much interested in seeing the procedure. She said this woman kept saying mournfully all through the trial that that jury would be sure to convict Carey and that you couldn't expect anything else from such a bunch of men. Mrs. L. finally got interested enough to inquire why, and the woman announced it was because they were all Methodists. She then launched forth into a tirade, explaining that she could always tell a Methodist when she saw one, and that there were eight on the jury. Mrs. L. was highly amused, and interested in the earmarks of a

Methodist, but the woman did not seem able to impart to anyone else her ability to spot a Methodist or her system for doing so. As a matter of interest, Mrs. Lovercheck inquired and found that there actually were three Methodists on the jury. She said that all through the trial this woman was a regular circus to others because of her comments on the Methodists and their ways.

My new dress has come and the lace part is lovely. The satin (charmeuse) part is not as good a material as one could desire, but the dress altogether is quite pretty. It has a cunning bunch of gold and silver and colored flowers at the belt, and silver and gold braid around the sleeves.

Monday, March 10, 1924

The children are happy, for Jackie Coogan is to be at the movie tonight in "Long Live the King," and they are to go. They want me to go too, and take Anne, but I think Anne and I will keep house and sit down and rest a bit while the rest go. It is really hard work to take all three of them out at night in the winter time. They all go to sleep on the way home, and my arm just about numbs off trying to hold them all up on the seat and keep them covered.

Friday, March 14, 1924

When the men came in for dinner they sniffed and sniffed and went about with such beatific expressions that I told them if I had a bouquet of roses they couldn't seem any more pleased. They responded that roses would fade, but the sauerkraut I was canning would last all summer. We made a four gallon jar of it several weeks ago and it is just "ripe" now, and I am canning it today. I canned four quarts and four pints this morning, have another pan ready to can now, and a third still in the jar. It is so handy to have it in the jars, and more economical, for if one leaves it in the big jar a little on top always spoils each time. This way there is practically no loss.

Friday, March 21, 1924

When I wrote you some time ago that I did not believe the price of my new lace and silk dress would cause any of the banks in Powell to go broke, I had no idea that in a few weeks the Powell National (Dowling's bank) would close its doors, which it did this morning, tying up whatever cash we have on deposit. Fortunately we had settled up all the bills owed, except to the bank, so we do not have more than a few hundred dollars on deposit. We have some checks on hand that we had not deposited, and have quite a bit of money yet outstanding for small lots of honey we had sold, so we are not worried about having a few dollars on hand for running expenses as needed. We were laughing this noon about how we could get along without cash for a while. We decided we had a cellar full of all sorts of meat, vegetables and fruit, an upstairs full of flour, plenty of lard, honey, milk, and eggs, so that we could get along for quite a while without buying anything from the grocery, and if we did want to, we could get it in trade for eggs. Postage stamps is about the only thing we absolutely have to have, except gasoline, and we thought we might be able to scrape up enough cash to provide those two items. If we run out of stamps, we will let you know, and you can send us postage for a return whenever you write us a letter.

John decided the other day he wanted to go to the Shriner minstrel next week, so he bought tickets for himself and Cecilia. He has been joking ever since we heard the bank was closed about having the tickets. Each time anything is said about what we have, he adds, "And two tickets to the vaudeville."

March 26, 1924

We have a new ice box, which is very nice. It has only two doors, one for the ice chamber and one for the food chamber. It is plenty large enough for us, as it has an ice capacity of 100 pounds, and in the food chamber has two shelves, so with the bottom there are three places for food. The food chamber is 24 inches wide, 13½ inches deep, and 20 inches high. It is all white enamel inside, and is very pretty. We have set it in the corner of the kitchen against the north wall, beside the window. John will connect the drain with the sink in the basement so we will not have to bother about emptying the pan. He will put a funnel on the top of the drain pipe and arrange it so that the drip will have to fall in the funnel. It will be so much handier than having to remember to empty the drain pan every day.

Monday, March 31, 1924

We are glad to say that the stockholders of the Powell National Bank expect to be able to reopen the bank soon. None of the depositors will lose anything, but I suppose the stockholders will be out something.

It is rather inconvenient to be short of cash, and we have had a lot of fun hunting up all the pocketbooks and billfolds on the place and searching out the various places where we have kept change, to gather it all up. Fortunately our honey orders have been increasing in the past couple of weeks—the fairies are on the job, you see—so we will not have any real difficulty, but as we have to pay the postage on the honey when it goes out and do not collect for it until it is delivered, we had to have a little money on hand. So many farmers have sold all they had to sell this season and have all the money tied up in the bank until things are straightened out there. I guess lots of folk who never asked for credit before are having to ask their grocers to advance groceries for a few weeks.

April 4, 1924

There was a terrible accident at the Star School yesterday, and the children were nearly scared to death. A new pupil brought some dynamite caps which he found in the granary of the place to which they had moved a day or two before. The child did not know what they were and gave one to Irvin Good, seven years old. Irvin remarked that he would make himself a whistle out of it, and before any of the older children could take it away or explain that it was dangerous, he stuck a nail in the end and banged it down on a rock to clean it out. Of course the shell exploded and tore off all the fingers and thumb of Irvin's right hand. The left hand was badly burned and his face was also slightly burned. Mr. Martin, the upper room tacher, at once applied first aid, using a tourniquet, or the child would have bled to death in a few minutes. Miss Godfrey ran to a telephone and got a doctor, who came in just a few minutes. Mr. Martin in the meantime got out his car and took Irvin home, half a mile away. After the doctor came and took care of the injury temporarily they took the child to the hospital, where they had to amputate the shattered bones and dress the wound. Everybody in the community is so shocked about it. It was absolutely no one's fault, for the boy who brought the shells did not know what they were, and his parents did not know he had them.

Wednesday, April 23, 1924

"Just when you think you got a thing, it ain't." And then when you are sure you ain't got it, it is. Measles, anyway. I was sure Cecilia was getting them last week and she did not. Then I thought she was all right. Yesterday afternoon her teacher had a neighbor telephone that Cecilia was sick, so I went right after her. She had a 101 fever and felt pretty miserable, but she was not really very sick, for the first thing she wanted when she got home was something to eat! We put her to bed and I have kept her there since. She is not very sick. This afternoon her temperature is 99.5, so you see she does not have enough fever to make her feel very badly. However, as long as the fever keeps up, I suppose the measles are incubating and will hatch out about tomorrow. I guess she will be exposed to measles off and on all through her school life, so she might as well have it over with. I confess I do not care to have Jules and Anne take them, but Dr. Graham says that if they are in the house, even though in a separate room, it is practically impossible to prevent the other children from getting them. Jules is well and strong, and Anne is still nursing, so I guess they would get along all right. I am not going to wean Anne entirely until this measley epidemic is over with, for a nursing baby seldom has a hard spell even if it does catch them.

Sunday, April 27, 1924

When Dr. Clark, the local officer, came today to quarantine us, I asked him if it would be safe for me to write letters. He said he was not putting a tight quarantine on now, and that we could send out mail. I then said what I wanted to know was if it would be safe for the people who got my letters, and he said that if I washed my hands before handling the letters there would not be any danger of my sending any germs along, especially as all the letter writing is done here in the office and Cecilia is in the bedroom. So it therefore appears all right for me to let you know that we are getting along all right.

There is something to be said for a quarantine, after all. It is quite comfortable to sit down with the floor "unswop" and the work not all done, and know that nobody will come in and surprise you. You don't have to have on a clean apron and your best smile all the time, but can sit down in peace and ease and read a paper if you want to, knowing that when you get ready you can go on with the work at your own convenience without consulting anybody else. I am enjoying today especially, for Mr. Bretney [the hired man] went to town this morning, and John did not want anything cooked at noon, so I just took my own time for everything. I washed, and baked and filled cream puffs, and baked bread, but through it all I have just loafed along and taken it easy.

Sunday, May 4, 1924

Well, I guess we are on the second lap of the measles. Jules and Anne both had fever last night, and neither is quite well today, though neither is very sick. We have tried to keep Jules in bed, but the nearest we have come to it is keeping him wrapped up in a blanket in a chair, or on our laps. Since he does not feel badly, of course he does not want to stay still. Dr. Clark was here today and extended the quarantine to cover the new cases. There has been one death here from measles, a child named Borders, in Powell — pneumonia complications. Dr. Clark says he now has about fifty families quarantined.

Friday, May 9, 1924

Anne is sleeping soundly, praise be, and Jules is wrapped in a blanket and sitting in a chair, so I will try to write to you while the writing is good. If anybody tells you you need not worry when the children get "only the measles" you politely — or otherwise — inform them they are a "nother." To be sure Jules and Anne have not had anything out of the way, but I must say that for making children uncomfortable and unhappy, if there is anything to beat measles I have not yet run across it. Fortunately Cecilia had a much lighter case than the babies, and she was not really sick at all. But the two little ones were as sick as I ever care to see children get. They did not have high temperature — luckily — nothing much over 102, and usually only around 100 to 101, but they were so achy and hot and itchy and when they did break out so completely covered that it made you sick yourself to see them. Jules was a sight. Dr. Graham told Mrs. Young that Jules was about the worst broken-out child he ever saw. His whole face was one solid red, and from the edge of his jaw to his collar bone you could hardly find a white place. The measles were in his hair clear to the top of his head. Then the next day they were on his body and his back was almost solid. When Cecilia saw it, she said, "Why, Mamma, he doesn't have red spots! He has only a couple of white spots on his back." And the red was so livid and stood up so that it really felt as if you could run your fingers over the ridges. Anne was nearly as completely covered, but hers did not stand out so high or look so angry. For two nights they were restless during the night, as well as in the day. Last night Anne fretted most of the time, unless she was held. In fact, John or I have held one or both of them for three days, it seems to me. Part of the time I held them both at once. I was worried about Anne Tuesday night, as she was so hoarse she could hardly cry. I greased her up, and by morning she was all right again, but we had the doctor come again Wednesday morning to be sure their lungs were still all right. All three have coughed so hard, all the time, and I have coughed with them, naturally. Poor Anne did hate the coughing so much. When she had to cough at first, before she felt too badly, she would just get hopping mad about it, but later she just looked miserable. Fortunately she is not coughing as much as Jules and Cecilia now so I hope she will soon be able to quit. I think by tomorrow both the babies will be about normal again.

Monday, May 12, 1924

We have just had a terrible loss. Our big shop caught fire from some unknown origin this noon and burned down entirely. Mr. Bretney was working there till about twelve o'clock. He came in to dinner, and about half past the neighbors called and said we had a fire. I ran out and the smoke was pouring out of the north side of the shop. We ran out to the building but it was all on fire on the north side, to the middle. We ran in and tried to get the extractor out, and got it pulled about half way to the door when we were driven out by the smoke. Later on, when most of the men in the country were here (about five minutes later, I guess) some of the boys jumped in the door and managed to get the extractor out the rest of the way. So we saved that, and that is absolutely all. It was a terribly hot fire, as you can imagine, for the whole shop was stacked full of thousands of supers and hive bodies with foundation and combs in them, and of course the wax made a terrible fire. In the east end was the ice house, and the sawdust around it made a heavy fire too, though it did not burn clear up, because it was damp from the ice. But the ice shows everywhere. I wonder if we can pack it somewhere else so as to have some for at least part of the summer.

John is at Casper at a Board of Agriculture meeting, and he will be just sick when he hears about the fire. Of course I wired him, because I thought that maybe he would not get back till Wednesday, and I want him to come tomorrow since this has happened. I am so sorry for him, for he will have such a terribly worried trip home, thinking about what he will see when he gets here. I am going to call Edith tonight and tell her about it and have her or Ted go to the train tomorrow and tell John some of the details, so he will know a little more by the time he leaves Greybull.

We have no idea whatever how the fire started. It began in the northeast corner, as the neighbors all said the smoke was pouring out of the driveway into the basement when they first saw it. Mr. Bretney was working there all morning, but was in the south part. He never smokes indoors, and when he smoked this morning he went outside while he was doing it. He does not smoke cigarettes at all, only a pipe. There has not been any fire in the boiler or any engine running in the shop for a long time—no fire for several months and no engine running in the shop since last week. So it is evident that we will never know just how the fire started.

We have all the insurance on the shop that we could get in the Mutual Company. John did intend to raise the amount the past few months, since he made so many improvements this spring, but he had never got that done. The insurance will about half cover the loss. That will be enough to give us a little start, but of course will not touch all the supplies and machinery we had.

All the men in the country and a lot from Powell came out, but there was nothing they could do to save the shop. However, if the wind had been toward the house, every one of them would have been most useful. The men from Powell gathered up all the fire extinguishers in town, I guess, for they had a car full of them. That was certainly good of them.

A number of the men are coming back this evening to see if there is anything that needs doing to safeguard the rest of the property. The fire was so hot they could not do anything this afternoon, and of course they were anxious to get back to their work when they could not be of any service.

I am so sorry it happened while John was away, for of course he will feel that if he had been here he could have done something. But I am sure he could not, for when Mr. Bretney and I got there we could not. Poor John, I feel so sorry for him because he has worked so hard this spring to get the shop just the way he wanted it, and used all the material from the old house to improve the extracting department.

However, it might have been much worse, for if the wind had been toward the house, as strong as it was, we might and probably would have lost everything. Then we would have been done for. Mr. Bretney feels so badly about it, for he says people might think that he smoked and was careless. The men who were here concluded that the fire must have started from an oil-soaked rag, or something else that caused spontaneous combustion. [An analysis of the origin of the fire showed that it had begun in the walls of the ice bin, where the wet sawdust had heated and expanded, and caused the spontaneous combustion.]

I am sorry this is such a gloomy letter, but I thought I had better let you know about it right away. Mr. Bretney and Ed Osborne are going to stay up tonight to see that nothing catches from the ruins. I will feel much safer if they do that. Helen Young has offered to come and stay with me, for fear I might be nervous. The neighbors are all so good.

Tuesday, May 12, 1924

Everything is quiet for a while, so I will try to write you a few words, as you will probably want to hear again after the letter I wrote you yesterday telling about the fire. Jules and Anne are asleep and Mr. Bretney is upstairs resting, if not napping. He is about worn out, as he was up nearly all night and he worked so hard yesterday. Then this morning he had to put up some temporary fencing to keep the cows in the pasture.

Last night, after the worst of the fire had burnt out, a number of men came back and they salvaged about 475 ten pound pails of honey from the basement. It was stacked all along the north wall, and being against the wall and stacked so closely together, it was not in the worst of the fire. In fact, some of the wooden cases in the lower layers were not burnt. Of course we do not know just how much good there is in this lot until we go over it, but at least it will be valuable for feeding the bees until the honey flow begins. You see, all the supers containing the combs of honey for spring feeding were burned, so we will have to use either sugar syrup or honey syrup, and it would be pretty expensive to have to buy sugar now. So I am very glad they were able to save that amount of honey. In fact, we would not have had any for the table or for any use if they had not got some out, for except the can or two we had in the house, it was all stored in the basement of the shop.

I wired John as soon as the fire was over, and was very much relieved to get an answer from him within about three hours. He wired back this: "Think we can rebuild better. Will be home tomorrow." I can't tell you how it cheered me to have him take such a cheerful view of the matter, for I was afraid he might feel especially badly since he was away at the time.

We have three thousand dollars insurance on the building and contents, and extra insurance on the honey. The building insurance is in the Farmer's Mutual Company; the special honey insurance is in some company Mr. Long, in Powell, represents. We always carry special insurance on the honey as soon as we get the crop in the house, and then usually have it cancelled when we ship, but this year we did not ship nearly all, so John let it run on. You may be sure we are glad now, for even if we get only a couple hundred dollars out of it, it will be just that much help. The insurance was taken out on 40,000 pounds, but there was probably only about 6,000 pounds in the basement yesterday.

John will be home on this evening's train. I am sure he will be glad to get here, and also sure I will be glad to see him.

However, we are all right, so you need not worry about us a bit, for worry can't do a bit of good. I have not worried myself, for there is no use in using up one's energy that way.

May 16, 1924

John and Mr. Bretney have worked all day today and most of yesterday taking care of the ice. They packed several tons in the cellar at the shop site, and over it put the sawdust that did not burn—over and under and around. They walled up a place with old boards so that it is really in a sort of house, with the basement wall for one side. They will pack straw over the sawdust. The rest of the ice they cleaned off and put in the cistern, which is empty and had to be filled today. We ought to have pretty good cistern water if there is a ton or so of ice in the cistern as the water runs in. We hope what they packed at the cellar will last a couple of months, at least.

Thursday, May 22, 1924

Thanks for your sympathy about the fire, Mamma. No, we have not worried, as you no doubt know before this from my letters. It wouldn't do any good, so why do it. It couldn't have been prevented, and even if John had been here it might have gone just the same. Yes, the children stayed in the house. Mr. Bretney was holding Anne when we found out about the fire. When Mrs. Young asked if something was on fire, I ran out to see, and came back in and said, "O, Mr. Bretney, the shop is on fire," for the smoke was just rolling out of the whole east end. He set Anne on the floor and ran out after me. Jules and Anne both stayed in the house. In just a few minutes Mrs. Osborne came, and she stayed with the children in the house for half an hour or so, and put Anne to sleep before she had to go over home to see about her youngster. After that I took Jules out in the yard with me, as he wanted to see the fire. He had been standing on the kitchen table, where Mrs. Osborne had put him so he could see the fire. No, I can't say I was so very frightened, for it was all so quick and so impossible to do anything that one couldn't get scared.

I think I have told you that we had about 15,000 pounds of honey in the shop, covered by extra insurance in the Fireman's Fund, at 10 cents a pound. John and Mr. B. went over it yesterday, and found that most of it is more or less damaged. John estimated that it is worth about $100, and offered to allow that much on the amount lost. Mr. Long, the local agent of the Fireman's Fund, was satisfied with John's estimate and so we will probably get $1400 insurance from them. That will be enough to pay for the new shop we will build right away, half as large as the one that burned. We will build it as large as the basement which was under half the old shop. We are certainly thankful we had the special insurance still on.

The 60 colonies of bees that were lost were totally destroyed — bees, hives, and everything. All that was left of the row was a pile of ashes. If John had been here, of course they would have been saved, for they could have been moved. But men in general are afraid of bees, and it was not until some men came who were used to handling bees that they tried to do anything. They carried out ten colonies, tearing the burning paper wrappings off the hives, but the fire got so hot that they were driven back and could not get the rest. Fortunately the wind changed a little, just enough to save the rest of the yard.

Tuesday, May 27, 1924

I must tell you what the neighbors did for us Saturday. Of course there was an awful mess of all sorts of debris after the fire. John and Mr. Bretney had hauled out truck load after truck load of pails and cans and such other light stuff as they could handle, and had the south part of the floor all cleaned up. But they could not get into the basement part because the wall on the south side of the driveway down into the basement had caved in from the fire, and the driveway was filled with concrete. It was too heavy for John to shovel. So the neighbors, led by Mr. Murray, arranged to come and help clear away. They hauled out wagon load after wagon load of concrete, cans, pails, tanks, and ashes, and got everything all cleaned up except the honey that was partly burnt, and was so sticky and hard they could not get it out in any way. Mr. Susterka brought a box wagon, Mrs. Wallace sent a beet wagon and a man to drive it, George Young brought a rack wagon; Mr. Murray, Bruce and Max, Corrie Lovercheck, Mr. N.S. Graham and his grandson, Delbert Coorough, all were here and worked all morning. By noon they were just about done, but loaded a truck load after dinner. Mr. Hoots came after dinner and drove the truck and he and Mr. Bretney took out two loads in the truck, finishing the job. You may be sure we appreciate the help very much, as it would have taken two men a week or more to do what the crowd did in a few hours.

John is working today trying to clean up the honey mess. There is a pile of partly burnt honey mixed with cans, charred crates, and ashes. The honey is burnt to a candy, so stiff and hard you can't dig it out. They finally concluded that the only way to get rid of it would be to try to burn it up, so John soaked the whole pile with kerosene last night and today they put some trash on it and set it afire. They are hoping the fire will burn the honey completely and they can then dig up the cans and ashes.

The pails of honey that were saved are partly good, but you can't tell by looking at them what they are worth. A can may look all right and be still completely granulated, and have the most bitter smoke taste you ever tasted. Some of the pails have burnt places that show dark while the rest is perfectly white. It does seem strange that the nasty smoke taste should have got clear through the cans, when there is nothing to show either in color or appearance of the honey. So we have to test every can before we can use it. Often, if we dig off an inch or two of the top we find the rest of the honey is all right.

Friday, June 6, 1924

The car of lumber came in yesterday and the men are hauling today. There are five wagons, and John hauled a load in the truck this morning. Having the insurance on the honey as well as on the shop and contents gives us enough that we can rebuild what we must have at once and replace what we need at once without borrowing any money. Of course we do not want to borrow any now, as we had been counting on paying off some with the returns on the honey that was in the shop. But we will not be able to now until we raise some more honey.

We have had quite a bother getting the insurance adjusted on the honey. Instead of letting the local agent adjust the matter, the company sent in a man all the way from Denver. He haggled and quibbled over the amount of honey in the shop, but as we knew exactly how much we had last fall and had a duplicate ticket for every pound we have sold all winter, and the bank record of the carlot, there wasn't much room for him to argue when John put the evidence before him. Finally the man got down to within eleven dollars of the correct amount, and argued for a long time that John would have to take that sum. But of course John stood firm. The adjuster probably thought he was going to run into a farmer who didn't know much about what he was doing and was probably rather surprised to find a business man with absolute and accurate records. At any rate, after they argued for an hour or two, the Denver man and the local agent went away, and as soon as they got to Powell they called and said if John would come in the next morning early, before train time, the check would be ready for him at John's price. Another funny thing about the whole business is that when the man first began to talk he offered to settle for $1500. Now John was asking only $1332. The adjuster had figured so many pounds at 12½ cents a pound, which amounted to $1750, and then he just clipped off $250 on general principles, I suppose, and offered $1500. John did not know then the adjuster meant to be so nasty, or he would simply have said all right to the first proposal. But you know how honest John is, and he did not want to take advantage of any mistake, so he expressed himself as perfectly satisfied with the insured value of the honey, which was 10 cents a pound. We would have been glad to accept that for the lot if we had been able to sell it any time in the past few months.

The insurance adjustment that the Denver man fixed up and sent here for John to sign allowed $10 more than John asked for. Now isn't it the limit for a man to act as ugly as he did and then not only give what was asked for but more? Why couldn't he act decent right along and maintain pleasant relations, instead of acting so bossy and saying that we were trying to collect on more honey than was in the fire, and then having to back down when we had all the papers and records to prove the exact amount. We would like to know what the local man told him. John thanked Mr. Long, the local agent, yesterday for whatever he had done, and Mr. Long would only answer that he had told the Denver man the fire was an honest one. He pointed to a building down the street and said that fire was not an honest one, and that the company had refused to settle promptly in that case. But we have a notion that as soon as the Denver man heard of John's activities in the mutual company, he was wise enough not to put any more arguments than necessary in John's hands against old line companies.

I have not told you yet that in a heavy rain storm Saturday afternoon, about two o'clock, lightning struck our new shop and tore out the northwest corner. The 2 x 4's were splintered, the walls torn loose from each other and from the roof, and part of the side walls splintered. Mr. Dawson and Mr. Hower and Oliver were in the basement at the time. Splinters and boards flew all around them, but no one was hurt or even stunned, for which we are duly thankful. The damage to the shop was not as large as we first thought. It looked as though it would take a long time to repair, but Mr. Dawson did it in less than half a day, so the damage did not amount to more than $25. We had applied for builder's risk insurance on the shop some time ago, but do not know if it would cover such a damage or not.

Tomorrow is the big day, ranking quite as important as Monday, which will be circus day. So you see how important a matter Aunt Cora's arrival is to the kindergarten, as well as to Edith and me. All the children, even Jules, insist they must go to meet Cora tomorrow morning when she arrives about five a.m. on the park train. We think that maybe we can slip off without Jules, but we are taking it for granted that Cecilia and Edith Rhoda will have to go. And of course Edith and I expect to, and this year I am not anticipating anything like the event that kept me home last year on the morning that Cora arrived.

We are so glad to have Cora here. I don't think we can let her go anywhere else, for she is the best put-a-baby-to-sleep-er that you ever saw. She can take Anne out on the lawn in the cart and get her to sleep in five minutes any time. For the rest of us, Anne wants to play. I asked Cora how she did it, and she says she sings and Anne goes to sleep rather than lie and listen. She advised me to try the singing too.

The children had such a great time when Aunt Cora unpacked. Aunt Cora always represents Santa Claus and a fairy godmother rolled in one when she arrives, for she has so many things long desired and so many they couldn't even think of wanting, that they are as rich as can be when they get all that she has brought.

We are to have an apprentice to learn the bee business. Mr. Herman Krueger, who taught the upper grades at the Star School last year, is to take vocational training beginning about September 1. He is a homesteader near Mantua. His farm is a little better than the average here, so he wants to hold on to it. He is a veteran of the World War, having been in Turkey with the aviation corps that served there. He has suffered from some trouble ever since the war but is getting better now. The man at the head of the vocational training for this territory was here from Casper and arranged with John for Krueger to work here for about a year. He will get his pay from the government and we are to pay him whatever we want. John is going to find out from some of the larger beekeepers what they pay student help and pay Mr. Krueger accordingly. But the nice thing will be that next summer we can get away for short trips, as we will have some one responsible to leave in charge. He is such a fine man. Everybody liked him so much as a teacher and we were all sorry that his health did not make it wise for him to teach again this past year. His sister is one of the best teachers in the Powell high school.

Wednesday, August 27, 1924

We had a great scare last night. I was in the basement, Cecilia was with me, and Anne was on the back porch. Suddenly I heard Anne making a queer noise and told Cecilia to run up and see what she was doing. Cecilia ran up to the porch and began to scream that Anne had got some gasoline. Norma had cleaned her suit with some gasoline in a cup and had set the cup away over on the porch rail. We did not know Anne could reach up there, but she did in some manner and either tried to drink the contents of the cup and then spilled it over herself or else she tipped it down over her face in trying to get the cup from the railing. When I reached Anne, she was gasping and choking, and for at least fifteen minutes she could not get her breath. John telephoned the doctor immediately and asked him what to do and told him to hurry out. The doctor said to make her vomit. We tried to make her drink milk, but she could not swallow any, she was choking so. I kept sticking my finger down her throat and making her vomit, but she did not throw up anything but a phlegm. By the time the doctor got here she was better and when she heard his car coming, she waved her hand and said "bye" and "car." But she still gasped for quite a while. However, her pulse and respiration were not bad, and he thought she would get along. He stayed for a long time to see that she kept getting better. We tried to get her to drink milk, but she would not touch it at all. Finally, about two hours after she got the gasoline, she ate a little macaroni and a bit of baked apple. Then she went to sleep and slept until about one o'clock. Then she threw up everything inside her as the doctor had said she probably would. Then, after playing a little while, she went to sleep and slept till about six this morning. She was a little peevish today but otherwise well as could be, and did not seem to suffer any ill effects whatever. The apple sauce gave her several good bowel movements and each of them, even this evening, smelled strongly of the gasoline. So she evidently got enough to have an effect. John and I were both scared nearly stiff, for we both remembered instantly that John's oldest sister lost a baby about Anne's age who got the cap off a gasoline can and sucked the spout. The baby died in about two hours, before they could get a doctor to West Franklin. Remembering that made us all the more scared about Anne. Twice Anne gasped and rolled up her eyes, and we just about stopped breathing ourselves. But you may be sure we did not stop praying.

Tuesday, September 16, 1924

John started to Douglas this morning for the State Fair. Going to a fair or anything that requires his being on his feet for some hours is about the hardest kind of work he can do, and I guess he finds it hard to understand that some people think it fun to go to such a place. The State Agricultural Board meets in Douglas during the Fair. This board has charge of the fair, hiring a man by the year who takes special charge of the fair. The appropriation the legislature has made in all previous sessions is not enough to pay for a good fair. Heretofore the fair managers have simply gone ahead and spent what they thought necessary, and then put in a bill to the next legislature for the overcharge. But as that is really against the law in this state, the present Board decided their fair manager could spend just the amount allowed and no more. So one thing the Board needs to do at this meeting is to decide whether it is wise to go on trying to give a fair with the present allowance, or whether they should quit trying, or try to persuade the legislature for a larger allowance.

Sunday, September 21, 1924

John had a nice trip to Douglas but was rather tired when he got home. He said he saw Governor and Mrs. Ross the first day he was there, as they were driving in their car near the fairgrounds and, seeing John, invited him to ride with them. The Kiwanis had a noon luncheon to which the dignitaries were invited, and various ones of them spoke on the subject of securing more funds for the Fair.

September 28, 1924

We were indeed sorry to hear of Governor Ross's serious illness, and hope very much he is improving. We have had no news since the Thursday paper, which was issued only a short time after the operation, so we do not know much about it except that he was very dangerously ill. The trouble was some abdominal one, under the general name, of course, of appendicitis.

October 2, 1924

No doubt you will have heard long before this letter reaches Indiana that Governor Ross died this morning. We are terribly sorry. Ever since we knew Mr. Ross was sick, John has been debating whether or not he would go to Cheyenne for the funeral in case the governor died. He has decided now that he will not, unless some special reason comes up to urge his presence. Of course he would like very much to go, but as it is so far it would take at least three or four days and be an expensive trip in money as well as time. John is so anxious to get all the honey extracted and as he is only about half done, he hates to lose the better part of a week again.

We are having gorgeous Indian summer now. I wish you could see our trees. The row of cottonwoods along the west end of the lawn are all golden yellow and so are the cottonwoods in the end of the row on the south side. The south row is still as green and white as in the middle of summer. I like the silver poplars so much better than the cottonwood poplars because the leaves stay green so much later in the fall. They come almost as early in the spring, though they do not grow large as fast; but in the fall it gives one such a feeling of reprieve to have the silver poplars all green and pretty after all the other trees are yellow and then bare.

Sunday night, October 5, 1924

The memorial service for Governor Ross this afternoon was very good. The Presbyterian minister presided, the Baptist minister gave the invocation and benediction and read the scripture, and the Methodist minister gave the main address. There were three addresses on the program: the one mentioned, and two shorter ones, one by Sheriff Loomis and the other by John. Both made very good talks. Mr. Loomis spoke of the sympathy and kindliness of Governor Ross in all his dealing with the sheriffs of the state in his law-enforcement campaign, and of his constant instructions to them to be fair in every way, be sure of their evidence, and then go ahead without stopping. John spoke of the honesty and fairness of Governor Ross and of the way in which he insisted that every appointee of his absolutely must stay within the appropriation for his work, and of the economy he constantly practiced. He also spoke of the consistent character of Mr. Ross, from his first public work until his death, and of the high ideals he had always shown. Rev. Alford spoke mainly of the value to the state of Governor Ross's law enforcement campaign and of the great need of the state for another man like Ross in the governor's chair. The Baptist minister read the Psalm No. 1, and compared Gov. Ross to the righteous man whose delight is the law of the Lord. He made a really beautiful invocation, in which he expressed the gratitude of the people of Wyoming for a man whose character was as high as the mountains to the east and the west, and whose life was full of good deeds like the streams that run down from the mountains and water the plains. Rev. Alford used as his text, "Know ye not that there is a prince and a great man fallen this day in Israel?"

I am sure Ted will be interested in the local rumor that State Senator S.A. Nelson is to be put up before the Republican state committee as a candidate for governor on the Republican side. You remember two years ago when Kindler was a candidate in the primaries, one argument much used was that this part of the state has never had its turn in supplying a governor. It may be that this argument will have some force now, for of course Nelson is an entirely different man from Kindler.

Mr. Nelson is the president of the First National Bank of Powell, a man who has been sent many times to represent the people of this community both to Washington in reclamation matters and as state senator to Cheyenne. Mrs. Nelson is one of the really fine women in Powell and would make an exceedingly fine governor's wife, I think.

I must tell you one of Governor Ross's favorite jokes that he always told when ministers were around. A young Episcopal couple desiring to be married arranged with the minister to have the service performed at the close of the regular Sunday service. During the closing hymn, the two were to come forward and stand ready for the ceremony at the close of the hymn. Just at the last, however, the clergyman thought it would look a little queer to have the young folk pop up unannounced, so he said, as he announced the closing hymn, "And will those who desire to be married come forward during the singing of this hymn." When the hymn was finished, he found to his amazement that there were thirteen women and one man standing in front.

Yes, Edith, I think it would be exceedingly clever to put Mrs. Ross on as a candidate for governor. On the other hand, it is evident that the Republicans are making every effort to prevent having any election, for if Mrs. Ross were a candidate, folks would have to be courteous enough to vote for her, so of course the Republicans can avoid having to do that by preventing any election at all.

We just heard that the Democrats have really nominated Mrs. Ross as their candidate for governor. We are so glad, for we think she is capable, and we believe she can be elected, and we are delighted that Wyoming will be one of the first states to have a woman governor. It really ought to, for it is really the original suffrage state since women have had suffrage since 1869, I believe it is. Mrs. Ferguson of Texas won't be the only governess after the November election.

John's state board meeting has been put off till the second week in December; so we have decided to start on November 5th when John goes to Thermopolis for the state beekeepers' meeting, and to go right on without stopping over at Thermopolis. Hotel bills for the whole family for three days count up and the trip will be so expensive that we must save every penny. We are due to arrive in Cheyenne on Thursday morning about four or five. The sleeper is set off there, so we will not have to get up till the regular time, which will be a great comfort to me, what with the children.

Joe O'Mahoney is going to meet me at the station and take me up to meet Mrs. Ross, and also the head of John's board, Comissioner Faville. We will leave Cheyenne over the U.P. at 12:34 noon Thursday and get to Chicago about 4:00 in the afternoon on Friday, and to Bloomington at 4:00 A.M. Saturday.

I am trying to sew, but I don't get to stick at it very long, it seems, for there is so much to do about the house. Then too, we have been going out at night, and one isn't so energetic after being out till eleven or one. Monday night I spoke for Mrs. Ross at a meeting in Garland where there was a bigger crowd than you ever thought could gather in this part of the woods. Last night we went to Powell to hear Mr. O'Mahoney and Mr. Wanerus and tomorrow night I am to speak again for Mrs. Ross at the North End Clubhouse. When the first thing Mr. O'Mahoney said to me last night was about what a fine speech I had made, and when Mr. Wanerus, the Democratic candidate for U.S. representative from this state, said the same thing to me, I began to think they really meant it, for if these two men who had come into the county only the day before had heard about it, people must have been talking. So of course I am quite puffed up.

Cheyenne, Wyoming
Thursday noon, November 6, 1924

Dear Daddy,

Just leaving Cheyenne. Had a lovely time here. Mr. O'M. wired me on the train at Casper that he would meet us this morning at 7 A.M. He took us to his house for breakfast. Later we went to see Mrs. Ross and had a lovely call. She wants to be remembered to you. Mrs. Faville came down to the depot to see us. Jules was in the car when we went to Ross's and she insisted on his coming in. She thought he was so nice and gave him a rose. Mrs. Ross is splendid.

Ce.

822 Atwater
Bloomington, Indiana
November 8, 1924

Dearest Johnny,

You will know that our train was on time when I tell you that after being due to arrive at 3:57 we were here at the house at 4:10, just 13 minutes later. The ride down from Chicago was very comfortable as all three children slept all the way. I got them all three awake and dressed and off the train without their making any noise whatever, so that no one else on the sleeper was aroused.

Pater and Mamma both look quite well to me, about the same as two years ago. I was afraid they would be much more feeble, but I can't see that they are. The new house is lovely, ever so much more comfortable than the old one, and even Pater is more satisfied here. It is funny, though, to hear him talk about "our old place" as if it really were the family ancestral home. We are having such a nice trip and we hope you are too. We are so glad our Daddy wanted us to have this trip.

West Franklin, Indiana
November 23, 1924

Here we are at West Franklin. Pacific and Clara came to Evansville for us this afternoon and on the way home took us through Howell and then to the river, past Dogtown and Parker Settlement. We went to the ferry so the children could see how the autos are ferried over the Ohio at Henderson. Then we went to the big dam on the river below Henderson, Dam #48.

Pacific says business here at West Franklin is at the lowest ebb it has ever struck. They usually have pretty good trade in December until Christmas, but this year it is as slack now as it usually is in January and February. They would like to get rid of the store. Clara says farmers here just simply don't have any money to spend.

December 1, 1924

We are on the train going back to Bloomington. We passed through Hazelton just a little while ago. Anne is now asleep. Cecilia is playing with her dolls and Jules is sleepy, but he is so naughty today and won't do anything he should. He has been so worn out the past three or four days he has been so cross there has been no living with him. I haven't been able to spank him the way he needed it, because we have been going to so many places where one could not have a rumpus. As soon as we get back to Bloomington and he gets rested up, he will be in for some good spankings if he doesn't straighten up. He has got to the point where he teases Anne all the time and makes her fall down. I really think he doesn't know what to do to pass the time. This continual changing is certainly hard on young-sters. Anne, however, has been just as good as gold and would go to anybody. She took a special liking to Aunt Lena and Uncle George and Emily, and when they were around wanted them to hold her all the time. Everybody wanted to keep her, she was so sweet and good.

I enjoyed the Evansville visit but I am glad it is over, for there are too many places to go. I will be glad for a chance to sit down and catch my breath. I think I told you Cecilia had a little spell of grippe, and I was up with her several nights. Anne has not been sleeping well at night, I think, because her hours have been so irregular, so that all in all I have not had more than five or six hours rest a night, and that broken, since we went to Evansville. Even at West Franklin I did not sleep well, and would sometimes be awake two hours at a stretch for no reason whatever. I am glad to say, however, that I have been feeling fine all the time. I have been, and still am, tired and sleepy, but otherwise have felt fine.

Jules says to tell you we have been passing a river. Jules also says to tell you he is going to be a good boy now.

822 Atwater, Bloomington
December 12, 1924

Cecilia certainly has the chicken pox. She is well broken out now, even having some on her head and face. But she is not sick and has had no fever since the first day. I suspect, however, the other children will get the chicken pox, too, in about ten days to two weeks. I am thankful that it is not worse. I guess it would have been better not to let Cecilia go to school [here] at all, for they all might have escaped it, but again they might not have. Well, she will be over with it, anyway.

Bloomington
Tuesday, December 16, 1924

I am sure if you had heard all the nice things said today about your three children, you would be proud as can be. We had our thimble party this afternoon, and everybody was more interested in the children than in anything else. We had quite a house full, having invited 45 ladies; but of course not all of them could come. Cecilia sat with Mrs. Edmondson most of the afternoon and of course had a splendid time. She got out her quilt blocks and sewed with the guests. Jules and Anne both behaved beautifully, I am glad to say, so everybody thinks we have not only beautiful and healthy children, but beautifully behaved children. I don't know of any time I'd rather have had them behave well than at this party, for all my old friends were here, and of course I wanted them to know I wasn't a complete failure in the job I took when I resigned here.

Bloomington
December 21, 1924

Anne has the chicken pox too. She is not broken out as much as Jules, but has a good case of it. I am afraid she won't be able to travel in just another week from now if she progresses at the same rate Cecilia did.

Bloomington
Christmas night, 1924

The great day is almost over. Such a good time as the children have had. They got up about eight this morning and had their stockings. Cecilia got a play wrist watch and Jules the purple beads and Noah's Ark he has been wanting. Of course they had candy and nuts and oranges. After the rest were up and breakfast over, we had the grand opening. I can't begin to tell you all the things we all got.

When Jules first woke up this morning he began to say daddy. Anne did too, so they both sat up in bed and called for you. They can hardly wait till they get back to where daddy is.

Just like me. We spoke of you many times, and wondered what you were doing. We guessed that you were eating candy and nuts and playing lots of music, especially Christmas music.

Jules and Anne look like wrecks, for their faces are all scabby from the chicken pox. Jules's sore places are beginning to dry up very nicely, so I think in another week they will be all right to travel. I hope so, for we must get back to you, and we want to, although we do hate to leave here. With love to our daddy, who was good enough to let us be here for Christmas.

Bloomington
December 27, 1924

A week from tonight I can "come home" to my lover. The children were talking today about being back home next Saturday. They hate to leave here, but will all be glad to be home again.

The children are about over the chicken pox now. Jules' scabs are practically all gone; Anne's still show but do not look like anything dangerous. What with this disease, the extreme cold, and mamma's not being well, I have not been able to do lots of things I should like to do. Mamma has been worse the past few days. The doctor says the trouble is her heart. I am glad I could be here to do a few things while she was sick and Cora working so hard on her textbook. Cora hopes to get the book off tomorrow; and she and Pater are working now proofing the final copy.

Honeyhill Farm
Tuesday, January 6, 1925

Mamma, we are glad you miss us, for we were afraid that maybe you were getting so sleepy you would be glad to be alone again. I really think that what you need is about 12 hours sleep every night, and I hope you will get it now that we are gone and Cora's book is done. I wish you wouldn't wait to see that everybody else is in bed before you go yourself.

We had such a lovely time with you we hate to have it over, and yet we felt as if we must get home to John. We thank you all for everything you did to make our visit possible and pleasant. We feel as if you gave us too much, but we appreciate every bit of it.

We have been working in the office lickety-split for several days. Yesterday we worked all day, not even stopping to do any cooking, but ate what I had prepared the day before. John had a lot of letters to get out, and we have the decks pretty well cleared now.

January 18, 1925

We have another turkey that ought to be eaten soon and we are thinking of inviting all the ministers of Powell, including the Catholic priest, to dinner. Only Rev. Walter has a wife; Rev. Winecoff is back to look after the Episcopal church for a while, and he, together with Rev. Schult of the Methodist church, Father Spillane, and Rev. Walter would be the men. The Baptists have no man here at present, the Rev. Price who came here from North Vernon, Indiana, having played out in less than a year. The Methodist minister is new here, having recently come from Illinois. The ministers have had a sort of informal ministerial association, and some of them are desirous of having an organization that is more formal. Maybe we can help along a little in forming such an organization if we get them all together at dinner.

January 30, 1925

I am taking advantage of Edith's being here to give the preacher party I mentioned some time ago. We are to have it tomorrow night. The Methodist minister is away now, so he will not be here, but the others will — Rev. Walter of our church, with his wife and her sister; Rev. Winecoff, the Episcopal lay missioner and scientist I told you about; and Father Spillane, of the Catholic church. I suppose some of the folk in southern Indiana would hold up their hands at the idea of entertaining a priest, buy why not. If churches are to live together in peace and do their work with all classes of people, surely the people have to be kind to each other. There was an excellent article in a recent *Digest* on the subject of religious tolerance. It said that the sooner people came to realize that there was a difference, and an unchangeable difference, between Protestant and Catholic, and learned to let each one hold his own belief without trying to change it, the sooner churches would flourish and people become more religious.

By the way, it is interesting that our old college friend, Everett Sanders, is to be President Coolidge's secretary. I have been thinking of writing Mrs. Sanders a letter. You know she and I played basketball together a great deal and were right good friends that one year.

Sunday night, March 1, 1925

Cora, I worked on the puzzle that you had marked 17 minutes, and found it took me 18 to do it. But as Anne trailed me to the office where I had taken refuge in order to be alone, and tried to show me all the envelopes in the drawer until I had to stop her, and them bumped her head and stood at my elbow and cried for about 9 of the 18 minutes, I think maybe I might be allowed the one minute as a handicap and not rate too terribly far behind you. I tried to time myself last night on a puzzle to send to you, and got it all but one word in ten minutes. Cecilia came and looked on about that time, and while I was puzzling my brain to think what under the sun the last word could possibly be, and had worked about two minutes on it, she spoke up and said that the word was muddy, which it was. So of course I could not send you that puzzle with time.

I have read Joseph Conrad's "The Rover" last week. It is the first Conrad book I have read. I felt rather ashamed at not having read any of his things, after all the praise he has received. The book is certainly wonderfully written. It is not alarming in plot, and yet when one goes over it afterward, it is keen as a sharp sword. I was amused at myself while reading. I was reading one morning while I was eating my breakfast. Suddenly I heard the morning train whistle. I thought, "Why, there is no train on Sunday. I wonder what has happened that there is a train today." Then I realized that the day was Tuesday, and not Sunday at all, and finally realized that I was reading about Sunday in "The Rover," and was so immersed in the story that I really thought it was Sunday. That, it seems to me, is pretty much praise for a book.

"The Hoosier Schoolmaster" is to be at the movie tomorrow night, and so the family is to have a theatre party for my birthday. Won't that be nice? Wish you were all here to go along.

Thursday, March 5, 1925

John has to go to Hyattville to see after the bees there that we bought from Mr. Hower.* Mr. Hower promised to go with him, and they are to go Friday morning and come back Saturday. He will go through Greybull, and while he does not want to take time to stop, he will at least see you or talk to you, Edith, and find out how you are.

In regard to your question as to who asked the blessing at our ministerial dinner party, I may say that I brought up the subject beforehand with John, and he decided that our own minister should be the one. At the dinner, after that rite had been finished, I told the assembly the story of the little boy at whose house several ministers were dining during a church conference. The father there had not considered the matter previously, and when time came to sit down and have grace said, he suddenly realized that there were several professionals

---

*The beeyard at Hyattville, near the foot of the Big Horn Mountains, about 100 miles east of Powell, was established to provide an isolated environment for the development of queen bees of the Italian strain, thought to be gentler than the Caucasian strain owned by most of the beekeepers near Honeyhill. The absence of wild bees and other beeyards in the Hyattville area meant little chance of foul brood developing among the bees; and the absence of Caucasian crossbred drones for mating assured that more queens of the pure strain could be raised and then moved to other Honeyhill beeyards. Trips to Hyattville had to be made every few weeks during the season, over poor dirt and gravel roads which presented all manner of difficulties.

at the table. His small son, noticing his momentary hesitation, said, "Wait a minute, Dad, I'll fix it," and proceeded to count: eeny, meeny, miny, mo, and soon decided which one should say the grace.

Tuesday, March 24, 1925

Mamma, we are glad that you and Pater got the kind of flowers you liked best for the wedding anniversary. It is so hard at this long range to order anything that suits. We are glad you took the trouble to go to Ellises florist shop yourself and pick out just what you found there that you like. The green wrapper with the cerise ribbon the same color as the cyclamen flowers must make a lovely showing. Cecilia remarked that she wished daddy and I would get that sort of flower when we had an anniversary. I told her that when I was a little girl, mamma always got me either a cyclamen or a cineraria for my birthday present. I remember I always liked the cinerarias best, but a cyclamen would do. I don't know how long it has been now since I have seen a real live cineraria.

Tuesday, April 7, 1925

We can hardly wait to have Mamma come back with Ted. I have thought so many times of the time when Pater came back with Ted. I knew Pater was expecting to come, and that he was planning to do so, but we had wanted so many times for him to come and he had never been here that I was afraid something would happen at the last minute to keep him from coming that time. I never will forget how when we met the train at Garland, I was holding my breath for fear he would not be on the train, and when the train actually stopped and Ted got off, I was afraid to look to see if Pater was there, for I would have been so disappointed if he had not been. And when he was really there I was so glad I couldn't do anything but cry. Even if he did not get to stay as long as we wanted, he at least was here long enough to see where we all live, so that now when we talk about anything, we know Pater knows just where the place is and how it looks. So we are more than anxious for Mamma to come this time, so she can find out just where we live and all about us. There never was a better chance, for the time between Ted's getting back and Edith's going east is so short that Mamma would hardly know she had been away from home. So please, please, Mamma, come to see us now. You never will have such a good opportunity to be personally escorted, or to make the trip without having to spend a long time away from home.

Monday noon, April 13, 1925

We got your telegram this morning saying, "Can not come. Sorry to disappoint you. Have wired Ted. Mother." We surely are disappointed. I had my hopes all built up this time and really felt that you would come, Mamma. Edith says she did not really think so, so she is not so much disappointed. We did so much want you to see where we live, and this would have been such a good chance to come out with Ted and go back with Edith. John is as disappointed as I am, for he wants you to see our place. I guess he wants you to see for yourself that we have a most comfortable and convenient place in which to live, as well as a beautiful view. We are anxious to get your letter to find out just why you can not come. We hope it is not because you are not feeling well.

Tuesday, April 28, 1925

Ted was to be at Powell last night for a Lions Club meeting. Yesterday afternoon Mr. Dowling, the president of the Powell National Bank, called me up and said the Lions were to have a dinner and wanted me to come. I thanked him kindly but said that Jules was sick and I could hardly get away. He laughed, and went on to say that they had invited Governor Ross, who is at Cody this week, to the dinner, that she was to be the only special woman guest, and that they wanted to have another woman to keep her company. They had asked her whom to invite, and she had asked for me. Mr. Dowling then laughed again and said, "The boy's not so sick now, is he?" Of course I had to admit that under the circumstances there was nothing for me to do but appear and that I would be there. I appreciated the invitation very much and I told Dowling that for any ordinary occasion I would not try to leave home, but that this one seemed to be quite special. As John had to stay with the children, especially Jules, I had to drive the car myself. It was a nasty, windy, stormy, cold night and I hated to go in the open car but I did it none the less. I put the car in a garage, so it would be ready for me whenever I was ready to go home without my bothering to get someone to crank it.

Ted was at the Wyoming Hotel when I got there and we had a nice little visit. I was invited for 6:45 as the dinner was to be at seven. At the speakers' table Ted was seated at the head since he is the Lions' District Governor, Mrs. Ross was next to him, I was next her, and Rev. Walter was next me. Mr. Dowling was next Ted on the other side, and Dr. Winecoff, the Episcopal lay missioner, was also at this table, as well as various others.

After the dinner, Mrs. Ross made a nice speech and was much amused when the men sang, after she had been introduced, and before she could say anything, their song about the kind of speech she should make—"Make it brief, sister, make it brief, make it snappy and witty and short," or something like that. At the beginning of the dinner, Ted introduced Mrs. Ross to the crowd and they all sang, "Howdy-do, Gov. Ross, Howdy-do," and all the rest about being glad to see her. He also introduced Avery Haggard, the Cheyenne lawyer who is the only international director Wyoming has ever had in the Lions. Then Ted also introduced me, and I felt quite set up when the men all sang "Howdy-do, Mrs. Hendricks, howdy-do" and all the rest of it, while I stood up ready to make my little bow and say thank you.

Mr. Dowling had arranged to have a little reception for Mrs. Ross in the lobby of the hotel. When we left the dining room, Mr. Dowling came out to the lobby with Mrs. Ross and me. He introduced Mrs. Ross to Mrs. Ice, who introduced her to the ladies present. Of course all the elite of the city were on hand, of all political parties, and you can guess that I didn't just exactly hate to be the only woman with Mrs. Ross coming from the dining room and walking out into the crowd. After she had met all those present and walked over to one corner of the room, and there was a pause, I suggested to her that I knew the ladies would like to hear some of the interesting things that had come up in her work. She had just told about a number of these in her talk to the men. Once when she stopped and seemed done, one of the town women called to me to ask if I couldn't think of something else for the governor to speak about as they didn't want her to stop.

You can guess that I enjoyed the whole evening very much. I don't want to boast, but it sort o' gives one a comfortable feeling to sit at home and tend to her own business for many years, not breaking her neck or making any effort whatever to break into the "elite" society of the town, and then when some one in high position comes along, to be asked not just to be among those present, but to be the only one.

Friday, May 8, 1925

Jules is finally very much better. I really think he is all right, but want to knock on wood to say it. His neck has gone down entirely. This morning I suspected that it showed a little swelling, but I think I imagine it. You know how easy that is to do when you are looking for trouble, after having had it for some time, and he has been running this pesky high temperature for nearly three weeks. The main thing is that he has not had any fever—that I know of—since last Sunday, so I think he is all right. He is hungry as a harvest hand, and that is a good sign.

May 29, 1925

Did I tell you that Mr. Krueger bought about a hundred colonies of bees this spring? John has about 600, so they now have about 700 to look after, and by the end of the season, what with the increase they expect to make, should have about a thousand colonies between them. So you see they won't have so much idle time on their hands they will get into mischief. I expect to begin work in the shop in another week or so, as there is lots of nailing to do.

Excuse me for laughing. You would too, if you were here. I was interrupted while writing this letter by an agent, who wished to show me the most !!!!!????? — put in the adjectives for yourself — kind of enlarged pictures, both scenic and human. They got the first prize at the state fair, as per the certificate he showed me, but he did not specify what state nor leave the certificate in my sight long enough for me to discover myself. The price, I believe he said, is $30, but in order to introduce his work into the best (ahem) families, he is taking a few photographs as a special favor, to get his work shown in the community. I did not ask him how much you had to pay for the favor, as we did not get that far. He showed me what he had to show, and some of the photographs he has collected from the neighbors. I assured him I was not interested in having members of my family adorning my walls. Then he showed me some pictures he had, done on fine German linen. One was a Christmas Eve snow scene, one of the Castle of Chillon, and one of morning in some valley in Colorado. All had the most lurid coloring. He demanded if I did not think them lovely, and wanted to know which one I wanted at only $1.10 each. I replied that they were all too highly colored and I did not care for any of them. He craved to know what I did like, and I told him only standard pictures in good coloring, such as I had on the walls. He thereupon noticed the pictures on the walls, advised me that he usually carried the sepia prints, and *always* did in the *cities*, but that I was one person in a hundred in my likes and dislikes in the country; and he packed up his stuff so fast he hardly said anything else, except could he go out the front door — he had come in the kitchen door. So, naturally, you see, I had to laugh. Wouldn't you?

John is at Hyattville this week. He started Tuesday morning and may get home tomorrow night or it may be the next night. He said not to look for him till we see him and not to worry if he did not come till Friday. I am getting along splendidly with the chores, the milking being the only thing that really amounts to anything. I did have a swarm of bees to hive this morning, but that is only a few minutes work, if the swarm is where it can be got at. The cow gives so much milk one's wrists get pretty tired, when one is not used to milking. This morning I got 23 pounds and this evening 26, which makes 49 pounds today, or 49 pints, which is 6¼ gallons. If you want to know how much I got this evening, just take a look at a 14 quart bucket, if you have one such, and imagine it full of milk almost to the top, and the foam sticking up the way the foam does on a soda at the drug store. This is the way my bucket looked when I got done milking this evening, as I had 3 gallons and a quart of milk, plus the foam.

Thursday, July 23, 1925

The box with the dresses arrived yesterday. Mamma, I certainly think you have enough to do without making dresses for me, and I wish you would not use up your strength doing that in this hot summer weather. Of course I love the dresses you make, but I don't feel right about letting you sew for me when you have a dozen times as much work as you ought to be doing without sewing. But I am like the woman with Aunt Barbara Schueler's doughnuts. *"Das ist zu viel,"* she said, but she swept the whole pan-full into her apron and carried them home. If anything were needed to argue me into being glad you do send me clothes, it is that you always find just the thing I have been seeing in my mind's eye all the time and never located either in a store or a catalogue. I wanted a figured voile dress and have read every catalogue three times but never saw one that I liked. And now you sent it to me. Thanks ever and ever so much. I have been staying at home pretty closely as there is so much to do in the canning work and in the shop, but I am afraid from now on I shall be looking up places to go so I can show off my clothes.

You would have thought I had very nice children if you had heard how interested they were in the arrival of the box with the dresses for me. They always spoke of the package as coming with mamma's dresses. But they knew that Grandma always sent something for them in a package, and that is why they could hardly wait for it to arrive. Yesterday they were sitting out at the mailbox waiting for the carrier to come. He had tire trouble down the road a ways, where they could see him, and they could scarcely contain themselves till he got the tire fixed and came on. They watched all the operation, and when he got to the point of pumping up the tire they began to jump up and down, for they knew he would soon be on the way and here. Naturally they were not surprised to find the chocolate, though of course it was a surprise as to the actual article for them.

I am sure you will enjoy Mr. Krueger, when you get here, Co, for he is an even more interesting talker than Mr. Carr was, with the added advantage of being a fine character and a clean, open-as-day man. I am sorry he is not about ten years older, for if he were, we could at last tell you to come on, we had found *him* for you. But he is, unfortunately for you, only 31. He was an ace in the war, flying all over the southern war zone, with headquarters in Italy. He almost died from flu—he says he would have if he had not become conscious when about to die and found everybody was expecting him to die and had a priest there ready to say the service over the dying, which made him so mad he rallied and stayed alive. But the work and the illness left him weak, and he had chronic bronchial trouble which threatened to turn into T.B., so that he was an invalid for several years after the war. He is now well but, like John, not as strong as he was before he was injured. He has a homestead near Mantua, but does not expect to stay there. He has had more and more varied experience than you could listen to, as he jogged around a lot as he was growing up and tried for a time almost every occupation there is, even undertaking, just for the experience.

Mr. Werts just called to say he had heard over the radio that William Jennings Bryan died suddenly this afternoon. I suppose the excitement of the Scopes trial was too much for him.

No, we do not camp out when we go to Hyattville, Mamma. The bees are on a place where there is quite a large, two-story house, right on the bank of the creek. We have a gasoline stove and cook on it, and have bedding and some beds and mattresses. Come out and go along.

Wednesday, August 6, 1925

I am so sleepy I don't know if I will stay awake to write or not. I was awake till after twelve last night — went to chautauqua — and got up at five this morning to help John off for Hyattville. I worked in the shop all morning and nearly went to sleep then. I am afraid I will go to sleep this afternoon when the music begins at the chautauqua.

I sometimes think I'll never again try to go to chautauqua. The one this year is a seven-day session, which is really too long. However, since John is gone, I shall not try to go again at night. I shall miss the play, "Daddy Long Legs" which I should really like to see, but it is not worth the effort when you have to take two babies along. Jules always goes to sleep before Anne does, and the seats are so narrow one has to watch him or he will roll off. Anne does not go to sleep but wants to roam around, and by the time you take a youngster out and in and carry her around a few times, you'd rather be at home. The local committee has hired two very capable women and they have a nursery in the high school building right next to the tent, so there is a place where the children can play and not get lost or in danger. Anne enjoys it for half an hour or so, and then she is ready to move on.

This is one day I don't have to look at the calendar to find out the date. Anne was terribly interested in her first birthday cake and told us just how she wanted it decorated. We had only a small cake today and will have a big birthday cake Sunday when Co and all of you from Greybull are here. Of course today's had candles and flowers on it, but it was not a large cake. Otherwise it filled all the necessary requirements. I made a cake this morning to take to a house where we went to a funeral this morning and made enough dough for the small cake here.

Douglas, Wyoming
Friday, September 18, 1925

I am in the office of the Wyoming State Fair secretary and will take advantage of my opportunity with a typewriter to say a few words about our trip here. As you probably know, we arrived about 10:30 Wednesday night, having left the children at Greybull.

Yesterday was the big day at the Fair. Thursday is always Governor's Day, and Mrs. Ross was here. She was escorted to her box by two companies of cavalry soldiers from Fort Russell, who are here giving drills and exhibitions in the program. The board members and their wives had a box close to the governor's, and Dr. Hylton, who is the Democratic state chairman for this state now, suggested that we all go and visit in the governor's box, so we did; and she insisted that Mrs. Rollins, the wife of the president of the Board, and I stay there. There were a number of other women in the box, and from time to time various prominent men, such as Congressman Winter and other men who are prominent in the state. In the box next, which was the military box, were General La Trobe and Major Attis, and various other militaries in command of the cavalrymen here. After we got in the governor's box another man came into the military box and I was told he was Mr. Robert S. Ellison, vice president of the Midwest Refining Company at Casper. He was looking for me, but of course did not know me on sight. I was looking for him, but did not know him. (I had corresponded with him when I was Wyoming chairman for the I.U. memorial fund drive three years ago, but we had never met.) So as soon as I discovered who he was, I asked to be introduced to him, and he and I had a great time. He was sitting right next where I was, with only a flag draping between. We talked all afternoon, not just to each other, but to the others, too. The other women in the box wanted to know about Mr. Ellison and me, and I was greatly amused to hear Mrs. Ross explain that Mr. Ellison and I were graduates of the same university and were having a reunion. I told the women that Mr. Ellison and I had a date to meet at the fair and they thought that was very amusing. Ellison is really a great man out here. The crowd cheered for three persons during the afternoon: Governor Ross, Congressman Winter, and Mr. Ellison. I don't know when I had such a good time as I did, and Mr. Ellison seemed to also.

Last night we were all in boxes again to see the fireworks and hear the band concert. There is a very elaborate display of fireworks each night, a good many set pieces, and various sky rockets and chasers and everything one could think of. One of the pieces last night was an Arab riding a camel, coming up to a little tent on the desert. There were other conventional designs that were quite pretty. The show ended with one called "Smashing the Hindenburg Line." It shows a long row of houses and church and various buildings and then a battle beginning until a number of the houses were shot down. The fireworks display in this, in color, noise and light, was very fine, and we enjoyed it all.

John is having a Board meeting now and I am waiting for him here in the secretary's office. Last spring when this secretary was appointed John was the only man on the board who stood for him first to last and wanted him to have the same salary his predecessor had. But the fair this year beats anything any other secretary has done, and proves this man is the proper man for the place. Naturally, since John was for him all the time, John can have anything he asks for or doesn't even ask for, while we are here at the fair.

Mamma, we have planted apple trees — several times. We have some now that are still alive and that is about all one can expect of them for about the first five years. If they stay alive that long, then they may start to grow. The trees the apples came from that Cora brought home are 15 years old and this is the first time Bygrens have had enough apples from them to talk about. Hart's orchard is the same age, and they had a good crop last year for the first time. To grow an orchard here you must first grow a grove that entirely protects the orchard. You can't just set out a tree and then pick the fruit. Hart's protective trees are now about forty feet high practically all around the orchard. Bygren's are the same, on two sides and part of a third. So you see it takes pretty nearly a child's lifetime to get a tree to bearing. It is cheaper for us to buy the fruit each year than to raise it. Of course a child enjoys picking fruit from its own trees, and we have tried all the time to get some trees here for that purpose. We have a number of plums and some apples. We also tried grapes, but we can't get anywhere with them. The plum tree that had such a nice top and was loaded with plums last summer was all dead down to the roots this spring, and had to start all over again. That is what happens again and again.

Edith, I certainly am grateful to you for all you did in looking after the children so I could go to Douglas. Jules thinks he would like to come to see you again, especially if he could leave Anne at home this time. You did a lot more than you should have. Think of it, Mamma, she not only returned the children washed and clean but all their clothes likewise. Jules had a great time and has been telling us all about it.

John came in the other day with his chest all chesty and strutted around like a pouter pigeon. I wanted to know what was up now, and he announced that at last he had attained equality with his wife. Of course I was anxious to know what he was doing now, and he said that at last he was a university professor too, so that he was on an equal with me. He finally explained that the Veteran's Bureau at Casper, on Mr. Krueger's request, was giving Krueger another year of training under John, the advanced training being under the jurisdiction of the state university and the practical men giving the work being listed as members of the faculty for this work. They actually receive pay for it, about $20 a month during the school year. The money for the salary comes from the Veteran's Bureau, of course, but it is paid over to the University and paid by the University to the training teachers. I asked John if I should call him Prof. or Doc., but he refused to answer.

Wednesday, September 30, 1925

Jules is happy. For some time John has been singing to him that old crazy song about the preacher and the bear. Do you remember it?

> A preacher went out hunting,
> 'Twas on a Sunday morn,
> And though 'twas against his religion,
> He took his gun along;
> He shot himself some very fine quail,
> And a little bit of a measley hare,
> And on the way back to his home,
> He met a great Big Grizzley Bear.

The preacher then reminds the Lord of all the assistance He gave Jonah and the Hebrew children and Daniel and various others, and ends by saying, "And O Lord, if you can't help me, For mercy sake, don't you help dat bear." Then he tries to talk to the bear, but the bear only growls, which the children think is very funny. Anne goes into peals of laughter every time the bear growls. Well, Jules wanted John to take him to Werts to hear the whole record, as John did not remember all the story, so we sent for the record. It came yesterday, and you should have seen Jules when he heard what it was. He made more noise than a whole pack of bears, and has been so tickled ever since he does not know what to do. Of course the record has been playing most of the time.

I am sure you will be glad to hear that I am to have steady help. Wanda Shaulis told me the other day that she wishes she could go to high school again this winter, to take some of the subjects she did not have that she needs for entrance in the nurse's training course she wants to take at the hospital of the University of Denver. So I suggested that she go to school and stay here this winter. She is such good help and gets up so early in the morning and does so much in a short time that she can do up practically all the morning work before she goes to school. Then on Saturday and in the evenings she can do nearly everything else. So we offered her half wages if she would stay this winter. We have been paying her six dollars, so that will make three.

We told her if she would stay with us till she goes to school next September we could pay her three dollars this winter and then raise her wages to a dollar more than we had been paying for during the summer. I think that is reasonable enough for as much work as she does. I certainly am glad to have some one, for it makes it much easier for me and insures our having a clean house no matter what else I have to do. I sometimes think I am terribly lazy to need help, and then again I decide that it is so much better for me to use what strength I have in things that some one else can't do. When we talked it over, I told John I didn't know whether or not we could afford it, but he said he thought we couldn't afford not to have the help in the house. When I think of so many women around who do all their work and a lot more, I get ashamed of myself; and then when I think how their houses look except on special occasions, I feel that maybe after all a woman can't do more than so much, and it is worth a lot to her to be able to do other things and at the same time have a livable house all the time. Some men never notice if a house looks nice or not, but John does; and if we are alone and I get swamped he always does some of the work in the house, and I hate for him to use his energy that way. So we are very much pleased to have good help all the time for at least another year.

Mr. Krueger said a very lovely thing the other day about John's professor work. He laughed until he could hardly stop at your suggestion, Cora, that he charge a commission. He said he hadn't thought of that, and appreciated the suggestion. John said something about this being one windfall he had never expected and the first windfall that had ever come to him, and that he did not know if he could deliver the goods in return. Then Mr. Krueger said, "Perhaps the service has already been rendered."

Sunday night, December 6, 1925

If you don't get any letters from me in the next week, you will know why. Tomorrow is the day my division of the Aid serves the men's brotherhood banquet and I have to be at the church from early in the morning until the last dish is put away at night. We have to get the turkeys ready to roast, stuffing and all, but we shall have the baker shop roast them, which takes a lot of work off our hands. Tuesday I must wash and iron and do some baking. Wednesday I entertain the E.E.E. Club at an all day meeting here, which means the ladies come anywhere from ten o'clock on and stay till five, bringing their own dinner. I will make rolls and have coffee, mashed potatoes, etc. Thursday morning we start to Greybull, so you can see that times for much writing in the next three days will be few and far between.

If I had thought of it in time, I should have included in my Santa Claus list an encyclopedia of etiquette that Mont Wards are making a special on. It is by Emily Holt (whoever she is) and is called "Encyclopedia of Etiquette." It contains 500 pages and the present price is only 98 cents. I really think somebody ought to hand out copies of some book on the etiquette of dress to all the women who work in Powell. Yesterday afternoon while we were there we saw a dentist office girl down the street, without coat or hat, evidently on a short errand. She had on a black panne velvet dress trimmed in fur. Think of it. The dress was made with a long waist that was pointed front and back, and the sides gathered rather full over the hips, so as to make a circular skirt that had at the bottom a wide border of fur. In all my life I have never had a dress of such fine material, and she was wearing it in the office. About half an hour later we saw her on the street again, and she had on a *different* dress, this time a silk crepe light brown in color, of material not quite so rich as the black one, but the dress even more elaborately made. I wonder how many times a day she changes her costume. A little later we went into one of the hard-ware stores where there is a large display of toys. The wife of the proprietor was clerking there for the day—Saturday. She is a tall woman, rather homely in feature, but very nice looking. And she had on a silk crepe dress in two shades of gray. The underskirt and part of the bodice and overskirt were of a darker gray, and the fronts and sleeves of a very delicate gray, the overskirt being trimmed with a stencilled pattern of the darker color. She had on pale gray silk hose and very elaborate high-heeled, cut-out, gray suede slippers. For serving tea at an elaborate afternoon party she would have been perfect, but think of selling hardware store things in such an outfit.

I certainly hope that Mamma is feeling better and getting strong. Somehow I felt quite worried about you all afternoon, Mamma, but along about nine o'clock this evening I happened to find an old letter of yours the children had pulled out from somewhere, and after I read it I felt much better. Take your time and don't try to do too much. Don't worry about being Santa Claus. If you are well, we won't ask for anything else for Christmas.

Dear Everyone at Honeyhill:

We arrived here all right at 6:30 last night. Pater and Myrtle Woerner were at the station to meet us, the Colemans having driven out in their car to bring us home.

Aunt Cora says to tell you that Grandma got to see her Christmas present [that you children made for her]. They did not wait till Christmas morning, as Grandma was not strong enough to have it all at once. So they opened a few packages at a time. Grandma liked Buster Bear so much, and examined him carefully, looking at all the different colors to figure out what each was. Grandma felt weak Wednesday and Thursday and stayed in bed. Friday she sat up a while in the morning. About three in the afternoon she wanted to go to the bathroom. Cora helped her there, and she almost fell when she got there. Cora helped her to sit down and called Grandpa. He came at once and held Grandma while Cora telephoned for the doctor and the Colemans. Just after Cora got back to the bathroom Grandma dropped her head, and Grandpa said, "She is gone." When the doctor came he said the same. Grandpa said Grandma did not speak but nodded her head when he asked her some questions. So she was conscious till the end, and went as peacefully as going to sleep. She looks so lovely. She has on a lovely gray silk georgette dress, and has a pink rose in her hand. Grandpa went right down to the green house and picked out a rose for her as soon as she was gone.

There will be a service here in the morning at 10:30. We plan to leave for Evansville tomorrow afternoon. Pater will not attempt to make the trip and of course Cora will stay with him. Edith and the children and I will go to Evansville. There will be a service there some time Thursday. The Evansville folk wanted Grandma to be there one evening before the service so all her old friends could come to see her.

We think we will come back to Bloomington Saturday or Sunday. Then we will talk it over and see how long Pater and Cora want us to stay.

We are at French Lick, waiting for the train to Evansville. We left Bloomington at 2:05 and got here at four. We leave at six, and have to change again at Huntingburg, arriving at Evansville at 9:45.

The service at Bloomington this morning was so beautiful. I wish you could have been there. The house was full of friends. The minister read the 23rd Psalm and said a prayer, then he read the obituary we had prepared, and preached a 15 minute sermon. Mamma looked perfectly beautiful. Cora had put a notice in the paper requesting no flowers, but of course a number of the most intimate friends sent flowers anyway, and there were a large lot of beautiful sprays of white chrysanthemums, narcissus, carnations, roses, and others. Mamma was so peaceful and sweet. After all the others had gone, we girls stood and looked at her a while before she went out. But when she went out the door we did not feel at all as if she had gone, but felt that she was still with us the same as ever.

The doctor would not let Pater go to Evansville or to the funeral at the house. Pater and Janet and Anne spent the morning next door at Prof. Hanna's and did not come home till Cora went for them. Mrs. Hanna's elderly father is there and Pater enjoys talking to him. The folk say Pater looked awful the first few days, but since we have been here he has improved wonderfully and looked fine this noon, stronger than he did a year ago. But the doctor says he must not have any overstrain or shock.

I hope you all have a nice time at Thermopolis. Tell all the folk I am sorry I can not be there.

Bloomington, Indiana
January 9, 1926

Dear Daddy and Jules and Cecilia:

I got your letters from Thermopolis. We were very glad to know the bear was awake and likes candy. I hope Jules' suit got there all right and also the other package with the butterfly balloon and the cardboard oil pumping station.

Pater and I have been talking all evening. I asked him all about his Civil War record and want to write it down so we won't forget it. He enlisted April 19, 1861, for 3 months, and was in the service 3 years and 3 months, when he was too sick to stay any longer. His first engagement was at Rich Mountain. He was in the campaign through West Virginia and Virginia, starting in near Parkersburg. He fought through Maryland, too. He was captured at the battle of Fredericksburg and placed on parole the next day. Then he was sent to Annapolis, Maryland, to the parole camp there, and then after some months sent to Columbus, Ohio, and finally to Indianapolis. While there he got a month's furlough and returned to Evansville to find his father had died a few days before and had just been buried. After returning to Indianapolis he was sent to Madison, Indiana to a parole camp, and after a few months there exchanged. He got back to his company the day before the Battle of Gettysburg, in which he was on the right wing in the hardest of the fight. He was in all the battles and finally had to quit just before the Battle of the Wilderness.

Honeyhill Farm
Monday afternoon, January 18, 1926

Dear Everyone:

I will address my faithful typewriter again and say a few words to let you know how we are and hope you are the same — as the children always start their letters. John and Cecilia and Jules met us at Deaver yesterday, and they were right glad to see us, too. Jules nearly hugged the life out of Anne. I did not know how much he had missed her. He insisted on sitting beside her on the way home and ever since he has stayed right with her. He says he was lonesome for us while we were away. I asked him what he did when he was lonesome, and he said sometimes he went over to Gimmeson's and sometimes he went out to the shop and stayed with daddy.

Friday night, January 22, 1926

We have been working today on our 1925 accounts. At the end of the year we always go over all our checks — we do practically all our business by check — and find out what our expenditures were in household, personal, bee business, truck and car expense, general upkeep, and general expenses. We keep the lists from year to year posted in a ledger, so we can refer to them if necessary. We found one rather comforting thing, and that was that we had put about $800 into replacing necessary equipment lost in the shop fire and that means, of course, that we saved the equivalent of that much money. We really put about half again that much into replacement, but the rest has not been paid for.

February 3, 1926

Cora, in case you are wondering what to give me for Christmas next, I tell you that you can put down a P.E.O.* pin for me. I think I'll be eligible to wear one by that time. Miss Krueger called me up the other day and wanted to know when I would be at home, as she wanted to see me on business. We arranged a time and she came after school yesterday, accompanied by Miss June Selby, the normal training teacher here. The business, it developed, was an inquiry as to whether or not I would be interested in becoming a charter member of a chapter of P.E.O. if they organized one in Powell. Naturally I

*The P.E.O. sisterhood is a philanthropic and educational organization interested in bringing to women increased opportunities for higher education. P.E.O. was founded as a college sorority at Iowa Wesleyan College, January 21, 1869, and later changed from a college to a community group.

accepted. Miss Selby and Mrs. S.A. Nelson, the banker's wife, are members, and one other woman. They interested Miss Krueger, and she and they have asked me and one other woman in Powell to get together and start to organize. The P.E.O. Sisterhood is really the only thing I care very much about belonging to, as it is the really highbrow organization here in the West, as Edith can attest. When only three women were selected, I felt rather set up to think I was one of them. Especially since I have not been a member at all of any of the pseudo "high-brow" clubs in Powell and never tried to "climb" at all into the self-elected "elite."

February 19, 1926

I don't know when I had more fun than last night when we judged the essays in the American citizenship contest the state women's club started. The local women's clubs raised enough money to give two prizes in the high school and one in the upper grades. The prizes were $10 and $5 in the high school and $10 in the grades. There were 18 essays submitted in the high school and 11 in the grades. The work was very easy in judging, as two of the high school essays were remarkably fine. The subject was "How can I train myself to become a loyal Wyoming citizen." Most of the papers talked on a hundred points. The two winners emphasized the few things that made Wyoming different from all other states, took for granted the points in common with all other states, and played up the highlights in Wyoming history as being essential to becoming a loyal *Wyoming* citizen. There were so many funny statements in the grade papers that we shouted over and over. One paper said, in enumerating all the things a child should do to become a better citizen, that if there was a policeman in the town, the child should be courteous to him. Another said it was necessary to pay one's taxes and other debts, for one felt so much better when his debts were all paid. Another said if one was driving a fine, shining, lovely, high-powered, big car, he should not break the speed limits. (Nothing was mentioned about a Ford's exceeding the limit.) Another said that if you put money in the bank, you should be honest and not try to cheat the bank. One said that you must be honest and truthful and that Abraham Lincoln would have been a good "Wyoming citizen." Another said you had to be a Christian, like Theodore Roosevelt, to be a good citizen. Another said that conservation of natural resources was essential, and that you must never let the water run from the faucet or leave the gas burning when you did not need it. Another mentioned that you must "get acquainted with the mayor, president, and firemen" in the town where you live, so that if anybody does anything to violate the law you will know to whom to report him. Another said that if you catch a merchant not dealing fairly in business you must report him to the proper authorities. One said every child must obey the law and must observe the rule for "no whispering and no drinking during school hours." Evidently the teacher had told them to get their drink of water at recess time. One erudite youth spoke at length of our Wyoming delegation in Congress and said that these men were not only there to draw their money, but so we could follow their examples. One said that we should always be interested in learning about citizenship, and that if we ever found any unfortunate person who did not know about it, we should stop and teach him, for no matter how old the person might be, it is never too late to repent. Another said that he would like to go so far as to say he had been born, had lived, and would die in Wyoming, but he could not say he had been born here. However, he could say that he would live and die in Wyoming. All these I have mentioned were in 7th grade and 8th grade essays. None of the high school ones were so refreshing to the judges. Fortunately, we did the high school ones first.

February 20, 1926

At the E.E.E. Club meeting yesterday Miss Rokahr, state home economics specialist, and also Miss Eells, the county special agent, were present. Miss Rokahr has been giving talks and demonstrations on living room and general house furnishings, and this week gave a whole afternoon in Powell, taking the crowd from one house to another, discussing what was right and wrong in the various places they visited, after having had a lecture on the general principles of household art. She was laughing yesterday about having suggested at one place that a certain picture did not look well at the place it was hung, and suggsted that it should be somewhere else. She asked the householder if she had any special reason for putting the picture where it was, and the woman answered, "Yes, there is a hole in the wall that the picture hides." Yesterday at Youngs she spoke of the curtains at one window in the living room. The window was a cross-wise one. It probably was just an ordinary window put in sideways instead of up and down. The curtain was a figured net, two strips. One strip was very long, coming below the bottom of the frame. The other was very short, coming about half way down the glass part of the window. She asked Mrs. Young if she had any particular reason for making the curtain like that, and Mrs. Young replied it was all the goods she had. Of course we all laughed, for it probably was the truth. Miss R. then went on to suggest very tactfully that if the one long strip had been split in two, and one put at either side of the window, with the shorter length in the middle as a valance, the arrangement would be much improved. She also said that if she had a window with as lovely a view as that one had, she would dress it so that she could look out at all times without having to lift the curtain to see out. I was much amused and much interested in the whole discussion to see how she would handle a situation of criticizing an actual room without hurting the owner's feelings. She did some really constructive work and answered a lot of practical questions as to color of woodwork, paint vs. other finishes for floors, wall paper, kalsomine, drop ceilings or not, pictures and the way they were hung, and various other things. That she was helpful and not merely critical is evidenced by the fact that various women wished the meeting could have been held at their houses so she could have told them what to do with their rooms. So I take my hat off to her.

February 27, 1926

Jules is too happy for words. Ever since Cecilia got the game of Authors for Christmas, he has been wanting a game too. The four-book authors are just a little too difficult for him, although he knows a good many of the cards. So I got some seed catalogues with colored pictures and made him a set of vegetable and flower cards, in sets of two each. I have twenty or so different kinds of flowers and about the same number of vegetables, chickens, and fruits. To play, we give each person five cards and put the rest of the deck on the table. One person begins, and asks some one else for a card to match something he has. If he gets it, he asks again, until he does not get what he wants. Then he draws the top card from the deck to add to his hand. The next has a turn, in the same way, and so on. You would be surprised how fast Jules has learned the different objects. He does not know all the various flowers, as I have calendulas, poppies, snapdragons, scabiosa, phlox, wool flower, and many others that he has never seen. But by starting with only a few flowers that he knew, and then adding a few cards from time to time, he learns them all soon. All of us played last night, with Anne to receive the "books" as they were laid aside, and we had lots of fun.

Friday, March 5, 1926

It never rains but it pours. Mrs. Voss, who was supposed to be chairman for the Garland Ladies' Aid committee to serve the banquet for the Garland Men's Community Club next Monday night, says she gets so nervous she can't be in charge of such an affair, and begged me to take her place, so I agreed to help. Well, yesterday Mrs. Jump called me and announced that Wednesday night is the time our division serves the banquet for the Men's Brotherhood at Powell. I agreed to be chairman, as I thought, for the turkey banquet in December. She now informs me that the appointment as chairman is for the year! Nothing like keeping in practice! The dinner at Garland is to have as its piece de resistance a whole roast suckling pig, donated by — hold your breath — Mrs. Wallace!! However she happened to offer it I do not know, but she did. However, they tell me that she always has given rather liberally to the church at Garland, though she never attends. In addition to the roast pig, which we will have the baker in Powell roast, we will have mashed potatoes, sauerkraut, apple sauce, brown raisin and white bread, gravy, pickles, jelly, and blackberry pie.

Hear the joke! You know how little trouble I take to make bread. Most women fool around with it all day, never putting it in the pans till it has risen twice, and they make a sponge to start with before they stir it up stiff. Well, the state home economics director is to be here this coming week, and among other things is to give a demonstration on how to judge bread and cake, training some of the local women so they can do the work properly at the county fair next summer. So she wants a number of loaves of bread and cake to practice on. At our E.E.E. club yesterday the president announced that each woman's club was to send in one cake and one loaf of bread. Well, you should have heard the discussion. Of course the best bread bakers were asked to take a loaf, but they had such good excuses — mainly that their husbands had not brought home the best quality flour this time, and they could not use anything else because the bread would not be as white as possible. Several gave that reason. They insisted that I should send in a loaf of bread to represent this club. Think of it, I, who stir up every-thing at once, let it rise, and put it right in the pans, without monkeying around or using any great amount of time or energy! And they requested a loaf of my graham bread as the sample! I don't know when anything has given me such a kick as to be asked to set up my baking against the community when every other woman goes to twice the trouble I do in baking, and they all know it. Besides, if I can get it, I prefer the lower grades of flour, as they have such a fine flavor. To be sure, my being willing to send in a loaf may be only another instance of rushing in, but at least I was willing to do what the club president asked me to. Co, do you remember when you enjoyed the home made bread at a club meeting here only to find out afterward that it was Powell bakery bread. Well, some one suggested yesterday that we might send in a loaf of bakery bread.

By the way, does either of you girls use a sanitary apron? Nearly everyone uses one nowadays to keep the back of silk dresses from getting wrinkled. I got one from Sears R. that is the nicest thing I ever saw. It has a net top, and a rubber lower part. The rubber is some patent material that can be laundered and, if desired, even boiled without damaging the goods. And the apron is simply huge, too. Not like those microscopic ones that slipped aside every time you sat down. And the price, most wonderful of all, is only 59 cents.

Friday, March 18, 1926

I see that the author Hergesheimer is writing up the movie colony in the *Post*. The articles have been running for an issue or two. I tried to read one yesterday, and although I did manage to get through it, it was heavy swimming. I never did care for his writing, and always will. Give me somebody like Ben Ames Williams. Don't you like him, Edith? I really think he is one of the best writers of current fiction. You can measure him up alongside of such used-to-be models as George Eliot and Thackeray and find he stands pretty well. Of course he may not come up to some of the moderns in suggestiveness (unpleasant things, I mean) but in character work and plot I consider him unusually fine. I keep looking each time I find a serial of his to see if it is the American novel every one is always looking for. He almost gets there, but hasn't quite yet. But I am betting on him.

March 19, 1926

The unitholders are going to have to send three men to Washington, D.C. to deal with the Reclamation Service over the matter of our new contract with the government. John's Relief Committee of fifteen met last night and selected S.A. Nelson to represent them. The main contention, among other important ones, is what is called the joint-liability clause. Commissioner Mead, who seems to have pretty much to say about what the contract shall call for, seems to be adamant on the score that it shall call for joint liability. That means that every farmer here is responsible not only for his own farm, but that of everybody else. When a farm is neglected, the expense of the construction charges of that farm are to be added to the general account, and the people who stick on their farms will be charged with all the expenses of all the abandoned farms. Inasmuch as there is so much bad land here, so many farms that never will be worth anything, the farmers feel that they can not pay for anything except each one his own farm. John said when he got home last night that all the men on the committee agreed that if we had to have joint liability, in ten years there wouldn't be anybody left, and the best thing to do would be to quit right now before we put any more money into our places. Of course if the land here were anything like uniformly good, joint liability might be assumed without bankruptcy to the unitholders. But with so many bad units, it simply can't be done. And anyway, why should we farmers pay for the mistakes of the government engineers? We didn't hire them.

March 26, 1926

John was out this morning marshalling up telegrams to send to the chairman of the House Committee on Interstate and Foreign Commerce. It seems that there is a bill up in Congress to make it possible to adulterate honey with corn sugar without the necessity of so labeling the result. That is, the honey could be adulterated and then sold as pure honey, without any mention on the label of the corn sugar. Of course that would knock the honey business sky high. So the honey producers here are protesting its passage. Anybody who wants to can put all the corn sugar he wants to, or anything else he wants to in honey, but he should be required to label it accordingly, and not as pure honey. The bill passed the Senate before anything got out about it. The honey people all over the country are now working against it. Of course the same thing was fought out over glucose years ago. I can't see why the corn sugar wouldn't come under the pure food law the same as glucose, which is corn syrup, but it seems not. Corn sugar is a new thing commercially.

Wednesday, April 7, 1926

There is an article in the *Saturday Evening Post* of April 10 that I have enjoyed immensely. It is by Elizabeth Jordan, on the subject of "On Being a Spinster." It seems to me the best thing I have ever read on the subject. Read it, Co, for it is worth while. I have laughed a great deal at some of the statements becaue they are so true, and probably never said before. For instance:

"Of all the medieval notions cherished today about spinsters, the strangest is the notion that the poor thing never had a chance to marry. There's hardly a spinster anywhere sound in mind and body, who has not had at least one chance, and many of them have had dozens. No sane observer of the married women of his or her acquaintance can doubt that acquiring a husband is a comparatively easy achievement. It is reasonably clear that not all married women won their men by pulchritude or charm." (That last sentence is rich!)

And again: "Another thing the spinster gets out of the experience of having suitors appear is the conviction that all the men worth while are married. Almost every spinster gives voice to this opinion at intervals; and it appears to have some foundation. Most of us know several men, any one of whom we would ruthlessly have annexed if he had not been previously captured. Their wives earnestly assure us that these men, when roaming wild in bachelorhood, were not the perfect specimens they are today. It has taken years of patient, wifely training, they maintain, to whip those husbands into shape. A casual inspection of men still at large gives one a persistent impression that this may be true."

And this, too: "The starved nature of the spinster seems to be greatly distressing everyone but the spinster herself. She will admit what a tragedy it is to go through life without children of one's own, and she may sigh and add philosophically that one can't have everything. She will mention in passing, however, the trouble most of her friends are having with their children, grown or growing. But so far as her starved nature is concerned, the cold, dispassionately told truth is that the active, independent, busy spinster of today doesn't know she has a starved nature. Theoretically, of course, she must have one. All the rules of the game of life demand that she should have one. All the married men and women she knows insist that she has one. But she hasn't! It is very puzzling!" (But read the whole article. It has lots of good sense in it, as well as cleverness.)

April 21, 1926

If you had craved excitement, you could have had plenty of it here today. In the first place, The Star School Club met here for an all-day meeting, to have Miss Eells, the county home demonstrator, demonstrate the use of milk in cooking. We had a large crowd, about 20 grown-ups and as many children, or more. We had dinner, and then had the club business meeting, after which Miss Eells gave a talk to sum up the cooking she had done. While we were having the business meeting, we heard the awfullest groans you ever heard, and Vera Rickard, a 16-year-old girl who has been in very poor health all winter, came in the kitchen door from where she had been playing with the children, pulling them in the wagon on the lawn. I never heard anybody groan like that. She got to the chest in the dining room, and fell on it and nearly fainted. By that time a number of women, including her mother, had got to her. We gave her ammonia to smell and took her to the bedroom and put her to bed with a hot water bottle, when it developed she was suffering with a severe pain in her tummy. She gradually grew better, and in an hour or so was up again.

We then went on with the meeting and Miss Eells began her spiel. Before she was quite done, the children came running in to say there was a fire at the shop. I ran out to see, and met

John running in to say it was so. I rushed to the telephone and called for help on the line, and called central and asked her to give a general alarm on the nearby lines. The women grabbed buckets, even coal buckets, and carried water to the shop. As soon as I got out I got some tubs, and they carried water in tubs. By that time Mr. Gimmeson, who was at work in the field, had come, and it just happened that Mr. Young came driving by, and he came in. Soon the Loverchecks were here, as Frank was working in their field, and his mother (who was here) yelled at him. The Werts soon came, too, so there were six men, counting John. By that time the women had carried enough water to the shop, although the men carried a little more.

John had been burning weeds, below the bee yard, a long ways off, but evidently a spark had blown up and caught in behind a bench on which there was some lumber and under which some small sticks were piled. The fire started just east of the door at the west corner of the shop. The door was burned, and about an equal space of the wall, all on the south side. The fire had burned through it, as it was between the wall board ceiling and the roof of the shop. John says there is about 300 feet of wall board destroyed, partly from fire and partly torn off to get at the fire.

Merle, the little boy across the road, saw it first, and told John. John had watched the weed fire until he thought all danger was past, and had come to the house. The first three buckets of water got the fire checked, so that with the remainder of the water, it could be put out. But if there had not been a crowd here to carry water, we couldn't have saved the shop. And in the shop is the honey we are to load tomorrow. If we had lost the shop this time, and the honey in it, we would have been completely done for. John says he doesn't know what we would have done then.

April 25, 1926

I am pleased to state that we got a telegram this morning from New Orleans ordering a car of honey. We had a wire from this firm last week offering us 7-3/4 cents a pound after we had quoted them eight cents. We certainly needed to sell most awfully bad, but we decided we would not cut the price below 8 cents and wired back that we could not accept anything less than the 8 cents we had quoted them previously. This morning they came back accepting the 8 cents. One of the biggest honey producers in Montana said recently he couldn't get anything over 7½, so we felt rather shaky at turning down the 7-3/4, but we did it anyway, feeling that our good fairies were on the job as usual. And you see they were. Honey has been so slow in movement this year. We got 8-3/4 for the first car we sold, so you see the price has dropped considerably. We had offered that car for nine cents and got an offer back of 8½. We refused, but wired that we would take 8-3/4. That was accepted. We have been luckier than most beekeepers, as most of them did not get more than 8½ then, and less than 8 now.

Do you remember reading "The Plastic Age" several years ago? It has been translated into German under the title of "Studenten Jahre." In the *Literary Digest* Book Review is an interesting bit about this translation. Once when the hero is three sheets in the wind, he is maudlin enough to crave suicide, and laments, "Oh, oh, I wish I didn't use a shafety-razhor!" In the German edition, this becomes, "Ach je, ach je, wenn ich nur einin Sicherheitrasierapparet hat!" The author, Dr. Marks, in writing to his publishers, telling the translation, says, "Can you imagine any one, German or American, when he is drink-fuddled, rolling forth a word like that? Try to say it sober."

May 7, 1926

We are going to a political banquet tonight. I have not got very enthusiastic yet about campaigns. It is too early, I suppose. Some day, when the children are older, I am going to run for the legislature, just for the experience (of being *in* the legislature, I mean, not of *running*). There is no hurry about it, however, as one can be of any age to do that. I flatter myself that I could be elected in this county, tho of course I may be mistaken. John cut down the ordinary Republican majority from about 700 to 150 when he ran, and I believe that being a woman, and perhaps the first woman from this county to run (if I am), I could get elected. But as I said, I don't intend to take up that sort of business till all three children are sizable. However, it is interesting to have something of the sort in the future to look forward to occasionally. It makes life more interesting. I wouldn't care for politics as a steady diet, but an occasional fingering into the subject is refreshing.

May 9, 1926

We had a very good dinner and a very good time at the Democratic county banquet the other night and I was glad I was there. The main speaker of the evening was Barry Marshall of Sheridan. I had met him four years ago, and he remembered me. (By the way, it was he who delivered to John at the convention at Casper the telegram telling that our shop had burned two years ago.) Mr. Marshall was much interested in learning that Ted and I are related. He spoke earnestly about the wonderful and unbelievable record Ted has made as district governor for Lions and could not say enough about what splendid work Ted has done.

A very funny thing happened during the speeches at the banquet. A jazz band played while we were eating, but they were mercifully stopped when it was time for the toastmaster to take charge. He first called on the leading man in the county, John Cook of Cody, to give a statement of the why and wherefor of this meeting. After Mr. Cook finished, the toastmaster then said, as we understood it, "Now we want to hear from Mr. John Hendricks." We were at the opposite end of the table at which the toastmaster sat. John got up, made the usual proper bow and address to the toastmaster, "Ladies and gentlemen," and was clearing his throat to sail into a speech, when the toastmaster halted him with the statement that he had called on *Mrs.* Hendricks, not Mr. Of course everybody roared. Naturally the joke was on John, and there was nothing for him to do but to bow to me and invite me to stand up. I really thought the toastmaster *had* called on John, and so did the folk around us. I made my little speech, and then the toastmaster invited John to speak. John had a really good talk ready and proceeded to give it. That it was good is evident by the fact that nearly all the later speakers referred to what John had said and approved of his point. The toastmaster called on half a dozen other prominent Democrats, and then Mr. Marshall made his talk.

When I talked I started out by telling the story of the Czechoslovakian at Casper who came up before the judge for citizenship papers a year ago. The judge asked him as a first question what was the government of this country. The man responded promptly, "Nellie Ross." The judge decided the man did not know enough to become a citizen, so he gave the man a year in which to study up and told him to come back then. Recently, the man appeared again. This time the first question asked him was who discovered America. Again, and as promptly, the response was "Nellie Ross." And the man has another year in which to learn about conditions. I then went on to say that we good Democrats were a good deal like the Czechoslovakian. Of course we did not go as far as to say or believe that Nellie Ross discovered America and was the whole government, but, etc., etc., for about two sentences. Then I told the story of the old maid who was present when proposals were being discussed — the old, "but once a man asked me to walk in the moonlight" story, and concluded by saying that anything I might say at this time would be as far away from the excellent speech I knew Mr. Marshall would make as being asked to take a walk in the moonlight was from a real proposal.

I was rather flattered at being the only woman asked to talk, and also at being the first one called on. Of course this latter might be for either of two reasons, not so flattering: 1. because they believed in ladies first, and 2. because they wanted to get me done and out of the way. But at all events, it is rather interesting to be the only woman in the county asked to say anything. One has evidently made her existence known, at least, and that is something. This was not just a local meeting, but was to represent the entire county, and there were many people there from Cody, Meeteetsee, Sage Creek, and various other corners of the county, and also from Lovell. Of course the whole county is a small enough puddle, but at all events we have splashed a little! Naturally, I wouldn't want to say anything about it except in the family, but I can tell you about it.

May 23, 1926

We have had some very nice compliments on our honey recently. We have sold a car the past two seasons to Dadant and Sons, the firm that is about the most expert in the whole country on honey business. They make and sell supplies and publish the *American Bee Journal.* Some time ago they wrote us about the cars of honey they got from us in 1924 and 1925, asking just what system of heating we used, as the honey did not granulate for months and months. As this honey here will granulate in two weeks after extracting if not heated when extracted, they thought we had a pretty fine system to accomplish what we did. In another letter we got just a few days ago, they spoke again of our honey and said they would want another car this year. So you see we can sell at least one car, if we have it, and we hope to have about three or four this year.

The Sweetens were here last night and took us riding in their new Chrysler coach. It is a beauty. I told John afterward that they would never in a million years have been able to get such a car if they had stayed in Indiana. He said, no, and they wouldn't either if they had stayed on their farm here! He said maybe we'd better move off the farm, too. As Edith said some time ago, we have the consolation of knowing that Joe has got a college education, and Mina a start. Probably they would have gone on till they would have got an education, but I am positive that without your influence, Cora, that got Joe the job he has had, his struggles would have been much harder.

There was the largest crowd yesterday at the meeting that ever gathered in the state for a Democratic rally. We did not call the meeting a convention, for a very good reason. You see, we have a state primary law in this state, providing a primary for the nomination of candidates. Last week the Republicans had a meeting, which they called a convention. They actually made out a state ticket, and issued it as the state candidates for the Republican ticket. The Repub. bosses for some years have been trying to get rid of the primary law, because they cannot control nominations under it. They introduced a bill in the last legislature abolishing the primary, but the bill was overwhelmingly defeated. Naturally, the large rank and file of the Rep. party is opposed to boss rule and wants the primary law kept and observed.

The Democrats, profiting by this, naturally avoided everything at their meeting that would in any way seem to steam roller things. Consequently nothing was done except to endorse the administration of Gov. Ross and to discuss the matters that were considered important in the affairs of the state. Naturally, the people who intend to be candidates let it be known informally so that the gathering could look them over.

The five men who were from here insisted on putting me on the program committee. We met both before and after lunch and arranged for all the matters to be considered by the meeting. In the afternoon there were speeches by Attorney General Howell, who reviewed the present state administration and outlined the matters the party ought to stand for; and by Mr. O'Mahoney, who spoke of both national and state affairs, the Democratic prospects this year, and also what the party ought to advocate. Governor Ross then spoke on her administration and the aims she and her associates had in carrying on the state government, and pledged the same for the future.

Then the chair called for Barry Marshall of Sheridan, one of the most prominent men in the state besides Howell and

O'Mahoney. Mr. Marshall made a nice little speech. Then the chairman began to speak of a lady present who had been a candidate on the state ticket four years ago. I was sitting with Mrs. Haggard of Cheyenne, who had come at Gov. Ross's request as her companion on the trip. When the chairman began to speak, Mrs. H. turned to me and said, "He means you." I stared at her and answered, "O no." She said, "Yes, he does." By that time he spoke my name, and she said "Stand up, of course that's you." So there was nothing for me to do but to walk down front and say something. I said I had had no intention whatever of making a speech and not the slightest idea I would be called on. I had nothing to say, and would say it. As Mr. O'Mahoney and Mr. Marshall had just said, the party that does not serve the people is put into the discard. I was very proud to be a member of a party that served the people themselves. The Democratic party has not been in power in this state and has had time and opportunity to study what the people need, and see that they get it. We have issues and good people for candidates. I can see no reason why there should not be a Democratic victory in this state this fall. I thank you.

The state committee wanted me to run again for state superintendent, but I declined absolutely. I told them I couldn't afford financially to make the race and I actually did not want the office because I did not care for the work, but that some time in the future I want to get into the Legislature.

The Powell men have been very nice to me, especially Mr. Werts and Mr. Keyser. I have not bothered them at all, as fortunately I am not afraid to chase about in a strange place. Mr. Werts told me he wanted to take me to lunch yesterday but couldn't find me. I am quite sure it didn't lower their idea of my ability for me to be pretty independent of the need of their attentions and for them to see I knew various people from various places.

I am proud of being able to hold my own in such a gathering, and to do the family credit. No small part of my assurance is due to the feeling of being dressed with perfect taste and suitability for each occasion. When I spoke I had on the dark blue, with one streamer fastened high about my neck. I wore a black and white hat, light hose, and black patent leather pumps. Without the dresses and coat you sent, Cora, I couldn't have been so confident.

Wednesday, June 23, 1926

I hope you got the letters I mailed from the train and Thermopolis to you at 822, telling all about my trip. I enjoyed it immensely. As I told you, they wanted me to run again on the state ticket, but I refused. In the first place, I do not care for the state sup't office, as that is not the line of work I really care to do. In the second place, the money would probably be wasted, for I believe it would be very hard and probably impossible for anybody to defeat Mrs. Morton, the present incumbent, as she has been very popular. I rather hated to spend the money necessary to go to Thermopolis, as we need all we have, because our expenses are heavy, our farm loan is overdue, and until we can get some definite action from the government we do not know where we are nor what we can count on. But after I was called on to speak from the floor of the meeting—the only person in the state beside Barry Marshall of Sheridan, except the regular speakers on the program—I felt it was worth going to have had that bit of publicity, even if I do not mean to take political advantage of it now. At all events, going on such a trip gives one something to think about, and I guess there isn't really anything worth money—possibly even worth more money—than something worth while to think about.

Monday, June 28, 1926

We are girl-less. Wanda got a wire yesterday from a girl friend who is working in the Park, offering Wanda a job as waitress at Mammoth. Wanda is hoping it is at the hotel, for she says the camp guests don't tip. She left on the night train last night to go by way of Billings and Gardiner. Of course I hate to lose a girl who is trained to do my work, but I wouldn't for anything try to hold a girl who wanted to get away.

Of course you did not expect me to write you a letter yesterday, inasmuch as it was circus day. About 4:30 yesterday morning John said he guessed he would get up and milk Susannah, so as to have it done before the circus train came in. Cecilia got up at the same time and looked out the dining room window. Over the hill north toward Mantua she saw train smoke, so John got out the car instead of milking the cow, and we all hustled into some clothes and went to Powell to see the circus unload. It was really worth seeing. I wouldn't have missed it for anything. The circus does not have a parade here, but they use elephants to pull various wagons and cages from the railroad to the circus grounds, as well as about 30 of the finest draft horses you ever saw, and a funny little caterpillar tractor that hauls what it would take eight horses to do. It really is wonderful to see the organization with which the big cages and wagons and all the other things are unloaded from the cars and pulled from the track and taken far enough that horses or elephants or a tractor can be hitched on, and then the load pulled off. We stayed till after seven and then came home for breakfast and to do the chores so we could go back again before noon, as we wanted to be there early.

The circus itself was really "bigger and better" than ever! Even if you saw it last time, two years ago, you would enjoy it again. There were many new acts, and more performing animals than ever. We especially enjoyed the performing lions, tiger, leopard, polar bears, seals, zebras, and horses. There was some very fine acrobatic work and strong-man stunts. At one time there was a group of trapeze performers all around the tent, about ten or twelve, all performing the most hair raising stunts. There was some lovely dancing. The center ring was filled with girls dressed like butterfles, while the two end rings had a background of dancing girls in spangled costumes, with a platform at the front occupied by a girl in white draperies who did a swirling costume dance. There were sticks or wires attached to the wing parts of each costume, and the whole thing kept in motion, while colored lights played. I enjoyed that very much.

There was a lot of performing on horseback, good as usual. I really don't believe there was ever a better, cleaner, more interesting show than Barnes.

As for some of the highlights, to us, of course, the elephant herd always attracts, because one of their largest elephants is named Jules. Jules and Anne and Cecilia fed all the elephants peanuts and a pocketful of pretzels which John had taken along. Anne also enjoyed feeding the big ostriches, which stood about eight feet tall. They had to stick their heads through the lower part of the pen for Anne to feed them. She thought they were the biggest chickens she ever saw. But the most interesting thing was a baby monkey and its mother. The baby was a real baby, about the size of a half-grown kitten. The mother was perhaps two feet tall. The baby could run and climb everywhere but was evidently quite as timid as any human child in a crowd. One time the baby wanted to have the mother hold it. The mother would put it down, but the baby would run to her and throw its arms around her neck and whimper. The mother would pat it and put it down again. The baby would then fairly howl, and try to follow the mother; but the mother would not hold it until one time when the baby came close to the front of the cage, and John stuck out his finger and touched it. The mother was way at the back of the cage, but quick as a flash she was at the front, grabbed the baby in her arms, hugged it tight as could be, and gave John the awfullest look! We just howled.

Do you remember, Co, how Jules and Anne and Janet stick out their lips when anything peeves them? Yesterday there was a large ape, advertised always as "Joe Martin." He was dressed in full evening dress, top hat and all. I saw his keeper sitting with him, between performances, talking to him. The ape sat there and stuck out his lip! And what do you think the keeper did? He put out his finger and flipped the monkey's lip, just the way we do to the children! So the next time any of the youngsters sticks out its lip, I guess we'll have to call him or her "Joe Martin."

So, the horoscope is rich. I am glad to find out what the stars (according to Miss Adams) say I am like. Edith, the horoscope gave quite a lecture to March folk on their need of being able to concentrate. Begoora, however, after 12 years of housekeeping and nearly ten years of knowing 24 hours a day what babies are doing, maybe I do need some advice on concentrating, for as I see it, the chief asset of a housekeeper is to be able not to concentrate on one thing, but to run about six rings at the same time. My chief difficulty has been that I will start half a dozen things and then forget about them until I smell the oven or hear something boil over on the stove. O, of course, not all the time, but frequently.

The other morning, when we watched the circus unload we saw the general laborers come off the train and start for the grounds. We happened to be parked near the canal, and that was the bathroom for the roustabouts. One of the men who attracted our attention particularly was a very large, tall, very black Negro with the most magnificent whiskers I ever saw. The shaving people ought to have his picture for their ads. The whiskers were long, full, and black as the ace of spades. The man performed his matutinal ablutions in the canal, wiped his face with a blue handkerchief, meanwhile laying down his bundle and on it a half-smoked cigar, which he guarded as a cat would a mouse while he was washing; and then he struck out for the grounds, his little bundle under his arm and the cigar in his mouth. Well, a little later, as we passed the grounds, we saw him driving tent stakes. In the afternoon, in the grand parade of all nations, who should appear but this same Negro, with his whiskers bigger and blacker than ever. He was dressed as a ruler of some oriental or African tribe. He had on a large, fancy turban crown, and a robe made of striped material. The robe was very large and full, with flowing sleeves and a long, long train, which was carried some six or eight feet behind him by a black boy dressed as a slave. Talk about airs! Any monarch who could put on the strutting and dignity that he showed would go down in history.

I was picking strawberries yesterday afternoon when I heard a car honk. I couldn't see it, as the house was between us. But in a second Jules came running and said Aunt Edith and Uncle Teddy were here. Just then a perfectly huge, gorgeously spiffy sedan drove around the house to the back porch. I hustled to the house and immediately recognized the license number and then Ted. So it was they, sure enough. You should see the car this family can boast of now. If anybody says anything about automobiles, just speak casually of the Nash four door sedan your sister and brother-in-law have, with gorgeous gray plush upholstery throughout, and every convenience known to human beings. Ted and Edith drove on to Cody, leaving the children here. They got back about eleven and spent the night here, starting home about eight this morning. After they went away today, Anne came in and said, "When will we get our new car?" I told her to ask that question of daddy. She came back shortly and said, "Daddy said not today," and was perfectly content.

Tomorrow I have two meetings, one in the afternoon and one at night. The evening meeting is the special meeting of P.E.O. for the convention report. The afternoon meeting is one for the purpose of federating the women's clubs here on the Flat. There are some nine or ten women's clubs all told. Only one of them, the Library Club, belongs to the State Federation. As the annual dues per member for belonging to the State Federation are fifty cents, that counts up too high, especially as most of the clubs do not have any dues at all locally. Naturally the members would balk at paying out half a dollar per for membership which means practically nothing to them individually. So some of the Library Club bright ladies conceived the idea of having a federation of our own here, to consist of three members from each of the local clubs. This would make membership of some thirty. As each club sends three delegates, the cost per club would be $1.50 per year. Then this federated local club is to become federated with the State Federation and in that way each local club will get as much benefit from its $1.50 as it would if it paid fifty cents for each member on its list. In addition, the local federated club will serve as a sort of clearing house for all sorts of local movements that can best be carried on by the women's clubs. The plan is such a clever one I am sorry I didn't think of it myself.

Friday afternoon, July 16, 1926

I was at Burke's at a meeting of the Star Club the other afternoon, when John called me to say there was a long distance telephone call for me from Cheyenne. The telephone line was so bad I could not even hear the Powell central, but I did understand enough to find out that it was Mr. O'Mahoney calling. So I went to Garland to get the call on the direct long distance phone there. But when I got there, the Cheyenne central could not get Mr. O'M, and after wasting more than an hour I came on home and finally got the call about eight o'clock last night.

When I was at Thermopolis, Mr. O'M. wanted me to let my name come up again for state superintendent. I refused, as I do not want to run, and do not want the office. When he called he said he understood entirely that I did not want the place, and did not want to make any campaign, but that if I would only consent to allow my name to appear on the ticket it would be a very great help to the party. It seems that there is a man in Goshen County who wants to run for the office. He is not the least big qualified and they do not want to have him, but of course there is no way to prevent his filing for nomination at the primaries except by making him think he would not be nominated. So the state committee begged me to let my name come up again, just to prevent this man from filing. I had told Mr. O'M. at Thermopolis that we did not have any money to spend on politics, so he knew that. He told me over the phone that if I would let my name come up for filing, they would see to the filing fee. When they wanted me to run so badly that they would pay the piper, I decided that since there is no more chance for my being elected than for me to become president of the U.S., I might as well render the party the little service of using my name. When things are handed out on a silver platter with a bill marked paid, one can't very well refuse. So here I am, against my wishes entirely, in politics again. Can you beat it? However, I hope Mrs. Morton will beat me, for I would have as much use for the office of state sup't as the dog would have for the train he was running after, if he caught it.

John has no objections to my running, but he certainly does to my being elected! He wakes up every once in a while to inquire what in the world we would do if I were elected? Well, I am not worrying about that, for I do not think anybody could defeat Mrs. Morton. But it certainly would be a terrible joke on us if by any slip I were elected. Now isn't that a rich situation — to be offered a chance to run for the job that hundreds of folk in Indiana — and various other states — would give their eye teeth for, and not only refuse to make any campaign but even hope to be defeated?

Thursday, July 22, 1926

So, I am glad to hear you say you object to the routine of housework. The housekeeping magazines and manuals ding dong away constantly at having a schedule, and following it daily. I sometimes think I must be an animal of a very low order, at least as a housekeeper, for I certainly would go mad and bite something if I had to do the same thing at the same time every day. But if I stopped to think that at nine o'clock every morning and four o'clock every afternoon I had to hang up my dish cloth and start the evening fire, I think I'd croak. I don't mind work — it's a good thing I don't for I get plenty of it this summer, it seems — but I do hate monotonous repetition. It's a good thing I married a man who doesn't mind and rather enjoys irregular breakfasts and suppers. If I had to cook three meals every day including Sunday I think I'd have struck long since. And that in spite of the fact that I really like to cook.

Ihappened on a diary that I kept the first year I taught school. It tells at length how homesick I got all the time and how much I was helped by your visits on Wednesdays and at other times during the week. Under the date of October 9, 1901, I found this entry:

> Cora came to see me tonight, all alone. Mamma is in town. Aunts Lizzie and Lena have gone to St. Louis, and Cora was to have stayed with Grandma, but Grandma has been sick, so Mamma took her place. Cora is housekeeper at home this week. She has to do the cooking, housework, and all, and papa has two men working, stripping cane. Pretty hard on Cora. She didn't want to come out today — thought she couldn't spare the time — but papa knew me, and made her. Before she started she asked papa what she should take to me.
> "Our love," he replied.
> "Oh," Cora said, "she can't eat that!"
> "Well," papa answered, "if she doesn't like it raw, she can preserve it."

Isn't that just like him? You may be sure I did preserve it, as well as eat it up raw, and I am glad to say that today we preserve it more than ever.

Itold you some time ago that Mrs. Clark, the doctor's wife, had conceived of the idea of having a local federation of women's clubs, to be composed of three delegates from each of the 12 women's clubs in the community, this central club to federate with the State Federation. I represented the Star Club in the federated meeting today, and to my surprise was elected temporary president and then permanent president. I never hankered much to be president of one of the clubs, tho I have served a number of years as such, but I confess I really feel flattered to be the president of the club of the clubs. Maybe I like the places of honor too much, but when one is handed out, unsolicited, and unexpected, I guess I might as well take it.

Sunday, August 8, 1926

We have to go to Hyattville tomorrow. I'd rather go to Hyattville and help there than to stay home and do the chores, especially as June has wrecked three of her teats and is a real problem to handle. She never did like me anyhow — maybe it is reciprocal — and I do hate to have to wrestle her. I don't mind milking Susannah but I do June. Mr. Maloy, the hired man, can stay here and work in the shop and I can do the work necessary at Hyattville.

I suppose you are happy, Ted, over Emerson's nomination for governor. Well, there is this comfort in it to all of us, outside of our personal interest on your account — that no matter which ones becomes governor this fall, the incumbent will be decent, clean and honest, as well as efficient.

Thursday, September 2, 1926

The children talk of nothing but going to Douglas and to Bloomington. Jules is somewhat confused and thought we would stay on the train overnight to go to Douglas the same as to go to Indiana. However, if he can eat on the train on the Douglas trip, it will be all right! We told them of the fine melons we had last year on the diner, and of course they are counting on having some this year. We will be on the train for two meals each way, lunch and dinner on the way down, and breakfast and lunch coming back. I think I shall take along lunch on the way down to eat at noon, as the children are so fond of cheese and a few other articles that are easy to pack and not expensive. But on the way back, we'll have two meals on the diner. It will be a rather expensive trip, as the railroad fare for Cecilia and me, even at special fare-and-a-third rates will be about $25. However, John may not be on the Board again, if Mrs. Ross is not reelected, and it seems too good an opportunity to miss. If we figured up what the admission fees would be for all of us, not counting the grandstand box and all the other complimentary tickets we get, it would take a big check to pay for it all. So we might as well take advantage of our opportunity while it is there. It is rather nice to have a lot of the prominent men of the state meeting the train for you and chasing around with their autos all the while you are in town to see if there is anything they can do or any place you want to go. With all the new clothes you sent me, Pater, I can dress the part, so I might as well be one of those present, especially this year when I am in politics. And as for the children, nothing they ever go to will remain more in their memory than their first state fair and rodeo. I guess a lot of folk around here think we are extravagant to spend so much railroad fare and go so many places, but when I think of how much it means to children and how much they learn that way, I feel it is money well spent, and worth more than almost anything else they can have.

Friday, September 10, 1926

Mrs. Gimmeson and Mrs. Voss have their hair bobbed now, so there are only a few of us "old" ladies in the community — Mrs. Murray, Bygren, Lovercheck and I. From the way some folk speak, it is no particular honor to be in the class with these, but I should worry about what folk think of me! I told George Young this noon, when he was teasing me about getting mine bobbed, that I had lived with my hair long enough to know more about it than anyone else, and I knew why I did not want it bobbed. In this dry climate, it stays too dry and soft to look well bobbed. I washed it a week ago yesterday, and it is only now getting so I can make it look like anything. When I get to Indiana, it gets oily in two weeks or so, as usual, but out here I think I could go seven months without its ever getting oily. My scalp does not get dirty either, and when I wash my head the water is not as soiled after a couple of months as after a week or two in Indiana. Naturally, I do not wash my hair very often. When I wanted my hair clean (?) to go to Douglas next week I washed it last week! If I had washed it any later than that, I could not have made it stay anywhere after it was dressed. The curl won't stay in it, and the hair is so soft it falls everywhere except where it should.

Here we are, having a fine time. The children are seeing so much they can hardly contain it all. However, there are naturally various things they enjoy more than others, and they go back again and again to see them. One is an exhibit of silver fox puppies. Another is a gopher display by the state department of rodent control. There is a tall, narrow display case with a live gopher in it that burrows back and forth through the ground. He digs a while with the claws of his forefeet, then turns around and pushes the loose earth away up the burrow with his back feet, working backward. The children never tire of watching that. Another is a forest fire exhibit. There is a large frame, like a movie screen. In it you see a picture of a camp in a forest, with a camp fire in the foreground. Pretty soon the camp fire starts to burn up, and pretty soon the whole forest is on fire. Then the end shows the burned off stumps of the trees. Pretty soon it changes back again and starts all over. The thing is worked electrically and there is lots of smoke and apparent flame when the fire burns up. There is a health food display with a moving cow whose milk goes through tubes to the various milk products and then to the people they feed. As the figures move continually and the cow chews all the time, there is plenty of action and the children run through the industrial building every time we go back and forth anywhere to see that exhibit.

We sat in the governor's box a long time yesterday afternoon and of course had a nice time. Jules and Cecilia think they are quite important as they met Senator Kendrick and Congressman Winter and sat with Gov. Ross a long time.

I have been wearing the dark blue georgette and the dotted silk, the former in the morning and the latter in the afternoon. I feel quite comfortable in any company. Mrs. Morton, my opponent, is here and although she is good looking, I am sure — and John agrees — that I make as good an appearance. Clothes count so much.

I did a little politicking while I was there, but not much. I had a conference with the state chairman and talked with Gov. Ross and some of the other state candidates. The state chairman is sure Mrs. Ross will be reelected by a very large majority — greater than any Democrat ever received before. He thinks some of the rest of the state ticket may be elected, too. I rather think one man, Mr. McWhinnie, who is at present commissioner of public lands, and is running for treasurer, has a good chance, as he is well known through his present office. But I don't think the rest of us have any show.

Thursday, September 23, 1926

I am sure you will be glad to learn I am to have help in the house again. Mrs. Murray called the other day to ask if I wanted a high school girl named Mary Busch. It seems that Mary's mother formerly lived at Powell and then married and went to live up in the mountains somewhere near Shell. When Mary was ready for high school she came to Powell, as she had no high school nearby, and besides her stepfather did not care for her to stay at home. She worked for Mrs. Oviatt for her board last winter and has also stayed at Dr. Gould's. All she wants is a place to stay for her board. However, as she is 18 years old, we feel that she ought to have more than that, especially as she has absolutely nothing to go on. The Mother's Circle of the Methodist church kept her in clothes last winter. So we are going to wait to find out what she can do, and then pay her a dollar or two a week in addition to her board. I feel sorry for a girl who hasn't a penny of her own, and I would rather give her a regular small wage and then let her administer her own finances than to pay for things she needs, such as school supplies and the like.

September 24, 1926

We had word yesterday that the annual meeting of the state beekeepers' association is from November 30 to December 3. So I think we had better plan to go to Thermopolis and then on to Indiana, which will bring us there early in December. We can then spend Christmas with you, Co and Pater, if you think you can stand the commotion of three youngsters on that occasion.

I have thought all the time I should not leave here before election, just as a matter of appearance, though of course I could get an absent vote by arranging for it beforehand. But I do not think it would look well, even though the state committee agreed when I allowed my name to go on the ticket that I would not make an active campaign. I had so much encouragement when I was at Douglas that if I really wanted the office I would be tempted to prowl over the state quite a bit.

Edith, I never did get to tell you that I had such a nice time with the Browns on the train the day we went to Douglas. They thought their visit at Greybull was the best part of their whole trip and they were wild about you and Ted and the children and the house and the dinner you served them. I was amused at them about my political connections. When I told her about being candidate for state superintendent, she was quite excited over it, exclaiming that she must tell Mr. B., she must tell Mr. B as he would be so interested. When he came along, she told him. He stopped short, looked queer, straightened up, and said stiffly, "Yes, I know all about it. Ed told me. He doesn't approve at all. He says he won't vote for her." (I was also amused at Judge Harding's comment on our return trip. He assured me he wished he could vote for me, and was considering coming back for election just so he could. He said Ted insisted that he wouldn't but that Ted was a great talker and that I need not worry about what Ted *said*.)

To return to the Browns. There were some girls on the train going to Laramie to college. During the evening, Mr. B. came in from the platform quite wrought up, and announced that the girls were out there smoking. He gave quite a dialectic on the conduct of such girls and the probability of their parents' going to great sacrifice to send them to college. Then he said, "They are all nice looking, too. But THINK of KISSING a girl whose lips tasted of TOBACCO!" I replied mildly, "But think of all the girls who have had to kiss men whose lips tasted of tobacco." He stiffened like a soldier on parade and bristled as Jack the dog would at the approach of an agent, and shouted, "Mrs. Brown never had to do that!" "Well," I said, "neither did I, thank fortune, but think of the great majority of girls who have always had to." And he said not another word on the subject of smoking. Not that I approve of it, but it seemed to me that sauce for the goose was sauce for the gander.

Monday, September 27, 1926

We like our new girl very much. If Wanda was the prettiest girl on the Flat, Mary Busch could qualify for pretty much the opposite. She is rather short, and heavy and freckly, and red haired, and large nosed, and round faced. But she has a pleasant expression and is cheerful as can be, and a more than willing worker. She went right ahead without being told more than once, and hardly that. I am offering her $2 a week and her board during the winter, and $6 if she stays next summer. She seems very well satisfied.

Friday, October 1, 1926

I don't know that I have anything worth while saying to put a two cent stamp on. It is too bad we can't stamp our letters according to the value that is in them. It wouldn't cost us so much for postage. But perhaps the government postal deficit would be too great and Uncle Sam would have to quit carrying mail altogether if every letter were charged for on the basis of what it said inside.

I haven't said much about politics in my letters, because I can't say anything in the letters that go to Greybull, except matters of general interest. You know Ted is working tooth and nail for Emerson, Mrs. Ross's opponent. Ted told me all about his connection with Emerson. He said it was his work at the Republican state convention, more than anybody's else, that got the nomination for Emerson. You can see that with Ted working for Emerson and we for Gov. Ross, we can't say much

about what we are doing. Ted asked me to hold off Emerson in
any campaigning I might do, and not to do anything that
would keep Emerson from getting votes. Naturally, I won't do
anything to slam Emerson, but I certainly will do everything in
my power to get votes for Gov. Ross. We are interested,
personally, too, for if Gov. Ross is not reelected, John won't be
on the state agricultural board for another term. So it is about
half of a dozen one way and six the other.

October 10, 1926

Have you read "Babbitt?" It is a pretty good book, rather
tiresome at times with all the sordid details of a man's life,
but quite real, it seems to me. The author is certainly down on
the Citizen's Defense League and the Pentecost fold, and
scarcely less kind in his remarks about churches and Y.M.C.A.'s.
I think he is picturing only one very small side of church work
in the church he describes and the religion of its pastor. However, he does picture a true case, one must admit. The theme
of the story, as it seems to me, is excellent — that a man who is
unhappy at home, whether actively or passively unhappy, is a
regular breeding place for discontent of all sorts. When Babbitt
and his wife get things straightened out again, he is able to get
his life in order again on all sorts of things, whether real estate,
boosting the town, being a good fellow, or whatnot. Of course,
one might argue that when he does, he becomes narrow and
intolerant again, and that dissatisfaction with one's own condition
is the best argument for socialistic ideas, or even tolerance.
Maybe if he had had team work at home from the start, he
wouldn't have been so smug. But he never had courage enough
to start out after what he wanted, and his very marriage was
merely an occurrence that happened because he did not have
strength enough to make clear what he did want. However, at
the end of the book, he does have courage enough to back his
son in getting what the son wants, so maybe the son will have
a happier and more successful life.

I, too, was greatly interested in learning what becomes of permanent waves. They just roll on, it seems. If such is the case, I do not think I shall accept your kind invitation to have a permanent when I get to Indiana. I was telling John about it this noon, and what happened to the wave, and how much it costs. He said, "O my, if I had that much money I would buy myself a suit of clothes!" He really needs a new suit before he goes to Thermopolis and to Cheyenne in December, and we have been trying to see where the wherewithal to get one would come from. Our bank balance had just slipped to the red two weeks ago when we got an unexpected order from an old customer for $45 worth of honey, pay in advance. Paraphrasing the "Storm at Sea," John waved the check and remarked, "We are saved, the captain shouted."

Tuesday morning, October 11, 1926

Next week Governor Ross is to be in this part of the state. I am invited to be the guest of Sen. and Mrs. Cook at Cody while Gov. Ross is there Tuesday. Wednesday I'll come with them to Powell, for the Chamber of Commerce dinner at noon, at which Gov. Ross has been invited to speak, and for the evening meeting. Thursday she goes to Lovell and Cowley, and Friday to Greybull and Basin. I want to go with her as far as I can, but I have promised to go to Meeteetse Saturday night to a county Democratic rally and make the main speech for Governor Ross. So I can't stay too long with the traveling party.

Tuesday morning, October 19, 1926

Here I sit with my dress suit on, waiting for Werts to come along, for us to go to Cody to meet the Governor and her party. Senator and Mrs. John Cook invited me to stay at their house tonight, and come to Powell with them tomorrow or else with the Governor.

I think I told you about the doings in Powell: tomorrow the Chamber of Commerce luncheon at noon, the non-political reception in the afternoon, and the political meeting at night.

As the luncheon at noon is in the Methodist church, we had planned to hold the afternoon reception in the basement of the Presbyterian church. But yesterday two of the men, one a member of the church, and the other merely one who sometimes comes, made a fuss about "Profaning the House of God" by holding the reception there. Rev. Walter said he had told the committee they could use the basement for the reception, and he would stay by his word. But of course as soon as the Democrat men heard the two Republicans were stirring up a fuss, they told Rev. Walter they would not cause him any trouble for the world, and rented the Lyric Theatre hall in which to hold the reception. Inasmuch as the ladies who are assisting at the reception are the presidents of the various women's organizations about here — clubs, church aids and altar societies, fraternal and American Legion auxiliaries, including Eastern Star, Rebeccas, etc., you can see that the reception really is non-party, for the majority of these women are Republicans. Mrs. S.A. Nelson, wife of the man who has always been the leader in Republican affairs here, is to help in the receiving line, introducing people to the Governor. As a matter of fact, people are so peeved at the two men who started the trouble that the whole thing is making votes for Governor Ross. If we had planned to do anything that would make votes for her, we couldn't have thought of anything that would be so successful. So we are laughing up our sleeves at the usual boneheadedness of the two men. I really believe that more votes are made by the boners that are pulled by each party than by all the solicitation and advertising by each party for its own candidates. One man told me last night this fiasco means 400 additional votes here for Governor Ross.

Cody, Wyoming
October 20, 1926

I had the rather unusual experience last night of sitting on a platform and hearing one of the most prominent men in the U.S., a senator, praise me as I have never been lauded before! It happens that this is the first time Senator Kendrick ever heard me make a real speech. He has been speaking in my behalf over the state, but only from hearsay. After I got done speaking, he leaned over to me — we were sitting next each other on the stage — and demanded to know why he had never known before what I could really do. I never had more earnest praise for a talk I made. Then later when he got up to talk, he said the most complimentary things about me you can imagine, and so did Gov. Ross.

I really must say I did make a good speech. I'll tell you some time what I said. I don't know how many folk told me how well I said what I did, and how good it was. Please understand I am not boasting. You really know when you have an effect, and I did last night. It is always interesting to prove one's ability to a group of prominent folk who hope you are able but don't know for sure.

Lovell, Wyoming
October 22, 1926

I am really politicking this week, and when I get back I am sure my family will have to be introduced to me again.

I wrote you from Cody. We went to Powell the next day and had the scheduled meetings there.

The afternoon reception was a huge success, with a large crowd, mostly ladies. The evening meeting was a wow. You never saw such a crowd. Every seat was full, nearly an hour before time. Even the stage was filled, and every chair they could get was brought in. There were a hundred folk standing at the back, and at least 200 were turned away. You can guess I felt mighty proud to preside at such a meeting, and if I do say so, it went off with a bang.

Yesterday morning we started again. John took me to Garland where I joined the party. I took Jules and Anne to be introduced to Gov. Ross and Sen. Kendrick, and Mr. and Mrs. Kimball. Then John took them home with him. We stopped at Garland and Gov. Ross spoke to the school children, then we went to Byron and had a big meeting where we all spoke. Then we were entertained at dinner by the mayor of

Byron, Mrs. Pryde — the mayor herself, not the mayor's wife. We then drove to Deaver and Gov. R. spoke at the school. We came to Cowley to an afternoon reception for ladies. In the evening we had meetings at Cowley and Lovell. Each of us spoke at each place, someone with an auto standing waiting to rush us the six miles to the other town as soon as we were through.

Today we go to Burlington, over on Germania Bench, for an eleven a.m. meeting, to Manderson for an afternoon meeting, and to Basin and Greybull for night meetings, shifting as we did last night. Saturday morning I'll take the stage to Meeteetsee to speak for Gov. Ross. Then Sunday I hope to get home to my family again.

Sunday night, October 24, 1926

I got home about one this afternoon and my loving family has scarcely let loose of me since, much less let me get out of sight. I did not know they could be so glad to have me at home again. Cecilia insisted I had been gone over a week, when it really was only since Wednesday morning, and then amended it by saying it seemed six years. Anne told me a million times "I'm so glad you came home," varied only with "Please don't go away again." Jules wanted to sit on my lap, and so did the others, and I had from one to three most of the time.

I enjoyed so much getting to be with you and Ted, Edith, and am so glad my schedule allowed that.

Friday evening we had meetings at Greybull and Basin, [nine miles apart] each of us speaking at both places. Unfortunately for me, or my audience, Governor Ross, who spoke first at Basin, talked longer than Senator Kendrick, who was first at Greybull. Several local non-partisan speakers (Mrs. Van Devener for county superintendent, and Judge Metz for district judge) were in the audience and were asked to speak briefly. They did so, but used up only a little time. The chairman then introduced me, and it was up to me to talk till the Governor arrived. I had been speaking from 6 to 9 minutes in giving my own speech, and I had to keep on talking about 20 minutes before I saw the governor come into the lobby, and I could not begin to use the end of my speech until I knew she was there. That was my first experience at talking to keep an audience from going home before the real speaker arrived. Edith assured me that everything was all right, and that she still admits she is my sister, so I guess I did not disgrace the family.

Last night I made the big speech at Meeteetsee to a crowd of several hundred. Paul Greever was supposed to make the speech for the state ticket. He came to Meeteetsee but did not show up at the meeting, so I had to talk his speech and my own, too. I spoke for perhaps ten minutes, and the crowd, which stopped dancing to listen to me, was perfectly quiet and attentive, which you must admit is rather a compliment.

I decided tonight that I would go to Casper and join the Governor's party for the meetings at Casper, Salt Creek, Glenrock, and Douglas, and various intermediate points. I hate to spend the money, for it will take about $35 for the trip and we do not have it to spare. As a matter of fact, we do not have it at all now. We have a check for $15 we were counting on for running expenses for the next week. That will pay my fare to Casper, so I am going to use it, and I have written to the state Democratic committee saying I want to borrow fifty dollars from them for this trip, with the privilege of repaying it whenever we can. They are to get the money to me at Casper. I will start Tuesday morning and come back Saturday. I hate to leave the family, but John says go, so I shall do so. Edith, can you come to see me Tuesday when the train goes through Greybull?

Hotel Henning
Casper, Wyoming
October 27, 1926

We had a wonderful meeting here last night at the big Elk's Hall. The hall must seat seven or eight hundred, and more than a hundred stood up. There was an overflow meeting of 300 in another hall, and Governor Ross went there first to speak.

On the way down I got off at Greybull and visited while

the train stopped. Edith was not feeling well enough to come down, as the day was raw, but Ted and Edith Rhoda came to the train and I talked to Edith over the telephone. Of course Ted wanted to bet a pair of $10 shoes vs. a new dress that Emerson would beat Gov. Ross, but I wouldn't bet. When we got on the train Ted said, as usual, "Well, Cecil, I'm sorry I can't vote for you." Of course I replied, as usual, that was too bad. (This is our stereotyped conversation every time we meet.) After we got in the train I was laughing with the two Wyoming University extension workers with whom I had been sitting at what Edward said, and Mr. Bowman said to me, "It is too bad, but he winked at me with *both* eyes when he said it."

Yesterday we had meetings all day. Governor Ross made seven speeches and I made four. The rest of the crowd made two and three each. At each meeting there were from 50 to 600 people present. Our schedule was so heavy we could not get places on time, as we had 15 and 20 minute drives between meetings over roads that were awful from rain.

You know in the beginning, and all the time, in this campaign the Republicans have constantly argued that no matter how well Governor Ross had done, the Gov's office is no place for a woman, but is a man's job. Our speakers have been telling this, and then after telling of the schedule she has been filling—more strenuous than any man candidate ever had, because the people everywhere took matters in their own hands and arranged for two or three extra meetings each day—they say they are sure it is not a man's job, for no man could stand up under such a strain, and no one but a woman could meet all the requirements placed on her everywhere.

November 3, 1926

Well, the smoke has about cleared away, and although we do not have complete returns on all the offices, it is very apparent, as John remarked at noon, that he would not have to be a bachelor again for the next four years. My family is greatly relieved, although I must confess that the suggestion of

$4,000 a year was quite a drawing card in their considering permitting me to depart from my role as housekeeper. Cecilia asked the other day if we could get a new car if I were elected, and although she had insisted up to that time that she wished she was old enough to vote for my opponent, she began to say she might consider voting for me.

Cora, the fortune you got for me is rich. I got a lot of kick out of that and told everybody about it. I assured them I thought it was much better as a pre-election forecast than as a post-election statement. Mrs. Werts explained as you did, however, that whichever way the election went, I had "become prominent in public affairs." Edith, the fortune is one from the weighing machine Cora has as a particular friend. Maybe she told you, but I'll say that she carried with her all the extra baggage she could get hold of, and weighed for me, to see what fortune she would receive for me, and the wording on the card is as follows:

> You take a keen interest in everything and everyone about you, and are destined to become prominent in public affairs.

Can you beat that? I am afraid the weight marked, 105 pounds, is pretty light for me. I am extra thin right now, folk tell me, but I think I'd require about ten more pounds than the 105 listed to balance me. However, it was the turn at the scale and not the weight that determined the fortune, wasn't it?

November 7, 1926

John has forecast this election since the Democratic meeting in June in Thermopolis. When I came home and told him what that meeting had done, he said at once he did not think the party could possibly win in November for the simple reason that it had done nothing. The normal Republican vote in this state is about 35,000; the normal Democratic about 33,000. In addition to this there is an independent vote of about 10,000, of which about 2200 are so-called progressives. Whenever there is a special issue at stake, the 10,000 get out and vote; when there is not, they do not. But this year, when there was nothing especial in the Democratic platform (if any) to attract the progressives, they did not vote at all, and the Republicans got their normal 35,000 and the Democrats their 33,000 with the result that Emerson was elected by 1460 votes, with only a few scattered small precincts out. It is evident that good people on a ticket is not a sufficient appeal to the ordinary voter. There must be issues or the result is that people vote according to party, and the independents do not vote at all.

Wednesday, November 10, 1926

Tell Ted I appreciate very much his having voted for me, which I expected all the time.

I am interested to hear that my after-election letter sounded meek. I did not realize when I wrote it that it would sound that way, but as a matter of fact I was so tired when I wrote it that it is a wonder it sounded at all. I don't know when I have ever been so perpetually and unspeakably weary as I have this fall. I wake up at night too tired to lie the way I am and too weary to move. I told John several times that if I stayed this tired the next 45 years of my life I was afraid I'd go to sleep and not bother to wake up after 35 or 40 years more. I am not a bit sick, but just don't seem to get rested. I don't know what I'd do if I didn't have Mary. I am ashamed of myself the way I let her do most of the work, and go to bed before she does, and lie in bed long after she is up in the morning.

November 12, 1926

Pater, I think I have told you that we have not yet sold any honey, and consequently do not have any money on hand. I hate to have to tell you, but I do not have the money to buy our tickets to Indiana. As you know, railroad tickets take cash. I don't know if you will get your money's worth by having the children and me come to visit you, but we are willing to take the trip if you are willing to risk that much on us. You don't need me to tell you how much we want to come.

We would have to have the money here about November 26 or 27 in order to make arrangements for starting December 4, as I have to be at Thermopolis from November 30 to December 3.

Sunday morning, November 21, 1926

The storm is over and the snow has quit. There must be five or six inches of snow on the ground, and the trees and bushes are lovely this morning against the white earth and the gloriously blue sky. It was foggy early this morning and the moisture stuck to the trees and made all of them look like silver Christmas trees of spruce. The cloud of fog was not very high, and you could see the top of the hills surrounding this valley, the ones to the north and west particularly. Ordinarily, when you can see the mountains to the other side of these near hills, the hills do not look very high. But I wish you could have seen them this morning. The cloud of fog lying from their base about three-fourths of the way up showed just their tops, and you got an idea how high they really are. I guess it is a good deal like our ordinary life. With the usual background of hum-drum existence we do not realize how large our daily blessings are until we see them suddenly all by themselves, and then we discover they are veritable mountains.

John was lucky enough to be in Cheyenne when the Russian Symphonic Choir under the direction of Basile Kibalchich gave a concert there. He says it was the most wonderful music he ever heard. The literature describing the choir says that the conductor long ago abandoned the usual division into four parts and selected his singers as an orchestra leader selects his instru-ments—for timbre and range. Every voice has a characteristic value of its own, just as every instrument in a symphony does. Each is an individual instrument in the hands of the conductor. There are eleven male and eleven female voices. There is no instrumental accompaniment. When I asked John about that, he said, "Does an orchestra need an accompaniment?" John said not a word was spoken from the time the concert began till it ended. The conductor said not a word to the singers or to the audience. No one was introduced. The programs contained all the information the audience needed. There was a single sheet of program with the particular selections for that evening, and a large booklet giving the history of the choir, pictures, and a short summary and translation of all the foreign songs they used. In fact, they sang entirely in Russian. John said they assumed no attitudes and did no stunts, but sang just as a bird would, simply opening their mouths and letting the melody out. There were no encores, except the repeating of a piece of two that received special applause. The program included all sorts of music, from ancient Greek church melodies to voice arrangements from famous orchestral symphonies, such as Beethoven's Fifth and Rubenstein's landscape music. John said the finest music, in his opinion, was church music such as the Pater Noster and the Credo, and Chant of the Cherubims, and other mass and festival day songs, including the Gloria Patri. Their general program included such well known songs as the Pilgrim's Chorus from Tannhauser, and Nevin's The Rosary. Practically every singer in the ensemble was a soloist at some theatre in Europe. Don't you wish you could have heard them?

822 Atwater, Bloomington
Tuesday morning, December 7, 1926

Dearest Daddy,

We arrived by bus only an hour later than we would have by train, and an hour earlier than the folk thought we could get here. In fact, when we rang the bell, and Cora let us in, Pater came to see who it was, with his dirty shirt still on and his clean shirt in his hand. So I got to put the cuff buttons in his shirt for him to greet us! Pater looks fine—better than ever, and the first thing he asked was how is John? He is so delighted to see the children.

That was a nice letter from Governor Ross to me.* I wonder if she has written you. I suspect she is somewhat afraid of anything radical, not because she is a standpatter, but because she is timid about starting anything new; and afraid of not being able to make a go of it.

I was glad to know that "Good Housekeeping" would be interested in an article on "When a Woman Governor Campaigns." I have been working at the article and have it about half done. Working at it has kept me from writing you as much as I wanted to.

I was also delighted with the letter from Senator Kendrick. I have thought out what I want to say to him in reply, and here is what I decided on:

Dear Senator Kendrick:

Your letter of Dec. 6 followed me here. Thank you for your sympathy in my defeat at the election. As you know, I did not expect anything else, so I was not disappointed for myself, although the more I knew of the situation and the need for efficient administration in the office of the state dep't of education, the more willing I became to undertake the work at whatever personal sacrifice. I believe if the Democratic party found an able candidate who really wanted the place and would cover the state campaigning, that four years from now we could elect a state sup't. I heard a good bit of comment to the effect that one person could hold an office too long, and by the time Mrs. Morton has been in office 12 yrs. a good many people will be ready for a change.

I was tremendously disappointed that Gov. Ross was not reelected and could scarcely believe the returns. I can't help feeling that a good deal of the blame goes back to the lack of any stand on any subject at the state Dem. meeting in June. I was present at the meeting, and was disappointed that no definite platform was adopted, and especially so when I learned that the

---

*Cecilia had received letters from Governor Ross and Senator Kendrick expressing their disappointment in the outcome of the election.

so-called Progressives had waited, before holding a meeting of their own, to find out what platform we had adopteod. If we could only have had their 500 votes in November, the story would have been different. I did so hope that Gov. Ross & Mr. Kimball would be in office, for the good of the state as well as for the honor of our party.

Mr. Hendricks has written me of your kind interest in his pension claim and of the work you are doing to forward his case. Please allow me to add my thanks to those of my husband for your help. No one knows as well as I do how much he suffers, both in actual discomfort and pain, and also in the suffering that comes from being unable to do the things he longs to do. A man pays a heavy penalty in lowered income when he must hire done all heavy manual work, and when he is limited in the occupations he can enter. But that is small in comparison with the disappointment he has in giving up his life's ambition (John's was to be a physician), at losing a college education, and in general, in a loss of nerve energy that debars him from doing fully the things that are most interesting to him. If he could only have had a living wage pension 25 years ago, he could have been spared nine tenths of his present suffering, both physical and mental, and could have realized most of his ambitions. Since the gov't did not give him the help at the time he needed it most, when with it he could have prepared himself to be independent, he naturally feels that something is due him now to make up for that lack.

A thoughtful wife has more opportunity than any one else to size up a man's real worth. I know that Mr. Hendricks is a very able man who would have done things of real worth. As it is, whatever he accomplishes is under great handicap. I know of no one who really is more entitled to an adequate pension.

One of my pleasantest campaign memories is the becoming better acquainted with you. I know now why everybody has such love and respect for you.

With very best wishes, I am

Sincerely yours,

I haven't got much of anything done this afternoon and evening because Pater has been sitting and telling me all sorts of things, some business and some just general information. However, to talk to Pater is mainly what I came for, isn't it? He is applying for an invalid pension and wants a statement from Dr. Graham as to the condition of his heart when Dr. G. treated Pater at our house on June 8, 1919. Pater can get a $90 a month pension by asking for an invalid pension, or so the circular from the Pension Bureau seems to indicate. Total disability or blindness, either one, is sufficient, and Pater is certainly totally disabled from heart trouble, and he has been blind in one eye since about 1910.

I do so hate to be away from you on Christmas Day, heart's dearest. I shall be thinking of you and giving thanks that we belong to each other. I am so glad we do. I'd rather be with you than any place else I know.

The great day is over and the children are all in bed. They had a great time most of the day, and only a few times wished they were home. They did once this afternoon, however, when the chimney caught on fire, and they were all scared for a little while. I put salt in the fire right away, and watched the roof, and also got up into the attic to make sure everything was all right. Fortunately Pater was asleep and he knows nothing about it. Also fortunately, it has been snowing all day and there were several inches of snow everywhere, so the sparks were not likely to do any damage.

Of course we had a grand opening this morning and again after the mail came today. The children were very good about the opening, even though they were sorely tried because Pater wouldn't let them touch things, and also when he began to shave just after the parcel post came, and they had to wait till he finished that—which took about an hour—and also until we ate dinner before he would open the package.

Poor Jules is so homesick. The sun has shone only two days in three weeks, and there has been rain or snow all the time. The children can't get out to get exercise, and Jules doesn't know what to do. They have loads of toys and games but nothing to work off their energy. He had to throw up Christmas night. I gave him pepsin several times, and tonight gave him a dose of mineral oil. He said tonight, "If I could go home I'd be all right. My tummy would be all right and my head would be all right, and everything. But if I came back here I'd be mizzerble again." No one had said anything to him about going home and we try to keep him cheerful, but he certainly wants to be at home. Maybe he'll have more chance to work off his surplus energy at West Franklin. I hope so, for he certainly is "mizzerble."

My neighbors are still losing their farms.

4

1927–1931

I have been interested in reading the *Unity* Magazine, but I confess I can't go all the way. One of the numbers that discusses the difference between Unity, ordinary Christian Science, and orthodox sects, says this: "Christianity believes in a God whose presence is separate and distinct from his universe. Unity teaches that God is the immanent, indwelling spirit of man and the universe, not a personality." And again: "We believe that Jesus Christ is the God of this planet; that he returned to the Father in the fourth dimension in order that he may be everywhere present in the realms of spiritual consciousness." In another issue there is a discussion of the creation the way the Unity folk believe it as compared with the orthodox interpretation. As I understand it, Unity's idea is that there is an impersonal spirit that started the ideas resulting in the various and innumerable solar systems and organizations of planets in existence everywhere, and a somewhat personal God in each of the systems or planets, just as above. Jesus is given as being the God of this planet. The first two days of creation, according to the Bible story, represent this general, impersonal deity; the rest of the days tell of the result in concrete form of the thought expressed in the first two days, or the thought started to work.

I confess I am orthodox enough not to want to lose the idea of personality in the God in which I believe — in the entire God, I mean, and not just part of Him. One of the most forceful arguments always given for believing at all in a God is that when we see the wonders of everything, we are forced to the conclusion that there is a Mind behind it all, not just chance. In exactly the same line of argument, personality being after all the most forceful thing of which we know, I feel that it must be an attribute of that Mind.

I went to town this afternoon for the monthly meeting of the Federated Club. The thing has sifted down to a permanent basis now, and six of the twelve clubs are members. Not bad for a start. I think after a year to two, when the other clubs find out we can really accomplish something, they will all want to join. One of the first things we are going to do is to get out a list of good subjects for programs for women's clubs here. Having been on the program committee of various clubs, I know how hard it is for a committee to make up a program worth working on. Another thing we want to do is to have a committee that reports each month on the worthwhile things in the magazines. Every little while there is a magazine article really worth reporting to a woman's club, but very few people think of it in that connection.

By the way, I was interested in these statements in the January *Unity*: "The purpose of Unity is not to found a new sect but to give the people a practical application of what they already have through their church affiliations," and "We suggest that you accept in our literature what appears to you to be the truth and that you let the remainder rest until you understand it better." Certainly fair enough, isn't it?

J ohn starts for Casper in the morning for grand jury duty. Of course he does not have any idea how long he will stay. He may not be accepted at all as a juror and be home Wednesday. And then he may be kept for part of the time, or for all. However, it will be a pleasant little jaunt for him and he can get away from his work all right at this time of year.

Cora, do you want to laugh? Not long ago, Mrs. Wallace called me up to say that she had heard I was home again and that it was only after I had been gone a month or more that she learned I was away. She inquired very earnestly after your good health, and then went on to say that she had been thinking perhaps it was to attend your wedding that I had gone to

Indiana. When I assured her that you were still holding on to your regular job, she advised that it was never too late, and one should always have hope. She wanted to know when you were coming out here again and went on to say I should tell you to be sure to come out, and "who knows, we might have a wedding yet." I was too much amused to ask her to elucidate her statement, so you may put any construction on it you please. But now that Walter is unattached, it sounds suspiciously like a declaration that she would be pleased to play Naomi to your Ruth! I think I told you that she has Walter's six year old boy now. She told me she is happy as can be since she has the grandson. Some one else told me that she looks like a different woman since the boy is with her. But I can't help thinking it must be hard on the child.

February 11, 1927

I had a letter from John yesterday saying there were only three jury cases — one had already been disposed of — so that he thought he would be sure to get home by Saturday. We were very much surprised, therefore, when a car stopped in front of the house about 5:30, to see John alight. He had the good fortune to be drawn on the jury for the second case, and as soon as that was over the judge excused the men on that list, as the ones who had served in Case No. 1 were empanelled for Case No. 3. Jules was greatly pleased with a pair of new shoes Daddy brought him, and Cecilia with a hair barrette set with stones the same color as her hair. Anne got a bunch of valentines, and I candy. John nearly always brings me the same kind of candy when he returns from a trip — French nougat with lots of nuts and fruit in it. Yum, yum. Eating it is like having cream candy and nuts all at once, not to mention candied cherries and pineapple and ginger.

There is an article in the new *Woman's Home Compannion* by
Sophie Kerr on "Married Woman and the Job" that has
started me to writing a similar article. Nerve? That's me all
over, Mabel. Miss Kerr's article is about girls in a large city
who want to marry and keep on with their job. The conclusion
she comes to is that it is possible, but not easy, to run a house
and work in an office, but that it is practically, if not absolutely,
impossible to have any children. When I got to thinking over
the situation, I came to the conclusion, rather surprising, I
believe, that in smaller towns it is possible for a woman to run
a house, do the equivalent of office work, *and have children, too.*
For instance, yourself, Edith. You do as much typing as any
stenog Ted would have in the office, and by having the telephone
arranged as you do, take care of the office when Ted is not
there. What more could any office girl do? Even the best paid
private secretary couldn't handle the work as efficiently or with
as much interest. So I am going to write an article and state
the opinion that it can be done, and is done, in smaller towns.

Edith, I think you hit the Unity nail on the head when
you say the results come from the efforts of the person himself,
rather than through what is done at Unity headquarters. In
fact, the February issue of *Unity* says so in these words: "You
should conceive of a larger idea of prosperity than that symbol-
ized in the possession of money or things . . . . The course of
individual prosperity is in individual consciousness of the
resources of the invisible. . . . Your latent forces, thus spiritually
quickened, will bring compensation. Have faith in the invisible
possessions, and they will be brought forth into the visible . . . .
What ever finds its way into your consciousness from this
unlimited source must, through divine law, find expression in
the without, for the divine urge is for expression." I think there
is a lot in the above, for one never would get anything done if
he didn't have faith enough—or conceit—to believe he could do
it. I have come to the conclusion one might as well try big
things as little. Why spend time writing little 50 cent articles?
Why not try $50 ones?

We had such a scare the other morning, and I did not know what it was till the danger was over. Jules and Merle Gimmeson have got into the habit of holding on the back of a car when it starts off and running along with it a little way. I scolded Jules for it and told him he should not do it again, as soon as I found out about it. The other morning John started to Garland, and when he drove from the yard here, Merle caught on the brace rod that runs across the back of the car from fender to fender and started off with the car. Jules did not do it, I am glad to say, but Anne, seeing Merle do it, grabbed hold with her little paws and started along too. Jules called to her to quit, but she did not. When the car got to the gate at the road, Merle let go and stopped. But Anne held on, explaining afterward, "Daddy was driving so fast and the road was running away under me so fast I couldn't let go." When John slowed up at the bottom of the hill to cross the bridge, he heard Anne crying. He did not know where she was, but knew she was caught behind the car somewhere. You can guess his heart stopped beating. He stopped the car as fast as possible, but by the time he had got out, Anne was starting back up the hill. She was glad to let go as soon as the car stopped! John was so relieved she was all right he did not even scold her. Her knees were skinned and she was dusty from head to foot, for she had been dragged down the hill. Her feet couldn't possibly go fast enough to run. Of course what saved her was her holding on to the rod so tightly, for if she had been thrown off she could have been badly hurt from hitting a rock in the hill. I heard Jules calling and ran out to see what was the matter, but by that time John was coming this way with Anne. Jules ran to meet her and led her home, as John had to go on. It certainly taught all three children a lesson, and I don't think any of them will hold on the back of a car again. As this seems to be a hospital bulletin, I might as well finish this part by telling you that our arms are progressing very nicely from our smallpox vaccinations. I have suffered quite a lot with mine, and so have Mary and Cecilia. Jules' just started to bother last night. Anne's is festering but she declares it does not hurt. I wish I could say that. John's does not show much indication of anything. I have the honor of being able to produce the largest red area, running all the way from shoulder to elbow. I think mine is about at the worst, for it seems completely festered. I hope so — I think I shall not celebrate washday tomorrow, nor until my arm is all right.

March 29, 1927

I wrote to Governor Ross about my article for the *Good House-keeping*, when I found that she is writing for that magazine, and was leaving April 1 for an eastern trip. I am quite sure she will go to the offices of the magazine while she is east, for the article I read in the Cheyenne *Eagle* said she had been working during the past month on the articles she was writing for *Good Housekeeping*. I sent her a copy of my article, saying I wanted to be sure she approved of it before it was published, and asking for her comments. I got [a] letter from her yesterday [saying that she thought the article was splendid and cleverly written, and that I had treated her with generosity. She did suggest that I say "sometimes" instead of "usually" in referring to women presiding over meetings.] That was the only change she suggested. I wanted to make sure that if she was shown my article when she gets to the offices of *Good Housekeeping* she can assure the editors that she had already read it and approves. Surely she will give it a good word after the letter [she wrote]. I feel therefore that I shall be able to market the article. However, I do wish the editors would hurry up and let me know, for I want the money pronto.

April 4, 1927, Monday morning

I told you I was looking for an April Fool letter from *Good Housekeeping*. Well, I got it all right. They sent my article back. Now what do you think of that! I immediately sent it on to *The Saturday Evening Post*, Edith, as per your advice. If it comes back from there, I'll send it to *The American*. I am fully convinced it is a good article, and I think it ought to strike some editor the same way. The letter that came with the return was quite long, and incidentally very badly written, with erasures, and words run together in several places. The letter is signed by the editor himself, W.F. Bigelow, without any stenog initials anywhere on it. Well, at least it is something to have an editor write you that the only reason he has turned your stuff down was that he accepted the same stuff from a famous person!

The other day Jules said, "I haven't made up my mind completely as to what I'll be when I am big, but I think now I'll be a man who studies stars. Then maybe I can tell you all about them." Thereupon Anne piped up with, "When I am big, I will be a dressmaker and make dresses, and then I'lll make you lots of pretty dresses." She did not state whether or not she thought I needed them, but was sure she would make them for me. This morning Jules announced to me, "Merle and I have quite a lot of girls picked out to go with before we are married." This was evidently a result of a discussion we had some time since, when he asked me whom he would marry when he was grown, and I told him I had no idea, that he should wait and see, and have a good time with a whole crowd of folk till he found the one girl he was sure he wanted. He takes things so seriously. I think my main task with him will be to give him a sense of humor to keep him from being too serious. Anne, the little rascal, was lucky enough to be born with a sense of humor, and Cecilia has a pretty fair amount, too. We were all convulsed at Anne the other day. John was feeling specially bad, and the noise the children made disturbed him. Then when they started scrapping, he objected and made a remark that it seemed almost impossible to live in the house with them. Anne began to laugh (we were at dinner) and said, "Well, Daddy, you said once you guessed you'd have to go to the barn to live." Badly as he felt, John couldn't help shouting with the rest of us. Anne took it so absolutely for granted that the children wouldn't be the ones to leave the house. John said he guessed Ted was right when he said Anne has a sense of humor, for she certainly knows the right time to bring in a quotation.

Pater, I wish you were here to teach John how to play solitaire. He has been feeling so punk he can't read much or work very much, and he needs something to quiet his nerves. Billiards used to do it when he was in the Soldier's Home, but we don't have a billiard table here. He works at that crazy puzzle attempting to draw a line through all the lines in the figure and says he can do that without using up any energy. He also works cross word puzzles. I am sure that solitaire would be the thing for him. He said the other day he almost wished he had something to play solitaire with, and that is a big admission for him, for he always disliked cards so much, what with his stern Methodist upbringing.

I must tell you, Co, that I have followed your example and sent to Unity for a prosperity bank.* However, one might as well adventure a little, and not think he knows everything. Of course anybody knows that there is no use in depending on others alone, but maybe others can help along when one does all he can himself.

John has been feeling so badly and doesn't seem to get any rest. He is as tired in the morning as in the evening, or more so. I thought maybe some of the articles in the *Unity* Magazine might help him—they really do me—but he can't see anything in them. He says he tried out that kind of thing years ago when he was in such poor health and couldn't get anything out of it. He says if I think I can do him any good, without his assistance, to go ahead and do anything I can. So I promptly wrote to Unity and also sent for a bank. I know there is a lot in mental healing, for I know how it helps me, but I don't know enough about it to make it help someone else.

---

*According to the Unity School of Christianity, the prosperity bank is intended to "help people build into their consciousness the truth that God is the source of all supply and that there is no lack of any good thing." A prayer is to be repeated when depositing a coin in the bank, and the money collected is returned to the Unity School to finance its work.

Wednesday, April 13, 1927

The *Sat. Ev. Post* sent my Ross article back. I thought at first I'd send it to the *American* when it came back, if it did, but I decided I'd write a letter to the editor of the *Christian Science Monitor* to ask if he would like to see the article. I told him how I happened to write it, and that I knew he was interested in "authentic accounts of unique events," but that I did not know whether or not he cared for such long articles, 5500 to 6000 words. If he says so, I'll send it for him to see; if not, I'll save a lot of postage.

April 27, 1927

John is sitting at his desk playing sol. Never did I think this day would arrive! I certainly am glad he has agreed to his need of sol, for I am sure it will do his nerves more good than anything else. I did not suggest it, either. He did himself. But you can bet I encouraged him in it. This morning when he started to town he wondered if some one might possibly send him a deck of cards, or if he should buy one for himself right now. I told him he'd better get a deck this morning, and he did so. I know it will relieve his nerves. At night he can't read because it wears him out, and there isn't anything to do but go to bed. When you go to bed at 7:30 and don't sleep more than half a dozen hours during the night, it gets pretty tiresome just staying in bed. So maybe if he plays sol till he is really sleepy, he will go to bed and sleep more hours and get better rest.

I must tell you that I got a check yesterday from the Wyoming *Tribune* for my March stuff, amounting to $10.50. Think of it! Also I had a letter with this statement: "Your work this past month covering the correspondence from your community was so excellent that we cannot but help comment in sending you this monthly remittance in payment of the string you sent us on April 1." Ha! If I can't sell stuff to *Good Housekeeping*, I can at least sell it to the tune of $10.50 a month to the *Tribune*, and in the course of the year that will pay several grocery bills and pairs of shoes and overalls. I have developed a regular smeller for news affecting people from this part of the state who are known in Cheyenne or who occupy prominent positions, appointive or elective, in the state.

By the way, the check for $10.50 from Cheyenne came in the same mail yesterday with my prosperity bank. That's a good starter, isn't it? I'll be looking for the mail every day.

Friday, May 5, 1927

I know you will laugh when I tell you I got in another three dollar check yesterday for an article. I am sure my rating is $3. Well, that's better than 30¢, isn't it — ten times better! I did not wait till the three months was up to send in the $3 for the prosperity bank, but sent it the other day, less than a month after I got it. I had been saving one $3 check to pay for it, and decided I might as well cash it and send the money right along — "anticipating a greater blessing," as one correspondent quoted in Unity said in doing the same thing!

I have been checking up my April clippings from the Cheyenne *Tribune*, and find that I have 105 column inches, counting headings and all, or 75 inches if the headings do not count. They pay 10¢ a column inch, with a 10% additional allowance to pay for postage and stationery; so you see my pay this month should be $8.25 if heads are not counted, and $11.55 if they are. That is not bad for the amount of time I put in it.

May 22, 1927, Sunday

John has been just about killed over the outcome of his pension application. The Pension Bureau ruled that veterans who were receiving a pension under the General Law did not come in under the automatic increase decreed by Congress in its bill of May 1, 1926. Inasmuch as the men who are receiving pensions under the General Law are those who have had pensions for more than seven years, you can readily see they are the ones who needed pensions from soon after the Spanish War, and obviously are the ones most seriously injured. In spite of this evident fact, the Bureau ruled that the new law applied only to those getting their pensions under the act of June, 1920. These persons received the automatic increase. All others had to apply for an increase, first making application for pension under the act of June, 1920. Sen. Kendrick and Cong. Winter both urged John to apply under the new act, and he finally did so. Sen. Kendrick has done a lot all along to help matters move faster. Under the old law, John was getting $30, which was the *maximum amount* for physical disability of the nature of his. Last week Sen. Kendrick wrote us that the Bureau had increased John's pension to $40. But under the new law, $50 represents the same disability that $30 did under the old law, so that while the Bureau increased his pension $10 a month it *decreased* his rating. This is what has hurt him so. For what he suffers, he really does not have as high a rating as he should, and then to have it decreased nearly made him ready to quit living entirely. As I said above, he received the maximum rating for physical disability such as his, but that takes into consideration only the condition of the injured leg, and not of the crutch paralysis he has in his arms, and weakness in other parts of the body resulting from the injury to the leg and nerve trunks. Under the new law, he really should get $65 to have an adequate rating according to the amount of injury he suffers.

One thing that is as much of a slap in the face to a veteran as not giving the proper rating, is the statement that if he thinks he does not receive the proper amount, he can apply again in six months. The way the thing is stated, it makes one wonder if the Bureau just takes it for granted they won't rate a man properly the first time, as a matter of principle. Maybe they have to keep each case, going over and over it so many times, to keep their clerks busy. If they used real business methods they'd probably run out of work for their many clerks.

John has refused entirely to accept the new rating, and has returned through Senator Kendrick the communications that have come from the Pension Bureau about the matter—returned them unopened, checks and all. We had a letter from Sen. Kendrick a day or two ago in which he said, "I believe Mr. Hendricks is entitled to the highest rating under the new law just as he was under the old. I told this to the Commissioner of the Bureau of Pensions in a formal letter and followed it up with a request for a personal conference regarding the matter. I shall do my utmost to advance his rating and shall write him as soon as I have anything new to offer." John has in a slight measure got over his first hurt about the matter, and his chief desire now is to be able to get our income to the point where he can refuse to accept any compensation at all, even the old $30 one, unless the Bureau gives him a just rating without any further fight on our part.

Sunday, June 19, 1927

Co, I found your scarf and check awaiting me when I got home from Hyattville. Thanks ever so much for the scarf. I never hoped to possess such a gorgeous one that was so lovely. I have often wished for one but never expected to have one. As for the check, if the money is from Pater, I shall be more than glad to take it. But if it is from Cora, I can not, because I think you have enough and more to do to take care of the expenses of the house and everything connected with that. But Pater, your money is yours to do whatever you want with it, and if you get any pleasure from sending some to us, why we are glad, although it seems to us that the proper memory gem is "The pleasure is all ours." Not having sold last year's honey yet has run us more closely than we ever have been. Some weeks we actually have to figure to know if we can buy any groceries. We have never gone hungry yet, and never expect to, but we have never lived on such close rations and such staple food as we have this summer. Our garden is beginning to yield now, so we will have more variety. It took John 12 hours instead of eight to make the trip home from Hyattville yesterday with the truck because we can't finance proper tires as yet, and have lots of tire trouble. But things will soon take a turn, I am sure, and in the meantime, this fifty helps wonderfully. We are more grateful than I can say.

Edith, John says he did not know anything could taste so good as the loganberry juice you gave him to drink when he stopped at your house yesterday. He was so hot and tired, and worried over the accident to the truck, that he felt like a different person after drinking the loganberry. He did not say how much he drank, but I suspect you began to think he must be a camel before he had enough.

Poor John certainly had a hectic day yesterday. He left Hyattville about four in the morning and should have been home long before noon. As it was, it was nearly nine thirty at night when he arrived. Just before he got to Basin a bolt came loose in the engine somehow, and broke the engine to pieces. There wasn't anything to do but get another engine at Basin. Fortunately he was able to find a good second hand one at a garage in Basin for $60, and he had that put in. The road between Greybull and Lovell is being changed across the desert, and there are frequent detours that are dusty and bumpy and hard to travel. One place they are putting in a new bridge, and you have to drive down into a gully and up the other bank. It took John *three hours* to make this place, and he had to have help to get out. He was just about all in when he got home last night, as such a day's work is entirely more than he can stand. It is a marvel that he could do it in his present condition. Fortunately it was a warm, clear day, when he feels better than at any other time. His arm is lame today from cranking the truck so much.

Ted, John says he may have to use the check you gave him, but will hold it up as long as possible. He doesn't have enough in at present to cover the cost of the new engine, but won't use your check unless it is absolutely necessary. I can't tell you how much we appreciate your help. John was so worried over the whole matter and then needing the extra money made it all the worse. Your offer to help took the edge off the trouble and was a great comfort.

There is so much to thank you both for that I hardly know where to begin.

Pater, you surely will have several extra bright stars in your crown for relieving John's mind of the worry he has had recently, because the taxes were overdue, and the notice of sale had come just a few days before we received Cora's letter saying you were sending the drafts. We had till July 20 to pay the taxes before the sale was advertised. To be sure, there are so many others here who are delinquent in their taxes that it is not likely there will be much bidding in at the tax sale, and of course one always has a chance later on to redeem the property, but that all costs extra money and means extra worry. Then too, the nicest places are always the ones that are most in danger, and our place is so good looking, with the nice house and pretty yard, that anybody looking for tax sales would think of our place. The taxes in this county are around $113, and in Bighorn County (for the bees at Hyattville) are $9.

When John had the breakdown with his truck two weeks ago, and had to buy a new engine he didn't have enough money in the bank to pay for it, and Ted lent him $60. Now we can pay Ted back at once, for which we are glad.

Times have changed since Squire Stebbins made his famous remarks. You remember:

Some times we send a present down to the boys, you know,
Like a barrel of potatoes, a peck of beans, or so.
Sometimes we get a letter, a-statin' times is bad,
Which means about ten dollars, from the pocket of their dad.
Why dum it, mother's sent 'em, in good clean hard earned cash,
Not a-countin' pork and 'taters, butter an' eggs, and all such trash,
But in good, clean, hard-earned dollars, got from the stuff we've sold,
From this here old deserted farm, more'n a 'tater sack would hold.

Nowadays it is the folks on the farm who have to have the help, it seems!

Co, the box with the wonderful dresses for Cecilia, Anne, and me came, and we are all delighted. Mine is certainly lovely — such a nice dress that I shall use it for afternoon wear for a while before using it for a house dress. Cecilia has been wanting a Peter Pan print and when she found the name on the label, she fairly exploded. Every time she went to town she looked at the Peter Pan prints in the stores and would tell me about the different patterns. I wish you could have seen Anne with the blue flowered dress. I told her she could wear the new dress for the P.E.O. picnic here, and when she got up Thursday morning she insisted on putting the dress on right then. She wore it all day and for the evening too, and it was still clean enough that she wore it another day. She told everybody about it as soon as they arrived — as soon as they got out of the cars, and before they got in the house! During the afternoon she had gone to Gimmeson's and in a little while came home as indignant as could be. When I inquired the cause of her peeve, she informed me that Billy (the two-year-old) had thrown some dust on *her new dress*, and he was a very *very* naughty boy!

July 29, 1927

I must tell you about a speech I heard the other day at the Chamber of Commerce meeting, the day my division served the dinner. The session was rather long and tiresome, and just when everybody thought the president was going to adjourn, he got up and said there was a man present who had been away but had come back to Powell to live again, and in a speech that lasted at least three minutes and seemed like ten or fifteen, he introduced Mr. Lehman, an old German tailor, one of the most public spirited people who ever lived here, who is always giving something for some public good — as for instance, a huge silk flag to the high school, and such like. Well, people of course were glad to have Mr. Lehman back, but they groaned inwardly at the thought of the speech he might make. He did not get up at once, but finally when they applauded, he did. And this is what he said: "Well, I ain't much on dis speech making business. But I choost vant to say dis: DOMMED GLAD TO BE WID YOU AGAIN. Ain't dot enough?" And he sat down. Of course everybody yelled, and Mr. McElvain got up and moved that this speech be recorded in the minutes as a model speech, and everybody required to follow it hereafter in speaking before the Chamber of Commerce. The thing that tickled me so much was the discussion the women had over what he really did say. They insisted he had said, "I'm *dumb* glad to be with you." But knowing German, I knew that what he had said was the German equivalent for damned—damnt. Of course I did not say so to them.

Co, thanks ever so much for the cone-and-pop money. The children are delighted. Jules immediately announced the first thing he would have is a bottle of pop. We will take the dollar along when we go to Hyattville and they can all have a treat at Greybull. One of the stores there has what they call an ice cream pie. The shell is made of the same dough as a cone, but is about $3 \times 6 \times 2$ inches in size, and a slice of ice cream or sherbet about the size of a slice of brick ice cream is slipped into it. Another store here serves the same slice of cream between two slices of nabisco—like the ice cream sandwiches you get at the ten cent store. Each of these is a nickel at Greybull. When you get a slice of pineapple or raspberry sherbet inside, the sandwich is really fine.

August 7, 1927

Bady, I took your advice and wrote to various magazines telling them I would submit my Governor Ross article to them if they are interested. I even wrote to the *Sat. Ev. Post* again, since they wrote me earlier they thought the article interesting but could not make a place for it. I said that since the public was interested in Gov. Ross through her memoirs in *Good Housekeeping* and since several months had passed, maybe they would be interested in using the article now. I also wrote to the *Atlantic, Scribner's*, and had written to the *Woman's Home Companion*. There is no use in writing to the *American* or *McClure's* or the *Ladies' Home Journal* because they are all published by the various firms to which I had already written, and it would scarcely do to offer the same article twice to the same firm at the same time, would it?

Cora, I can report that we certainly got a lot of pleasure out of the dollar you sent, which afforded the following: ice cream all around for us all on the way home from Hyattville, wieners twice for dinner, and a movie for Cecilia and Jules. So you see you provided 20 treats!

I am sure you will all be glad to hear that Mr. Robert Bridges, editor of *Scribner's Magazine*, [replied to my letter of inquiry, saying that] they would be interested in reading my article on Gov. Ross. I at once recopied the article double space and sent it on. I certainly hope it makes the grade, don't you? Scribner's seems interested in women in politics, as they publish the articles by the woman commissioner of labor in Missouri on her work and also on women in politics.

We are hoping to see the Sanders at Cody tomorrow when they are there with President Coolidge's party. We sent them a wire to the Park day before yesterday, saying, "Edith and I and our husbands are looking forward to seeing you both at Cody. We hope you can stop off to visit us for a few days." Of course we do not have any idea that Everett can get away, but I should think Ella could, and I wish she would, for it would be lots of fun to see her again.

We had a return wire this morning from Mr. Sanders from Lake Camp in the Park, saying "Will arrive at Cody about 12:30 Saturday. Mrs. Sanders and I hope to greet you there. Bring this wire for identification."

I have been amused to pieces over what Mr. Baird, the local newspaper editor, told me this morning. Everybody here has been trying to find out when the President would come through here, and no one has been able to get any definite word. I called Mr. Baird the other day to ask what he knew about it, for we wanted to know ourselves when to go to Cody and were not sure that the Sanders would answer our message. Mr. Baird said he would tell me as soon as he heard anything, and wanted me to do likewise. I called him this morning after getting the wire, and after I read it to him (except the last sentence) he said, "Well, WELL. Well, that ought to be pretty definite information oughtn't it?" It amused me to hear how pleased he was to find out something that was real information.

August 28, 1927

How I wish you could all be here for a few days. Then maybe I could tell you most of the things that happened at Cody the other day when we went to see the Sanders. I don't think I can ever tell it all in letters.

We drove to Cody Saturday morning, and talked with the superintendent of the special train which was waiting then at the depot. He told us the President's party would be at the new Buffalo Bill Museum at twelve o'clock, and we had better go right there. We did, and as soon as we arrived, we hunted up Colonel Starling, chief of the secret service men, and presented our telegram. He looked at it and remarked, "Yes, I was right there when this message was dictated." I said, "You know then that it is authentic." He laughed and said we had better go right into the museum and stay there till the party arrived. The museum, by the way, is well worth seeing, as it has Buffalo Bill's personal belongings, guns, etc., and also many mounted animals from all over the world—birds, fishes, furniture of note, and lots of other things.

It was twelve-ten when the President's party drove in from the canyon. They went first to see the Buffalo Bill monument and then came to the museum. In the meantime, policemen had moved everybody from the museum outside the ropes surrounding it except the reception committee and John and me. We waited till the Sanders came along, and went in with them.

The party spent about 15 minutes in the museum and wished they could stay an hour or more. They were all very much interested and looked at everything in every room, but of course hurriedly. Mr. Sanders introduced us to the President as an old classmate of his, and Mrs. S. to Mrs. Coolidge and their son John. We received a very cordial handshake from each of the three. We did not talk with them, as they were interested in seeing everything in the museum. We were also introduced to Colonel Blanton Winship, the President's military aide, a very large, handsome and dignified gentleman with yards of heavy gold braid hanging all over his uniform. He was very spiffy. [We also met] Major Coupal, the President's medical aide, Superintendent Albright of Yellowstone Park, and maybe some others I don't recall.

We visited with the Sanders as they walked through the museum, and talked of everything under the sun. Ella spoke of her visit at Bloomington at commencement and what a rare time she had; of seeing you girls, and how natural you looked — no older than when she saw you before. When it was time to leave, they told us to meet them again at the depot and visit some more till the train pulled out. We were the first ones away from the museum and got to the Burlington station almost before the president's party had left Cody. Again we had to show our telegram to be allowed to the platform beside the train, but as soon as the secret service men saw the message they were courtesy itself. The superintendent told us to stand right beside the steps of the observation car where the party would board the train. As soon as the Sanders came, we again visited with them until they had to get on the train.

We had planned to give them a pail of our honey. The day before, President Dowling of the Powell National Bank asked me if we would like to supply some honey for the whole party, and I assured him we would. He said the Powell Chamber of Commerce had tried to think of the nicest product raised here to give President Coolidge and his party and couldn't think of anything finer than honey. The Chamber of Commerce offered to pay for it, but of course neither Mr. Hardy nor we would take anything for it. President Coolidge was given a case of six ten-pound pails, and each of the men in his immediate party was given a pail, and there were two pails for the press representatives. When the party reached the Burlington station Messrs. Dowling and Thomson had the honey on a stand right at the corner, with a large placard on it telling all about where it was produced. When Mr. Coolidge arrived, he was escorted to the place by Colonel Starling, and Mr. Thomson made a short speech of presentation. Mr. Coolidge smilingly accepted the honey, which a porter immediately carried on board the train. The men had interviewed the chef and the steward, and they had promised to serve cakes and honey for breakfast Sunday morning.

Monday, August 29, 1927

For your own good as well as the general welfare of your domiciles, I advise all of you, individually and collectively, to *sit down* before you proceed with this epistle. Are you all sot? If not, don't say I didn't warn you.

[I have a letter from Robert A. Bridges of *Scribner's* saying that he read my article with interest and that it is, as the magazine likes them, personal and picturesque. He says they will be glad to have "When A Woman Governor Campaigns" for the magazine and expect to pay me $200 for it. He also asks for photographs of the trip and of Governor Ross and for biographical information about me.]

Sisters, ahoy. The family is started. Where do we go from here, and who will be the next to go?

Dot's all I got to say dis time. Ain't dot enough?

September 8, 1927

Again I say for the general good you'd better all sit down while you peruse this epistle. If you don't take my advice, don't try to collect damages from my $200 — when I get it. [I have had a letter from Nellie Tayloe Ross, written ten minutes before she was due to leave New York for Cheyenne. Governor Ross was in New York when she received my letter to Mr. O'Mahoney asking for photographs of her; and so she went to the Scribner's office immediately and not only gave Mr. Bridges the photographs he had requested but spoke glowingly of my abilities.]

Well, you know it doesn't hurt your standing any with an editor to have a personage such as the first woman governor in the U.S. hurry to the editorial sanctum as soon as she hears from you that your article has been accepted, does it? Wasn't it nice for our family fairies to be on the job, and have my letter reach Mrs. Ross while she was right in New York, with time enough to go to see Mr. Bridges, and to write me a letter with ten minutes to spare?

September 20, 1927, Tuesday

I am sure you will be interested in knowing that I got the check for $200 from Scribner's. It certainly comes in at an opportune time! We had been wondering if we could get any fruit to can, and various other things that we really needed, and now we can. I had told Mr. Krueger some time ago about selling the article, but had not told him the price. When I told him that the other day, after the check came, he said, "Gee, I bet that looks like a million dollars right now." It certainly does!

We have also sold a car of last year's honey, for which praise be. We have not shipped yet, but will as soon as we can get a car, which John ordered yesterday. The new Mountain States Honey Producers' Association has sold the honey for us. We do not know yet what we will get, but it will be the best the market allows, we know that. The joke is that it is sold to a firm in New York that has bought our honey several times, and has written us that ours is the finest honey they ever got anywhere. Of course we tried to sell to them several times in the past season, but they would not pay what we wanted. Now that all this intermountain honey is pooled under the direction of the new association, they have to pay the best price or not get any of it.

With all due appreciation of your placing a ten cent value on my utterances, I think your arithmetic is wrong. When I went to school 5,000 words for $200 did not count more than about 4 cents a word. You may be interested in knowing what I have cashed in on this year—so far: Cheyenne *Tribune*

$14.50; Casper *Herald* $13.25; Scribners $200.00; Christmas gift verses $3.00; Puzzles $6.50; "When Naptime Comes" $3.00. January to September 1—8 months—Total $240.25. The Cheyenne paper is not taking much of anything, but I earn about 50¢ a day now from the Casper paper. I certainly am thankful for this extra money this lean year. It has bought many a sack of flour and gallon of gasoline!

Friday morning, October 14, 1927

Edith, I told you when you were here that I had joined the "Faery Queene Club" in Scribner's, didn't I? I have been meaning for several years to write Mr. Phelps and tell him how I read the Faery Queene and everything else of Spenser's while I was eating my noon lunch when teaching at School No. 3. I finally did it a few weeks ago, when I was writing to Scribner's. I told Mr. Phelps about how my landlady used to give me cold oatmeal for lunch, cooked with milk and served with sugar and no cream. Strange as it may sound, it was immensely good, and as I read Spenser I ate the oats, until now whenever I think of the Faery Queene I think of that oatmeal, and the longer I think about it, the richer they both grow in flavor. I have a letter from Mr. Phelps in acknowledgment of my letter. It is on buff colored paper, about 7 inches square, folded once through the center to fit a large, oblong envelope. Both paper and envelope are embossed in dark blue (Yale blue!)

Wednesday afternoon, November 9, 1927

John's pension claim has progressed to the point where a special examiner was appointed to come to investigate. Through Senator Kendrick and Theodore Wanerus, who is Sen. K's secretary, the Pension Bureau finally agreed to appoint a special examiner. That was three months ago. It took that long for him to get here. Not only did the Bureau delay that long in sending him after they said they would, but they have held up the pension entirely during this time. That is one reason why we have been so close run for cash, not getting in any pension for three months.

The examiner got here yesterday noon from Denver and went away this morning. He came out here yesterday afternoon but we were in town. When he got back to town he found John and wanted to go into the hotel for ten minutes and have it all over with. But John refused, saying that he wanted me present at the hearing, and also wanted Mr. Murray, Mr. McMath (our mail carrier), and Mr. Krueger to give their opinion of his disability. So the man came out here last night. I never saw anything work in such lightning fashion. The first thing he said was that he was going to get John the limit there was. He brought along a Corona, set it up on the dining table, and typed faster than lightning, reading what he said after every paragraph or two. He knew when he arrived just what he was going to put down for each of us to sign, apparently, for he did not ask us questions, and anything we wanted to say we had to get in edgewise. But you never read such positive statements as he typed for us to sign. He knew more about John's disability than you do yourself. The thing was that he had all the letters we have ever written to the Pension Bureau, and all those that Senator K. ever wrote, and he had evidently studied them all very carefully until he knew every argument we ever put out. You would have thought he was our lawyer trying to set forth our side of the case. He did not argue a thing, except to make it stronger than we did ourselves. When he left here, he said again that he was going to get the limit for John, and when John saw him at the train this morning, that was the last thing he said again. So we are anxious to hear from the Bureau to see what his idea of the limit is.

The thing that makes you despise the Pension Bureau is that you have to fight like fury to get a special examiner, and then when you do, all he does is to present to the Bureau in his report exactly what you have said all the time in your letters. Why the Bureau couldn't accept it without the expense of a special examiner is a mystery, except of course, that such is the way in which government bureaus function. I suppose it will be two or three months before we hear now what the Bureau's action is on his report. But when we finally do hear, we ought to get a couple hundred dollars of back pension, counting the increase, which should date from last December a year ago.

Tuesday night, November 15, 1927

I got my first check today from the Billings *Gazette*. I was interested in getting it to see how they would pay. I do not have to clip the stuff in the *Gazette*, so I do not keep an actual measurement of inches printed. I began to write for them on October 20, and the check says it pays in full to October 31, which is about 11 days. The check is for $15.30, so you see I made a little over a dollar a day on the stuff I sent in. I got a check yesterday for the month of October from the Casper paper for $12.80, and the check is due tomorrow from Cheyenne and should be for $8.50. So you see my newspaper correspondence during October brought in $36.60. My desk is piled with stuff now to write up. People are begining to call me up and give me items.

Pater, thanks immensely for the offer to pay my way home any time. I'd like to come, but don't see how I can do so this winter. You have had us all so regularly lately I'd think you and Co would be like Aunt Lizzie — glad to be alone for awhile. John has been in such miserable health I wouldn't want to be away from him till he is stronger. He is planning to go to Thermopolis soon for two weeks, and I hope that will start him toward more strength. The children all want to be at home for Christmas this year, and are already making great plans. Anne plays hanging up stockings daily now already, and hands out the empty stockings with the command to see what good candy, oranges, and nuts are in them. We all dutifully eat Barmicide feasts from the stockings.

Thursday night, November 17, 1927

Pater, thanks greatly for the check. John will enjoy using it when he goes to Thermopolis for the baths. He has been needing a new suit for some time, but did not see his way clear to getting it until recently. So we have been having a great time picking out the suit to order. We found several in a special sale catalogue reduced $6 or $7 in price, and he likes one of these very much.

Have you noticed the recent development in the Andy Gump comics? Uncle Bim, the millionaire uncle from Australia, has set aside a billion dollars for helping people, and Andy is administrator of the fund. Pater, I don't think the Gumps have anything on you when it comes to giving folk things to make them happy. You are the original yourself. You are always doing something for us all that makes us feel like a million dollars.

We have had word that the Pension Bureau has finally allowed John the full rating on his pension under the new act. That gives us $50 a month. Senator Kendrick kept after the Bureau until they got the special examiner on the case, and the examiner's report was so positive the Bureau at once granted the full amount. The case has a funny side, however. More than a year ago, when the application was first made, we wrote to Senator Warren and Congressman Winter, as well as to Senator Kendrick, but they did not take up the claim. We have not heard from them for more than a year, except that when the $40 rating was allowed last May, the one we refused, we got a telegram from Congressman Winter saying he was pleased to inform us that the pension was increased to $40, and that was followed by a statement in a few days in the Cheyenne *Tribune* that Congressman Winter had secured a $10 increase in pension for John Hendricks of Powell. From that day to a few days ago we had never heard from him, and he probably did not know that John turned down that amount. Then last Wednesday while John was at Thermopolis I got a telegram from Winter saying "Your application for pension increase granted at new rate of $50 effective from today." I knew that we had applied a year ago, and we were both concerned over what that might mean—"effective from today." Then yesterday we got a letter from Senator Kendrick saying the increase had been allowed, effective from December 14, 1926. It just happened by sheer coincidence that the date of filing of the old claim was December 14, 1926 and the date it was allowed was December

14, 1927. Winter (or his clerks) evidently did not notice the year and sent out the wire to say "effective today," which of course shows up his lack of knowledge in the case. John says he supposes that in a few days the Cheyenne *Tribune* will say that Congressman Winter has secured an increase of pension to $50 for John Hendricks of Powell. Senator Kendrick wrote the loveliest letter telling of the increase, in which he said in part, "It has been a long, hard struggle but since it has been in behalf of a friend in whose welfare I was specially interested I have enjoyed pressing your claim for you. This increase is undoubtedly due entirely to the recent visit which the special examiner paid to your home. If in any further way I can cooperate with you, please let me know."

Thursday, December 22, 1927

I don't know yet whether to say goodbye till I see you and tell you the rest personally, or to say I'll keep on writing it in letters. Sometimes Anne does not cough at all, for hours and hours, and we think I will start as per schedule next Tuesday. Then she will cough, and we'll give up planning entirely. So I guess the only thing to do is for you to look for us when you see us. I would like to start on Dec. 27 so as to get the excursion rates, as it will make a difference of some dollars on the trip. But if we can't start then, we'll just have to go later.

The children can hardly wait for tomorrow. They want the room decorated and the tree trimmed. Anne asks a dozen times a day when it will be time to decorate the room. Ever since our children have been big enough, we have let them help trim the tree ahead of time. Why should John and I stay up all night to do something they love to do? The tree means so much more to them when they decide where to hang the various ornaments. We have had the ornaments out for a couple days, and they have got reacquainted with them.

Dear Daddy and Sister and Jules,

We made our connections nicely at Billings last night. Mr. Roach carried our big suitcase off the train for us. When I asked for our reservation I found that the tourist sleeper had been taken off and that we had to take an upper in the regular Pullman as that was all that was left.

Anne coughed quite a bit during the night, although I gave her both kinds of medicine regularly. When we came from breakfast this morning the Pullman conductor asked me if Anne had the whooping cough, saying the other passengers were alarmed at her coughing. I told him the doctor had said not. He wanted to know if I would move to a compartment instead of staying in the regular seat, for the peace of mind of the other passengers. So here we are in Compartment B, occupying it in state all by ourselves. As long as they give it to us for the same price as an upper berth we are having a good bargain.

Dearest Daddy and Cecilia and Jules,

Anne was greatly delighted when she found that the letter we got from you this morning said, "My dear big girls." She laughed and laughed about it. She will not let Pater call her a little girl at all. When she does something he does not approve of, he calls her baby. Then she knows she should not do that! Pater is greatly amused at her calling herself a woman with the grown ups, and usually asks her how the women are this morning.

You can't imagine how much time it takes to wait on Pater. Since he can't walk around as usual, he needs so many things. I try to get some work done and have to stop a dozen times while washing a few dishes and walk in the other room to answer his call. If we don't hurry when he calls he is likely to try to get up and go after what he wants. We are afraid he might fall and break a bone if he does that, so we run as soon as he calls.

It certainly is a good thing I came. Cora is not a bit well and she said the other day that she believes she would have had a breakdown if I hadn't come to help her out right now. She has had the flu so many times that her heart is affected, and she has to be very careful. With Pater's irregular hours, she does not get enough sleep and that is what she needs most of all to correct the heart trouble. So you see I am glad I came when I did. I hate to be away from you all and make extra work for you to do, but I believe right now that I am more needed here even than at Honeyhill. I certainly am thankful that you are so good at getting along yourselves.

Bloomington, January 22, 1928

Cora and I are going out to dinner this noon with Miss Berry and Miss Conklin. We are having a student girl come and stay with Anne while we are away. Pater is napping in his chair now and I must stop and put him to bed. He always needs help. We take off his collar and tie and shoes, get the hot water bottle in the bed, and then help him in. One of us usually stays up at night till we get him to bed. As he usually stays up till midnight or later, you can see why I have had to stay in bed half the morning once in a while to catch up on my sleep. When Cora is in school, I try to get her to bed and I stay up to put Pater to bed, as she has to get up at seven or earlier. I usually try to get up about 6 or 6:30 and make all three fires, and then go back to bed. Yesterday and this morning, when Cora did not have to go to school, I slept late.

My Dear Sweet Big Girls:

It is mighty fine of Pater to want to give you a new car. It hardly looks like the thing for him to do when he and Cora neither have a car for themselves. Looks to me like they are entitled to one themselves, and that before he gives one to you.

However, you do whatever you want to about accepting it. If Pater wants to do so and can afford to do it I see no reason why you should not accept it. With the setback that the fire gave us and the almost complete failure of the honey crop last year it may be some time before we can drive a new one from our own income. With a slight displacement of the right elbow and a lame back, both of which have doubtless come from cranking these two old Fords for the last ten years I am hardly in shape to discourage your accepting the present of a new car with a starter if Pater wants to give it to you.

If we were buying a new car ourselves we could not consider anything but a Ford Fordor, the Sedan. The Fordor has plenty of leg room for me. The Sedan may not have as much as the Coach, but if it does not we can remedy that by putting an additional cushion in the front seat for the driver.   — Daddy.

Dear Sweet Big Girls:

I ran the figures of last year's business over the adding machine at Murray's this morning. The grocery list showed only $151.29. Personal $395.50. Bees, seasonal $488.41. Bees, permanent $478.37. Postage $81.59. Household labor. $92.50. That item does not seem large enough. Even with the time out for Mary's being sick it ought to have shown more than that. There must have been a lot of cash payments that we have no record of. General expense $233.97. Life insurance $204.99. Car upkeep, $58.55. Truck $155.88. Household, $32.70. The mattress was the greater portion of that item. Gasoline, $193.75 — 738 gallons. That is a little better than 60 gal. a month. We will probably use considerably less this year as we will not run the saw much. Farm, $936.83. There was almost two years' interest in this account this time. Dairy $156.25. This item includes an estimate of $70.00 for pasture and $70.00 for hay. We probably will not use all the hay charged against the dairy. Garden $23.24. $15.00 of Maloy's labor is charged against this item. Coal for the house, $96.31. Coal for the shop, $12.20. Bank deposits (income) $4,367.60.

Your lovers all,
Daddy, Sister, and Jules

Friday, February 17, 1928

When John met me at the station he told me that Mrs. Werts and Mrs. Cubbage had both been wanting to get me, and wanted to see me as soon as I got home, as they wanted me to help with a dinner at the church today. With John's hearty agreement I balked at such immediate service. But after I was home about an hour, Mrs. Werts called me and said they did not want me to come to the church to help, but to make enough rice pudding for fifty dinners at home, and they would come by for it. So I arose early this a.m. and made a dishpan and a baking pan full of raisin-pineapple-custard rice pudding. By the time Mrs. Werts came for it at 9:30 it was baked. I suppose I am easy, but you know we will all do something when we feel flattered. Once last fall when my division of the Aid had to serve dinner, I made a dishpan of rice pudding, thinking the men must be tired of the everlasting pie at the commercial club dinner every week. I did so with fear and trembling, however, not knowing how rice pudding would take, for no one had ever served it or even thought of it before. The men (and women) licked up every grain, and the women had several servings. The dinner today was for the extension division workers here from Laramie and Washington, D.C., and the local people attending the agricultural survey conference being held here today and tomorrow. Naturally, when the church women asked me to make my rice pudding for such a distinguished assemblage, I fell for it, being flattered. The pudding really is good. I use 2 pounds of rice, a package of seedless raisins, a can of crushed pineapple, honey to sweeten, vanilla flavor, 12 eggs, and a gallon and a half of milk. We serve it with real cream, not too thick.

Pater, if you could for just half an hour sit in the sunshine here in this office, you'd forget that you ever had such a thing as sciatica, and would go jumping about like a spring lamb. I wish you were here.

Sunday afternoon, February 20, 1928

Ifound a big job of reporting ready for me to write up on the economic conference that was held here Friday and Saturday. I have sent in yards by mail and yesterday afternoon after the closing session I talked for twenty minutes over long distance reporting the results to the Billings paper. There were present at the meeting federal, state, and county agricultural workers from Washington, D.C., Salt Lake City, Laramie, Billings, and all over Wyoming, from various counties. This is the first conference of this kind held in Wyoming. The findings are most interesting, and, to me, revolutionary at least in the way they comment on what the reclamation service has always said about farming on irrigated land.

Two of the chief men here were connected with the Bureau of Reclamation as demonstrator on reclamation projects and field agent for the Department of Agriculture in western states. You know the units here were all laid out in 40 and 80 acre tracts, 40 acres for the best land and 80 acres for everything else, and the contention was always made that 40 acres of good land was enough for anybody to farm of irrigated land. Well, what this conference did was to take all the available data on farming here, from the records in the reclamation office, from farmers, and everybody else who was reliable, and then after studying the data, make a report on the conditions and necessities and future possibilities. And what do you suppose the report of the committee on farm management and organization reported as a result of its study? They recommended and insisted that not less than *100* acres of *cropped* land is necessary to support an average sized family (5 people) in this irrigated country! Think of it!

The committees on home management found from their study of present conditions that it took $1190 to support an average family of five for one year, and that to produce that much the crops from 100 acres of intensively cultivated land were necessary. Another result I think astounding is the statement that a study of the actual crops produced here for nine years past showed that the price received for alfalfa does not pay the cost of production. Alfalfa always has been and always must be the chief forage crop and chief soil improver here, and yet it costs more to produce than the receipts. When you stop to consider that 50% of the cultivated area here is in alfalfa, which costs more to produce than farmers get from it, you can see why farmers here are getting poorer every year. All the government advice has been to keep on planting alfalfa.

The report showed that potatoes lead in being the best paying cash crop raised here. Sugar beets are one of the safest cash crops. That is, the season has a lot to do with whether or not your potato crop is a success, and also the market conditions, while the season does not affect beets so much and the market is always established before the crop is raised, by the contract with the sugar company. In 1927, beans paid more than the cost of production. As I said above, 50% of the cropped area is in alfalfa, 10% in beans, 10% in beets, and 5% in potatoes, the remaining 25% in small grains and pasture.

Friday, February 24, 1928

My family was invited to various oyster feeds among the neighbors while Anne and I were in Indiana, and tonight is our turn to return the compliment and give a feed for all the rest. Bygrens, Gilletts, Vosses, Gimmesons, and ourselves constitute the bunch that has been getting together. The count is 25 grownups and children, besides the two small babies. If everybody eats as much as some of the men, the soup will have to be made in a washboiler. Mary said that last time one of the men used a large vegetable bowl for a soup dish, and had it filled twice and a half. As the bowl must have held at least a quart, you can easily figure how much he took care of. If all the 25 ate that much, you would have to use an adding machine to find out how much to make.

However, I am going to have escalloped oysters as well as soup, and figure that the soup consumption will thereby be lessened. I am figuring on about a quart for each person, which, considering that four or five of the children will probably not eat more than a pint, if that, ought to allow half a gallon for some of the men. I shall make three large pans of escalloped oysters, and also serve cabbage slaw, hot rolls, butter, honey, apple butter, pickles, coffee, sassafras tea, and two kinds of cake. John got a gallon of oysters this morning. I'll use half in the stew and half in the scallop. You have to order oysters here special, as the dealer has to order at least three gallons at a time and doesn't have a sale for very many. These are fine, as they came direct from the eastern coast, without coming through the hands of several dealers. They came in a gallon bucket with a friction top lid, and cost $4.25.

Sunday Afternoon, March 18, 1928

Our pie supper at the Star School was a huge success for we made almost $30 with practically no work. Last time we had a chicken supper and all of us worked for several days doing all the necessary cooking and preparing, and we didn't make much more either, for at 50¢ a dinner you have to serve a lot of meals to make $30. We were all surprised at the prices paid for the pies as most of them sold for about a dollar each. We thought the men would pay only about half that much, but they certainly bid up. Mr. Cubbage from the grocery at Garland was the auctioneer. He is so funny; but the crowd was just as funny. The bids usually started about 25 or 30¢ and went up a nickel or a dime at a time. Once when the bid was

80¢, Cubbage begged the crowd to make it a dollar. One of the men shouted, "O, earn your money," and bid 85¢. They all expected to pay a dollar but made the auctioneer draw it out a nickel at a time. Once they bid by one cent raises, just to kid Mr. Cubbage, and the final bid was 99½¢. But he got back at them by accepting it and saying "Pay the clerk and he will make the change."

The program was excellent but the hit of the whole evening was Anne's reciting. She said "Puppy and I," and for an encore "The Brownie." She got up like a drum major, and talked louder than anybody else of the children, so that all could hear. I had to laugh, for when she finished the first verse, about meeting the man, the crowd laughed and began to applaud, thinking that was about the size of a poem a child of her age could say. When she went on to tell about meeting the horse and the woman and the rabbits and the puppy, four more verses, they couldn't believe it, and then when she said a poem with two verses more for an encore, they nearly raised the roof. She said the poem, too, with full expression. Her "No, not I," in every verse was worth going a long way to hear, and when she came to "I'll go with you, Puppy," the words fairly tumbled out over each other. When she returned for the second piece, she announced, "Now I'll tell you about a Brownie," and proceeded to do so, giggling delightfully when she said "They're all so tickly." I do wish you could have heard her. Jules did well, too. He said "I Had a Penny." I wish you could have heard him say, "I *do* like rabbits," and "I hadn't got nuffin, no I hadn't got nuffin." He always insists on saying, "I hadn't got nuffin, *no Sir*, I hadn't got nuffin." Co, you certainly deserve a medal for finding these Milne poems.

Tuesday, March 20, 1928

It does not seem to me that I have been married very long, but now I know I have. If you want to be convinced also, please glance over the enclosed pages from a Sears R. catalogue that came one of the first years I was out here. And didn't we think we were dressed up when we had the long skirts and the up-and-coming hats! I think the thing that amuses me the most is the pictures of the bloomerettes with either ruffles to the ankles or ankle cuffs. Honest, did we ever wear our dresses that long? No one can tell me that modern styles are bad compared with these.

Friday night, March 23, 1928

Dear Pater,

I have made out the orders for the furniture and other articles you told me to order, and am enclosing them herewith, so you can see what the articles are. There are two orders: one to Sears Roebuck and one to Montgomery Ward, both to Kansas City.

I hope I have not ordered too much. The furniture in both orders will give a wicker set for the library, 2 rockers and two straight chairs and a bench for the living room, and the fernery. The bench I will use either beside the furnace register or the fireplace. It is just a nice size and height for the children.

I didn't know I could get so excited over anything as I am over getting the living room all fixed up. If only you could come to see it our joy would be complete. We can't thank you enough.

The new carpets came today that I picked out at Olson's in Chicago on the way home. The large 9 × 11 rug has the lovely flower and bird pattern in two opposite corners and so has the small 26 × 33. The 4 × 11 rug does not have the pattern. All three rugs are the same color, with the same kind of deeper colored border. We took the rugs upstairs and laid them out on the floor in the east room. I don't think I'll use them in the living room till I get a vacuum sweeper to clean them with. We use our living room so much the carpets get very hard wear, and about the hardest part is the cleaning, even though we always use a soft fibre brush and never a harsh broom. Mrs. Nelson, wife of the president of the First National Bank, told me last night she has just sent off some old rugs to Olson's to have them made into a new rug. So you see, Pater, we are in the class with the banker's wife, with our new carpets.

The April number of the *Household* Magazine has a double page of pictures and write-ups about various kinds of mothers, as for instance, the nagging mother, the old-fashioned mother (who doesn't bother to look well dressed), the ambitious mother, the tearful mother, the severe mother, the saccharine mother, the gad-about, the quarrelsome, the bragging, the slacker, the housekeeping mother. The heading is "Which Mother Are You?" I was very much interested in showing the pages to the children and asking them which one I was. I was quite relieved to find that they could not locate me on the pages. It seemed to me that at times I was a good deal of various ones of the kinds listed, and I was glad to know they had not recognized me as such. Then I asked them which kind they thought was the *worst* kind of mother to have and was greatly edified at their answers. Cecilia said the worst kind was the bragging mother who was always boasting of what her children could do. Jules thought that the worst kind of mother would be the one who was always severe, while Anne thought that the slacker mother, who was indifferent to what her children did or wanted, was the very worst of all. I suspect one who did not know the ages of the children could guess how old they are by their classification of the worst mother. To a child Cecilia's age, the worst possible embarrassment comes from being paraded in public.

The other night Anne was playing in the kitchen, where Mary was washing dishes. John was in the office and I in the living room. I heard a queer sound from the kitchen but did not think anything of it, till I saw John start in a hurry from the office. Then I heard Mary say, "She is choking." I hurried to the kitchen and found Anne choking and coughing, or trying to, and vomiting. I hurried her to the coal bucket, and held her. She was a "whay-all" violently, and choked and could not get her breath for several minutes. She gasped and gasped. Finally she got a little breath, sat up in my lap, laughed merrily, and said, "I ate some shampoo." Then she choked again, and it was several minutes before she could get enough breath again to answer our questions. She was playing with a shampoo bottle that was empty, supposedly, but had a little of the liquid still in it. She had filled the bottle with water, poured the water on some snow she had, and sucked the snow! There was enough of the shampoo to make her nauseated. After she got it all thrown up, and drank several glasses of water, she was perfectly all right again. But the thing that got us was her seeing the joke on herself and laughing about it with the little wisp of breath she was able to catch between chokes and vomitings. Most children would have come up weeping, but not Anne. Since then, she has giggled every time she has thought about it, and we have had lots of fun offering her shampoo for her meals. What makes it all the funnier is that she pronounces shampoo as if it were spelled "shampoo-ah."

Sunday, April 1, 1928

Pater, I stopped writing long enough to read the Palm Sunday lesson with the family before they all went to bed. We read the proper chapter, and played "The Palms" on the victrola. The children got out the Bible scroll you sent and turned to the picture of the Triumphal Entry while the song was being sung. They know all the pictures, their titles, and their story.

We are loading a car of honey. I am glad to say that last year's crop is sold, through the Mountain States Honey Producers' Association. This car will take all we have, all Mr. Krueger has, all Mr. Graham has, and 40 cases of Mr. Johnson's. So you see that all of us had very small crops, as we ourselves usually have a great deal more than a carload to ship. The carload goes to Birmingham, Alabama. The freight on the car will be about $570, and the honey is worth $30,000. We do not know yet just what price we will get.

Sunday night, April 22, 1928

John is taking such delight in the self starter that is on the truck now, Pater, and says that your helping us so much made it possible to get that put on the truck. He can't tell you how much comfort it is to him not to have to crank. I think as much of it as he does, for I can drive the truck now, and since the car is out of commission, and the new car not yet here, it makes it mighty handy for me to be able to take the truck out by myself.

The county superintendents of the four Big Horn Basin counties are having a meeting at Basin today to decide about the teacher's institute for next fall. The four counties always have a joint institute. I called Mrs. Anderson, the superintendent from this county, and put in my bid to be one of the instructors. If they accept me, I'll have a lot of work to do, but I think it will be worth while to do it. And I am sure I can give a series of lectures that will be worth something to the teachers and will help them in their own writing and speaking of English. So if any of you have any suggestions as to what errors teachers make in their speech and writing, please let me know so I can discourse on them. The Powell Chamber of Commerce voted yesterday to invite the teachers to have the institute here this fall. If they do, and I can give the lectures right here, I won't be at any expense, and I'll have the new car to make the trips in and can do it without bother. Maybe if I get the course really worked up, I can get a chance to deliver the lectures at other teachers' institutes in this and nearby states.

The Powell paper tells of a girl who lives on a ranch up in the Sunlight country who came to Powell recently to have her first baby. She was Edith Wallis of Chicago, and lived here with Mrs. Steinbarger before she married Heber Ward and went to live on the ranch in the mountains. When she got ready to come here to await the stork, she had to travel 25 miles *on skis* to get to Sunlight to the stage. Her husband accompanied her this much of the trip, and then she came on by stage and train the rest of the way alone. The baby, a boy, came just a week after she got here. There isn't any auto road or even a horse trail in the winter to their place. How do you like that?

The entertainment Friday night by the grade school was splendid.* The first grade gave a symphony orchestra concert of several numbers. The children had bells, tambourines, sticks, blocks of wood, and drums, with which they kept time and produced some interesting "music." Other of the lower grades gave folk dances, some in Kate Greenaway costumes, others in aprons and overalls. One class wound the Maypole perfectly. I never saw a pole where the ribbons were woven so perfectly. One class gave a box of dolls, that was as pretty as anything I ever saw. A high packing box, lying on its side, with the top open side to the audience, was discovered full of Japanese dolls when the curtain rose — six boys and six girls, all in kimonas, packed closely in the box. They stepped out and began to talk about their trip over the sea. The clock struck twelve, and they came alive for a while and sang songs and did cunning drills and dances. Then they became dolls again and were repacked in the box when the curtain fell. It was too cunning for words. Another grade did a march of the wooden soldiers, with singing, the boys being dressed in red and black uniforms and the girls in fancy costumes being lined up at the back to form a frame for the dances, and doing the singing. The cantata Cecilia was in, "In Foreign Lands," had scenes by Japanese, Romanians, Spanish, and Egyptians. Each did characteristic dancing and sang songs. The costumes were lovely and really difficult, they were so well planned. The whole thing ended with America, the melting pot, and singing of patriotic songs and flag waving.

Everything was lovely, except for one thing. The Egyptians wore typical costumes, very beautifully made. They were all girls in the sixth grade. In keeping with their Egyptian costumes, they wore breastplates of gilt, trimmed in beads. The girls made the plates, one for each breast, the teacher gilded them, and the girls sewed on the beads themselves. It was really very well done. But it happened that Mrs. Murray, whose daughter

*Cecilia, Jr. moved from Star School to the Powell school in the fifth grade.

was in the first grade toy orchestra, had such pride in her child (who merely thumped a tambourine in the back row) that she went to the afternoon rehearsal as well as to the evening performance. In the afternoon she saw these Egyptians and stirred up a fuss about their costumes, declaring the breastplates were immodest and immoral and everything else. She complained so to the grade school principal that the latter had to go to the teachers in charge of the costumes and tell them they'd better omit the breastplates. The teachers, however, who had really studied costumes, insisted there would be no point in the whole thing if the costumes were not true to type. In the evening, Mrs. Murray went to the teachers and made a fuss right in the auditorium where the performance was going on, but the teacher who was responsible for the costuming, although she wept over the situation, remained firm, and the girls went on in the costumes as planned. Everybody who heard about it of course sympathized with the teacher, and I suspect Mrs. Murray has had more unkind things said about her in the past couple days than anybody else in the community. I was not surprised at her disapproval of the costumes, but did think she would have sense enough not to try to manage everything. Mr. Murray is on the school board, however, and ever since that she has carried the burden of the whole school system on her shoulders, and thinks she has been elected to manage all school affairs. And as for disapproving of the costumes, what can you expect of a person who thinks O'Henry's books are so immoral she will not allow one of them to be brought into her house?

May 14, 1928

"Seventh Heaven" is here tonight and I want John to take Jules and Cecilia. I think they will enjoy it. Edith, did you get to see it? I think it received more favorable comment from Indiana University people than anything that was in Bloomington when I was there.

I got my monthly news checks the other day, and as usual the one from the Casper paper was $12.50. I was much pleased to find that the one from the Billings *Gazette* was $40.50, so you see my salary last month was $53. Not so bad, eh? I bought myself some bloomers and a pair of shoes on the strength of the extra amount, as well as shoes for Cecilia and Anne and trousers for John—no, pants—they cost less than $2.00, two cents less—they were everyday jeans—work pants.

May 17, 1928

Pater, the grand opening took place yesterday when the order from Sears Roebuck arrived. I wish you could see the things in our living room now. I don't which is prettier, the carpets, the chairs, or the draperies, or the new electric light fixtures. We are wild about them all, and the nicest thing is that they all go so beautifully together. The new wicker furniture is light green in color, with striped cushions and back cushions of cretonne. The cretonne has a stripe about three inches wide that looks like a moire ribbon in dark colors, and another stripe about ten inches wide with patterns of autumn leaves and flowers in bright colors. The mahogany rocker has a very pretty tapestry seat, and the two arm chairs are simply lovely. On the back of each chair there is a bowl of flowers in two shades of red, two shades of brown, two of tan, and black, with a little blue at the edges and in the pattern of the rest of the tapestry. These colors go just right with the black and rose of the drapes, and the black, rose and blue of the valances. I have the chairs standing on each side of the front door, beneath the two windows, and they seem to have grown there they look so natural.

The new shades came the other night, and they looked so interesting that John got the necessary tools and put them all up that same evening. They are lovely. The children are wild about them, and so are the rest of us. Mrs. Gimmeson came over to see them, saying that her children talked so much about them she had to see them herself. She had never seen the Austrian plisse kind, and did not know you could get them. I had the drapes and other curtain all ready so we put them all up too, and you would hardly know the place. The room looks like a different one.

I've caught the position of institute instructor for the Bighorn Basin teacher's institute here at Powell next week, and now I have to think about what I will do now that I have it.

Sunday night, May 20, 1928

We were much surprised and greatly delighted to have Ted and Edith and the children and Jack, the dog, and the lamb drive in last night just about supper time. We did not think they were coming this weekend. They did not expect to either, Edith said, but about three o'clock Ted called up and said, "Let's drive to Powell," and of course she said she was ready. We had such a good time. Ted wanted to see some men in Powell, so we all drove up in the evening, and had a good time.

I hate to think of their going away from Greybull, but of course there is no reason for their staying if Ted can get something better elsewhere. At any rate, he might as well try it. Personally, I do not think he will be satisfied at all in the East and will be headed West again in a few years. But the only way to make him know for certain is for him to try it out. I remember he said once, years ago, that he would never let his wife live in the East again, where men's opinion of women was so different from what it is in the West. Maybe he has forgot that, but when he gets east again he'll probably remember it.

June 4, 1928

This is an important occasion, of course. A seven-year birthday is very important, as you may be sure. I am to bake an angel food cake this afternoon and make ice cream. Jules wants to ask the Gimmeson children to eat ice cream and cake this evening, but we will not have a regular party.

June 15, 1928

Jules is quite aged in his announcement regarding what he is doing these days. I was talking to Mrs. Richards over the telephone, and he said he wanted to tell her something. He began, "Do you know what I am doing these days? I am going into the bee business." Then he proceeded to tell her what he was going to do. I made him a suit of light colored coveralls to wear to the bee yard and John fixed the screen for a bee veil and bought him a pair of white cotton gloves. I'll make the veil and also a pair of over-sleeves with the gloves sewed to them, and he will work the smoker and help John a lot in the bee yard, especially at Hyattville, where they expect to go Monday to work that yard and bring home a load of bees.

Cecilia is quite enthused over their girls' 4-H club, which will take up sewing this summer. Mrs. Richards is going to be the leader, to their great delight. Miss Eells, the county home demonstrator, brought Cecilia her books and instructions today, and I had to sit down with her and go over them all — and learn how to make all the stitches and finishes and how to darn and patch. The booklets illustrate it all. The girls will first make a bag for their sewing, then hem a towel, and make various simple things, and finally a nightie or dress for themselves. It will be fine training. They learned a lot last summer in their cooking club and will this summer in the sewing. One of the girls in the bunch doesn't want to take the sewing. She said she started once to take it, and had to rip out everything she sewed. Cecilia told her if she had done it right in the first place, she wouldn't have to take it out. I told Cecilia I knew the motto for the club all right; it should be "As ye sew, so shall ye rip." Mrs. Richards shouted when I told it to her.

Friday, June 29, 1928

I received yesterday two copies of the July *Scribner's* from the editors and had the pleasure of seeing my name in print. Quite pleasant, isn't it?

I dread to think of Edith's going away from this part of the country. It doesn't seem possible that she won't be at Greybull, as usual. The place will be dead to me now when we pass through. It was always an interesting half way point to Hyattville, but now it will only be so many miles from somewhere else.

I am sure you will be glad to know that John is feeling much better than he has for several years. He still gets pretty tired when he does as much work as he wants to, but he seems to recover now in a way he did not last year. He is cheerful now and full of plans for the bee work next year. Last year he was so blue he never mentioned the next year except to wonder if there would be one. This evening he sang all the while he was doing the chores, the first time I have heard him sing like that for months and months. He plays with the children and even with the dogs and enjoys it all. He has played more in the last month, I think, than in the past year. For all of which you may be sure I am thankful.

John is so pleased over the way the Hyattville yard has come up this spring and thinks that now since we have built it up about where we want it, next year should be the most interesting year of beekeeping he has ever had. We have brought down about $1500 worth of bees from that yard this summer and that means a profit of about $10 per colony there, on bees. We may get a little honey, too.

Murrays got their new car today. It was one that was sent to Cody for the stampede there over the 4th of July. This car was on display during the stampede, having been driven up from Denver for that occasion. Mr. Murray says everybody who saw it is wild about it, people who have been used to higher priced cars being the most enthusiastic. Murrays had ordered a dark blue, but this car is a light green. It seems that almost every car that is sent out is a different color, of these first lots. When Mr. Murray got his car, he found that the price is about $50 higher than they told him at first. They paid $795 for the car, fully equipped, and including a set of tire chains which he bought extra.

July 15, 1928

The children had a great time at the Christy Brothers circus. The advertisements called for a huge street parade, *two miles long*, and a *five* ring circus. We went up when the train came in about seven in the morning and stayed till about eleven. Then we came home and ate a snack, and went back at twelve, staying all afternoon for the performance. The show itself was very good, with some of the best acrobatic work I have ever seen. There were really five rings to the circus, with something going on in most of them all the time.

The children were very sensible about not wanting anything at the circus in the way of drinks or cones. When they found they could get three cones at the drug store for what one cost at the circus, they at once decided to wait till afterward. They took a bottle of pop each along, and we had a bucket of ice water in the truck, so they did not eat anything at the circus except the peanuts we bought in the morning and took with us. There is so much dust and dirt at the circus, and the cold drink and ice cream cone vendors look so dirty I can't believe their stuff would taste good or be clean.

I suppose Ted has gone on to New Jersey and the rest of you are in Bloomington. I hope he finds out exactly what his brother John has for him, and that it promises well. I think you are very wise to know definitely before moving your lares and penates that far from where they are now.

Sunday night, August 5, 1928

The other day when Cecilia was in town with Ivy, John's niece who is visiting us, Ivy treated her to an ice cream soda. That is, she asked Cecilia if she wanted one and was surprised (as I was later when they told me) to find that Cecilia had *never had* an ice cream soda in her life! Cecilia thinks it is about the best thing she ever tasted. But as you probably know, a soda costs 15¢ here, which amount will provide cones or eskimo pies or dixies for all three of the children. So naturally we generally get the three. Then too, it is very, very seldom that we go into a store and sit down to eat ice cream. We usually get something for the youngsters to eat on the way home.

Ted surprised us by coming up Monday for Jack. He and the young man who is to go into his office arrived about six o'clock. We were glad to see Ted and meet McHale, who seems to be a very nice young chap, and we liked him very much. I told Ted I would go to Greybull some time next week to help him pack whatever he wanted me to supervise. If you have any instructions, Edith, write them to me at Greybull and I'll have them when I get there.

I am on my way to Greybull to help Ted start east. I don't know just how much help I'll be, but he seemed to feel the need of moral backing, at least. I wish you were here, Edith, to decide what to take and what not — or would you say leave all the what-nots? I think we'll just pack up the things you may want if you come back West some time and store them at Honeyhill, for we have plenty of closets upstairs where things can be stored.

John got a new Root Extractor yesterday. It is a dandy — one of the new kinds that holds 45 frames of honey at one time. Instead of baskets in which to put the frames there is just one big basket the size of the extractor with rabbets to hold the frames all the way round. It is so much simpler and better and faster than the older types of extractors. It cost $190. John wants to start extracting Tuesday, as we need the supers. We keep thinking the honey flow surely won't go on any longer, but the bees keep piling in the honey. We are quite sure we already have 20 tons of honey. After the small crops of 1924–1925–1926 and the practical failure of 1927 we have to pinch ourselves to make sure we are seeing right.

I had a nice time at Greybull when I didn't stop to think of your going away, Edith. We certainly did a lot of work in the short time. Sunday night we had Motts to dinner and the whole house was lovely as usual, except that Ted had most of the books packed. Monday we packed the dishes from the china closet; Tuesday we packed most of the linens and some of the beddings and clothing, the curtains, pictures, and a little of everything. Wednesday we finished up. The house didn't look so bare until I took down all the curtains and then it certainly did look like no place at all.

I think Ted was wise to sell off all the furniture he could. You can take the amount he got for the furniture and make first payments on about all the furniture you will need in your new place.

We brought home a whole truck load, and the children have been in seventh heaven all morning. I tried to send on all the toys that were worth shipping, and that the youngsters wouldn't get a whole train load like again next Christmas. I did take all the things you can easily replace at the first ten cent store you get into, such as paper napkins and paper lace doilies, and tissue paper and candles. Ted gave us the camping equipment, stove, tent, and arm chairs and cots. We hope to start camping next summer, and it will be a joy. We will use it whenever we need it, take good care of it, and store it in a dry place; and any time you come out this way again and want it, it's yours.

Well, if you were to step in right now, you would find a very clean house, all spick and span. We are all ready for our institute guests, who will arrive tomorrow morning, having stopped in Lovell to visit today and tonight.

This institute business is going to be too easy for words. Instead of five or ten lectures I am to have only two, and the welcoming address. I have learned now that each of the two lectures I am to give is to be to a different section, which means that I need only one lecture. I give the welcome tomorrow at ten, have a section Tuesday at ten, and another Wednesday at 10:45.

We had to desecrate the sabbath today by cleaning the house. John helped. I had not expected to have him help, but as I could not do it myself, was more than glad for his assistance. You remember that when I was home last winter I celebrated violently at regular intervals. After I got back here, it was just the opposite — barely enough to make sure it was happening. This kept up for some months, then last month I nearly ran away. It was while Ivy was here, and she did the work, and I just stayed quiet. I was not a bit sick but so weak I couldn't walk without effort. Day before yesterday I started to perform again. I could not do a thing yesterday, and that is why we had to clean up the house today. By noon today I felt all right again.

Sunday night, September 3, 1928

We had a very fine county fair here this year. I enjoyed the visit we made there Friday afternoon. Our Star Club entered a community club display and got third in both size of exhibit and artistic display.

I wish you could have seen one farm display, Pater. It belonged to George Bullock, who lives north of town. He had a whole booth filled with things he grew in his own garden. He makes rather a specialty of market gardening, and he told me he had 62 different farm and garden products on display in his booth. He had ten different kinds of apples and crab apples, 2 kinds of currants, Veda grapes, gooseberries, plums, red raspberries, four kinds of cherries — compas, sand, Zumbra, and mountain cherries (not one of which is a real cherry, I might say); he also had string, shell, and lima beans, celery, lettuce, potatoes, kohlrabi, corn and pop corn, onions, rhubarb, tomatoes, melons, turnips, squashes, cucumbers, beets, parsley, parsnips, and cabbage. He had some Gano apples from last year's crop that were in perfect condition and just nice for eating. He said he had just kept them in his cellar on the farm, the same as we used to do when we lived on the farm near Evansville.

We have had a number of kinds of fruit from our little orchard this year—red raspberries, gooseberries, black and yellow currants, also red and white currants, and plums—Sapa and Opata. One of our apple trees is growing nicely now. From now on we should have all the black, yellow, red, and white currants we can use.

So you have a radio, Cora and Pater. Ted offered us his, but John said if Ted could get anything out of it, he'd better sell it. One reason we have never been terribly keen about having a radio is that John has to go to bed too early to get a great deal of benefit from it. However, the children are getting to the age now where they want one, or will pretty soon, so I suppose eventually we will have to get one. We have just put the idea away, in the past, for the reason that we felt we could not afford to spend money for a radio as long as we were so handicapped in the business by the lack of the rest of the shop, and we made up our minds that we would do without luxuries until after we had replaced the rest of the shop. The crop this year is the first one we have had since the shop burned that is at all like normal.

Tuesday, October 23, 1928

Anne is coming along fine with her broken arm. I'm not sure I told you the details—that she and Billy and Mary Alice Gimmeson were all riding one of their work horses down the hill, bareback, hanging on to each other, and that they all three slid off. She fell on the rocks and got what Dr. Graham called a "green stick" break—the bone in her lower arm just looking humped up and bent a little bit. Dr. Graham came and bandaged it heavily and put it in a sling. After Anne had gone to bed last night and the two other children and I were talking, I remarked, "Anne doesn't make any fuss at all about her arm, does she? I believe if it were either of you two that had the broken arm, you'd make three times as much." Jules was looking at a catalogue and pretty soon he looked up from the page and said, "Three times nothing is nothing." Then he resumed his catalogue study. Of course there was nothing for me to do but laugh too. I am afraid Jules will be a statistician when he is grown. I am glad to say that Anne's arm does not hurt her at all; in fact, you would never know it was hurt. She jumps and hops about in a way that would jar anybody else, and she can move her fingers and straighten them out without its hurting, and her hand is not the least bit swelled any more.

November 8, 1928

That is hard about Ted's having nothing definite in Trenton. You know, I think he really ought to look about, now that he is footloose, and get a try-out job in some large manufacturing establishment in the personnel department. With his perfect gift for letter writing, there is no reason why he shouldn't put it to account in writing letters in a claim department, and with his ability to handle men, he surely ought to be an A-1 man in that line. So I would earnestly suggest that he try out that line of work now and see if he would really care for it. With his Lions connections, he could pick out some big firm that really had oceans of work in claims, and get recommendations to give him a real position, not that of merely a clerk. If Ted waits a few months, I have no doubt whatever but that he will find some good opening in some western town, a really big town. So I wouldn't be worrying about losing time now, but take things as they come and play a little waiting game. Of course it is monotonous, but probably will pay in the long run.

November 11, 1928

Save a thing long enough and it is in style again. So, I see by the fashion notes that silk lace is the most stylish material of all this season for dinner and evening gowns. Don't you want your Spanish lace evening dress again? It certainly is a beauty.

I wore it last night to a dinner given by Dr. and Mrs. Perry J. Clark in honor of Dr. Crane, president of the state university.

He is here to give the Armistice Day address this morning. In spite of the fact that all the other ladies present had on high necked, long sleeved silk or wool dresses, I did not feel that I was not properly clad, for certainly a seven o'clock Sunday night dinner for the president of the state university is a place, if any, to wear a dinner dress. We had a lovely time. The guests were mostly Powell people, excepting Mrs. Pearson and her daughter from Clarks Fork. She was formerly assistant dean of women at the university and the daughter is a graduate. The others were Attorney and Mrs. Homer Mann, who were entertaining Dr. Crane at their home, state senator-elect and Mrs. R.A. Allan, Mr. and Mrs. W.A. Longley, Dr. and Mrs. Clark and their son Wynn, a graduate of the university, and I. John was invited but felt too all in to go. I hated to have him miss it but concluded he would be too tired to enjoy it, and that it would be no pleasure to him. He did go to bed about dark, as I found when I got home.

The dinner wasn't exactly a pure, unadulterated social affair, but had a raison d'etre. People from here have been greatly interested for some time in having a refund of traveling expenses — more properly, railroad fare, for students attending the state university. There used to be a regulation like that in force whereby all railroad fare over $15, I think it was, was refunded to the student. This made the university equally available to students all over the state. The result of the present situation is that students from here — 500 miles from Laramie — and from Sheridan and that part of the state, go to schools in other states that are nearer, either in miles or railroad fare. The bill was brought up at the last legislature but lost out. So we got Dr. Crane while we could, to find out what was the matter with the bill and what to do to make a new one that could pass. The university is very much in favor of such a bill, if it is properly prepared, and Dr. Crane offered to help in any way by revising or suggesting improvements on any bill we got up.

A freight train came in this morning about nine o'clock and John came in to tell the children that our new Ford was coming into the valley. Cecilia waited a while and then tried to call the Ford service station to see if the car had really come in, and what color it was, but could get no answer. Either they were all over at the freight yards, or else, it being Armistice Day, they were closed. You can guess that the children are greatly excited and can hardly wait. They can't see why we couldn't have got the car today while they had no school and are seriously considering staying home from school tomorrow to help get the car, if it is ready then. I'll let you know as soon as we hear anything definite about the car. The whole neighborhood is excited about our new car.

Friday, November 16, 1928

Dear Pater,

I have had a ride in the new car myself now. I certainly wish you could be here to ride with us. The car is such an easy riding one. The children exclaim all the way about how the bumps have been taken out of the road since we have the new car.

The other night when we were riding, I wish you could have heard the conversation. Jules said, "It just doesn't seem possible that Grandpa could have given us such a fine new car." John said, "No, it doesn't seem as if it really could be true." Jules said, "It seems just like a dream, or like something magic." John said, "It is a dream, but we are all dreaming the same thing."

Of course we all agreed that we hoped we would not wake up from the dream. We were anxious to know what color it would be. The two cars that had been delivered so far—Murray's and the American Legion's—are both a light green, and ours is too. We had much rather have had either a dark blue or an Arabian sand, but were glad to get any color just so we got the car. We have been quoting President Wilson's favorite limerick about "My face I don't mind it, for I am behind it, It's the folks out in front that I jar."

We went to church this morning in the new car and I drove it myself both ways. It is a beauty to drive. Of course I have to get used to the different driving, for in the new car you have to do just opposite with your feet that you did in the old Ford—in the old car you pushed in with your left foot to get more power, and in the new one you have to let the clutch come out to apply the power. However, I think I shall soon transfer my reflex action to my feet and have no trouble whatever in driving.

John says there is no reason why I shouldn't go anywhere I want to now, since I have a car of my own to drive. He had the bill of sale and all the papers made out in my name and jokes about "Mother's Car." Of course he is just as delighted as the rest of us and can hardly sit still and let some one else handle the wheel. In fact, he couldn't keep his hands off the gear shift and frequently would shift the gears before I could do so when I stopped the car or when I wanted to change the power.

Has Ted found anything yet worth taking? I am sure there are lots of places, if he can just get his finger on one. Our family fairies have seemed to be on the job so well that I am sure things will work out beautifully in the end. It isn't every man who can have his wife and children and likewise himself serve as a family benefactor while changing positions. You don't know how much relief and comfort it is to me to have Edith able to spend so much time at 822. I know how much comfort and relief it is to Cora and Pater to have you there. I have felt for a long time that it is too much for Co to have the house and her work, too, but there wasn't anything we could do about it, except to give her a kind thought occasionally. There never was a time, I reckon, when Co really needed some one more, or Pater needed company more. So you see everything seemed to come about right, and eventually will turn out in fine shape.

Do you remember the quotation you sent me, Edith, from Charles Cooley's "Life and the Student: Wayside Notes," that reads: "There are two conditions of success difficult to combine:

one the power to think clearly and decisively at the right time, the other the power to leave things undecided, without worry, at other times." That seems to fit right now, doesn't it? So take your time and keep your eyes open, but don't be in too big a hurry. All of us are so glad you can stay at 822 this winter and be company for Pater and a help for Cora.

November 24, 1928

I think I have been away from home more in the past ten days since the new car came than in the past ten weeks before that. It certainly is fine to be able to do the things you want to. Of course I have done in the past ten days all the things I wanted to do for months and couldn't because I had no good way to go. I visited Cecilia's school and have invited the teachers out for dinner Monday night, six of them. I also called on Mrs. Marschall, wife of our new high school principal. She graduated from Indiana in 1917.

Tuesday, December 11, 1928

I am enclosing a clipping from the Wyoming *Eagle*, the state Democratic paper, that may be of interest to you. Of course you never know what a governor will do about an appointment, but it would be right nice to be on the board of trustees of the university, wouldn't it? Both the Republican and the Democratic Park County committees have written to the governor urging my appointment, the State Democratic Committee has been doing some work, and both Republicans and Democrats in the Big Horn Basin have written Gov. Emerson. The women's clubs have also written him. As long as you were in the state, Edith, I felt that any appointment from a Republican governor should go to you, but since you are away, I am a perfect Barkis. And of course, since there are Democratic members to be appointed, naturally I am desirous that there be Democratic candidates. No use letting the governor think no one but a Republican wants it. No, of course I have said nothing to the governor myself. But my good friends apparently have used up a good deal of postage.

I had a letter yesterday from Mr. John Cook of Cody which interested and amused me very much, in regard to the university trustee appointment. Senator Cook enclosed a letter from Governor Emerson which read, "Dear Senator Cook: I am pleased to acknowledge receipt of your letter of December 3, whereby you endorse Mrs. Cecilia Hendricks of Powell for appointment as a Trustee of the University of Wyoming, to fill the vacancy caused by the death of Mrs. Haggard. If circumstances were different, I would be glad to give Mrs. Hendricks consideration for appointment to this position, as I am convinced she is well qualified to discharge the duties encumbent upon a Trustee. However, the fact that Mr. J.M. Schwoob of Cody is at this time a member of the Board seems to make her selection illogical, in that it would mean a second member from the same county. Thanking you for your interest in the matter, I am, Sincerely yours, Frank C. Emerson, Governor."

Now what tickled me was the note Mr. Cook enclosed, which says, "This letter from the Governor is just what I expected and in no way prevents him from further consideration of your application. Anyway we can still hope for the best and do all we can. Judge Fourts from Lander is here holding court. Is a good friend of mine and close to the Governor. I helped in forming the judicial district that gave him the judgeship. I was talking to him yesterday and he told me he would write to the Governor regarding you and the appointment. Also I will see Howard Bell again to be sure he did not forget to write, for that kind of endorsement counts. Very truly yours, John F. Cook."

Whereby you will see that Senator Cook is not only a good politician but a good Democrat, who does not expect to get what he goes after the first time he asks for it. I suppose if this were a bread-and-butter matter, I would take it more seriously, but as it is, I see the humor in the situation.

I feel as if I am about to begin a serial that will last for many issues. At least, to tell you how much we have enjoyed (already) the contents of the wonderful box we opened this morning, and how much we shall continue to enjoy them, would take a serial article.

I don't see how I can write enough to tell you all about it. In the first place, your boxes from 822 and Greybull are always the official Christmas boxes. Since both came together this year, the huge box was a perfect marvel.

We had a wonderful day. Everything was perfect. Everybody felt fine and we had loads of fun, now that we all are over the flu. Of course the children were ready about five-thirty this a.m. to get their stockings, but they went back to bed with them and did not really get up till about six, when the house was warm. All the things we had for each other and that "Santa Claus" brought, were in or tied to the stockings at the fireplace. The packages from 822 and elsewhere we saved for the grand opening later. By six-thirty the children couldn't wait any longer for me to come to see what was in my stocking, so of course I rolled out. I would have to be deaf and blind not to have known what was going on for the past few weeks, but of course I was much surprised to receive a pair of sport galoshes from John, a pyrex dish from Cecilia and a much needed address book she had made me, and a china bowl from Jules. Jules got his greatly desired football, and Anne a little dustpan that is the joy of her life. It is ten-thirty, or later, and as I have been up since six-thirty this a.m., I must remain.

Before I start to town I'll write you a few lines. I have to go in tonight for a meeting with the local state senator and representative about the student refund bill the local federated club hopes to get through the coming legislature. It will refund all railway fare to students of the state university except $10, on one round trip each year, or one trip during the summer to attend summer school. This, you will see, puts each student within about 250 miles of the university.

Fifteen years ago tonight John and I were on our way to Evansville at this time. My, it does not seem like fifteen years ago that we were married. I can't figure up how it can be more than about ten years since I came west. But when I look at the size of Cecilia, I am convinced. She is getting so big.

I must get ready now and go to town. I'd rather stay home, but as this meeting has been postponed before when I couldn't go, I must go this time. Happy New Year to you all.

January 18, 1929

I had a nice surprise the other day. The St. Louis Press Reporting Syndicate has a contest in which it offers prizes for the best letters telling why and how you benefitted from their instruction. Of course I sent one in, quite a while ago, and as I had never heard anything after many months, I forgot about it. The other day I got a $5 check as third prize. I think the children were even more delighted. They have been wanting skates all winter, but we have been too close run to spare the money for them. As soon as this unexpected check came, I told them they could have the skates, and we sent for them right away.

I checked up the other day on the receipts from my newspaper work during the past year. I got $249.35 from the Billings *Gazette* and $150 from the Casper paper, which totals 65¢ less than $400 for the two for my year's news, or more than a dollar a day. This and John's pension have kept us going the past year, for our 1927 honey crop was so small we would have been up against it a good many more times than we were if it had not been for the monthly news and pension checks. The 1928 crop was pretty good, but we are trying to pay off as much as we can at the bank and the monthly checks will keep us going.

We had a real blizzard yesterday. The wind began blowing Saturday morning and drifted the old snow everywhere. We had to shovel to get to town Saturday afternoon, the wind having drifted shut tracks made only a couple hours before. Saturday night was worse, and then yesterday morning the wind blew really hard and about noon it began to snow in great clouds. You couldn't see any distance at all, it "snew" so hard. I don't know how many inches fell, but enough to cover the ground several inches deep everywhere, in spite of all the snow that went into the drifts, that are the worst we have ever known here. The school board decided the school trucks could not get through today and called off school. The truck drivers can go through their routes empty today and break the road for tomorrow. The drifts just north of this house and the old house are three feet deep in many places. Over at the corner toward Gimmeson's there is a long drift even deeper than that. At Lovercheck's corner the road was drifted shut, and also between Lovercheck's and Werts'. The east and west roads are simply impassable everywhere, and the north and south ones bad enough. The road to Deaver is blocked just north of Garland, over the top of the hill near the coal mine. The road to Elk Basin is closed now until someone digs through. The road to Cody is passable, but three-foot drifts in many places make pretty slow going and cause a lot of trouble to cars. A truck that left Casper Friday got to Powell yesterday — Sunday — taking about three times as long as usual to make the trip. So you see we are for once having the kind of weather that most folk think we have in Wyoming all the time during the winter months.

The children are building a snow fort in the drift toward Gimmeson's on our field. They simply dig out, as for a cave, and don't have to pile up at all. The sun is bright and warm this morning and now at noon it is up to 15 below. You probably won't believe it, but the snow on the south slopes of the roofs is melting and dripping from the eaves.

Whenever there is no school, as today, our house seems to be the gathering place for the entire neighborhood. Saturday the Gillett and Gimmeson children were here, and today the Gimmesons worked with our youngsters in making the snow fort, and now the whole bunch is busy in the kitchen making candy. As whatever amount they make of any kind of candy is eaten up at once as soon as cool enough, I general limit the amount of sugar to be used in cooking the candy.

No one from here got to Sunday school yesterday, so we had it at home. We all studied a lesson from Cecilia's quarterly, with Jules looking up all the geography matters in the atlas. The lesson was the visit of the Queen of Sheba to Solomon, involving quite a journey, which gave plenty of geographical references. Cecilia played for us and we sang "Brighten the Corner," "Jesus Loves Me," etc. Then we read a sermon from the book of children's sermons you sent, Co, and let Rodeheaver, etc. do the rest of the singing on the victrola. I am quite sure the children learned as much — maybe more — than if we had gone to town.

February 3, 1929

I have just written Ted a letter at Greybull. I thought maybe he might be glad to hear from some one in this part of the country, to let him know we are glad he is back in our midst.*

We got an advance payment of $1307.60 on our carlot shipments of honey Friday and will be rich for a few days. We have been busy all afternoon writing letters and addressing envelopes containing the checks John wrote all last evening, and will pay the rest of the money on a note at the bank, so you see our affluence is short lived. The checks we are now sending out are for life insurance premiums, veterinary bill, hay grinding, interest, Literary Digest, and "sichlike." However, we are delighted to be able to pay up our bills, even if the money does depart faster than it came. If you have any bills to present to this firm, you'd better get them in pretty soon, while we are solvent. It may be several months until we get any more payments on the two cars of honey we shipped out.

---

*Ted's job prospects in New Jersey didn't materialize; he and Edith were considering moving back west.

February 20, 1929

Every time I think of how Ted can pick up business when he is there in person, I have to hand him another bouquet. But of course he could not do it where he was a stranger. His being able to do it is a result of his having proved his ability in the past ten years to the people there. I really think he ought to hold on to the business in Greybull to the extent of being there in person every little while so that people will realize it is still his ability that is looking after their interests. I rather think he would like to live in Greybull again, from what I gathered while he was here last week. He seems to like it best of any place he has known.

You are right about funeral services in small towns. They are barbaric. How the family sits there and listens (but maybe they don't listen!) to the ordinary funeral sermon without going mad is more than I can see. If the sermon is good, it is harrowing, and if it is bad, it hurts their feelings not to have a nice service. The thing that gets me, though, is their having to sit there while the undertaker ushers the whole church full of people past the coffin and then for the family to walk to their autos with the whole crowd watching them. It always seems to me it would show more respect and consideration if the audience would get into their own cars and let the mourners come out unwatched.

March 3, 1929

I assure you, Edith, that I did not encourage Ted just to settle down in Greybull and not look elsewhere. Now that he is foot loose he ought to run down every possibility. I urged him to go to Boulder and to Montana to see what possibilities there were in those places. But at the same time I do think he should hold on to the Greybull office until he is sure it is on a paying basis. With $4,000 worth of assets there, he can't afford to let things go without making sure he will get his money out of it, for he has worked ten years to earn the assets he has there. What I urged Ted to do was to try to find a place close enough that he could go to Greybull every few months and make sure that the office was being run right. Ted said that if he could be assured of the $50 a month regularly from the Greybull office he would not be afraid to start in anywhere and go through the necessary building up period, but that without some steady income he did not want to take his family to a new place without pretty good assurance that he could make a living from the beginning. And of course a new lawyer in a town can not pick up business right off. He has to make contacts and prove his ability as Ted has done in Greybull. That is why I said, and why I think Ted should continue to spend as much time as necessary in Greybull in the next year or two to train McHale properly.

Tuesday, March 5, 1929

The chinook blows and the snow is fast melting. In many places now the ground is bare, but the heavy drifts are merely sinking. Even so, the drift that runs from the gate into the pasture here at the house is still several feet deep. It was more than three feet deep—four feet in places—for about six weeks. We have not driven along the driveway to the north door of the garage all winter but around the east end of the old house and then into the garage from the front of the old house. Today was the first day for about three months that we could let the chickens out of the chicken house. They were glad to be out and chased everywhere, singing and cackling. I hope the exercise produces some eggs.

Thursday, March 7, 1929

I had a letter from Ted yesterday. Says he made a splendid buy in a Chevrolet coupe. John had some chains off our old car he offered Ted if he could use them and Ted said he'd be glad to have them if they would fit the Chevy. Ted also said he's cleaned up all the mess McHale had got the firm into and that he'd been too busy even to think of future plans until he got all the things there straightened out. He certainly has done a Herculean job since he landed in Greybull.

Sunday night, March 17, 1929

The children were very much delighted when I went to Sunday school with the family this morning. They seemed to think it quite an occasion. They told me everybody would stop, look, and listen when I arrived, but I assured them I did not think myself or my presence or absence so important. This is the first time I went to Sunday school since last fall, I think! When I am so tired and miserable as I have been so much this winter, it does me more good to stay at home all alone while the rest of the family goes rather than to hustle around to get things done and ready, and then be in a crowd at the church. One really does not learn a great deal from the class discussion that he could not get by studying the lesson at home by himself.

March 27, 1929

Ted told me last week when he called that he expected to get away from Greybull before long to go to Boulder to look things over there. He will be so glad to have you with him again. He has been so lonesome. It gets rather monotonous to work all the time and have no one to talk with. I think that is why he called me up last week — he wanted some one to talk to.

Friday morning, April 12, 1929

Again I take my carbon in hand to write two letters at once. It is a long time since I have done that. We are all glad that Ted has found an opening that seems worth taking up, and in such a fine place to live as Boulder. Ted and Edith, I hope you find everything works out lovely and that you find just the kind of house you want at the price you want to pay. Let me know if there is anything here you want. Come up as soon as you can and stay as long as you can. We have about a year's talking to do, you know.

Our diptheria prevention clinic was a great success, we think. About 300 school children and 100 children below school age took the serum. We had to do some tall stepping to get that done, as when the state health officer arrived he informed us he had to go on to Cody that same afternoon instead of staying here all day as we had planned. We got Dr. Mills and Dr. Clark to look after the afternoon hours as we had announced pre-school children and adult hours from 2:30 to 4:30, and could not change that, as we had no way to let people know. Next week, for the second clinic, we have planned it all in the morning. The work was muchly complicated because last week a family here broke out with small pox after having been in school, in town, and every where over the country, thinking they had the chicken pox. So the local health officer declared all school children would have to be vaccinated for small pox, and that was done at the same time and place as our diptheria vaccination. Next week we won't have this extra confusion.

Last Wednesday we went to the American Legion banquet and I gave a talk on Paul V. McNutt.* People really seemed to enjoy it very much. I told of his high school and college work and said practically nothing of his military career, for of course the Legion paper has had that. I tried to tell the personal interest things that biographies leave out. For instance, I told of his little girl's illness, which no one seemed to know about. Mrs. McKemey told me the child's picture has been in the Legion paper but she had no idea such a pretty, bright looking child was an invalid. I summed up by giving as the reasons for Paul's success his handsome appearance, his bright mind, his magnetic personality, and his hard work. Of course I told them he was the best bluffer that ever went to I.U. and

---

*McNutt was the national commander of the American Legion and later governor of Indiana and high commissioner of the Philippines.

that a person who did as much out-of-class activity naturally couldn't always be prepared and had to bluff sometimes. I told them how he would persuade me to serve as prompter for Strut and Fret after I had decided I wouldn't spend the time again doing it. I said some people called him a snob because he often paid little attention to people until he wanted something and then was so nice you couldn't refuse, but that men who accomplish things usually have to concentrate on their own interests. I told them about having prompted for the plays and that therefore I could truthfully say that I used to tell their national commander what to say. Of course that got a laugh, as did the part about his being such a good bluffer. As for the presidency of Michigan, I quoted an Associated Press report of recent date in which McNutt said he would accept the presidency if offered. I thought that was perfectly safe to say.

Thursday, May 16, 1929

Have you ever heard the words of "The Prisoner's Song" that has been so popular the past few years? Cecilia borrowed a copy from one of the girls and the children sing it endlessly. Do you remember the old maid who sat weeping at the grave of a child because she was thinking how sad she would feel if she married and had a baby and it died? Well, I am sure that the prisoner is that baby grown up, and after reading his maudlin words one can't help being sorry the old maid's fears were not realized. The song starts out:

> Oh! I wish I had some one to love me,
> Some one to call me their own,
> Oh! I wish I had someone to live with
> For I'm tired of living alone.

After begging some one — anybody — to meet him in the moonlight to hear his sad story, that never has been told, he ends:

> Now if I had the wings like an angel
> Over these prison walls I would fly,
> And straight to the arms of my darling,
> And there I'd be willing to die."

Inasmuch as the whole thing starts out wishing for some one to love, the darling is evidently like the old maid's child. Verily, the great American desert is well located by O'Henry, or else why should a song with no more sense than that sweep the whole country and be so popular. Of course the music has a sad note that saxophones can moan out perfectly. That may have something to do with the popularity.

Wednesday, May 22, 1929

Monday night we had our new minister, Reverend Wills, out for supper and the evening. He is a dear fellow, nice as can be. Anne fairly fell in love with him and he with her. From the first time she saw him she kept remarking what a sweet face he has. He is 28 years old, just graduated a few weeks ago from McCormick. He is an English boy, from Northhampton. His father was killed in the World War when he was about 14 years old. He came to this country when he was sixteen, telling his mother he would stay here two years and earn a thousand dollars to come back to England to go to college to study for the ministry. He has been here ever since. He went to high school and college in Ohio and to Chicago for the last two years of the seminary training. He is going back to England the first of July for a two month's visit and hopes to bring his mother and younger sister and brother back with him when he comes.

Sunday night, June 9, 1929

If you want to read a perfectly darling book, read "Messer Marco Polo" by Donn Byrne. It is supposed to be the story about Marco Polo told by an old Irishman. The Irish constructions in the story are perfectly lovely. There is a passage in the book that describes the effect the whole book has on the reader. Marco Polo is talking about Venice and its beauty, and he says, "One summer's day...I took out my little boat and went out on the water to compose a poem for a lady, and the water was blue—oh, as blue as the sky's self, and the sands of the

Lido were silver, and the water shuffled gently over them, as gently as a child's little feet. And there was a clump of olive trees there so green as to be black, and there alighted before it a great scarlet Egyptian bird. And the beauty of that brought tears to my eyes." The book is like that scene—the beauty of it brings tears to your eyes. It has a keen undercurrent, too. Marco Polo goes to convert the people of Kubla Khan's regions to Christianity, sent specifically by the Pope, at the request of the Khan. The only convert Polo makes is the girl there, the daughter of the Khan, who falls in love with Polo. The effect of the appearance of Christianity on the Chinese is wonderfully told. The comparison of the virtues of the Christian and other religions is so well done. The Pope does not expect Polo to make converts when he sends him. "Now in the matter of converting the Great Khan and his numerous millions—I have little hopes," the Pope says to Polo. "The Khan wants to be argued into it, you see. Religion is not a matter of argument. It is a wisdom that surpasses wisdom. It drifts in man's souls as the foggy dew comes unbidden to the trees. It is born before our soul, as the horned moon is born before our eyes. And now, my child, you might say, what is the use of sending me to China if he knows I can not bring these millions into the fold? My dear son, there is the wisdom surpassing wisdom. A great and noble thought must not die. Things of the spirit we can not reckon as a husbandman reckons his crops....Now you'll think it's the queer Pope I am to be telling you things like this instead of demanding converts....I will not keep you any longer, only to say this, and this is the chiefest thing: Never let your dream be taken from you, your dream of beauty."

Co, do you see the *Weekly Unity*? There was an article in the children's day number that I simply shouted at. The article told a number of remarks made by children to an old lady who was a sort of confidante of the whole community—not a regular healer, but a helper of the whole town, who was always preaching the principles of Unity. The particular story that struck me so keenly was about ducks. This woman had some ducks, whom she says she trained to do as she told them simply by expecting them to do it. One day the ducks got out of their pen and started toward the front gate. She went to the door and called, "Where do you ducks think you are going? You'd better come right back where you belong." The ducks knew her voice and came back. Some children were playing in her yard and heard what she said. She overheard their comments. One child, who apparently was not from the neighborhood, said, "Why she talked to those ducks nicer than my mother often talks to me, and they understood just what she meant. Those ducks must understand English." Whereupon another child, a neighbor girl, replied, "Of course they do. Do you suppose Mrs. W. would have dumb ducks? Why she believes in universal intelligence!" I think the story will be much comfort to me. I sometimes get discouraged over the way the children don't come up to what I think they should and wonder if they are really as bright as I think they should be. But now I'll just say to myself, "Of course they are. Do you think I'd have dumb kids? Why of course not. I believe in universal intelligence." And when I get a pain somewhere, I'll say, "Do you think I'd have a dumb body that has something wrong with it? Of course not. I believe in universal intelligence." Incidentally, I hope I have enough of that intelligence myself to use a plentiful supply.

Thursday, June 13, 1929

After having firmly refused to be a delegate to the state P.E.O. convention, behold me now expecting to go. But there is a difference, I think, in going to represent your own chapter as a delegate and going to serve as a state officer, with all your expenses paid. The state recording secretary can not go to the convention and the state president wrote to me asking if I would serve in her place. Some women work for years to get on the list of state officers, and here it is handed out to me, without any great desire on my part to be one.

Anne is taking music lessons. She has learned to play so many tunes with one finger that I thought she ought to know something of the proper way to play, even if she is only five.

She learned the first lesson, which uses both hands, but only one at a time, in less than no time, and now knows three exercises in less than a week. I don't think a child of her age makes much headway, but she might as well know the proper method. I thought I'd have her take lessons until she starts school in the fall. Of course if she turns out to be an infant prodigy (!) we may scare up the money to have her take lessons right along, but I suspect it won't be necessary, although she is unusually good at it.

> *The Ranger Hotel*
> *Lusk, Wyoming*
> *Wednesday, 7 a.m., June 19, 1929*

I am sure there is no one at this convention who has more clothes or more good looking ones, thanks to Edith's generosity, and your good taste, Cora, in helping her pick out the contents of her wardrobe. I had to laugh (to myself, of course) when Mrs. Loy, a past state president, gave me a message to send Edith in response to Edith's greeting to her. She inquired about how E & E like Boulder and then said, "Well, you tell her that her mantle has now descended on you, since she is out of the state." I thought to myself, "Madam, it wasn't just the mantle — it was the whole wardrobe!"

I know you will be interested in knowing that I was elected to the office of state recording secretary. My name was nominated for some of the other offices, but there is a rule that to be president, any vice president, or organizer of the state chapter one must have been president of her own chapter. I have not, so I was not eligible to those offices. I haven't time to tell you all the praise I got for my work as secretary of the meeting. I had my minutes all typed at the beginning of each session, even just over noon, so that the minutes of the last session could be read and approved each time at the beginning of the following session.

We have about 15,000 pounds of honey in our warming room now and have about 10,000 pounds ready to come in as soon as there is room for it. The honey flow is practically over in this locality now. We had quite a frost last night and the temperature fell as low as 26. It looks as though the crop might be pretty close to 60,000 this season.

September 11, 1929

We can hardly believe yet that you have both actually been here, Pater and Cora. It was such a joy to see you and have you here. We hope you will come every summer now, and plan to stay all summer. It certainly gives Cora a chance to get enough strength to go on with her work. She has about three jobs to carry on all the time, and that takes a lot of strength to do. We don't see how you do all you accomplish, Cora. Only about one woman in a thousand could do it. I don't believe I could. Pater, you should have stayed a while longer, for the weather is getting nicer every day. Today is a regular Indian summer day, and the sun is almost too warm to stay out in. I hope you had a nice visit with Edith. I am so glad she has a big, nice house to live in now.

September 22, 1929

Uncle Joe Sweeten is improving rapidly. One doctor still insists he did not have cancer at all and has every chance of complete recovery. Joe expects to go back to work the first of November. The company will give him a pleasant, light job in the distilling house where they distill all the water for their operation at Elk Basin.

Sunday night, September 29, 1929

I am glad this past week is over. I don't want too many like it. We had company from Friday till Tuesday. Wednesday afternoon I had to entertain the Powell Presbyterian Aid, and as there was a canned food shower for the minister's bride, we had a large crowd. Thursday afternoon our Federated Club had the reception for Miss Eells, at which eleven women's clubs joined. Friday I was invited out for the afternoon, but declined. I did a little washing in the morning, took Anne to school when she missed the bus, went to Garland, and did some canning. Saturday I also canned, baked, and various other things. Every chance I had during the week I canned — tomatoes, pears, and tomato and pear preserves. I have at last finished the main part of the canning. I don't know exactly how many cans I did can during the past week, but in the past ten days I have put up 30 cans of pears, 40 of tomatoes, a gallon or so of peach preserves, the same of tomato preserves, and a gallon and a half of pear preserves. Just before that I put up 60 quarts of peaches, so you see you can come to see us this winter and be sure of something to eat. This past week's work wouldn't have seemed so heavy if I had not had another spell of flowing, and for two days really felt weaker than the proverbial cat.

I was tickled at Anne when she missed the bus. She was taking a bath, and had plenty of time, as she dawdled along for more than half an hour. I guess the bus was a little early, but anyway, as Anne was sitting by the fire with her birthday dress on, and her union suit in her hands ready to put it on, Jules announced that the bus was at Gimmeson's corner. The two older children grabbed their lunches and ran. Anne looked too funny for words, sitting there almost speechless, with one foot in her underwear. She simply couldn't do a thing, as she couldn't get ready in time. I told her I would take her, but I had to write a letter for John and get out some news before I could go, as I had to make the morning train with the mail. Anne got scared she would be tardy, and pretty soon began to cry. She had finished dressing, even to her hat and coat, in record time. I thought it wouldn't do any harm to let her cry a bit, even when she said the other children would tease her for missing the bus. She decided for a while she was sick — her tummy hurt, she said — and she guessed she'd better not try to go to school at all! But when I got my typing done, I took her and she was on time, of course. I have an idea after this she won't play around so getting dressed.

The Baptist women's society gave a play two nights last week, put out under the direction of a representative of the Universal Producing Company of Fairfield, Iowa. The woman came here for a little more than a week and trained the bunch. It was a large cast—about a hundred people. The play was mighty poor, and the stage setting absolutely nil. I suppose the trainer concentrated on the lines that had to be spoken, but a little work on scenery would have helped tremendously.

I understand that the local organization got half the profits and the producing company the other half. The play was put on two nights and netted, I heard, $300. So the Baptist ladies paid $150 for the work the representative did. Well, that's a good deal of money to give away. I know I could write a better play and train the cast as well or better, and I know I could have some real stage effects.

I was much edified to hear one of the Baptist ladies tell what the director had insisted on for success. One thing was that they have a large crowd of children in the play, so all their families would buy tickets. Another was to get as many of the prominent business men as possible to get that crowd interested. Another was to have the leads in the play taken by the most prominent young people and to have these young people also in the choruses. The thing to avoid was to confine the cast to any one organization or group, but to draw from every part of the community. If I do go ahead and make up a play for the P.E.O.'s, I shall observe all the above rules! But I shall certainly see to it that all these people are in acts that are connected with the main plot of the play and contribute something to the working out of the plot.

John said the other day that if he gets done extracting this week, and the weather stays nice, we would take a trip somewhere to celebrate the finish of the season. The children have been wanting all year to go to Billings, so I think that is where we'll go if the weather is fit, a week from next Saturday. John suggested a trip up South Fork, above Cody, as we have never been very far up that way, but the bright lights of the city held such attraction for the children — though it was really the dime shop — that they would not hear to another rural trip, having had so many of these during the summer.

We expect to hear our first "talkie" tomorrow night. We had thought all sumer we would go to Billings some time for a talkie, but now that the Powell theatre has installed the talking pictures we do not have to go to Billings to hear them. The first one was on tonight, but we never go to the movie on Sunday, just as a matter of principle. The play for tonight and tomorrow is "The Drag," being the story of a young newspaper man who against his desire found himself married to his employer's daughter, with her entire family attached. The play is on his attempt to shake them loose, and is said to be full of funny lines and scenes.

October 20, 1929

Aren't women funny? I don't know which are queerer, men or women, but I sometimes think the women get the palm. The other week when I had to look after the Chamber of Commerce dinner, I planned a regular man meal. The salad was to be plain lettuce and tomato, just a nice crisp lettuce leaf with several large slices of tomato, and the salad dressing passed separately. After it was ready it looked lovely. Then the women wanted to know why not put the pretty salad dressing on the red and green, as the yellow looked so pretty with the two other colors. I said I did not think many cared for the dressing. One woman, the president of the Aid, said her husband would not eat it if it had dressing on, as he never used anything but sugar on his fresh tomatoes, but she thought the colors were so pretty together we should put the dressing on anyhow. Can you beat it! I notice that her husband did not eat any salad at all, but pushed it aside because he could not eat the dressing. Another objection they raised to serving the dressing separately was that the men never passed things, and just set the dish down without seeing that the next fellow got any. I had the idea that the reason we had waitresses was to see that everybody was served, but when the president and the other older women insisted on putting the salad dressing on the salad, of course I said no more and let them go ahead. But it seems to me that if I knew what my husband liked, I'd try to get it for him, and if I knew what he particularly did not like, I'd not try to force him to eat it, or waste it.

Monday afternoon, October 28, 1929

We certainly chose the right time to make our trip to Billings. Saturday was a gorgeous day, lovely and warm, with enough clouds to keep the sun from being too glaring. Yesterday afternoon a storm blew down, and we were surely glad we were not on the road then. The roads were perfect, except for a good deal of dust where there was beet hauling.

The children had the time of their lives. We spent a lot of time in Hart Albins, the ten cent store, Mont. Wards, and the Sawyer grocery. We had dinner at the Princess, and the youngsters all thought they never tasted anything so good as the halibut, roast pork, and veal with vegetables we had there, not to mention bean soup with tomatoes in it, and real French buns with crust half an inch thick. Of course the most fun was the Woolworth store, where we spent two whole hours. Anne summed it up by saying there were just too many things to see. I bought a lot of Christmas gifts for youngsters here, and am delighted to have the articles all ready, which will save much time and thought later on. I struck some good bargains at Hart Albins. I read their ad in the paper before we started and found they had a sale on children's flannelette pajamas, which was what Anne and Jules needed. I had some goods already bought to make some, but when I found I could get lovely one-piece ones with drop seats for 48 cents a suit, you may be sure I invested. I also struck a bargain counter of odds and ends, where I got some 65 cent white charmeuse bloomers for 19 cents, and lovely, lace-trimmed, ribbon-drawn, one-piece underwear for children at the same price. These suits were marked 98¢ and are lovely. I shall use some of them for Christmas gifts, too. We were disappointed in not being able to get Jules a suit. Hart Albins advertised 4-piece suits for boys — a coat, vest, long and short pants — in broken sizes, for only $3.69. But when we got there they had nothing in his size, having sold the last one of size 11 just before we arrived.

John has just gone to Garland with the wax that has been rendered from this season's crop. Now that he has shipped it, the season's work is all done except finishing packing some of the bees for winter. The wax comes from the cappings that are cut off when the honey is extracted. We should have eight or nine hundred dollars' worth of the wax this year and hope to have more than enough to pay for the supplies we need. We ship the wax to Dadant & Sons at Hamilton, Ill., and get from them the foundation and other supplies we need for next season.

I went to a quilting party yesterday, but not Aunt Dinah's. It was at Mrs. Werts'. She had two quilts she wanted quilted, so she furnished the dinner for the E.E.E. Club and the Aid, and the ladies did the quilting. Both quilts were what is called postage stamp quilts, in which the blocks of cloth used are the size of an ordinary postage stamp. Fancy cutting that many pieces and then sewing them all together again!

At the quilting party Mrs. Gillett got to telling about what happened once when she went east for a visit, leaving Mr. G. and their five sons at home. The boys ranged in age from 8 to 20 years. One of them was a good cook, so she did not worry about leaving them. A week after she left, he broke his arm and had to go stay with a neighbor to have it cared for. One day the two older boys wanted cake. She had left simple recipes, one for a one-egg cream cake. They not only decided to bake a cake, but to run a race to see who could bake the most in the shortest time. To have oven room for their contest, they used both oil stove and range. Before they stopped, they had baked *nine* cakes, and baked them in all sorts and kinds of pans. There wasn't room to turn them out on the table, so they had them on chairs all over the kitchen. It was summer time and they got so hot they opened up everything they could, including a door on which there was no screen. When their last cake was out of the oven, they went out into the yard to play baseball and cool off, forgetting all about the door without a screen. When they came back in, the kitchen was full of chickens and there was not a crumb left of their nine cakes.

The house caught fire three times while Mrs. G. was away. Once might have been pretty serious. Mr. G. and the older boys went to chautauqua, leaving the 9 and 11-year-olds at home alone one evening. As it got dark, the boys lighted a lamp. They set it on a chair beside their bed so they could read. It was a very hot night and they went to bed without the formality of a nightie, there being no mother around to see they observed the proprieties. After a while it got cool, as Wyoming nights often do in summer, and they pulled up some cover. Still later they awoke to find the lamp turned over and the room on fire. The rug on the floor was burned, the curtains were burned from the window, the part of the cover that hung over the side of the bed was burned, and the top of the cover over them was aflame, but it was filled with wool, which kept it from burning through. The boys kicked off the cover, chased out of the house and down the road to the nearest house, a quarter of a mile away. The people there had just driven into the yard, coming from chautauqua, as the boys ran into the yard. The boys shouted their news and then, not wishing to lose the excitement, started back toward their house while the neighbor turned his car around and went, without waiting for anybody to get out of the car. The two little boys had a slight start, and they kept ahead of the car all the way down the road the quarter of a mile. The neighbor's wife said that if the whole country had burned, she would still have laughed at the sight of those two little figures, absolutely naked, chasing down the road ahead of the car with the full glare of the headlights on them all the way. Isn't that a peach of a story? I think I'll have to write it up into a real story, to show what happens when mother goes away from home. You couldn't ask for better material.

Monday, November 25, 1929

We went to Gimmeson's Friday night to listen to their radio and hear Mina sing in the Atwater Kent competition but they could not get the station in very well.* So we hitched up the Ford and drove down to Werts to see what their radio would do. We finally got the contest all right and heard five or six girls sing. As there apparently were 19, we missed more than we got. At least we heard No. 19, so assumed there were that many. We thought we heard Mina but were not sure.

Heretofore we have never been very anxious for a radio of our own, but lately all of us have wanted a radio very much. I have wanted to wait till we could get an electric like yours, but it seems there is no hope of getting electricity for a good while to come [and our electric plant won't work a radio]. The company that wants to put in the lines here is taking a year or two, it looks like, to make a complete survey of the entire project, and goodness only knows when they will be ready to deliver the juice. What would you think, Pater, of getting a cheap Sears Roebuck battery radio in the meantime? Mr. Werts has one and it certainly gives splendid service. He gets stations all over the western half of the U.S. and yesterday had Cincinnati. When there is anything really worth wanting from the eastern stations, there is a national hook up, and he can get the program from some station in the west. He gets Chicago, Texas, and Pacific coast stations all the time, and practically everything in between. The church services broadcast from Shreveport, La., are always extra good, and he gets that station regularly. So I should think a radio of that type would give plenty of service, don't you, as long as one has to use batteries. We can keep our storage battery charged along with our light plant batteries, and be sure of good working order and plenty of battery current in that way.

---

*Mina Sweeten was now a music student at Indiana University, where she was selected to compete in the national Atwater Kent vocal competition. Her brother Joseph had attended Indiana earlier, receiving his B.S. in Business in 1926.

I see by the paper that Mina did not win out at Chicago. The *Gazette* said yesterday that a girl from Ohio was ahead, but that as the last girl got shut off before she finished, because the radio time was up, they would have a sing-off soon in Ohio, since both were from that state. Well, even if Mina did not get to go to New York, she made a fine record and I should think winning the state audition will be of help to her in her future work.

I got a letter from the Billings *Gazette* yesterday saying they were changing the plan of news from out-of-town communities and wanted to pay a regular salary each month instead of by-the-inch according to news published. They have listed this community as a $15 one for news service and want to know if that will be acceptable to me. Inasmuch as they will do what they please about paying for news, of course it has to suit me. I used to get $30 and $35 a month, but since there has been a change in managing editors they don't use all that I send. But if they send $15 and the Casper paper $14, I can earn enough for gasoline all right, and an occasional pair of shoes for the children. And that is a great help, I'll tell you, when honey is lower in price than we have been expecting. Our return on the 1928 honey pool is about $500 less than we had expected, and the price on the 1929 probably won't be as high as we were led to think from earlier reports.

We can all hardly wait till the radio comes. The children ask many times each day when it will be here, and all I can say is that they know as much about it as I do. They know John does not like jazz, and the other night they had a discussion as to whether or not we would ever tune in for such music. They thought they would tire of always hearing classical stuff, and I told them of course we would want to hear all kinds of music, but that we would probably find that a small amount of jazz would go a long way. They were pleased to know they could try it out when they wanted to, and I have an idea they will be the first to tune in for something different after a little of the noise. Familiarity breeds contempt; if they couldn't have it, they would want it.

So, your letter today was a complete surprise as regards my coming to Bloomington this winter. I had not thought about it at all. When you left Pater said as you had both been here so late in the summer I would not need to come this winter. So I had not considered going at all. I hardly know what to say. John says, though, that if it will give Pater pleasure for Anne and me to come, we had better go for a short time at least. So if you really want us to come, we'll do so. Do you think we could manage to stay about a month so as not to leave the folk here alone so long?

Cecilia and Jules want us to go, and they do not. Cecilia of course would not want to miss school to make a trip herself, so she has no feelings on that score. But she hates for me to be away very much while she is in the last half of the 8th grade, for she says she can do much better work when I am here to help her at home, and she is trying so hard to be on the honor roll when the class graduates in the spring. Poor Jules feels quite deserted. He wept over the matter, for he would like to go too! He says he just doesn't know when he will ever get to Indiana again! If we are not gone much more than a month, I do not worry about leaving John and Jules and Cecilia, for John can look after the house during January and the older children are big enough to take care of themselves pretty well.

We are planning to start east tomorrow afternoon, by way of Billings. We have 35 minutes to make connections there and that should give us plenty of time to step from one train to another. I hope you will not be disappointed when I tell you we have decided to bring Jules. When we got to thinking it over, we found that he has not made the trip since he was five years old, and really does not have a very good idea of things in Bloomington. If he can go this year he is old enough to remember everything, and know just what we talk about afterward when we mention various things there. Then too, he can miss school all right this year, and in another year or two he ought not. Of course he is perfectly delighted. Cecilia thought she would be lonesome without him, but told him to go.

Honeyhill, December 31, 1929

Dear Mamma, Jules and Anne:

We received today the letter that you mailed at St. Paul. We were glad to learn that Jules and Anne were having such a fine time, but sorry that our sweet mamma was so train sick. Son, I am mighty glad that you looked after Anne so well on that train. I am sure that was quite a help for Mamma.

I got your books, son, and mailed them to you yesterday afternoon. When I asked Mrs. Cubbage for your reader she said that it was hard to keep Jules in something to read as he goes through a book so quickly. I was mighty well pleased, Son, to learn that you can read so fast already. It is a wonderful blessing to be able to do that and I hope you will continue to gain speed in your reading. It shows mental activity above the average. I am not a fast reader myself, therefore I know just how much it will mean to you later to be able to read fast. When you were born and we named you Jules I told Mamma that I hoped you would grow up to have the physical strength of your Grandfather Hendricks, the mental strength of your mother, physical courage of Lt. Ord for whom you are named, and the moral courage of your father. You certainly show the mental strength of your mother when you can read so fast, and I hope that you will eventually acquire the other three kinds of strength that I have always hoped you would have.

I suppose you have heard before this evening about Joe. I got a letter from Carrie today. She said that Joe had developed toxic poisoning and that the doctor had said that it was only a question of a short time. She said that she had wired Joe and Mina and that the best she could hope for was that he would still be here when they arrived in Billings Thursday. I am so glad you are close enough to be able to go to the funeral.

Your lovers,
Daddy and Sister

West Franklin, Indiana
January 9, 1930

Dear Daddy and Sister:

How we do wish you could be here with us. Pacific has been telling stories of all the pranks the boys here used to play, especially Charlie Sweeten and Jim Brown, who were the most mischievous of the bunch. He thinks the story of how they stole a bunch of ducks and put them in Mr. Hightower's smoke house, to make it appear that he stole them, is as good a story as anyone could think up. Pacific told how they tried to scare you by rolling a burning barrel of straw down the hill, but you wouldn't scare. And there were many more good stories.

It rained hard all day yesterday and was a bad day for a funeral. In spite of that, there was a huge crowd for Joe's service. We were glad we could be here. Carrie is fine, and taking it all very sensibly, without any fuss at all. She is cheerful and enters into the reminiscing the same as the rest.

Honeyhill Farm
January 21, 1930

Our Dear Sweet Ones:

Sister said to tell you that we heard something this morning that we never hope to see: King George V. opening the Naval Limitations Conference in the Chamber of the House of Lords, London. We got the announcement last evening over a couple of stations so I planned to get up in time to listen in. The last announcement said that it would be at 5:40 E.S. time instead of six. That means 3:40 for us. It was 3:50 when I awoke. I had the radio set for KSL at Salt Lake, so as soon as

I switched it on we heard the Marsielles [sic]. There were several other numbers rendered by what I considered a very fine band. Then a period of waiting, and then the King's address. After a brief pause a Frenchman began to talk, and as we could not understand him we switched off and went back to bed. We were mighty glad that we could hear it. It came as clear and distinct as it possibly could.

Your lover,
John Hendricks

Honeyhill Farm
Tuesday, March 4, 1930

Dear Pater and Cora,

Your letter and check came yesterday. Thanks greatly. I think you should not have sent that much. After all you did for us in the past months you shouldn't have made this check for so much. If I send you one in return will you cash it? Edith sent me a lovely apron and box of chocolates and mints for my birthday.

I haven't been feeling very well since I got home and have to stay in bed right now. I got a catch in my hip last night and can't use my left leg. Dr. Graham came last night and says I'll be all right soon.

March 10, 1930

I think I am lots better this a.m. We had the doctor again yesterday morning after I had a most painful night Friday. He gave me some more medicine and it is helping greatly. The pain I had was exactly like after pains, which are the most devilish pains ever invented, only Friday night it was continuous and not in flashes. I guess maybe my present condition is somewhat similar to that which produces after pains in that the uterus in this change of life business should be shrinking and isn't. Otherwise there is no similarity. The medicine I am now using is a uterine sedative and is very helpful. I have pain tablets too, but have had to use very few of them since I have this new medicine. I think it is doing the work and that I can get up soon.

The woman we got today is excellent. She cleaned the house and did a lot of ironing and cooked the meals without asking me more than half a dozen questions beyond what I told her. Her little youngster is a cute child, quite talkative, but very good and cheerful all the time.

I certainly ought to be ashamed to stay in bed. I haven't had any pain for two days now, and I don't see any reason why I shouldn't get up and do all the work. But I just don't want to! Isn't that a great state for a husky female to be in! After I am up a little while I get tired and want to lie down again, so I just decided I'd stay in bed till I wasn't tired any more, now that we have this woman to relieve John. With the typewriter here on my wonderful bed table that John made me, which I can set down over my knees, I can do writing and have been keeping up my news. I have also written one little story that I think I'll try out on the *Parents'* Magazine. It really happened since I have been sick, between Jules and me. I decided if I stay in bed a few days and finish up some of the writing on hand I'll make more than if I get up and try to do the housework myself right now.

Today food really tasted pretty good, and I ate the nearest to a meal since last Thursday a week ago in North Dakota, on the way home. I had for dinner tonight a cup of broth with rice, a glass of sauerkraut juice, a slice of toast, some mashed potatoes and creamed carrots. Living for the past ten days on milk of magnesia and oranges I haven't got fat—especially when using the two together.

Every time John goes to the bank and has any dealings with young Gerald Williams we remember what you said Edith— that if he is a banker you are the Prince of Wales. John took to the bank yesterday the $1200 that the Telephone Company lent us on our stock so we could pay off that much on a note at the bank. We owed $2300 at the bank, with about $10,000 security. A couple of months ago the bank told John he'd have to pay off something. John told them he was planning to pay off $500 as soon as his check got in from the honey association. Now among his assets he had listed was our stock in the local telephone company. It was not in the mortgage, but just in a list of securities we own. When John said he would pay off $500, the bank said all right, that would suit them, but he would also have to increase his security by including the telephone stock. Now it did not look reasonable that we should decrease the loan and increase the security, especially as we have at times in the past owed the bank as much as $4200 on the same securities. John made up his mind right away he wasn't going to let the bank get its hands on that telephone stock, and decided it would be better to sell his telephone stock to the company for the $1700 par value, and borrow enough from a private party where he could get the money to clean up the debt entirely at the bank and be entirely out of their clutches. At the annual meeting, the other stockholders decided they did not want to lose John from the company and offered to lend him $1200 on his stock with which to pay off that much at the bank. They offered it for 8% and we pay 10% at the bank. Of course John was pleased at their desire to have him stay in the company and also at the lower rate of interest and decided if he could pay off all but $1100 at the bank the banker surely couldn't insist on increased securities.

Well, this is a long financial extra, but I knew Ted would enjoy the story and that Co and Pater would enjoy the end of it, having had the first chapter before I left Indiana. I knew too that Ted would be glad to hear that the Telephone Company is doing so well. You remember John and eleven other local men bought it thirteen years ago when, as a cooperative exchange, it had failed. Not one man put in one actual penny of money— they pooled their credit. They have now paid off entirely the cost, built up the system three or four times the original size, and provided a safe sinking fund. The gross income of the company during the past year was $18,300.

Honeyhill Farm,
Powell, Wyoming,
April 7, 1930

The Stockgrowers' National Bank,
Cheyenne, Wyoming.

Dear Mr. Cronland:

Last December, at the annual meeting of the Wyoming State Beekeepers' Association, the manager of the Mountain States Honey Producers' Association told us that the Association would be in position to advance 5 cents per pound on the 1929 crop to its members by the first of February. February and March have both gone, and this advance has not been made. I have written several times to the Association to find out why, and my letters have not been answered. Therefore I would like to ask you if you could not write to the Boise Trust Company, of Boise, Idaho, which bank acts as treasurer for the Association, to find out why this promised advance has not been made.

If the advance had been made at the time it was promised, I would have enough to make a $500 payment on my loan to you, in addition to paying the interest. But inasmuch as I have not received the advance, I have nothing to turn over to you at this time.

I had expected, as I had previously told you, to have $500 to apply on this debt when final settlement was made on the 1928 crop. Final settlement was made in December on the 1928 crop, but when the statement came, it disclosed the fact that the expenses of the Association on the 1928 crop amounted to exactly a cent a pound more than on the 1927 crop. This extra cent a pound was just enough to consume the $500 I thought was still coming to me and why I had planned to apply it on my indebtedness with you.

This extra overhead expense of the association brought the net price of honey to the producer down to 6 cents per pound. The association has also notified us that 6 cents per pound is as much as we can expect on the 1929 crop. When this fact was made known to me I at once realized that I would have to depend on something else beside my annual production to reduce my indebtedness. Therefore I planned to do two things just as soon as they can be done: First, to sell the small piece of farm land I own in Indiana; second, to dispose of my stock in the local Telephone Company and apply the proceeds on my indebtedness.

One of my brothers in Indiana has agreed to buy my Indiana holdings, but because of poor crops and low price he received for his 1929 crop, he can not do it from the proceeds of last year's farming. He hopes to be able to do this out of the present season's farming operations. It will be approximately another year before I can realize on this piece of property.

The manager of our Telephone Company has had a tentative offer within the past month for the sale of the property. He expressed the opinion that if the deal did go through it would be several months before it is finally closed. If this sale can be made (and practically all the stockholders are willing) I should have about $500 from this source to apply on my indebtedness with you.

There is yet one other thing I have in reserve to apply on this indebtedness in case of emergency. I can cash in on my life insurance. I am writing to the company today to find out what the cash value of my policy would be in case I must cash in on it.

Inasmuch as the manager of the Mountain States Honey Producers' Association has not answered my inquiries about this advance which was promised for February 1, I do wish you would write the Boise Trust Company and find out the reason why the advance was not made. We were told last December that arrangements had been made for securing a loan of $135,000 from the Federal Farm Loan Board, and that when this money was received, the association would then go on a cash basis. But the advance has not been made, and we have not been told that the loan did not go through.

My 1929 crop amounted to 54,000 pounds, and the Association has received all but a very small portion of this. It was shipped several months ago.

Very truly yours,
/s/ John Hendricks.

JH:C

The Stockgrowers National Bank,
Cheyenne, Wyoming.

Dear Mr. Cronland:

I wish to thank you for your kind letter of a few days ago [suggesting that if I could pay $1000 on my loan at The Stockgrower's National Bank, I might be able to get a state farm loan at a low interest rate to pay off the balance.] In reply I wish to state that I have looked into the matter of securing a state loan.

I am personally acquainted with the local appraiser of the state farm loan board. He is a particular friend of mine. He has told me that under the instructions the board gives him, that it would be useless for him to recommend more than a $4,000 loan on my place. He also expressed the opinion that they might not allow more than $3500. Since he has told me this, I think it would hardly be worth while applying for the loan until I have enough cash in sight to reduce my loan with you $2,000. I do not understand why the state farm loan board will not lend more than that, because my improvements alone have cost me $11,000, and I carry approximately $8200 worth of insurance on my buildings. However, I expect to let go of both my telephone stock and the small property in Indiana just as soon as I can without making unnecessary sacrifice.

I am therefore very hopeful that within the next twelve months I can reduce my loan with you to where the state loan board will take over the balance.

Very truly yours,
/s/ John Hendricks.

JH:C

Tuesday night, April 22, 1930

If you were here now you would think we lived in a large city. The Taggart Construction Company, which has the contract for resurfacing about ten miles of the road between Deaver and Powell, has bought gravel from the dry hillside just across the road west of us. They are setting up their gravel digging and crushing machinery and expect to start work in another day or so. They have their cook tents and a bunk house and one tent beside our well at the foot of the hill. Their three sleeping tents, big ones, are set up in our pasture east of our barn. Mr. Taggart asked John to put the tents there so they would be handy for the men and yet not so close to the machinery. What we will do when they start up I don't know. They plan to run day and night for six weeks, moving 300 tons of gravel every day. With the digger and crusher working right opposite our bedroom windows, about as far across on the other side of the road as our house is on this side, we will feel that we are living beside the L in Chicago, especially at night. We may have to move to the east side of the house upstairs to sleep.

Thursday, April 24, 1930

The gravel machinery is about installed across the road from us, and the night won't be musical from now on. The children enjoy talking to the cook and visiting the cookhouse. The cook is a rather young woman, about 25 or so, I should guess. It is hard to guess, as she has all her front teeth out. She cooks for 25 men! How'd you like her job? Worse than that, she has to get four meals each 24 hours—breakfast and supper for the whole bunch, and dinner at noon and midnight for half of them, as one crew works at night and one in the daytime and each crew has to have dinner in the middle of its working hours. I really don't see how she can get enough sleep. If I had to get dinner at midnight and wash the dishes afterward (even if they were granite dishes for table use) I don't believe I'd want to have breakfast ready at 6:30.

Pater, I am glad you like the Herbet cakes. Be sure to let me know when the supply begins to run low and I'll send some more. I was reminded while making them of what Grandma Thuman told me once when she had made a batch of cookies, and I asked her, "Grandma, what do you mix in your cookies to make them so good?" I must have been about as big as Ruddy* then. She answered, with her usual eye twinkle, "Why, I mix them with brains!" I remember it took me about half a minute to see what she meant, for she did such unusual cooking I wouldn't have been the least surprised to know she put brains in the cookies. I wish we could remember more of her clever sayings. She had about the biggest sense of humor of anybody I have ever known. I suspect that is where we get some of ours.

April 27, 1930

The children get great fun from going down to the tent settlement and watching the workers. The woman doesn't do all the work. Her husband is the chief cook and she is his assistant, and the two of them do the camp work and cooking. However, they have their hands full, for they do all their own bread baking, cake making, bake doughnuts, and everything of the sort. Doesn't it seem impossible for a crew of men like that to have fresh homemade bread all the time? The woman was here today and told me they bake 8 loaves of bread every other day, using Fleischmann's yeast. Today they made doughnuts for supper, for Cecilia and Lucille Gimmeson went down and helped fry them. The girls think it great sport to go and help cook and wait table. They like to help wash dishes, too, and I guess the woman enjoys it. She is really only a girl. She was married right after graduating from high school, and she and her husband have been cooking for work crews all the time. The reason she has her teeth out is that she was in an auto accident last fall and got the teeth knocked out. She is getting new ones soon, she said today. She told Cecilia they get 50¢ a

---

*A nickname for Edith Rhoda.

meal from the workmen for their meals, out of which they have to buy the food. Whatever they have left they can keep, and the two together get $150 a month for their work. Their grocery bill last week was $105. She said it usually takes all but five or six dollars to pay for the necessary groceries and supplies, so they don't clear much on that part of the deal.

> Honeyhill Farm,
> Powell, Wyoming,
> May 5, 1930

The Stockgrowers National Bank,
Cheyenne, Wyoming.

Dear Mr. Cronland:

I am glad that you wrote the Boise Trust Company in inquiry. Shortly after you did that, the manager of the Mountain States Honey Producers' Association wrote me a very lengthy letter, explaining why the Association had not made the five cents per pound advance that the manager promised last December. I thought he should have written this to me long ago in reply to my own inquiries, but it seems that it took your inquiry to bring forth the information.

The manager claims that the Association has never secured the $135,000 loan from the Federal Farm Board, nor the money that had been promised from the Intermediate Credits banks, because the association has been unable to move its honey into bonded warehouses. This latter movement was held up because some of the eastern railroads will not consent to allowing extracted honey to have a storage-in-transit privilege. With the present low market price for honey, our product can not stand a freight rate to the bonded warehouses, and then another separate frieght rate from there to market, which two rates combined make a much higher rate than the through rate from the territory to eastern and seaboard markets.

I will write the Association giving them an order to deliver to you the next payment they will have for me as soon as the money is available. However, I will not be able to make it quite a thousand dollars. Basing my calculations on the statement the manager gave us that we need not expect more than 6¢ on last year's crop, there will not be a thousand dollars that I can apply on my obligation with you. From this 6¢ must be deducted the price of my cans and cases for this year's crop. I am ordering the Association to send you enough to pay first the interest due April 1 and then a payment of $500 on the principal. I had to borrow $500 from the local bank to take care of my taxes this past month. I must take up this note out of returns of honey shipped last season. . . .

Very truly yours,
/s/ John Hendricks.

JH:C

Tuesday, May 13, 1930

Cecilia is getting more and more excited about her commencement from junior high school, though it is hardly possible for her to be any more happy than when she found she would actually get the watch she has been wanting for so long. You all sent such generous checks that there is enough to get both the wrist watch and the camera she wants almost as badly. Co, your check and Edith's make thirteen dollars, and by the time we put our share in we can get her both.

Saturday, May 17, 1930

This certainly has been one round of school activities the past week—something every day or night or both. Last night I was too tired to go, but lay down a while and rested while the children did the dishes, and then Cecilia and I went. Dr. Crane, president of Wyoming U., gave the speech for the high school commencement, and I felt I ought to go. John was suffering from the weather and went to bed about 6:30. I was glad I went, for various reasons. I got to sit next to Carrie and we had a good visit. She is delighted over Mina's Mortar Board election. Dr. Crane's talk was as excellent a one as I ever heard, and well worth going for. He is such an alive, normal person, and throws such homely, understandable illustrations into everything he says that every crowd loves him from the start. You know, when a university prexy, who is a pretty big person to a crowd of ordinary, small town mortals, says things that are everyday experience to them, they don't stop to realize that he is ordinary, but think they are akin to greatness.

After the exercise I spoke to him. I wanted to tell President Crane what Governor Emerson said to me when he was here last summer about our bill to refund student railroad fares. You remember we got the bill passed by the legislature only to have it vetoed by Gov. Emerson. Emerson explained at length to me that it was economy that required the veto and hoped we would bring the matter up again at the next session. He said he did not want to make any absolutely hard and fast promises, but that if we did, he was sure we would get good treatment from him, which is about as definite as a politician can state anything. Dr. Crane had not talked with Emerson about the matter and was very much interested in hearing that the Governor had made the statement to me. He felt that if the bill would meet with a veto again it would be silly to get it passed again by the legislature, but of course this puts a different light on the matter.

I had to laugh at John. When we sat down to dinner the day after Cecilia had her commencement John winked at me and remarked that he was so glad I had a *high school* girl to help me now, for it was always so much easier for me when I had a high school girl staying here to help with the housework. Cecilia had to laugh and then she said, "Snicker, snicker."

May 25, 1930

John has decided to give up the Hyattville bee yard. There is so much foul brood in that neighborhood we just can't keep our bees there. There are so many people there with a few hives, and one commercial beekeeper who always has a lot of the disease. John thinks that he can plan his work here somewhat differently and get along just as well or better than if we keep the bees up there. When we started that yard there was no early bloom here at all. Now there are oceans of dandelions here that bloom almost as early as the ones at Hyattville. We thought for a number of years we could get good queens mated at Hyattville but with the other bees there now we can not depend on getting pure queens of the Italian stock we want, and have concluded it is cheaper to buy the queens than to try to raise them at Hyattville ourselves. We have been doing business the past two years with a queen breeder in Texas who gives us splendid prices and excellent service, and waits till our crop is sold to get him money. With that arrangement, we can buy queens cheaper than we can raise them. John says if we do away with the Hyattville yard we'll have more time to make some trips we want to instead of always having to go to Hyattville.

It is after eleven, the lights are getting dim, I do not want to have to start the engine any more tonight, and it is time anyway for me to get to bed — so good night, if you're still reading.

Tuesday, June 3, 1930

We drove down to visit old Mr. Nauser on Sunday, and he surely was glad to see us. He lives on his place, all alone, as usual, and evidently doesn't get to talk with very many people, for he simply would not let us go, and even after we had started he stood with his foot on the car's running board until John stopped the engine and started it several times before we finally managed to get away. He talked politics and religion and exploration and family and farming and everything under the sun. The man really reads a lot and knows more about what is going on in the wide world than most of his neighbors all put together. He is 73 and thinks that is pretty ancient; however, he is doing all the work on his farm this year, work that would be hard for a younger man.

He told us about going to Billings to have his eye taken out a year ago. After his eye was all right again, and ready, as he thought, for a glass eye, the doctor fitted one in, and then told him it would never stay in unless Mr. Nauser had another operation to take up the slack in his eyelids. He said it had to be done. The doctor went to another room, and while he was gone the nurse came up to Mr. Nauser, put her arm around him, and told him not to believe the doctor, that all he wanted was Mr. Nauser's money. Mr. Nauser thought so himself, but when the nurse told him, he was sure, so he told the doctor to go to, and he came on home. He wears dark glasses, with the glass over the lost eye darkened still more, and does not look any worse than he did before the operation. You recall he never was a raging beauty, since he got kicked in the face by a mule years ago and his face dented the wrong way.

Cora, are you sitting down? If not, please do before you read this. Mr. Nauser inquired especially about you, as he always does, and wanted to know if you are married yet. He was interested to find you are not, and wanted to know if you do not want a man. He went on to say if he were not quite so old and not quite so homely since he lost his eye, he would make the trip to see you to see if you wouldn't come out here with him. So any time you want a man, here is one waiting for you. He told me that when I was talking with him, and just before we started home he said it again and told both John and me he would like to go to see if you wouldn't come out and be his house-keeper! He asked especially how old you are, and if you have got stout and big, or if you are still slender as you were when he saw you 16 years ago. I told him you looked as slender as when you were 18, and not any older. He says the oil business is likely to boom again and he hopes to get some more money before long by leasing some more of the land he owns.

June 6, 1930

I have to go to Buffalo, starting on Wednesday morning, June 18, for the P.E.O. state convention. We'll probably drive home the following Sunday. I do not expect to take my car this year, and much prefer not to, as I am not so keen about driving a great deal, although for the last few weeks driving does not hurt me at all, the way it did the first month or two after I was back from Indiana. After I was sick, both driving and riding did not seem to do me any good, and I did very little of either, but I think now I am better than ever. Mrs. Nelson is planning to take her car, which is a Cadillac, or perhaps a Cadillac's younger sister, if there is such.

I never did answer your question, Cora, about the pony. Unfortunately this has been such a bad season here for alfalfa we are afraid to get any extra stock now for fear we won't have feed for it next winter. The hay fields, for some unknown reason, nearly all died out during the winter. Most people plowed up great acreages of it, and the prospects are that hay will be out of sight in price this fall and winter. Jules has been wanting a wrist watch (of course, since Sister has one) so I told him you had sent two dollars to save toward his watch, and he was greatly pleased. The watch he has been looking at in the Mont Ward cat costs about $4.75.

Monday, June 16, 1930

Pater, I see President Hoover signed the bill increasing the pensions to Civil War soldiers. Will that affect your pension? I hope so. I guess he was afraid not to sign the bill after the slap the Congress gave him over the Spanish War veterans' bill, when Congress passed the bill at once by an overwhelming majority after Pres. Hoover had vetoed it. We thought one or two of Hoover's points about vicious habits formed after the dismissal from service were well taken, but when everybody knows that one of the main reasons why Hoover, standing in with the big business interests, wants to keep expenditures low is that taxes on big business can be kept low, his argument rather loses force. Big business has always been the chief factor in holding down generous pensions. It has been hard enough for veterans to prove their disability without making them prove their poverty also. If a man had to prove that he and his family could not exist unless he got the government pittance, that would be a nice state of affairs. When this bill was passed over the president's veto, John wrote Senator Kendrick to ask if it would be necessary for a veteran to undergo another medical examination to get the increase the new bill provides. Sen. K. wrote back he understood no further examination was necessary, only a formal filing of an application blank, which he enclosed. We filled it out, and are waiting to see how long it will take to get the increase of $10 a month under the new law. If we get it, that will give John $60 a month, which will certainly be a help to us.

Co, when I was writing about the money you sent for a pony, I did not get to finish, and you probably wondered why we told Jules you had sent only two dollars. As a matter of fact, shortly after Pater's check came we were absolutely strapped for cash. We were overdrawn at the bank and had nothing coming in, and had some extra expense. We simply had to use the extra you sent to tide us over. One reason we have been so close run is that for about three or four months we have not had any cream to sell and for several months have had to buy even butter. We plan to have at least one cow milking all the time, but plans sometimes "gay agley" and this time they certainly did. Now we have two fresh cows almost at once, and the cream will not only furnish us with plenty of butter but more than pay our grocery bills for months to come. All of which makes a good deal of difference when you haven't realized anything on last year's honey crop and don't know when you will. When you have to go twelve or more months without getting any money on your business, it takes just about all you can scrape together to keep things going and the business still running.

John has been trying to realize something on some of the property he has, but until just now has not succeeded. Now his brother Lincoln, who lives on the family farm in Posey County, has agreed to buy John's share. The share is really worth $2,000 but Lincoln could not see his way clear to paying that much, what with the present prices of farm products and the poor crops in recent years. Finally John lowered the price to $1700 and Lincoln wrote a few days ago he would take the share at that figure and would get the money about the first of

August and send it to us. We are hoping we can pay, counting that, enough on our farm mortgage here to reduce the amount to the place where we can get a state loan. During the past few months John has felt many times that he would have to cash in one or both of his insurance policies to keep going, unless he could dispose of either the Indiana farm share or the telephone stock.

The main reason the association has not been able to pay for the honey is that it can not borrow from the federal farm loan board as originally assured. The plan of the association was to store the honey in bonded warehouses and secure government loans on it to advance to the producers. Before this could be done, however, it was necessary to have the privilege of this storage in transit. Freight rates are so high we could not afford to ship the honey to warehouses and then reship it elsewhere. The western and central trunk lines have agreed to the storage in transit privilege but the eastern trunk lines have refused to concur. As most of our honey goes to the eastern seaboard, it is necessary for the concurrence of the eastern trunk lines. John did not know about this until a month or so ago and since then we have done a good deal of letter writing, and I believe, have the problem well on the way to solution. We are now waiting for more information from the association before going ahead with the line we have started, which is reaching the Interstate Commerce Commission through Senator Kendrick.

With the money from the sale of the Indiana farm share to reduce our interest on the mortgage here, and the cream checks now to pay our grocery bills we are on easy street now. Then if John gets the $10 a month pension increase, we will have to have a family conference to decide what to do with all our income! I might remark, as to grocery bills, that we could have run an account, but have never done so and hated to start, so we just took in our extra eggs and up to date have never gone hungry, and never expect to.

Well, this seems to be a financial extra, and you are probably weary of the subject of our finances. But having started to explain where the pony money went, I got on such a long trail I just kept going.

It certainly wouldn't bankrupt anybody to buy the stamps for all the letters that this family has exchanged in the past few weeks. Being at Hyattville most of the week before last and at Buffalo most of last week put such a crimp in my work that I have been trying vainly to get done just the things that had to be, and by that time I tumbled into bed half asleep. John was in Hyattville part of this week and that gave me two cows to milk, and made me get up at least an hour earlier every morning, which is no joke to me, for being an early riser was not one of the gifts the fairies left at my birth.

I told you last week I'd tell you about the auto accident we had on the way to Buffalo that caused me to sport a gorgeous black eye all through the P.E.O. convention, as well as sundry bruises in various places over my anatomy.

We were in Mrs. S.A. Nelson's car and she was driving along on the highway between Lovell and Greybull, which is simply perfect now. We were going about 45 miles an hour, when we had a flat tire. The car skidded slightly and she shut off her gas and tried to slow down but just then we started down a rather steep hill and the car did not slacken speed. She thought we were going into the ditch and put on her brakes to stop the car, and the car naturally stopped too quickly for safety. We all felt the car going over, and then the next thing any of us knew we were all still in the car, which was standing still in the middle of the road with the engine running and the gear in neutral. But in the meantime the car had turned a complete somersault and end for end in the road, so that we were facing back toward Lovell. As we were riding along, Mrs. Nelson and Mrs. Peterson were in the front seat, Mrs. Scott and I in the back. When the car turned over, Mrs. Peterson was thrown into the back seat with us and Mrs. Nelson left in the front seat with her long legs wrapped around the steering wheel.

I could not open the door beside me nor could we get two other doors open, so much out of plumb the top of the car was from the turnover. Mrs. Peterson climbed back into the front seat, opened her door, got out and opened our doors, and I helped Mrs. Scott out while she helped Mrs. Nelson out. Mrs. Scott had a cut place across the bridge of her nose from her glasses and her nose was bleeding. We got a box and a pillow from the car and seated her at the side of the road, but she insisted she was all right. Mrs. Nelson had a bump on her head that knocked her out, but she came to just a little after I did. Each one of us insisted she was all right. As a matter of fact, I did not know until after I had helped Mrs. Scott out that I had been bumped hard. Then my head felt queer. I put my hand up to my forehead and over my right eye there was a hump from the eye clear up into the hair, that stood up like a mountain ridge. The skin about my eye and ear was more or less cut. I then recalled that when the car started over I had felt just the way I do when I go under an anesthetic, and that I had wondered where I would wake up! I remembered praying to God to take care of us all, and then the next thing, we were all sitting in the car, right side up.

Well, we then looked to see which tire had caused the trouble, and proceeded to change the tire and put on the spare. We had it about half changed when the first car came along, two men. When they saw our car and heard what had happened, they were simply scared stiff. For a little they couldn't do anything but stare and gasp. Then they proceeded to finish changing the tire. By that time there was a whole procession of cars and help a-plenty. Some of the men drove our car up and down the road a little to make sure it was safe to drive. Then we all got in again and went on to Greybull. I admit we were all pretty shaky for a while when we realized just what had happened, but not one in the crowd made any fuss.

We could not get any repairs at Greybull and went to Basin. We took Mrs. Scott to Mrs. Leo Werts' house and I stayed there with her while Mrs. Nelson and Mrs. Peterson went to the garage. The car certainly was a sight. The windshield was smashed out entirely, the left front door window was broken out and the right back window beside where I was sitting was out. The frame was knocked about three inches out of square, and listed over to the right side. Only one door would go shut, the others hanging two or three inches away from the frame at the bottom when pushed shut. But the engine wasn't hurt in the least nor did the fenders show more than a bump or two. We did not know if the car would be all right to go on to Buffalo in, but decided we would take the word of the Ford garage at Basin, as we knew they are reliable. They straightened out the frame of the car, stood it on end and examined every bolt and screw, took it out on the road and drove it a while and reported that it was as safe as a new car, in spite of its looks. Mr. Werts went down to the garage and looked the car over himself, before he was willing for us to go on.

Mrs. Scott really was quite badly shocked over the accident and as she had wrenched her back in addition to cutting her face, she decided she did not want to go on. So Mrs. Werts and I put her on the northbound train at one o'clock and I tipped the porter to look after her. Mrs. Werts called Mrs. Scott's son and had him meet her at Deaver.

The garage at Basin did not have any windshield to fit the car, and we had to drive 30 miles clear to Worland to get one. We had a flat tire between Basin and Worland and had to wait in Worland while they repaired the tire and put in the windshield. We started from Basin about two o'clock and it was after four when we got away from Worland. We thought we would drive to Tensleep at least that night, and the rest of the way to Buffalo next morning. It is 69 miles from Worland to Tensleep, and about as much farther to Buffalo. But we got to Tensleep so early according to the sun that we concluded we would go on, and we did, arriving in Buffalo at 9:30. We had to drive the last twenty miles after dark, but the road was perfectly safe, although quite downhill, as there is a drop of 4,000 feet in this distance. The road over the Big Horn mountains is perfectly marvelous. There are no really steep places and we did not go in low once over the entire way; but of course we went miles and miles and miles in second, both up and down, and we did not know the road and preferred to drive safely. Also, driving in second saves brakes, and we'd had enough experience that morning with brakes!

Of course the folk at the convention made a lot of fuss over us when they found what had happened and that we had continued on the trip. Mrs. Nelson, however, is the one that deserves the credit, for she was driving and it was her car. She explained that she felt that if she went right on, she would always be willing to drive, but that if she stopped and did not, she would probably never be able to get up nerve enough to drive a car again. She and Mrs. Peterson took turns driving that day. I couldn't, as I could not see out of my right eye, having it bandaged. But by the time we came home, I took my turn, too.

I had to sit quite lightly for several days, as I had the most dramatic black and blue spots on my hips you ever heard of, both in size and color. My right shoulder also sported a lovely bruise. The way I got the spots on my hips was that when the car turned over, the cushion on the back seat flew up against the back of the seat and when Mrs. Scott and I came down we sat on the iron framework.

Well, the moral is that when you have a flat tire and your car starts veering, don't put on your brakes. That is what turned us over, and that is what turned John over at almost the same place in the road last winter. I said to John that it is almost impossible not to put your foot on the brake when you want to stop the car and know something is the matter, but he opined that after you turned over once, your foot didn't work so automatically to push the brake.

The children are playing crokinole or carroms, and having a great time. Willard and Lucille Gimmeson are here. A few weeks ago Max Murray came over and brought their crokinole board along, and Jules got so enthusiastic about the game he simply couldn't exist without a board of our own. So he and I went out to the shop and got a sheet of wallboard and cut one out. By the time we had it half done, John got interested too, and helped finish it. We put regular pockets in the corners so they can play carroms, and they have been having lots of fun with it. You would have laughed to see the whole family working to make that board, but I guess that is what keeps children at home. They'll never get more pleasure from the most expensive board made than they do from this homemade wallboard one. We had a set of the carrom rings, as I got them several Christmases ago when we expected to make a board and did not get it done.

July 17, 1930, Thursday night

We had a very interesting visitor today. He is M. Jean Chaneaux, beekeeper, vice president of the Apis Club, Les Arbures, Jura, France. He is spending this season in the U.S. studying honey production methods all over the country. He has been all across from Alabama to southern California and in most of the northern part. He is specially interested in beekeeping methods in this intermountain region, as his home in France is along the Swiss border, about the center of eastern France. He came here with letters of introduction to Mr. Hardy from some of the bee supply manufacturers. M. Chaneaux reminds one somewhat of Mr. Krueger, and is a most interesting, pleasant person. He is polite to excess, but not offensively so. We invited him to come and spend a couple of days here next week while John will be going through the outyards, as that is the kind of experience he wants — actual field work. M. Chaneaux told us that he works with three other men in his honey work, and that the four of them turn out 1,000 pounds of extracted honey a day. John usually works at the rate of 6,000 pounds a day, by himself. Of course John's equipment is in proportion. But that is what the French gentleman wants to learn — better methods of field work and shop work.

August 2, 1930

We got the money last week on the sale of John's share of the Indiana farm to his brother. John applied $1500 at once on the farm mortgage and is using $200 to clear up some local bills he wants out of the way. We hope now with that much paid on the farm mortgage that we can get a state loan for the rest, which will reduce the interest very greatly as we have been paying 8% on the mortgage.

We took our entries to the fair this morning. We are wondering if Jules' pumpkins are not likely to get a prize. When I took them in, the county agent asked me if he could take those pumpkins to Billings for the Midland Empire Fair, as they were the most uniform in size and quality of any he had seen. We could have got bigger ones, but hunted over and over the patch to get three of as near as possible the same size, color and shape. Beside the pumpkins we took half a dozen white onions (Anne's entry) and a dozen white eggs and a dozen brown eggs. We also took butter. Cecilia and I churned yesterday and she made one pound and I made one. She molded hers in the regulation oblong commercial shape, in a mold, while I did mine by hand into a round shape with little fancy decorations on the top, a la the butter we used to get in Indiana when I was a child. Ours was the only butter entered when we were there, but of course more may have come in later. Anybody has to hurry to get better butter than ours, as the flavor is simply perfect.

The fair was pretty good, but was spoiled, in the opinion of many of us, by a large carnival company which is inside the grounds and of course attracts more attention from the majority of the people than the exhibits. I think it is a mistake to combine the two. The young people will really look closely at the exhibits and learn a lot, if there is nothing else to distract them; but when there are merry go round, ferris wheels large and small, fortune tellers, athletic contests, bird and monkey and other shows, and about two dozen different booths where you throw rings or balls or spin wheels to get gim cracks of a dozen different kinds, there is too much to see there to spend time looking at the exhibits. I hope next year there will be nothing but a fair. The local variety store manager got the concession for selling refreshments, and instead of selling at usual prices he has downtown, he doubled the prices for only the simplest things and explained that he had to use the same prices the carnival company had.

Jules got first prize on his pumpkins and he has grown an inch, I think, in pride. Cecilia's butter took second prize and mine got nothing. I got first prize again on white eggs. Isn't that a joke? But I like jokes to the tune of $1.50. I got third on my brown eggs but there is no cash premium for that.

The Power company workmen have been working all day today and have the electric line up to our house and even the wires up into the house where they connect with the house wiring system. They brought the bulbs this morning that we ordered, so as soon as they get the line connected we can change bulbs and turn on the lights. They started this afternoon to set the poles and string the wire to Gimmeson's, and they may not turn our current on until they get that done. But it will take only two more poles and a short wire, so they should finish that tomorrow.

Monday, September 2, 1930

We had a telegram from Senator Kendrick this a.m. saying that John's pension has been increased to $60 a month, according to the new law passed by the recent Congress. John applied in June, so the increase will take effect as of June 19.

Sunday night, September 7, 1930

I have been much amused at something Janet said the other night when I heard the girls say their prayers before going to sleep. When she said her prayer, Janet remembered all her family, and Grandpa and Aunt Cora, and then she stopped, evidently feeling that it was not exactly polite to mention various persons and not those present. She said she would like to put in all my family, but it took so long to say so many names. (Time is evidently precious to her.) I told her that when I said my prayers, I always wanted to mention all the family, so I always just said, "And please take care of all our dear people everywhere." She agreed that was quite simple and effective but was far more interested in the fact that I said prayers too. She asked to whom I said my prayers when I said them, and I answered that I said them to the Lord. She said she knew that, of course, but what she meant was, "Who holds your hand when you say your prayers?" And she was greatly edified and amused when I told her that Uncle John did!

Sunday, September 21, 1930

John decided Friday that yesterday would be the day for us to go to Billings on our annual pilgrimage to the ten cent store. We started about 6:45 Saturday morning and got to Billings just at ten. We went to Mont Wards, Hart Albins, Yegen's and the ten cent store. We had a merchant's dinner at the Princess, and of course that was one of the most important parts of the day. We went by way of Frannie and returned by way of Elk Basin. We went to the Deaconess Hospital to see Mary Busch, who has passed her probationary period and is on the first term of her regular nurse's training work. She was delighted to see us, for she has very little company. She is a great deal thinner and seems to be getting along all right in her work.

I wish you could have seen John yesterday, what with the new gray suit he had on and the gray hat he has that just matches the suit. He looked just too spiffy for words. Really, I have never seen him look so well in any suit he has ever had since I have known him. You'd be sure if you saw him walking down the street that he was a professional man of great success. I had to laugh at him today. The Sunday school superintendent called on John to give the morning prayer in Sunday school, and John wondered if he was called on because he looked so fine. As a matter of fact, he made one of the most beautiful public prayers I have heard for a long time — nothing stereotyped, but practical and natural in expression, yet dignified. When I told him so, after he wondered if the sup't called on him because of his clothes, he wondered if his words lived up to his suit!

The children certainly had a grand time yesterday, and we all enjoyed the whole day. After we left Billings John announced that he was thirsty and that we would stop in Laurel for something to drink. With our usual good luck, we stopped right in front of a drug store that was having a one-cent sale! And what do you suppose? They had a 1¢ price on *ice cream* as well as on drugs! We each had a drink (root beer and the best Green River I ever tasted in all my experience) and then we got the ice cream and took it along to the car. The price of a pint was 25¢ and of a quart was 26¢. Of course we got the quart. We had some cups along and we had bought some small spoons in Billings, so we sat in the car and ate up that whole quart of ice cream. It served for supper, and no one was at all hungry even when we got home.

September 30, 1930

Yesterday morning I heard a car honking in our driveway, and looking out the dining room window I saw a new car with a man and woman in it driving in. I thought it would be you, Edith, up again. I glanced through the kitchen window as the car passed there and thought I recognized John's sister-in-law. I went out on the back porch and sure enough, there were Clara and Pacific. I was so glad to see them. They and John haven't seen each other since 1919, when John was last in Indiana. They went to Elk Basin last night to see Carrie but will be back here later.

October 7, 1930

The folks are talking so fast in the living room I don't believe they will miss me. You can guess how much John and Pacific and Clara have to talk about, considering they haven't seen each other for 11 years. Carrie was prevented from coming from Elk Basin today by a heavy rain.

Pater, I think Pacific and Clara have got about as much pleasure as you used to from watching the car lights all over the country, especially as they come down the bench hill from Elk Basin and from above Garland. They simply won't believe they can see as far as they do. They tell with glee how they drove over a hill into sight of Colorado Springs, and then drove for two or three hours without getting any closer, though they thought it was only a few miles into the center of the town. They are having the time of their lives, and I am so glad they came.

October 9, 1930

Pacific and Clara ought to be in the Black Hills today. They started yesterday morning from Elk Basin. They certainly had a good time here. John and Pacific fairly beamed every time they saw each other. I was rather amused at Pacific. He somehow got the idea that John was about as decrepit as a man of a hundred, and that he had at least one foot in the grave. I believe from what Clara said they were afraid to wait another winter before one or the other of them visited for fear one wouldn't be there. Of course we never know what will happen, but I am sure since they saw John they feel he is not any older than his age, if that. In fact, Pacific is quite gray, and John is hardly gray at all—just a little on the temples! John was in town when they came, and when he came back in the truck with some ground grain for dairy feed he drove to the barn and unloaded the sack before coming to the house. When they saw him coming, Pacific and Clara stood on the back porch to watch him, and they both exclaimed over how well John could handle himself, and fairly gasped when he grabbed the sack of grain and hauled it into the barn. They both said over and over that John is much better and stronger than they expected to find him, and gets about so much better than they had any idea. They remember him the way he was in Indiana when he had to use two crutches all the time, or at least a crutch and a cane. I am certainly glad they came, for they feel much more easy about John.

October 19, 1930

John finished extracting a few days ago. He was so glad to have it finished before the weather got really cold as the honey works so much better when it is naturally warm. If the weather is fit tomorrow he'll begin wrapping the bees for the winter and get that done before really cold weather sets in. Our crop this year is not so large — about 45,000 pounds, of which we shall have to keep some for spring feeding. There is a crop shortage over the country in general and a tremendous demand for honey this fall. All we have extracted has been shipped out as fast as we could get it ready, all but the last few days' work. Of course we haven't got any money on it yet (we haven't got the returns on last year's crops yet, either) but there is no question of its coming eventually and we are glad to have the honey shipped out this early, because it saves having to get insurance on it here.

November 5, 1930

Pater, you certainly are a jewel to tell us to get a radio, and we lost no time in going to the local Majestic dealer to see what he has. After looking over the models we found one that comes apart so we can set the radio part on the pedestal in our living room, where we really prefer to have the machine, as it is so convenient there and sends the music and speaking into the part of the room where we want it. It is called "The New Majestic Perfected Screen Grid Superheterodyne, tremendously powerful, extremely selective, yet so compact it fits any room easily."

Thursday, November 6, 1930

I am sure you would have laughed to see the way I hopped out of bed this morning, me, who usually requires a derrick to get me started in the morning. John finished his chores and got back into the house a little before seven. As usual, he turned on the radio when he got in, and what do you suppose I heard, for the first time since I left 822 last year? One who calls himself Cheerio! I tried all last winter to get that but could not find it, and here it is, on the Majestic. We got it at the San Antonio station. You may be sure we'll be on the lookout for it after this. I could not find where to get it before, and of course with the battery machine we could not range far in the morning. This morning I got any number of west coast stations any time I wanted, and earlier John got Cleveland, Ohio. We have not yet located Cincinnati on this dial, but will as soon as I have time.

November 7, 1930

Dear Cora,

Your wire has come, and Anne and I will plan to start next Saturday, November 15. There is such a difference in rates it is well worth waiting, unless in emergency. If we leave here on Saturday afternoon by Billings and St. Paul we get to you on Monday evening. Won't that be nice? By staying here until then I can get done all the odds and ends I really ought to attend to before starting.

Anne can hardly wait to start. Jules and Cecilia would like to come too, but they don't really think they should miss school. John says for Anne and me to come at once and stay as long as you want us. His outside work is all done, much earlier than usual, and he is feeling fine. The new radio is all-day company and he wants us to be with you.

November 10, 1930

This radio is certainly a wonder. We got the football game Saturday afternoon between Wyoming and the Colorado Aggies, and heard the reports of the scores all over the country. Co, we knew by four-thirty that Indiana got beat by Northwestern and how much. Isn't it marvelous to know these things as soon as the people who are actually there? That evening at five o'clock Cecilia turned the dial to see what she could get, and she could bring in 45 stations that time of day! Think of it! We can get stations all over the west in the morning and forenoon, too. And of course from five o'clock on in the evening we can get practically anything there is. Last night John said about nine o'clock he guessed he'd go to bed, when Seth Parkers were through. The announcer said the Russian Symphony choir would sing, and of course John couldn't miss that. Then the cowboys came on at Denver and of course he had to stay for that. Then I don't know what else, but anyway it was eleven when he finally pulled himself away. John says if we can get everything now, what can't they get during the winter when radioing is really good!

Pater, do you still have the girl who was so good at house work? If not, don't lose track of her, for after Anne and I are there it would be fine to have her do the work and leave us free to do what we wanted to to have a good time with you. I never have had to look after the furnace in the morning and do such things about the house. It would be fine if I could have plenty of time for writing and sewing when I get there, and not have to do all the cooking and such necessary work that anybody can do who has the time. I don't care how late I stay up at night if I can sleep late in the morning, and if there is some one else there to do the morning work I'm sure I'd get a good rest, which I admit I rather need. And of course Cora can't do good work at school if she has to do so much at home before she starts that she is tired when she goes.

822 Atwater
Bloomington, Indiana
Monday, November 17, 1930

Dearest Three:

We arrived all right on schedule. Cora was at the train to meet us. I don't know which was gladder to see us, Pater or Cora. Pater looks as well as ever, I think. I can't see any difference from last year, except, of course, he can not see. I think he hears as well as ever.

Pater just told me how anxious he was for me to come for Cora's sake. He says Cora has been on the verge of a nervous breakdown from loss of sleep and having all the cooking to do, and that he and Cora both were on the verge of a breakdown and certainly needed me. He says the thing that bothered him about the hired girl was that she either talked over the telephone or played the radio, and when he told her not to run the radio she would sit waiting for him to go to sleep or go outdoors so she could run the radio.

Our Dear Sweet Mamma and Anne:

We went to the Byrd movie last night and were more than pleased with it. Every picture they showed was interesting. We would not have missed it for anything. The house was well filled. I wish you could have been here to have gone with us. Anne, I know you would have enjoyed seeing the penguins, whales, and puppies.

Notice came in Saturday's mail from the State Farm Loan Board that my application has been acted on favorably to the extent of $2500.00. That is a thousand less than I had hoped for. That will leave $1500.00 after the honey association pays the $500.00 I have ordered them to pay from last year's crop. I expect to write Mr. Cronland at the Cheyenne bank today of the action of the state board, and see if he can carry the other $1500.00 until it can be paid out of the honey crops. Beginning with next year's crop we should be able to apply nearly all the honey returns on this debt until it is paid.

A circular letter came in yesterday's mail from the Mountain States Assn. [saying that] about one third of last year's crop was yet unsold the 30th of Sept. The circular stated that this would have to be sold before settlement in full could be made to the members. As usual the circular left us up in the air. We cannot tell from this statement whether or not anything will be distributed before all this surplus is sold.

Dearest Three:

Cecilia, your letter about the good Thanksgiving dinner came this morning. We were all anxious to hear how you came out with the turkey roasting and are glad it proved a success.

Cora said you had no need of me, if Jules raised the turkey, John dressed it, and Cecilia cooked it. Well, I could have helped eat it!

I think every day I'll write you a longer letter, but every day takes my time with Pater so I just can't get it done. Now it is time to get this over to the cafe or the mail will go without it. But I never forget to think of you. You are in my thoughts day and night.

Honeyhill Farm
December 5, 1930

Our Dear Sweet Mamma and Anne:

It seems that the State loan will be held up for a while. I got a letter from Pacific today saying that Miss Anne* was afraid to release the mortgage that she holds on the loan we made from her some years ago. He thought that she might have done it if both our names were on the note. The one I sent with the letter was only to be held until I could get one to you to sign and until the State loan was finished. I could not very well make out another mortgage until the first one was made because we could not get it properly worded, for I do not know what to say it is second to until the other note and mortgage is made out. I judge from Pacific's letter that she might have the fear of the hard times on her mind. Then too, it might be that she thinks that the loan has stood long enough and would like to have her money.

Do you suppose that you could find some one back there from whom the thousand dollars could be borrowed? After we cash in on our telephone paper the bees could be used as security. Also after another season the honey crop could be put in the chattel mortgage, for even with a crop next year no larger than this year's crop we should have enough to pay the balance at Cheyenne. The honey that I shipped Pacific will reduce this

---

*Miss Anne Brown was an old friend and former teacher of John's who lived in West Franklin, Indiana. He had borrowed $2000 from her when he and Cecilia were getting started in Wyoming.

year's interest $12.00, so there will be $1068.00 to pay Miss A. before the mortgage could be released. I will enclose the blank release with this so in case you could secure the amount back there you could send it direct to Miss Anne and have her release the mortgage. I will write Pacific tonight and tell him that we will make an effort to raise the amount that we owe her as it looks as if that is the only thing to do.

Bloomington, Indiana
Tuesday, December 9, 1930

Dear Everybody:

I am enclosing the note with my signature. I hope that will be sufficient for Miss Anne until the mortgage can be cleared up and another one issued in place of the one she holds. People here are all so scared over the unemployment and the hard times they have lost all their confidence in humans. I have no idea where I could borrow the thousand, but will keep my eyes open and let you know if anything turns up. I am sure the matter will work out properly without our worrying, but of course we must use all our powers and ability to help along, and have faith for the rest of the way.

Honeyhill Farm
December 12, 1930

Our Dear Sweet Mamma and Anne:

I am real sorry to learn that you think that there is no chance of your raising the $1000.00 for Miss Anne. It looks to me like the only thing to do is to raise the money some how. I will look up the life insurance letters that we got last spring and see how much it is that we can raise by cashing in on both policies. The $200.00 premium due the first of January, added to the cash value of the policies ought to go a long way toward making up the $1000.00 that we must raise. Perhaps if we get that much Miss Anne will let the balance ride until we can get returns from this year's crop. Or the balance that will be left from the Phone paper when we cash in on it and pay the bank will be enough to make up the balance for Miss Anne. This is the only course that I can see open to us just now.

The radio is coming in fine tonight. Amos 'n' Andy time, so that is stopping time.

Your lovers,
Daddy, Sister and Jules.

Honeyhill, Wyoming
December 14, 1930

Our Dear Sweet Mamma and Anne:

Jules wanted to know yesterday if I had written you about what we found scribbled in the back of one of the song books in the church last Sunday. I told him I thought that I had not so he insisted that I tell you. Someone had written on the back fly leaf with a pencil: "Wake the honey man." Evidently some one had observed me at my Sunday morning rest.

I looked up the insurance letters and find that the cash value is almost $500.00. In fact it may total that much. This, coupled with the $200.00 that would be necessary to pay the next premium if we continue the policies, will leave only $300.00 more to raise. We should be able to save that much out of the sale of the 'phone paper after paying the bank. This would mean that we would have to do without some things that we need, among other things a new cream separator and a set of teeth for the man of the house. But I think that it is the best thing to do much as I regret to do so. We just cannot carry all the things that we are loaded with and support our home and family with honey at the price it is now. And we do not know how long the low prices will prevail. I think the thing to do is to get rid of the debts that we have carried about eight years longer than we expected to have to carry them even if it does mean sacrificing things that we do not want to sacrifice.

Dear Everybody:

Aunt Cora looks so much better everybody tells her about it, and tells me too. She says it nearly saved her life to have me come, so it is a good thing I did. But I hate to be away from you three and our own dear home. I have been trying to do all I can to help Cora and take things off her hands.

Daddy, Cora says she will make application for a loan on her insurance immediately, as soon as we hear from you. She says there is no reason why we shouldn't use it, as it is doing no one any good where it is, and you must not lose your insurance when this might as well be used. So let us know right away how much and she will apply at once.

Dear Sweet Mamma and Anne:

It certainly is fine of Cora to offer to raise the money for us to meet Miss Anne's note. But I believe that we could meet the note without that if Miss A. would give us sufficient time. I think that the thing to do is to cash in on the insurance and apply that money on this note. We have too big a load to carry with honey at 6¢. The premiums are just about due and there is no money to pay them. The condition we are in financially we can use that money to better advantage than by putting it in cold storage for the future. For about six years we have not been able to buy the things for the house that we have needed. True we have got them but it was by gifts from other people. The same is true of the children's clothing. And twice I have been unable to buy tires when I needed them. If we could have these two hundred dollars each year to use in our business it could soon be made to return more than the insurance will and we can have it when we need it. Besides, if I live longer than you, it is just so much money wasted so far as we are concerned, and if you live to be my widow there will by that time be

$50.00 per month, at least, awaiting you. So what is the use of hoarding this when we need it so badly.

I shall write the insurance companies in a week or ten days notifying them that I must cash in on the policies. This ought to get us the money early next month. Of course if Cora could see fit to raise the balance for us there would then be no question about getting Miss Anne to release the mortgage at once.

Bloomington, Indiana
December 26, 1930

Dearest Daddy,

Cora made application for a loan of $1200 on her insurance, as she needed a little money herself. So you can surely have the full amount you need to finish paying Miss Anne after what you realize on the insurance you cash in. It will take about $600, won't it?

As for turning in your insurance, my dear, it is all right with me. You do what you figure is best. I felt while the children were small that I ought to be protected in case you left us suddenly. But they are big enough now that I could take care of them and work if necessary. I have no fear of the future, so far as finances are concerned. When you first suggested letting your insurance go it did not seem wise to me, because it seemed like failing to insure protection for the children. Of course the pension would help, but as we have learned from experience, even $600 a year doesn't go terribly far in supporting a family.

The more I thought and prayed about it, the more I came to see that if religion means anything it must include complete trust in God's taking care of our needs as they arise. I think this includes His teaching us to make the best and wisest use of whatever assets we have. So if you have gone over the whole matter and decided that it would be wiser to stop putting the $200 each year in cold storage and use it to bring better returns, that is the thing to do. It is certainly fine that we have this saved up now and get enough more from Cora to take care of

Miss Anne's note. It seems to me that shows Providence has helped us to meet this need when it arose unexpectedly, and I believe fully that if we have complete confidence in God's help and provisions we will have plenty for every need as it arises. I have had enough experience to learn that if I tell God my need and trust in his providing, all the time using (of course) all the wisdom He has given me, the supply will be on hand when the time comes. If I were not fully convinced of this I would be afraid to let your insurance go. But since I know that God is our help in every need, I know He will always provide, and I would much rather you would be able to drop a little of the burden you have been carrying and get some of the things that have been needed.

It is so hard to be away from you so long at a time, but even that works for our good, for if I had not been here we probably couldn't have known about getting the loan from Cora. I love you, my dearest, and will be so glad when we can be together again.

Sister, I wish I could have seen the play and heard you recite. You certainly must have been fine. Do you think by the time I get home you'll be able to manage the kitchen fire as well as you recited? Building a fire and controlling it is not easy job, but one that takes study and attention. But it is a valuable asset.

So you think, Daddy, that your Christmas gift to me "is a lot of housework more or less done." That is surely a fine gift from you and also from Cecilia and Jules, for if it were not for my loving family I couldn't be here where I am so much needed. Anne gave me a similar gift for Christmas—she learned to put on her own stockings over the long underwear. Well, there is no gift like service. Material things can be bought, but loving service is above all price.

Our Dear Sweet Mamma and Anne:

I have finally got the bookkeeping work done. Following are some of the facts from last year's business. Our living cost us $1056.75. Of this amount $100.00 is chargeable to garden sass, $180.00 to milk (6,000 lbs @ 3¢ per lb.), cash expenditure items of $738.71. This item includes personal, groceries, laundry, music, coal for house and $50 worth of gasoline. The pension came within $73.71 of providing what the cows and garden did not furnish. Your writing brought in more than enough to pay the balance. So if we had only the cows and a garden spot we would actually have a better living than the business is bringing at present. But when these debts are reduced, as they will be by the first of April, there should be a different story.

The cows did not do so well this year. Only 15,858 pounds of milk from the three. In money credits from milk, cream, and three heifer calves @ $25.00, the dairy shows $429.81. Total expense chargeable against the dairy is $241.96, leaving a net book credit of $187.85 to the three cows for the year.

The coal bill for the house is smaller this time than usual, being only $87.55. But, oh, that truck. We spent $227.40 on it the past year. The transmission repairs last spring, and the new transmission this fall, and six new tires and the new jack were the main and most costly items.

We spent $104.88 with M.W. & Co., $121.60 with S.R. & Co., and $9.04 with N.B.H. & Co. Bank deposits totaled $6114.19. This includes $1700 from the Indiana property and $1200 from the Telephone Co. Interest and principal paid totals of $3854.70, and that helps a lot.

The total income including the non-cash items from farm and dairy is $6,990.50. Total expense items that would be deductible on an income tax assessment amount to $3791.50. This leaves a net income of $3198.69. Not enough to have to pay Federal Income tax, but if we had a state income tax that would get us this time.

Honeyhill
January 21, 1931

Dear Sweet Mamma and Anne:

Here is my contribution to the work of the committee appointed by the mass meeting to work against the proposed school bond issue. It is what I want addressed to the ex-soldiers.

Do the ex-soldiers of this community who are now enjoying the benefits of the law exempting us ex-soldiers from paying taxes on $2,500.00 worth of property realize that such men as our late friends, Ed., O.K., and Adolf Anderson and Wm. Kimmett gladly consented to this law for our benefit? These men are not here now to help decide the coming bond election, but their widows are with us and are having a hard enough time to meet their present load of taxes, especially if they own a farm or live in Powell and run a rooming house and have to pay water rent. Is it the manly thing for us ex-soldiers to do now to say by our votes in this coming bond election that these widows of our late friends should have no relief from their load of taxes, but that we desire to increase their burdens for them while ours is lightened yearly to the extent of from $50.00 to $125.00. For those of us who have accumulated enough property that we can enjoy this exemption would it not be the soldierly thing for us to do to say by our votes that these widows, and our other friends, should not have their tax burden increased until our state gives us an income tax law that will give all those of us whose incomes might be large enough to be taxed the privilege of paying our proportionate share of the community's expense?

As for me, my vote shall not be cast to tax these widows additional at this time in order that my son, being reared on a farm, might have a building in town in which to exercise.

822 Atwater, Bloomington
January 23, 1931

Dearest Three:

I was very much surprised to get [a wire from Jack Lewis of the American Legion and Wm. Castberg, president of the chamber of commerce, asking me to wire my support for the new building]. I did not know just how to answer it as I did not know, Daddy, what stand you were taking on the matter. I knew you were on the committee from all organizations that was to meet, but you have never mentioned anything about a meeting or anything about the bond election. Of course it is necessary that the district does not lose its rating in the North Central Association, or our children will have to take examinations when they want to enter college anywhere, and that would be an awful nuisance. Then too, complete consolidation can probably be effected better when there is a junior high building in Powell. So I sent the following answer:

> Imperative we maintain North Central Association rating. New building necessary for present requirements and eventual complete consolidation with resulting benefits.
>
> CHH

This this morning I had your letter saying a meeting was held the first Monday in December and a committee appointed. As I do not see the Powell paper except once in a great while when Mina happens to be here, I did not know there was any opposition to the bond issue. You speak of making a statement about an income tax law. Do you mean that the bond issue for a school building should wait until the funds can be raised through an income tax law? Or is it that those who are in favor of the bond issue should also be in favor of an income tax law? I do not even know when the bond election is to take place. Mrs. Marschall sent me a clipping from the January 8 *Tribune* saying the school board had decided to have a vote, but the date was not set, excepting that it would be late in January or early in February. I rather suspected from the telegram yesterday the date must be soon or they would have written me instead of wiring. But as yet I do not know. By the way, what was the mass meeting held in December? Who called it and what was done beside appointing a committee? How many were there and what were the arguments beside economy? I wish I were there so we could talk it over as it is so hard to know what to do when I don't know what is going on.

I hope you are all right. You can't imagine what a fright I had when I got a telegram from Powell yesterday. I was shaky for a long time afterward.

Dearest Three:

The letter you asked Senator Robinson to write Pater regarding his pension has come. I don't know what to say. Everybody insists Pater should have more pension. The last letter he had from his old army pal, Mr. Warren, at Evansville said he ought to have more and was entitled to more. Co says Pater has known before he would not have to apply and he has refused to let even a doctor's statement be sent. It has always been such a point of honor with him to accept only what every other soldier his age gets that Co thinks it would not be right to do anything without his knowing what was done. We'll try to talk to him to see if maybe Mr. Warren's opinion won't change him. If we find we can do anything we'll write, or if it seems best to have the letter go from you, we'll let you know. I think Pater is wrong, but of course there isn't any use in arguing that. Thanks, Co says, for the start you made, and we'll try to follow it up.

Our Dear Sweet Mamma and Anne,

The mail brought three letters from you today. Sister and I thought it strange that you did not know that I was against the bonds after all that I have written. However, I am glad that you did not know for then you might have considered that you were not free to use your own judgment. I sent you a copy of the letter that I took to the *Tribune* Thursday of last week, and I am glad to say that Baird published it last week. It certainly will be interesting now to see what the Legion will do with your telegram.

I am against the bonds because I have not been able to clothe my children since the shop burned, because I have not been able to pay for the furniture we have needed in the house since that fire, and because the business has not been sufficient to buy a new car when we needed it nor a truck since we have been needing one for the past four years. And I am against them because during the past six months my business could not keep me from sacrificing my Indiana property, my telephone stock and my life insurance and because my neighbors are still losing their farms. Mr. Murray and E.S. Lynd have just lost theirs. How many others on the Flat have lost theirs the past season I do not know.

822 Atwater, Bloomington
January 29, 1931

Dearest Three:

Pater had a lovely birthday yesterday. Of course Cora got him the usual rose he always likes, a red one, as that is the kind he wants. We had a birthday cake — an angel food from the bakershop. We put four rose candle holders on each side of the oblong cake and then nine candles down the center for the nine single years to make the 89 total. Pater could see enough to count the lights, as he can see dark and light. He blew all but one out the first blow.

I am so sleepy I could go to sleep standing up, I think. For weeks I have not been in bed before about one o'clock and sometimes later. I have slept fairly late in the mornings this week, but somehow that doesn't seem to rest one as sleep earlier in the night does. What makes one so extra tired is not being able to sleep more than about four or five hours at a stretch without getting up, but of course when Pater gets up one of us has to get up too to put him back to bed in his chair.

Dear Sweet Mamma and Anne,

I worked a few hours yesterday afternoon in the territory assigned me by the committee and did not find a person who said that they were for the bonds. I worked about half of my assignment and will try to do the balance this afternoon. There was a circular in the mail yesterday boosting for the bonds. It was unsigned, so the identity of the persons responsible is not known. I venture that the material we put out can be traced to the authors somehow. It may be signed by the chairman of the Committee of Eighteen, or it may be signed by the three who are in charge of assembling it.

Why don't you have the doctor make the certificate about Pater's blindness and send it to Sen. Robinson and ask him to write Pater when it is allowed. The senator need not tell Pater anything about the Dr.'s certificate. He need only state that under the law Pater is entitled to the new rating. Or you could send in the certificate to Sen. Robinson and never let P. know that the increase comes. Cora needs every penny for running the home and taking care of it, and when P. won't take what he should have and help Cora with it, it is time for you two to supply the guardianship management that the case needs.

Dearest Three:

Too bad Murrays are losing their place. The farm really is a very poor one. But it does seem queer they should prefer Willwood, doesn't it?

We thought, too, it was queer you hadn't mentioned you were against the bonds when the telegram came. The wire came to me on Thursday morning. Friday I got a letter from you with the first mention of the bond election in it. I have been wondering what Castberg and Lewis will do with my answer. Of course if I had known you were opposed I would not have answered as I did. The reason I thought the bonds were necessary was on the score of the accrediting of the Powell high school. I understood we simply had to comply with the requirements of the North Central Association or else our graduates could not enter college without exams. You see, my own experience here gave me the college side of students who come from non-accredited high schools. They never have the first-class chance in college that students do who come from accredited schools. For a high school grad to have to take entrance exams means extra study and perhaps tutoring, for a student does not remember freshman algebra four years later. Each exam means a separate fee and it all amounts up to a goodly sum. I had all this in mind when I thought of the necessity of maintaining Powell's rating. It is, of course, obviously ridiculous for a student to have to take exams in Latin and algebra and English and history and geometry just because his high school did not have a gym, but such are the rules and all our argument doesn't get around it. With college only a few years off for Sister the move is a vital one with us. She will have to go away from home soon enough at best, and I'd hate terribly for her to have to go to Boulder for her senior year of high school just so she could graduate from an accredited high school with full college entrance privileges.

822 Atwater, Bloomington
February 1, 1931

Dearest Three:

Anne is still homesick and is always talking about going home so she can see Jules. Yesterday when she said she wanted to go home I asked what for, and she said, "To see Jules." Then she said, "Do you think he'll kiss me and let me kiss him when we get there?" She misses Jules more than all the rest of the children at school.

Anne is not the only one who misses Jules and all of you. I miss the hugs and caresses, and I hope you are giving my share to each other while I am away. A little praise and loving goes a long way toward happiness in the home, and you know you can catch a lot more flies with molasses than with vinegar! Let's have "honey" in the house as well as in the shop!

822 Atwater, Bloomington
February 5, 1931

Dearest Three:

Daddy, I just got your letter asking if the loan money had come. You must have missed a letter of mine, for I wrote you a week or more ago that it was here and ready for your orders. If you want me to send this at once, and if there is time to get it done and the papers back from Mt. Vernon in time for this month's state board meeting, perhaps you had better wire me how much to send and I will get it done at once and ask Pacific to rush the release to you.

So the bonds carried. Well, I hope my part did not have any effect in influencing votes. With farm finances the way they are it does not look as if people could stand any more taxes or even as much, but on the other hand the education we can give our children is about the only thing they really have that is permanently theirs. Pater sold his farm to get us through college and I wouldn't trade my education for any farm any-where. I regret very much that your first letter telling of the fight over the bond election did not get to me *one* day sooner, for then I would never have sent the telegram I did. I think it was certainly mean of the city bunch to take advantage of me the way they did. Well, you and your committee certainly worked hard and did everything you could, and if the majority of the farmers wouldn't go to the trouble to register their protest, they have only themselves to blame.

I have some good news for you, something you have accomplished. Pater is willing for us to write Senator Robinson about his pension increase. When the pension check came yesterday I mentioned that Mr. Warren, Pater's old friend at Evansville, thought he ought to get more pension. Pater said as usual he would not accept a disability pension and then I told him you had seen an article about Sen. Robinson's new bill and had written Sen. R. and had an answer from him. I read Pater *parts* of the Senator's letter to show the increase would be for natural infirmities due to age, and he insisted he had never heard of that bill and there was no reason why he shouldn't have that, as any veteran his age could get it. So this morning I asked what to write Sen. Robinson and Pater told me he wanted me to write as your wife and his daughter, referring to your letter. It certainly is strange. Heretofore he has never wanted to admit he was blind or needed help, but now he says to tell Sen. R. both. I read the part about no application being necessary, and explained that the veteran had to take the initiative of reporting his condition if he was eligible for the increase. *But*, I did *not* tell Pater that the doctor's certificate must be sent. We'll just send that along and ask Sen. Robinson not to refer to it in his reply. My, I am surely thankful to accomplish this on this trip. It is almost worth the trip, isn't it? The $300 increase in the year's pension will pay for a good many things. I am so glad you started the matter and that Mr. Warren's letter came in just right, and I was here to explain that the new law is of a service nature for age infirmity and not war disability. But you deserve the main credit.

Sister, I am so sorry to hear you could not sleep. Write and tell me all about it, won't you? I hate terribly being away for I miss you so much and all the good times we have talking over everything that happens in school. Aunt Cora and I both enjoyed your long letter and read it over and over and between the lines, too.

822 Atwater, Bloomington
February 13, 1931

We have learned of a splendid masseuse here who does marvels for sick people. The woman certainly is good, for she found every sore spot on me without my telling her. She would rub her fingers over me and say O my or Um-um and every time it was a place I have been having trouble. Cora was so surprised at what happened. When we first went, she was so completely worn out she could not keep going, and I felt about the way I have for the past few years. When Mrs. Parmer gave Cora her treatment she told Co there was nothing wrong with her but overwork, but she couldn't see how I had kept going in the condition I was in. Cora said afterward here she thought she was all in and I had come from Wyoming to rescue her and then the doctor said there is nothing the matter with her but that I was a fright! I have had five treatments now and will have two more. Today the doctor says it is remarkable how much better I am and she thinks a couple more will set me up so I'll be all right when I get home, if I don't do any heavy lifting. So Jules, my dear, I'll count on you to carry up the coal. I am so glad I'll have so much help, so I'll be entirely well soon.

822 Atwater, Bloomington
February 14, 1931

Dear Everyone:

We were very glad to get your letter this morning telling the exact amount to send Miss Anne. We went to the bank this afternoon and got a cashier's check made out to Pacific for $597. I suppose you have told him, but I mentioned to him that he should send the mortgage release papers to you. Do you want the note we give Cora made out for $597 or for an even amount, $600. We'll have to pay 6% on it as that is what she pays the insurance company. It will be much simpler, of course, to have the note for the even amount, but we'll do just as you say.

822 Atwater, Bloomington
February 17, 1931

Dearest Three:

Daddy, I was delighted to get the letter you sent from Dean Maxwell's office at the University of Wyoming. That is the best information yet, don't you think? Indeed, it has come out just recently that the North Central Association is a voluntary organization and does not absolutely control the accrediting of students to higher institutions of learning. The whole point I had about the necessity of keeping up our high school rating had to do with making it possible for our children to go to college without being under a serious handicap. The necessity of taking college entrance examinations is bad enough, as it requires a great deal of extra study and tutoring and expense, but the worst phase of the whole thing is that for several years at college a student from a non-accredited high school is always considered under-prepared and never receives the same consideration from faculty members as a student who is known to come from an accredited school. But now that the University of Wyoming says there is no danger of losing our rating on that point, the other points are not important. Of course I never did think much of making a point of wasting money on a gym. You certainly are clever and thorough, Daddy, to get this letter from Dean Maxwell's office, and I hope you will see that it gets widespread advertising, as people will understand the situation.

> 822 Atwater, Bloomington
> February 22, 1931

(From Cora)

Dear John:

Don't you think it's about time I'm writing to thank you for letting us keep Cecil this long? I just don't know what would have become of us if she and Anne hadn't come when they did. I didn't really mean for them to have to stay so long, but for a month or so Cecil hasn't been at all well. [She had to spend several days in bed with a severe cold and has been miserable since then with sciatica and some heart palpitations], so we thought she'd better stay on awhile to take the treatments from Mrs. Parmer. The treatments have been helping her a great deal, but she is still far from well and will have to be careful for quite awhile.

It certainly is fine of you to be willing to have Cecil away for so long. It hasn't been easy, I know, and I imagine that many a time you've had to keep going when you didn't feel like it. It's quite an achievement for a man and fourteen-year-old girl and nine-year-old lad to keep house all alone for so long. You can certainly be proud of the youngsters, can't you? Everybody here thinks it's marvelous that Cecilia can go ahead as she can and that you and Jules are so willing to do the extra work that accumulates so rapidly and bobs up so regularly.

We've been enjoying Sunday evening at Seth Parker's. I imagine you and Cecilia and Jules, and Edith and the others at Boulder are hearing it too. Doesn't it give one a sense of nearness and unity?

Thanks again for Cecil and Anne.

As ever,

Cora.

822 Atwater, Bloomington
February 23, 1931

Dearest Three:

This is the last letter we'll write you on this trip. Aren't you glad? I certainly am. We'll be so glad to get home again, for it is as hard for me to be away from you all as for you to get along without Anne and me. If I had my choice I would never have gone, but of course we had to come to the rescue here when Pater and Cora both needed help. The other day Cora was counting up her bank balance. Anne said, "Aunt Cora, what would you have now if you hadn't sent us the money to come here on?" And Cora replied quickly, "Nervous prostration."

I can hardly believe we'll be home again by the end of this week. It has been so hard to be away from all three of you all this time.

822 Atwater, Bloomington
February 25, 1931

Dear Cecil:

Pater has been talking intermittently since I got home from
the train about how much better we all are than when you
came, about the pension increase ("which we wouldn't have
known about if it hadn't been for you") and about the check he
gave you (he's had his money's worth out of the last already).
He was smoking when I got home; he wasn't in condition to go
to bed after the excitement of having you leave and was
smoking to get calmed down.

Thanks again for coming. I imagine you'll have had a big
time the day this letter arrives or the days preceding, as the
case may be. I expect to mail this early in the a.m. Thursday.
Let me know when it arrives.

Remember you mustn't work too hard and you mustn't be
under nervous strain. So rest a lot and have the family keep
things moving as calmly as possible. I hope you'll keep on
improving rapidly.

I'll wager you got a royal welcome home. It's nice to have
a family to welcome one back, isn't it?

And so thanks again and good night.

Lovingly,

Co

Honeyhill Farm
Sunday night, March 1, 1931

Dear Co: (Read and burn)

Everything is lovely and the goose hangs high—whoever that
is. Anyway, it isn't I!

The folk here are really glad to see me at home again.
They are so glad that they keep on doing the work so I won't get
tired out right away. That is about as much proof as anybody
could desire. When we got home, we found a huge box on the
library table on which there was a card saying "Celebrating the
return of Mother and Anne, and Mother's birthday." When I

opened the box I found it was a *five* pound box of chocolates! Think of it!

John was considerably worried over whether I would be arriving in a wheeled chair or on my own feet, after getting your and my last letter. He got up at 5:30 Saturday morning and did all the washing so I wouldn't have any excuse for starting in to work Monday morning. The day before he had scrubbed the whole house, oiled the floors, washed the windows, and even the woodwork in the bathroom. Everything is so clean I am afraid I can't keep it that way. After we got home and had things unpacked, and I asked about what they wanted for dinner, he announced that he was going to cook the dinner, which would be waffles. He did, and I never tasted such crisp waffles as he produced. He washed up the milk things that had been left from morning, and did just about everything there was to do. This noon we all sat in the living room a while after dinner and he brought me the article he is still working at for me to rewrite so he can take it around tomorrow for signatures and present it to the school board tomorrow night at their monthly meeting. While I was working on that he and the children did up all the kitchen work. He said at noon we should plan not to do any cooking on Sunday, after this, but have Sister bake a cake on Saturday and have cold meat ready and salad and milk and fruit. I feel rather wicked to be the object of such worry and attention, but I guess if I make use of my opportunity now I'll really get well enough so I won't have to be so careful after a while.

It really is almost pathetic how glad John is to have me here. I told you before I left that where there is real love between two people, misunderstandings clear away as soon as there is a chance for talking things over. And of course that is what has happened. I certainly am thankful I know how to practice Unity, at least to some extent, for I think after this I shall never again doubt that all one needs to do is to put all his affairs lovingly in the hands of the Father.

John is happy today. He went to town this morning to make final arrangements for selling his telephone stock and using the money to pay off what we have been owing at the bank here. The amount will also just about cover the taxes and the cost of the motor we bought last fall from the electric light company. John says he does not know just how he can fitly celebrate the condition of not owing the bank here any money, and since the change in ownership he is very glad to get out.

You may be sure there was excitement when your letter came yesterday saying Jules is to have a bicycle for his birthday. I think you must be mind readers. Just a few days ago I was watching some of the neighbor children with a bicycle and wishing our family had one. Now it comes. It is getting so I will be afraid to wish for anything soon, for fear it will come right away. At any rate, I'd better not wish for sausage on the end of anybody's nose! Jules has been studying catalogues to see which bicycle he will choose when the check comes. Several of the boys of the neighborhood have bicycles and they have such good times with them.

This is a special letter which you had better read over yourself, Cora, before telling Pater about it, and then pass on whatever you think best. I am glad Edith is there so you can talk over together what we have to say in this.

I'll tell first the general situation and then explain particulars. The question is this: Would you like to have me there for the entire school year, bringing all three children with me to go to school in Bloomington?

From what you said in the letter that came yesterday, you are not getting any more rest at proper hours than last year. You can't go on alone, of course. I expect to help out again, as usual. But the problem is this: It is too much for John to look after the things here and also the children. They can't shift about for a few months of the year and get anything from their school work. It is too expensive a trip to take them for so short a time. So we concluded that if you need me and want me, we might as well spend the whole winter in Bloomington and have the children go to school there.

There is a very particular reason besides being with you. Because of the financial depression in agricultural matters, we are up against it. We have not received all that was supposed to be due on the 1929 honey that we shipped, and we have had practically nothing on the 1930 crop. Now we have learned through the man who represents Wyoming on the board of the honey selling association that probably there will be nothing coming. This is not generally known, as the association has not sent out the information yet. The drop in prices was so great and the market so poor, both at home and abroad, that the association has not sold last year's honey and still has some on hand of the year before. Now the fact is that the storage charges and the other incidentals have amounted to enough to eat up whatever we will have coming if the honey ever is sold. By the time the association pays the cost of taking care of this honey, there won't be any money left to go to the producer. We wouldn't be any better off if we had not shipped through the association, for the market has been so bad the individual producer has not done any better. It is the same with all farm crops. I think perhaps I told you that last fall when our beans were harvested, we received what was supposed to be an advance of 3¢ a pound from the bean marketing association, the remainder to come later in the winter when all the beans were sold and the pool closed. When I came home in February the market price of beans was $2.60 per hundred, or 40 cents a hundred less than the advance we had received in the fall. Farmers who stored their potatoes last fall instead of accepting from 90¢ to $1.85 a hundred, sold them this spring for 65¢ a hundred, after all the work of storing and culling, and the shrinkage loss.

Well, after all this explanation, what I want to say is this. We can not get enough to live on from our possibilities here at the present time. I need to earn some money to help along until this depression is over and we can again realize on our crops, farm as well as honey. There is nothing I can do here to earn money, except the news writing, and the papers have cut down on that until it is not worth much any more. The Casper paper has cut out correspondents entirely and the Billings paper won't pay more than eight or nine dollars a month no matter how hard I work.

We have been thinking of what Miss Berry said last spring about my getting work as a substitute in the English Department if I were in Bloomington for any length of time. Do you suppose that would be possible? With as many freshman English instructors as are now necessary, it really is needed to have some one who can fill in, and the substitute could probably get a good deal of work to do. I feel sure I could do that work again, for while it has been a good many years, I haven't exactly been rusting in my mind all the time. I hope that I can get to writing and earn an income from that eventually, but right now we need to have something more definite. If I could get enough work in the English Department to take care of the expenses of the children and me while we are in Bloomington, John could get along on his pension and pay the running expenses of the farm and business besides from the pension. In addition we need money for interest and taxes. If we can keep things going for the coming year, we think we can weather the financial depression safely. But if we get behind during the coming year, no telling what would happen, and we do so want to hold on to the place here, for it is home and the nicest place we know of to live right along.

Of course we realize it will be a great burden on you, Cora, to have such a family descend upon you for a school year. But we would try to make it as easy as possible, and there is this side of it—that if the children and I were all there, you could get away any time you wanted for as long as you wanted, and could be much freer than if you were alone. If we came before the city schools start, you would have almost three weeks to do as you please before college begins in September. We would, of course, expect to pay our share of the living expense, with so many of us. Then too, Cecilia can do the work you usually hire a student to do, and Jules can take care of the wood and kindling and ashes, and run errands. He can also do the yard work. And I am rather used to cooking for a family, so that part won't be anything different than regular for me.

I do not feel that it is right for you to face the winter alone, even if Pater's sight is improving. You simply can't take care of him and the house and do your college work. You need me, that I know. My family also needs me. John feels that I can do the most for all concerned, including him if I take the children with me and help you and Pater. John says he can manage all right by himself, and he is willing to do so. He says the biggest problem before us is to safeguard our investment here, and that if I can help at that by earning some money this coming winter to help along, he can stand being alone for a while. He says it is better to suffer that now than to face the probable loss of our home.

Please think it over and let us know. If we do plan to be there the whole school year, there aren't many weeks left to arrange. This has come up suddenly, for until a few days ago we still thought we could count on getting money out of previous honey crops, enough to tide us over. But now we know there is none to come, and this year's prospect isn't much better.

July 8, 1931, Wednesday

We are looking for an answer soon to my letter asking what you think of our spending the winter at 822. Of course we all are anxious to hear. It will make a good deal of difference in my canning arrangements, as well as various other household matters whether we'll all be here or most of us in Indiana. When the subject of being in Bloomington for the school year was first broached to Cecilia, she wept bitterly at the idea of being away from Powell, but the more she thinks of it the more advantages she sees in the plan and the more things she thinks of that she wants to do in Bloomington. She has a whole book of reasons now why she would like to go. We have not told anybody here of our tentative plans, and won't, of course, till we are all set either way.

When I got home from town yesterday afternoon John met at the gate and announced: "The letter is here. Come and see what Cora has to say." You may be sure we lost no time in reading your epistle, and we were all greatly pleased that you are willing to have us descend upon you for the whole school year. You say we are good sports to plan as we have, but we think you are the real sport to put up with a whole family. To be sure, you will enjoy the children when you have time, but the trouble is they will be there all the time.

In writing to Dr. Carter and the others I'll simply say that since I find it necessary to be in Bloomington the entire school year I would like to have work. I won't say anything about hard times, but I think to Dr. Carter, who does not know my record, I'll mention that I have two degrees in English and taught in the department six years. I think I'll write to Mr. Cravens, Miss Berry, Dr. Hale, and Dr. Howe, and also Mrs. Teter, and perhaps Dr. Bryan. I thought at first I'd wait till I heard from Dr. Carter before writing the others, then decided that he might ask them soon about me and I'd better have them forewarned. Thanks for the suggestion, Edith, that I apply for a regular job. Perhaps if I do that and there isn't any to be had, Dr. Carter would be more interested in giving me substitute work. However, I feel that there is something there for me to do, and it will work out all right with financial returns that will take care of all our needs.

Jules did not really believe we might go for the year until yesterday, and he is taking it hard—the way Cecilia did when I first told her about it several weeks ago. I thought at first I would not say anything to them until all plans were made.

Then when I merely hinted at it, and Cecilia took it so hard I decided they should have some time to be prepared. Yesterday when she knew the letter had come, Cecilia quoted Jacob in "One Must Marry," and said she really wanted to go now, and she hoped you would say we could come. I am sure Jules will arrive at the same point as soon as he has had time to think things over, but yesterday the only thing he could think of that he wanted to do when he got to Bloomington was to come back home again! However, I think perhaps his views were somewhat warped at the moment by his big sister's suggestion that if he went to Bloomington and lived in town, he would have to stay dressed up all the time and not live in overalls the way he does here! Jules hasn't reached the stage Cecilia has of *desiring* to be dressed up all the time. All three of the children are eagerly looking forward to having all the oranges and bananas they want, and to having grapefruit for breakfast any time during the winter. This noon they all got quite excited over Anne's suggestion that there would be pears on the tree and grapes on the vines in the back yard!

I was quite interested yesterday in something that happened. One of the Powell girls who is a junior in college is taking some English by correspondence. She got stuck and asked me for help. The work was on late 18th century poets, leading up to the period of Romanticism. When she showed me her outline and questions, I hadn't thought of Crabbe and others leading up to Burns, for years and years. I was pleased to find that before I had talked with her five minutes I recalled the essential points and was able to get her started right. You remember several years ago when the Big Horn Basin Teachers Association held its institute in Powell I was on for some work. I was anxious to find out if I could still get up without undue embarrassment and worry and direct a class of grown-ups in English and I found, to my delight, that it did not bother me at all. I made out my lesson plans and had no trouble at all in putting them across to the teachers. All of which gives me some confidence in undertaking to teach again in college, for after all, 18 years is a long time to be out of a line of work and then drop back in.

I got a letter from Dr. Carter yesterday, and I was more than delighted with his letter, for it says more than we could ask for right off the bat. He certainly answered immediately. One would hardly expect there would be a vacancy at this time of year, but of course there may be even yet, and his letter is worded in such a way that it appears I would have first chance in case one happens. Anyway, he himself has now suggested that I am to have whatever substitute work comes up, and that is better than for me to ask for it. What with the scarcity of jobs in general right now, and also considering that it is now nearly *18* years since I resigned my job in the Department, it certainly is fine to get a letter like this from the present head. Of course anybody knows the most of it is due to the wonderful work Cora has done in these years. Wasn't it dear of Prof. Stephenson to hustle right over to Dr. Carter and say a good word for me? Stevie always did like me, you know. You remember he wouldn't let anybody poke a nose into his picturemaking lab in the English Dept., where he made enlargements for the walls of the department and stereoptican and movie film, and used to call me in and show me all his results, and then when he went away for a year gave me carte blanche in the lab to use all his supplies and do anything I wanted.

Co, I do not think you need to worry about what people here will say about my teaching again. I have told several, and the general comment is, "You are lucky to have something to fall back on. I wish I had." Several women have told me they have wished they could find something to do to help along. Mrs. Murray told me the other day about their having to give up their place. She said she had always thought she would never live through having to give up that place and start another, but there wasn't any use lying down and dying as that wouldn't help anyone. She said there were months when neither she nor Mr. Murray slept while they were fighting through deciding to let the place go, but that now they had decided and quit suffering by just giving up and letting it go at that. She said Bruce would go to college in September from this place and come back at Christmas to the new one on the Willwood. After all, that can't be as hard as having to help move. She says Max is taking it very hard as he is just realizing now what the move means in giving up the good house. As a matter of fact, they don't know yet where they will get the money to build the little shack they will have to have. She said the banker said there is always money in the bank, but if crops turn out no better this year than last, no one will have any money. John heard the other day they are trying to rent a place on this side of the river next to their farm on the south side of the river, as the place on this side has a good house on it, small, but in good repair.

Thursday, July 23, 1931

Cora, we will start whenever it is necessary for us to arrive in time for you to go to Boulder with Edith. I had been wishing all along you could get away for awhile, and if you will stay away a week or two or three after school starts and get a real rest, so much the better. As for our leaving early, a few days or weeks either way won't make any difference after we are started. It is just starting that is hard. After we get settled, there will be a routine that will keep us all busy and I know we will enjoy the year. It will be nice to have a few weeks in Bloomington before school starts to get things all settled and perhaps some things about the house done before the children start school.

There just seems to be every reason why we should spend this winter in Indiana. Pater needs me for a while, you certainly need someone for more than a while (even though you don't like to admit it) and we need to help ourselves. So if spending the year in Bloomington will serve all three needs at once, it surely is the thing to do. Of course John hates for us to be away, but there are many reasons too why this year is the best one for us to be away. For one thing, the crop is very light, and he will have only half as much work to do this fall as usual, or maybe less than that. He will not have to work so hard or so long, and can get along by himself this year, whereas ordinarily he would have to have a lot of help. John has been so worried since so many people around us have lost their places that he is more than glad we can do something to help. Losing good neighbors like the Youngs, Bygrens, and Murrays has made us feel badly, and we are only too thankful there is some way we can keep going without having to face what they have gone through. Since we have found that I can get some work in the English Department, what with that help and our other opportunities, John looks and feels years younger, for he is sure we will pull through in fine shape. And of course your generous offer [to send us $100 a month from Pater's pension or your income] has cheered him greatly, even though he does not want to accept it.

We have been away so much for such varied lengths of time that going away now isn't as hard as if we never had been parted. If John were a helpless soul who had to go to a restaurant every time he wanted something to eat, of course it would be different. But he is a good cook and housekeeper, and in the winter has time, so he gets on famously.

We are planning to go to the Park Saturday morning and get back some time Monday afternoon or evening. I am so glad we can all make the Park trip together now, and that we have this nice car to travel in. The new road over Sylvan Pass is said to be marvellous—wide and lovely grades, so you go in high all the time. It is about an hour shorter in time than the old road.

Wednesday, July 29, 1931

We had a marvellous trip to Yellowstone Park and, thanks to your generosity, Co, without having to worry about finances. We wouldn't have missed it for anything. We all agreed it will be a lovely memory to think of this winter when we are away from the mountains.

I guess it is settled now that we'll leave here on the evening train, Tuesday, August 11, due in Chicago on Thursday morning about nine, and in Bloomington via Indpls about 6:30 that evening. I am trying to get things done up this week so John will have as little as possible of extra things to do. I'll be all right if no one insists on having any parties or special leave takings. I have nipped one in the bud and refused an invitation to a music recital as a special farewell, explaining that I appreciated the wish as much as if I could accept the invitation. The last week is worth more to me at home than sitting around with people for whom I care only a little.

So you think anybody who would choose Indiana is a raving maniac, Edith? Well, the family says to tell you it is not exactly by choice that we are all descending on Cora, but we are certainly glad we have the opportunity of doing so since we need it.

Out of Frannie,
August 11, 1931

Dearest Daddy,

We have been on the observation platform and have seen the Mantua bee yard and all the houses along the way. Both Cecilias felt pretty weepy when we watched Honeyhill out of sight. We are going back to the section now and go to bed. It is 8:30. I wonder if you are going to bed now.

We all love you, dearest, and dread being away from you, but we are glad you are brave enough to face the winter alone so we can go. I am sure only good will result for all of us.

Your Ce.

In Minnesota
August 12, 1931

Anne has had a fine birthday. We gave her some of the little packages of cakes this morning before breakfast and she was much pleased. She thought that was her birthday present. While the children changed their clothes to go to the diner for lunch, I took the real presents and gave them to the steward. He was much interested. When we got to the diner, the little packages were in the center of the table, hid by the menu cards. When Anne saw them her eyes were big as saucers and she could not figure how they knew it was her birthday, until we told her. The steward told me when we began to eat that the chief cook had made Anne a birthday cake, and sure enough, when the table was cleared the waiter brought in a *whole* cake. The first layer was covered with crushed pineapple. The top and sides were spread with marshmallow icing and then covered with crushed nuts. I never ate a lighter, nicer cake. There was no charge for it, and the steward apologized because they did not have any candles to put on the cake. The dinner cost $3 including tip. We ordered two luncheons at a dollar each — soup, fish, potatoes, carrots, bread and butter, milk, and ice cream. The two were enough to serve the three children. I had a combination salad — head lettuce, tomatoes, cucumbers, radish, and peas, enough to serve all four of us. I did not want anything else but bread and butter. We ordered one extra dessert so each of the children had ice cream. They all ate so much they at once decided they didn't want much for supper. The waiter asked me if we wanted to take the cake along with us, but of course I said no. We ate only about a fourth of the cake. It was a real birthday party and all the people in the diner were interested.

Honeyhill Farm
August 11, 1931

My Dear Sweet Family,

When you get this you will either be there or on your way down from Indianapolis in Uncle Teddy's car. And I hope you will be having a fine time.

I wonder this morning where you will be Wednesday morning when you see daylight and the sun. And I wonder if you will see the sun when you see daylight Thursday morning.

All three of you children must be as good and as helpful to Mamma during the next nine months as you can possibly be, because if Mamma works in the University she will have to work awfully hard.

Sister: You must not boss and banter too much!

Jules: You must not tease too much!

Anne: You must always answer as soon as you are called, and always be good — as you can be.

And all three of you must be on hand when either Grandpa, Aunt Cora, or Mother wants you and must do cheerfully and gladly what you are asked to do.

I hope all three of you children will get to go to Evansville. I will send a letter so that it will get to Uncle Pacific by the middle of next week when you should be there. Mother and Grandpa can have a fine visit by themselves while you are at West Franklin.

Your lover,
Daddy.

Bloomington
Saturday, August 15, 1931

The Boulderites and Cora started west this morning shortly after five o'clock. They expected to be in St. Louis by noon and goodness knows where tonight. You can guess that from the time we got here Thursday night until they started this morning there was not much time for letter writing. Cora had exam papers to mark and grades to make out, all her things to pack, and directions to leave about all sorts of matters, as well as finances to be arranged for while she was gone. We get our first salary checks October 3.* I had $37 left, she has about $65, and that is all there is in sight until October 3 unless we use the pension check Pater gets September 4, which we expect to do. I guess it is a good thing in one way that I am here, for Pater seldom gives Cora any of his pension checks unless she

---

*Dr. Carter had written to Cecilia in August to say that one of the professors in his department had resigned and that he could offer her full-time work instead of substitute work.

asks specially for it, and of course she ought to have the money regularly since she pays all the expenses.

Dr. Carter was as lovely as could be. He told me all about the courses and gave me the books he had on hand and called the University bookstore to have them give me the others. He showed me all through the new building the English Department is in and explained about offices and class rooms, and all. There are about a half dozen women teachers in the department, and to my pleasure I found he had allotted me in the same office with Miss Edna Johnson, who ranks highest in the department of any of the women. We think that quite an honor.

He told me all the men in the department who knew me had recommended me most highly, and mentioned them by name. He said that when he went to Dr. Bryan to speak to him about putting me in the vacant place, Dr. Bryan was very enthusiastic about it and recommended me most warmly, as did many others in the departments and the university office.

Then he said something that completely bowled me over. He told me that the man whose place I take has gone back where he used to teach in college to accept a promotion he had long wished for, and then said that there would have been no difficulty in finding someone to take his place, as there are many, many persons wanting positions whose qualifications and training and experience are beyond question. Then he said, "But no matter how well qualified an instructor may be, there is always that indeterminable thing we call personality that no one can read from the finest of qualifications, and Dr. Bryan and all your friends assure me that you have that essential and highly desired quality in fullest measure, and we are very happy to have you. I feel the Department is very fortunate in having you on hand to step into this vacancy when we need someone." What do you think of that? Isn't that a wonderful recommendation from President Bryan and the others who knew me? I did not write to President Bryan, you know, so I feel all the more honored at his fine compliment.

Tuesday, August 18, 1931

Just a week ago we were starting. In some ways it doesn't seem that long, but in the main it already seems like a year.

I took the children to a movie yesterday. In the middle of it the picture made me homesick for you when two lovers kissed and one patted the other's cheek the way you do. The girls wanted to see the show twice but I didn't want to cry twice.

Wednesday, September 9, 1931

I have a telephone call in for Cora while I am writing this. Pater insists she must come home at once before school starts. Of course we knew he would do that! If I say she is not well and needs the rest and the change, he insists all the more she must come home and let him doctor her. He wanted me to wire her today to come home at once. I am going to tell her to tell me to tell Pater that she is on leave of absence to do some observation in the mathematics department of the university at Boulder and that it may take some weeks. It does no good to tell him she needs the change. He simply says she does not, and that is all there is to it. He is certain he is the only one who knows how to treat all the diseases and gets peeved if you tell him what any doctor said. He thinks no doctor knows anything. For that reason, illness, no matter how real, is no argument to him because he simply says the doctor doesn't know anything. It makes it hard, Daddy, to have to begin telling untruths at my age! I hate to have the children know about it, but can't keep it all from them. Pater won't admit that anybody needs a vacation. He thinks that is all nonsense. Two or three weeks he thinks is more than enough for anybody.

Thursday, September 10, 1931

I must tell you what happened after I called Cora last night. I was not far wrong in my scheme to tell Pater that Cora was to visit the mathematics department of the university in Boulder, for when I talked with her she said the head of her dep't had really suggested she do that and also that she investigate what the Association of University Professors was doing in the Boulder chapter. Well, after I finished talking with Cora and told Pater that she would not come back because she was to visit the university there and it did not start until college did here, he asked all about it. Cecilia and I sat holding our breaths to see if the explanation would be accepted, for Pater had worked himself up until he was all sick. He sat and pondered a bit, and then remarked, with a chuckle: "Well, the bluff did not work— that time." Sister and I nearly shouted we were so tickled. The bluff did not work! Sister thought maybe Pater did not realize he had said it out loud. Maybe not, but we heard it. I am not sorry I called, for now he seems perfectly satisfied and is all right. It is worth $2 to me to have Pater content and quiet.

Wednesday, September 16, 1931

I taught my first class today. It seemed perfectly natural to be back at it again. My classes will all be in the afternoon. Three days a week—Monday, Wednesday, and Friday—I'll have a literature class at one o'clock. Two days each week— Tuesday and Thursday—I'll have composition classes at one, two and three o'clock. In addition I'll have office hours and conference hours with students. All Cora's classes are in the morning and we can therefore divide the home work between us very nicely. Of course there will be frequent occasions when she will have to go in the afternoons and I in the mornings, but we can arrange that to suit our convenience.

I have the full schedule of four classes, so we ought to be able to count on the $1800 for the year.

I made the rounds of the merchants here who would be interested in potatoes, as you ask. They all told me I should go to Indianapolis, as these potatoes are too fine for local trade. They did not think there would be enough demand to pay what these potatoes are worth. All the men frankly admitted they never saw potatoes like these.

When I got back from Indianapolis this afternoon at five I stopped at the Western Union and wired you as follows: "High freight prohibits sale here or Indianapolis. Mailing details tonight." I thought I'd better let you know so you would not hold up the cars as they were loaded.

I went to the Pennsylvania freight office first after I got to Indpls and found that the freight from Powell to Indpls would be 91 cents a hundred, as close as they could figure it without a lot of checking.

I then went to the Atlantic and Pacific general offices, on South State Street, just off East Washington in the 1700 block. The manager there was very nice and we talked a long time. He finally said they did most of their buying through the Atlantic Commission Company, and called up the man and talked to him. Then he sent me to see him. I was not so keen on his service, however, as he charges $15 a car for selling, and if we are going to pay that we might as well sell to Bever at home.

I then went to see some wholesale buyers, three in all. One firm was not buying potatoes at all at present. Another said offhand the market was too unsteady to buy now. The third discussed the whole potato situation with me but said at once the freight rate was prohibitive. The second also told me the whole potato market, from New York to Chicago is poor and that this market can not take our potatoes, no matter how fine they are, because the freight makes the cost too high. They all knew the potatoes at once as Triumphs, and admired them greatly. The general market here does not know the late fall Triumph, and the only potato that can command a higher price at this time of year is the Idaho Russet. They do not know that the western Triumph is a baking potato, as the southern early Triumph is decidedly not. They all said there is no use trying to educate the market here as it is too slow a process.

I am sorry this is the situation, but it is well to find it all out. As one wholesaler said to me today, "You are just out of luck on your freight, and there isn't anything you can do about it." I hated to spend the money necessary for a trip to Indpls, but I decided right now is the time to find out just what we can do, and if there was any chance at all to break into this market.

Cora is home again and she looks fine and feels fine except for a cold which all of us are going through right now. She is glad to be back. After she taught the first morning she came in and said, "My, but I love to teach college math!" Her students have told her that they have understood more in two days of her teaching than in the three weeks before. She gave me quite a compliment after I told her something about the classes and courses I have. You know she is said always to be the best teacher in the University. Well, she told me that if I keep on the way I am doing, before the end of the year she is afraid she won't be the best teacher in the University!

So you think of me all the time. So do I of you. It gives us something to look forward to as well as something to fall back on for comfort. I dreamed the other night that I was tired, and you came up behind me and put your arms around me, holding my breasts in your hands, one on each side. It gave me such a feeling of strength and rest in the dream, and many times since.

Last night the Faculty Women's Club, the organization of wives of faculty men, and women of the faculty, gave their annual formal reception to new members of the faculty. Of course I received a special invitation. This is one of the most important social affairs of the year. Everything was lovely. All the people were so nice to me and gave me such a hearty welcome.

We were so delighted over what President Bryan said. We went up to speak to him — Cora went first, and he greeted her in the usual manner. Then he saw me. He put out his hand quickly and said, "O, Mrs. Hendricks, I am *so glad* you are with us again." Then he went on, with a laugh, "You know, when Dr. Carter came to me about the middle of the summer, saying he wanted to talk about an appointment for Mrs. Hendricks, the name at first did not mean anything to me, for I did not connect it with you immediately. Dr. Carter is very conservative, and so am I. Then suddenly I made the connection. I threw up my hands, and said to Dr. Carter, "O, Mrs. *Hendricks*! Of course we want *her*!" He threw up his hands to illustrate. Isn't it lovely to have him say it himself? You know Dr. Carter told me that Dr. Bryan had recommended me. It is nice to hear his side of it. Cora thinks it wonderful for the President to be so enthusiastic over a faculty member.

Friday, October 30, 1931

Ienclose a check for you to deposit. We ran out of money here and found it necessary to trade checks for $100. That is, I gave Cora a check for $100 to deposit here. I am enclosing a check for $150, but that of course means only $50 after the $100 is taken out that I gave Cora. I believe the $50 will be the amount I'll send you for deposit in Powell out of the salary check I get November 6, unless you particularly need more right now. Cora and Pater have taxes and insurance payments to meet now and Co is behind on the rent and must pay some. Pater sent us his July and August pension amounts, and $50 more of Cora's to pay our railroad fare here, so they did not have that money to use for expenses here. Then, Sister and I both had to have coats. I had to have new spectacles, Jules and Anne needed shoes, and Jules must have an overcoat, as he has none at all. There are so many little expenses that don't seem much when considered singly, but all together they count up. We try to be as careful as possible, but somehow the money goes. Living is expensive with $50 a month house rent, and every bit of food bought. However, as you have said a number of times, we are fortunate to be able to have the children where they get the right food and schooling.

One of my students yesterday asked to be excused from class today. He had just learned that the bank at his home town, Logansport, had failed, and in this bank was all the money he had saved to go to college this year, and all his father's money, too. He thought he could fix it up so he could stay in school if he could go home over the weekend to arrange it. The same day another student explained his absence at a previous recitation by saying he had lost the job on which he was depending to earn his room and board. He was entirely without money and had to stay out of class and hunt a job so he could eat. Yesterday morning he heard his father was taken to the hospital for an operation. So other people have their troubles, too.

Honeyhill
November 15, 1931

My Dear Sweet Family,

Even with all that you can earn and put into the business here we will be mighty close run to pay what we have to pay and get what we need. I am pretty well satisfied that if we do not get any thing more from the honey association we had better give up the idea of buying a new truck and get a used one at Bloomington or Indianapolis when I come east in the spring. We must have one that I will not have to crank, but we can get along with a used one and especially so if a satisfactory one can be bought back there at a reasonable price. We will at least have the Farm Loan Board payment to take care out of what you can earn and that must be paid the first of April. And we need a new separator and the old house should be covered. And we will have to renew our insurance on the house next summer. There is also the washer note that must be paid about the first of January. There is Mrs. Dungan's bill and we owe the Home Lumber Co. close on to $90.00 yet. But first of all Nelson must be paid. There is now left on his note a balance of a little less than $120.00. I told him we would have enough to take that up when you sent the next check the first of the month. The bean check amounted to $142.21. There is yet about $30.00 coming on the seed beans that Simon saved and a little more on the potatoes that he has in the cellar, but the cow feed is to be paid out of that. And when this is paid for there will not be much left. All of this and taxes will have to be taken care of somehow, so we better not buy me a new coat just now. I wanted you to get one only if you could get a serge one for a good price. My plain one will be sufficient for winter wear now that we have the closed car. If not, the big one will keep me warm any where I may want to go. And for work coats I have plenty for this winter.

I fear that the loss of their peas has put Richards in a very bad shape. Their beet check did not suffice to pay all they owed Nelson, and they have nothing to pay their grocery bill at Cubbages. It makes me feel bad to realize that they are in such bad condition financially. I have always thought so much of both of them because it seemed to me they had a better understanding and appreciation of your abilities and character than any others in the community. It is therefore disagreeable to have to realize that they may be the next ones in this neighborhood to lose their place. And they stand a good chance to do so, unless some of their people can come to their assistance. Mr. R. told me yesterday that his annual payment on his state loan is now due and they have nothing to meet it with.

822 Atwater, Bloomington
November 28, 1931

Yes, my dear, it is hard to be away from a comfortable home. We have decided that we can't stand this house any longer as it is. Co and I went to see Mr. Cravens and Dr. Bryan this a.m. to say we'd have to move, but that if the University would fix up the house so it was really comfortable we'd move back. We are now looking for a place and expect to move before long. Pater is willing to go as the floor has sunk so there is always a draft. We'll know in a few days what the University intends to do, and we'll then know whether to take a house to stay in or only a temporary one until this is ready. We insisted on a real basement and complete remodeling. We have had to heat with the gas oven and the fireplace for some time.

There has been so much to do the last couple of days I am not sure how much I have told you about moving. Pater mentioned last week he would be willing to move out of this house. We lost no time hunting another. We called real estate men and walked the streets in this part of town. We looked at lots of places, none of them suitable. All the while we knew Miss Berry has a house near here, but we did not want it because it is right across the street from Stone's Restaurant, where the radio plays most of the night. We had no idea her house was large enough, anyway. When we went to see Mr. Cravens and Dr. Bryan to tell them this university-owned house is no longer habitable, they agreed for us to move out at any time, with first chance at moving back in if the house suits us when it is remodeled. Since the remodeling ought to take not more than two or three months, we decided if we could move somewhere near it would be easy to move back again. So we went to look at Miss Berry's house and to our surprise found it much larger than it looks, and very conveniently arranged. There are five large rooms and a bath on the first floor; the upstairs is one large room, but with three alcoves; the basement is very large, light, and completely finished. The rent is $40, ten dollars less than this house. There is nearly twice as much room, considering basement and upstairs.

So we are all set to move tomorrow. We had a man and his wife clean the house today so it will all be ready. The moving men set up the beds and put everything in place. The moving car men say we do not need to pack anything as it is such a short way—just across the street and around the corner—that they will carry the china and breakables in tubs.

We are moving almost next to where we used to be on East Third Street—about half way between here and there. Our new number is 324 South Woodlawn Avenue. As we have the same mail carrier, we'll be sure to get our mail addressed either way.

In spite of the extra work and expense (it cost about $50 to get moved) we are delighted to be moved. This house is too comfortable for words. We can't believe yet we can go anywhere in the house in comfort! There is a big upstairs where the children sleep—all in one room, but really three rooms without partitions. Cora and I are in the downstairs bedroom. Pater's room was the dining room, and we have a living room and a music room. The basement is large, dry, and all finished. And the furnace heats as well as a Mont Ward one. In ten or fifteen minutes the fire burns up enough to heat the whole house. There are many other advantages, and we are so glad we are here.

We have been interested in Cecilia's changing attitude toward the possibility of our being here another year. She told Co the other day she *almost* hoped we would! She asked me if I remembered how she cried one day at noon when you mentioned there was a chance we'd be here for two years, and made the comment now that being here another year isn't such a calamity as it seemed then! She is enjoying everything immensely, especially her library work at school. She isn't doing anything marvelous in Latin yet, but we think she will pass all right. Her teacher told her the trouble was not with her—that her other grades showed she was bright enough and that she studied enough. The trouble was that she had not had the necessary first year work.

The surprise package came this morning. We are all delighted. The children think the heart immense. The store here has calf hearts that are quite small. Jules says he is going to take this heart to the store to show the men there what kind of beef hearts we raise in Wyoming. The T-bones are lovely, and we'll all enjoy them.

I have read over all the letters in the file for the past couple weeks. I hardly know how to plan about finances except to say that we are trying to get along so as to send you $100 a month now to apply in any way you think best. We get paid ten months during the year—I have had three checks now and there are seven more to come, or approximately $700. I think you had better plan how to use the money as you understand the whole matter. There is $36 interest due on the $600 Cora borrowed on her life insurance for us, and that must come out of the January check. Even the $100 a month from my salary doesn't seem to take care of everything we have to pay, does it? But it helps a lot, and without it we would be worse off than we are. I suspect we might as well count on our being here another year, and by that time we ought to come out all right, don't you think? I hate to be apart from you, but there are so many advantages to be gained we can't let the personal longing deter us from what is best. And you *must* have a truck by spring.

Jules has been wishing for years for an erector set and a steam engine. We have priced them and looked them up in the cat, and are sending to Mont Wards. With the erector set he can build machinery for the engine to run. The engine runs by electricity, which is safer than alcohol. We are planning to get Anne a doll house, her great desire, as we now have a place for it. Sister's gifts will be mainly wearing apparel she needs and wants, and the magazines you have sent her, which are coming. We all enjoy them.

Honeyhill
December 10, 1931

My Dear Sweet Family,

Well, "thim's that." The fruit cakes are in the oven, six of them. The pans are all cleaned, and that means all that were available, and put away. The kitchen floor is swabbed and mobbed. And the fruit cakes are half baked. That is, they have been in the oven 1½ hours. My, how good it smells to open the oven door now. If they only end well and are really fit to eat that will be fine. If they are good I shall take one of them to Richards with me when I go there for Christmas dinner.

This morning was the frostiest morning of any this winter. The telephone wires looked like cables at least an inch thick. I had forgot to get nuts for the fruit cake mixture yesterday so had to go to Powell again this morning. So I concluded to get a film for the camera and try to get some pictures. Shortly after I got home the sun burst through the fog so I could get a good exposure of the house and the trees together.

I would be glad, Mother Dear, if you could get your position in the University again next year, so that the children might have the benefits of the schools there, especially the high school. So long as you will need to be there during the winter to be with Pater I think you might as well spend the school year there if you could get the regular work that you now have. It is not as good a home for me as I would like, to be separated from the children and their good mother all this time. But by securing that work and taking the children there again it would be giving the children more than we could give them here. The hope of some day being able to hear their voices was the thing that enticed and lured me from a life of idleness and ease in the Soldiers' Home. And now that we have those Voices there is nothing within my power to do that I would not do to give them the best that we can give them. And so long as they can have an advantage by going to school in Bloomington and at the same time be with you I can afford to do without them a few months each year while you need to be in Bloomington.

324 South Woodlawn, Bloomington
December 16, 1931

Yes, dearest, it is comfortable to know the note at the bank is all paid. I am sure we'll come out fine by the end of the year and in another year we ought to be pretty clear of everything pressing. Too bad all our good neighbors can't say as much.

I did not show the children the letter with the financial matters in it. I suspect you'd better write me a separate note when there are such matters. If you put my name on the note the children will hand it right to me if they open the envelope.

324 South Woodlawn, Bloomington
Sunday, December 20, 1931

Dearest Daddy,

We mailed Christmas packages yesterday. They should reach Wyoming and Honeyhill in plenty of time, we think. We sent a package to Gimmesons, Gilletts, Murrays, and Richards. Cecilia sent the Bygren twins and Celeste Beacock and Mary Elizabeth Webb little gifts, and Anne sent to Emily Susterka, Mary Kawano, and Mary Jean Beacock. We did not get expensive gifts—mainly practical things to wear, and we watched the bargain counters, too, and got many dollar articles for a quarter.

Cora thought your package did not have much in it as gifts. Cecilia wanted to buy you a dollar book, but I insisted you would rather use the dollar to pay some one we owe. I know you will accept their desire to send something as valuable as the articles they might have sent. We all had to laugh at Cora, even tho what she said made me homesick enough to cry the next minute. She said all you could do would be to eat some candy and nuts, play a game of sol, use a new handkerchief to blow your nose and wipe your eyes, and then Christmas would be over for you as there would be nothing else for you to do.

We had a letter yesterday from Richards telling us not to send them anything for Christmas, as they could not send us any. We already had gifts for them all wrapped and ready to send, so of course we sent them. I hope they will not feel that they must send us some now. Anyway, Cora and I have jobs to go on and can surely spare a little for others. Too bad their peas blew away. You know how it feels to have a crop blow away, don't you.

If we could all have been together nothing more could be desired. You may be sure we thought of you every minute of the day. The children did not seem homesick, I am glad to say. As for me, the feel of your arms around me and the touch of your lips would be all I would ask for on Christmas, or any other day.

The children are happy with the many gifts from all the relatives and friends. Of course your name is in with ours, Cora's and mine, on all the gifts "Santa Claus" brought. Jules is happy with the erector set and Anne with the doll house they have wanted for several years. Jules has made various things — engines and derricks and what-nots — with the erector set. Anne's doll house is a large, beautiful one with six rooms. It came flat from Mont Wards and we had the fun of putting it together and fastening it with gummed paper tape. We wish you were here to have the fun with us.

I had a lovely time from 5:30 till six this evening. I sat at the radio in the music room all alone. Pater was asleep and the others gone. It was dark outside and the moon just coming up — a full moon, lovely as could be. I had the Christmas tree lights on part of the time, but mostly I just sat in the dark room and watched the moon. I walked through all the house at Honeyhill and looked out all the windows. I thought of all the neighbors — Murrays losing their good home; Richards with nothing to go on; other families nearby with personal problems — and I realized again how fortunate we are. I stood (in thought) at the dining room windows, looking at the moon rising over the Big Horns. I watched you coming up the hill from doing the chores. Dearest, I am so glad you are our Daddy and Lover, and that I am

Your Sweetheart.

My Dearest Sweetheart:

Eighteen years ago now we were on the way to Evansville, just you and I. We were happy then, and our love was beautiful. But in these eighteen years it has grown much more beautiful and wonderful. It was then just a new plant; now it is a large, lovely tree, in whose shelter not only we two, but three others find heaven on earth. Today I have lived through the whole day all that happened on our wedding day, and have felt you very near. I hope you have felt me near you too.

Your darling letter came yesterday. It is a more valuable anniversary remembrance to me than gold or silver or precious stones. For you to write such evidence of your love and esteem honors me more than anything else you could send. I have read your letter again just now. Your understanding of the call here for my help, and your unselfish willingness to lend your family show your bigness and strength of character. You are able to see through the present discomfort to the future value that will result for us and our children. It takes a real man to be able to do that. I told you long ago that I knew a *M*an when I saw one, and now I know it is all the more true.

I love you, dearest, more and more every day. I tell you so many times every day and night. Do you hear me say it? I imagine I feel your dear arms around me, and they rest me when I am tired, and give me strength when I need it. They give me joy and happiness at all times. Sometimes I dream of you and wake refreshed and happier from having been with you.

The children are well and happy. They are really enjoying their life here. Even Jules is now glad to be here. He has a fine boy for a special chum and several others who come often. I can hardly believe that eighteen years have gone by, and that we really have three such splendid children. The years have been happy ones, and have gone quickly. These few that we must be apart will go quickly too, I am sure, and will leave valuable gifts. Then we'll have many lovely, happy years together again, with interesting and profitable work together.

Goodnight, my sweetheart, and God bless you. I am so thankful that you wanted me to be yours, and happy that I can be

Your,   Ce.

Postscript

Our Wyoming years came to an end, but our association with Honeyhill and with friends in the Shoshone Valley continued. The economic situation stabilized, and the farm was not lost. We eagerly looked forward each year to spending summer in Wyoming and visiting the Ellises in Colorado; but autumn brought us back to Indiana, and winter brought John east to spend several months with his beloved family.

Pater continued to be a semi-invalid, needing round-the-clock care from his daughters until finally, in 1933, after much soul-searching, they settled him in the home of a practical nurse. He died at ninety-two, in January 1934.

By this time John had developed angina problems and had to limit his activities. He had assistance with the work in the apiary and leased the farm. His physical problems and the absence of his family depressed him, but he kept busy with his community activities and planned for the summers when everyone was together at Honeyhill. In December 1936, the angina, complicated by pneumonia, caused his death. He was sixty-two — an old man to his children — and old by that decade's standards. When he became ill, Cecilia traveled from Bloomington to be with him in the hospital at Billings, Montana; and then, alone, traveling the same route as their honeymoon trip, she brought him back to Indiana to be buried at West Franklin where three of his brothers and sisters still lived.

Cecilia was fifty-three when she was widowed. The faculty position at Indiana University enabled her to continue doing what she did best: teach and provide for her family. She taught survey courses in literature for business students — to give them a basis for expanding their horizons later in life, she always said. She and Cora loved the teaching. They could hardly wait for their new students to appear every semester so they could share their enthusiasm for literature and correct grammar and writing, and for the excitement and the discipline of mathematics. They were inspirational teachers as well as demanding ones, and they continued to support their Alma Mater enthusiastically all their lives. Cecilia helped found the I.U. Writer's Conference and served on its administrative committee for many years, and she was secretary and then president of her Phi Beta Kappa chapter.

Late in her career, in 1950, Cecilia took a sabbatical and traveled to the Palau Islands in the Western Pacific where she developed an English-Palauan dictionary that was helpful in the island schools administered by the United States as part of a United Nations trusteeship. She retired from Indiana University in 1953 as Associate Professor Emeritus of English, and after retirement spent a year at Coe College, Iowa, as a John Hay Whitney Foundation exchange professor. She was also a consultant for a U.S. Veterans Writing Project, corresponding with hospitalized veterans after the Korean War to help them develop writing skills. In 1960 she was named a Distinguished Alumnus of Indiana University.

Cora died after a brief illness in 1947, and by that time Jules and Anne and I had finished college, were married, and had started our own careers. Our mother shared her house near the campus with graduate students, becoming their friend and counselor much as her mother had done with their student roomers fifty years earlier. She managed Honeyhill long-distance until shortly before her death and continued to make frequent summer trips to Wyoming and Colorado. She continued her numerous writing projects, working on historical material for the university and for the Shoshone Valley's fiftieth anniversary and, as "Nana," she made her house headquarters for all her children and grandchildren. She filed their letters, just as her family had kept hers: letters from my husband Henry and me in the western Pacific while he was in the Navy and in the administration of the Trust Territory of the Pacific Islands; letters from Jules and Lois in Austria, where Jules finished his Army service, and later from Afghanistan where he served on an Agency for International Development contract; and from Anne and John DeCamp at Purdue University where John was director of the educational radio station. Ultimately Jules and Lois and Henry and I came home from our travels to work on the staff of Indiana University, continuing the love of university life we had all inherited from our mother.

We all urged Cecilia to travel to England and the Continent, where the roots of her beloved literature lay, but she was content to be with the family and to be at home. Her Great Journey had been taken when she went to the western mountains under rugged conditions — as far from home in the early 1900s as were her children's later travels to the faraway places around the world. The details of our lives are not so well preserved because communication has become less written and more verbal. Cecilia's correspondence files were kept by the family until her death at eighty-six, in 1969, and they are now in the archives of Indiana University.

Like our mother, we walk through the rooms at Honeyhill often in our minds. The shining mountains surround us and the valley is open and green and fruitful. We are children again in a happy home, with a father who laughs heartily but who spanks with a big and heavy hand, and a mother who keeps us busy and happy and interested in everything around us. The telephone wires sing in the cold wintertime under heavy hoar frost. In summer the strawberries are ripe, the sweet peas bloom in the garden, and the yellow, old-fashioned rosebush blooms by the front steps. The lawn is green at Honeyhill, nurtured by the irrigation water that stands on it in summer nights, and a tall row of cottonwoods and silverleaf maples surround the yard. The Park train goes whistling by early in the morning, and we watch cars coming down the Garland hill, several miles away, wondering who might be coming to our house. And Honeyhill is a happy, comfortable haven where children can grow and wonder, and look to the wider world beyond the Big Horns and Heart Mountain.

A poem my mother wrote some time after she left Honeyhill seems a fitting conclusion for this volume of letters, for it bespeaks her life beautifully.

Cecilia Hendricks Wahl

Homesteading

I have watched fields grow where there were no fields,
Fields that I laid out myself.
I have built irrigation ditches for the life-giving water
Through desert of sagebrush and cactus.
I planted wheat and potatoes, alfalfa and oats,
I watered and I tended them,
They grew.
Now my tilled fields lie before me
Squares in a living checkerboard.
They are food for man and stock.
They are satisfaction through achievement.
They are a constant challenge,
My fields.

I have watched trees grow where there were no trees,
Trees that I planted myself,
My trees.
Small shoots, saplings without a fork,
I watered and I tended them,
They grew.
Leaves came, and twigs, and branches,
They spread upward and outward.
Now they stand against the sky in ordered rows.
They are a grateful shade,
They are a tracery of lace against blue velvet,
They are comfort and beauty and joy,
My trees.

I have watched children grow where there were no children,
Children I bore myself.
My children.
Small scions, buds not yet unfolded,
I nursed them and I tended them,
They grew.
They walked, they talked, they reasoned,
They developed senses, minds, and hearts.
Now they stand before me tall and beautiful.
They are a present strength,
They are myself projected into the future,
They are love and faith and hope,
My children.

Cecilia H. Hendricks

INDEX

manuscript, 546; accepts article for publication, 549

Brown, Mr. and Mrs. (Ellises' Greybull friends), 510

Brown, Anne (West Franklin, Indiana friend), 640, 641, 643, 653, 655

Brown, Mr. and Mrs. Walter, 131, 378

Bryan, William Lowe (president, Indiana University), 664, 672, 676

Buffalo, Wyoming, 622, 626

Buffalo Bill Museum: Hendrickses join Coolidge party at, 547

Bullock, George, 577

Burlington, Wyoming, 516

Busch, Mary, 509, 511, 520

Butchering, 93, 104, 159

Butter, 24

Bygren, Levi, Ida, and family, 103, 106, 184, 429, 473, 561, 684, 668

Byrne, Donn, 594

Byron, Wyoming, 267, 285, 332, 515

Callahan, Mr., 310

Calling cards, 118

Camping, 64

Canning, 30, 74, 104, 380, 599

Carr, Mr. (hired man), 276–78, 282, 285–90, 295, 297, 300, 302, 304, 305, 321

Carr, Grace, 289–91, 296–99, 302, 304

Carter, Henry H. (chairman, Indiana University English Department), 664, 666, 671, 672

Casper, Wyoming, 517, 531

Casper *Herald*, 569, 586

Castberg, William, 651, 648

Catholic church, 460

Cattle, 31, 124, 159, 506

Chautauqua, 315, 373, 422, 470

Cheyenne, Wyoming, 220, 223, 228, 455, 882

Cheyenne *Tribune*, 426, 539, 550, 554–55

Chicago, Burlington & Quincy Railroad (CB&Q), 203; daily trains on line, 302; freight rate hearing, 365; equitable shipping rates, 409, 413

Chickens, 112, 118, 124, 176

Chinook, 158, 590

Christian Science Monitor, 538

Christmas, 87, 90, 152, 202, 251, 328, 356, 404, 458, 525, 555, 585, 684

Christy Brothers Circus: at Powell, 574

Circus, 448, 499, 501, 574

Cistern, 171

Citizenship essay contest, 482

Clark, Perry J. and Mrs., 437, 505, 579

Clocks, 18, 89

Clothing, 65, 176, 185, 292, 426, 437, 477, 487, 498, 508, 563, 579, 602

Clover, 75, 93, 136, 139, 140, 160, 188, 200, 202, 207, 244, 247, 269

Coal, 43, 203, 227

Cody, Wyoming, 3, 70, 378, 421, 546

Coe College, 688

Collins, Mr. and Mrs. Harry, 118, 338

Colorado Honey Producers Association, 76, 92, 162, 426

"Company Dinners" (poem), 150

Conklin, Jotilda (Indiana University French professor), 557

Conrad, Joseph: *The Rover*, 461

Contractors' Lumber Supply Company, 309

Cook, Mr. and Mrs. John (Cody laundryman, county Democratic chairman), 493, 513, 584

Coolidge, Calvin: visits Cody, 547–48

Coorough, Delbert, 445

Corkins, Mr. (state entomologist), 426, 429

Country Sales, 39, 47, 105, 160

Cowley, Wyoming, 266, 269, 516

Cox, James M. (presidential candidate), 320

Crane, Arthur Griswold (president, University of Wyoming), 428, 579, 620

Cravens, John (Indiana University bursar), 664

experience, 480; 505, 510, 520, 522, 525, 537, 541–43, 553, 556–57, 558, 564, 566, 570; new car for Hendricks, 581; visit at Honeyhill, 598; 605, 610, 617, 636, 638, 649, 650, 651, 653; health a factor in Cecilia's return to Indiana, 663, 667; 673, 679; failing health, death, 687

Hennel, Will, 5

Hergescheimer, Joseph, 487

Hired girls: Norma Myers, 419; Wanda Shaulis, 475, 498; Mary Busch, 509–11; 611

Hired men: "Ozarks," 76; beet workers, 127; Vern Newcomb, 164, 165, 168; Mr. Carr, 276–321; Mr. Bretney, 439; Mr. Maloy, 559

Hoffman, Mr. and Mrs., 192

Homesickness, 15, 16, 91, 100, 122, 242

Homesteading, 3, 335, 690

Honey: crop not sold, 27, 28, 29, 32, 33; 43, 71; advertising, 72; 73–76; 81; 140–41, 185–88, 189, 213–16, 223, 239; newspaper article on wartime shipment, 249; 252, 274, 275, 279, 285, 302; honey tariffs, 332, 333, 346, 341, 365, 380; shipping rates, 409, 413; 421, 425; shop destroyed by fire, 439–46; 488, 490, 491, 495, 541, 548, 550, 566, 575, 586, 588, 598, 603, 614, 635

Honeyhill Farm, 1, 19, 68, 81, 93, 115; future planning, 254; 368, 385–86, 405, 407, 419, 427; shop destroyed by fire, 439–46; minor shop fire, 491; new furniture, 564, 570; gathering place for neighborhood children, 587; 616, 660, 685, 687, 689

"The Hoosier Schoolmaster," 462

Hoots, Mr. John, 445

Hoover, Herbert, 623

Horn, Mr. and Mrs. Anton, 177, 318, 429

Horoscopes, 501

Horses, 53, 177, 221

Hospitals, 243, 430

House, 19, 30, 33, 54, 68, 79, 125, 152, 171; plans for new house, 211; 246, 308, 309, 312; construction of, 316, 318, 321, 325, 328, 330, 331; electricity for, 386; 434, 564, 570

Household Magazine, 565

Housekeeping, 37, 40, 43, 66, 238, 504

Howe, Will D. (I.U. professor and *Scribner's* editor), 664

Howell, Mr. (Wyoming attorney general), 496

Hower, Oliver (president, Wyoming State Farm Bureau; Cowley resident), 378, 447, 462

Hyattville, Wyoming: Hendricks beeyard at, 462; 468, 470, 506, 573, 620, 626

Ice: packing year's supply, 22, 101; ice house inside shop, 427; 441, 434, 443

Ice, Dr. and Mrs. Thew Joseph, 465

Income, 124, 140, 150, 211, 213, 216, 223, 252, 254, 285, 383, 427, 435, 481, 513, 539, 541, 543, 549, 551, 553, 558, 569, 586, 588, 606, 624, 630, 646, 660, 667

Indiana Club, 23, 128, 141, 142, 143, 146

Indiana University: Hennel sisters enter, 5; 145; Cecilia applies for teaching position, 661, 666, 671; 676, 677, 687, 688, 689

Ingram, Mrs. (nurse), 339, 342

Insurance: formation of cooperative company, 123, 164, 167, 188; 189; on shop fire, 440, 442, 444, 446; need to cash policies, 625, 641, 642, 643

Ironing: electric iron, 409

Irrigation: Shoshone Dam, 3; 123, 138, 143, 162, 214

251; flu epidemic, 280, 284; 288; electric streetlights, 315; 336, 368, 385, 409, 448, 452, 476; reception for Governor Ross, 513; economic conference, 560

Powell *Leader*, The, 250, 265

Powell National Bank, 434, 435

Powell Telephone Company, 131, 210, 218, 611, 614, 660

Powell *Tribune*, 426, 546, 567, 649

"The Preacher Went Out Hunting," 474

Price, Rev. J. Allen, 460

"Prisoners Song, The," 593

Prohibition party, 79

Pryde, Marion (Mrs. Robert), 516

Pryor Mountains, 335

Rabbits, 159, 198

Radios, 578, 605, 606, 609, 636, 637, 642

Railroads, 203, 211, 409, 412, 413, 625

Rauchfuss, Mr., 76, 381

Reading, 255, 285, 320, 325, 335, 404, 461, 489, 512, 533, 565, 594

Reclamation Service, U.S., 3, 123, 138, 212, 214, 217, 406, 487, 560

Red Cross, 237, 238, 250, 253, 259, 260, 261

Reese, Mrs., 130, 253

Relief Committee of Fifteen, 487

Republican party, 320, 378, 395, 399, 422, 496, 519, 583

Richards family, Ernest, 77, 79, 130, 135; daughter born, 174; 194; German book burning incident, 263, 265, 313; 353, 679, 684, 685

Rickard, Harvey, 368, 490

Ries, Mr. and Mrs. Joseph, 177, 185, 222

Roach, Mr. and Mrs., 107, 109, 212, 213, 385, 556

Robinson, Mr. (U.S. Senator, Indiana), 651, 653, 654

Rokahr, Miss (state home economics specialist), 483

Ross, Nellie Tayloe: nominated to replace husband as governor, 453, 454; 455, 464-65, 471; running for reelection, 496; 508, 513, 515, 516; loses election, 518, 519; 523, 535, 549

Ross, William B.: candidacy for governor, 377; wins primary, 383; 387, 394; wins election 397-98; 415; 451; illness and death, 451, 452, 453

Russian Symphonic Choir, 882

St. Louis Press Reporting Syndicate, 486

Salesmen, 163, 178, 467

Sanders, Mr. and Mrs. Everett (secretary to President Coolidge), 461, 546, 547-48

Saturday Evening Post, 487, 489, 535, 538

Saxe, Mr. and Mrs., 131

Schools, 120, 226, 263, 313, 344, 371, 408, 431, 482, 567, 568, 576, 592, 619, 647, 648, 653

Schult, Reverend Ernest E., 460

Schwoob, Jake (Cody resident): chairman of arrangements for Coolidge visit, 547, 584

Scott, Hazel, 626

Scribner's Magazine, 545, 546; accepts Cecilia's article, 549; 551; 572

Sears Roebuck, 83, 89, 563, 564, 570, 646

Sedwick, William, 139

Selby, June (Powell school teacher), 481

Sewing. *See* Clothing

Shaulis, Wanda, 475, 498, 511

Sheep, 429

Shop, 265; destroyed by fire, 439, 440, 445; struck by lightning, 447; minor fire at, 491, 578

Shoshone Dam, 3, 54, 547

Shoshone Farmers Mutual Protective Association: formation, 164, 167; 188

Shoshone Farmers Union, 45; John